Using Computers
A Gateway to Information
WORLD WIDE WEB *Edition*

Gary B. Shelly
Thomas J. Cashman
Gloria A. Waggoner
William C. Waggoner

Contributing Authors
John F. Repede
Misty E. Vermaat
Tim J. Walker

Visit Shelly Cashman Online at
http://www.bf.com/scseries.html

boyd & fraser publishing company
An International Thomson Publishing Company

Danvers • Albany • Bonn • Boston • Cincinnati • Detroit • London • Madrid • Melbourne
Mexico City • New York • Paris • San Francisco • Singapore • Tokyo • Toronto • Washington

SHELLY
CASHMAN
SERIES®

Special thanks to Dennis Tani for outstanding cover designs.

Special thanks go to the following reviewers of *Using Computers: A Gateway to Information, World Wide Web Edition*:

Paula Bell, Lock Haven University; **Catherine J. Brotherton**, Riverside Community College; **Deborah Fansler**, Purdue University Calumet; **Kenneth Frizane**, Oakton Community College; **E. Colin Ikei**, Long Beach City College; **Gary L. Margot**, Ashland University; **Harry J. Rosenblatt**, College of the Albemarle; **Althea Stevens**, Mid-Plains Community College, McDonald/Belton Campus; and **Mike Waggoner**, Educational Consultant.

 © 1996 boyd & fraser publishing company
A Division of Course Technology
One Corporate Place • 55 Ferncroft Road
Danvers, Massachusetts 01923-4016

 Course TECHNOLOGY

I(T)P International Thomson Publishing
boyd & fraser publishing company is an ITP company.
The ITP trademark is used under license.

Printed in the United States of America

For more information, contact boyd & fraser publishing company:

boyd & fraser publishing company
A Division of Course Technology
One Corporate Place • 55 Ferncroft Road
Danvers, Massachusetts 01923-4016, USA

International Thomson Editors
Campos Eliseos 385, Piso 7
Colonia Polanco
11560 Mexico D.F. Mexico

International Thomson Publishing Europe
Berkshire House
168-173 High Holborn
London, WC1V 7AA, United Kingdom

International Thomson Publishing GmbH
Konigswinterer Strasse 418
53227 Bonn, Germany

International Thomson Publishing Asia
Block 211, Henderson Road #08-03
Henderson Industrial Park
Singapore 0315

Thomas Nelson Australia
102 Dodds Street
South Melbourne
Victoria 3205 Australia

International Thomson Publishing Japan
Hirakawa-cho Kyowa Building, 3F
2-2-1 Hirakawa-cho, Chiyoda-ku
Tokyo 102, Japan

Nelson Canada
1120 Birchmont Road
Scarborough, Ontario
Canada M1K 5G4

ISBN 0-7895-1185-1

3 4 5 6 7 8 9 10   BC 0 9 8 7 6

Contents

Using Computers • A Gateway to Information
WORLD WIDE WEB Edition

CHAPTER ONE

An Overview of Computer Concepts

SPECIAL FEATURE

The Evolution of the Computer Industry

CHAPTER TWO

Computer Software Applications: User Tools

3

Input to the Computer

4

The System Unit

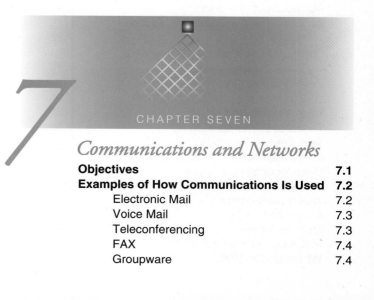

CHAPTER NINE

Information Management: Files and Databases

CHAPTER TEN

Information Systems

CHAPTER ELEVEN

Information Systems Development

Preface

In 1994, the Shelly Cashman Series team produced one of the most successful computer concepts textbooks ever. The title of the textbook was *Using Computers: A Gateway to Information*. We could have rested on our laurels and revised it in 1997, following the typical three-year-revision cycle of higher education publishers. Two major events occurred in the computer industry in 1995, however, that propelled us to revise this best seller after just one year. The two events were the phenomenal acceptance of the World Wide Web as a depository of useful information and the long-awaited release of Microsoft Windows 95.

Using our bestseller as a basis, we developed *Using Computers: A Gateway to Information, World Wide Web Edition*. An instructor using the earlier edition need not create new lecture material when moving to this new edition. What we have done is, taken the identical material from the previous edition and presented it using Windows 95 figures. We also have incorporated Windows 95 and World Wide Web exercises into the end-of-chapter material. A few paragraphs and tables and the Timeline have been updated. Other than these changes, the new edition is the same as the previous edition, even to the point of having identical pagination.

Combining the earlier edition and the latest revisions, this book was developed with five goals in mind: The material must

- represent the latest in computer technology, particularly with respect to personal computer hardware and software.
- recognize that personal computers have become the backbone of the computer industry and emphasize their use as both stand-alone devices and networked devices.
- focus on using the computer as a productivity tool.
- present the material in an interesting, exciting manner with a format that invites the student to learn. This includes new, color photographs and unique, state-of-the-art drawings that augment the text material.
- provide exercises and lab assignments that allow the student to interact with a computer and actually learn by using the computer.

Therefore, not only do we discuss the latest in computer equipment, computer software, and personal computer applications, but we also explain the processes required to successfully use these tools to produce useful information. The result is a complete treatment of computers and the computer industry.

Merely explaining topics without allowing a student to interact with a computer, however, would deprive the student of an essential experience. Therefore, at the end of each chapter, we have included a series of *In the Lab with Windows 95* and *Where on the Web* exercises that direct the student to use a computer to learn Microsoft Windows 95 and access information on the World Wide Web using Netscape Navigator. In addition, a series of special Shelly Cashman Series Interactive Labs allows students to learn computer skills and gain computer knowledge in an online, interactive setting.

Each of the sections of the book, together with the extraordinary instructor's materials, are explained in the following paragraphs.

Objective of the Textbook

Using Computers: A Gateway to Information, World Wide Web Edition is intended for use in a one-quarter or one-semester introductory course whose purpose is to provide students with a firm foundation in computer technology, computer nomenclature, and the use of computers as productivity tools, including access to the World Wide Web. Although each of the fourteen chapters in the book addresses a specific topic, the fundamental computer concepts are actually integrated throughout the textbook in a manner that first presents an overview of the material and then, in subsequent chapters, moves to more in-depth coverage. Therefore, it is suggested that the book be used in a sequential manner, from beginning to end, with a minimum of jumping to chapters out of sequence.

When a student has completed a course using this book, he or she will have a thorough understanding of computers, computer technology, computer hardware and software, and how computers can be used to produce meaningful information. With the experience gained via the *In the Lab with Windows 95* and the *Where on the Web* sections at the end of each chapter, the student should be proficient in using computers running Windows 95 and Netscape Navigator.

Chapter Organization

Each chapter within the book is organized to present the optimum amount of material in the most effective manner possible. The text is presented in concise, clearly identified sections and subsections so the student is easily guided through the chapter. Figures (pictures and drawings) are visually separated from the text so the student can read without being encumbered by confusing text, graphics, arrows, and drawings.

Each chapter is organized into the following sections:

- **Objectives** The objectives for the chapter are clearly stated on the first page of the chapter so the student has an overview of the subject matter.
- **Chapter Introduction** Each chapter has an introduction that briefs the student on the material within the chapter and the reason the material is important.
- **Chapter Text, Pictures, and Drawings** The major learning material in the chapter is presented as text, pictures, and drawings. The pictures have been chosen for their pedagogical value and provide a valuable addition that allows students to see the actual hardware, software, and other subjects being described in the text. The drawings, created with the latest state-of-the-art drawing capabilities of computers, specifically illustrate concepts that are understood more easily through the use of drawings. The combination of drawings and pictures used in this book sets a new standard for computer textbooks.
- **Computers at Work** At the end of each chapter, an example of computers being used for interesting applications is presented. These examples illustrate points made within the chapter.
- **In the Future** This feature, which appears at the end of each chapter, points out an application or applications that will occur in the future using technology discussed in the chapter.
- **What You Should Know** This clear, step-by-step summary of the material in the chapter will help students review the chapter and prepare for examinations.
- **Terms to Remember** This listing of the key terms found in the chapter together with the page on which the terms are defined will aid students in mastering the chapter material. A complete summary of all key terms in the book, together with their definitions, appear in the Index at the end of the book.
- **Test Your Knowledge** Fill-in and short answer questions, together with a figure from the chapter that must be labeled, help focus the student when reviewing the material within the chapter.
- **Points to Ponder** The computer industry is not without its controversial issues. At the end of each chapter, six scenarios are presented that challenge the student to critically examine the computer industry and rethink his or her perspective of technology in society.
- **Out and About** Computers are found everywhere. This section, appearing at the end of each chapter, provides multiple projects that send the student out of the classroom and into the world where interesting discoveries about computers will take place.
  - **In the Lab with Windows 95** Students must interact with and use a computer to complete their introduction to computers. At the end of each chapter, a series of Windows 95 Lab exercises are presented for student use. Beginning with the simplest exercises within Microsoft Windows 95, students are led through a series of activities that, by the end of the book, will enable them to be proficient in using Windows.
- **Where on the Web** In this section that ends each chapter students learn how to access information from the World Wide Web using Netscape Navigator.
- **Shelly Cashman Series Interactive Labs** These unique exercises, developed specifically for this book, are hands-on exercises that use the computer to teach about the computer. The Labs are described in detail on page xvi.

This chapter organization and the material presented provide the most in-depth treatment of introductory computer subjects ever found in a textbook. Students will finish the course with a complete understanding of computers, how to use computers, and how to access information from the World Wide Web.

Contents of *Using Computers: A Gateway to Information, World Wide Web Edition*

A brief explanation of each of the chapters in this book follows:

Chapter 1 – An Overview of Computer Concepts Introduces the student to the fundamentals of a computer, including the information processing cycle. When the student completes the chapter, he or she will have a firm understanding of the basics of computer processing and will be ready for the more in-depth treatment of subjects in subsequent chapters.

Chapter 2 – Computer Software Applications: User Tools Provides a complete explanation of application software available on computers, with an emphasis on personal computer software that students are likely to use. Numerous examples of the use of software such as word processing, spreadsheets, database, presentation graphics, data communications, electronic mail, and others in a Windows 95 environment are included.

Chapter 3 – Input to the Computer Presents the manner in which data is entered into the computer for processing, with primary attention to personal computers. In addition to the keyboard and mouse, pointing devices, scanners, voice input, and other means of entering data into personal computers are closely examined.

Chapter 4 – The System Unit   Offers a detailed look inside the system unit. Topics include the motherboard, processors, memory, ports, and other elements that make a personal computer run.

Chapter 5 — Output from the Computer   Explores the many means for obtaining useful information from a computer, including printers, display devices, voice output, and plotters. Included is an explanation of the types of output from personal computers, such as reports, graphics, audio output, video output, multimedia, and virtual reality.

Chapter 6 – Secondary Storage   Discusses the manner in which data is stored on a computer. Included are diskettes, hard disks, and cartridge tape systems, among others, together with an explanation of such storage issues as defragmentation and compression.

Chapter 7 – Communications and Networks   Covers communications and networks from a user's perspective. All important subjects are explained, with a special emphasis on local area networks and personal computers.

Chapter 8 – Operating Systems and System Software   Teaches students about operating systems such as Windows 95, OS/2, and DOS. A clear explanation of difficult subjects such as multitasking and multiprocessing contributes to a student's overall understanding.

Chapter 9 – Information Management: Files and Databases   Emphasizes the care and treatment of data, with particular attention on databases and the capability of accessing data to create meaningful information.

Chapter 10 – Information Systems   Explains that when the computer is used as a tool within an organization, be it small or large, the information from the computer must be organized and presented in its most useful form; details the information needs of various people within an organization.

Chapter 11 – Information Systems Development   Identifies the processes necessary to analyze, design, and implement an information system because effective use of computers and application systems does not happen by accident.

Chapter 12 – Program Development and Programming Languages   Presents all the steps required to produce a robust, functioning program. In addition, the student is exposed to the multitude of available programming languages.

Chapter 13 – Security, Ethics, and Privacy   Explores the effects of computers within society. It also looks at security issues with computers, and in particular, how to ensure that data and programs on a computer are not rendered useless by viruses.

Chapter 14 – Your Future in the Information Age   Examines career opportunities in the computer field and discusses the future of computers in our society.

Special Features   Within the book, the special features sections provide an in-depth look at certain aspects of computers. The six special features are:

- The Evolution of the Computer Industry
- Making a Computer Chip
- The Internet
- How to Purchase, Install, and Maintain a Personal Computer
- Multimedia
- Virtual Reality

These contents, together with *In the Lab with Windows 95* and *Where on the Web* and other projects within this book, present a thorough course on computers and computer usage.

Instructor's Support Package

The most comprehensive instructor's support package ever developed accompanies *Using Computers: A Gateway to Information, World Wide Web Edition.* The elements of this package are as follows:

- **Annotated Instructor's Edition (AIE)**   The AIE for *Using Computers: A Gateway to Information, World Wide Web Edition* is designed to assist you with your lectures by suggesting transparencies to use, summarizing key points, proposing pertinent questions, offering important tips, and incorporating the answers to the student activities. The several hundred annotations in the AIE fall into three major categories:
    - **Teacher Notes**   Suggest ways to convey an idea effectively; point beyond what is covered in the book; describe the latest uses of computers; explain misconceptions; include quotes, show and tell suggestions, and interesting sidelights
    - **Discussion Topics**   Include questions to ask students that result in classroom discussion
    - **Transparency References**   Recommend transparencies to use at key points in the lecture presentation
- **Instructor's Manual**   The Instructor's Manual includes the following:
    - Detailed lesson plans, including objectives, overviews, and lecture outlines with transparency references for each illustration in each chapter of the book
    - Black and white transparency masters
    - A test bank of True/False, Multiple Choice, and Fill-in questions

- A lesson plans and test bank diskette, called Elec-Man, that includes the detailed lesson plans and test bank for customizing to each instructor's needs
- Answers to all student activities
- Black and white transparency masters for every drawing in the textbook and actual color transparencies of selected drawings for use in lectures
- A lab solutions diskette that contains all the answers to the *In the Lab with Windows 95* and *Where on the Web* exercises in the book
- **Color Transparencies** One hundred of the figures and tables in the textbook are available as color transparencies with accompanying lecture notes.
- **MicroSWAT III** MicroSWAT III, a computerized test-generating system, is available free to adopters of any Shelly Cashman Series textbook. It includes all the questions from the test bank previously described. MicroSWAT III is an easy-to-use, menu-driven software package that provides instructors with testing flexibility and allows customizing of testing documents.
- **NetTest IV** NetTest IV, available at no cost, allows instructors to take a MicroSWAT III file made up of True/False and Multiple Choice questions and proctor a paperless examination in a network environment. The same questions display in a different order on each personal computer in the network. Students have the option of instantaneous feedback. Tests are electronically graded, and an item analysis is produced.
- **Video Tapes to Augment Lectures** Complimentary selections from the three series, *Computer Applications*, *The Machine That Changed the World*, and *The Computer Revolution*, are available to qualified adopters of *Using Computers: A Gateway to Information, World Wide Web Edition*.
- **Multimedia Lecture Presentation System** The multimedia lecture presentation system was prepared specifically for use with *Using Computers: A Gateway to Information, World Wide Web Edition*. The multimedia lecture presentation system is available on CD-ROM and includes chapter highlights, pictures, and more than one hour of video clips. The pictures and video clips can be viewed during lecture at the discretion of the instructor.

Student Study Guide

This highly popular supplement contains completely new student activities to help solidify the concepts and techniques presented in the text. The Study Guide compliments the end-of-chapter material with short answer, fill-in, and matching questions and other challenging exercises.

Acknowledgments

The Shelly Cashman Series would not be the most successful computer textbook series ever published without the contributions of outstanding publishing professionals. First, and foremost, among them is Becky Herrington, director of production and designer. She is the heart and soul of the Shelly Cashman Series, and it is only through her leadership, dedication, and untiring efforts that superior products are produced.

Under Becky's direction, the following individuals made significant contributions to this book: Ginny Harvey, series administrator and manuscript editor; Peter Schiller, production manager; Tracy Murphy, series coordinator; Nancy Lamm, proofreader; Sarah Evertson and Sarah Bendersky, photo researchers; Marilyn Martin, photo credits; and Cristina Haley, indexer.

Our sincere thanks go to Dennis Tani, who together with Becky Herrington, designed this book. In addition, Dennis performed all the layout and typography, executed the magnificent drawings contained in this book, designed the cover, and survived an impossible schedule with goodwill and amazing patience. We salute Dennis's superior work.

We appreciate the assistance of Kenneth Frizane, Harry Rosenblatt, and Althea Stevens in preparing the Annotated Instructor's Edition.

The efforts of our three contributing authors, John Repede, Tim Walker, and Misty Vermaat, on the chapter ending material helped make this book extraordinary. As always, special recognition for a job well-done must go to Jim Quasney, who quarterbacked this book from its beginning to its final form. Thanks to Tom Walker, president and CEO of boyd & fraser publishing company, for his vision and support of this project.

We hope you find using this book an enriching and rewarding experience.

Gary B. Shelly
Thomas J. Cashman
Gloria A. Waggoner
William C. Waggoner

Shelly Cashman Series – Traditionally Bound Textbooks

The Shelly Cashman Series presents computer textbooks across the entire spectrum including both Windows- and DOS-based personal computer applications in a variety of traditionally bound textbooks, as shown in the table below. For more information, see your Course Technology representative or call 1-800-648-7450.

COMPUTERS	
Computers	Using Computers: A Gateway to Information, World Wide Web Edition
	Using Computers: A Gateway to Information, World Wide Web Brief Edition
	Using Computers: A Gateway to Information
	Using Computers: A Gateway to Information, Brief Edition
	Exploring Computers: A Record of Discovery with CD-ROM
	A Record of Discovery for Exploring Computers
	Study Guide for Using Computers: A Gateway to Information, World Wide Web Edition
	Study Guide for Using Computers: A Gateway to Information
and Windows Apps	Using Computers: A Gateway to Information and Microsoft Office (also in spiral bound)
	Using Computers: A Gateway to Information and Microsoft Works 3.0 (also in spiral bound)
and Programming	Using Computers: A Gateway to Information and Programming in QBasic
and World Wide Web	Using Computers: A Gateway to Information and Netscape Navigator 2.0 World Wide Web Edition

WINDOWS APPLICATIONS	
Integrated Packages	Microsoft Office 4.3 running under Windows 95: Introductory Concepts and Techniques (also in spiral bound)
	Microsoft Office: Introductory Concepts and Techniques (also in spiral bound)
	Microsoft Office: Advanced Concepts and Techniques (also in spiral bound)
	Microsoft Works 4.0 for Windows 95* ₁ Microsoft Works 4.0 for Windows 95—Short Course
	Microsoft Works 3.0 (also in spiral bound)* ₁ Microsoft Works 2.0 (also in spiral bound)
	Microsoft Works 3.0—Short Course
Windows	Microsoft Windows 95
	Microsoft Windows 3.1 Introductory Concepts and Techniques
	Microsoft Windows 3.1 Complete Concepts and Techniques
Windows Applications	Microsoft Word 2.0, Microsoft Excel 4, and Paradox 1.0 (also in spiral bound)
Word Processing	Microsoft Word 7* ₁ Microsoft Word 6* ₁ Microsoft Word 2.0
	WordPerfect 6.1* ₁ WordPerfect 6* ₁ WordPerfect 5.2
Spreadsheets	Microsoft Excel 7* ₁ Microsoft Excel 5* ₁ Microsoft Excel 4
	Lotus 1-2-3 Release 5* ₁ Lotus 1-2-3 Release 4*
	Quattro Pro 6 ₁ Quattro Pro 5
Database Management	Microsoft Access 7* ₁ Microsoft Access 2*
	Paradox 5 ₁ Paradox 4.5 ₁ Paradox 1.0
	Visual dBASE 5/5.5
Presentation Graphics	Microsoft PowerPoint 7* ₁ Microsoft PowerPoint 4*

DOS APPLICATIONS	
Operating Systems	DOS 6 Introductory Concepts and Techniques
	DOS 6 and Microsoft Windows 3.1 Introductory Concepts and Techniques
Integrated Package	Microsoft Works 3.0 (also in spiral bound)
Word Processing	WordPerfect 6.1 ₁ WordPerfect 6.0
	WordPerfect 5.1 Step-by-Step Function Key Edition
	WordPerfect 5.1 Function Key Edition
	Microsoft Word 5.0
Spreadsheets	Lotus 1-2-3 Release 4 ₁ Lotus 1-2-3 Release 2.4 ₁ Lotus 1-2-3 Release 2.3
	Lotus 1-2-3 Release 2.2 ₁ Lotus 1-2-3 Release 2.01
	Quattro Pro 3.0
	Quattro with 1-2-3 Menus (with Educational Software)
Database Management	dBASE 5 ₁ dBASE IV Version 1.1 ₁ dBASE III PLUS (with Educational Software)
	Paradox 4.5 ₁ Paradox 3.5 (with Educational Software)

PROGRAMMING AND NETWORKING	
Programming	Microsoft Visual Basic 3.0 for Windows*
	Microsoft BASIC
	QBasic
	QBasic: An Introduction to Programming
	Structured COBOL Programming
Networking	Novell NetWare for Users
	Business Data Communications: Introductory Concepts and Techniques
Internet	The Internet: Introductory Concepts and Techniques (UNIX)
	Netscape Navigator 2.0 Windows 95 Edition ₁ Netscape Navigator 2.0 Windows 3.1 Edition
	Netscape Navigator: An Introduction

SYSTEMS ANALYSIS	
Systems Analysis	Systems Analysis and Design, Second Edition

*Also available as a Double Diamond Edition, which is a shortened version of the complete book

Shelly Cashman Series – **Custom Edition** Program

If you do not find a Shelly Cashman Series traditionally bound textbook to fit your needs, boyd & fraser's unique **Custom Edition** program allows you to choose from a number of options and create a textbook perfectly suited to your course. Features of the **Custom Edition** program are:

▸ Textbooks that match the content of your course
▸ Windows- and DOS-based materials for the latest versions of personal computer applications software
▸ Shelly Cashman Series quality, with the same full-color materials and Shelly Cashman Series pedagogy found in the traditionally bound books
▸ Affordable pricing so your students receive the **Custom Edition** at a cost similar to that of traditionally bound books

The table on the right summarizes the available materials. For more information, see your Course Technology representative or call 1-800-648-7450.

For Shelly Cashman Series information, visit Shelly Cashman Online at http://www.bf.com/scseries.html

COMPUTERS	
Computers	Using Computers: A Gateway to Information, World Wide Web Edition
	Using Computers: A Gateway to Information, World Wide Web Brief Edition
	Using Computers: A Gateway to Information
	Using Computers: A Gateway to Information, Brief Edition
	A Record of Discovery for Exploring Computers (available with CD-ROM)
	Study Guide for Using Computers: A Gateway to Information, World Wide Web Edition
	Study Guide for Using Computers: A Gateway to Information
	Introduction to Computers (32-page)

OPERATING SYSTEMS	
Windows	Microsoft Windows 95
	Microsoft Windows 3.1 Introductory Concepts and Techniques
	Microsoft Windows 3.1 Complete Concepts and Techniques
DOS	Introduction to DOS 6 (using DOS prompt)
	Introduction to DOS 5.0 (using DOS shell)
	Introduction to DOS 5.0 or earlier (using DOS prompt)

WINDOWS APPLICATIONS	
Integrated Packages	Microsoft Works 4.0 for Windows 95*
	Microsoft Works 4.0 for Windows 95—Short Course
	Microsoft Works 3.0*
	Microsoft Works 3.0—Short Course
	Microsoft Works 2.0
Microsoft Office	Using Microsoft Office (16-page)
	Object Linking and Embedding (OLE) (32-page)
Word Processing	Microsoft Word 7* ₁ Microsoft Word 6* ₁ Microsoft Word 2.0
	WordPerfect 6.1* ₁ WordPerfect 6* ₁ WordPerfect 5.2
Spreadsheets	Microsoft Excel 7* ₁ Microsoft Excel 5* ₁ Microsoft Excel 4
	Lotus 1-2-3 Release 5* ₁ Lotus 1-2-3 Release 4*
	Quattro Pro 6 ₁ Quattro Pro 5
Database Management	Microsoft Access 7* ₁ Microsoft Access 2*
	Paradox 5 ₁ Paradox 4.5 ₁ Paradox 1.0
	Visual dBASE 5/5.5
Presentation Graphics	Microsoft PowerPoint 7* ₁ Microsoft PowerPoint 4*

DOS APPLICATIONS	
Integrated Package	Microsoft Works 3.0
Word Processing	WordPerfect 6.1 ₁ WordPerfect 6.0
	WordPerfect 5.1 Step-by-Step Function Key Edition
	WordPerfect 5.1 Function Key Edition
	Microsoft Word 5.0
Spreadsheets	Lotus 1-2-3 Release 4 ₁ Lotus 1-2-3 Release 2.4 ₁ Lotus 1-2-3 Release 2.3
	Lotus 1-2-3 Release 2.2 ₁ Lotus 1-2-3 Release 2.01
	Quattro Pro 3.0
	Quattro with 1-2-3 Menus
Database Management	dBASE 5 ₁ dBASE IV Version 1.1 ₁ dBASE III PLUS
	Paradox 4.5 ₁ Paradox 3.5

PROGRAMMING AND NETWORKING	
Programming	Microsoft Visual Basic 3.0 for Windows*
	Microsoft BASIC
	QBasic
Networking Internet	Novell NetWare for Users
	The Internet: Introductory Concepts and Techniques (UNIX)
	Netscape Navigator 2.0 Windows 95 Edition
	Netscape Navigator 2.0 Windows 3.1 Edition
	Netscape Navigator: An Introduction

*Also available as a mini-module

Shelly Cashman Series Interactive Labs

Each of the chapters in this book concludes with hands-on exercises, which consist of *In the Lab with Windows 95* and *Where on the Web*. The purpose of these hands-on exercises is to allow students to use computers so they learn firsthand how computers work. The exercises solidify and reinforce the computer concepts presented in each chapter in a way unparalleled in previous computer textbooks. Students completing these exercises will have a firm understanding of how to use computers with Windows 95 and Netscape Navigator.

Of particular interest in the section titled *In the Lab with Windows 95* are the Shelly Cashman Series Interactive Labs (below), which help students gain a better understanding of a specific subject covered in a chapter.

Shelly Cashman Series Interactive Labs

Lab	Function	Page
Using the Mouse	Master how to use a mouse. The Lab includes pointing, clicking, double-clicking, and dragging.	1.30
Using the Keyboard	Learn how to use the keyboard. The Lab discusses different categories of keys, including the edit keys, function keys, ESC, CTRL, and ALT keys, and how to press keys simultaneously.	1.30
Scanning Documents	Understand how document scanners work.	3.30
Understanding the Motherboard	Step through the components of the motherboard and build one by adding components. The Lab shows how different motherboard configurations affect the overall speed of a computer.	4.33
Setting Up to Print	See how information flows from the system unit to the printer and how drivers, fonts, and physical connections play a role in generating a printout.	5.36
Configuring Your Display	Recognize the different monitor configurations available, including screen size, display cards, and number of colors.	5.36
Maintaining Your Hard Drive	Understand how files are stored on disk, what causes fragmentation, and how to maintain an efficient hard drive.	6.33
Connecting to the Internet	Learn how a computer is connected to the Internet. The Lab presents using the Internet to access information.	7.41
Evaluating Operating Systems	Evaluate the advantages and disadvantages of different categories of operating systems.	8.27
Working at Your Computer	Learn the basic ergonomic principles that prevent back and neck pain, eye strain, and other computer-related ailments.	8.27
Designing a Database	Create a database structure and optimize a database to support searching.	9.31
Choosing a Programming Language	Differentiate between traditional languages and newer object-oriented languages.	12.34
Keeping Your Computer Virus Free	Learn what a virus is and about the different kinds of viruses. The Lab teaches how to prevent your computer from being infected with a virus.	13.31
Exploring the Computers of the Future	Learn about computers of the future and how they will work.	14.33

An Overview of Computer Concepts

1

Objectives

After completing this chapter, you will be able to:

- Define computer and information literacy

- Explain the four operations of the information processing cycle: input, process, output, and storage

- Explain how speed, reliability and storage make computers powerful tools

- Identify the major components of a computer

- Identify the categories of computers

- Explain the difference between system software and application software

- Describe how the six elements of an information system work together

Computers play a key role in how individuals work and how they live. Today, even the smallest organizations have computers to help them operate more efficiently. Computers also affect people's lives in many unseen ways. Buying groceries at the supermarket, using an automated teller machine, or making a long-distance phone call all require using computers.

As they have for a number of years, personal computers continue to make an increasing impact on our lives. At home, at work, and in the field, these small systems help us do our work faster, more accurately, and in some cases, in ways that previously would not have been possible.

Computer and Information Literacy

Today, most people believe that knowing how to use a computer, especially a personal computer, is a basic skill necessary to succeed in business or to function effectively in society. Given the increasing use and availability of computer systems, such knowledge will continue to be an essential skill. Is just knowing how to use a computer, sometimes called **computer literacy**, enough? Many people now believe that a person should be *information literate* as well as *computer literate*. **Information literacy** is defined as knowing how to find, analyze, and use information. It is the ability to gather information from multiple sources, select the relevant material, and organize it into a form that will allow you to make a decision or take a specific action. For example, in shopping for a new car, one approach would be to visit several car dealers and talk to the salespeople about features of the model car in which you are interested. You can take written notes but your information will be limited to what you are told. An information literate person, however, will obtain relevant information about specific vehicles from a variety of sources before making any purchase decision. Such information might include vehicle list price, dealer cost, available options, repair history, and whether or not there have been any recalls. This type of information is available in several consumer-oriented publications and automobile magazines. With these facts, the car buyer is able to make a more informed decision on what car to buy (or not buy). How then do computers relate to information literacy?

They relate because increasingly, information on cars and other products, as well as information on finances, upcoming events, travel, and weather, is available from information sources that can be accessed using computers. With communications equipment and software, computers can connect with information sources around the world. Using a computer allows you to obtain up-to-date information in a fast, efficient, and cost-effective manner. Computers have become the tools people use to access and manage information.

The purpose of this book is to give you the knowledge you need to understand how computers work and how computers are used by people and organizations to gather and analyze information to make better decisions.

Chapter 1 gives you an overview of computer concepts. You will begin to learn what a computer is, how it processes data into information, and what elements are necessary for a successful information system. You will also begin to develop a basic vocabulary of computer terminology. While you are reading, remember that this chapter is an overview and that many of the terms and concepts that are introduced will be discussed in more detail in later chapters. *Figure1-1* shows a variety of computers including personal computers and their applications. As you can see, the use of computer technology is widespread in our world. New uses for computers and improvements to existing technology are continually being developed. Computers affect your life every day and will continue to do so in the future. Learning about computers and their applications will help you to function more effectively in the world.

Figure1-1
Computers being used in a wide variety of applications and professions; new applications are being developed every day.

What Is a Computer?

The most obvious question related to understanding computers and their impact on our lives is, "What is a computer?" A **computer** is an electronic device, operating under the control of instructions stored in its own memory unit, that can accept data (input), process data arithmetically and logically, produce output from the processing, and store the results for future use. While broader definitions of a computer exist, this definition includes a wide range of devices with various capabilities. For example, the tiny microprocessor shown in *Figure 1-2* can be called a computer. Generally, the term is used to describe a collection of devices that function together to process data. An example of the devices that make up a computer is shown in *Figure 1-3*.

What Does a Computer Do?

Whether small or large, computers can perform four general operations. These operations comprise the **information processing cycle** and are: input, process, output, and storage. Collectively, these operations describe the procedures that a computer performs to process data into information and store it for future use.

All computer processing requires data. **Data** refers to the raw facts, including numbers, words, images, and sounds, given to a computer during the input operation. In the processing phase, the computer manipulates the data to create information. **Information** refers to data that has been processed into a meaningul and useful form. The production of information by processing data on a computer is called **information processing**, or sometimes **data processing** (DP). During the output operation, the information created is put

Figure 1-2
Small enough to fool a bumblebee, this microprocessor contains the electronic circuits that perform the operations of a computer.

Speaker   **Monitor**   **System Unit**   **CD Rom**   **Speaker**   **Keyboard**   **Mouse**

Figure 1-3
Devices that comprise a personal computer system.

into some form, such as a printed report, that people can use. The information can also be stored electronically for future use.

The people who either use the computer directly or use the information it provides are called **computer users**, **end users**, or **users**. *Figure 1-4* shows a computer user and demonstrates how the four operations of the information processing cycle can occur on a personal computer. (1) The computer user inputs data by pressing the keys on the keyboard. (2) The data is then processed by the device called the system unit. (3) The output, or results, from the processing are displayed on the screen of the monitor or printed on the printer, providing information to the user. (4) Finally, the output is stored on a disk for future reference.

Figure 1-4 ▶
The use of this personal computer illustrates the four operations of the information processing cycle: input, process, output, and storage.

Why Is a Computer so Powerful?

The input, process, output, and storage operations that a computer performs may seem very basic and simple. However, the computer's power derives from its capability to perform these operations with speed and reliability and to store large amounts of data and information.

Speed

In a computer, operations occur through the use of electronic circuits contained on small chips as shown in

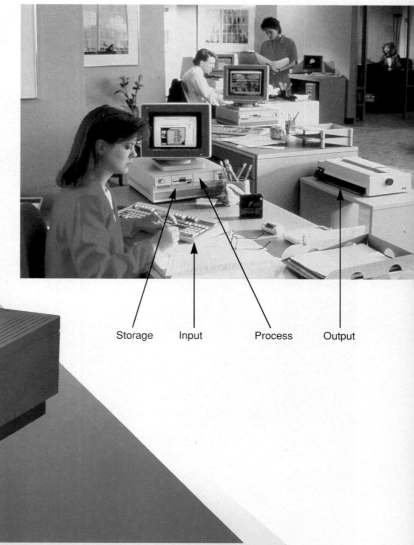

Storage   Input   Process   Output

Printer

Figure 1-5 When data flows along these circuits it travels at close to the speed of light. This allows processing to be accomplished in billionths of a second.

Reliability

The electronic components in modern computers are very reliable and seldom fail. In fact, most reports about computer errors are usually traced to other causes, often human mistakes. The high reliability of the components enables the computer to produce accurate results on a consistent basis.

Storage

Computers can store enormous amounts of data and keep that data readily available for processing. Using modern storage methods, the data can be quickly retrieved and processed and then re-stored for future use.

The speed, reliability, and storage capabilities of the computer make it a powerful tool for information processing.

How Does a Computer Know What to Do?

For a computer to perform the operations in the information processing cycle, it must be given a detailed set of instructions that tell it exactly what to do. These instructions are called a **computer program**, **program instructions**, or **software**.

Before the information processing cycle for a specific job begins, the computer program corresponding to that job is loaded into the computer's memory. Once the program is loaded, the computer can begin to process data by executing the program's first instruction. The computer executes one program instruction after another until the job is complete.

Figure 1-5
Inside a computer are chips and other electronic components that process data in billionths of a second.

Chips

The Information Processing Cycle

Your understanding of the information processing cycle introduced in this chapter is fundamental to understanding computers and how they process data into information. To review, the information processing cycle consists of four operations. They are: input, process, output, and storage.

The first three of these operations, **input**, **process**, and **output**, describe the procedures that a computer performs to process data into information. The fourth operation, **storage**, describes a computer's electronic storage capability. As you learn more about computers, you will see that these four operations apply to both the computer equipment and the computer software. The equipment, or devices, of a computer are classified according to the operations they perform. Computer software is made up of instructions that describe how the operations are to be performed.

What Are the Components of a Computer?

Data is processed by specific equipment that is often called computer **hardware**. This equipment consists of: input devices, a system unit, output devices, and secondary storage devices *(Figure 1-6)*.

Input Devices

Input devices are used to enter data into a computer. Two common input devices shown in *Figure 1-7* on the next page are the keyboard and the mouse. As the data is entered on the **keyboard**, it is temporarily stored in the computer's memory and displayed on the screen of the monitor. A **mouse** is a type of pointing device used to select processing options or information displayed on the screen. The mouse is used to move a small symbol that appears on the screen. This symbol, called a **mouse pointer** or **pointer**, can be many shapes but is often in the shape of an arrow.

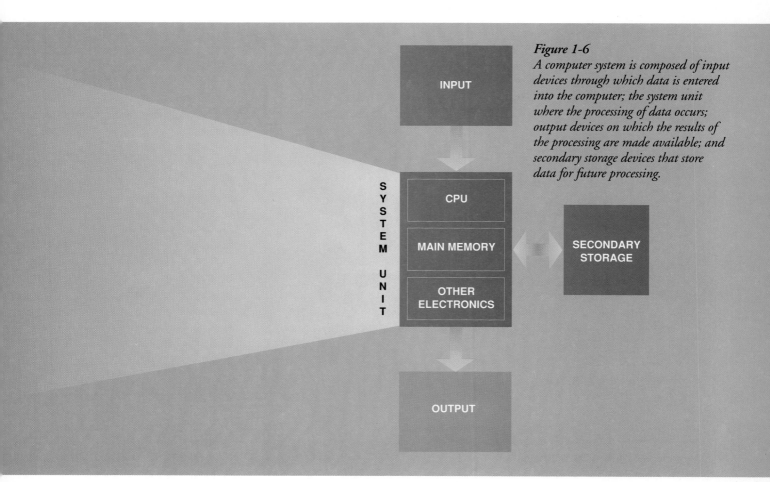

Figure 1-6
A computer system is composed of input devices through which data is entered into the computer; the system unit where the processing of data occurs; output devices on which the results of the processing are made available; and secondary storage devices that store data for future processing.

System Unit

Figure 1-6 on the previous page and *Figure 1-7* show the **system unit** of a computer, which contains the electronic circuits that actually cause the processing of data to occur. The system unit includes the central processing unit, main memory, and other electronic components. The **central processing unit** (CPU) contains a **control unit** that executes the program instructions and an **arithmetic/logic unit** (ALU) that performs math and logic operations. **Arithmetic operations** include numeric calculations such as addition, subtraction, multiplication, and division. Comparisons of data to see if one value is greater than, equal to, or less than another are called **logical operations.**

Main memory, also called **RAM (Random Access Memory)** or **primary storage,** temporarily stores data and program instructions when they are being processed.

Other electronics include components that work with the input, output, and storage devices and optional components that enable the computer to communicate with other computers.

Output Devices

Output from a computer can be presented in many forms. The two most commonly used **output devices** are the **printer** and the **monitor** shown in *Figure 1-7.* Other frequently used names for the monitor are the **screen,** or the CRT, which stands for **cathode ray tube.**

Figure1-7
The components of a personal computer system perform the four operations of the information processing cycle.

Input

KEYBOARD AND MOUSE

Process

MONITOR

Secondary Storage

SYSTEM UNIT

Output

HARD DISK DRIVE

DISKETTE DRIVE

PRINTER

Secondary Storage Devices

Secondary storage devices, sometimes called **auxiliary storage devices,** shown in *Figure 1-7,* store instructions and data when they are not being used by the system unit. A common secondary storage device on personal computers is a diskette drive, which stores data as magnetic areas on a small plastic disk called a **diskette.** Another secondary storage device is called a hard disk drive. **Hard disk** drives contain nonremovable disks and provide larger storage capacities than diskettes.

As you can see, each component shown in *Figure 1-7* plays an important role in information processing. Collectively, this equipment is called a **computer system,** or simply a computer. The term computer is also used to refer to the system unit where the actual processing of data occurs. The input devices, output devices, and secondary storage devices that surround the system unit are sometimes referred to as **peripheral devices.**

Categories of Computers

Figure 1-8 shows the following five major categories of computers: personal computers, servers, minicomputers, mainframe computers, and supercomputers.

Computers are generally classified according to their size, speed, processing capabilities, and price. However, rapid changes in technology make firm definitions of these categories difficult. This year's speed, performance, and price classification of a mainframe might fit next year's classification of a minicomputer. Even though they are not firmly defined, the categories are frequently used and should be generally understood.

CATEGORY	PHYSICAL SIZE	SPEED*	NUMBER OF ONLINE USERS	GENERAL PRICE RANGE
Personal Computer	Hand-held to desktop or tower	1 to 100 MIPS	Usually a single user	Hundreds to several thousand $
Server	Tower or small cabinet	25 to 200 MIPS	2 to 1,000 users	$5,000 to $150,000
Minicomputer	Small cabinet to several large cabinets	Hundreds of MIPS	2 to 4,000 users	$15,000 to several hundred thousand $
Mainframe	Partial to full room of equipment	Hundreds of MIPS	Hundreds to thousands of users	$300,000 to several million $
Supercomputer	Full room of equipment	Thousands of MIPS	Hundreds of users	Several million $ and up

*speed rated in MIPS; each MIP equals one million instructions per second.

Figure 1-8
This table summarizes some of the differences between the categories of computers. Because of rapid changes in technology, these should be considered general guidelines only.

Personal Computers

Personal computers (PCs), shown in *Figure 1-9*, also called **microcomputers** or **micros**, are the small systems that have become so widely used. Classifications within this category include hand-held, palmtop, notebook, subnotebook, laptop, pen, desktop, tower, and workstation. Hand-held, palmtop, notebook, subnotebook, laptop, and pen computers are considered portable computers. Depending on their size and features, personal computer prices range from several hundred to several thousand dollars. The most expensive personal computers are generally under $10,000.

Hand-held computers *(Figure 1-9a)* are usually designed for a specific purpose such as meter reading or inventory counting and are used by workers who are on their feet instead of sitting at a desk.

Palmtop computers *(Figure 1-9b)* often have several built-in or interchangeable personal information management functions such as a calendar to keep track of meetings and events, an address and phone file, and a task list of things to do. Some palmtop computers also have limited capabilities to write correspondence and perform financial analysis. Palmtop computers do not have disk storage devices and usually have a nonstandard keyboard, meaning that the keys are not arranged like a typewriter.

Notebook computers *(Figure 1-9c)* are small enough to be carried in a briefcase but are often transported in their own carrying case. Notebooks are general-purpose computers in that they can run most application software packages. They have standard keyboards and usually have at least one disk drive for storage. Notebooks usually weigh between four and eight pounds.

Subnotebook computers *(Figure 1-9d)* are smaller versions of notebook computers and generally weigh less than four pounds. To save weight and space, some subnotebooks do not have disk drives and use special-purpose memory cards for storage.

Figure 1-9
Personal computers come in many shapes and sizes.
Shown in these photos are
(a) hand-held,
(b) palmtop,
(c) notebook,
(d) subnotebook,
(e) laptop,
(f) pen,
(g) personal digital assistant (PDA),
(h) desktop,
(i) tower, and
(j) workstation.

1-9a

1-9c

1-9b

1-9d

Laptop computers *(Figure 1-9e)* are larger versions of notebook computers that weigh between eight and fifteen pounds. The extra weight comes primarily from large-capacity disk storage devices and larger display screens.

Pen computers *(Figure 1-9f)* are specialized portable computers that use a pen-like device to enter data. Sometimes the pen is used to write information on a special input screen and sometimes it is used as a pointing device to select a processing choice presented on the screen. Pen systems have successfully replaced many applications that previously required the user to fill out a form or checklist. The unique feature about pen systems is the special software that allows the system to recognize handwritten input. One type of small pen input system is called a **personal digital assistant** (PDA) or **personal communicator**. These hand-held devices are designed for workers on the go and often have built-in communications capabilities that allow the PDA to use voice, fax, or data communications. Apple's Newton PDA *(Figure 1-9g)* has built-in intelligence that assists the user in making entries.

Desktop computers *(Figure 1-9h)* are the most common type of personal computer and are designed to fit conveniently on the surface of a desk or workspace. Desktop computers have separate display screens.

Tower computers *(Figure 1-9i)* are personal computers in an upright case. A full-size tower case provides more room for expanding the system and adding optional equipment. The most powerful personal computers are sometimes only available in tower cases. A mini-tower case, approximately half the size of a full tower case, usually has less expansion room than a desktop computer but takes up less room.

Workstations *(Figure l -9j)* are expensive high-end personal computers that have powerful calculating and graphics capabilities. Workstations are frequently used by engineers to aid in product design and testing. The term workstation is sometimes used to refer to a personal computer or terminal connected to a network.

1-9e
1-9g
1-9i
1-9f
1-9h
1-9j

Servers

Server computers, shown in *Figure 1-10,* are designed to support a computer network that allows users to share files, applications software, and hardware such as printers. The term server really describes how a computer is used. Technically, the term could be applied to any of the other categories of computers if they were used to support a network of other computers. However, in recent years manufacturers have built computers specifically designed for network use and the term server is becoming widely used to describe this type of computer. Server computers usually have the following characteristics:

- designed to be connected to one or more networks
- most powerful CPUs available
- capability to add more than one CPU to divide the processing tasks (one manufacturer's server can use up to 32 CPUs)
- large memory capacity
- large disk storage capacity, usually comprised of numerous small disks instead of several large disks
- high-speed internal and external communications

Small servers look like high-end personal computers and are priced in the $5,000 to $20,000 range. The most powerful servers look and function more like minicomputers and are priced as high as $150,000.

Minicomputers

Minicomputers, shown in *Figure 1-11,* are more powerful than personal computers and can support a number of users performing different tasks. Originally developed to perform specific tasks such as engineering calculations, their use grew rapidly as their performance and capabilities increased. Today, many businesses and other organizations use minicomputers for their information processing requirements. These systems can cost from approximately $15,000 up to several hundred thousand dollars. The most powerful minicomputers are called superminicomputers.

Figure 1-11
Minicomputers can perform many of the functions of a mainframe computer but on a smaller scale.

Figure 1-10
Server computers are designed to support a network of other computers. Servers allow the other computers to share data, applications software, and hardware resources such as printers. Small servers are simply powerful personal computers dedicated to a server function. The most powerful servers, however, are more like minicomputers. High-end servers contain multiple CPUs, numerous large-capacity disk drives, and large amounts of memory.

Figure 1-12
Mainframe computers are large, powerful machines that can handle many users concurrently and process large volumes of data.

Mainframe Computers

Mainframe computers, shown in *Figure 1-12,* are large systems that can handle hundreds of users, store large amounts of data, and process transactions at a very high rate. Mainframes usually require a specialized environment including separate air conditioning, cooling, and electrical power. Raised flooring is often built to accommodate the many cables connecting the system components underneath. The price range for mainframes is from several hundred thousand dollars to several million dollars.

Supercomputers

Supercomputers, shown in *Figure 1-13,* are the most powerful category of computers and, accordingly, the most expensive. The capability of these systems to process hundreds of millions of instructions per second is used for such applications as weather forecasting, engineering design and testing, space exploration, and other jobs requiring long, complex calculations *(Figure 1-14)*. These machines cost several million dollars.

Computers of all categories, especially personal computers, are sometimes connected to form **networks** that allow users to share data and computing resources such as software, printers, and storage devices.

Figure 1-14
This simulated weather pattern was calculated on a supercomputer.

Figure 1-13
Supercomputers are the most powerful and expensive computers.

Computer Software

As mentioned previously, a computer is directed by a series of instructions called a computer program *(Figure 1-15)* that specifies the sequence of operations the computer will perform. To do this, the program must be loaded into the main memory of the computer. Computer programs are commonly referred to as computer software. Many instructions can be used to direct a computer to perform a specific task. For example, some instructions allow data to be entered from a keyboard and stored in main memory; some instructions allow data in main memory to be used in calculations such as adding a series of numbers to obtain a total; some instructions compare two values stored in main memory and direct the computer to perform alternative operations based on the results of the comparison; and some instructions direct the computer to print a report, display information on the screen, draw a color graph on a screen, or store data on a disk.

Most computer programs are written by people with specialized training. These people, called **computer programmers**, write the instructions necessary to direct the computer to process data into information. The instructions must be placed in the correct sequence so the desired results will occur.

Complex programs may require hundreds or even thousands of program instructions. Programmers often follow a plan developed by a **systems analyst** who works with both the user and the programmer to determine and design the desired output of the program.

Computer software is the key to productive use of computers. With the correct software, a computer can become a valuable tool. Software can be categorized into two types: system software and application software.

System Software and Application Software

System software consists of programs that are related to controlling the actual operations of the computer equipment. An important part of the system software is a set of programs called the operating system. The instructions in the **operating system** tell the computer how to perform functions such as how to load, store, and execute an application program and how to transfer data between the input/output devices and main memory. For a computer to operate, an operating system must be stored in the main memory of the computer. Each time a computer is turned on, or restarted, the operating

Figure 1-15
A computer program contains instructions that specify the sequence of operations to be performed. This program is written in a language called QuickBASIC. The program prompts the user for data and then calculates and prints a sales commission amount.

Program

```
REM Program 1-15
REM Determining a Salesperson's Commission
REM Dave Brame, CIS 204, Div. 01
REM September 30, 1996
REM ****************************************
REM Clear Screen
CLS
REM Request Data from Operator
INPUT "Commission rate =====> ", Rate
INPUT "Week 1 sales ========> ", Week1
INPUT "Week 2 sales ========> ", Week2
INPUT "Return sales ========> ", Returns
REM Calculate the Earned Commission
Commission = Rate * (Week1 + Week2 - Returns)
REM Display the Earned Commission
PRINT
PRINT "Earned commission ===>"; Commission
END


[run]
```

Results

```
Commission rate =====> 0.15
Week 1 sales ========> 1200
Week 2 sales ========> 1500
Return sales ========> 75

Earned commission ===> 393.75
```

system is loaded into the computer and stored in the computer's main memory. Many different operating systems are available for computers. Today, many computers use what is called an **operating environment** that is part of or works with the operating system to make the computer system easier to use. Operating environments have a **graphical user interface** (**GUI**) that provides visual clues such as symbols, called icons, to help the user. Each **icon** represents an application software package, such as word processing, or a file or document where data is stored. Microsoft Windows 95 *(Figure 1-16)* is the latest version of Microsoft Windows, the most widely used graphical user interface operating system for personal computers. Apple Macintosh computers also have a graphical user interface built into the Macintosh operating system.

Application software consists of programs that tell a computer how to produce information. When you think of the different ways that people use computers in their careers or in their personal lives, you are thinking of examples of application software. Business, scientific, and educational programs are all examples of application software.

Application Software Packages

Most end users do not write their own programs. In some corporations, the information processing department develops custom software programs for unique company applications. Programs required for common business and personal applications can be purchased from software vendors or stores that sell computer products *(Figure 1-17)*. Purchased programs are often referred to as **application software packages**, or simply **software packages**.

Personal Computer Application Software Packages

Personal computer users often use application software packages. Some of the most widely used packages are word processing, desktop publishing, electronic spreadsheet, presentation graphics, database, communications, and electronic mail.

Figure 1-16
A graphical user interface, such as Microsoft Windows 95, makes the computer easier to use. The small pictures, or symbols, on the screen are called icons. The icons represent different processing options that the user can choose.

Figure 1-17
Many programs commonly required for business and personal applications can be purchased from computer stores.

What Are the Elements of an Information System?

Obtaining useful and timely information from computer processing requires more than just the equipment and software described so far. Other elements required for successful information processing include accurate data, trained information systems personnel, knowledgeable users, and documented procedures. Together these elements are referred to as an **information system** *(Figure 1-18).*

For an information system to provide accurate, timely, and useful information, each element in the system must be strong and all of the elements must work together. The equipment must be reliable and capable of handling the expected work load. The software must have been carefully developed and tested, and the data entered to be processed must be accurate. If the data is incorrect, the resulting information produced from it will be incorrect. Properly trained

information systems personnel are required to run most medium and large computer systems. Even small networks of personal computers usually have a system administrator to manage the system. Users are sometimes overlooked as an important element of an information system, but with expanding computer use, users are taking increasing responsibility for the successful operation of information systems. This includes responsibility for the accuracy of both the input and output. In addition, users are taking a more active role in the development of computer applications. They work closely with information systems department personnel in the development of computer applications that relate to their areas of work. Finally, all information processing applications should have documented procedures covering not only the computer operations but any other related procedures as well.

Figure 1-18

An information system requires computer equipment; software that runs on the equipment; data the computer processes; people including both computer personnel who manage the equipment and users who use the information the equipment produces; and finally procedures, that help the entire system run efficiently.

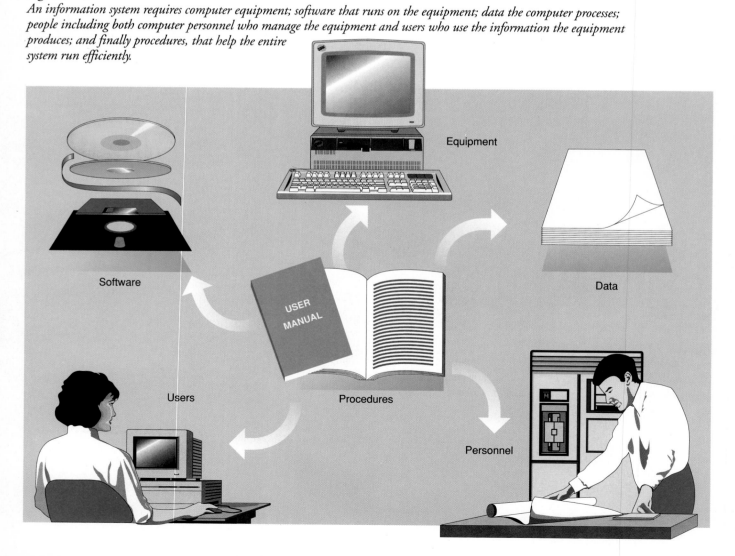

Software

Equipment

Data

USER MANUAL

Users

Procedures

Personnel

Connectivity

Connectivity refers to the capability to connect a computer to other computers. The connection may be temporary, such as when a computer is connected to an online information service provider, or permanent, such as when a computer is connected to a network of other computers. For many years, computers were used as stand-alone devices, limited to the hardware and software resources contained in that computer. Stand-alone computers are becoming the exception. Most business computers are connected to other computers as part of a network. Even home computers are increasingly used to access other computers to transfer data or to obtain information on practically any subject. You may have heard about the *Information Highway,* the United States government's plan to bring information access into the home of every citizen. This ambitious plan will create a high-speed network that will allow people, with a computer, to access government and other information. Today, millions of people use the Internet, a global network of computers, to obtain information, send messages, and obtain products and services *(Figure 1-19).* Many people believe that the computer eventually will be used for all forms of communication; written, visual, and sound.

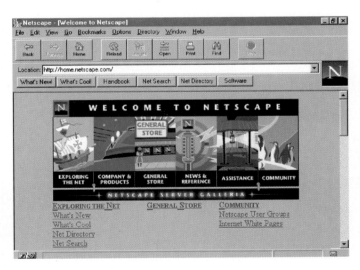

Figure 1-19
Use of the Internet has been made easier with browser *programs such as Netscape Navigator. Browsers allow users to access World Wide Web (WWW or Web) sites that have text, graphics, video, and sound and have hypertext links to other information and Web sites. This screen shows how Netscape Navigator displays the first page of information (called a* home page*) located at the Web site of Netscape Communications Corporation, the developer of Netscape Navigator.*

An Example of How One Company Uses Computers

To show you how a typical mid-sized company might use computers, this section will take you on a visual and narrative tour of Hayden Corporation, an automobile parts manufacturer. All of the computers at Hayden are joined together in a network that allows the computer users to communicate with one another and share information.

Receptionist

One of the things you notice when you enter the main lobby of Hayden is the computer sitting on the receptionist's desk *(Figure 1-20).* Outside calls are answered by the receptionist who transfers them to the appropriate employee. If an employee doesn't answer his or her phone, the receptionist can use the computer to determine the location of the employee. When employees leave their work area for a meeting, lunch, or to travel away from the office, they record their destination or reason for being away using their computer terminal. An employee can also record any special instructions to the receptionist, such as when he or she will return or to hold calls. If a caller wants to leave a voice message, the company phone system, which also uses a computer, can record the message and play it back for the employee when he or she returns or calls in for messages.

Figure 1-20 The receptionist uses the computer system to locate employees away from their desks, to record messages, and to help with general correspondence.

Sales

The Hayden sales department consists of two groups; in-house sales representatives that handle phone-in and mail-in sales orders and the field sales force that makes sales calls at customer locations. The in-house sales staff use headset phones *(Figure 1-21)* so their hands are free to use their computer keyboards. Using the computer while they are on the phone with a customer allows them to check product availability and the customer's credit status. A computer program also recommends products that compliment the products ordered by the customer and displays information on special product promotions. Field sales force representatives use notebook computers and special communications equipment and software to communicate with the Hayden main office. As with the in-house sales staff, they also can check

product availability and customer credit status. If they receive a customer order, they can enter it into the Hayden computer system while they are still at the customer site. In addition, the field sales representatives can use the electronic mail capability to check for or send messages.

Marketing

The marketing department uses the computer system for a number of purposes. Desktop publishing, drawing, and graphics software is used to develop all marketing literature *(Figure 1-22)*. Product brochures, print advertising, and product packaging are all produced in-house, saving considerable time and money. The customer service representatives all have computer terminals that allow them to record a variety of customer inquiries. Recording the nature of each customer service inquiry provides for better follow-up (less chance of forgetting an unresolved inquiry) and enables the company to summarize and review why customers are calling. This helps the company identify and resolve potential problems at an early stage. The marketing department also uses a calendar program to schedule product promotions and attendance at trade shows *(Figure 1-23)*.

Figure 1-21
Order entry personnel use the computer to check if the products requested by the customer are in stock. The system automatically displays additional products the customer might need and information on special product promotions.

Figure 1-22
Many companies now use desktop publishing and drawing software packages to create product literature and advertising materials.

Figure 1-23
Calendar programs help users plan their schedules.

Shipping and Receiving

The shipping and receiving department uses the computer system to enter transactions that keep Hayden's inventory records accurate *(Figure 1-24)*. Inventory receipts are first checked against computer records to make sure that Hayden receives only what was ordered. If the received goods match what was ordered, only a single entry has to be made to update the on-hand inventory and purchasing records. Shipping transactions are also efficient. If all requested items were in stock, only a single entry is required to decrease the inventory and create the information that will be used to prepare the billing invoice. Shipping information such as the method and time of shipment can be added to the transaction record so the computer system can be used to provide up-to-the-minute status of the customer's order.

Manufacturing

The manufacturing department uses the computer to schedule production and to record the costs of the items produced. Special manufacturing software matches the availability of production resources such as people, machines, and material against the desired product output. This information allows Hayden to efficiently schedule production and tells them when and how much to buy of the raw materials they need to produce their products *(Figure 1-25)*. Actual labor, material, and machine usage is recorded on the manufacturing floor using special terminals designed to be used in industrial environments *(Figure 1-26)*. This information is automatically entered into the computer system to update inventory, production, payroll, and cost accounting records.

Figure 1-25
Special software helps the company manufacture products.

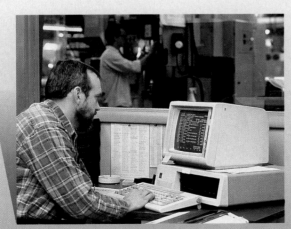

Figure 1-24
Computers help companies keep accurate inventory records.

Figure 1-26
Some computer terminals have been specially designed to withstand the heat, dust, and other conditions of a factory floor.

Engineering

The engineering department uses computer-aided design (CAD) software to design new products *(Figure 1-27)*. CAD software allows the engineers to design and review three-dimensional models of new products on the computer before expensive molds are required. If a design is approved, the CAD software can automatically produce a list of the required parts.

Accounting

The accounting department is one of the largest computer system users. Many of the accounting records are the result of transactions entered in the user departments, such as shipping and receiving and manufacturing. These records are used to pay vendor invoices, bill customers for product sales, and to process the Hayden employee payroll *(Figure 1-28)*. The accounting transactions are automatically summarized to produce Hayden's financial statements that are used internally to monitor financial performance and given to outside organizations such as banks.

Human Resources

The human resources department uses the computer system to keep track of information on existing, past, and potential employees *(Figure 1-29)*. Besides the standard information required for payroll and employee benefits, the system keeps track of employees job skills and training. This information enables the human resource department to review the records of existing employees first when a new job becomes available.

Information Systems

A primary responsibility of the information systems department is to keep the existing system running and to

Figure 1-27
Computer-aided design (CAD) software is used to design new products. As with word processing software, CAD programs make the design process easier by allowing the user to make many changes until they are satisfied.

Figure 1-28
Accounting departments were one of the first users of computer systems and still rely heavily on computers to summarize the numerous financial transactions.

Figure 1-29
Human resource departments use computers to keep track of past, present, and potential employees.

determine when and if new equipment or software is required. To help answer these questions, the information systems personnel use diagnostic and performance measurement software that tells them how much the system is being used and if system problems are being encountered *(Figure 1-30).* A systems analyst works with users to design custom software for user applications for which application software packages do not exist. A computer programmer uses the design to write the program instructions necessary to produce the desired processing results and output.

Executive

The senior management staff of Hayden Corporation (the president and three vice presidents) use the computer for an executive information system (EIS). The EIS summarizes information such as actual sales, order backlog, number of employees, cash on hand, and other performance measures into both a numeric and graphic display *(Figure 1-31).* The EIS is specifically designed for executives who do not regularly work with computers and who only want to see summarized information.

Summary of How One Company Uses Computers

The computer applications just discussed are only some of the many potential uses of a computer within Hayden Corporation. In addition, employees in each of the departments would use the computer for preparing correspondence, project and task management, budgeting, and sending messages via electronic mail.

As you can see in the Hayden Corporation example, computers are used throughout an organization. Employees use computers to perform a variety of tasks related to their job area. Because of the widespread use of computers, most organizations prefer to hire employees with computer experience and knowledge.

Summary of an Overview of Computer Concepts

This chapter presented a broad introduction to concepts and terminology related to computers. You now have a basic understanding of what a computer is, how it processes data into information, and what elements are necessary for a successful information system. You also have seen some examples of different types of computers and how they are used. Reading the overview of computer concepts in Chapter 1 will help you to more easily understand topics as they are presented in more detail in following chapters.

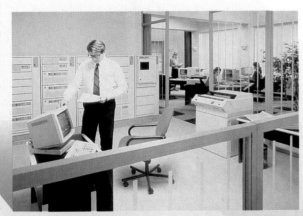

Figure 1-30
Information system personnel check on how much the computer system is being used with performance measurement software.

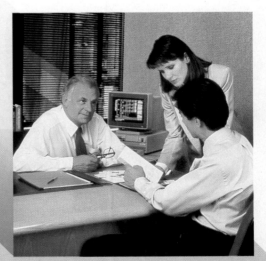

Figure 1-31
Executive information system (EIS) software usually includes graphics to convey information to users who do not frequently use the computer and who want summarized information.

C O M P U T E R S   A T   W O R K

Carnegie Mellon University: Information at Your Dorm Room

Students at Carnegie Mellon University (CMU) can access the latest in research reference materials from the comfort of their dorm rooms. CMU has long been recognized as a leader in computer science education and their Library Information System (LIS) is one of the first decentralized electronic library applications. Using nearly any type of personal computer, CMU's 5,000 students can log into a network that provides information from numerous journals on computer science, artificial intelligence, and other subjects. Eventually, CMU plans on having more than 600 journals available for review online. Some publishers, however, have been reluctant to permit their material to be added to the system. These publishers are concerned about improper use of their materials and loss of subscription revenue. But with the strong overall trend towards electronic publishing, CMU officials are confident that these issues will eventually be resolved. Students without their own personal computers can use systems in the library and at several other locations around the campus. The LIS runs on a campus-wide network supported by seven server computers. Future plans for the LIS include additional server computers, a natural language interface that will make the system easier to use, and expansion of the network to include outside resources such as commercial online services and the Internet.

Figure 1-32

IN THE FUTURE

Information Appliances

Many believe that today's personal computer will evolve into an information appliance. This device will serve as a master control for all your home systems as well as allow you to access and process information from around the world.

Numerous changes will have to take place before any one device can control so many aspects of daily life, but the trend in that direction seems to be firmly established. For one thing, computers can handle different types of information more easily than ever before. Originally limited to text and numbers, computers can now handle sound, sophisticated color graphics, and still images. Movie-length, full-motion video will be available in the near future. Entertainment, hardware, software, and communications companies are forming partnerships to provide video entertainment to individuals on demand. This merging of industries and products is sometimes referred to as digital convergence, the conversion of all types of data into digital input that can be processed and stored by a computer. All forms of voice communications are now heavily computerized, including wireless communication from almost any location on earth.

Even everyday household appliances such as washers, driers, and refrigerators are becoming smarter. These and many other products now use embedded computer chips to help them work more efficiently. Eventually, these embedded computers will be capable of communicating with and be controlled by computers. This will enable you to start dinner and turn on the home air-conditioning before you leave the office; if you work in an office, that is. Another change computers have enabled is working away from the office. With existing communications capabilities, many people work at home and commute to the office electronically.

Can you imagine having to use a remote control to visually search through the 500 or more TV channels that will be available or to look through the directories of five online databases to find information on a single topic? New ways of presenting information will be developed so users can quickly make informed selections from expanded information choices. Smart software will be developed that will perform the necessary research to meet our information requests. Computers will undoubtedly be used to help users sort through all of the information, entertainment, and communications options.

Figure 1-33

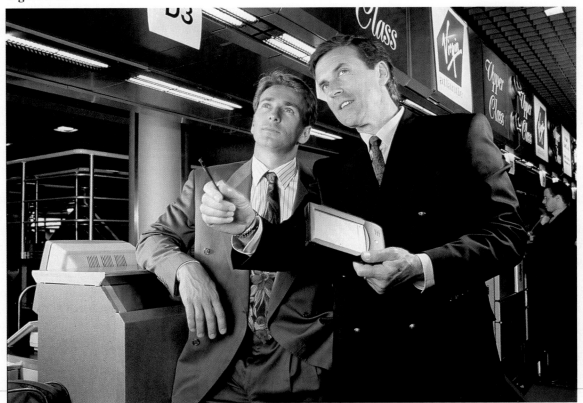

File   Edit   Section   Page   Tools   Options   Help

What You Should Know

1. **Computer literacy** is knowing how to use a computer and **information literacy** is knowing how to find, analyze, and use information.

2. A **computer** is an electronic device, operating under the control of instructions stored in its own memory unit, that can accept data (input), process data arithmetically and logically, produce output from the processing, and store the results for future use.

3. The **information processing cycle** is composed of four general operations: input, process, output, and storage.

4. All computer processing requires **data**–raw facts, including numbers, words, images, and sounds, given to a computer during the input operation. In the processing phase, the computer manipulates data to create **information**–data that has been processed into a form that has meaning and is useful.

5. **Information processing**, sometimes called **data processing (DP)**, is the production of information by processing data on a computer.

6. People who either use the computer directly or use the information it provides are called **computer users**, **end users**, or **users**.

7. A computer's power derives from its capability to perform input, process, output, and storage operations with speed and reliability and to store large amounts of information.

8. A **computer program**, also called **program instructions** or **software**, is a detailed set of instructions that tell a computer exactly what to do.

9. The first three operations of the information processing cycle, **input**, **process**, and **output**, describe the procedures that a computer performs to process data into information. The fourth operation, **storage**, describes a computer's electronic storage capability.

10. Data is processed by specific equipment that is often called computer **hardware**.

11. **Input devices** are used to enter data into a computer. Two common input devices are the **keyboard** and the **mouse**. The mouse is used to move a small symbol, called a **mouse pointer** or **pointer**, that appears on the computer screen.

12. A computer's **system unit** contains the electronic circuits that actually cause the processing of data to occur. The system unit includes the central processing unit, main memory, and other electronic components.

13. The **central processing unit** (CPU) contains a **control unit** that executes the program instructions and an **arithmetic/logic unit** (ALU) that performs math and logic operations. **Arithmetic operations** include numeric calculations such as addition, subtraction, multiplication, and division. **Logical operations** are comparisons of data to see if one value is greater than, less than, or equal to another.

14. **Main memory**, also called RAM (**Random Access Memory**) or **primary storage**, temporarily stores data and program instructions when they are being processed.

15. **Output devices** present the output from a computer. The two most commonly used output devices are the **printer** and the **monitor**, also called the **screen** or the CRT (which stands for **cathode ray tube**).

16. **Secondary storage devices**, or **auxiliary storage devices**, store instructions and data when they are not being used by the system unit. Common secondary storage devices on personal computers store data as magnetic areas on a **diskette** or **hard disk**.

17. Collectively, the equipment that performs the four operations of the information processing cycle is called a **computer system**. The input devices, output devices, and secondary storage devices that surround the system unit are sometimes referred to as **peripheral devices**.

18. The five major categories of computers are: personal computers, servers, minicomputers, mainframe computers, and supercomputers. Computers are generally classified according to their size, speed, processing capabilities, and price.

19. **Personal computers**, also called **microcomputers** or **micros**, are the small systems that have become so widely used in recent years. Depending on their size and features, personal computer prices range from several hundred to several thousand dollars. Classifications within this category include **hand-held computers**, **palmtop computers**, **notebook computers**, **subnotebook computers**, **laptop computers**, **pen computers**, (such as a **personal digital assistant** (PDA) or **personal communicator**), **desktop computers**, **tower computers**, and **workstations**.

20. **Server** computers are designed to support a computer network that allows users to share files, applications software, and hardware. Small servers look like high-end personal computers and are priced in the $5,000 to $20,000 range, while the most powerful servers look and function more like minicomputers and are priced as high as $150,000.

21. **Minicomputers** are more powerful than personal computers and can support a number of users performing different tasks. These systems cost from approximately $15,000 to several hundred thousand dollars.

22. **Mainframe** computers are large systems that can handle hundreds of users, store large amounts of data, and process transactions at a very high rate. The price range for mainframes is from several hundred thousand dollars to several million dollars.

23. **Supercomputers**, the most powerful category of computers and, accordingly, the most expensive, are capable of processing hundreds of millions of instructions per second. These machines cost several million dollars.

24. Computers of all categories, especially personal computers, are sometimes connected to form **networks** that allow users to share data and computer resources.

25. Computer programs, commonly referred to as computer software, specify the sequence of operations the computer will perform. **Computer programmers** write the instructions (computer programs) necessary to direct the computer to process data into information. Programmers often follow a plan developed by a **systems analyst**, who works with both the user and the programmer to determine and design the desired output of the program.

26. **System software** consists of programs that are related to controlling the actual operations of the computer equipment. The instructions in the **operating system**, a component of system software, tell the computer how to perform functions such as how to load, store, and execute an application program and how to transfer data between the input/output devices and main memory.

27. Today, many computers use an **operating environment** that works with the operating system to make the computer easier to use. Operating environments have a **graphical user interface** (GUI) that provides visual clues, such as symbols called icons, to help the user. Each **icon** represents an application software package or a file or document where data is stored.

28. **Application software** consists of programs that tell a computer how to produce information. Programs required for common business and personal applications can be purchased from software vendors or stores that sell computer products. Purchased programs are often referred to as **application software packages** or simply **software packages**. Some of the more widely used packages for personal computer users are: word processing, desktop publishing, electronic spreadsheet, presentation graphics, database, communications, and electronic mail software.

29. In addition to a computer system and software, other elements required for successful information processing include accurate data, trained information systems personnel, knowledgeable users, and documented procedures. Together these elements are referred to as an **information system**.

30. **Connectivity** refers to the capability to connect a computer to other computers. The connection may be temporary or permanent.

31. A typical mid-sized company might use computers in a variety of areas, including: the receptionist, sales department, marketing department, shipping and receiving department, manufacturing department, engineering department, accounting department, human resources department, information systems department, and executive level.

32. Because of the widespread use of computers, most organizations prefer to hire employees with computer experience and knowledge.

File   Edit   Section   Page   Tools   Options   Help

Terms to Remember

arithmetic/logic unit (ALU) (1.8)
application software (1.15)
application software package (1.15)
arithmetic/logic unit (ALU) (1.8)
arithmetic operation (1.8)
auxiliary storage device (1.9)

cathode ray tube (CRT) (1.8)
central processing unit (CPU) (1.8)
computer (1.4)
computer literacy (1.2)
computer program (1.6)
computer programmer (1.14)
computer system (1.9)
computer users (1.5)
connectivity (1.17)
control unit (1.8)
CPU (central processing unit) (1.8)
CRT (cathode ray tube) (1.8)

data (1.4)
data processing (DP) (1.5)
desktop computer (1.11)
diskette (1.9)
DP (data processing) (1.5)

end users (1.5)

graphical user interface (GUI) (1.15)
GUI (graphical user interface) (1.15)

hand-held computers (1.10)
hard disk (1.9)
hardware (1.7)

icon (1.15)
information (1.4)
information literacy (1.2)
information processing (1.5)
information processing cycle (1.4)
information system (1.16)
input (1.7)
input device (1.7)

keyboard (1.7)

laptop computer (1.11)
logical operation (1.8)

main memory (1.8)
mainframe (1.13)
micro (1.10)
microcomputer (1.10)
minicomputer (1.12)
monitor (1.8)
mouse (1.7)
mouse pointer (1.7)

network (1.13)
notebook computer (1.10)

operating environment (1.15)
operating system (1.14)
output (1.7)
output device (1.8)

palmtop computer (1.10)
PC (personal computer) (1.10)
PDA (personal digital assistant) (1.11)
pen computer (1.11)
peripheral device (1.9)
personal communicator (1.11)
personal computer (PC) (1.10)
personal digital assistant (PDA) (1.11)
pointer (1.7)
primary storage (1.8)
printer (1.8)
process (1.7)
program instructions (1.6)

RAM (Random Access Memory) (1.8)
Random Access Memory (RAM) (1.8)

screen (1.8)
secondary storage device (1.9)
server (1.12)
software (1.6)
software package (1.15)
storage (1.7)
subnotebook computer (1.10)
supercomputer (1.13)
system software (1.14)
system unit (1.8)
systems analyst (1.14)

tower computer (1.11)

users (1.5)

workstation (1.11)

Test Your Knowledge

Fill in the Blanks

1. A(n) _____ is an electronic device, operating under the control of instructions stored in its memory unit, that can accept input, process the input arithmetically and logically, produce output from the processing, and store the results for future use.

2. The four operations of the information processing cycle are: _____, _____, _____, and _____.

3. During information processing, the computer manipulates _____–raw facts given to a computer during the input operation–to create _____–input that has been converted into a form that has meaning and is useful.

4. The central processing unit (CPU) contains a(n) _____ that executes program instructions and a(n) _____ that performs math and logic operations.

5. Collectively, the equipment that performs the four operations of the information processing cycle is called a(n) _____, and the input devices, output devices, and secondary storage devices that surround the system unit are referred to as _____.

Short Answer

1. What is the difference between computer literacy and information literacy? How do computers relate to information literacy?

2. What three characteristics make the computer such a powerful tool? Describe each.

3. How are computers generally classified? What are the five major categories of computers? Briefly describe each. Why is it difficult to make firm definitions of these categories?

4. What is computer software? How is system software different from application software?

5. What is an information system? How do the six elements of an information system work together?

Label the Figure

Instructions: The figure below represents a computer system. In the spaces provided, label the components of the system.

File   Edit   Section   Page   Tools   Options   Help

Points to Ponder

1

Cynics once said that it's not *what* you know, it's *who* you know that is important. With the increasing emphasis on information literacy, however, it might be argued that now it's not *what* you know, it's *how you can find out* that is most significant. What do you think? What changes, if any, should schools make to better address information literacy? How should computers be used in schools to enhance information literacy?

2

Some technological innovations, such as the telephone and the automobile, have had a significant impact on society at large, in both positive ways and negative ways. Together with a classmate, present a debate on the ways computers have affected society. One of you should argue that the impact of computers has been primarily positive and the other that the impact has been primarily negative. When the debate is over, and your classmates have had their say, see if you can reach a consensus on whether, overall, society is better off, or worse off, with the proliferation of computers.

3

Despite the reliability of computers, everyone has heard of "computer errors." Describe a situation you are familiar with (either through reading or personal experience) in which a "computer error" occurred. Who, or what, do you feel was responsible for the error? What steps do you think could be taken to ensure that the error does not happen again?

4

Your school has been given a grant to purchase a supercomputer, a mainframe computer, several mini-computers, and a number of personal computers. How do you think each category of computer would be best used in your school? Who should have access to each computer? If the money for personal computers had to be spent on three different types of personal computers, what kind do you think should be purchased and how should they be used?

5

This chapter describes how computers are used in the Hayden Corporation, an automobile manufacturer. You have been hired as a consultant to the Hayden Corporation and asked to provide a worst-case and a best-case scenario. If, due to financial difficulties, the computers in one part of the organization have to be moved to another department, which part of the organization do you feel could best withstand the loss? Why? If, as a result of increased profits, the Hayden Corporation is able to purchase additional computer equipment, where should the equipment go to most benefit the corporation as a whole? Why?

6

From the timeline presented following this chapter, you can see that many of the most notable developments in the computer industry took place over the past thirty years. Draw a hypothetical timeline that chronicles the computer industry over the next twenty years. On your timeline, place and describe at least six developments you think will have a significant impact on the computer industry during the next two decades.

File   Edit   Section   Page   Tools   Options   Help

Out and About

1. Visit a library or book store and examine at least three different current magazines aimed at computer users. Write down the name of all three magazines and make a list of the titles of articles in each. Look at the advertisements. What is the most expensive computer equipment advertised? What is the least expensive? What, in your opinion, is the most unusual computer equipment advertised? Do you think each magazine is intended for a particular type of computer user? Why or why not?

2. Interview a person who uses a computer every day at work, and prepare a report on that person's feelings about computers. Some of the questions you might ask are: How is the computer used? Did the person feel any anxiety when first confronted with the computer? What type of computer training did the individual receive? How does the computer make this person's job easier? How does the computer make this person's job more difficult? What kind of computer education would this individual recommend to students interested in going into the same field?

3. Visit a computer vendor and interview the manager or a salesperson. Based on your interview, prepare a report on the demographics of the typical computer buyer at that store. Find the answers to such questions as: What gender are most computer purchasers? In what age range are the buyers? What is their average age? What seems to be the characteristic educational level of a computer buyer? Approximately what is their average income? Why do most purchasers buy a computer?

4. Rent a videotape in which a computer plays a major part–some examples are *2001: A Space Odyssey, War Games,* and *Short Circuit.* Watch the videotape, then prepare a report on how the movie makers view computers. What part did the computer play in the movie? In general, was the computer a hero, a villain, or simply the tool of a human character? Why? What was the theme of the movie? What role, if any, did the computer play in promoting the theme?

5. Prepare a detailed report on one of the individuals or events depicted on the timeline following this chapter. Describe the impact the individual or event has had on the computer industry. How do you think the computer industry would be different if the individual had never existed or if the event had never taken place?

6. Visit a store that sells computer software and examine the application software packages. Make a list of at least five application packages you would like to have on your personal computer. Most application software is written for a specific operating system (system software). Write down the name of the operating system with which each of the application packages you selected is designed to work. If one (or more) of your applications does not work with the same operating system as the others, try to locate a similar application package. Your goal is to find five application packages that all work with the same operating system. Make a list of your final five application packages, and note the operating system that they all use. What features, if any, did you have to give up to find five applications that use the same operating system?

Start   1:04 AM

File   Edit   Section   Page   Tools   Options   Help

In the Lab with Windows 95

1 **Shelly Cashman Series Mouse Lab**   Click the Start button on the taskbar, point to Programs on the Start menu, and then click Shelly Cashman Series on the Programs submenu. When the Shelly Cashman Series Labs screen displays *(Figure 1-34),* if Using the Mouse is not selected, use the UP or DOWN ARROW key to select it. Press ENTER. When the introductory screen displays, carefully read the objectives. With your printer turned on, press the P key on the keyboard to print the questions for the Mouse Lab. Fill out the top of the Questions sheet and answer the questions as you step through the Mouse Lab. Click the Exit button to close the Shelly Cashman Series Labs.

2 **Shelly Cashman Series Keyboard Lab**   Follow the instructions in Windows 95 Lab 1 to display the Shelly Cashman Series Labs screen. Click Using the Keyboard. Click the Start Lab button. When the initial screen displays, carefully read the objectives. With your printer turned on, click the Print Questions button. Fill out the top of the Questions sheet and answer the questions as you step through the Keyboard Lab. Close the Shelly Cashman Series Labs.

3 **Learning the Basics of Microsoft Windows 95** Click the Start button on the taskbar, and then click Help on the Start menu to display the Help Topics: Windows Help dialog box. Click the Contents tab, double-click Introducing Windows, double-click Welcome, double-click A List of What's New, and then double-click A new look and feel. When the Windows Help window displays, click the Options button, click Print Topic on the Options menu, and then click the OK button to print the topic. One by one, click

each topic button and read the information. Using pencil and paper, answer the following questions as you step through this Lab: (1) describe three uses of the taskbar; (2) explain how a file can be moved or copied using Windows Explorer; (3) describe what characters can be used in filenames; (4) explain how you can access an item's properties; (5) identify the term used for folders in previous versions of Windows; (6) explain how you can view a shortcut menu; (7) draw the button used to close a window; (8) explain how Help can be obtained in dialog boxes. Click the Close button on any open Help window's title bar to close the window(s).

4 **Improving Mouse Skills**   Click the Start button on the taskbar, point to Programs on the Start menu, point to Accessories on the Programs submenu, point to Games on the Accessories submenu, and then click Solitaire *(Figure 1-35)* on the Games submenu. When the Solitaire window displays, click its Maximize button. Click Help on Solitaire's menu bar and then click Help Topics. Click the Contents tab and then double-click How to play Solitaire. Read and print the topic by clicking the Options button, clicking Print Topic, and then clicking the OK button. Click the Help Topics button to return to the Contents sheet. Double-click Scoring information. Read and print the topic. To close the Solitaire Help window, click its Close button. Play the game of Solitaire. To quit Solitaire, click the Solitaire window's Close button.

Figure 1-34

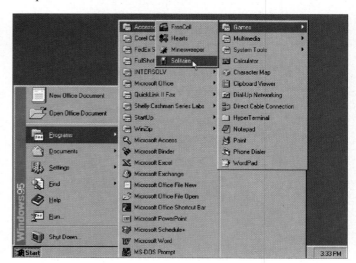

Figure 1-35

File   Edit   Section   Page   Tools   Options   Help

Where on the Web

1 **Use Yahoo Directory**   Programs for common business and personal applications often are referred to as application software packages. Complete the following steps to increase your understanding of the number of different types of application software packages and the companies that create them. With Netscape on the screen (*Figure 1-19* on page 1.17), click the Net Search button. Click Yahoo. Scroll down and click Computers. Scroll down and click Software. Click File on the menu bar. Click Print on the File menu. Click Pages and then type 1 in the To text box to print just the first page. Click OK. Write the three categories of most interest to you on the printout and hand it in.

2 **Choose a Car on the Web**   Information literacy is knowing how to find, analyze, and use information. Complete the following steps to find information on the Internet about your favorite car. With Netscape on the screen, type http://www.dealernet.com in the Location text box and then press ENTER. Click New Cars. Scroll through the list of manufactures and click the check box next to one you are interested in. Scroll down and click the Submit button. Click one of the models. Click one of the dealers for more information, such as that shown in *Figure 1-36*. Click Print on the File menu. Click the Print button on the Netscape toolbar and then type 1 in the To text box. Click OK. Hand in the printout.

3 **Monitor Info**   The monitor is one of the two most commonly used output devices of a computer. Complete the following steps to learn more about monitors.

With Netscape on the screen, type http://www.nec.com in the Location text box and press ENTER. Scroll down and type monitors in the NEC SITE SEARCH box. Click SEARCH. Scroll down the page and click one of the monitors listed. Click Print on the File menu. Click OK. Hand in the printout.

4 **Map the Internet**   Connectivity refers to the capability to connect a computer to other computers. Complete the following steps to learn more about the connectivity of World Wide Web servers across the Internet. With Netscape on the screen, type http://www.vtourist.com/webmap in the Location text box and then press ENTER. Scroll down and click North America on the map. Click United States. Scroll down and click the state you are in. Click your city or region. Click Print on the File menu. Click OK. Hand in the printout.

5 **Shelly Cashman Online**   Additional exercises for this chapter are available at the Shelly Cashman Online World Wide Web site *(Figure 1-37)*. Perform the following steps to access these exercises. With Netscape on the screen, type http://www.bf.com/scseries.html in the Location text box and then press ENTER. Click Student Center. Scroll down and click Using Computers: A Gateway To Information World Wide Web Edition. Scroll down and click Chapter 1. Complete the activities listed.

Figure 1-36

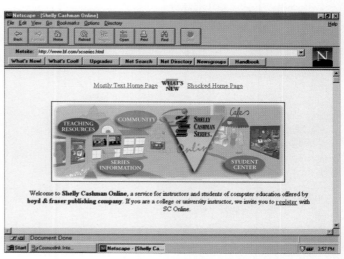

Figure 1-37

Start   1:06 AM

The Evolution of the Computer Industry

The electronic computer industry began more than fifty years ago.

1937

Dr. John V. Atanasoff and his assistant Clifford Berry designed and began to build the first electronic digital computer during the winter of 1937-38. Their machine, the Atanasoff-Berry-Computer, or ABC, provided the foundation for the next advances in electronic digital computers.

1943

During the years 1943 to 1946, Dr. John W. Mauchly and J. Presper Eckert, Jr. completed the ENIAC (Electronic Numerical Integrator and Computer), the first large-scale electronic digital computer. The ENIAC weighed thirty tons, contained 18,000 vacuum tubes, and occupied a thirty-by-fifty-foot space.

1952

In 1952, Dr. Grace Hopper, a mathematician and commodore in the U.S. Navy, wrote a paper describing how to program a computer with symbolic notation instead of the detailed machine language that had been used.

Dr. Hopper was instrumental in developing high-level languages such as COBOL, a business application language introduced in 1960. COBOL uses English-like phrases and runs on most computers, making it one of the more widely used languages in the world.

1953

The IBM model 650 was one of the first widely used computer systems. Originally, IBM planned to produce only 50 machines, but the system was so successful that eventually it manufactured more than 1,000.

Core memory, developed in the early 1950s, provided much larger storage capacities and greater reliability than vacuum tube memory.

This timeline summarizes the major events in the evolution of the computer industry.

1945   1951   1952

In 1951-52, after much discussion, IBM decided to add computers to its line of business equipment products. This led IBM to become a dominant force in the computer industry.

Dr. John von Neumann is credited with writing a brilliant report in 1945 describing several new hardware concepts and the use of stored programs. His breakthrough laid the foundation for the digital computers that have since been built.

J. Presper Eckert, Jr., standing left, explains the operations of the UNIVAC I to newsman Walter Cronkite, right. This machine was the first commercially available electronic digital computer.

Public awareness of computers increased when, in 1951, the UNIVAC I, after analyzing only 5% of the tallied vote, correctly predicted that Dwight D. Eisenhower would win the presidential election.

1957   1958   1959

By 1959, more than 200 programming languages had been created.

FORTRAN (FORmula TRANslator) was introduced in 1957, proving that efficient, easy-to-use programming languages could be developed. FORTRAN is still in use.

In 1958, computers built with transistors marked the beginning of the second generation of computer hardware. Previous computers built with vacuum tubes were first-generation machines.

1960

1964

1965

From 1958 to 1964, the number of computers in the U.S. grew from 2,500 to 18,000.

Third-generation computers, with their controlling circuitry stored on chips, were introduced in 1964. The IBM System/360 computers were the first third-generation machines.

In 1965, Dr. John Kemeny of Dartmouth led the development of the BASIC programming language. BASIC is still widely used on personal computers.

1969

1970

1975

In 1969, under pressure from the industry, IBM announced that some of its software would be priced separately from the computer hardware. This "unbundling" allowed software firms to emerge in the industry.

The fourth-generation computers built with chips that used LSI (large-scale integration) arrived in 1970. The chips used in 1965 contained as many as 1,000 circuits. By 1970, the LSI chip contained as many as 15,000.

The MITS, Inc. Altair computer, sold in kits for less than $400, was the first commercially successful microcomputer.

ETHERNET, developed at Xerox PARC (Palo Alto Research Center) by Robert Metcalfe, was the first local area network (LAN). Originally designed to link minicomputers, ETHERNET was later extended to personal computers. The LAN allows computers to communicate and share software, data, and peripherals such as printers.

1967

Digital Equipment Corporation (DEC) introduced the first minicomputer in 1965.

PASCAL, a structured programming language, was developed by Swiss computer scientist Niklaus Wirth between 1967 and 1971.

1968

The software industry emerged in the 1960s. In 1968, Computer Science Corporation became the first software company to be listed on the New York Stock Exchange.

1969

In 1969, Dr. Ted Hoff of Intel Corporation developed a microprocessor, or microprogrammable computer chip, the Intel 4004.

1976

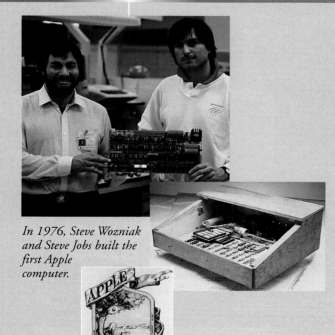

In 1976, Steve Wozniak and Steve Jobs built the first Apple computer.

1979

The first public online information services, CompuServe and the Source, were founded.

The VisiCalc spreadsheet program written by Bob Frankston and Dan Bricklin was introduced in 1979. This product was originally written to run on Apple II computers. Together, VisiCalc and Apple II computers rapidly became successful. Most people consider VisiCalc to be the singlemost important reason why personal computers gained acceptance in the business world.

1980

In 1980, IBM offered Microsoft Corporation's founder, Bill Gates, the opportunity to develop the operating system for the soon-to-be announced IBM personal computer. With the development of MS-DOS, Microsoft achieved tremendous growth and success.

1981

The IBM PC was introduced in 1981, signaling IBM's entrance into the personal computer marketplace. The IBM PC quickly garnered the largest share of the personal computer market and became the personal computer of choice in business.

1982

More than 300,000 personal computers were sold in 1981. In 1982, the number jumped to 3,275,000

1984

Apple introduced the Macintosh computer, which incorporated a unique graphical interface, making it easy to learn.

1987

Several personal computers utilizing the powerful Intel 80386 microprocessor were introduced in 1987. These machines handled processing that previously only large systems could handle.

1983

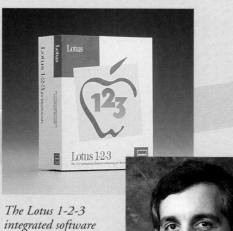

Instead of choosing a person for its annual award, TIME magazine named the computer "Machine of the Year" for 1982. This event acknowledged the impact of the computer on society.

The Lotus 1-2-3 integrated software package, developed by Mitch Kapor, was introduced in 1983. It combined spreadsheet, graphics, and database programs in one package.

1984

IBM introduced a personal computer, called the PC AT, that used the Intel 80286 microprocessor.

1989

The Intel 486 became the world's first 1,000,000 transistor microprocessor. It crammed 1.2 million transistors on a sliver of silicon that measured .4" x .6" and executed instructions at 15 MIPS (million instructions per second) — four times as fast as its predecessor, the 80386 chip. The 80 designation used with previous Intel chips, such as the 80386 and 80286, was dropped with the 486.

1990

Microsoft released Windows 3.0, a substantially enhanced version of its Windows graphical user interface first introduced in 1985. The software allowed users to run multiple applications on a personal computer and more easily move data from one application to another. The package became an instant success, selling hundreds of thousands of copies.

By 1990, more than 54 million computers were in use in the United States.

1992

Apple introduced a personal digital assistant (PDA) called the Newton MessagePad. This 7 $^1/4$ -by-4 $^1/2$ -inch personal computer incorporates a pen interface and wireless communications.

1993

Several companies introduced computer systems using the Pentium microprocessor from Intel. The Pentium chip is the successor to the Intel 486 microprocessor. It contains 3.1 million transistors and is able to perform 112 million instructions per second (MIPS).

1993

The Energy Star program, endorsed by the Environmental Protection Agency (EPA), encouraged manufacturers to build computer equipment that meets strict power consumption guidelines. Manufacturers meeting the guidelines can then display the Energy Star logo on their products.

1995

Intel begins shipment of the Pentium Pro microprocessor, the successor to its widely used Pentium chip. The Pentium Pro microprocessor contains 5.5 million transistors and is able to perform 250 million instructions per second (MIPS).

1995

Microsoft releases Windows 95, a major upgrade to its Windows operating system, the leading graphical user interface for PCs. Windows 95 consists of over 10 million lines of computer instruction developed by 300 person-years of effort. Over 50,000 individuals and companies tested the software before it was released.

"The personal computer industry is on the verge of a new revolution that will bring dramatic changes to the way people work by making software much more personalized and by providing easier access to online sources."

More than 50 million PCs were sold worldwide in 1995, Over 250 million are in use.

In the U.S. 2 out of 3 employees have access to a PC. 1 out of every 3 homes has a PC.

Bill Gates
COMDEX '95

Computer Software Applications: User Tools

Objectives

After completing this chapter, you will be able to:

- Identify the most widely used personal computer software applications

- Describe productivity software

- Define and describe a user interface and a graphical user interface

- Explain the key features of each of the major applications

- Explain the advantages of integrated software

- List and describe learning aids and support tools that help users to use personal computer software applications

Today, understanding the applications commonly used on personal computers is considered a part of being computer literate. In fact, a working knowledge of at least some of these applications is now considered by many employers to be a required skill. Because of this, personal computer software applications are discussed early in this book. Learning about each of the most widely used applications will help you understand how people use personal computers in our modern world. Before discussing the applications, the user interface is explained. The user interface controls how the user works with the software and applies to all the applications. After learning about individual applications, you will learn about integrated software; the combination of several applications into a single software package. Finally, some of the aids and tools that are available to help you learn and use software applications are discussed.

Productivity Software

This chapter will introduce you to nine widely used personal computer software applications:
- Word processing
- Desktop publishing
- Spreadsheet
- Database
- Presentation graphics
- Communications
- Electronic mail
- Personal information management
- Project management

These software applications are used by a wide range of organizations and individuals. Because these applications help people perform their work more efficiently, they are sometimes referred to as **productivity software**.

Although these applications are discussed as they are used on personal computers, they are actually available on computers of all sizes. The concepts you will learn about each application package on personal computers will also apply if you are working on a larger system.

User Interface

To more easily learn about productivity software, you need to understand some of the features of a user interface. A **user interface** is the way the user tells the software what to do and the way the computer displays information and processing options to the user. One of the most common user interfaces is the graphical user interface (GUI). The **graphical user interface**, or **GUI** (pronounced gooey), combines text and graphics to make the software easier to use. Graphical user interfaces include several common features such as windows, icons, menus, and buttons.

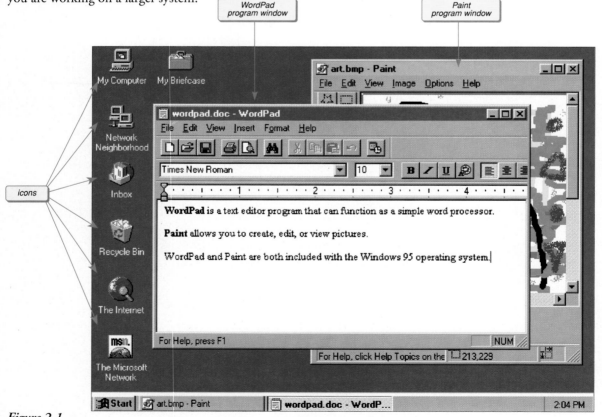

Figure 2-1

Two key features of a graphical user interface (GUI) are windows and icons. Windows are rectangular areas that present information. Icons are symbols that represent processing options or documents. In this screen, two windows are open; the WordPad program window in the foreground and the Paint program window in the background. Several windows can be open at the same time and moved from back to front so all information on a window can be seen. The icons along the left side of the screen represent other applications that can be started.

A **window** is a rectangular area of the screen that is used to present information *(Figure 2-1)*. They are called windows because of their capability to see into another part of a program. Many people consider windows to be like multiple sheets of paper on top of a desk. In the same way that each piece of paper on the desk contains different information, each window on the screen contains different information. Just as papers can be moved from the bottom of a pile to the top of the desk when they are needed, windows can be created on a screen and moved around to show information when it is needed. The term Windows, with a capital W, refers to **Microsoft Windows,** the most popular graphical user interface for personal computers. **Windows 95** is the most recent version of Windows.

Icons are pictures or symbols that are used to represent processing options, such as an application or a program, or documents, such as a letter or spreadsheet *(Figure 2-1)*.

A **menu** is a list of options from which the user can choose. **Commands** are instructions that cause the computer software to perform a specific action. *Figure 2-2* displays commands associated with the Windows 95 Start menu.

A **button** is an icon (usually a rectangular or circular shape) that causes a specific action to take place. Buttons are selected using a pointing device such as a mouse, and many can be activated by using the keyboard. *Figure 2-3,* shows several different types of buttons.

The features of a user interface make it easier for the user to communicate with the computer. You will see examples of these features and how they are used as you learn about the various personal computer applications.

Figure 2-2
A menu is a list of commands from which the user can choose. Some commands are followed by a right arrow. A right arrow indicates that a submenu of additional commands exists. A command followed by an ellipsis (...) indicates that additional information will be requested before the command is executed. On the screen shown in this figure, the Start menu is shown on the left and the Settings submenu is shown to the right.

Figure 2-3
A button is an icon that causes a specific action to take place. This screen shows several types of buttons. Many applications contain a row of buttons with icons called a toolbar. The icon indicates what happens when the button is clicked. For example, the first four buttons on the top toolbar shown on this screen perform the following tasks; start a new document, open an existing document, save the document, and print the document, respectively. Option buttons modify the action that will take place, such as printing all or a range of pages. Stand-alone buttons can contain text or icons and are referred to as command buttons.

Word Processing Software

The most widely used computer application is word processing. **Word processing software** enables a computer to produce or modify documents that consist primarily of text. Millions of people use word processing software every day to create letters, memos, reports, and other documents. A major advantage of using word processing to produce a document is the capability to easily change what has been done. Because the document is stored electronically, you can add, delete, or rearrange words, sentences, or entire sections. The document can be printed as many times as you like with each copy looking as good as the first. With older methods such as using a typewriter, making changes and reprinting a document take much more time. Using word processing software is also an efficient way of storing documents because many documents can be stored on a disk or diskette. If computers are connected in a network, stored documents can be shared among users.

Today, most people perform word processing using personal computers or larger computer systems such as minicomputers or mainframes. These computers are also used for other applications. **Dedicated word processing systems**, used only for word processing, also exist.

Producing a document using word processing usually consists of four steps: creating, editing, formatting, and printing. A fifth step, saving the document, should be performed frequently throughout the process so work will not be lost.

frequently throughout the proc

Creating

Creating a word processi text, usually by using the keybo features used during the creatin scrolling, and moving the curso

- Word Wrap. **Word wrap** pro when the text reaches a certa such as the right-hand margi user can continue typing and return or line feed key.
- Scrolling. **Scrolling** is the pr so the user can view any por documents as having been cr paper *(Figure 2-4)*. The scree window that allows a portion The document can be moved the screen window. For wide scrolled left and right, as wel
- Moving the Cursor. The **curs underline character, rectangle where on the screen the next

cursor control keys, on the **ke** character or line at a time. If movement is repeated until th efficient ways to move the **cu** using the Page Up and Page I so work will not be lost.

ocument involves entering

. Key word processing

ep include word wrap,

es an automatic line return

osition on the document,

Jnlike a typewriter, the

es not have to press a

s of moving the document

. Think of multipage

ed on a continuous roll of

an be thought of as a

the document to be seen.

rolled) up or down behind

cuments, the screen can be

is a symbol, such as an

vertical bar that indicates

racter will appear. The

ard, move the cursor one

keys are held down, the

ey is released. More

farther and faster include

vn keys to move a page (or

Creating

Creating a word processing document involves entering text, usually by using the keyboard. Key word processing features used during the creating step include word wrap, scrolling, and moving the cursor.

- Word Wrap. **Word wrap** provides an automatic line return when the text reaches a certain position on the document, such as the right-hand margin. Unlike a typewriter, the user can continue typing and does not have to press a return or line feed key.

- Scrolling. **Scrolling** is the process of moving the document so the user can view any portion. Think of multipage documents as having been created on a continuous roll of paper *(Figure 2-4)*. The screen can be thought of as a window that allows a portion of the document to be seen. The document can be moved (scrolled) up or down behind the screen window. For wide documents, the screen can be scrolled left and right, as well.

- Moving the Cursor. The **cursor** is a symbol, such as an underline character, rectangle, or vertical bar that indicates where on the screen the next character will appear. The cursor is moved by using the mouse or keyboard. The cursor control keys, on the keyboard, move the cursor one character or line at a time. If the keys are held down, the movement is repeated until the key is released. More efficient ways to move the cursor farther and faster include using the Page Up and Page Down keys to move a page (or screen) at a time and the Home and End keys to move to the beginning or end of a line. Other key combinations can be used to move to the beginning of words, paragraphs, or the start or end of the document.

Figure 2-4
Scrolling is the process of moving the document so the portion you want to see is displayed on the screen. It's as if the document had been created on a continuous roll of paper. The limited size of the screen only allows you to see a portion of the document. The document can be moved (scrolled) up or down and right or left so any portion of the document that will fit on one screen can be seen.

Editing

Editing is the process of making changes in the content of a document. Word processing editing features include cutting, copying, and pasting, inserting and deleting, and searching and replacing. Advanced editing features include spell checking, using a thesaurus, and grammar checking.

- Cut, Copy, and Paste. To **cut** involves removing a portion of the document and electronically storing it in a temporary location called the **Clipboard.** Whatever is on the Clipboard can be placed somewhere else in the document by giving a **paste** command. When you **copy,** a portion of the document is duplicated.
- Insert and Delete. When you **insert,** you add text to a document. When you **delete,** you remove text. Most word processors are normally in the *insert mode,* meaning that as you type, any existing text is pushed down the page to make room for the new text. However, word processors can be placed in a *typeover mode* (also called *overtype mode*), where new text replaces any existing text.

- Search. The **search** feature lets you find all occurrences of a particular character, word, or combination of words. Search can be used in combination with **replace** to substitute new letters or words for the old.
- Spelling Checker. A **spelling checker** allows you to review individual words, sections of a document, or the entire document for correct spelling. Words are compared to an electronic dictionary included in the word processing software. Some spelling checker dictionaries contain more than 120,000 words. If a match is not found, a list of similar words that may be the correct spelling is displayed *(Figure 2-5).* You can select one of the suggested words displayed, ignore the suggestions and leave the word unchanged, or add the unrecognized but properly spelled word to the dictionary so it will not be considered misspelled in the future. Many users customize their software dictionaries by adding company, street, city, and personal names so the software can check the correct spelling of those words.

While spelling checkers can catch misspelled words and words that are repeated such as *the the,* they cannot identify words that are used incorrectly. A thesaurus and grammar checker will help you to choose proper words and use them in a correct manner.

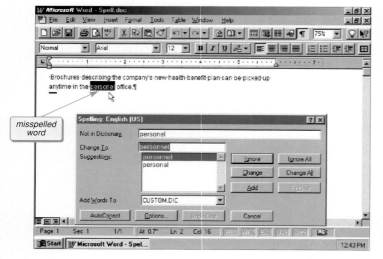

Figure 2-5
A spelling checker identifies words that do not match entries in the spelling checker dictionary. Alternative words are suggested and can be substituted for the unidentified word.

Figure 2-6
Grammar checking software identifies grammar, writing style, and sentence structure errors. As shown on this screen, most grammar checkers offer a possible solution when they detect a problem.

- Thesaurus. A **thesaurus** allows you to look up synonyms for words in a document while you are using your word processor. Using a thesaurus is similar to using a spelling checker. When you want to look up a synonym for a word, you place the cursor on the word to check, and activate the thesaurus with either a keyboard command or by using a pointing device. The thesaurus software displays a list of possible synonyms. If you find a word you would rather use, you select the desired word from the list and the software automatically incorporates it in the document by replacing the previous word.
- Grammar Checker. A **grammar checker** is used to check for grammar, writing style, and sentence structure errors *(Figure 2-6)*. This software can check documents for excessive use of a word or phrase, identify sentences that are too long, and find words that are used out of context such as *four* example.

Formatting

To **format** means to change the appearance of a document. Formatting is important because the overall look of a document can significantly affect its capability to communicate. For documents being sent to clients, it is not unusual to spend more time formatting the document than in entering the text. Word processing features that can be used to format a document include the following *(see Figure 2-7):*
- Typeface, Font, and Style. A **typeface** is a specific set of characters that are designed the same. Helvetica and Times New Roman are examples of typefaces. The size of a typeface is measured in points. Each **point** is approximately 1/72 of an inch. The text you are reading in this book is ten point type. A specific combination of typeface and point size is called a **font,** though it is common to hear and read of typefaces being called fonts. A particular **style,** such as **bold**, *italics,* or underlining, can be applied to a font to make it stand out.

Figure 2-7
Examples of word processing formatting features.

- Margins and Justification. **Margins** specify the space in the border of a page and include the left, right, bottom, and top margin. **Justification**, also called **alignment**, deals with how text is positioned in relation to a fixed reference point, usually a right or left margin. **Full justification** aligns text with both the left and right margins. Left justification and right justification align with the left and right margins only. Centered justification divides the text equally on either side of a reference point, usually the center of the page.
- Spacing. **Spacing** deals with how far apart individual letters (horizontal spacing) and lines of text (vertical spacing) are placed. With **monospacing**, each character takes up the same amount of space. With **proportional spacing**, wide characters, such as a W or M, are given more space than narrow characters, such as an I. **Line spacing** increases the distance from the bottom of one line to the bottom of the next line. Single and double line spacing are the most common, but exact distances can also be specified in some word processing software.

- Columns, Tables, and Graphics. Most word processors can arrange text in two or more columns, like a newspaper or magazine. The text from the bottom of one column automatically flows to the top of the next column. Tables are a way of organizing information in rows and columns. Word processors that support tables enable the user to easily add and change table information and move the entire table as a single item, instead of as individual lines of text. Although word processors are primarily designed to work with text, most can now incorporate graphics such as drawings and pictures. Some graphics are included in word processing packages, however, graphic items are usually created in separate applications and imported (brought into) the word processing document.
- Borders and Shading. Borders and shading can be used to emphasize or highlight sections of a word processing document. A **border** is a decorative line or box that is used with text, graphics, or tables. **Shading** darkens the background area of a section of a document or table. Colors can be used for borders and shading but will print as black or gray unless you have a color printer.

Portrait Orientation

MEMORANDUM

TO:　　　　　All Village Creek Employees

FROM:　　　　Christine Reddings, Training Supervi

DATE:　　　　December 1, 1995

SUBJECT:　　**Computer Training Seminars**

On Monday, January 2, 1996, we will begin using new versions cessing and electronic spreadsheet software. To prepare you fc we are offering the following training seminars.

Word Processing *(December 8, 1995, 1:00 p.m. - 4:30 p.m.)*

This seminar focuses on the new word processor features. Thro and hands-on exercises, you will create, edit, format, save and p Bring a blank formatted disk to the seminar.

Electronic Spreadsheets *(December 12, 1995, 8:00 a.m. - 11.*

This seminar addresses the new features of the electronic sprea ware. During the session, you will build worksheets with calculat graphs. Bring a blank formatted disk to the seminar.

Integrating Your Software *(December 15, 1995, 2:00 p.m. - 4.*

This seminar illustrates how to merge worksheet data and graph processing documents. Bring a disk containing one word proces one electronic spreadsheet file.

These training seminars will be held in Room C-312. Once you h selections(s), please check with your supervisor and then call m 290 to make a reservation.

Landscape Orientation

Village Creek Industries
Personnel Database

Last Name	First Name	Hire Date	Age	Gender	Education	Department	Title	Salary
Hoika	Janice	11/12/71	60	F	BS	R&D	Engineer	52,500
Webb	Marci	2/4/95	34	F	AAS	Computer	Programmer	36,500
Ling	Jodi	2/26/92	25	F	MS	Computer	Analyst	47,400
Webster	Jeffrey	5/22/84	47	M	AAS	R&D	Technician	36,250
Sabol	Lisa	7/15/94	52	F	BS	Marketing	Manager	47,500
Chin	Ben	1/5/89	22	M	HS	Administration	Clerk	18,500
Brown	Jeremiah	9/4/87	29	M	PhD	R&D	Engineer	48,900
Sobalski	Joseph	9/2376	44	M	BS	Marketing	Telemarketer	29,700
Raih	Niki	5/18/79	36	F	AAS	Administration	Receptionist	24,300
Nyguen	Sue	1/17/82	32	F	BS	Computer	Programmer	43,200
Stephens	James	6/22/84	31	M	HS	Mail Room	Clerk	17,400
Rae	Amy	11/26/92	57	F	MS	Production	Manager	52,200
McCarthy	Kevin	1/11/80	62	M	MA	Personnel	Director	57,600
Dolar	Laura	11/2/85	46	F	AA	Production	Supervisor	46,000

Figure 2-8
Most correspondence is printed in portrait orientation; printing across the narrower portion of a sheet of paper. In landscape orientation, the printing goes across the wider portion of the paper.

- Page Numbers, Headers, and Footers. Most word processors can automatically apply page numbers to any location on the page. Page numbers can be started at a particular number and can appear in a font different from the main body of text. **Headers** and **footers** allow you to place the same information at the top or bottom of each page. A company name, report title, date, or page number are examples of items that may appear in a header or footer.
- Style Sheets. A **style sheet** lets you save font and format information so it can be applied to new documents. A style sheet can save you considerable time if you use different formatting techniques on frequently created documents. Company letterhead, a memorandum, or a report that is prepared each month are examples of items that could use style sheets.

Printing

Most word processors give the user many options other than printing a single copy of the entire document.
- Number of Copies and Pages. The capability to print individual pages and a range of pages (for example, pages 2 through 7) is usually available. In addition, the user can specify how many copies are to be printed.
- Portrait and Landscape. **Portrait** printing means that the paper is taller than it is wide. Most letters are printed in portrait orientation. **Landscape** printing means that the paper is wider than it is tall. Tables with a large number of columns are often printed in landscape orientation. See *Figure 2-8* for examples.
- Print Preview. **Print preview** *(Figure 2-9)* allows the user to see on the screen how the document will look when it is printed. In print preview you can see one or more pages. Even though the text may be too small to read, you can review the overall appearance and decide if the page needs additional formatting.

With the features available in word processing packages, users can easily and efficiently create professional looking documents. Packages such as WordPerfect and Microsoft Word may contain enough features to satisfy the desktop publishing needs of many users. However, the document design capabilities of desktop publishing packages still exceed the capabilities of word processing software.

Figure 2-9
Print preview allows you to see on the screen how the document will look when it is printed. This feature helps you decide if the overall appearance of the document is acceptable or if the document needs more formatting.

Desktop Publishing Software

Desktop publishing (DTP) software allows users to design and produce professional looking documents that contain both text and graphics *(Figure 2-10)*. Examples of such documents include newsletters, marketing literature, technical manuals, and annual reports. Documents of this type were previously created by slower, more expensive traditional publishing methods such as typesetting.

Whereas word processing software is designed to manipulate text, DTP software focuses on page composition and layout. **Page composition and layout**, sometimes called **page makeup**, is the process of arranging text and graphics on a document page. The text and graphics used by a DTP program are frequently imported from other software packages. For example, because text manipulation capabilities of word processing packages exceed those offered in DTP packages, text is usually created with a word processor and then transferred into the desktop publishing package. Graphics objects, such as illustrations, and photographs, are also imported from other software packages. Illustration software that is designed for use by artists, such as Corel Draw and Aldus Freehand, is often used to create graphics for DTP documents.

Business\Credit   Business\Globe   Business\File

Business\Head   Business\Dice

Figure 2-11
Clip art consists of previously created illustrations that can be added to documents. Clip art usually comes in collections of individual images that are grouped by type. These clip art examples are from a business collection.

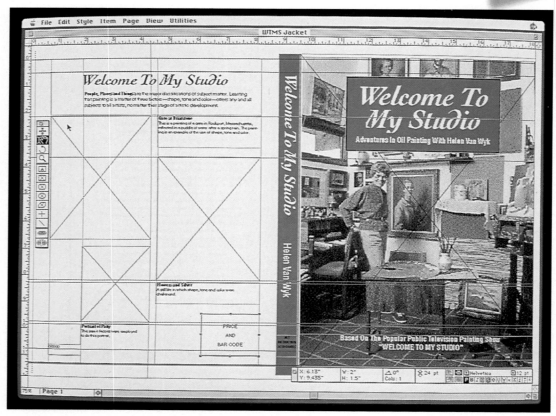

Figure 2-10
Desktop publishing software is used to create professional looking documents that combine text, graphics, illustrations, and photographs.

In addition, DTP documents often make use of pre-viously created art, called **clip art**, that is sold in collections. Collections of clip art contain several hundred to several thousand images grouped by type, such as holidays, vehicles, or people. *Figure 2-11* shows examples of different clip art. Input devices, called scanners, can also be used to import photographs and art into DTP documents.

To aid the user in the process of page layout and design, all DTP programs display information on the screen exactly as it will look when printed. This capability is called WYSIWYG (pronounced whiz-e-wig). **WYSIWYG** is an acronym for What You See Is What You Get. Although many application programs now offer the WYSIWYG feature, DTP software packages were among the first.

Some of the other page composition and layout features that distinguish DTP software include the following (some of these features are illustrated in *Figure 2-12*):

- Capability to increase or decrease the size of graphic objects
- Capability to rotate text and graphics objects
- Backgrounds of different shades, colors, and textures
- Large page sizes (up to 18" by 24")
- Capability to flow text around irregularly shaped objects
- Capability to easily add or delete entire columns or pages
- Rulers and guides for aligning text and graphics
- Precise horizontal and vertical spacing control
- Color control

The capability to print DTP documents relies on a page definition language. A **page definition language**, such as **PostScript**, describes the document to be printed in language the printer can understand. The printer, which includes a page definition language translator, interprets the instructions and prints the document. Using a page definition language enables a DTP document created on one computer system to be printed on another computer with a different printer, as long as the second printer has a compatible page definition language.

With desktop publishing, users can now create profes-sional looking documents on their own computers and produce work that previously could only be done by graphic artists. By using desktop publishing, both the cost and time of producing quality documents is significantly decreased. Popular desktop publishing packages include PageMaker, QuarkXpress, and Corel Ventura.

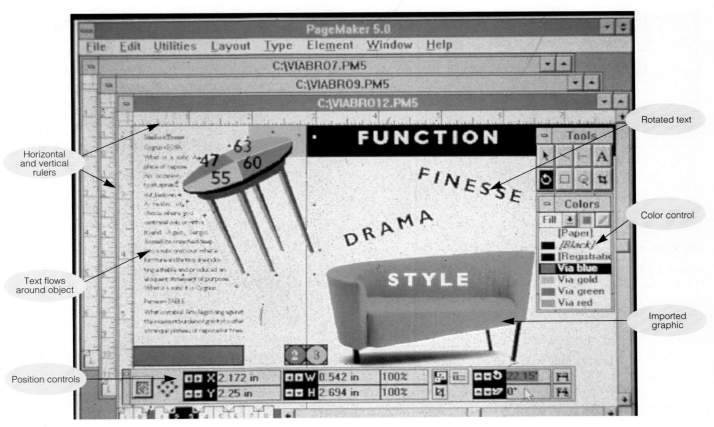

Figure 2-12
Some of the features available in the PageMaker desktop publishing software package are shown in this screen.

Spreadsheet Software

Spreadsheet software allows you to organize numeric data in a worksheet or table format called an **electronic spreadsheet** or **spreadsheet**. Manual methods, those done by hand, have long been used to organize numeric data in this manner *(Figure 2-13)*. You will see that the data in an electronic spreadsheet is organized in the same manner as it is in a manual spreadsheet. Within a spreadsheet, data is organized vertically in **columns** and horizontally in **rows**. Columns are usually identified by a letter and rows by a number. The intersection where a column and row meet is called a **cell** *(Figure 2-14)*. Cells are named by their location in the spreadsheet. In *Figure 2-14,* the cursor is on cell C2, the intersection of column C and row 2.

Cells may contain three types of data: labels (text), values (numbers), and formulas. The text, or **labels**, as they are called, identify the data and help document the worksheet.

Good spreadsheets contain descriptive labels. The rest of the cells in a spreadsheet may appear to contain numbers, or **values**. However, some of the cells actually contain formulas. The **formulas** perform calculations on the data in the spreadsheet and display the resulting value in the cell containing the formula. Formulas can be created by the user or can use functions that come with the spreadsheet software. **Functions** are stored formulas that perform common calculations, such as adding a range of cells, or generating a value such as the time or date. *Figure 2-15* is a list of functions found in most spreadsheet packages.

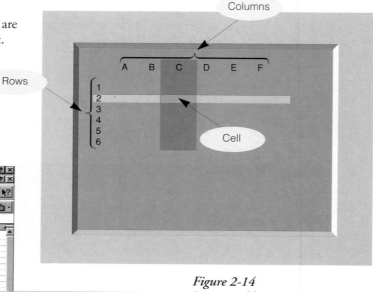

Figure 2-14
In a spreadsheet, columns refer to the vertical lines of data and rows refer to the horizontal lines of data. Columns are identified by letters and rows are identified by numbers. The intersection of a column and row is called a cell.

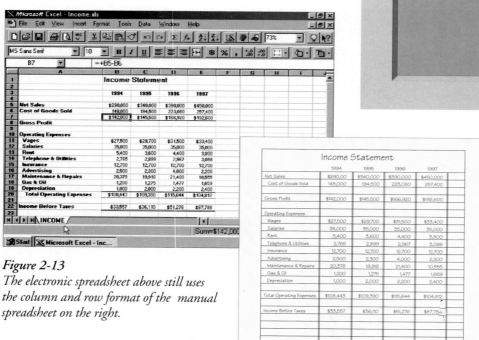

Figure 2-13
The electronic spreadsheet above still uses the column and row format of the manual spreadsheet on the right.

By developing a simple spreadsheet to calculate the profit and profit % from three months of revenues and costs, you will see how a spreadsheet works. As shown in *Figure 2-16,* the first step in creating the spreadsheet is to enter the labels, or titles. These should be short but descriptive, to help you organize the layout of the data in your spreadsheet.

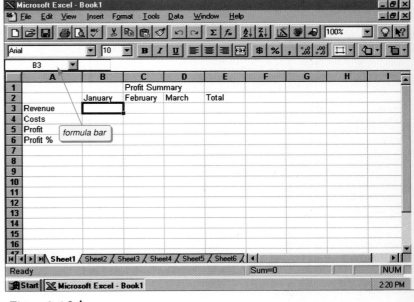

Figure 2-15 ▼
Spreadsheet functions are predefined formulas that perform calculations or return information based on given data. This is just a partial list of some of the more common functions. Probably the most often used function is SUM, which is used to add a range of numbers.

Figure 2-16 ▲
Labels such as January, February, Revenue, and Costs are entered in the spreadsheet to identify columns and rows of data. The formula bar shows the address and contents of the active cell. Here, the active cell is B3 (column B, row 3). Nothing has been entered for this cell, so the formula bar shows only the cell address.

SPREADSHEET FUNCTIONS

FINANCIAL
FV (rate, number of periods, payment)	Calculates the future value of an investment.
NPV (rate, range)	Calculates the net present value of an investment.
PMT (rate, number of periods, present value)	Calculates the periodic payment for an annuity.
PV (rate, number of periods, payment)	Calculates the present value of an investment.
RATE (number of periods, payment, present value)	Calculates the periodic interest rate of an annuity.

DAY & TIME
DATE	Returns the current date.
NOW	Returns the current date and time.
TIME	Returns the current time.

MATHEMATICAL
ABS (number)	Returns the absolute value of a number.
INT (number)	Rounds a number down to the nearest integer.
LN (number)	Calculates the natural logarithm of a number.
LOG (number, base)	Calculates the logarithm of a number to a specified base.
ROUND (number, number of digits)	Rounds a number to a specified number of digits.
SQRT (number)	Calculates the square root of a number.
SUM (range)	Calculates the total of a range of numbers.

STATISTICAL
AVERAGE (range)	Calculates the average value of a range of numbers.
COUNT (range)	Counts how many cells in the range have entries.
MAX (range)	Returns the maximum value in a range.
MIN (range)	Returns the minimum value in a range.
STDEV (range)	Calculates the standard deviation of a range of numbers.

LOGICAL
IF (logical test, value if true, value if false).	Performs a test and returns one value if test is true and another value if test is false.

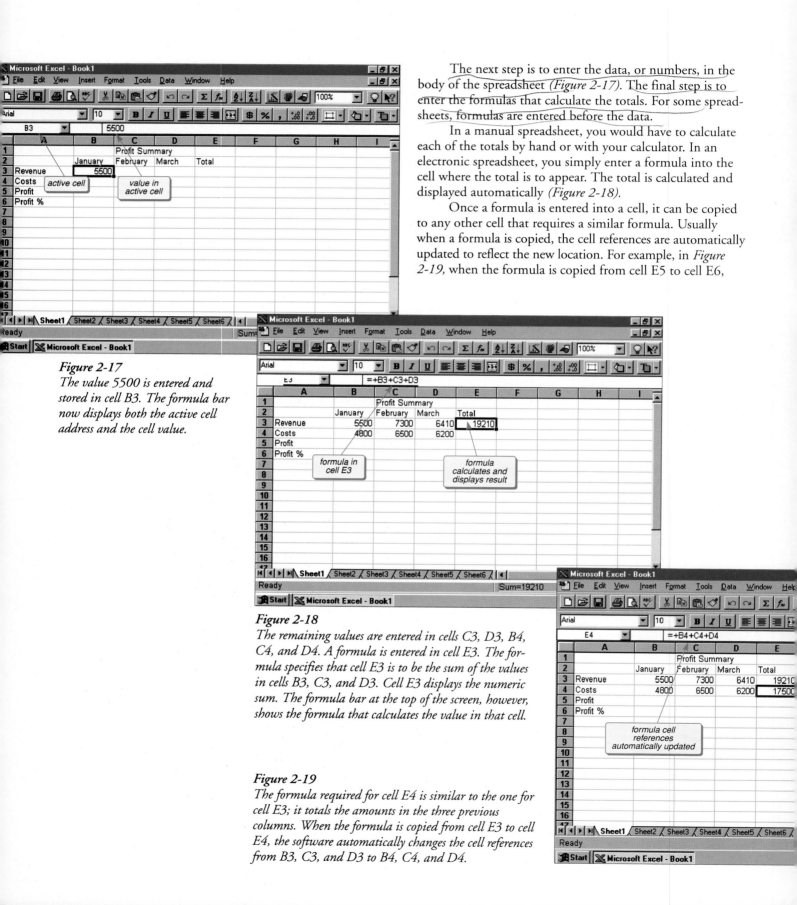

The next step is to enter the data, or numbers, in the body of the spreadsheet *(Figure 2-17)*. The final step is to enter the formulas that calculate the totals. For some spreadsheets, formulas are entered before the data.

In a manual spreadsheet, you would have to calculate each of the totals by hand or with your calculator. In an electronic spreadsheet, you simply enter a formula into the cell where the total is to appear. The total is calculated and displayed automatically *(Figure 2-18)*.

Once a formula is entered into a cell, it can be copied to any other cell that requires a similar formula. Usually when a formula is copied, the cell references are automatically updated to reflect the new location. For example, in *Figure 2-19*, when the formula is copied from cell E5 to cell E6,

Figure 2-17
The value 5500 is entered and stored in cell B3. The formula bar now displays both the active cell address and the cell value.

Figure 2-18
The remaining values are entered in cells C3, D3, B4, C4, and D4. A formula is entered in cell E3. The formula specifies that cell E3 is to be the sum of the values in cells B3, C3, and D3. Cell E3 displays the numeric sum. The formula bar at the top of the screen, however, shows the formula that calculates the value in that cell.

Figure 2-19
The formula required for cell E4 is similar to the one for cell E3; it totals the amounts in the three previous columns. When the formula is copied from cell E3 to cell E4, the software automatically changes the cell references from B3, C3, and D3 to B4, C4, and D4.

the formula changes from B5+C5+D5 to B6+C6+D6. This automatic updating of the formula is called **relative referencing**.

If you are going to copy a formula but always want the formula to refer to the same cell location, you would use **absolute referencing**. For example, if you had a single tax rate that was going to be used to calculate taxes on the amounts in more than one cell, you would make an absolute reference to the cell containing the tax rate. To make a cell an absolute reference, you place a dollar sign in front of the column and row. E5 in a formula would be an absolute reference to cell E5. As the formula is copied, the formula calculations are performed automatically. After entering the remaining formulas, the spreadsheet is complete *(Figure 2-20)*.

One of the more powerful features of the electronic spreadsheet occurs when the data in a spreadsheet changes. To appreciate the capabilities of spreadsheet software, consider how a change is handled in a manual system. When a value in a manual spreadsheet changes, you must erase it and write a new value into the cell. You must also erase all cells that contain calculations referring to the value that changed and then you must recalculate these cells and enter the new result.

For example, the row totals and column totals would be updated to reflect changes to any values within their areas. In a large manual spreadsheet, accurately posting changes and updating the values affected would be time consuming and new errors could be introduced. But posting changes on an electronic spreadsheet is easy. You change data in a cell by simply entering in the new value. All other values that are affected are updated automatically. *Figure 2-21* shows that if you change the value in cell C3 from 7300 to 8000, five other cell values will automatically change. On a computer, the updating happens almost instantly.

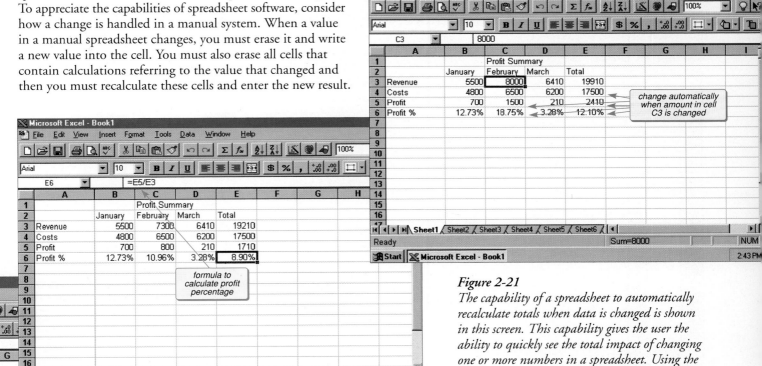

Figure 2-20
In the completed spreadsheet, the value in cell E6 is derived from the formula in the formula bar, which specifies that the value in cell E5 is to be divided by the value in cell E3 (the slash character indicates division).

Figure 2-21
The capability of a spreadsheet to automatically recalculate totals when data is changed is shown in this screen. This capability gives the user the ability to quickly see the total impact of changing one or more numbers in a spreadsheet. Using the spreadsheet shown in Figure 2-20, one number was changed; the Revenue amount for February. This one change results in five numbers automatically recalculating in the spreadsheet.

A spreadsheet's capability to recalculate when data is changed makes it a valuable tool for decision making. This capability is sometimes called **what-if analysis** because the results of different assumptions ("what-if we changed this ...") can be quickly seen.

A standard feature of spreadsheet packages is the capability to create **charts** that graphically present the relationship of numerical data. Visual representation of data in charts often makes it easier to analyze and interpret information. The types of charts provided by spreadsheet packages are sometimes called **analytical graphics** or **business graphics** because they are primarily used for the analysis of numerical data by businesses. *Figure 2-22* shows the chart types offered in one spreadsheet package.

Most of these charts are variations on three basic chart types; line charts, bar charts and pie charts. Line charts are effective for showing a trend as indicated by a rising or falling line. If the area below or above a line is filled in with a color or pattern, it is called an area chart. **Bar charts** display bars of various lengths to show the relationship of data *(Figure 2-23)*. The bars can be horizontal, vertical (sometimes called columns), or stacked one on top of the other. **Pie charts**, so called because they look like a pie cut into pieces, are effective for showing the relationship of parts to a whole. Pie charts are often used for budget presentations to show how much each part of the budget is a percentage of the total. To improve their appearance, most charts can be displayed or printed in a three-dimensional (3-D) format.

Figure 2-22
Spreadsheet data can be used to create numerous types of charts. This screen shows 15 types of charts that are available with the Microsoft Excel spreadsheet package.

Figure 2-23
A simple bar chart can be created from spreadsheet numeric data as shown in this Excel screen.

Besides the capability to manipulate numbers, spreadsheet packages have many formatting features that can improve the overall appearance of the data. These include typefaces, sizes, and styles, borders and lines, and shading and colors to highlight data. *Figure 2-24* shows the spreadsheet with some of these features added.

Spreadsheets are one of the most popular software packages and have been adapted to a wide range of business and nonbusiness applications. Some of the popular packages used today are Lotus 1-2-3, Microsoft Excel, and Quattro Pro.

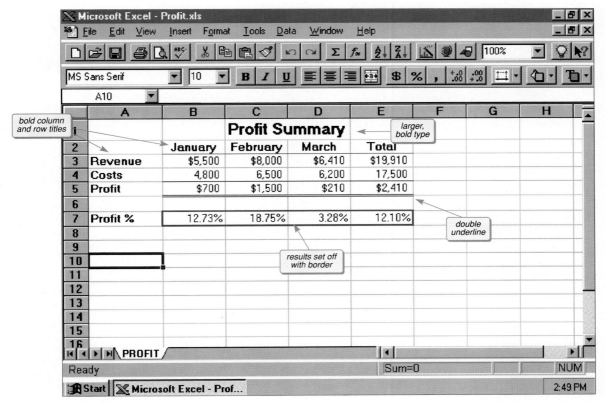

Figure 2-24
This formatted spreadsheet shows how the formatting features improve the appearance of a document.

Database Software

A **database** refers to a collection of data that is stored in files. **Database software** allows you to create a database and to retrieve, manipulate, and update the data that you store in it. In a manual system *(Figure 2-25)*, data is recorded on paper and stored in a filing cabinet. In a database on the computer, the data will be stored in an electronic format on a secondary storage device such as a disk.

Figure 2-25
A database is similar to a manual system; related data items are stored in files.

When you use a database, you need to be familiar with the terms file, record, and field. Just as in a manual system, the word **file** is a collection of related data that is organized in records. Each **record** contains a collection of related facts called **fields**. For example, an address file might consist of records containing name and address information. All the data that relates to one name would be considered a record. Each fact, such as the street address or phone number, is called a field.

The screens in *Figures 2-26* through *2-29* present the development of a database containing information about the members of a school band booster club. The booster club members donate money to help fund band activities. Besides keeping track of each member's name, address, and phone number, the band director wants to record the amount of money donated and the date the money was received.

A good way to begin creating a database is to make a list of the information you want to record. Each item that you want to keep track of will become a field in the database. Each field should be given a unique name that is short but descriptive. For example, the field name for a member's last name could be LNAME. The field name for a member's first

Figure 2-26
One of the first steps in creating a database is to make a list of the items that will be included in the database. The list should include the item description, a short, one-word field name that will be used by the database, the length of the item, and the data type. Most databases allow you to add or delete fields after the database is created.

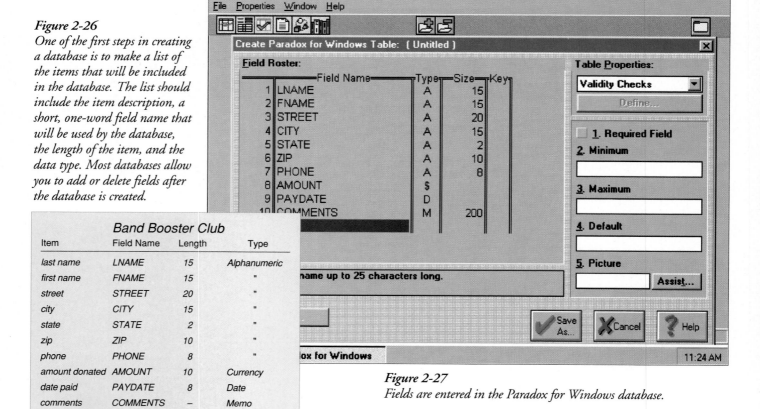

Figure 2-27
Fields are entered in the Paradox for Windows database.

name could be FNAME. Additional information that needs to be decided is the length of each field and the type of information that each field will contain. The type of information could be any of the following:
- **Alphanumeric** – letters, numbers, or special characters
- **Numeric** – numbers only
- **Currency** – dollar and cents amounts
- **Date** – month, day, and year information
- **Memo** – free form text of any type or length

A list of the information necessary for the band booster club is shown in *Figure 2-26*.

Each database program differs slightly in how it requires the user to enter the file and field information. A field entry screen from the Paradox for Windows database software package is shown in *Figure 2-27*.

After the database structure is created by defining the fields, individual database records can be entered. Usually, they are entered one at a time by using the keyboard. However, most database programs also have the capability to import data from other files. The information specified for each field helps the user in entering the data. For example, designating the DATE PAID field as a date field prevents

the user from entering anything other than a valid date. Comparing data entered against a predefined format or value is called **validation** and is an important feature of database programs. *Figure 2-28* shows the entry screen for the band booster club data.

After the records are entered, the database can be used to produce information. All or some of the records can be selected and arranged in the order specified by the user. This is one of the most powerful features of a database; the capability to retrieve database information based on criteria specified by the user. For example, suppose the band director wanted to personally call and thank all the booster club members who donated more than $100. A report, called a **query** could be produced that listed the members names, phone numbers, and the amounts and dates donated. An example of such a report is shown in *Figure 2-29*.

As shown in the band boosters club example, database software assists users in creating files and storing, manipulating, and retrieving data. Popular software packages that perform these functions include dBASE, FoxPro, Microsoft Access, and Paradox.

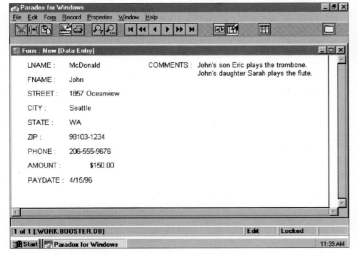

Figure 2-28
Once the database fields are defined, data can be entered. Most database programs automatically create a data entry form based on information that was entered for the fields. This Paradox for Windows data entry form lists each of the database fields in the order they were entered. Advanced database features can be used to design more complex data entry forms.

Figure 2-29
Database software packages can produce reports based on criteria specified by the user. For example, this screen shows the result of a request, called a query, that specified the name and phone number of each booster club member that contributed $100 or more. The amount and date of the contribution were also requested. The results of the query can be displayed on the screen or printed.

Presentation Graphics Software

Presentation graphics software allows the user to create documents, called **slides**, that are used in making presentations before a group *(Figure 2-30)*. The slides can be displayed on a large monitor or projected on a screen. Presentation graphics goes beyond analytical graphics by offering the user a wider choice of presentation features. Some of the features included with most presentation graphics packages include:

- Numerous chart types
- Three-dimensional effects for charts, text, and graphics
- Special effects such as shading, shadows, and textures
- Color control that includes preestablished groups of complementary colors for backgrounds, lines and text, shadows, fills, and accents
- Image libraries that include clip art graphics that can be incorporated into the slides; the image libraries are usually business oriented and include illustrations of factories, people, money, and other business-related art

Besides the slides, presentation graphics packages create several other documents that can be used in a presentation *(Figure 2-31)*. *Outlines* include only the text from each slide, usually the slide title and the key points. A *notes page* is used

outline

handout

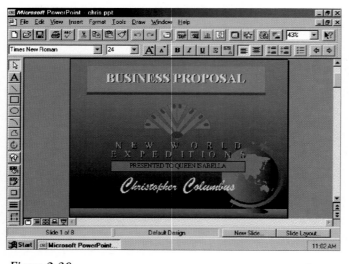

Figure 2-30
Presentation graphics software is used to prepare slides used in making presentations. The slides can be displayed on a computer, projected on a screen, or printed and handed out. The presentation graphics software includes many features to control graphics objects and color to make the slides more visually interesting.

notes page

Figure 2-31
Documents that can be created with presentation software packages.

transparency

by the speaker making the presentation and includes a picture of the slide and any notes the speaker wants to see when he or she is discussing the slide. Audience *handouts* include images of two or more slides on a page that can be given to people who attended the presentation.

To help organize and present the slides, presentation graphics packages include slide sorters. A slide sorter presents a screen view similar to how 35mm slides would look on a photographer's light table *(Figure 2-32)*. By using a mouse or other pointing device, the user can arrange the slides in any order. When the slides are arranged in the proper order, they can be displayed one at a time by clicking the mouse or using the keyboard. The presenter can also set up the slides to be automatically displayed with a predetermined time delay between each slide. Special effects can also be applied to the transition between each slide. For example, one slide might slowly dissolve as the other slide comes into view.

Using presentation graphics software allows you to efficiently create professional quality presentations that help communicate information more effectively. Studies have shown that people are more likely to remember information they have seen as well as heard and that they recall 25% more information when it is presented in color. Popular presentation graphics packages include Microsoft PowerPoint, Aldus Persuasion, Lotus Freelance Graphics, and SPC Harvard Graphics.

Figure 2-32
This slide sorter screen shows a miniature version of each slide. Using a pointing device or the keyboard, the slides can be rearranged to change their order of presentation.

Data Communications Software

Data communications software is used to transmit data from one computer to another. For two computers to communicate, they each must have data communications software, data communications equipment, and be connected by some type of link such as a telephone line. Features that most data communications software packages include are:

- A dialing directory of phone numbers that can be used to automatically connect with other computer systems *(Figure 2-33)*
- Automatic redial that lets the user set the number of times the computer will keep trying to connect with another computer if the line is busy; a time delay between call attempts can also be set
- Automatic answer if another user tries to call your computer
- The capability to send or receive one or more data files

Communications software is frequently used by employees that are away from the office. Using communications software (and sometimes other packages such as E-mail), remote employees can check their messages, send messages to other employees, check the quantity of inventory on hand, and enter orders that they have just received from customers.

Communications software is also used to access online services for news, weather, financial, and travel information. Online service companies such as Prodigy and America Online provide a wide range of information for a small monthly fee *(Figure 2-34)*. Other service companies provide detailed information in subject areas such as medicine, finance, or specific industries. Shopping is also available from several services. Online shoppers can read a description and, in some cases, see a picture of a product on their screen. Using a credit card, the product can be ordered. More banks are now offering online banking. The user can review recent financial transactions, transfer money from one account to another, and even pay bills using his or her computer. All of these activities are made possible through the use of data communications software. Popular communications software packages are Crosstalk and Procomm Plus.

each icon represents a remote computer that can be called

Figure 2-33
Communications programs include dialing directories that make it easier to connect with other computers. In this screen from Crosstalk for Windows, each icon represents a computer that can be called. To make the connection, the user selects the icon with a pointing device or the keyboard. The communications software then dials the other computer using a prestored phone number and establishes the connection.

Figure 2-34
Online information services such as America Online offer a wide variety of information to their subscribers. The user needs to have a computer and a modem, a piece of communications equipment that enables the computer to use a phone line to connect to the online service. Communications software is usually provided by the information service.

Electronic Mail Software

Electronic mail software, also called **E-mail,** allows users to send messages to and receive messages from other computer users *(Figure 2-35)*. The other users may be on the same computer network or on a separate computer system reached through the use of communications equipment and software. Each E-mail user has a mailbox and an address to which the mail can be sent. To make the sending of messages efficient, E-mail software allows the user to send a single message to a distribution list consisting of two or more individuals. The E-mail software takes care of copying the message and routing it to each person on the distribution list. For example, a message sent to the Department Supervisors distribution list would be routed to each of the department supervisors. E-mail systems usually have a mail waiting alert that notifies a user through a message or sound that a message is waiting to be read even if the user is working in another application.

Although E-mail is primarily used within private organizations, several communications companies (such as MCI) and online services providers (such as Prodigy and America Online) have established public E-mail facilities. For a small monthly fee, users can receive mail from and send mail to other users of the service. E-mail can be especially useful to people whose job keeps them away from the office. Remote workers can dial into their E-mail and send and receive messages at any time of the day. Because of its widespread use, informal rules, called E-mail etiquette, have been developed. These mostly common-sense rules include:

- Keep messages short and to the point.
- Avoid using E-mail for trivia, gossip, or other nonessential communications.
- Keep the distribution list to a minimum.
- Avoid using all capital letters – it is considered the same as yelling.
- It's okay (OK) for you (u) to (2) abbreviate as long as the abbreviation can be easily understood.
- Make the subject as meaningful as possible. Many E-mail systems list a summary of the mail and only show the subject, date, and sender.
- Read your mail regularly and clear messages that are no longer needed.

Popular E-mail packages are Microsoft Mail, Lotus CC:Mail, and Da Vinci eMAIL.

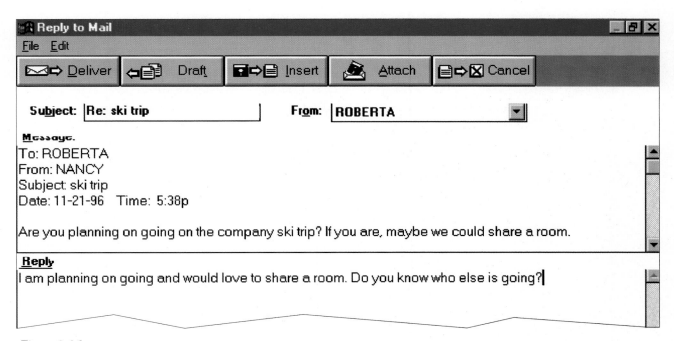

Figure 2-35
Electronic mail allows users to send and receive messages with other computer users. Each user has an electronic mail box to which messages are sent. This screen shows how a user can add a reply to a received message and then send the reply back to the person who sent the original message.

Personal Information Management

Personal information management (PIM) software helps users keep track of the miscellaneous bits of personal information that each of us deals with every day. This information can take many forms: notes to ourselves or from others, phone messages, notes about a current or future project, appointments, and so on. Programs that keep track of this type of information, such as electronic calendars, have been in existence for some time. In recent years, however, such programs have been combined so one package can keep track of all of a user's personal information.

Because of the many types of information that these programs can manage, it is difficult to precisely define personal information software. However, the category can be applied to programs that offer any of the following capabilities: appointment calendars, outliners, electronic notepads, data managers, and text retrieval. Some personal information software packages also include communications software capabilities such as phone dialers and electronic mail.

Appointment calendars allow you to schedule activities for a particular day and time *(Figure 2-36)*. Most of them will warn you if two activities are scheduled for the same time. Outliners allow you to *rough out* an idea by constructing and reorganizing an outline of important points and subpoints. Electronic notepads allow the user to record comments and assign them to one or more categories that can be used to retrieve the comments. Data managers are simple file management systems that allow the input, update, and retrieval of related records such as name and address lists or phone numbers. Text retrieval provides the capability to search files for specific words or phrases such as *Sales Meeting*. Two popular personal information management packages are Ecco and Commence.

Figure 2-36
Personal information management (PIM) software helps organize and keep track of the many different types of information that people encounter each day. This screen shows the ECCO PIM software. In addition to text, graphics objects, such as the map, can be inserted in the calendar portion of the software.

Project Management

Project management software allows users to plan, schedule, track, and analyze the events, resources, and costs of a project *(Figure 2-37)*. For example, a construction company might use this type of software to manage the building of an apartment complex or a campaign manager might use it to coordinate the many activities of a politician running for office. The value of project management software is that it provides a method for managers to control and manage the variables of a project to help ensure that the project will be completed on time and within budget. Popular project management packages include Timeline and Microsoft Project.

Integrated Software

Software packages such as databases and electronic spreadsheets are generally used independently of each other; but what if you wanted to place information from a database into a spreadsheet? The data in the database would have to be reentered in the spreadsheet. This would be time consuming and errors could be introduced as you reentered the data. The inability of separate programs to easily communicate with one another and use a common set of data has been overcome through the use of integrated software.

Integrated software refers to packages that combine applications such as word processing, spreadsheet, and database into a single, easy-to-use set of programs. Many integrated packages also include communications capabilities. The applications that are included in integrated packages are designed to have a consistent command and menu structure. For example, the command to print a document looks and works the same in each of the integrated applications. Besides a consistent look and feel, a key feature of integrated packages is their capability to pass data quickly and easily from one application to another. For example, revenue and cost information from a database on daily sales could be

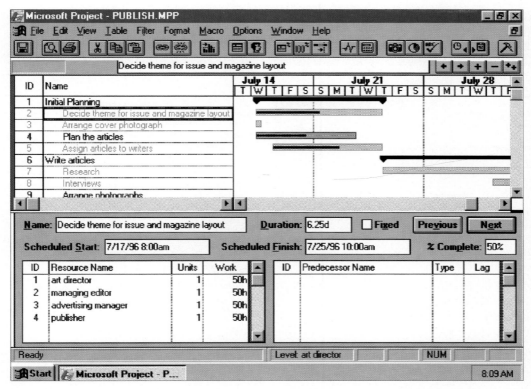

Figure 2-37
Project management software helps you plan and keep track of the tasks and resources necessary to complete a project. This screen shows part of a project plan for publishing a magazine. The most important tasks are listed in red. The bars in the upper right corner, called a Gantt chart, graphically indicate the duration of each task. The bottom portion of the screen identifies the resources required for the highlighted task; in this case, the hours needed from specific individuals.

quickly loaded into a spreadsheet. The spreadsheet could be used to calculate gross profits. Once the calculations are completed, all or a portion of the spreadsheet data can be passed to the word processing application to create a narrative report.

In their early days, integrated packages were criticized as being a collection of good but not great applications. To some extent this is still true. Users who need the most powerful word processor or spreadsheet will probably not be satisfied with the capabilities of an integrated application. For many users, however, the capabilities of today's integrated applications more than meet their needs. Besides the advantages of working well together, integrated applications are less expensive than buying comparable applications separately. Two popular integrated software packages are Microsoft Works and ClarisWorks.

Similar to integrated software are software **suites**; individual applications packaged in the same box and sold for a price that is significantly less than buying the applications individually. Although the use of suites was originally just a pricing strategy, it is becoming more and more like integrated software. First the individual packages were just bundled together for a good price; now they are being modified to work better together and offer the same command and menu structures. For the developer, the advantages of products that look and work the same include shorter development and training time, and easier customer support. Another advantage is that customers who have learned one application package are more likely to buy a second package if they know it works in a similar manner. Popular software suites include Microsoft Office, Lotus SmartSuite, and Novell PerfectOffice.

Figure 2-38
Four ways to learn application software packages.

Figure 2-38a
Software tutorials help you learn an application while using the actual software on your computer. This screen shows how the Quicken financial management software teaches how to set up a new account.

Figure 2-38b
Online help provides assistance without having to leave your application.

Learning Aids and Support Tools for Application Users

Learning to use an application software package involves time and practice. In addition to taking a class to learn how to use a software application, several learning aids and support tools are available to help you including: tutorials, online help, trade books, and keyboard templates *(Figure 2-38)*.

Tutorials are step-by-step instructions using real examples that show you how to use an application. Some tutorials are written manuals, but more tutorials are software based, allowing you to use your computer to learn about a package.

Online help refers to additional instructions that are available within the application. In most packages, a function key is reserved for the help feature. When you are using an application and have a question, pressing the designated *help* key will temporarily overlay your work on the screen with information on how to use the package. When you are finished using the help feature, pressing another key allows you to return to your work.

The documentation that accompanies software packages is frequently organized as reference material. This makes it very useful once you know how to use a package, but difficult to use when you are first learning it. For this reason, many **trade books** are available to help users learn to use the features of personal computer application packages. These books can be found where software is sold and are usually carried in regular bookstores.

Keyboard templates are plastic sheets that fit around a portion of your keyboard. The keyboard commands to select the various features of the application programs are printed on the template. Having a guide to the commands readily available is helpful for both beginners and experienced users. Many application software packages include keyboard templates.

Summary of Personal Computer Software Applications

In this chapter, you have learned about user interfaces and several widely used personal computer applications. The chapter covered the learning aids and support tools available for applications software. Knowledge about these topics increases your computer literacy and helps you to understand how personal computers are being used.

Figure 2-38c
Trade books are available for all popular software applications.

Figure 2-38d
Keyboard templates give you quick reference to software commands.

COMPUTERS AT WORK

Productivity Software Use High in Business

According to a recent report, more than $2 billion of productivity software applications are sold each year. By far, the largest user of this software is business, although home use is increasing. In a survey of 1,000 large businesses, nearly 100% of the companies said they used word processing and spreadsheet software. Close behind at approximately 95% are four applications; database, presentation graphics, communications, and electronic mail. Rounding out the applications were desktop publishing at 84%, project management at 72%, and personal information management at 48%. A survey of smaller businesses ranked the applications in the same order with slightly lower percentages. These results make it clear that productivity software is an essential part of business. Companies and individuals are turning to these software applications to work efficiently and become more productive. Project management is one of the fastest growing applications. Nowadays, practically every manager is a project manager. Likewise, many individuals are now using personal information management (PIM) software to manage their day-to-day activities.

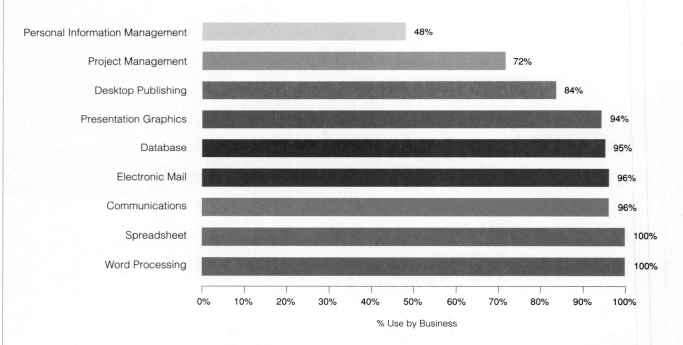

Productivity Software Use

Personal Information Management — 48%
Project Management — 72%
Desktop Publishing — 84%
Presentation Graphics — 94%
Database — 95%
Electronic Mail — 96%
Communications — 96%
Spreadsheet — 100%
Word Processing — 100%

% Use by Business

Figure 2-39

IN THE FUTURE

Will There Eventually Be Only One Software Superapplication?

Some people believe that individual software applications such as word processing and spreadsheets will eventually be replaced by a single *super*application that has the combined features of today's separate packages. They believe that the current software applications technology will become more standardized and thus easier to use for different document tasks. Some describe this evolution as a switch from application-oriented computing to document-oriented computing. The idea is that you shouldn't have to worry about what your document might contain before you start working on it. Even though the document may contain text, graphics, a spreadsheet, a chart, sound, or video, the necessary tools should be available as you need them.

Many worry that the trend toward superapplications will lead to less competition in the productivity software industry. Individual application developers will have a hard time competing against suites of applications that offer the user a common interface and one-call support. However, others see a continuing market for applications and individual tools that can be integrated with the superapplication. The same standardization that will enable the individual applications to be combined will enable independent developers to create tools that can replace or be added to the tools of the superapplication. For example, an artist may want a more powerful illustration tool than the one that comes with the superapplication. A salesperson who calls on five customers per day may want a more powerful personal information manager than a salesperson who makes one sales call per week. Other tools, such as a dictionary or a thesaurus, may be customized for specific professions such as law or medicine.

The trend toward the so-called superapplication was started with integrated software. Software suites with common toolbars and menus are the second step. How long will it be before we see ads for DocumentPerfect 1.0?

Figure 2-40

What You Should Know

1. Applications that help people perform their work more efficiently are sometimes referred to as **productivity software**.

2. A **user interface** is the way the user tells the software what to do and the way the computer displays information and processing options to the user. A **graphical user interface** (GUI) combines text and graphics to make software easier to use. Graphical user interfaces include several common features such as icons, windows, menus, and buttons.

3. **Icons** are pictures, or symbols, used to represent processing options. A **window** is a rectangular area of the screen that is used to present information. The term Windows refers to **Microsoft Windows**, the most popular graphical user interface for personal computers. A **menu** is a list of options from which the user can choose. In a graphical user interface, menus often contain a list of related **commands**, or instructions, that cause the computer software to perform a specific action. A **button** is an icon that, when selected, causes a specific action to take place.

4. **Word processing** involves the use of a computer to produce or modify documents that consist primarily of text. Although most people perform word processing using personal computers or larger computer systems that can also be used for other applications, **dedicated word processing systems**, that can only be used for word processing, also exist.

5. Producing a document using word processing usually involves the following steps: creating, editing, formatting, printing, and saving.

6. Creating a word processing document entails entering text, usually by using the keyboard. Key word processing features used during this step include **word wrap**, **scrolling**, and moving the **cursor**.

7. **Editing** is the process of making changes in the content of a document. Word processing editing features include **cut** (which electronically places text in a temporary storage location called the **Clipboard**), **paste**, **copy**, **insert**, **delete**, **search**, and **replace**. Other editing features include using a **spelling checker**, **thesaurus**, and **grammar checker**.

8. To **format** means to change the appearance of a document. Word processing features that can be used to format a document include **fonts**, a specific combination of **typeface** and **point** size, and **styles**, such as **bold**, *italic*, or <u>underline</u>. Formatting can also involve setting **margins**, changing **justification** or **alignment**, using **full justification**, altering the **spacing** between characters (using **monospacing** or **proportional spacing**), and adjusting **line spacing**. Most word processors can arrange text in columns, organize information in tables, and incorporate graphics. Word processors can also use a **border** or **shading**, and create **headers** and **footers**. A **style sheet** lets you save font and format information so it can be applied to new documents.

9. Most word processors give the user many printing options including number and copies of pages, **portrait** or **landscape orientation**, and **print preview**.

10. **Desktop publishing** (DTP) software allows users to design and produce professional looking documents that contain both text and graphics.

11. DTP software focuses on **page composition** and **layout**, sometimes called **page makeup**, which is the process of arranging text and graphics on a document page. The text and graphics used by a DTP program are frequently imported from other software packages. DTP documents often make use of previously created art, called **clip art**.

12. All DTP programs display information on the screen exactly as it will look when printed, a capability called **WYSIWYG** (an acronym from What You See Is What You Get).

13. The capability to print DTP documents relies on a **page definition language**, such as **PostScript**, which describes the document to be printed in language the printer can understand.

14. **Spreadsheet software** allows you to organize numeric data in a worksheet or table format called an **electronic spreadsheet** or **spreadsheet**.

Windows 95

Start

15. Within a spreadsheet, data is organized vertically in **columns** and horizontally in **rows**. The intersection where a column and row meet is called a **cell**.

16. Cells may contain three types of data: **labels** (text), **values** (numbers), and **formulas** that perform calculations on the data in the spreadsheet and display the resulting value. **Functions** are stored formulas that perform common calculations. When formulas are copied to another cell, the formula can be automatically updated to the new location (**relative referencing**) or continue to refer to the same cell locations (**absolute referencing**).

17. A spreadsheet's capability to recalculate when data is changed, sometimes called **what-if analysis**, makes it a valuable tool for decision making.

18. A standard feature of spreadsheet packages is the capability to turn numeric data into a **chart** that graphically shows the relationship of numerical data. The types of charts provided by spreadsheet packages are sometimes called **analytical graphics** or **business graphics**, and most are variations on three basic chart types: **line charts**, **bar charts**, and **pie charts**.

19. A **database** refers to a collection of data that is stored in files. **Database software** allows you to create a database and to retrieve, manipulate, and update the data that you store in it.

20. A **file** is a collection of related data that is organized in records. Each **record** contains a collection of related facts called **fields**. A field can contain any of the following types of information: **alphanumeric**, **numeric**, **currency**, **date**, or **memo**.

21. Comparing data entered against a predefined format is called **validation** and is an important feature of database programs.

22. The capability to retrieve database information in a report, called a **query**, based on criteria specified by the user is one of the more powerful features of a database.

23. **Presentation graphics software** allows the user to create documents called **slides** that are used in making presentations before a group to help communicate information more effectively.

24. Some of the features included with most presentation graphics packages include: numerous chart types, three-dimensional effects, special effects, color control, and image libraries. In addition to slides, presentation graphics packages create outlines, notes pages, and audience handouts. Presentation graphics packages also include slide sorters to help organize and present the slides.

25. **Data communications software** is used to transmit data from one computer to another. Features that most data communications software packages include are: a dialing directory of phone numbers, automatic redial, automatic answer, and the capability to send or receive one or more data files.

26. Communications software is frequently used by employees who are away from the office. It is also used to access online services for news, weather, financial, and travel information.

27. **Electronic mail software**, also called **E-mail**, allows users to send messages to and receive messages from other computer users. Although E-mail is primarily used within private organizations, several communications companies and online services have established public E-mail capabilities.

28. **Personal information management** (PIM) **software** helps users keep track of the miscellaneous bits of personal information that each of us deals with every day. The category can be applied to programs that offer any of the following capabilities: appointment calendars, outliners, electronic notepads, data managers, and text retrieval.

29. **Project management software** allows users to plan, schedule, track, and analyze the events, resources, and costs of a project.

30. **Integrated software** refers to packages that combine applications such as word processing, spreadsheet, and database into a single, easy-to-use set of programs. The applications have a consistent look and feel and the capability to pass data quickly from one application to another. Similar to integrated software are software **suites**; individual applications packaged in the same box and sold for a price that is significantly less than buying the applications individually.

31. Several learning aids and support tools are available to help you learn to use an application package including: **tutorials**, **online help**, **trade books**, and **keyboard templates**.

2:00 AM

File   Edit   Section   Page   Tools   Options   Help

Terms to Remember

absolute referencing (2.15)
alignment (2.8)
analytical graphics (2.16)

bar chart (2.16)
bold (2.7)
border (2.8)
business graphics (2.16)
button (2.3)

cell (2.12)
chart (2.16)
clip art (2.11)
Clipboard (2.6)
column (2.12)
command (2.3)
copy (2.6)
currency (2.19)
cursor (2.5)
cut (2.6)

data communications software (2.22)
database (2.18)
database software (2.18)
date (2.19)
dedicated word processing system (2.4)
delete (2.6)
desktop publishing (DTP) software (2.10)

E-mail (2.23)
editing (2.6)
electronic mail software (2.23)
electronic spreadsheet (2.12)

field (2.18)
file (2.18)
font (2.7)
footer (2.9)
format (2.7)
formula (2.12)

full justification (2.8)
functions (2.12)

grammar checker (2.7)
graphical user interface (GUI) (2.2)

header (2.9)

icon (2.3)
insert (2.6)
integrated software (2.25)

justification (2.8)

keyboard template (2.27)

label (2.12)
landscape (2.9)
line chart (2.16)
line spacing (2.8)

margins (2.8)
memo (2.19)
menu (2.3)
Microsoft Windows (2.3)
monospacing (2.8)

numeric (2.19)

online help (2.27)

page composition and layout (2.10)
page definition language (2.11)
page makeup (2.10)
paste (2.6)
personal information management (PIM) software (2.24)
pie chart (2.16)
point (2.7)
portrait (2.9)
PostScript (2.11)
presentation graphics software (2.20)

print preview (2.9)
productivity software (2.2)
project management software (2.25)
proportional spacing (2.8)

query (2.19)

record (2.18)
relative referencing (2.15)
replace (2.6)
row (2.12)

scrolling (2.5)
search (2.6)
shade (2.8)
slides (2.20)
spacing (2.8)
spelling checker (2.6)
spreadsheet (2.12)
spreadsheet software (2.12)
style (2.7)
style sheet (2.9)
suites (2.26)

thesaurus (2.7)
trade books (2.27)
tutorials (2.27)
typeface (2.7)

user interface (2.2)

validation (2.19)
values (2.12)

what-if analysis (2.16)
window (2.3)
Windows 95 (2.3)
word processing software (2.4)
word wrap (2.4)
WYSIWYG (2.11)

File   Edit   Section   Page   Tools   Options   Help

Test Your Knowledge

Fill in the Blanks

1. The nine most widely used personal computer software packages are: _____, _____, _____, _____, _____, _____, _____, _____, and _____.

2. Applications that help people perform their work more efficiently are sometimes referred to as _____.

3. A(n) _____ is the way the user tells the software what to do and the way the computer displays information and processing options to the user.

4. _____ refers to packages that combine applications such as word processing, spreadsheet, and database into a single, easy-to-use set of programs.

5. Four learning aids and support tools available for application users are: _____, _____, _____, and _____.

Short Answer

1. What is productivity software? Briefly explain why each of the nine widely used personal computer software applications described in this chapter can be considered productivity software.

2. What is a graphical user interface (GUI)? Describe the several common features included in most graphical user interfaces.

3. How is word processing software different from desktop publishing software (DTP)? Describe some of the major features of each type of software. In what way are word processing software and desktop publishing software used together?

4. What is the purpose of spreadsheet software? Briefly describe an electronic spreadsheet. How can a spreadsheet be a valuable tool for business decision making?

5. How is presentation graphics similar to analytical graphics? How are they different? Briefly describe the materials that can be created with presentation graphics packages. In what way do presentation graphics packages help communicate information more effectively?

Label the Figure

Instructions: The figure on the right shows Productivity Software Use. In the spaces provided label the bars.

_____

_____

_____

_____

_____

_____

_____

_____

_____

Productivity Software Use

48%
72%
84%
94%
95%
96%
96%
100%
100%

0% 10% 20% 30% 40% 50% 60% 70% 80% 90% 100%

% Use by Business

Points to Ponder

1

Many people believe that word processing software greatly improves the quality of written material by making it easier to create, edit, and print documents. Some word processing software even provides templates–patterns or blueprints for a document–that can be used to produce reports, memos, cover letters, resumes, legal pleadings, even letters to mom! Yet, other people argue that word processing software has become a crutch, making it unnecessary for students to learn the rudiments and nuances of language. These people feel that much of the work produced with word processors is indeed "processed," lacking the beauty, artistry, and individuality of great literature. What effect do you think word processing software has on written communication? Does it result in better work or simply more correct mediocre work? What word processing features, if any, do you feel are particularly valuable to an author?

2

Johann Guttenberg's invention of printing from moveable type had a profound impact on Western thought, making books that were previously available only to a privileged elite accessible to a much wider audience, thereby facilitating the distribution of knowledge. Will desktop publishing (DTP) software have a similar impact? Will previously unpublished writers use desktop publishing software to produce professional looking works that are widely circulated? What effect, if any, do you think desktop publishing will have on the ability of people to produce and gain access to material that reflects unconventional, or not generally accepted, ideas?

3

Your Aunt Agatha has offered to buy you some computer software for your birthday. Because she places a great deal of importance on organization (her socks are stored in alphabetical order by color), she will purchase only database software or personal information management software. How could you use both types of software now? How could you use both types of software in the future? If Aunt Agatha asks you which type of software you would rather have, what would you answer? Why?

4

An increasing number of employees are working at home, using data communications software to transmit data from their personal computer to a computer in the central office. What do you think are the advantages of working at home? What are the disadvantages? Do you feel a worker is likely to be more productive at home or in the office? If you could attend school at home, communicating with your teachers through your personal computer, would you? Why or why not?

5

A woman was once fired when she used her office electronic mail system to complain about her boss. Although she felt her E-mail conversations were private and would not be monitored, she learned, to her chagrin, that she was wrong. Do you think employers have the right to "listen in" to electronic mail conversations? Why or why not? If you "overheard" a fellow employee criticizing your boss on her E-mail system, would you tell your boss? What if you heard the same employee planning a theft of company products? Where do you draw the line?

6

One of the catch phrases in education today is "learning styles," the belief that different people learn things best in different ways. How do you learn things most effectively? Of the four learning aids described in this chapter (tutorials, online help, trade books, and keyboard templates), which fit your learning style best? Why?

Out and About

1. Unlike a graphical user interface, which combines text and graphics, a text interface uses only text, or commands, to communicate with the computer. Many software packages have one version written for use with a graphical user interface (such as Microsoft Windows) and another written for use with a text interface (such as DOS). Visit a computer store and find a software package that has a version written for both types of interfaces (such as WordPerfect for Windows and WordPerfect for DOS). Try out each version. How are they similar? How are they different? Which version is easier to learn? Why? If you were going to buy this software package, would you buy the version used with the graphical user interface or the version used with the text interface? Why?

2. Interview someone who regularly uses one of the productivity tools discussed in this chapter in the course of his or her work to find out his or her feelings about the software. For what purpose is the software used? Why does this person use the particular software package? What does he or she like about the software? What does the individual dislike? How did the person learn to use the software? If free to choose another software package to perform the same task, would this person choose one? Why or why not?

3. Many bookstores and software vendors carry trade books that can help users learn the features of personal computer application packages. Pick a productivity tool, such as spreadsheet software, and visit a bookstore or software vendor to survey the trade books on that tool. For what particular spreadsheet package (e.g., Lotus 1-2-3, Excel, or Quattro Pro) are the most titles available? How difficult do you think it would be to learn each software package using the available trade books? Which trade book do you think is the best? Why? If you were going to purchase a software package solely on the basis of the available trade books, which package would you buy? Why?

4. Make a list of the features listed in this chapter that are provided by word processing or spreadsheet software. Visit a computer vendor and compare two word processing or spreadsheet packages in terms of the features you have listed. Which package is easier to learn? Why? Once you have learned it, which package allows you to do more? If you were to purchase one of the two packages, which would you buy? Why?

5. Do some research on presentations. Make a list of the characteristics of effective presentations, in order from most important to least important. Which of these characteristics can be enhanced through the use of presentation graphics software? How much of a difference in the overall quality of a presentation do you think presentation graphics software can make? Do you think presentation graphics are more helpful in certain presentations than in others? If you had to give a presentation on your favorite subject, would you like to use presentation graphics software? Why or why not?

6. Uncle Ulysses has agreed to buy you an integrated software package of your choice. Visit a software vendor and compare integrated software packages. Which would you ask Uncle Ulysses to buy? Why? If Uncle Ullysses is willing to buy any applications, or a software suite, that are the same price or less than the integrated software package, which would you prefer? Why?

File Edit Section Page Tools Options Help

In the Lab with Windows 95

1 **Creating a Word Processing Document**   Click the Start button on the taskbar, point to Programs on the Start menu, point to Accessories on the Programs submenu, and then click WordPad on the Accessories submenu. Type the first three paragraphs on page 2.4 under the heading Word Processing Software and as shown in *Figure 2-41*. Press TAB to indent the first line of each paragraph. Only press ENTER to begin a new paragraph. Do not bold any words in the paragraphs. At the end of the third paragraph, press ENTER twice and type your name.

To correct errors in your document, use the mouse to move the I-beam to the location of the error; and then click to move the insertion point to the error. To erase to the left of the insertion point, press BACKSPACE; to erase to the right of the insertion point, press DELETE. To insert character(s), move the insertion point immediately to the left of the point of insertion and begin typing.

When your document is correct, save it by inserting a formatted floppy disk in drive A and then clicking the Save button on the toolbar. When the Save As dialog box displays, type a:windows 95 lab 2-1 in the File name text box and then click the Save button. With your printer turned on, click the Print button on the toolbar to print the document. Close WordPad by clicking the Close button on its title bar.

2 **Formatting a Word Processing Document**   Insert the floppy disk with Windows Lab 1 in drive A. Start WordPad as described in Windows 95 Lab 1. To open the document you created in Windows 95 Lab 1, click the Open button on the toolbar. When the Open dialog box displays, type a:windows 95 lab 2-1 in the File name text box and

then click the Open button. Move the mouse pointer to the far left of the window in front of the first character of the first paragraph. With the mouse pointer in the shape of a block right arrow, drag the mouse pointer down the left side of the document to highlight the three paragraphs of text. Click the Font Size box arrow on the format bar and then click 12. Click anywhere in the document to remove the highlight. Practice using the scroll bar to scroll through the document.

Move the insertion point to the upper left corner of the document and press ENTER twice. Reposition the insertion point in the upper left corner of the window. Click the Font Size box arrow on the format bar and then click 14. Type WORD PROCESSING SOFTWARE as the title. With the insertion point in the title, click the Center button on the format bar to center the title.

Drag the mouse over the first three words, Word processing software, in the second sentence. Click the Bold button on the format bar. Click anywhere in the document to remove the highlight *(Figure 2-42)*.

Click File on the menu bar, and then click Save As to save the document with a new filename. When the Save As dialog box displays, type a:windows 95 lab 2-2 in the File name text box. Click the Save button. Print the document. Close WordPad.

Figure 2-41

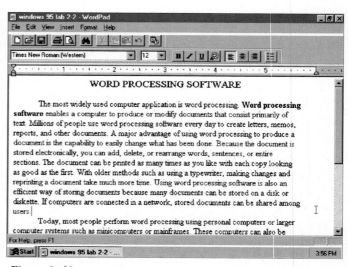

Figure 2-42

Start   2:05 AM

Where on the Web

1 **Microsoft Office Online**   Software suites are similar to integrated software; individual applications packaged in the same box and sold for a price that is significantly less than buying the applications individually. Complete the following steps to learn more about the Microsoft Office Suite *(Figure 2-43)*. With Netscape on the screen, type `http://www.microsoft.com/msofc` in the Location text box and then press ENTER. Click any item that seems of interest to you. Read the page you selected. Click Print on the File menu. Click OK. Hand in the printout.

2 **Looking Behind a Web Page**   Word processing involves the use of a computer to produce or modify documents that consist primarily of text. Complete the following steps to see how a word processor can be used to create a Web page. With Netscape on the screen, click the Home button. Click Document Source on the View menu. Read through some of the text. Click the Close button in the upper right corner of the document source window. Click Print on the File menu. Click OK. Write a brief description of what the source text for the Web page looked like. Hand in the printout.

3 **Web Comics**   Similar to word processors, Netscape gives the user many printing options including print preview. Complete the following steps to see a demonstration of these features. With Netscape on the screen, type `http://www.unitedmedia.com/comics/dilbert` in the Location text box and then press ENTER. Scroll down to view a Dilbert comic *(Figure 2-44)*. Click Print Preview on the File menu. Click the Zoom In button. Click the Next Page button. Click Print. Click OK. Hand in the printout.

4 **Cool Word of the Day**   Editing features of many word processors include a spelling checker, thesaurus, grammar checker, and dictionary. Increase your vocabulary and your familiarity with the World Wide Web by visiting a Web dictionary site. With Netscape on the screen, type `http://www.dsu.edu/projects/word_of_day` in the Location text box and then press ENTER. Click Definition. Read the definition of the Cool Word of the Day. Scroll down and type a word in the Lookup text box. Click the Look Up Definition button. Click Print on the File menu. Click OK. Hand in your printout.

5 **Shelly Cashman Online**   Click Using Computers: A Gateway To Information, World Wide Web Edition on the Shelly Cashman Student Center Web page (`http://www.bf.com/scstudnt.html`). Scroll down and click Chapter 2. Complete the activities listed.

Figure 2-43

Figure 2-44

Input to the Computer

3

Objectives

After completing this chapter, you will be able to:

- Review the four operations of the information processing cycle: input, process, output, and storage

- Define the four types of input and how the computer uses each type

- Describe the standard features of keyboards, and explain how to use the cursor control and function keys

- Explain how a mouse works and how it is used

- Describe several input devices other than the keyboard and mouse

- Explain the three types of terminals and how they are used

- Explain multimedia input devices

- Describe procedures used to ensure data accuracy

The information processing cycle is basic to all computers, large or small. It is important that you understand this cycle, for much of your success in understanding computers and what they do depends on having an understanding or feeling for the movement of data as it flows through the information processing cycle and becomes information. This chapter discusses the information processing cycle and describes some of the devices used for input. Certain devices that can be used for both input and storage, such as disk and tape drives, are covered in the chapter on secondary storage.

Overview of the Information Processing Cycle

As you saw in Chapter 1, the information processing cycle consists of four operations: input, processing, output, and storage *(Figure 3-1)*. Regardless of the size and type of computer, these operations process data into a meaningful form called information.

The operations in the information processing cycle are carried out through the combined use of computer equipment, also called computer hardware, and computer software. The computer software, or programs, contain instructions that direct the computer equipment to perform the tasks necessary to process data into information. In the information processing cycle, the input operation must take place before any data can be processed and any information produced and stored.

Figure 3-1
A computer consists of input devices, the system unit, output devices, and secondary storage devices. This equipment, or hardware, is used to perform the operations of the information processing cycle.

What Is Input?

Input refers to the process of entering data, programs, commands, and user responses into main memory. Input also refers to the media (e.g., disks, tapes, documents) that contain these input types. These four types of input are used by a computer in the following ways:

- **Data** refers to the raw facts, including numbers, letters, words, images, and sounds that a computer receives during the input operation and processes to produce information. Although technically speaking, a single item of data should be called a *datum,* it is common and accepted usage to use the word data to represent both singular and plural. Data must be entered and stored in main memory for processing to occur. Data is the most common type of input.
- **Programs** are instructions that direct the computer to perform the necessary operations to process data into information. The program that is loaded and stored in main memory determines the processing that the computer will perform. When a program is first created it is usually input by using a keyboard. Once the program has been entered and stored on secondary storage, it can be transferred to main memory by a command.

Input

KEYBOARD AND MOUSE

Process

Secondary Storage

HARD DISK DRIVE

DISKETTE DRIVE

SYSTEM UNIT

MONITOR

Output

PRINTER

- **Commands** are key words and phrases that the user inputs to direct the computer to perform certain activities. Commands are usually either entered from the keyboard or selected from a list.
- **User responses** refer to the data that a user inputs to respond to a question or message from the software. One of the most common responses is to answer "Yes" or "No" to a question. Based on the answer, the computer program will perform specific actions. For example, typing the letter Y in response to the message, Do you want to save this file?, will result in the file being saved (written) to the secondary storage device.

The Keyboard

The **keyboard** is the most commonly used input device. Users input data to a computer by pressing the keys on the keyboard. Keyboards are connected to other devices that have screens such as a personal computer or a terminal. As the user enters data through the keyboard, the data displays on the screen.

Keyboards are usually similar to the one shown in *Figure 3-2*. The alphabetic keys are arranged like those on a typewriter. A **numeric keypad** is located on the right-hand side of most keyboards. The numeric keys are arranged in an adding machine or calculator format to allow you to enter numeric data rapidly.

Figure 3-2
A typical keyboard used on personal computers.

Keyboards also contain keys that can be used to position the cursor on the screen. A **cursor** is a symbol, such as an underline character, rectangle, or vertical bar, that indicates where on the screen the next character entered will appear. The keys that move the cursor are called **arrow keys or cursor control keys**. Cursor control keys have an UP ARROW (↑), a DOWN ARROW (↓), a LEFT ARROW (←), and a RIGHT ARROW (→). When you press any of these keys, the cursor moves one space in the same direction as the arrow. In addition, many keyboards contain other cursor control keys, such as the HOME key, which when you press it can send the cursor to a beginning location such as the upper left position of the screen or document. The numeric keypad can also be used to move the cursor. With most keys, if you hold them down they will automatically start to repeat.

Some computer keyboards also contain keys that can alter or edit the text displayed on the screen. For example, the INSERT and DELETE keys allow characters to be inserted into or deleted from data displayed on the screen.

Function keys are keys that can be programmed to accomplish certain tasks that will assist the user. For example,

a function key may be programmed for use as a help key when using software such as a word processor. Whenever the function key is pressed, messages will appear that give helpful information about how to use the word processing software. Function keys can also save keystrokes. Sometimes several keystrokes are required to accomplish a certain task, for example, printing a document. Some application software packages are written so the user can either enter the individual keystrokes or press a function key and obtain the same result.

Status lights in the upper right corner of the keyboard indicate if the numeric keypad, capital letters, and scroll locks are turned on.

The ESCAPE (ESC) key is often used by computer software to cancel an instruction or exit from a situation. The use of the ESC key varies among software packages.

The disadvantage of using a keyboard as an input device is that training is required to use it efficiently. Users who lack typing ability are at a disadvantage because of the time they spend looking for the appropriate keys. While other input devices are appropriate in some situations, users should be encouraged to develop their keyboard skills.

Pointing Devices

Pointing devices allow the user to control an on-screen symbol called the **mouse pointer**, or **pointer**, that is usually represented by an arrow-shaped marker (⬉). The pointing device is used to move the cursor to a particular location on the screen or to select available software options.

Mouse

The mouse is a unique device used with personal computers and some computer terminals to select processing options or information displayed on the screen. A **mouse** is a small, lightweight input device that easily fits in the palm of your hand *(Figure 3-3)*. You move the device across a flat surface such as a desktop to control the movement of the pointer on a screen.

The mouse is usually attached to the computer by a cable but wireless mouse devices also exist. On the bottom of the mouse is a device, usually a small ball, that senses the movement of the mouse. Electronic circuits in the mouse translate the movement of the mouse into signals that are sent to the computer. The computer uses the mouse signals to move the pointer on the screen in the same direction as the mouse *(Figure 3-4)*. When you move the mouse left on the surface of the table or desk, the pointer moves left on the screen. When you move the mouse right, the pointer moves right, and so on.

On top of the mouse are one or more buttons. By using the mouse to move the pointer on the screen and pressing the buttons on the mouse, you can perform actions such as making menu selections, editing a word processing document, and moving data from one location on the screen to another.

The primary advantage of a mouse is that it is easy to use. With a little practice, a person can use a mouse to point to locations on the screen just as easily as using a finger.

There are two disadvantages of the mouse. The first is that it requires empty desk space where it can be moved about. The second disadvantage is that the user must remove a hand from the keyboard and place it on the mouse whenever the pointer is to be moved or a command is to be given.

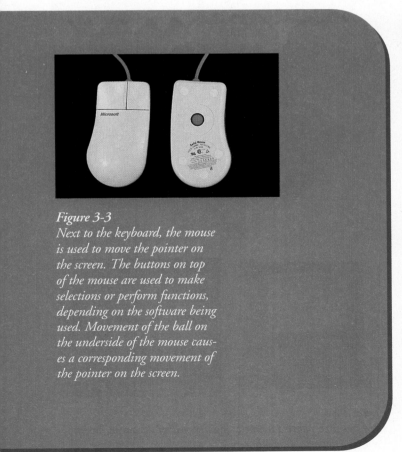

Figure 3-3
Next to the keyboard, the mouse is used to move the pointer on the screen. The buttons on top of the mouse are used to make selections or perform functions, depending on the software being used. Movement of the ball on the underside of the mouse causes a corresponding movement of the pointer on the screen.

Figure 3-4
As the mouse is moved diagonally across a flat surface, the mouse pointer on the screen moves in a similar direction.

Trackball

A **trackball** is a pointing device like a mouse only with the ball on the top of the device instead of the bottom *(Figure 3-5)*. To move the pointer with a trackball, all you have to do is rotate the ball in the desired direction. With a mouse, you have to move the entire device. To accommodate movement with both the fingers and palms of a hand, the ball on top of a trackball is usually larger than the ball on the bottom of a mouse. The main advantage of a trackball over a mouse is that it doesn't require clear desk space. Smaller trackball units have been designed for use on portable computers *(Figure 3-6)*.

Joystick

A **joystick** uses the movement of a vertical stem to direct the pointer. A full-size joystick, often used with computer games, is usually large enough for the user's hand to wrap around it *(Figure 3-7)*. Full-size joysticks usually have buttons you press to activate certain events, depending on the software. Much smaller joysticks, without buttons, have been incorporated into some portable computers *(Figure 3-8)*. The small joysticks look like a long pencil eraser stuck between the keys. Pressure on the joystick from the user's finger causes the pointer to move.

Figure 3-7
Joysticks are often used with computer games to control the actions of a vehicle or player.

Figure 3-5
The trackball is like a mouse turned upside down. The user rotates the ball to move the cursor and then presses one of the keys shown at the top of the trackball.

Figure 3-6
Smaller trackball units are often used on portable computers. Sometimes the trackballs are attached to the side of the computer as shown here, and other times they are built into the computer case.

Figure 3-8
IBM has incorporated a type of joystick, called a trackpoint, into their line of portable computers.

Pen Input Devices

Pen input devices have become increasingly popular in recent years and may eventually be part of most, if not all, computers. Almost all of the personal digital assistant (PDA) class of personal computers use a pen. One advantage is that people who have never used a computer adapt naturally to using a pen as an input device *(Figure 3-9)*.

Pen input devices allow the user to use the pen in three ways; to input data using hand-written characters and shapes the computer can recognize, as a pointing device like a mouse to select items on the screen, and to gesture, which is a way of issuing commands.

Pen computers use special hardware and software to interpret the movement of the pen. When the pen touches the screen, it causes two layers of electrically conductive material to make contact. The computer determines the coordinates for the contact point and darkens that location on the screen. The darkened area on the screen is referred to as **ink**. Hand-written characters are converted into computer text by software that matches the shape of the hand-written character to a database of known shapes. If the software cannot recognize

a particular letter, it asks the user to identify it. Most **hand-writing recognition software** can be taught to recognize an individual's unique style of writing. In addition to working with character input, graphic recognition software used on pen input devices improves drawings by cleaning up uneven lines. Wavy lines can be straightened and circles can be made perfectly round. Perhaps the most natural use of the pen is as a pointing device. When used this way, the pen functions as a mouse. Pressing the pen against the screen once or twice is the same as using the buttons on a mouse.

Gestures are special symbols made with the pen that issue a command such as delete text. As shown in *Figure 3-10*, many gestures are identical to those used for manual text editing. Gestures can be more efficient than using a mouse or keyboard because they not only identify where you want to make a change but also the type of change to be made.

Pen input devices have already been adapted to many applications that were previously not computerized. Any application where a form has to be filled out is a candidate for a pen input device. One of the largest markets for pen input devices is mobile workers, who spend most of their time away from their desks or offices.

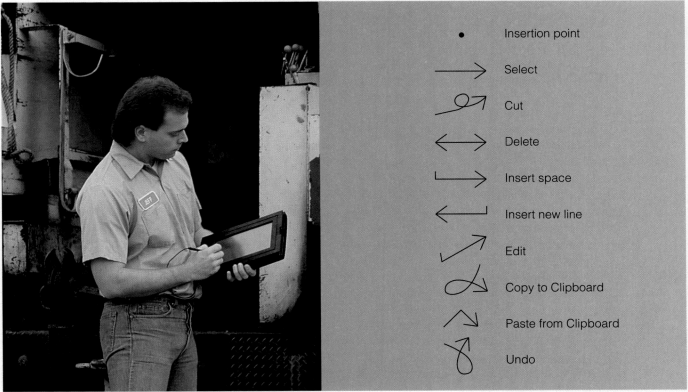

•	Insertion point
→	Select
	Cut
↔	Delete
	Insert space
	Insert new line
	Edit
	Copy to Clipboard
	Paste from Clipboard
	Undo

Figure 3-9
Pen input systems allow the user to use a pen to enter data or select processing options without using a keyboard. This method is easy to learn by individuals who have worked with a pencil and paper.

Figure 3-10
Gestures are a way of issuing commands with a pen. Gestures not only tell what you want done but also where you want to make a change. The arrows indicate the direction of the pen movement.

Touch Screen

A **touch screen** allows users to touch areas of the screen to enter data. They let the user interact with a computer by the touch of a finger rather than typing on a keyboard or moving a mouse. The user enters data by touching words or numbers or locations identified on the screen.

Several electronic techniques change a touch on the screen into electronic signals that are interpreted by the computer software. One technique uses beams of infrared light projected across the surface of the screen. A finger or other object touching the screen interrupts the beams, generating an electronic signal. This signal identifies the location on the screen where the touch occurred. The software interprets the signal and performs the required function.

Touch screens are not used to enter large amounts of data. They are used, however, for applications where the user must issue a command to the software to perform a particular task or must choose from a list of options. Touch screens have been successfully installed in kiosks used to provide information in hotels, airports, and other public locations *(Figure 3-11)*.

There are both advantages and disadvantages to touch screens. A significant advantage is that they are very natural to use; that is, people are used to pointing to things. With touch screens, users can point to indicate the processing they want performed by the computer. In addition, touch screens are usually easy for the user to learn. As quickly as pointing a finger, the user's request is processed. There are some disadvantages to touch screens. First, the resolution of the touching area is not precise. Thus, while a user can point to a box or a fairly large area on the screen and the electronics can determine the location of the touch, it is difficult to point to a single character in a word processing application, for example, and indicate that the character should be deleted. In cases such as these, a keyboard or mouse is easier to use. A second disadvantage is that after a period of reaching for the screen, the user's arm could become tired.

Figure 3-11
Touch screens are frequently used for information kiosks. Users touch the screen and receive information about the chosen topic.

Figure 3-12
The light pen can be used to make selections or to draw directly on the screen. A light cell in the tip of the pen can detect where on the screen the pen is touching. Light pens are often used in engineering applications.

Light Pen

A **light pen** is used by touching it on the display screen to create or modify graphics *(Figure 3-12)*. A light cell in the tip of the pen senses light from the screen to determine the pen's location. The light pen can be used to select processing options or to draw on the screen.

Digitizer

A **digitizer** converts points, lines, and curves from a sketch, drawing, or photograph to digital signals and transmits them to a computer *(Figure 3-13)*. The user indicates the data to be input by pressing one or more buttons on the hand-held digitizer device.

Graphics Tablet

A **graphics tablet** works in a manner similar to a digitizer, but it also contains unique characters and commands that can be automatically generated by the person using the tablet *(Figure 3-14)*.

Figure 3-13
Digitizers are used to create original drawings or to trace and reproduce existing drawings. When buttons on the hand-held device are pushed, the location on the drawing is input to the computer. Special software can link the points together to create a drawing that can be modified.

Figure 3-14
The color template on the graphics tablet allows the user to select processing options by placing a hand-held device over the appropriate location on the tablet and pressing a button.

Source Data Automation

Source data automation refers to procedures and equipment designed to make the input process more efficient by eliminating the manual entry of data. Instead of a person entering data using a keyboard, source data automation equipment captures data directly from its original form such as an invoice or an inventory tag. The original form is called a **source document**. In addition to making the input process more efficient, source data automation usually results in a higher input accuracy rate. The following section describes some of the equipment used for source data automation, which is sometimes called **source data collection**.

Image Scanner

An **image scanner**, sometimes called a **page scanner**, is an input device that electronically captures an entire page of text or images such as photographs or art work *(Figure 3-15)*. The scanner converts the text or image on the original document into digital information that can be stored on a disk and processed by the computer. The digitized information can be printed or displayed separately or merged into another document such as a newsletter. Hand-held devices that scan a portion of a page are also available *(Figure 3-16)* as well as color scanners.

Image processing systems use scanners to capture and electronically file documents such as legal documents or documents with signatures or drawings. These systems are like electronic filing cabinets that allow users to rapidly access and review exact reproductions of the original documents *(Figure 3-17)*.

Figure 3-15
The scanner inputs text, graphics, or photographs for use in word processing or desktop publishing applications.

Figure 3-16
A hand-held scanner enters text or graphics less than a page wide. Software allows you to join separately scanned items to make up a complete page.

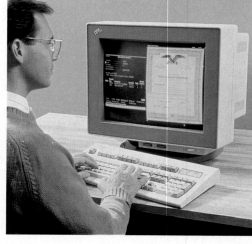

Figure 3-17
Image processing systems record and store an exact copy of a document. These systems are often used by insurance companies that may need to refer to any of hundreds of thousands of documents.

Optical Recognition

Optical recognition devices use a light source to read codes, marks, and characters and convert them into digital data that can be processed by a computer.

OPTICAL CODES

Optical codes use a pattern or symbols to represent data. The most common optical code is the bar code. A **bar code** consists of a set of vertical lines and spaces of different widths. The bar code is usually either printed on the product package or attached to the product with a label or tag. The bar code reader uses the light pattern from the bar code lines to identify the item. Of the several different types of bar codes, the most familiar is the **universal product code** (UPC). The UPC bar code, used for grocery and retail items, can be translated into a ten-digit number that identifies the product manufacturer and product number *(Figure 3-18)*.

Optical code scanning equipment includes light guns that are aimed at the code and wands that are passed over the code. Grocery stores often use stationary units set in a counter. *Figure 3-19* shows several different types of bar code readers.

Figure 3-18
Bar codes are a type of optical code found on most grocery and retail items. The universal product code (UPC) bar code is the most common. The numbers printed at the bottom identify the manufacturer and the product and can be used to input the item if the bar code reader fails.

Figure 3-19
Three different types of bar code readers are shown here: a hand-held gun, a hand-held wand, and a stationary reader set in the counter of a grocery store.

OPTICAL MARK RECOGNITION

Optical mark recognition (OMR) devices are often used to process questionnaires or test answer sheets *(Figure 3-20)*. Carefully placed marks on the form indicate responses to questions that are read and interpreted by a computer program.

OPTICAL CHARACTER RECOGNITION

Optical character recognition (OCR) devices are scanners that read typewritten, computer-printed, and in some cases hand-printed characters from ordinary documents. OCR devices range from large machines that automatically read thousands of documents per minute to hand-held wands.

An OCR device scans the shape of a character, compares it with a predefined shape stored in memory, and converts the character into the corresponding computer code. The standard OCR typeface, called OCR-A is illustrated in *Figure 3-21*. The characters are read easily by both people and machines. OCR-B is a set of standard characters widely used in Europe and Japan.

OCR is frequently used for **turn-around documents**, documents designed to be returned *(turned around)* to the organization that created them. Examples of such documents are billing statements from credit card companies and department stores. The portion of the statement that you send back with your payment has your account number, total balance, and payment information printed in optical characters.

Figure 3-20

Optical mark recognition devices are often used for processing questionnaires and test answer sheets. For test scores, the reader marks the incorrect answers and reports the number of correct answers and the average score of all tests.

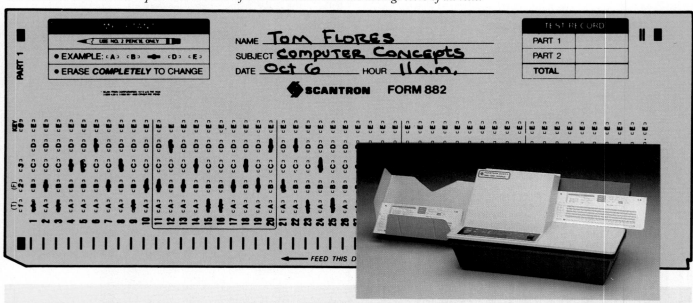

Figure 3-21

In this portion of the OCR-A character set, notice how the characters B and 8 and S and 5 and the number 0 and the letter O are designed differently. Thus, the reading device can easily distinguish between them.

OCR SOFTWARE

OCR **software** is used with image scanners to convert text images into data that can be processed by word processing software. OCR software works as follows: First the entire page of text is scanned. At this point, the page is considered a single graphic image, just like a picture, and individual words are not identified. Next, the software tries to identify individual letters and words. *Figure 3-22* shows how one OCR software package displays the status during this process. Modern OCR software has a very high success rate and can usually identify more than 98% of the scanned material. Finally, the OCR software displays the text that it could not identify. When the user makes the final corrections, the document may be saved in the word processing format of the user's choice.

Magnetic Ink Character Recognition (MICR)

Magnetic ink character recognition (MICR) characters use a special ink that is magnetized during processing. MICR is used almost exclusively by the banking industry for processing checks. Blank (unused) checks already have the bank code, account number, and check number printed in MICR characters across the bottom. When the check is processed by the bank, the amount of the check is also printed in the lower right corner *(Figure 3-23)*. Together, this information is read by MICR reader-sorter machines *(Figure 3-24* on the next page) as part of the check-clearing process.

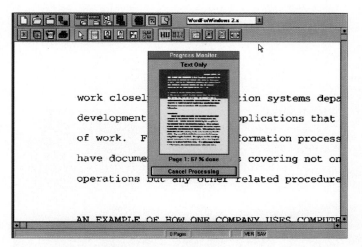

Figure 3-22 ◀
OCR software in the process of converting a page of scanned text into data that can be input to word processing software is shown in this screen. The entire page of text was converted in less than one minute; much faster than the text could be entered using the keyboard.

Figure 3-23 ▼
The MICR characters printed along the bottom edge indicate the bank, account number, and amount of the check. The amount in the lower right corner is added after the check is cashed. The other MICR numbers are preprinted on the check.

BBS
16 WILEY STREET
GLOUCESTER, MA 01930
S.S.# 026-26-8219
PH: (508) 283-2367

DATE	INVOICE	AMOUNT
	BB70	

53-229/113

763

PAY ___ THE SUM 75 DOLS 09 CTS ___ DOLLARS

TIME WK'D	DATE	TO THE ORDER OF	GROSS AMOUNT	INCOME TAX	SOC. SEC.	MEDI-CARE	STATE TAX	NET AMOUNT
	7/8/94	The Office Center 11 Pleasant Street Gloucester, MA 01930	Jank Supplies	Acct# BB70				75 09

GLOUCESTER BANK & TRUST COMPANY
GLOUCESTER, MA

BEVERLY SAUNDERS
PUBLIC ACCOUNTANT

⑆000763⑆ ⑆011302292⑆ 1018512406⑆   ⑆000000750⑆

Check number   Bank and account numbers   Check amount

Data Collection Devices

Data collection devices are designed and used for obtaining data at the site where the transaction or event being reported takes place. Oftentimes, data collection equipment is used in factories, warehouses, or other locations where heat, humidity, and cleanliness are difficult to control *(Figure 3-25)*. Data collection equipment must be rugged and easy to use because it is often operated by persons whose primary task is not entering data.

Figure 3-24
This MICR reader-sorter can process more than a thousand documents per minute. After the documents are read, they are sorted into the vertical bins on the right side of the machine. The reader-sorter is connected to a computer so the data is input as the documents are read.

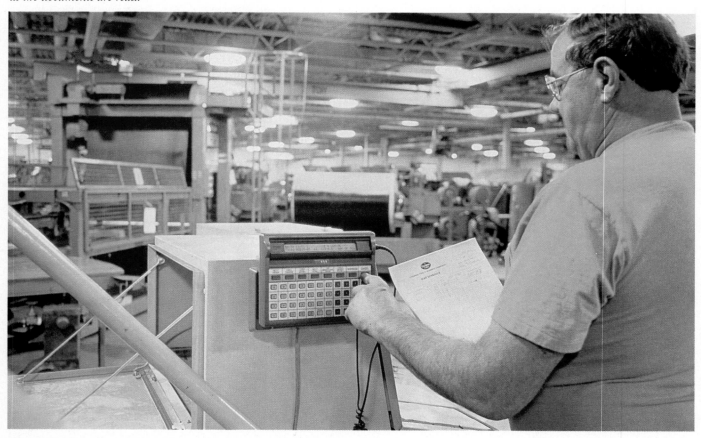

Figure 3-25
Data collection devices are often used in factories and warehouses where heat, humidity, and cleanliness are difficult to control.

Terminals

Terminals, sometimes called **display terminals,** or **video display terminals** (VDTs), consist of a keyboard and a screen. Terminals differ from monitors that only have a viewing screen and no keyboard.

A **dumb terminal** consists of a keyboard and a display screen that are used to enter and transmit data to or receive and display data from a computer to which it is connected. A dumb terminal has no independent processing capability or secondary storage and cannot function as a stand-alone device *(Figure 3-26)*. Dumb terminals are often connected to minicomputers, mainframes, or supercomputers.

Intelligent terminals have built-in processing capabilities and often contain not only the keyboard and screen but also secondary storage devices such as disk drives. Because of their built-in capabilities, these terminals can perform limited processing tasks when they are not communicating directly with the central computer. Intelligent terminals are also known as **programmable terminals** or **smart terminals** because they can be programmed by the user to perform many basic tasks, including arithmetic and logic operations. Personal computers are frequently used as intelligent terminals when they are connected to larger computers.

Special-purpose terminals perform specific jobs and contain features uniquely designed for use in a particular industry. The special-purpose terminal shown in *Figure 3-27* is called a point-of-sale terminal. **Point-of-sale (POS) terminals** allow data to be entered at the time and place where the transaction with a customer occurs, such as in fast-food restaurants or hotels, for example. Point-of-sale terminals serve as input to computers located at the place of business or elsewhere. The data entered is used to maintain sales records, update inventory, make automatic calculations such as sales tax, verify credit, and perform other activities associated with the sales transactions and critical to running the business. Point-of-sale terminals are designed to be easy to operate, requiring little technical knowledge. As shown in *Figure 3-27*, the keys are labeled to assist the user.

Figure 3-26
Dumb terminals have no independent processing capability and cannot function as a stand-alone device. They are usually connected to larger computer systems.

Figure 3-27
Point-of-sale terminals are usually designed for a specific type of business such as a restaurant, hotel, or retail store. Keys are labeled to assist the user in recording transactions.

Multimedia Input Devices

Multimedia is the combination of sound and images with text and graphics. To capture sound and image data, special input devices are required. For personal computers, these input devices consist primarily of electronics contained on a separate card, such as a **sound card** or **video card**, that is installed in the computer.

Sound Input

Sounds are usually recorded with a microphone connected to the sound card or by directly connecting a sound device such as an electronic music keyboard to the sound card. Sound editing software *(Figure 3-28)* allows the user to change the sound after it is recorded.

Voice Input

Voice input, sometimes referred to as speech or voice recognition, allows the user

to enter data and issue commands to the computer with spoken words. Some experts think that voice input may eventually be the most common way to operate a computer. Their belief is based on the fact that people can speak much faster than they can type (approximately 200 words per minute speaking and only 40 words per minute for the average typist). In addition, speaking is a more natural means of communicating than using a keyboard, which takes some time to learn.

Figure 3-28
Sound editing software allows the user to change sounds that have been digitally recorded. Sounds can be duplicated, speeded up, slowed down, or have special effects such as echo or fade added. This screen represents the sound of chimes.

Four areas where voice input is used are data entry, command and control, speaker recognition, and speech to text.

In many voice data entry applications, it is as if the user is verbally filling out a form. Standard questions are verbally completed, usually with a limited number of acceptable responses. For example, voice data entry systems are used for product inspections in manufacturing companies. Instead of manually recording data or using a keyboard, the inspector dictates the completed product information into a microphone.

This is especially efficient when the inspector's hands and eyes must stay focused on the item being inspected.

Command and control applications use a limited vocabulary of words that cause the computer to perform a specific action such as *save* or *print* a document. Command and control applications are also used to operate certain types of industrial machinery.

Speaker recognition applications are usually security oriented such as restricting physical access to a particular area. Unless a person's voice matches a previously recorded pattern, he or she is denied entry. This type of application has been used in banks, government installations, and other high security locations.

Speech-to-text applications offer the most possibility for the widespread use of voice input. With speech-to-text applications, spoken words are immediately translated into computer text and usually displayed on the screen. One area where speech-to-text applications have been implemented is in medical reporting. Many health professionals now use speech-to-text systems to input the numerous reports that must be maintained on patients *(Figure 3-29)*.

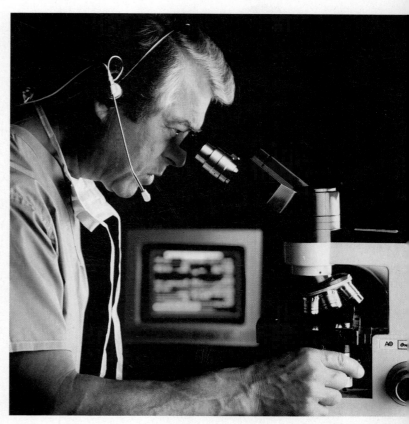

Figure 3-29
Many health care professionals use speech-to-text systems to record information while they are working.

Most voice input systems use a combination of hardware and software to convert spoken words into data the computer can process. The conversion process used by one voice input system developer, shown in *Figure 3-30,* is as follows:

1. The user's voice, consisting of sound waves, is converted into digital form by **digital signal processing** (DSP) circuits that are usually on a separate board added to the computer.
2. The digitized voice input is compared against patterns stored in the voice system's database.
3. Grammar rules are used to resolve possible word conflicts. Based on how a word was used, the computer can usually identify the correct word in cases of words that sound alike such as to, too, and two.
4. Unrecognized words are presented to the user to identify.

With many voice input systems, especially the lower cost systems with limited vocabularies, the user has to train the system to recognize his or her voice. For each of the words in the vocabulary, the user speaks the word. After each word has been spoken several times, the system develops a digital pattern for the word that can be stored on secondary storage. When the user later speaks a word to the system to request a particular action, the system compares the word to the words that were previously entered. When it finds a match, the software performs the activity associated with the word. Such systems are referred to as **speaker dependent** because each person who wants to use the system has to train it to his or her voice. With larger vocabulary systems containing up to 50,000 words, training on individual words is not practical. Instead, developers include multiple patterns, called **voice templates** for each word. These templates include male and female voices as well as regional accents. These systems are called **speaker independent** because most users will not have to train the system to their speech pattern.

Figure 3-30
This diagram shows how one speech recognition company, Kurzweil AI, Inc., converts spoken words to computer input.

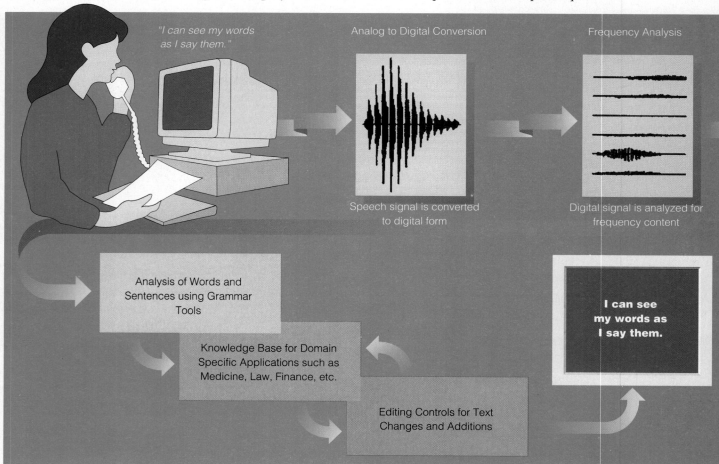

Most speech-to-text systems in use today use **discrete speech recognition** that requires the user to pause slightly between each word. **Continuous speech recognition** systems that allow the user to speak in a flowing conversational tone are not yet widely used because they require more complex software and hardware to separate and make sense of the words. Low cost continuous speech recognition systems are expected to be available for personal computers by the year 2000.

Beyond continuous voice recognition is what is called natural language voice interface. A **natural language voice interface** allows the user to ask a question and have the computer not only convert the question to understandable words but interpret the question and give an appropriate response. For example, think how powerful and easy it would be to use a system if you could simply ask, "How soon can we ship 200 red stainless steel widgets to Boston?" Think about how many different pieces of information the computer might have to pull together to generate a correct response. Such natural language voice recognition systems are not commercially available now but are being developed using powerful computers and sophisticated software.

Digital Camera

Digital cameras record photographs in the form of digital data that can be stored on a computer. No chemical based film is used. Some digital cameras are portable and look similar to traditional film cameras. Other digital cameras are stationary and are connected directly to a computer *(Figure 3-31)*.

Figure 3-31
The digital camera is used to record digital photographs of documents, products, or people. The camera is connected to a video board installed in the computer.

Many companies use digital cameras to record images of their products for computer based catalogs or to record photos of their employees for personnel records *(Figure 3-32)*.

Video Input

Video material is input to the computer using a video camera or a video recorder using previously recorded material. Video data requires tremendous amounts of storage space, which is why video segments in personal computer applications are often limited to only a few seconds. Improvements in video electronics and software and larger capacity storage devices will enable movie length video data to eventually become available. Video applications currently under development include video repair manuals. Rather that just looking at a photo or diagram, the user could view narrated video segments on how to disassemble and repair a piece of equipment.

The input devices discussed in this chapter are summarized in *Figure 3-33*. When any of these devices are used to input data, it is important that the data is entered accurately. Various procedures are used to help ensure data accuracy.

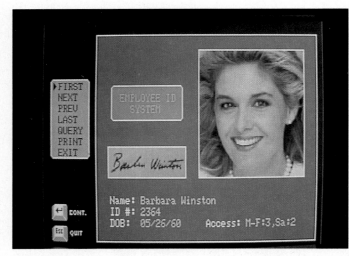

Figure 3-32
Digital cameras are often used to record photographs of employees that are added to their computer-based personnel records.

Data Accuracy

The procedures developed for controlling input are important because accurate data must be entered into a computer to ensure data integrity. Inaccurate information caused by inaccurate data is often worse than no information at all. The computer jargon term **GIGO** states this point very well; it stands for *Garbage In, Garbage Out.*

Because users are often interacting directly with the computer during the input process, procedures and documentation must be quite clear. Computer programs and procedures must be designed to check for accurate data and should specify the steps to take if the data is not valid. Although different applications will have specific criteria for validating input data, several tests can be performed before the data is processed by the computer. Some of these tests are:

- Tests for data type and format – If data should be of a particular type, such as alphabetic or numeric, then it should be tested for that. Often, a data type test is combined with a data format test. For example, in the United States, the ZIP postal code should either be five digits alone or five digits followed by a dash followed by four digits. Unless the data fits one of those two formats, it should be rejected.

DEVICE	DESCRIPTION
Keyboard	Most commonly used input device; special keys may include numeric keypad, cursor control keys, and function keys
Mouse or Trackball	Used to move pointer and select options
Joystick	Stem device often used as input device for games
Pen Input	Uses pen to input and edit data and select processing options
Touch Screen	User interacts with computer by touching screen with finger
Light Pen	Used to select options or draw on screen
Digitizer	Used to enter or edit drawings
Graphic Tablet	Digitizer with special processing options built into tablet
Image Scanner	Converts text, graphics, or photos into digital input
Optical Recognition	Uses light source to read codes, marks, and characters
MICR	Used in banking to read magnetic ink characters on checks
Data Collection	Used in factories and warehouses to input data at source
Sound Input	Converts sound into digital data
Voice Input	Converts speech into digital data
Digital Camera	Captures digital image of subject or object
Video Input	Converts video into digital data

Figure 3-33
A summary of some of the more common input devices.

- Tests for data reasonableness – A reasonableness check ensures that the data entered is within normal or accepted boundaries. For example, suppose no employee within a company is authorized to work more than 80 hours per week. If the value entered in the hours worked field is greater than 80, the value in the field would be indicated as a probable error.
- Tests for data consistency – In some cases, data entered cannot, by itself, be found to be invalid. If, however, the data is examined in relation to other data entered for the same transaction, discrepancies might be found. For example, in a hotel reservation system, both the check-in and check-out dates are entered. Each date should be checked to make sure it is valid. In addition, the check-out date should be later than the check-in date. If the check-out date is earlier than the check-in date, an error has been made when entering one of the dates *(Figure 3-34)*.
- Tests for transcription and transposition errors – The possibility always exists that an operator will make an error when entering data. A **transcription error** occurs when an error is made in copying the values from a source document. For example, if the operator keys the customer number

7165 when the proper number is 7765, the operator has made a transcription error. A **transposition error** happens when the operator switches two numbers. Such an error has occurred when the number 7765 is entered as 7756. Transcription and transposition errors are often difficult to detect. Usually, some other piece of information must be checked to verify that the data entered is correct. For example, when entering a customer number, the user should verify that the corresponding customer name is correct before proceeding.

Summary of Input to the Computer

Chapter 3 presented an overview of the information processing cycle and discussed how data is organized. Also discussed were the four types of input and a variety of input devices. Procedures used to ensure data accuracy were presented and explained. After reading this chapter, you should have a better overall understanding of computer input.

Figure 3-34
One way to check for data accuracy is to compare one piece of data with another and look for logical errors. In this example of a hotel reservation system, the system compared the check-out date with the check-in date. Because the check-out date was earlier than the check-in date, an error message was displayed and the user was asked to reenter the dates.

COMPUTERS AT WORK

Helping People with Special Needs

For physically challenged and disabled individuals, working with standard computers may be either difficult or impossible. Fortunately, special software and hardware, called adaptive, or assistive, technology enables many of these individuals to use computers productively and independently.

Adaptive technology covers a wide range of hardware and software products that help the user make the computer meet his or her special needs. For people with motor disabilities who cannot use a standard keyboard, there are a number of alternative input devices. Most of these devices involve the use of a switch that is controlled by any reliable muscle. One type of switch is even activated by breathing into a tube. The switches are used with special software to select commands or input characters. For those who cannot use their muscles to activate switches, a system exists that is controlled by eye movement. Called Eyegaze, the system uses a camera mounted on the computer and directed at one of the user's eyes. Using the movement of the user's eye, software determines where on the screen the user is looking to within $1/4$ inch accuracy. To activate a choice on the screen, the user has to stare at it for approximately $1/4$ second.

For blind individuals, voice recognition programs allow for verbal input. Software is also available that converts text to Braille and sends it to Braille printers. Both blind and nonverbal individuals use speech synthesis equipment to convert text documents into spoken words. For people with limited vision, several programs are available that magnify information on the screen.

The use of adaptive technology received further encouragement when the Americans with Disabilities Act (ADA) was enacted. Since 1994, the ADA requires that all companies with 15 or more employees make reasonable attempts to accommodate the needs of workers with physical challenges. Many employers are complying with the legislation through the use of personal computers and adaptive technology software and equipment.

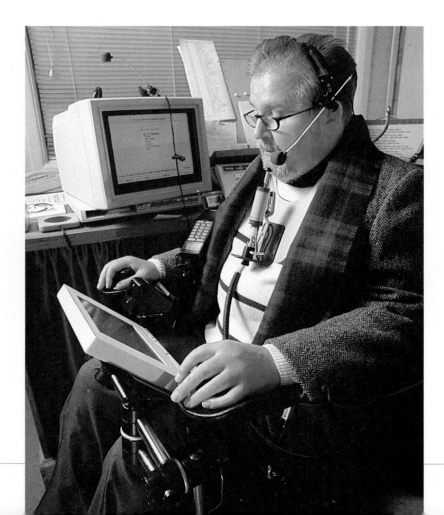

Figure 3-35

IN THE FUTURE

"Computer, tell me the status of . . ."

In many science fiction stories, humans have conversations with computers. The human speaks in a natural, conversational tone and the computer responds in a similar manner, sometimes asking questions to clarify the human's statement or request. Many experts believe that this type of natural language interface will one day become the way humans interact with a computer. To provide this capability, however, much more powerful and faster computers will have to be developed. In addition, voice recognition software will have to be significantly improved.

To understand human speech, a computer has to go through four steps: sound analysis, word recognition, sentence or thought construction, and statement context. Sound analysis is the easiest part. Sound waves are converted into the smallest units of speech, called phonemes. During word recognition, the phonemes are joined together to form words. This can be a difficult task because conversational speech often runs one word into another. The problem becomes more difficult during sentence and thought construction. During this process, the identified words are joined together to make a logical statement. As your high school English teacher may have told you, people do not always speak or write in a logical manner using correct grammar. Statement context involves using past statements to provide information about a current statement. For example, say an airline reservation agent told you there were no flights available on the day you wanted to leave, June 20. If you said, "How about the next day?", the computer should know that you now want to check the flights on June 21.

Some experts think that significant breakthroughs in natural speech recognition are just a few years away. Others think that easy to use systems will not be available until after the year 2000. The optimists, however, are already talking about the next human interface challenge; how to read lips!

Do you remember *HAL*, the computer in the movie *2001: A Space Odyssey*?

Figure 3-36

File   Edit   Section   Page   Tools   Options   Help

What You Should Know

1. The input operation must take place before any data can be processed and any information produced and stored. **Input** refers to the process of entering data, programs, commands, and user responses into main memory.

2. **Data** refers to the raw facts, including numbers, letters, words, images, and sounds a computer receives during the input operation and processes to produce information. **Programs** are instructions that direct the computer to perform the necessary operations to process data into information. **Commands** are key words and phrases the user inputs to direct the computer to perform certain activities. **User responses** refer to the data a user inputs to respond to a question or message from the software.

3. The **keyboard** is the most commonly used input device. The alphabetic keys are arranged like those on a typewriter, and a **numeric keypad** is located on the right-hand side of most keyboards. A **cursor** is a symbol that indicates where the next character typed will appear on the screen. Other keyboard keys include the **arrow keys** or **cursor control keys**, and **function keys**.

4. Pointing devices allow the user to control an on-screen symbol called the **mouse pointer** or **pointer** that is usually represented by an arrow-shaped marker.

5. A **mouse** is a small, lightweight input device that easily fits in the palm of your hand. Moving the mouse across a flat surface controls the movement of the pointer on the screen, and the buttons on top of the mouse can be used to select options displayed on the screen.

6. A **trackball** is a pointing device like a mouse only with the ball on top of the device instead of on the bottom.

7. A **joystick** uses the movement of a vertical stem to direct the pointer.

8. **Pen input devices** allow the user to use the pen in three ways; to input data using hand-written characters and shapes the computer can recognize, as a pointing device like a mouse to select items on the screen, and to gesture, which is a way of issuing commands. When the pen touches the screen, the computer darkens that location. The darkened area is referred to as **ink**.

9. Most **handwriting recognition software** can be taught to recognize an individual's unique style of writing. **Gestures** are special symbols made with the pen that issue a command.

10. A **touch screen** allows users to touch areas of the screen to enter data. A **light pen** is used by touching it on the display screen to create or modify graphics. A **digitizer** converts points, lines, and curves from a sketch, drawing, or photograph to digital impulses and transmits them to a computer. A **graphics tablet** works in a manner similar to a digitizer, but it also contains unique characters and commands that can be automatically generated by the person using the tablet.

11. **Source data automation**, sometimes called **source data collection**, refers to procedures and equipment designed to make the input process more efficient by eliminating the manual entry of data. Data is captured directly from its original form, called a **source document**.

12. An **image scanner**, sometimes called a **page scanner**, is an input device that electronically captures an entire page of text or images, such as photographs or art work. **Image processing systems** use scanners to capture and electronically file documents.

13. **Optical recognition** devices use a light source to read codes, marks, and characters and convert them into digital data that can be processed by a computer.

14. **Optical codes** use a pattern or symbols to represent data. A **bar code**, the most common optical code, consists of a set of vertical lines and spaces of different widths. There are several different types of bar codes, but the most familiar is the **universal product code** (UPC) used for grocery and retail items.

Windows 95

Start

15. **Optical mark recognition** (OMR) devices can read carefully placed marks on specially designed documents such as questionnaires or test answer sheets.

16. **Optical character recognition** (OCR) devices are scanners that read typewritten, computer-printed, and in some cases hand-printed characters from ordinary documents. OCR is frequently used for **turn-around documents** that are designed to be returned to the organization that created them.

17. **OCR software** is used with image scanners to convert text images into data that can be processed by word processing software.

18. **Magnetic ink character recognition** (MICR) characters use a special ink that can be magnetized during processing. MICR is used almost exclusively by the banking industry for processing checks.

19. **Data collection devices** are designed and used for obtaining data at the site where the transaction or event being reported takes place. They are often used in rugged locations, such as factories or warehouses, and operated by persons whose primary task is not entering data.

20. Terminals, sometimes called **display terminals** or **video display terminals** (VDTs), consist of a keyboard and a screen. A **dumb terminal** can be used to enter and transmit data to or receive data from a computer to which it is connected. It has no independent processing capability or secondary storage and cannot function as a stand-alone device. **Intelligent terminals**, also known as **programmable terminals** or **smart terminals**, have built-in processing capabilities, can be programmed by the user to perform many basic tasks, and often contain secondary storage devices. **Point-of-sale** (POS) terminals are special-purpose terminals that allow data to be entered at the time and place where the transaction with a customer occurs.

21. **Multimedia** is the combination of sound and images with text and graphics. Personal computers use special input devices consisting primarily of electronics contained on a separate card, such as a **sound card** or **video card**, that are installed in the computer to capture sound and image data.

22. Sounds are usually recorded by connecting a microphone or electronic music keyboard to the sound card. **Voice input** allows the user to enter data and issue commands to the computer with spoken words. The user's voice, consisting of sound waves, is converted into digital form by **digital signal processing** (DSP) circuits. Four areas where voice input is used are data entry, command and control, speaker recognition, and speech-to-text.

23. Voice input systems that must be trained to the voice of each person who wants to use the system are referred to as **speaker dependent**. Voice input systems that contain **voice templates** for each word are called **speaker independent**, because most users will not have to train the system to their speech pattern.

24. Most speech-to-text systems in use today use **discrete speech recognition** that requires the user to pause slightly between each word. **Continuous speech recognition** systems allow the user to speak in a flowing conversational tone but are not yet widely used. A **natural language voice interface** allows the user to ask a question and have the computer not only convert the question to understandable words but to interpret the question and give an appropriate response.

25. **Digital cameras** record photographs in the form of digital data that can be stored on a computer.

26. Video material is input to the computer with a video camera or a video recorder using previously recorded material. Video data requires tremendous amounts of storage space.

27. Inaccurate information caused by inaccurate data is often worse than no information at all. The computer jargon GIGO states this very well; it stands for *Garbage In, Garbage Out.*

28. Several tests can be performed to validate data before it is processed by the computer. Some of these tests are: tests for data type and format, tests for data reasonableness, tests for data consistency, and tests for **transcription errors** (errors made in copying values from a source document) and **transposition errors** (errors made by switching two numbers).

File   Edit   Section   Page   Tools   Options   Help

Terms to Remember

arrow keys (3.4)

bar code (3.11)

commands (3.2)
continuous speed recognition (3.19)
cursor (3.4)
cursor control keys (3.4)

data (3.3)
data collection devices (3.14)
digital camera (3.19)
digital signal processing (DSP) (3.18)
digitizer (3.9)
discrete speech recognition (3.19)
display terminals (3.15)
dumb terminals (3.15)

function keys (3.4)

gestures (3.7)
GIGO (Garbage In, Garbage Out) (3.20)
graphics tablet (3.9)

handwriting recognition software (3.7)

image processing systems (3.10)
image scanner (3.10)
ink (3.7)
input (3.2)
intelligent terminals (3.15)

joystick (3.6)

keyboard (3.3)

light pen (3.9)

magnetic ink character recognition
    (MICR) (3.13)
mouse (3.5)
mouse pointer (3.5)
multimedia (3.16)

natural language voice interface (3.19)
numeric keypad (3.3)

OCR software (3.13)
optical character recognition
    (OCR) (3.12)
optical codes (3.11)
optical mark recognition (OMR) (3.12)
optical recognition (3.11)

page scanner (3.10)
pen input devices (3.7)
point-of-sale (POS) terminals (3.15)
pointer (3.5)
programmable terminals (3.15)
programs (3.2)

smart terminals (3.15)
sound card (3.16)
source data automation (3.10)
source data collection (3.10)
source document (3.10)
speaker dependent (3.18)
speaker independent (3.18)

touch screen (3.8)
trackball (3.6)
transcription error (3.21)
transposition error (3.21)
turn-around documents (3.12)

universal product code (UPC) (3.11)
user responses (3.3)

video card (3.16)
video display terminals (VDT) (3.15)
voice input (3.16)
voice templates (3.18)

File   Edit   Section   Page   Tools   Options   Help

Test Your Knowledge

Fill in the Blanks

1. The information processing cycle consists of four operations: _____Input_____, _____Processing_____, _____Output_____, and _____Storage_____.

2. In the information processing cycle, the _____input_____ operation must take place before any data can be processed and any information produced and stored.

3. A(n) _____mouse_____ is a pointing device that, by moving it across a flat surface and pressing buttons, can be used to move the pointer and select options on the screen.

4. Three types of terminals are: _____Dumb terminal_____, which can be used to enter, transmit, receive, or display data but have no independent processing capability; _____Intelligent Terminal_____ which have built-in processing capabilities and often contain disk drives and printers; and _____Point of Sale_____, which allow data to be entered at the time and place where the transaction with a customer occurs.

5. _____Multimedia_____ is the combination of sound and images with text and graphics.

Short Answer

1. What is input? List the four types of input and briefly describe how the computer uses each type.

2. Although a computer keyboard is similar to a typewriter keyboard, a computer keyboard also has keys that are not found on the keyboard of a traditional typewriter. What are some of these keys? For what purpose are these keys used?

3. How are a mouse, trackball, and joystick similar? How are they different? What is the primary advantage of a mouse? What are the disadvantages? What advantage does a trackball have over a mouse?

4. What is a terminal? How is a dumb terminal different from an intelligent terminal? How is a point-of-sale terminal used?

5. Why is data accuracy important? What does the computer jargon term GIGO mean? Briefly describe three tests for data accuracy that can be performed before the data is processed by the computer.

Label the Figure

Instructions: The examples below show gestures; special symbols made with pen input devices. In the spaces provided, list the command issued for each gesture.

Gesture	Command	Gesture	Command
•	_____	←	_____
→	_____	↗	_____
↗	_____	∝	_____
↔	_____	∧	_____
→	_____	8	_____

 Start

 3:02 AM

Points to Ponder

1

The traditional arrangement of letters on a keyboard is sometimes called the QWERTY layout. The name QWERTY comes from the first six keys in the top row of letters. This layout was initially adopted by early typewriters to place the most commonly used letters in locations that were not easily reached, to slow typists down and prevent keys from jamming. Although keys jamming is no longer a problem, most keyboards still use the same design today. A different key arrangement, called the Dvorak layout, places the most commonly used letters on the home row, the row on which your fingers rest. What are the advantages of the Dvorak layout? What are the disadvantages? If a typist was trained to use both keyboard layouts, which do you think would result in faster data input? Why? Will the Dvorak layout ever be widely accepted? Why or why not?

2

At one time, the keyboard was the only means of inputting data into a computer. Although the keyboard remains the most commonly used input device, the mouse has also become almost essential; many makers of computer software require the use of a mouse with their application packages. What does the future of input devices hold? Thirty years from now, will a different pointing device be more popular than the mouse? Will the keyboard be replaced by another input device? Why? Will any input device become an historical oddity, seen only in museums? Why?

3

Pen input devices have been adapted to many applications and are currently being used by sales representatives, delivery services, nurses and doctors, and inventory takers. In what way do you think pen input devices are particularly useful in each of these fields? List some other areas that you feel could use pen input devices and briefly describe how they could be used in each. Do you think a pen input device would be valuable to a student? Why or why not?

4

A recent controversy in one county in New York state involved the use of optical code scanners in grocery stores. Scanners were being used at the check-out counters to determine the price of each purchase and, although prices were indicated on the grocery shelves, they were not marked on individual grocery items. Consumer groups argued that the shelf price tags were hard to read and not having price stickers on each item made it difficult to compare prices. In addition, they claimed that the databases from which the scanners obtained prices were not always accurate and frequently were not updated to reflect sale prices. The grocery stores maintained that the labor involved in individual item pricing would add to the item's cost, and that most of the time their scanned prices were accurate. What do you think? Should grocery stores be required to put a price on each individual item? Why or why not? Can you think of any other way to answer consumer concerns?

5

Although computers have become widespread, many people are still intimidated when forced to input data into a computer. Of the input devices discussed in this chapter, which do you feel would be the easiest to use for someone who is uncomfortable with computers? Why? Which input device do you think requires the most training? If a school decided every student must learn to use one input device, which device do you think should be taught? Why?

6

All input devices require some form of human interaction. A keyboard requires a great deal of human interaction because someone inputting data must not only read the data accurately but also locate and press the correct keys. In contrast, an optical code scanner requires a minimum of human interaction because the user need only pass the optical code in front of the scanner. Keeping in mind the tests described in this chapter, what impact do you think the degree of human interaction has on data accuracy? Why? List at least five input devices in order, from those that require the most human interaction to those that require the least human interaction. Which input devices do you think result in the most accurate input of data? Why?

File   Edit   Section   Page   Tools   Options   Help

Out and About

1. Although all computer keyboards may seem alike, the placement of special keys, the space between keys, the feel of the keys, and the noise produced when a key is pressed may vary. Visit a computer vendor and try at least three different types of computer keyboards. Evaluate each keyboard in terms of the suggested characteristics. Which keyboard do you like best? Why? Which keyboard do you like least? Why?

2. Visit a firm or organization that uses computers. Talk with a person involved with computer operations to find out what types of input devices are used. For what purpose is each device used? Has the firm or organization ever experienced problems as a result of inaccurate data being entered into the computer? If so, what kinds of problems? What measures were taken to insure that the problems did not happen again?

3. The wide range of input devices available for computers has helped many physically challenged individuals. Use a library to research the types of input devices that have helped people facing physical challenges. What types of input devices have been used? What input devices have been particularly helpful for people with specific physical disabilities?

4. Optical code scanners are used by retail stores, supermarkets, and libraries. Visit an organization that uses optical code scanners to find out how the scanners are used. What types of information are they able to record? How is the information used? In what way does the information obtained through the use of scanners benefit the organization or the organization's clientele? Were they able to keep track of the same information before they used scanners? Why or why not?

5. Visit a local bank and ask an employee about ATM (automatic teller machine) terminals. How are they used? What kind of information do they obtain? What security measures are provided? What precautions does the bank suggest to ATM users? Has the bank ever had any trouble with their ATMs? If so, what? After interviewing the bank employee, decide whether you think an ATM is a dumb terminal or an intelligent terminal. Why?

6. Visit a computer vendor and select a personal computer system displayed in the store. Make a list of the input devices that can be used with that personal computer, and provide a price for each input device. If you were to purchase that personal computer, which input device or devices would you want to purchase right away? Why? Which input devices do you think you might purchase at a later date? Why? Are there any available input devices that you think you would never buy? Why?

Start   3:04 AM

File   Edit   Section   Page   Tools   Options   Help

In the Lab with Windows 95

1 Shelly Cashman Series Input Lab   Follow the instructions in Windows 95 Lab 1 on page 1.30 to display the Shelly Cashman Series Labs screen. Click Scanning Documents. Click the Start Lab button. When the initial screen displays, carefully read the objectives. With your printer turned on, click the Print Questions button. Fill out the top of the Questions sheet and answer the questions as you step through the Input Lab. Close the Shelly Cashman Series Labs.

2 Scanning a Photograph   Bring a 3 1/2 x 5" (or larger) picture of yourself or family members to class. Ask your instructor for assistance in scanning the photograph to create a digital version on your floppy disk using your name as the file-name. Click the Start button on the taskbar, point to Programs on the Start menu, point to Accessories on the Programs submenu, and then click Paint on the Accessories submenu. To open the file containing your picture, click File on the menu bar and then click Open. In the Open dialog box, type a: followed by your filename in the File name text box and then click the Open button. Your Paint window should be similar to the one shown in *Figure 3-37*. To print your picture, click File on the menu bar, click Print, and then click the OK button. Close Paint.

3 Using the Mouse and Keyboard to Interact with an Online Program   Obtain information from your instructor on the location (path) of the file LOANCALC.EXE. Click the Start button on the taskbar, and then click Run on the Start menu to display the Run dialog box. In the Open

text box, type the path and filename loancalc. For example, type c:\sclabs\loancalc and then press ENTER to display the Loan Payment Calculator window. Type 100000 in the LOAN AMOUNT text box. Click the YEARS right scroll arrow or drag the scroll box until YEARS equals 15. Click the APR right scroll arrow or drag the scroll box until the APR equals 9.75. Click the Calculate button. Note the monthly payments and sum of all payments made *(Figure 3-38)*. Click the Clear button. What is the monthly payment and sum of payments for each of these loan amounts, years, and APRs? (1) 15000, 5, 6.25; (2) 55000, 30, 10.25; (3) 162500, 30, 8; (4) 75550, 15, 9.25; and (5) 9750, 3, 7.5. Click the About button. Who wrote this program? Click the OK button. Close Loan Payment Calculator.

4 More About Using Help   Click the Start button on the taskbar, and then click Help on the Start menu to display the Help Topics: Windows Help dialog box. Click the Contents tab, double-click How To…, and then double-click Use Help. One at a time, double-click the seven topics listed beneath Use Help. Read and print each one by clicking the Options button, clicking Print Topic, and then clicking the OK button. Click the Help Topics button to return to Help Topics: Windows Help. Close any open Help windows.

Figure 3-37

Figure 3-38

File   Edit   Section   Page   Tools   Options   Help

Where on the Web

1 The Amazing Fishcam   Digital cameras record photographs in the form of digital data that can be stored in a computer. Complete the following steps to see a "live" digital camera in action *(Figure 3-39)*. With Netscape on the screen, type www2.netscape.com/fishcam/fishcam.html in the Location text box and then press ENTER. Scroll down and click The Continuously Refreshing Fish Cam. Scroll down and watch the aquarium. Click Go Back To The Fish Cam. Scroll down and click About The Fishcam. Read about the fish cam. Click Print on the File menu. Click Pages and then type 1 in the To text box. Click OK. Hand in the printout.

2 Assistive Technology   For physically challenged and disabled individuals, working with standard computers either may be difficult or impossible. Complete the following steps to learn about how IBM Corporation is addressing these special needs. With Netscape on the screen, type http://www.ibm.com in the Location text box and then press ENTER. Click Products. Scroll down and click Technology for People with Special Needs. Read the first few paragraphs and then scroll down to Product Information. Click one of the products listed. Read about that product. Click Print on the File menu. Click OK. Hand in the printout.

3 Majestic Landscapes   Complete the following steps to visit the Kodak Web site and learn more about digital imaging. With Netscape on the screen, type http://www.kodak.com in the Location text box and then press ENTER. Scroll down and click Digital Imaging. Click Sample Digital Images. Scroll down and click How The Images

Were Prepared, and then read the first couple of paragraphs. Click the Back button on the Netscape toolbar. Click one of the sets of images listed under Photo CD Samples. Scroll down to the set of numbered images such as those shown in *Figure 3-40*. Click any one of the images. Click Print on the File menu. Click OK. Hand in the printout.

4 Voice Recognition Systems   Complete the following steps to learn more about voice input systems and speech recognition. With Netscape on the screen, type http://www.voila.com in the Location text box and then press ENTER. Scroll down and click Voice Input Solutions. Read about the types of voice recognition systems. Click Print on the File menu. Click Pages and then type 1 in the To text box. Click OK. Hand in the printout.

5 Shelly Cashman Online   Click Using Computers: A Gateway To Information, World Wide Web Edition on the Shelly Cashman Student Center Web page (http://www.bf.com/scstudnt.html). Scroll down and click Chapter 3. Complete the activities listed.

Figure 3-39

Figure 3-40

The System Unit

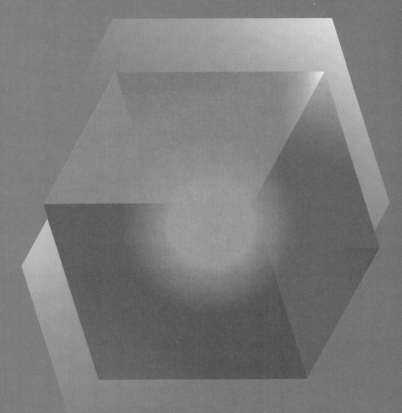

The information processing cycle consists of input, processing, output, and storage operations. When an input operation is completed and both a program and data are stored in main memory, processing operations can begin. During these operations, the system unit executes, or performs, the program instructions and processes the data into information.

Chapter 4 examines the components of the system unit, describes how main memory stores programs and data, and discusses the sequence of operations that occurs when instructions are executed on a computer. These topics are followed by a discussion of types of processing and number systems.

Objectives

After completing this chapter, you will be able to:

- Define a bit and describe how a series of bits in a byte is used to represent data

- Discuss how the ASCII and EBCDIC codes represent characters

- Identify the components of the system unit and describe their use

- Describe how the CPU uses the four steps of the machine cycle to process data

- Describe the primary use and characteristics of RAM and ROM memory

- Explain the difference between parallel and serial ports

- Describe a machine language instruction and the instruction set of a computer

- Describe various types of processing including pipe-lining, parallel processing, and neural networks

- Convert numbers between the decimal, binary, and hexadecimal number systems

What Is the System Unit?

*T*he term computer is usually used to describe the collection of devices that perform the information processing cycle. This term is also used more specifically to describe the system unit, because this is where the *computing* actually occurs *(Figure 4-1)*. It is in the **system unit** that the computer program instructions are executed and the data is manipulated. The system unit contains the central processing unit, or CPU, main memory, and other electronics *(Figure 4-2)*. To better understand how the system unit processes data, an explanation of how data is represented electronically follows.

How Data Is Represented Electronically

Most computers are **digital computers**, meaning that the data they process, whether it be text, sound, graphics, or video, is first converted into a digital (numeric) value. Converting data into a digital form is called **digitizing**. Other types of computers, called **analog computers**, are designed to process continuously variable data, such as electrical voltage.

You may be thinking that the digital values used by a computer are the numbers 0 through 9. In fact, only the numbers 0 and 1 are used. A 0 is used to represent the electronic state of *off* and a 1 is used to represent the electronic state of *on*. Each off or on digital value is called a **bit**, the smallest unit of data handled by a computer. Bit is short for *bi*nary dig*it*. The binary number system represents quantities by using only two numbers, 0 and 1 *(Figure 4-3)*.

By itself, a bit cannot represent much data. In a group of eight bits, called a **byte**, 256 different possibilities can be represented by using all the combinations of 0s and 1s. This provides enough combinations so a unique code can be assigned to each of the characters that are commonly used, such as the numbers 0 through 9, the uppercase and lowercase

Figure 4-2
The system unit contains the central processing unit (CPU), main memory, and other electronics. The system unit is connected to input devices such as a keyboard or mouse and output devices such as a monitor or printer. Secondary storage devices, such as a disk drive, can be located either inside or outside the system unit case.

Figure 4-1
The system unit is the metal or plastic case that contains the CPU, main memory, and other electronics that process information.

alphabet, foreign characters that require special accent marks such as umlauts (¨) and tildes (~), and special characters such as punctuation marks *(Figure 4-4)*. Several different coding schemes are used on computers.

ASCII and EBCDIC

Two popular codes that represent characters in memory and on secondary storage are the ASCII and EBCDIC codes. The **American Standard Code for Information Interchange**, called **ASCII** (pronounced ask-ee), is the most widely used coding system to represent data. Originally a seven-bit code, ASCII has been expanded to an eight-bit code. ASCII is used on personal computers and minicomputers. The **Extended Binary Coded Decimal Interchange Code**, or **EBCDIC** (pronounced eb-see-dick) is used primarily on mainframe computers. *Figure 4-5* summarizes these codes. Notice how the combination of bits, represented in binary, is unique for each character.

SYMBOL	ASCII	EBCDIC
0	01100000	11110000
1	01100001	11110001
2	01100010	11110010
3	01100011	11110011
4	01100100	11110100
5	01100101	11110101
6	01100110	11110110
7	01100111	11110111
8	01101000	11111000
9	01101001	11111001
A	01000001	11000001
B	01000010	11000010
C	01000011	11000011
D	01000100	11000100
E	01000101	11000101
F	01000110	11000110
G	01000111	11000111
H	01001000	11001000
I	01001001	11001001
J	01001010	11010001
K	01001011	11010010
L	01001100	11010011
M	01001101	11010100
N	01001110	11010101
O	01001111	11010110
P	01010000	11010111
Q	01010001	11011000
R	01010010	11011001
S	01010011	11100010
T	01010100	11100011
U	01010101	11100100
V	01010110	11100101
W	01010111	11100110
X	01011000	11100111
Y	01011001	11101000
Z	01011010	11101001
!	00100001	01011010
"	00100010	01111111
#	00100011	01111011
$	00100100	01011011
%	00100101	01101100
&	00100110	01010000
(	00101000	01001101
)	00101001	01011101
*	00101010	01011100
+	00101011	01001110

BINARY NUMBER	0	1
BIT	○	●
STATUS	OFF	ON

Figure 4-3
A bit, the smallest unit of data handled by a computer, can either be off or on. The binary numbers 0 and 1 are used to represent off and on, respectively.

0	1	0	0	0	0	0	1
○	●	○	○	○	○	○	●

8 – BIT BYTE

Figure 4-4
A graphic representation of an eight-bit byte with two bits on and six bits off. The off bits (open circles) are represented by the binary number 0 and the on bits (solid circles) are represented by the binary number 1. This combination of bits represents the letter A using the ASCII code.

Figure 4-5
Numeric, uppercase alphabetic, and several special characters as they are represented in ASCII and EBCDIC. Each character is represented in binary using a unique ordering of zeros and ones.

When the ASCII or EBCDIC code is used, each character that is represented is stored in one byte of memory. There are also other binary formats, sometimes used by the computer to represent numeric data. For example, a computer may store, or *pack,* two numeric characters in one byte of memory. These binary formats are used by the computer to increase storage and processing efficiency.

Parity

Regardless of whether ASCII, EBCDIC, or other binary methods are used to represent characters in main memory, it is important that the characters be stored accurately. For each byte of memory, most computers have at least one extra bit, called a **parity bit**, that is used by the computer for error checking. A parity bit can detect if one of the bits in a byte has been accidentally changed. While such errors are rare, they can occur because of voltage fluctuations, static electricity, or a memory failure.

Computers are either odd or even parity machines. In computers with **odd parity**, the total number of *on* bits in the byte (including the parity bit) must be an odd number *(Figure 4-6)*. In computers with **even parity**, the total number of *on* bits must be an even number. Parity is checked by the computer each time a memory location is used. When data is moved from one location to another in main memory, the parity bits of both the sending and receiving locations are compared to see if they are the same. If the system detects a difference or if the wrong number of bits is on (e.g., an even number in a system with odd parity), an error message displays. Some computers use multiple parity bits that enable them to detect and correct a single-bit error and detect multiple-bit errors.

Figure 4-6
In a computer with odd parity, the parity bit is turned on or off to make the total number of on bits (including the parity bit) an odd number. Here, the letters T and O have an odd number of bits so the parity bits are left off. The number of bits for the letter M is even, so in order to achieve parity, the parity bit is turned on.

The Components of the System Unit

The components of the system unit are usually contained in a metal or plastic case. For personal computers, all system unit components are usually in a single box. For larger and more powerful computers, the components may be housed in several cabinets. The components considered part of the system unit and discussed in the following sections include: the motherboard, the microprocessor and CPU, upgrade sockets, memory, coprocessors, buses, expansion slots, ports and connectors, bays, the power supply, and sound components *(Figure 4-7)*.

Figure 4-7
The components of the system unit are usually inside a plastic or metal case. This illustration shows how some of the components might be arranged on a typical PC.

Ports and connectors

Expansion boards

Expansion slots

Upgrade socket

Speaker

Memory

CPU

Motherboard

Power supply

Bays

Motherboard

The **motherboard**, sometimes called the **main board** or **system board**, is a circuit board that contains most of the electronic components of the system unit. *Figure 4-8* shows a photograph of a personal computer motherboard. One of the main components on the motherboard is the microprocessor.

Figure 4-8
The main circuit board (motherboard) of a personal computer.

Microprocessor and the CPU

On a personal computer, the CPU or central processing unit, is contained on a single integrated circuit called a **microprocessor** *(Figure 4-9)* that is located on the motherboard. An **integrated circuit**, also called a **chip** or an **IC**, is a complete electronic circuit that has been etched on a small slice of nonconducting material such as silicon. For mainframe and supercomputers, the CPU consists of one or more circuit boards *(Figure 4-10)*.

The **central processing unit** (CPU) contains the control unit and the arithmetic/logic unit. These two components work together using the program and data stored in main memory to perform the processing operations.

Control Unit

The control unit can be thought of as the *brain* of the computer. Just as the human brain controls the body, the control unit *controls* the computer. The **control unit** operates by repeating the following four operations, called the **machine cycle** *(Figure 4-11):* fetching, decoding, executing, and storing. **Fetching** means obtaining the next program

◀ *Figure 4-9*
A Pentium microprocessor from Intel Corporation. The microprocessor circuits are located in the center. Small gold wires lead from the circuits to the pins that fit in the microprocessor socket on the motherboard. The pins provide an electronic connection to different parts of the computer.

Figure 4-10 ▶
With PCs, the CPU is contained in a single microprocessor chip. With larger computers, the CPU operations are split among several chips and sometimes more than one circuit board.

instruction from main memory. **Decoding** is translating the program instruction into the commands the computer can process. **Executing** refers to the actual processing of the computer commands, and **storing** takes place when the result of the instruction is written to main memory.

System Clock

The control unit utilizes the **system clock** to synchronize, or control the timing of, all computer operations. The system clock generates electronic pulses at a fixed rate, measured in **megahertz** (abbreviated **MHz**). One megahertz equals one million pulses per second. The speed of the system clock varies among computers. Some personal computers can operate at speeds in excess of 100 megahertz.

Arithmetic/Logic Unit

The second part of the CPU is the **arithmetic/logic unit** (**ALU**). This unit contains the electronic circuitry necessary to perform arithmetic and logical operations on data. **Arithmetic operations** include addition, subtraction, multiplication, and division. **Logical operations** consist of comparing one data

item to another to determine if the first data item is *greater than, equal to,* or *less than* the other. Based on the result of the comparison, different processing may occur. For example, two part numbers in different records can be compared. If they are equal, the part quantity in one record can be added to the quantity in the other record. If they are not equal, the quantities would not be added.

Registers

Both the control unit and the ALU contain **registers**, temporary storage locations for specific types of data. Separate registers exist for the current program instruction, the address of the next instruction, and the values of data being processed.

Word Size

One aspect of the CPU that affects the speed of a computer is the word size. The **word size** is the number of bits the CPU processes at one time. The word size of a machine is measured in bits. CPUs can have 8-bit, 16-bit, 32-bit, or 64-bit word sizes. A CPU with a 16-bit word size can manipulate

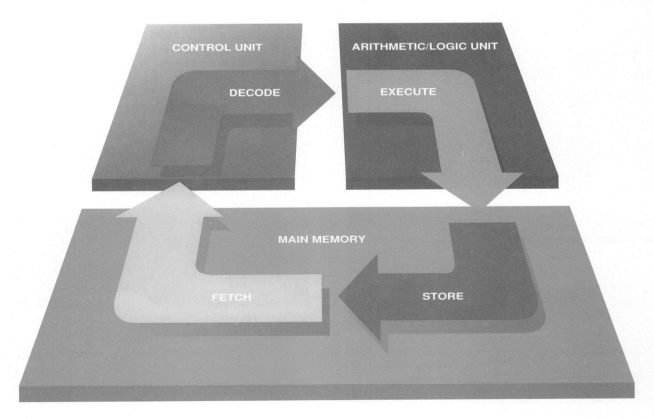

Figure 4-11
The machine cycle consists of four steps; fetching the next instruction, decoding the instruction, executing the instruction, and storing the result. Fetching and decoding are called the instruction cycle. Executing and storing are called the execution cycle.

16 bits at a time. Sometimes, the word size of a computer is given in bytes instead of bits. For example, a word size of 16 bits may be expressed as a word size of two bytes because there are eight bits in a byte. The larger the word size of the CPU, the faster the capability of the computer to process data.

Microprocessor Comparison

Personal computer microprocessors are most often identified by their model number or model name. *Figure 4-12a* summarizes some of the microprocessors currently in use. Microprocessors made by Intel come in several versions designated by letters after the processor name. *Figure 4-12b* explains the differences. Also, when discussing the three Intel processors prior to the Pentium, the "80" in the name/model number is usually not referred to. For example, the 80486 processor is usually referred to as a 486 processor.

Name	Date	Manufacturer	Word Size	Bus Width	Clock Speed (Mhz)	MIPS*
Pentium Pro	1995	Intel	64	64	133-150	250
Pentium	1993	Intel	64	64	60-150	150
80486DX	1989	Intel	32	32	25-100	20-75
80386DX	1985	Intel	32	32	16-33	6-12
80286	1982	Intel	16	16	6-12	1-2
PowerPC	1994	Motorola	64	64	50-133	150
68040	1989	Motorola	32	32	25-40	15-35
68030	1987	Motorola	32	32	16-50	12
68020	1984	Motorola	32	32	16-33	5.5
Alpha	1993	Digital	64	64	150-333	275-1332

MIPS: millions of instructions per second

Figure 4-12a
A comparison of some of the more widely used microprocessors.

486DX4	Internal speed of chip is three times faster than the speed at which the chip communicates with the rest of the system.
486DX2	Internal speed of chip is two times faster than the speed at which the chip communicates with the rest of the system.
486SX	Does not have internal math coprocessor like 486DX models. Slower and less expensive than DX models.
386SX	32-bit word length but only 16-bit data bus. Slower and less expensive than 386DX.
SL	Low voltage version of 386 and 486 chip. Used primarily in portable computers to extend battery life.

Figure 4-12b
Different versions of Intel microprocessors.

Upgrade Sockets

Some motherboards contain empty sockets, called **upgrade sockets** *(Figure 4-13),* that can be used to install more powerful CPUs or additional memory.

The CPU upgrade sockets enable a user to install a more powerful microprocessor and obtain increased performance without having to buy an entirely new system. With a CPU upgrade socket, the old microprocessor does not have to be removed. When the new microprocessor is installed, the old microprocessor is automatically disabled. Many, but not all, systems can install a more powerful microprocessor even if they do not have a separate CPU upgrade socket. For these systems, the old microprocessor is removed and replaced with the new microprocessor.

ZIF socket

Figure 4-13
This motherboard includes an upgrade socket that can accept a more powerful Intel microprocessor. This particular type of socket is called a zero insertion force (ZIF) socket. The ZIF socket uses a lever to clamp down on the microprocessor pins and makes the installation of the chip easier. Other types of upgrade sockets require the microprocessor pins to be forced into the socket.

Memory

Memory refers to integrated circuits that store program instructions and data that can be retrieved. Memory chips are installed in the system unit and also on circuit boards that control other computer devices such as printers. The two most common types of memory chips are Random Access Memory (RAM) and Read Only Memory (ROM).

Random Access Memory

Random access memory, or RAM, is the name given to the integrated circuits, or chips, that are used for main memory. **Main memory**, or **primary storage**, stores three items: the operating system and other system software that direct and coordinate the computer equipment; the application program instructions that direct the work to be done; and the data currently being processed by the application programs. Data and programs are transferred into and out of RAM, and data stored in RAM is manipulated by computer program instructions.

The basic unit of memory is a byte, which you recall consists of eight bits. Just as a house on a street has a unique address that indicates its location on the street, each byte in the main memory of a computer has an address that indicates its location in memory *(Figure 4-14)*. The number that indicates the location of a byte in memory is called a **memory address**. Whenever the computer references a byte, it does so by using the memory address, or location, of that byte.

The size of main memory is measured in either kilobytes or megabytes. A **kilobyte** (abbreviated as **K** or **KB**) is equal to 1,024 bytes, but for discussion purposes, is usually rounded to 1,000 bytes. A **megabyte** (abbreviated as **MB**) is approximately one million bytes. These terms are also used when discussing the storage capacity of other devices such as disk drives.

RAM memory is said to be **volatile** because the programs and data stored in RAM are erased when the power to the computer is turned off. As long as the power remains on,

Figure 4-14
Just as each house on a street has its own address, each byte in main memory is identified by a unique address.

the programs and data stored in RAM will remain intact until they are replaced by other programs and data. Programs and data that are needed for future use must be transferred from RAM to secondary storage before the power is turned off. A relatively new type of memory called **flash RAM** or **flash memory** can retain data even when the power is turned off. Flash memory is sometimes used instead of a disk drive in small portable computers.

Today, most RAM memory is installed by using a SIMM (single in-line memory module). As shown in *Figure 4-15*, a SIMM is a small circuit board that holds multiple RAM chips. Common SIMM sizes are 1, 2, 4, 8, and 16 megabytes of memory. A SIMM is installed directly on the motherboard.

Some computers improve their processing efficiency by using a limited amount of high-speed RAM memory between the CPU and main memory *(Figure 4-16)*. High-speed memory used in this manner is called **cache memory** (pronounced cash). Cache memory is used to store the most frequently used instructions and data. When the processor needs the next program instruction or data, it first checks the cache memory. If the required instruction or data is present in cache (called a *cache hit*), the processor will execute faster

than if the instruction or data has to be retrieved from the slower main memory.

As shown in *Figure 4-17*, memory on personal computers can be divided into four areas. **Conventional memory** is located in the first 640K of RAM and is used for the operating system, programs, and data. **Upper memory** is located between 640K and 1MB of RAM and is used for programs that control input and output devices and other computer hardware. **Extended memory** consists of all memory above 1MB and is used for programs and data. Not all programs are written to use extended memory. Older programs, including many games, must run in conventional memory space or use expanded memory. **Expanded memory** consists of up to 32MB of memory on a memory expansion board. A separate program called an *expanded memory manager* is used to access this memory 16K at a time and transfer the data into upper memory. Newer computers use extended memory and do not have expanded memory.

Figure 4-16
Some computers use high-speed cache memory to store frequently used instructions or data. If the required data or instructions are in cache, the processing will execute faster than if the instruction or data has to be retrieved from slower main memory or from secondary storage. Cache memory can consist of separate chips mounted on the motherboard or can be included in the actual CPU.

Figure 4-15
Most RAM memory is installed using a SIMM (single in-line memory module). SIMMs usually contain nine chips mounted on a small circuit board. Each chip represents one of the eight bit positions in a byte plus the parity bit. Common SIMM sizes are 1, 2, 4, 8, and 16 megabytes.

Read Only Memory

Read only memory (ROM) is the name given to chips that store information or instructions that do not change. For example, ROM is used to store the start up instructions and data used when a computer is first turned on. With ROM, data is permanently recorded in the memory when it is manufactured. ROM memory is described as **nonvolatile** because it retains its contents even when the power is turned off. The data or programs that are stored in ROM can be read and used, but cannot be altered, hence the name *read only*. Many of the special-purpose computers used in automobiles, appliances, and so on use small amounts of ROM to store instructions that will be executed repeatedly. Instructions that are stored in ROM memory are called **firmware** or **microcode**.

Memory Speed

Because of different manufacturing techniques and materials, some types of memory are faster than others. The speed of memory is measured in **nanoseconds**, one billionth of a second. Main memory is comprised of **dynamic RAM (DRAM)** chips that have access speeds of 50 to 100 nanoseconds. RAM cache memory is faster and is comprised of **static RAM (SRAM)** chips with access times of 10 to 50 nanoseconds. Static RAM chips are not used for main memory because they are larger than dynamic RAM chips and because they cost significantly more to manufacture. Registers designed into the CPU chip are the fastest type of memory with access times of 1 to 10 nanoseconds. ROM memory has access times between 50 and 250 nanoseconds. For comparison purposes, accessing data on a fast hard disk takes between 10 and 20 milliseconds. One **millisecond** is a thousandth of a second. Thus, accessing information in memory with a 70 nanosecond access time is 2,500 times faster than accessing data on a hard disk with a 15 millisecond access time.

Figure 4-17
Memory allocation on a personal computer.

Conventional Memory:
The first 640K of memory is called conventional memory. This space is used first for data and programs. A small amount of operating system instructions is also loaded in this area. Many older programs and games can only operate in conventional memory space, even if additional memory is available.

Upper Memory:
Upper memory runs from 640K to 1MB. Upper memory is reserved for programs that enable the computer to communicate with devices such as the monitor and the printer.

Extended Memory:
Extended memory is all memory above one megabyte. Most newer software and operating systems are designed to use extended memory.

Expanded Memory:
Expanded memory is used by older microprocessors that cannot directly access more than 1MB of memory. Up to 32MB of expanded memory can exist on a memory expansion board. A separate program called an expanded memory manager is used to transfer 16K of expanded memory at a time into a reserved area of upper memory where it can be used.

128MB

1MB

640K

EXTENDED MEMORY

UPPER MEMORY

CONVENTIONAL MEMORY

16K

EXPANDED MEMORY (UP TO 32MB)

Coprocessors

One way computers increase their productivity is the use of a **coprocessor**, a special microprocessor chip or circuit board designed to perform a specific task. For example, math coprocessors can be added to computers to greatly speed up the processing of numeric calculations. Other types of coprocessors are used to speed up the display of graphics and for communications. Some computers have coprocessors designed into the CPU.

Buses

As previously explained, computers store and process data as a series of electronic bits. These bits are transferred internally within the circuitry of the computer along paths capable of transmitting electrical impulses. Sometimes these paths are actual wires and sometimes they are etched lines on the circuit board or within the CPU chip itself. Any path along which bits are transmitted is called a **bus**. Buses are used to transfer bits from input devices to memory, from memory to the CPU, from the CPU to memory, and from memory to output devices. Separate buses are used for memory addresses, control signals, and data. One type of bus is called an expansion bus.

An **expansion bus** carries the data to and from the expansion slots (*Figure 4-18*). Personal computers can have different types of expansion buses. Some computers have more than one type present. It is important to know the type of expansion buses on your computer because some devices

Figure 4-18
Buses are electrical pathways that carry bits from one part of the computer to another. Different buses exist for data, addresses, and control signals. The expansion bus carries data to and from the expansion boards that control peripheral devices and other components used by the computer. Some computers have a special type of expansion bus called a local bus. The local bus communicates directly with the CPU at a much faster rate than the standard expansion bus. The local bus is used for devices that require large amounts of data quickly such as monitors and disk drives.

Figure 4-19
Types of expansion buses found on personal computers.

BUS NAME	TYPE	BITS
XT	standard	8
ISA	standard	16
EISA	standard	32
MCA	standard	16 or 32
VESA or VL	local	32
PCI	local	32 or 64
NuBus	standard	32

are designed to work with only one bus type. Most expansion buses connect directly to RAM. To obtain faster performance, some expansion buses bypass RAM and connect directly to the CPU. An expansion bus that connects directly to the CPU is called a **local bus**. *Figure 4-19* lists the most common expansion bus types on personal computers.

Buses can transfer multiples of eight bits at a time. A 16-bit bus has 16 lines and can transmit 16 bits at a time. On a 32-bit bus, bits can be moved from place to place 32 bits at a time, and on a 64-bit bus, bits are moved 64 bits at a time. The larger the number of bits that are handled by a bus, the faster the computer can transfer data. For example, assume a number in memory occupies four eight-bit bytes. With a 16-bit bus, two steps would be required to transfer the data from memory to the CPU because on the 16-bit bus, the data in two eight-bit bytes would be transferred in an individual step. On a 32-bit bus, the entire four bytes could be transferred at one time. The fewer number of transfer steps required, the faster the transfer of data.

Expansion Slots

An **expansion slot** is a socket designed to hold the circuit board for a device, such as a tape drive or sound card, that adds capability to the computer system. The circuit board for the add-on device is called an **expansion board**. Expansion boards are sometimes called **expansion cards**, **controller cards**, **adapter cards**, or **interface cards**. The expansion card is usually connected to the device it controls by a cable. The socket that holds the card is connected to the expansion bus that transmits data to memory or the CPU. *Figure 4-20* shows an expansion board being placed in an expansion slot on a personal computer motherboard.

A special type of expansion slot is the PCMCIA slot. PCMCIA stands for Personal Computer Memory Card International Association. This group has defined standards for a thin credit card-sized device that can be inserted into a personal computer *(Figure 4-21)*. **PCMCIA cards** are used for additional memory, storage, and communications.

DESCRIPTION
Developed for original IBM PC
Industry Standard Architecture, sometimes called AT bus
Extended Industry Standard Architecture developed by IBM clone manufacturers; backward compatible with ISA bus (ISA cards can run in EISA bus)
Micro Channel Architecture developed by IBM for high-end PS/2 systems
Local bus standard developed by Video Electronics Standards Association
Peripheral Component Interconnect local bus standard developed by Intel
High performance expansion bus used in Apple Macintosh computers

Figure 4-20
An expansion board being inserted into an expansion slot on the motherboard of a personal computer.

Figure 4-21
PCMCIA cards are not much bigger than a credit card and fit in a small slot, usually on the side of a computer. PCMCIA cards are used for additional memory, storage, and communications. Because of their small size, PCMCIA cards are often used on portable computers. The card shown in this photo is a fax/data modem that can be connected to a phone line.

Ports and Connectors

A **port** is a socket used to connect the system unit to a peripheral device such as a printer or a modem. Most of the time, ports are on the back of the system unit *(Figure 4-22)* but they can also be on the front. Ports have different types of couplers, called **connectors**, that are used to attach cables to the peripheral devices. A matching connector is on the end of the cable that attaches to the port. Most connectors are available in two genders – male or female. Male connectors have one or more exposed pins, like the end of an electrical cord you plug into the wall. Female connectors have matching receptacles to accept the pins, like an electrical wall outlet. *Figure 4-23* shows the different type of connectors you may find on a system unit. Ports can either be parallel or serial.

CONNECTORS

TYPE		USE
DB-9 9-pin male		serial port external modem
DB-9 9-pin female		EGA & CGA video
DB-15 15-pin female		VGA & EGA video
DB-25 25-pin male		serial port external modem
DB-25 25-pin female		parallel port printer tape backup
36-pin female mini ribbon		printer
5-pin 180° female DIN		keyboard MIDI
RJ-11 6-pin female modular telephone		telephone modem LAN
BNC male coaxial		LAN
6-pin male mini DIN		mouse keyboard

Figure 4-22
Ports are sockets used for cables that connect the system unit with devices such as a mouse, keyboard, and printer. Usually, ports are on the back of the system unit.

Figure 4-23
Examples of different types of connectors used to connect devices to the system unit. Adapters are available to join one type of connector with another.

Parallel Ports

Parallel ports are most often used to connect devices that send or receive large amounts of data such as printers or disk and tape drives. **Parallel ports** transfer eight bits (one byte) at a time using a cable that has eight data lines *(Figure 4-24)*. The electrical signals in a parallel cable tend to interfere with one another over a long distance and therefore, parallel cables are usually limited to 50 feet. Personal computer parallel cables are usually six to ten feet long. A special type of parallel port is the SCSI (pronounced scuzzy) port. SCSI stands for small computer system interface. A **SCSI port** can be used to attach up to seven different devices to a single port. The devices must be designed to connect to the SCSI port.

Serial Ports

A **serial port** transmits data one bit at a time *(Figure 4-25)* and is considerably slower than a parallel port. Cables connecting serial ports are smaller than parallel cables and do not generate as much electrical interference. Because of this, serial port cables can be up to 1,000 feet long. Serial ports are used for the mouse, the keyboard, and communication devices such as a modem. A special type of serial port is a MIDI (pronounced *midd-dee*) port. MIDI stands for musical instrument digital interface. A **MIDI port** is a serial port designed to be connected to a musical device such as an electronic keyboard or a music synthesizer.

Figure 4-24
Parallel ports transfer eight bits at a time using a cable with eight data lines.

Figure 4-25
Serial ports transfer only one bit at a time and are slower than parallel ports. Separate data lines are used to transmit and receive data. Pin 2 is used to receive data and pin 3 is used to send data.

Bays

A **bay** is an open area inside the system unit used to install additional equipment. Because they are often used for disk and tape drives, these spaces are also called **drive bays**. Mounting brackets called **rails** are sometimes required to install a device in a bay. Two or more bays side by side or on top of one another are called a **cage**. *Figure 4-26* shows a personal computer with a three-bay cage. *External bays* have one end adjacent to an opening in the case. External bays are used for devices that require loading and unloading of storage media such as diskettes, tapes, and CD-ROMs. *Internal bays* are not accessible from outside the case and are used for hard disk drives.

Power Supply

The **power supply** converts the wall outlet electricity (115-120 volts AC) to the lower voltages (5 to 12 volts DC) used by the computer. The power supply also has a fan that provides airflow inside the system unit to help cool the components. The humming noise you hear when you turn on a computer is usually the power supply fan. Personal computer power supplies are rated by wattage and range from 100 to 250 watts. Higher wattage power supplies can support more electronic equipment.

Figure 4-26
Bays, also called drive bays, are usually located beside or on top of one another. Each bay is approximately 1 3/4 inches high by 6 inches wide by 8 inches deep. Two or more bays together are called a cage.

Sound Components

Most personal computers have the capability to generate sounds through a small speaker housed within the system unit. Software allows users to generate a variety of sounds including music and voice. Some computers also have built-in microphones that allow users to record voice messages and other sounds. As you will see in the chapter on output devices, many users enhance the sound-generating capabilities of their systems by installing expansion boards, called sound boards, and by attaching higher quality speakers to their systems.

Summary of the Components of the System Unit

The previous sections have presented information about the various components of the system unit. You should now be able to identify these components and have a more complete understanding about how they operate. The next section will explain how the system unit processes data by executing machine language instructions.

Drive bays

Machine Language Instructions

The system unit gets its directions from programs permanently stored in ROM or temporarily stored in RAM. To execute, program instructions must be in a form, called machine language instructions, the CPU can understand. A **machine language instruction** is binary data that the electronic circuits in the CPU can interpret and convert into one or more of the commands in the computer's instruction set. The **instruction set** contains commands, such as ADD or MOVE, that the computer's circuits can directly perform. Most computers have hundreds of commands in their instruction sets and are referred to as **CISC** computers, standing for *complex instruction set computing* (or *computers*). Studies have shown, however, that as much as 80% of the processing is performed by a small number of frequently used instructions. Based on these findings, some manufacturers have designed CPUs based on RISC technology. **RISC**, which stands for *reduced instruction set computing* (or *computers*), involves reducing the instructions to only those that are most frequently used. Because a RISC computer is designed to execute the frequently used instructions, overall processing capability, or throughput, is increased.

A machine language instruction is composed of two parts. The first part is called an operation code or opcode for short. An **operation code** tells the computer what to do and matches one of the commands in the instruction set. The second part of the machine language instruction is an operand. An **operand** specifies the data or the location of the data that will be used by the instruction. A machine language instruction may have zero to three operands. *Figure 4-27* shows an example of a machine language instruction that adds the number 32 to a register in the CPU.

In the early days, computers actually had to be programmed in machine language instructions using mechanical switches to represent each binary bit. Today, program instructions are written in a readable form using a variety of programming languages. The program instructions are then converted by the computer into machine language instructions. Programming languages and conversion methods are discussed in the chapter on programming languages.

MACHINE LANGUAGE INSTRUCTION		
opcode	operand 1	operand 2
00000101	00100000	00000000
Addition command	the value 32	data register in CPU

Figure 4-27
A PC machine language instruction consists of an operation code (opcode) and up to three operands. This machine language instruction adds the value 32 to a register.

The number of machine language instructions a computer processes in one second is one way of rating the speed of computers. One **MIPS** equals one million instructions per second. Powerful personal computers today are rated at more than 100 MIPS. Another way of rating computer speed is the number of floating-point operations. Floating-point operations are a type of mathematical calculation. The term **megaflop** (**MFLOPS**) is used for millions of floating-point operations per second. **Gigaflop** (**GFLOPS**) is used for billions of floating-point operations per second. Giga is a prefix indicating billion.

Types of Processing

In the discussions thus far, the emphasis has focused on computers with single CPUs processing one instruction at a time. The following section presents variations from this approach.

Pipelining

In most CPUs, the system waits until an instruction completes all four stages of the machine cycle (fetch, decode, execute, and store) before beginning to work on the next instruction. With **pipelining**, a new instruction is started as soon as the preceding instruction moves to the next stage. The result is faster throughput, because by the time the first instruction is in the fourth and final stage of the machine cycle, three other instructions have started to be processed *(Figure 4-28)*. Some CPUs, such as the Intel Pentium, have two or more pipelines that can simultaneously process instructions.

MACHINE CYCLE (without pipelining):

Machine Cycle Stages

Fetch	Decode	Execute	Store
INSTRUCTION 1	INSTRUCTION 1	INSTRUCTION 1	**INSTRUCTION 1** (Results)

MACHINE CYCLE (with pipelining):

Machine Cycle Stages

Fetch	Decode	Execute	Store
INSTRUCTION 1 INSTRUCTION 2 INSTRUCTION 3 **INSTRUCTION 4**	INSTRUCTION 1 INSTRUCTION 2 **INSTRUCTION 3**	INSTRUCTION 1 **INSTRUCTION 2**	**INSTRUCTION 1** (Results)

Figure 4-28
Without pipelining, an instruction moves through the complete machine cycle before the next instruction is started. With pipelining, the CPU starts working on another instruction each time the preceding instruction moves to the next stage of the machine cycle. As shown in the illustration for pipelining, by the time the first instruction has reached the fourth stage of the machine cycle, the next three instructions have started the cycle. Some CPUs have more than one pipeline.

Parallel Processing

Most computers contain one central processing unit (CPU) that processes a single instruction at a time. When one instruction is finished, the CPU begins execution of the next instruction, and so on until the program is completed. This method is known as **serial processing**. **Parallel processing** involves the use of multiple CPUs, each with its own memory. Parallel processors divide up a problem so multiple CPUs can work on their assigned portion of the problem simultaneously *(Figure 4-29)*. As you might expect, parallel processors require special software that can recognize how to divide up problems and bring the results back together again. Parallel processors are often used in supercomputers. **Massively parallel processors** (MPP) use hundreds or thousands of microprocessor CPUs to perform calculations.

Neural Network Computers

Neural network computers use specially designed circuits to simulate the way the human brain processes information, learns, and remembers. Neural network chips form a interconnected system of processors that learn to associate the relative strength or weakness of inputs with specific results (output). Neural network computers are used in applications such as pattern recognition to correctly guess the identity of an object when only hazy or partial information is available. Other applications that use neural network computers are speech recognition and speech synthesis.

Figure 4-29
Parallel processors have multiple CPUs that can divide up parts of the same job or work on different jobs at the same time. Special software is required to divide up the tasks and bring the results together.

Number Systems

This section describes the number systems that are used with computers. Whereas thorough knowledge of this subject is required for technical computer personnel, a general understanding of number systems and how they relate to computers is all most users need.

As you have seen, the binary (base 2) number system is used to represent the electronic status of the bits in main memory. It is also used for other purposes such as addressing the memory locations. Another number system that is commonly used with computers is **hexadecimal** (base 16). *Figure 4-30* shows how the decimal values 0 through 15 are represented in binary and hexadecimal.

The mathematical principles that apply to the binary and hexadecimal number systems are the same as those that apply to the decimal number system. To help you better understand these principles, this section starts with the familiar decimal system, then progresses to the binary and hexadecimal number systems.

Decimal Number System

The decimal number system is a base 10 number system (*deci* means ten). The *base* of a number system indicates how many symbols are used in it. Decimal uses 10 symbols, 0 through 9. Each of the symbols in the number system has a value associated with it. For example, you know that 3 represents a quantity of three and 5 represents a quantity of five. The decimal number system is also a *positional* number system. This means that in a number such as 143, each position in the number has a value associated with it. When you look at the decimal number 143, you know that the 3 is in the ones, or units, position and represents three ones or (3 x 1); the 4 is in the tens position and represents four tens or (4 x 10); and the 1 is in the hundreds position and represents one hundred or (1 x 100). The number 143 is the sum of the values in each position of the number (100 + 40 + 3 = 143). The chart in *Figure 4-31* shows how the positional values (hundreds, tens, and units) for a number system can be calculated. Starting on the right and working to the left, the base of the number system, in this case 10, is raised to consecutive powers. The value 10^0, or 1, is the positional value for the units position. The value 10^1, or 10, is the positional value for the tens position. The value 10^2, or 100, is the positional value for the hundreds position. These calculations are a mathematical way of determining the place values in a number system.

DECIMAL	BINARY	HEXADECIMAL
0	0000	0
1	0001	1
2	0010	2
3	0011	3
4	0100	4
5	0101	5
6	0110	6
7	0111	7
8	1000	8
9	1001	9
10	1010	A
11	1011	B
12	1100	C
13	1101	D
14	1110	E
15	1111	F

Figure 4-30
The binary and hexadecimal representation of decimal numbers 0 through 15 are shown in this chart. Notice how letters represent the numbers 10 through 15 in the hexadecimal representation.

power of 10	10^2	10^1	10^0
positional value	100	10	1
number	1	4	3

$$(1 \times 10^2) + (4 \times 10^1) + (3 \times 10^0) =$$

$$(1 \times 100) + (4 \times 10) + (3 \times 1) =$$

$$100 + 40 + 3 = 143$$

Figure 4-31
The positional values in the decimal number 143 are shown in this chart.

When you use number systems other than decimal, the same principles apply. The base of the number system indicates the number of symbols that are used, and each position in a number system has a value associated with it. The positional value can be calculated by raising the base of the number system to consecutive powers beginning with zero.

Binary Number System

As previously discussed, binary is a base 2 number system (*bi* means two), and the symbols that are used are 0 and 1. Just as each position in a decimal number has a place value associated with it, so does each position in a binary number. To determine the place values for binary, the base of the number system, in this case 2, is raised to consecutive powers *(Figure 4-32)*. To construct a binary number, you place ones in the positions where the corresponding values add up to the quantity you want to represent; you place zeros in the other positions. For example, the binary place values are 8, 4, 2, and 1, and the binary number 1001 has ones in the positions for the values 8 and 1 and zeros in the positions for 4 and 2. Therefore, the quantity represented by binary 1001 is 9 (8 + 0 + 0 + 1).

Hexadecimal Number System

Many computers use a base 16 number system called hexadecimal. The hexadecimal number system uses 16 symbols to represent values. These include the symbols 0 through 9 and A through F *(Figure 4-30* on the previous page). The mathematical principles previously discussed also apply to hexadecimal *(Figure 4-33)*.

The primary reason why the hexadecimal number system is used with computers is because it can represent binary values in a more compact form and because the conversion between the binary and the hexadecimal number systems is very efficient. An eight-digit binary number can be represented by a two-digit hexadecimal number. For example, in the ASCII code, the character M is represented as 01001101. This value can be represented in hexadecimal as 4D. One way to convert this binary number to a hexadecimal number is to divide the binary number (from right to left) into groups of four digits; calculate the value of each group; and then change any two-digit values (10 through 15) into the symbols A through F that are used in hexadecimal *(Figure 4-34)*.

power of 2	2^3	2^2	2^1	2^0
positional value	8	4	2	1
binary	1	0	0	1

$(1 \times 2^3) + (0 \times 2^2) + (0 \times 2^1) + (1 \times 2^0) =$

$(1 \times 8) + (0 \times 4) + (0 \times 2) + (1 \times 1) =$

$8 + 0 + 0 + 1 = 9$

power of 16	16^1	16^0
positional value	16	1
hexadecimal	A	5

$(10 \times 16^1) + (5 \times 16^0) =$

$(10 \times 16) + (5 \times 1) =$

$160 + 5 = 165$

Figure 4-32
Each positional value in a binary number represents a consecutive power of two. Using the positional values, the binary number 1001 can be converted to the decimal number 9.

Figure 4-33
Conversion of the hexadecimal number A5 to the decimal number 165. Notice that the value 10 is substituted for the A during calculations.

Summary of Number Systems

As mentioned at the beginning of the section on number systems, binary and hexadecimal are used primarily by technical computer personnel. A general user does not need a complete understanding of numbering systems. The concepts that you should remember about number systems are that binary is used to represent the electronic status of the bits in main memory and auxiliary storage. Hexadecimal is used to represent binary in a more compact form.

Summary of the System Unit

This chapter examined various aspects of the system unit including its components, how programs and data are stored, and how the processor executes program instructions to process data into information. You have also studied various methods of processing and learned about the various number systems used with computers. Knowing this material will increase your overall understanding of how processing occurs on a computer.

positional value	8421	8421
binary	0100	1101
decimal	4	13
hexadecimal	4	D

Figure 4-34
Conversion of the ASCII code 01001101 for the letter M to the hexadecimal value 4D. Each group of four binary digits is converted to a hexadecimal symbol.

COMPUTERS AT WORK

Unparalleled Performance from Parallel Processors

One way of obtaining improved computer performance is by using more than one CPU. The theory is simple; if one CPU can do a job in one hour, then two CPUs could do the job in 30 minutes, four CPUs in 15 minutes, 60 CPUs in 1 minute, and so on. Although the results aren't as direct as the example (twice the CPUs does not reduce the time in half), significant improvements in performance can be obtained if the work to be done is divided into separate parts that can be worked on simultaneously. Some applications using this approach have been implemented on parallel processors for some time. These applications include automobile crash simulation and weather forecasting. With automobile crash simulation, parallel processors measure the impact and damage at multiple points on the automobile at the same time *(Figure 4-35)*. With weather forecasting, the effect of simultaneous temperature and pressure changes is calculated. Parallel processors are also being applied to commercial applications in several ways. Large-scale parallel processors are being applied to database searches. Kmart, WalMart, and Mervyn's are three retailers that use large parallel processors to sort through millions of transactions in hours to spot sales patterns and trends. For this type of application, the database can be divided among the number of processors available. On a mainframe, the same sales analysis application could take days. On a smaller scale, multiple processors are being implemented at the PC level. The most powerful server computers usually have four or more CPUs to handle the network requirements of up to several thousand users. Microprocessor designers are also incorporating parallel processor designs into the CPU itself. For example, Intel has plans to have four separate but linked CPUs in the chip it plans to build sometime around the year 2000 (see **IN THE FUTURE** on the next page). Existing microprocessor chips, such as the Intel Pentium, have some parts, but not all, of the CPU duplicated. Eventually, all computers will have multiple CPUs working in parallel to produce faster results than any single CPU system.

Figure 4-35

IN THE FUTURE

2,000 MIPS by the Year 2000

By the year 2000, Intel, the world's largest manufacturer of microprocessors, predicts it will have a CPU chip that can perform 2,000 MIPS; 2 billion instructions per second. This is almost ten times faster than microprocessor CPUs currently available. To reach this performance level, Intel will have to continue to pack more transistors onto the slice of silicon that becomes the heart of the microprocessor. Intel's Pentium processor has 3.3 million transistors. Their next generation processor, dubbed the P6, is predicted to have between 6 and 8 million transistors. The 2,000 MIPS processor will have between 50 and 100 million transistors spread among four integrated CPUs. To reach this level of transistor density, the size of the transistors will have to shrink below one-tenth of a micron. A micron is one-millionth of a meter. Current microprocessors have transistor sizes approximately six- to eight-tenths of a micron. For comparison purposes, an average human hair is 75 microns, or approximately 100 times the size of current microprocessor transistors. The clock speed of the microprocessor will also have to improve, probably to about 250 megahertz (each megahertz is one million cycles per second). Current microprocessors run at about 100 to 150 megahertz.

To reach these levels of transistor density and clock speed, microprocessor chip advances will have to continue to meet the prediction of Intel founder Gordon Moore. In 1965, Moore predicted that transistor density, and thus relative computing power, would double every 18 to 24 months. Called Moore's Law, this prediction has so far been amazingly accurate (see *Figure 4-36*). To reach Intel's goal of the 2,000 MIPS chip by the year 2000, the law will have to hold true for a few more years.

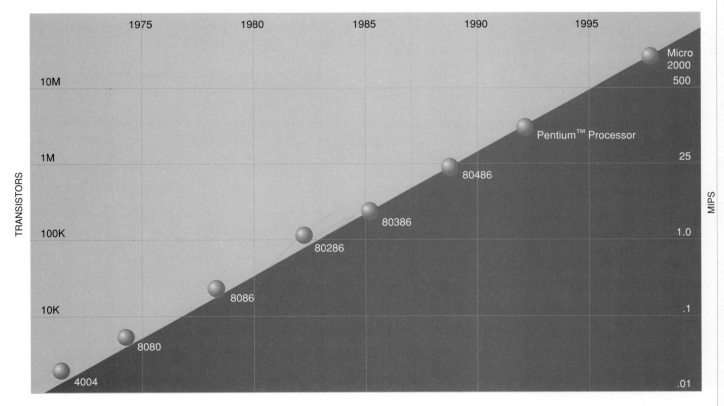

Figure 4-36

File   Edit   Section   Page   Tools   Options   Help

What You Should Know

1. It is in the **system unit** that the computer program instructions are executed and the data is manipulated. The system unit contains the central processing unit, or CPU, main memory, and other electronics.

2. Most computers are **digital computers**, meaning that the data they process is first converted into a digital (numeric) value. Converting data into digital form is called **digitizing**. Other types of computers, called **analog computers**, are designed to process variable data.

3. The digital values used by a computer are 0 (to represent the electronic state of *off*) and 1 (to represent the electronic state of *on*). Each off or on digital value is called a **bit**, which is short for *bi*nary dig*it,* the smallest unit of data handled by a computer. In a group of eight bits, called a **byte**, 256 data possibilities can be represented by using all the combinations of 0s and 1s.

4. Two popular codes that represent characters in memory and on secondary storage are the ASCII and EBCDIC codes. The **American Standard Code for Information Interchange**, called ASCII, is the most widely used coding system to represent data. It is an eight-bit code used on personal computers and minicomputers. The **Extended Binary Coded Decimal Interchange Code,** or EBCDIC, is used primarily on mainframe computers.

5. For each byte of memory, most computers have at least one extra bit, called a **parity bit**, that is used by the computer for error checking. In computers with **odd parity**, the total number of on bits must be an odd number. In computers with **even parity**, the total number of on bits must be an even number.

6. The components considered part of the system unit include: the motherboard, the microprocessor and CPU, upgrade sockets, memory, coprocessors, buses, expansion slots, ports and connectors, bays, the power supply, and sound components.

7. The **motherboard**, sometimes called the **main board** or **system board**, is a circuit board that contains most of the electronic components of the system unit.

8. On a personal computer, the CPU, or central processing unit, is contained on a single integrated circuit, called a **microprocessor**, that is located on the motherboard. An **integrated circuit**, also called a **chip** or an **IC**, is a complete electronic circuit that has been etched on a small slice of semiconducting material. The **central processing unit** (CPU) contains the control unit and the arithmetic/logic unit.

9. The **control unit** operates by repeating four operations, called the **machine cycle: fetching, decoding, executing,** and **storing**.

10. The control unit utilizes the **system clock** to synchronize all computer operations. The system clock generates electronic pulses at a fixed rate, measured in **megahertz (MHz)**.

11. The second part of the CPU is the **arithmetic/logic unit (ALU)**, which contains the electronic circuitry necessary to perform arithmetic and logical operations on data. **Arithmetic operations** include addition, subtraction, multiplication, and division. **Logical operations** consist of comparing one data item to another to determine if the first data item is greater than, equal to, or less than the other.

12. Both the control unit and the ALU contain **registers**, temporary storage locations for specific types of data.

13. One aspect of the CPU that affects the speed of a computer is the word size. **Word size** is the number of bits that the CPU can process at one time.

14. Some motherboards contain empty sockets, called **upgrade sockets**, that can be used to install more powerful CPUs or additional memory.

15. Memory refers to integrated circuits that store program instructions and data that can be retrieved. Memory chips are installed in the system unit and also on circuit boards that control other computer devices.

Windows 95

Start

16. **Random access memory**, or **RAM**, is the name given to the integrated circuits, or chips, that are used for main memory. **Main memory**, or **primary storage**, stores three items: the operating system and other system software, the application program instructions, and the data currently being processed. The number that indicates the location of a byte in memory is called a **memory address**. The size of main memory is measured in **kilobytes (K or KB)** or **megabytes (MB)**.

17. RAM memory is said to be **volatile** because the programs and data stored in RAM are erased when the power to the computer is turned off. A relatively new type of memory called **flash RAM**, or **flash memory**, retains data even when the power is turned off.

18. Today, most RAM memory is installed by using a **SIMM** (single in-line memory module). Some computers improve their processing efficiency by using a limited amount of high-speed RAM memory, called **cache memory**, between the CPU and main memory to store the most frequently used program instructions or data. Memory on personal computers can be divided into four areas: **conventional memory**, **upper memory**, **extended memory**, and **expanded memory**.

19. **Read only memory** (ROM) is the name given to chips that store information or instructions that do not change. ROM memory is described as **nonvolatile** because it retains its contents even when the power is turned off. Instructions that are stored in ROM memory are called **firmware** or **microcode**.

20. The speed of memory is measured in **nanoseconds**, one billionth of a second. Main memory is comprised of **dynamic RAM (DRAM)** chips that have access speeds of 50 to 100 nanoseconds. RAM cache memory is faster and is comprised of **static RAM (SRAM)** chips with access times of 10 to 50 nanoseconds. Registers designed into the CPU chip are the fastest type of memory with access times of 1 to 10 nanoseconds. ROM memory has access times between 50 and 250 nanoseconds. Accessing data on a fast hard disk drive takes between 10 and 20 **milliseconds** (a thousandth of a second).

21. One way computers can increase their productivity is through the use of a **coprocessor**, a special microprocessor chip or circuit board designed to perform a specific task.

22. Bits are transferred internally within the circuitry of the computer along paths capable of transmitting electrical impulses. Any path along which bits are transmitted is called a **bus**. An **expansion bus** carries data to and from the expansion slots. An expansion bus that connects directly to the CPU is called a **local bus**. Buses can transfer multiples of eight bits at a time.

23. An **expansion slot** is a socket designed to hold the circuit board for a device that adds capability to the computer system. The circuit board for the add-on device is called an **expansion board**. Expansion boards are also sometimes called **expansion cards**, **controller cards**, **adapter cards**, or **interface cards**. **PCMCIA cards** are used for additional memory, storage, and communications.

24. A **port** is a socket used to connect the system unit to a peripheral device such as a printer or a modem. Ports have different types of couplers, called **connectors**, that are used to attach cables to the peripheral devices. **Parallel ports** transfer eight bits (one byte) at a time using a cable that has eight data lines. These ports are most often used to connect devices that send or receive large amounts of data, such as printers or disk and tape drives. A **SCSI port** is a special type of parallel port that attaches up to seven devices to a single port. **Serial ports** transmit data one bit at a time and are considerably slower than parallel ports. These ports are used for the mouse, the keyboard, and communication devices such as a modem. A **MIDI port** is a special type of serial port designed to be connected to a musical device such as an electronic keyboard or music synthesizer.

25. A **bay** is an open area inside the system unit used to install additional equipment. Because they are often used for disk and tape drives, these spaces are also called **drive bays**. Mounting brackets, called **rails**, are sometimes required to install a device in a bay. Two or more bays side by side or on top of one another are called a **cage**.

26. The **power supply** converts the wall outlet electricity (115-120 volts AC) to the lower voltages (5 to 12 volts DC) used by the computer. The power supply also has a fan to help cool the system unit components. Personal computer power supplies range from 100 to 250 watts.

File   Edit   Section   Page   Tools   Options   Help

**What You
Should Know**
(continued)

27. Most personal computers can generate sounds through a small speaker housed within the system unit. Some computers also have built-in microphones that allow users to record voice messages and other sounds.

28. A **machine language instruction** is binary data that the electronic circuits in the CPU can interpret and convert into one or more commands in the computer's instruction set. The **instruction set** contains commands that the computer's circuits can directly perform. Most computers have hundreds of commands in their instruction set and are referred to as **CISC** computers, standing for *complex instruction set computing* (or *computers*). Some manufacturers have designed CPUs based on **RISC** technology, *or reduced instruction set computing* (or *computers*), which involves reducing the instructions to only those that are most frequently used, thus increasing overall processing capability.

29. The first part of a machine language instruction, called an **operation code**, tells the computer what to do and matches one of the commands in the instruction set. The second part of a machine language instruction, called an **operand**, specifies the data that will be used by the instruction. Although in the early days computers actually had to be programmed in machine language instructions, today program instructions are written in a readable form using a variety of programming languages.

30. The number of machine language instructions that a computer can process in one second is one way of rating the speed of computers. Powerful personal computers today are rated at more than 100 **MIPS** (million instructions per second). Another way of rating computer speed is the number of floating-point operations (a type of mathematical calculation). The term **megaflop** (**MFLOPS**) is used for millions of floating-point operations per second, and **gigaflop** (**GFLOPS**) is used for billions of floating-point operations per second.

31. In most CPUs, the system waits until an instruction completes all four stages of the machine cycle. With **pipelining**, a new instruction is started as soon as the preceding instruction moves to the next stage.

32. Most computers use a method known as **serial processing** in which one central CPU processes a single instruction at a time until the instruction is finished, then begins execution of the next instruction, and so on until the program is completed. **Parallel processing** involves the use of multiple CPUs, each with its own memory. Parallel processors, often used in supercomputers, divide up a problem so multiple CPUs can work on their assigned portion of the problem simultaneously. **Massively parallel processors** (MPP) use hundreds or thousands of microprocessor CPUs to perform calculations.

33. **Neural network computers** use specifically designed circuits to simulate the way the human brain processes information.

34. The binary (base 2) number system is used to represent the electronic status of the bits in main memory and secondary storage. The **hexadecimal** (base 16) number system, another number system commonly used with computers, represents binary in a more compact form. The mathematical principles that apply to the binary and hexadecimal number systems are the same as those that apply to the decimal system. The *base* of the number system indicates how many symbols are used in it. Each system is also a *positional* number system, meaning that every position in the number has a value associated with it.

File   Edit   Section   Page   Tools   Options   Help

Terms to Remember

adapter cards (4.13)
American Standard Code for
   Information Interchange
   (ASCII) (4.3)
Analog computers (4.2)
arithmetic operations (4.7)
arithmetic/logic unit (ALU) (4.7)
ASCII (4.3)

bay (4.6)
bit (4.2)
bus (4.12)
byte (4.2)

cache memory (4.10)
cage (4.16)
central processing unit (CPU) (4.6)
chip (4.6)
CISC (4.18)
connectors (4.14)
control unit (4.6)
controller cards (4.13)
conventional memory (4.10)
coprocessor (4.12)

decoding (4.7)
digital computers (4.2)
digitizing (4.2)
drive bays (4.16)
dynamic RAM (DRAM) (4.11)

EBCDIC (4.3)
even parity (4.4)
executing (4.7)
expanded memory (4.10)
expansion board (4.13)
expansion bus (4.12)
expansion cards (4.13)
expansion slot (4.13)
Extendend Binary Coded Decimal
   Interchange Code (EBCDIC) (4.3)
extended memory (4.10)

fetching (4.6)
firmware (4.11)
flash memory (4.10)
flash RAM (4.10)

gigaflop (GFLOPS) (4.19)

hexadecimal (4.21)

IC (4.6)
instruction set (4.18)
integrated circuit (4.6)
interface cards (4.13)

kilobyte (K or KB) (4.9)

local bus (4.13)
logical operations (4.7)

machine cycle (4.6)
machine language instruction (4.18)
main board (4.6)
main memory (4.9)
massively parallel processors
   (MPP) (4.20)
megabyte (MB) (4.9)
megaflop (MFLOPS) (4.19)
megahertz (MHz) (4.7)
memory address (4.9)
microcode (4.11)
microprocessor (4.6)
MIDI port (4.15)
millisecond (4.11)
MIPS (4.19)
motherboard (4.6)

nanoseconds (4.11)
neural network computers (4.20)
nonvolatile (4.11)

odd parity (4.4)
operand (4.18)
operation code (4.18)

parallel ports (4.15)
parallel processing (4.20)
parity bit (4.4)
PCMCIA cards (4.13)
pipelining (4.19)
port (4.14)
power supply (4.16)
primary storage (4.9)

rails (4.16)
RAM (4.9)
random access memory (RAM) (4.9)
read only memory (ROM) (4.11)
registers (4.7)
RISC (4.18)

SCSI port (4.15)
serial port (4.15)
serial processing (4.20)
SIMM (4.10)
static RAM (SRAM) (4.11)
storing (4.7)
system board (4.6)
system clock (4.7)
system unit (4.2)

upgrade sockets (4.8)
upper memory (4.10)

volatile (4.9)

word size (4.7)

File   Edit   Section   Page   Tools   Options   Help

Test Your Knowledge

Fill in the Blanks

1. Each off or on digital value is called a(n) _bit_, and a group of eight off or on digital values, called a(n) _byte_, can represent 256 different data possibilities.

2. _ASCII_, the most widely used coding system to represent data, is used primarily on personal computers and minicomputers, while _EBCDIC_ is a coding system used primarily on mainframe computers.

3. The four steps of the machine cycle are: _fetching_, _decoding_, _executing_, and _storage_.

4. The two parts of a machine language instruction are a(n) _operation code_ that tells the computer what to do and matches one of the commands in the instruction set and a(n) _operand_ that specifies the data or location of the data that will be used by the instruction.

5. The decimal number _13_ can be written as 1101 in the binary number system and as _D_ in the hexadecimal number system.

Short Answer

1. What is a parity bit? How are computers with odd parity different from computers with even parity? How are parity bits used to detect if one of the bits in a byte has been accidentally changed when data is moved from one location to another in main memory?

2. How is RAM memory different from ROM memory? For what purpose is each primarily used? What is flash RAM, or flash memory? What is cache memory?

3. How are parallel ports different from serial ports? For what devices are each type of port used? What is a SCSI port? What is a MIDI port?

4. What is an instruction set? How are CISC computers different from computers using RISC technology? Why does RISC technology increase overall processing capability?

5. What is pipelining? How is serial processing different from parallel processing? In what type of computer are parallel processors often used? What is a neural network computer?

Label the Figure

Instructions: Label the parts of the system unit in the spaces provided in the figure below.

Points to Ponder

1

Although the four operations in the machine cycle may seem new to you, in a sense you carry out these same operations each time you complete certain ordinary tasks. Think of a simple task in which you perform operations analogous to those in the machine cycle. Explain what parts of accomplishing the task would be considered fetching, decoding, executing, and storing.

2

Some of the terms in this chapter have another meaning in a different context. For example, a bus, any path along which bits are transmitted, can also be defined as a large, motor-driven passenger vehicle. In this case the meanings are similar because one involves the transfer of bits and the other the transfer of people. List some other terms in this chapter that have more than one meaning. Give both meanings. If the meanings are similar, explain how.

3

ENIAC, the first computer, filled an entire room, yet it was less powerful than today's laptop computers. As the processing power and memory of personal computers increases (during the 1980s, the power of PCs expanded tenfold, and over the past twenty years, the capacity of RAM has more than doubled every two years), it is becoming increasingly difficult to define "personal computer," and to separate it from its larger cousins. How do you define personal computer? Do you think your definition will still be valid twenty years from now? Why or why not?

4

Consider the differences between RAM and ROM. In terms of your own memory, what kind of information do you have in your "RAM" memory? What kind of information do you have in your "ROM" memory? What information, if any, do you have stored in your "cache" memory?

5

As a general marketing rule, higher quality results in higher prices. Computers appear to challenge this rule, however, as they become more powerful, smaller, faster, and *less* expensive. An Atari 800 purchased at a computer store in the early 1980s for more than $1,000 could, by the mid-1980s, be replaced by one bought at a toy store for about $70. What do you think will be the impact of the decline in the price of computers? Who will be using computers in the future? What effect will the greater affordability of computers have on education?

6

Because the instruction sets, or microcode, used with IBM computers are completely different from those used with Apple computers, unless special enhancements are made, software that is written for an IBM personal computer cannot be used on an Apple Macintosh computer. Recently, however, under an agreement with IBM and Apple, Motorola has created a new processor, called the PowerPC. This chip will enable IBM and Apple to produce software that takes advantage of each other's applications. IBM systems will be able to run Macintosh applications, and Macintosh systems will be able to run IBM software. Who will benefit from this new chip? Why? Will anyone be harmed by this new development? Why or why not?

Out and About

1. If you own a personal computer or have access to a personal computer, take the cover off the system unit. Make a sketch of the system unit and try to identify as many components of the system unit as you can. Be careful not to touch any of the components. By referring to the computer's *User Guide,* list the computer's specification for some of the components described in this chapter (for example, CPU, CPU speed, bus speed, cache, RAM type, RAM capacity, expansion slots, and power supply).

2. Make a copy of an advertisement in a newspaper or magazine for a personal computer. Highlight any terms in the advertisement that were discussed in this chapter. List the terms, and explain the meaning of each.

3. Visit a computer vendor and compare one of its less expensive personal computer systems to one of its more expensive computer systems. Make a table that shows the differences between their system units (type of microprocessor, RAM capacity, and so on). Do you think the differences justify the discrepancy in price? Why or why not? Are there any other factors (such as included software) that might also affect the price disparity?

4. Two of the earliest computers were the ENIAC (an acronym for Electronic Numerical Integrator and Computer) and UNIVAC I. Both of these computers were enormous – ENIAC filled an entire room and UNIVAC I weighed 16,000 pounds! Visit a library to research these early computers. What were their components? In what ways were they different from today's personal computers? What technological developments have led to laptop computers that have greater capabilities than either the ENIAC or the UNIVAC I?

5. It is sometimes said that, "Software drives hardware." Although this statement has several interpretations, when purchasing a personal computer, it means that the system unit and peripheral devices (hardware) you buy must be capable of running the application programs (software) in which you are interested. Visit a store that sells computer software and make a list of the application programs you would like now and those you may want in the future. Examine the software packages and note the system requirements. On the basis of your findings, what are the minimum system requirements you would demand in a personal computer?

6. The semiconductor industry continues to develop and introduce new microprocessor and memory chips. Using current computer magazines, explore the most recent advances in microchip technology. What are the latest advances? Where are they being made? How do you think these advances will affect the development of personal computers over the next decade? What impact, if any, will these advances have on the way computers are used?

File   Edit   Section   Page   Tools   Options   Help

In the Lab with Windows 95

1 Shelly Cashman Series Motherboard Lab   Follow the instructions in Windows 95 Lab 1 on page 1.30 to display the Shelly Cashman Series Labs screen. Click Understanding the Motherboard. Click the Start Lab button. When the initial screen displays, carefully read the objectives. With your printer turned on, click the Print Questions button. Fill out the top of the Questions sheet and answer the questions as you step through the Motherboard Lab. Close the Shelly Cashman Series Labs.

2 Setting the Date and Time   Double-click the time on the taskbar. When the Date/Time Properties dialog box displays *(Figure 4-37)*, click the question mark button on its title bar and then click the picture of the clock. Read the information in the pop-up window and then click anywhere to remove it from your screen. Repeat this process for the other areas of the dialog box. Answer the following questions: (1) What is the purpose of the clock? (2) What is displayed in the text box below the clock? (3) What is the purpose of the calendar? (4) How can you change the current time zone? Practice changing the system date and time. Click the Cancel button to close the Date/Time Properties dialog box.

3 Using Calculator to Perform Number System Conversion   Click the Start button on the taskbar, point to Programs on the Start menu, point to Accessories on the Programs submenu, and then click Calculator on the Accessories submenu. Click View on the menu bar and then click Scientific to display the scientific calculator *(Figure 4-38)*. Perform the following tasks: (1) Click Dec to select base 10. Enter 16384 by clicking the numeric buttons or using the

numeric keypad. Click Hex. Write down the number that displays. Click Bin. Write down the number that displays. (2) Convert the following base 10 (decimal) numbers to hexadecimal (Hex) and binary (Bin) and then write down the results of each conversion: 7, 16, 32, 64, 4096, and 8192. (3) Convert the following base 2 (binary) numbers to decimal (Dec) and hexadecimal (Hex) and then write down the results of each conversion: 100, 11111111, 1010, and 100000111000111. (5) Convert the following base 16 (hexadecimal) numbers to decimal (Dec) and binary (Bin) and then write down the results of each conversion: 64, 3AB, BBB, 49C2, FFFF, ACDB12, and 32AC. Close Calculator.

4 More About Using Help   Click the Start button on the taskbar, point to Settings on the Start menu, and then click Control Panel on the Settings submenu. Double-click the Regional Settings icon in the Control Panel window. Perform the following tasks: (1) Click the Time tab. Click the question mark button on the Regional Settings Properties dialog box title bar. Click the Time style box. Answer this question: Does your time display in 12-hour or 24-hour format? (2) Click the Date tab. Use the question mark button to identify the difference(s) between the Short date and Long date style. (3) Close the Regional Settings Properties dialog box. Close Control Panel.

Figure 4-37

Figure 4-38

Start   4:05 AM

File   Edit   Section   Page   Tools   Options   Help

Where on the Web

1 **Intel Corporation**   On a personal computer, the CPU, or central processing unit, is contained on a single integrated circuit, called a microprocessor, that is located on the motherboard. Complete the following steps to visit the Intel Corporation's Web site and learn more about the CPU. With Netscape on the screen, type http://www.intel.com/procs/homepc/buypc/smart in the Location text box and then press ENTER. Click Explore the PC. Click Processor. If a Plug In Not Loaded dialog box appears, click the Cancel button. Read and scroll down through the page. Click Print on the File menu. Click OK. Hand in your printout.

2 **Search the ZDNet**   Complete the following steps to learn more about the system unit from the ZDNet *(Figure 4-39)*. With Netscape on the screen, type http://www.zdnet.com in the Location text box and then press ENTER. Click Search. Scroll down to and click the Full Text Search text box. Type one of the Terms to Remember from the end of the chapter. Click the Start Search button. If the Security Information dialog box opens, click Continue. If no matches are found, click Return To Main Query Screen and type in another term. Scroll down the list of search results and click one that sounds interesting. Read and scroll down through the page. Click Print on the File menu. Click OK. Hand in your printout.

3 **Neural Networks**   Neural network computers use specifically designed circuits to simulate the way the human brain processes information. Increase your understanding of neural networks by completing the following exercise.

With Netscape on the screen, type http://www.mindspring.com/~zsol/nnintro.html in the Location text box and then press ENTER. Read and scroll down the Web page. Answer the following questions on a separate page (or use a word processor). What is a neural network? Why use a neural network? For what types of applications are neural networks well suited? Hand in the page of answers.

4 **Sun on the Net**   Complete the following steps to learn more about the system unit from Sun Microsystems *(Figure 4-40)*. With Netscape on the screen, type http://www.sun.com in the Location text box and then press ENTER. Scroll down and click SunWorld Online. Scroll down through the lists of article titles until you see a title that sounds interesting to you. Click the title. Read the article. Write a brief summary of the article on a separate page (or use a word processor). Include the name of the article on your summary and hand it in.

5 **Shelly Cashman Online**   Click Using Computers: A Gateway To Information, World Wide Web Edition on the Shelly Cashman Student Center Web page (http://www.bf.com/scstudnt.html). Scroll down and click Chapter 4. Complete the activities listed.

Figure 4-39

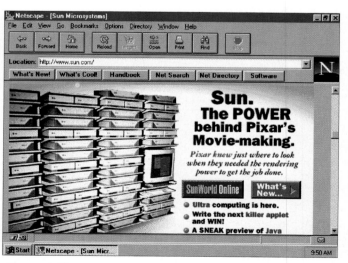

Figure 4-40

Making a Computer Chip

A computer chip is made by building layers of electronic pathways and connections using conducting and non-conducting materials on a surface of silicon. The combination of these materials into specific patterns forms microscopic electronic components such as transistors, diodes, resistors, and capacitors; the basic building blocks of electronic circuits. Connected together on a chip, these components are referred to as an integrated circuit. The application of the conducting and non-conducting materials to the silicon base is done through a series of technically sophisticated chemical and photographic processes. Some of the manufacturing steps are shown in the following photographs.

A computer chip begins with a design developed by engineers using a computer aided circuit design program (1). In order to better review the design, greatly enlarged printouts are prepared. Some chips only take a month or two to design while others may take a year or more. A separate design is required for each layer of the chip. Most chips have at least four to six layers but some have up to fifteen.

Although other materials can be used, the most common raw material used to make chips is silicon crystals (2) that have been refined from quartz rocks. The silicon crystals are melted and formed into a cylinder five to ten inches in diameter and several feet long (3). After being smoothed, the silicon ingot is sliced into wafers four to eight inches in diameter and 4/1000 of an inch thick.

Much of the chip manufacturing process is performed in special laboratories called clean rooms. Because even the smallest particle of dust can ruin a chip, the clean rooms are kept 1000 times cleaner than a hospital operating room. People who work in these facilities must wear special protective clothing called bunny suits (4). Before entering the manufacturing area, the workers remove any dust on their suits in an air shower (5).

After the wafer has been polished and sterilized, it is cleaned in a chemical bath. Because the chemicals used in the cleaning process are dangerous, this step is usually performed

6

7

by a robot (6). After cleaning, the wafers are placed in a diffusion oven where the first layer of material is added to the wafer surface (7). Other materials, called dopants, are added to the surface of the wafer in a process called ion implantation (8). The dopants create areas that will conduct electricity. Channels in these layers of materials are removed in a process called etching. Before etching, a soft gelatin-like emulsion called photoresist is added to the wafer. During photolithography (9), an image of the chip design, called a mask, is used as a negative. The photoresist is exposed to the mask using ultraviolet light. Ultraviolet light is used because its short wavelength can reproduce very small details on the wafer. Up to 100 images of the chip design are exposed on a single wafer. The photoresist exposed to the ultraviolet light becomes hard and the photoresist covered by the chip design on the mask remains soft. The soft photoresist and some of the surface materials are etched away with hot gases leaving what will become the circuit pathways (10). The process of adding material and photoresist to the wafer, exposing it to ultraviolet light, and etching away the unexposed surface, is repeated using a different mask for each layer of the circuit.

8

10

9

After all circuit layers have been added, individual chips on the wafer are tested by a machine that uses probes to apply electrical current to the chip circuits (11). In a process called dicing, the wafers are cut with a diamond saw (12) into individual chips called die (13). Die that have passed all tests are placed in a ceramic or plastic case called a package (14). Circuits on the chip are connected to pins on the package using gold wires (15). Gold is used because it conducts electricity well and does not corrode. The pins connect the chip to a socket on a circuit board (16).

Output from the Computer

Objectives

After completing this chapter, you will be able to:

- Define the term output

- Describe different types of printed output

- Describe multimedia and virtual reality output

- Explain the difference between impact and nonimpact printers

- Identify different types of display devices

- Explain how images are displayed on a screen

- List and describe other types of output devices used with computers

Output is the way the computer communicates with the user. Most people are familiar with computer printouts and information displayed on a screen, but computer output can take many other forms, as well. This chapter discusses different types of output and the devices computers use to produce output.

What Is Output?

Output is data that has been processed into a useful form called information that can be used by a person or a machine. Output used by a machine, such as a disk or tape file, is usually an intermediate result that eventually will be processed into output that can be used by people.

The type of output generated from the computer depends on the needs of the user and the hardware and software that are used. Two common types of output are reports and graphics. These types of output can be printed on a printer or displayed on a screen. Output that is printed is called **hard copy** and output that is displayed on a screen is called **soft copy**. Other types of output include audio (sound), video (visual images), multimedia, and virtual reality. Multimedia is an exciting method of communicating information that combines several types of output. Virtual reality also combines different types of output to create a simulated, three-dimensional environment that the user can experience using special equipment. Each of these types of output is discussed in the following sections.

Reports

A **report** is information presented in an organized form. Most people think of reports as items printed on paper or displayed on a screen. For example, word processing documents can be considered reports. Information printed on forms such as invoices or payroll checks can also be considered types of reports. One way to classify reports is by who uses them. An **internal report** is used by individuals in the performance of their jobs. For example, a daily sales report that is distributed to sales personnel is an internal report because it is used only by personnel within the organization. An **external report** is used outside the organization. Sales invoices that are printed and mailed to customers are external reports.

Reports can also be classified by the way they present information. The four types of common reports are: narrative reports, detail reports, summary reports, and exception reports.

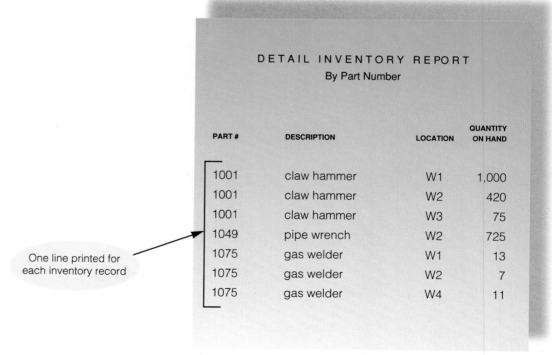

DETAIL INVENTORY REPORT
By Part Number

PART #	DESCRIPTION	LOCATION	QUANTITY ON HAND
1001	claw hammer	W1	1,000
1001	claw hammer	W2	420
1001	claw hammer	W3	75
1049	pipe wrench	W2	725
1075	gas welder	W1	13
1075	gas welder	W2	7
1075	gas welder	W4	11

One line printed for each inventory record

Figure 5-1
The data for this detail report was obtained from each inventory record.

Narrative reports may contain some graphic or numeric information but are primarily text-based reports. These reports, usually prepared with word processing software, include the various types of correspondence commonly used in business such as memos, letters, and sales proposals.

Detail, summary, and exception reports are primarily used to organize and present numeric-based information.

In a **detail report,** each line on the report usually corresponds to one record that has been processed. Detail reports contain a great deal of information and can be quite lengthy. They are usually required by individuals who need access to the day-to-day information that reflects the operating status of the organization. For example, people in the warehouse of a hardware distributor should have access to the location and number of units on hand for each product. The Detail Inventory Report in *Figure 5-1* contains a line for each warehouse location for each part number. Separate inventory records exist for each line on the report.

As the name implies, a **summary report** summarizes data. It contains totals for certain values found in the input records. The report shown in *Figure 5-2* contains a summary of the total quantity on hand for each part. The information on the summary report consists of totals for each part from the information contained in the detail report in *Figure 5-1*. Detail reports frequently contain more information than most managers have time to review. With a summary report, however, a manager can quickly review information in summarized form.

An **exception report** contains information that is outside of *normal* user-specified values or conditions, called the *exception criteria*. Records meeting this criteria are an *exception* to the majority of the data. For example, if an organization wants to know when to reorder inventory items to avoid running out of stock, it would design an exception report. The report would tell which inventory items fell below the reorder points and therefore need to be ordered. An example of such a report is shown in *Figure 5-3*.

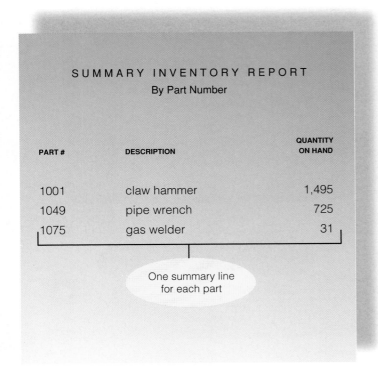

Figure 5-2
The summary report contains the total on-hand quantity for each part. The report can be prepared using the same records that were used to prepare the report in Figure 5-1.

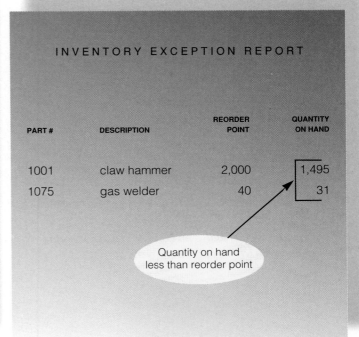

Figure 5-3
The exception report lists inventory items with an on-hand quantity below their reorder points. These parts could have been selected from thousands of inventory records. Only these items met the user's exception criteria.

Exception reports help users focus on situations that may require immediate decisions or specific actions. The advantage of exception reports is that they save time and money. In a large department store, for example, there may be more than 100,000 inventory items. A detail report containing all inventory items could be longer than 2,000 pages. To search through the report to determine the items whose on-hand quantity was less than the reorder point would be a difficult and time-consuming task. The exception report, however, could select these items, which might number 100 to 200, and place them on a two- to four-page report that could be reviewed in just a few minutes.

Reports are also sometimes classified by how often they are produced. **Periodic reports**, also called **scheduled reports**, are produced on a regular basis such as daily, weekly, monthly, or yearly. **On-demand reports** are created whenever they are needed for information that is not required on a scheduled basis.

Graphics

Computer graphics are any nontext pictorial information. One of the early uses of computer graphics was for charts to help analyze numeric information. Charts are now widely used in spreadsheet and presentation graphics software packages *(Figure 5-4)*. In recent years, computer graphics have gone far beyond charting capabilities. **Computer drawing programs** and **computer paint programs** allow an artistic user to create stunning looking works of art. These programs are frequently used for developing advertising and other marketing materials *(Figure 5-5)*. Clip art and photographs are also considered types of computer graphics.

Audio Output

Audio output, sometimes called **audio response**, consists of sounds, including words and music, produced by the computer. An audio output device on a computer is

Figure 5-4
A presentation graphics slide is an example of graphics output that combines text, charts based on numeric data, and art.

Figure 5-5
Computer drawing and paint programs are often used by professional artists to create advertising and marketing materials.

a speaker. Most personal computers come with a small speaker (approximately two inches) that is usually located behind an opening on the front or side of the system unit case. Increasingly, personal computer users are adding higher quality stereo speakers to their systems *(Figure 5-6)*. The stereo speakers connect to a port on a sound card that works with sound, voice, and music software.

Video Output

Video output consists of visual images that have been captured with a video input device, such as a VCR or camera, digitized, and directed to an output device such as a computer monitor *(Figure 5-7)*. As was mentioned in Chapter 3, some video input devices can digitize the image as it is captured. Video output can also be directed to a television monitor. Because standard televisions are not designed to handle a computer's digital signals, the video output has to be converted to an analog signal that can be displayed by the television. **High definition television** (HDTV) sets are designed for digital signals and may eventually replace computer monitors.

Multimedia

Multimedia is the combination of text, graphics, video, and sound. Some people have described it as a combination of traditional text-based computers and television. Multimedia is really more than just a combination of these previously separate information elements. Multimedia is different because it usually gives the user options on the amount of material to review and the sequence in which the material will be reviewed. For example, a typical multimedia presentation will display text material along with one or more photos or graphic images. Some sound or voice narration may also be provided. In addition, the screen will usually show icons that represent additional material, such as pictures, sounds, animation, or maps, that the user can also choose to review. Most multimedia presentations use a technique, called **hypermedia**, that allows the user to quickly move to related subject areas. An example of these features can be seen in *Figures 5-8* and *5-9* on the next page; screens from Microsoft's multimedia encyclopedia, Encarta. *Figure 5-8* shows text information about the famous jazz musician, Duke Ellington. The small icons at the top of the text material indicate there is an image item (represented by

Figure 5-6
To fully experience computer audio output, many users are adding or purchasing systems with stereo speakers.

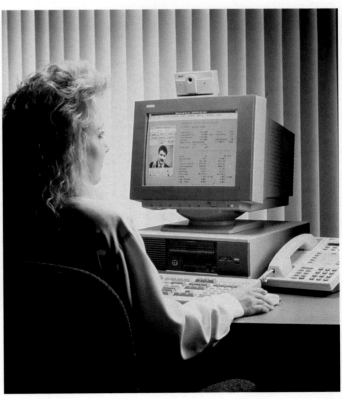

Figure 5-7
Use of video output is like a video telephone system; it allows company employees to see the coworker with whom they are talking.

the camera- shaped icon) and a sound item (represented by the speaker- shaped icon) that can also be reviewed. To see or hear these items, the user selects the icon with the mouse. To see related topics, the user can choose the See Also button at the bottom of the screen. When this is done, a list of the topics is presented *(Figure 5-9)*. The user can move directly to any of these topics by selecting one with the mouse.

The Microsoft Encarta multimedia encyclopedia, like most multimedia products available today, is stored on a CD-ROM disk. This type of storage device is required because of the large amounts of data that most multimedia applications require. For example, the Encarta encyclopedia takes more than 550MB of storage space. Full-motion video, which is used sparingly in most multimedia presentations today, can require more than 2 gigabytes of storage for each minute of video. These storage requirements can be reduced through the use of data compression techniques.

Currently, multimedia applications are primarily used in four areas; education, training, entertainment, and information. Information applications include multimedia kiosks that can be found in museums, airports, and hotels *(Figure 5-10)*. Eventually, multimedia techniques will be incorporated into most all software applications.

Figure 5-9
When the user chooses the Related Articles button at the bottom left of the screen, a list is displayed. The user can move directly to any of these topics by selecting one of them with a pointing device.

Figure 5-8
The Microsoft Encarta multimedia encyclopedia offers text, graphics, sound, and animation. The speaker-shaped icon above the main text indicates that a portion of one of Ellington's compositions can be listened to.

Figure 5-10
Coca-Cola uses multimedia kiosks to present information on their products and history at their Atlanta visitors center. Multimedia information kiosks are becoming a frequent site in hotels, museums, airports, and other locations where infrequent visitors need to obtain information.

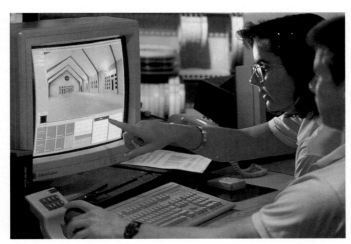

Figure 5-11
One of the first practical applications of virtual reality software was in the architectural profession. Architects use VR software to create a model of the project on which they are working. Clients can then walk through the virtual project and specify design changes before the project is built.

Virtual Reality

Virtual reality (VR) refers to the use of a computer to create an artificial environment that can be experienced by the computer user. In its simplest form, VR software displays what appears to be a three-dimensional view of a place, such as a landscape or a building, that can be explored by the user. Architects are using such software to show clients what proposed construction or remodeling changes will look like *(Figure 5-11)*. In more advanced forms, VR software requires the user to wear specialized headgear, gloves, and body suits to enhance the experience of the artificial environment *(Figure 5-12)*. The headgear includes displays in front of both eyes that project the artificial environment being experienced by the wearer. The glove and body suit sense the motion and direction of the user. Gloves allow the user to pick up and hold items displayed in the virtual environment. Eventually, experts predict, the body suits will provide tactile feedback so the wearer can experience the touch and feel of the virtual world.

Figure 5-12
The virtual reality body suit, called a "Datasuit" by developer VPL research, allows more than 50 different movements of the wearer to be interpreted by the VR software. The software then manipulates the image in the virtual environment, which is displayed in the headset.

Most experts agree that VR is still in its early stages and that practical applications are just now becoming available. The potential applications of VR, however, have many people excited and have kept millions of dollars flowing into VR research.

The general public's first encounter with VR will likely be through a three-dimensional electronic game. One such game is called Dactyl Nightmare *(Figure 5-13)*. Special visors allow the player to *see* the computer-generated environment. Sensors in the surrounding game machine record movement and direction as the player *walks* around the game's electronic landscape. The object of the game is to use a simulated laser gun to shoot other players before they shoot you. Players also have to avoid being snatched by giant green pterodactyls (prehistoric birds) that can carry them high into the sky before letting them crash to the ground. Because of their high cost (more than $50,000) and the special equipment required, VR games are not spreading across the land as fast as pin ball machines once did. Most major metropolitan U.S. cities, however, now have VR arcades installed or planned for the near future.

Commercial applications of VR include a virtual showroom and a virtual office. The showroom lets customers wander among available products and inspect those they find interesting. In the virtual office, created for an office furniture company, clients can see what their selected furniture will look like and can experiment with different furniture arrangements.

As computing power increases, VR applications will be able to be run on lower cost computers. This in turn will increase the number of commercial VR applications and make VR technology available for a wider number of users.

A variety of devices produce the output created in the information processing cycle. The following sections describe the devices most commonly used.

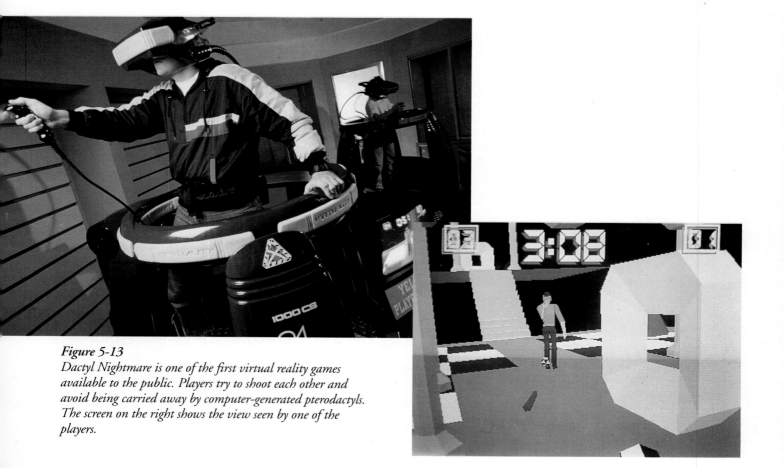

Figure 5-13
Dactyl Nightmare is one of the first virtual reality games available to the public. Players try to shoot each other and avoid being carried away by computer-generated pterodactyls. The screen on the right shows the view seen by one of the players.

Printers

Printing requirements vary greatly among computer users. For example, home computer users may only print a hundred pages or fewer a week. Small business computer users may print several hundred pages a day. Users of mainframe computers, such as large utility companies that send printed bills to hundreds of thousands of customers each month, need printers that are capable of printing thousands of pages per hour. These different needs have resulted in the development of printers with varying speeds, capabilities, and printing methods. Generally, printers can be classified into two groups, impact or nonimpact, based on how they transfer characters to the paper.

Impact Printers

Impact printers transfer the image onto paper by some type of printing mechanism striking the paper, ribbon, and character together. One technique is front striking in which the printing mechanism that forms the character strikes a ribbon against the paper from the front to form an image. This is similar to the method used on typewriters. The second technique utilizes a hammer striking device. The ribbon and paper are struck against the character from the back by a hammer to form the image on the paper *(Figure 5-14)*.

Most impact printers use continuous-form paper. The pages of **continuous-form paper** are connected together for a continuous flow through the printer *(Figure 5-15)*. The advantage of continuous-form paper is that it need not be changed frequently; thousands of pages come connected together. Some impact printers use single-sheet paper. The advantage of using single-sheet paper is that different types of paper, such as letterhead, can be quickly changed.

Figure 5-14
Impact printers operate in one of two ways; front striking or hammer striking.

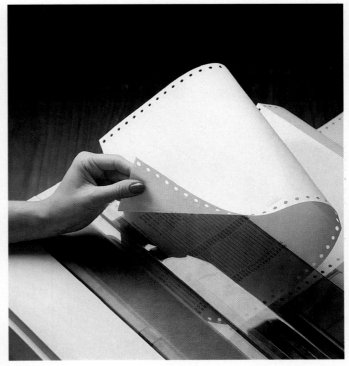

Figure 5-15
Sheets of continuous-form paper are connected together. Small holes on the sides of the paper allow sprockets to pull the paper through the printer. Perforations between each sheet allow the pages to be easily separated.

Dot Matrix Printers

A **dot matrix printer** produces printed images by striking wire pins against an inked ribbon. Its print head consists of a series of small tubes containing wire pins that, when pressed against a ribbon and paper, print small dots. The pins are activated by electromagnets that are arranged in a circular pattern. The combination of small dots printed closely together forms the character *(Figure 5-16)*. Dot matrix printers are used extensively because they are versatile and relatively inexpensive. The printer shown in *Figure 5-17* is a dot matrix printer used with personal computers. *Figure 5-18* shows a dot matrix printer frequently used with larger systems.

To print a character using a dot matrix printer, the character stored in main memory is sent to the printer's electronic circuitry. The printer circuitry activates the pins in the print head that correspond to the pattern of the character to be printed. The selected pins strike the ribbon and paper and print the character. Most dot matrix printers used with personal computers have a single print head that moves across the page. Dot matrix printers used with larger computers usually have fixed print mechanisms at each print position and can print an entire line at one time. Because the individual pins of a dot matrix printer can be activated, a dot matrix printer can be used to print expanded (larger than normal) and condensed (smaller than normal) characters and graphics.

Dot matrix printers can contain a varying number of pins, depending on the manufacturer and the printer model. Print heads consisting of 9 and 24 pins (two vertical rows of 12) are most common. *Figure 5-19* illustrates the formation of the letter E using a nine-pin dot matrix printer.

The speed of impact printers with movable print heads is rated in **characters per second (cps)**. Depending on the printer model, this speed varies between 50 and 300 cps. The speed of impact printers that print one line at a time is rated in **lines per minute (lpm)**. High-speed dot matrix printers can print up to 1,200 lpm. The speeds quoted by dot matrix printer manufacturers are usually for what is called draft-quality printing. **Draft-quality** printing uses the minimum

Figure 5-16
The print head assembly for a dot matrix printer consists of a series of pins that are fired at the paper by electromagnets. When activated, the pins push the ribbon into the paper forming an image made up of small dots.

Figure 5-17
Many different types of small dot matrix printers are available for use with personal computers.

number of dots to form a character and achieve the fastest printing speed. Draft quality is fine for internal reports but is not adequate for sending printed material to customers or other outsiders. To achieve a sharper, higher quality look, called **letter quality** (**LQ**) or **near letter quality** (**NLQ**), the printer overlaps the printed dots. Nine-pin print heads accomplish the overlapping by printing the line twice. The character is slightly offset during the second printing. This results in the appearance of solid characters *(Figure 5-20)*. Twenty-four-pin printers can accomplish the overlapping on a single pass because their multiple rows of pins are slightly offset *(Figure 5-21)*.

Dot matrix printers with movable print heads are designed to print in a **bidirectional** manner. That is, the print head, the device that contains the mechanism for transferring the character to the paper, can print as it moves from left to right and from right to left. The printer does this by storing the next line to be printed in its memory and then

Figure 5-18
Dot matrix printers used with larger systems often have print heads at each print position that allow them to print an entire line at a time.

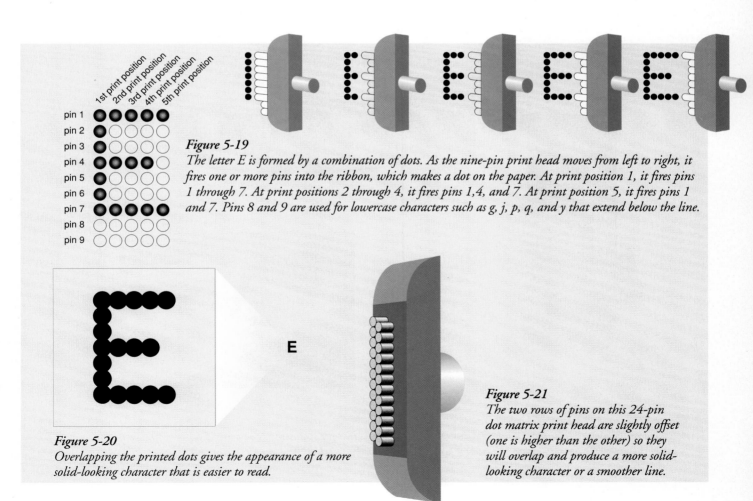

Figure 5-19
The letter E is formed by a combination of dots. As the nine-pin print head moves from left to right, it fires one or more pins into the ribbon, which makes a dot on the paper. At print position 1, it fires pins 1 through 7. At print positions 2 through 4, it fires pins 1,4, and 7. At print position 5, it fires pins 1 and 7. Pins 8 and 9 are used for lowercase characters such as g, j, p, q, and y that extend below the line.

Figure 5-20
Overlapping the printed dots gives the appearance of a more solid-looking character that is easier to read.

Figure 5-21
The two rows of pins on this 24-pin dot matrix print head are slightly offset (one is higher than the other) so they will overlap and produce a more solid-looking character or a smoother line.

printing the line forward or backward as needed. Bidirectional printing greatly increases the speed of the printer.

The feed mechanism determines how the paper moves through the printer. Two types of feed mechanisms found on dot matrix printers are tractor feed and friction feed. **Tractor feed mechanisms** transport continuous-form paper through the printer by using sprockets, which are small protruding prongs of plastic or metal that fit into holes on each side of the paper. Where it is necessary to feed single sheets of paper into the printer, **friction feed mechanisms** are used. As the name implies, paper is moved through friction feed printers by pressure on the paper and the carriage, as it is on a type-writer. As the carriage rotates, the paper moves through the printer.

Dot matrix printers are built with a standard, medium, or wide carriage. A standard carriage printer can accommodate paper up to 8 ¹/₂ inches wide. A medium carriage can accommodate paper up to 11 inches wide, and a wide carriage printer can accommodate paper up to 14 inches wide.

Some dot matrix printers can print in multiple colors using ribbons that contain the colors red, yellow, and blue in addition to the standard black. Color output is obtained by repeated printing and repositioning of the paper, print head, and ribbon. Such printers can be useful in printing graphs and charts, but other types of color printers offer a higher quality of color output.

Dot matrix printers range in cost from less than $200 for small desktop units to more than $10,000 for heavy-use business models. Most dot matrix printers are available for less than $1,000.

Band and Chain Printers

Band and chain printers are used for high-volume output on large computer systems. **Band printers** use a horizontal, rotating band containing numbers, letters of the alphabet, and selected special characters. The characters are struck by hammers located at each print position behind the paper and ribbon to create a line of print on the paper *(Figure 5-22)*.

Figure 5-22
A band printer uses a metal band that contains solid characters. When the character to be printed on the band comes by, print hammers strike the paper and the ribbon forcing them into the band to print the character.

Interchangeable type bands with different fonts can be used on band printers. A band printer can produce up to six carbon copies, has good print quality, high reliability, and depending on the manufacturer and model of the printer, can print in the range of 600 to 2,000 lines per minute.

The **chain printer** is similar to a band printer and contains characters on a rotating chain *(Figure 5-23)*. The chain consists of a series of type slugs that contains the character set. The character set on the type slugs is repeated two or more times on the chain mechanism. The chain rotates at a very high speed. Each possible print position has a hammer that can strike against the back of the paper, forcing the paper and ribbon against the character on the chain. As the chain rotates, the hammer strikes when the character to be printed is in the proper position.

The chain printer produces good print quality up to 3,000 lines per minute.

Nonimpact Printers

Nonimpact printing means that printing occurs without having a mechanism striking against a sheet of paper. For example, ink is sprayed against the paper or heat and pressure is used to fuse a fine black powder into the shape of a character.

Just as there are a variety of impact printers, there are also a variety of nonimpact printers. Ink-jet, small page printers, and thermal printers are frequently used on personal computers and small minicomputers. Medium- and high-speed page printers are used on minicomputers, mainframes, and supercomputers. The following sections discuss the various types of nonimpact printers.

Ink-Jet Printers

An **ink-jet printer** sprays tiny drops of ink onto the paper. The print head of an ink-jet printer contains a nozzle with anywhere from 50 to more than 100 small holes *(Figure 5-24)*. Although there are many more of them, the ink holes in the nozzle are similar to the individual pins on a dot matrix

Figure 5-24
The print head of an ink-jet printer contains many tiny holes that act as nozzles to spray drops of ink onto the paper.

Figure 5-23
The chain printer contains a complete set of characters on several sections of a chain that rotates at a high constant speed. Print hammers are located at each horizontal print position. The paper and ribbon are located between the hammers and the chain. As the chain rotates, the hammers fire when the proper characters are in front of their print positions.

Labels for Figure 5-23: Ribbon, Idler gear, Paper, Chain consisting of type slugs, 1 slug – each slug has 3 characters, Hammers, Drive gear printer. Just as any combination of dot matrix pins can be activated, ink can be propelled by heat or pressure through any combination of the nozzle holes to form a character or image on the paper. Ink-jet printers produce high-quality print and graphics and are quiet because the paper is not struck as it is by dot matrix printers. Good quality, single-sheet paper is usually used with ink-jet printers. Lower quality paper can be too soft and cause the ink to bleed. Transparency sheets can also be used. Ink-jet printers print at rates from 30 to 150 cps. Color ink-jet printers are also available *(Figure 5-25)*.

Page Printers

The **page printer** is a nonimpact printer that operates similar to a copying machine. The page printer converts data from the computer into light that is directed to a positively charged revolving drum. Each position on the drum touched by the light becomes negatively charged and attracts the toner (powdered ink). The toner is transferred onto the paper and then fused to the paper by heat and pressure. Several methods are used to direct light to the photosensitive drum and create the text or image that will be transferred to the paper. **Laser printers** use a laser beam aimed at the drum by a spinning mirror *(Figure 5-26)*.

Other page printers use light emitting diode (LED) arrays or liquid crystal shutters (LCS). With these methods, the light can expose thousands of individual points on the drum. Although the light exposure methods of LED and LCS printers are different from laser printers, they are often referred to and classified with laser printers. All page printers produce high-quality text and graphics suitable for business correspondence *(Figure 5-27)*. Color laser printers are available but are very expensive and not yet widely used.

An advantage of page printers is that they usually come with a large number of built-in fonts. As you recall from Chapter 2, a font is a specific combination of *typeface,* such as Courier, and *point size,* the height of the type. Although different fonts can be produced using software, documents using a printer's built-in fonts print faster.

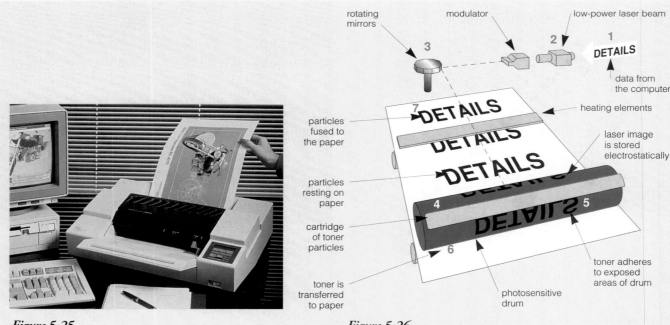

Figure 5-25
A color ink-jet printer.

Figure 5-26
Laser printers use a process similar to a copying machine. Data from the computer, such as the word DETAILS (1), is converted into a laser beam (2) that is directed by a mirror (3) to a photosensitive drum (4). The areas on the drum touched by the laser attract toner particles (5) that are transferred to the paper (6). The toner is fused to the paper with heat and pressure (7).

Page printers are rated by their speed and resolution. Speed is measured in **pages per minute (ppm)**. Page printers used with individual personal computers range from 4 to 12 ppm and start at less than $500. Page printers supporting multiple users on a network or larger computer range from 16 to 50 ppm and cost from $10,000 to $100,000. High-speed page printers costing as much as several hundred thousand dollars can produce output at the rate of several hundred pages per minute *(Figure 5-28)*. Page printer resolution is measured by the number of **dots per inch (dpi)** that can be printed. The more dots, the sharper the image. The resolution of page printers ranges from 240 to 1200 dpi with most printers currently offering 300 or 600 dpi. Page printers usually use individual sheets of paper stored in a removable tray that slides into the printer case. Some page printers have trays that can accommodate different-sized paper while others require separate trays for letter and legal paper. Most page printers have a manual feed slot where individual sheets can be inserted. Transparencies and envelopes can also be printed on page printers.

Thermal Printers

Thermal printers, sometimes called **thermal-transfer printers**, use heat to transfer colored inks from ink sheets onto the printing surface (*Figure 5-29* on the next page). Thermal printers can work with plain paper but produce the best results when higher quality, smooth paper or plastic transparencies are used. A special type of thermal printer using a method called **dye diffusion** uses chemically treated paper to obtain color print quality equal to glossy magazines. Dye diffusion actually varies the color intensity of each dot placed on the page. Most color printers merely alter the pattern of red, blue, yellow, and black dots to create the illusion of different colors. Thermal printers produce output at the rate of one to two pages per minute.

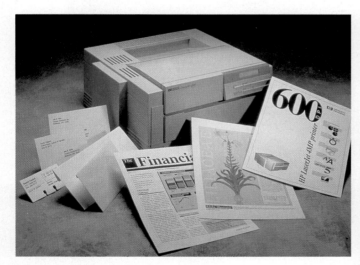

Figure 5-27
Page printers such as the laser printer can produce high-quality text or graphics output.

Figure 5-28
High speed laser printers can operate at speeds greater than 200 pages per minute. These printing systems can cost more than $200,000.

Other Types of Printers

In addition to the printers just discussed, there are a number of printers developed for special purposes. These include single label printers, bar code label printers, and portable printers. *Figure 5-30* shows examples of these printers.

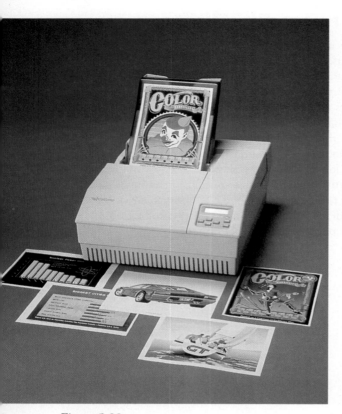

Figure 5-29
Thermal-transfer printers are used to produce high-quality color output.

Figure 5-30
Other types of printers, from left to right, include a bar code label printer, a single label printer, and a portable printer designed for use with portable computers.

Summary of Impact and Nonimpact Printers

Impact and nonimpact methods of printing each have advantages and disadvantages. Impact printing can be noisy because the paper is struck when printing occurs. Because the paper is struck, specially treated multipart paper can be used to create multiple copies of a report at one time, such as an invoice, that is routed to different people. Nonimpact printers are quiet, produce high-quality output, and have become the standard for business correspondence. They do not strike the paper, however, and can therefore create only one printed copy at a time. If additional copies are needed, they must each be printed separately. Color output is more attractive, but is slower and more expensive than black and white output for all printer types.

Considerations in Choosing a Printer

In addition to understanding the features and capabilities of the various types of printers that are available, you must consider several other factors before choosing a printer. These include factors such as how much output will be produced and who will use the output. Considering these and the other factors stated in *Figure 5-31* will help you to choose a printer to meet your needs.

Figure 5-31
Questions to consider when choosing a printer.

QUESTION	EXPLANATION
How much output will be produced?	Desktop printers are not designed for continous use. More than several hundred pages a day requires a commercial (business) grade printer. Check a printer's **duty cycle,** the recommended maximum number of copies per month and **mean time between failures (MTBF)**, the estimated time the before a component needs service.
What type of output will be produced?	Make a list of the types of output that will be produced (e.g., reports, transparencies, labels, charts, graphics) and match this list with printer capabilities.
Who will use the output?	Internal-only reports can be prepared on fast, draft-quality printers. External correspondence requires the letter-quality output of a nonimpact printer.
Where will the output be produced?	If the output will be produced at the user's desk or in an open office environment, a sound enclosure may be required to reduce printer noise.
Are multiple copies required?	Only impact printers can produce multiple copies on a single pass.
Is color required?	Color can enhance a document, but color printers are slower and cost more.
Are different fonts needed?	Most, but not all, printers have some built-in fonts. Page printers usually offer the most choices. Software-based fonts are also available.
Where will the printer be located?	Printers close (within 25 feet) to a computer use a faster parallel interface. Printers farther away will use a slower interface or use network cabling.

Display Devices

A **display device** is the visual output device of a computer. The most common type of display device is a monitor. A **monitor** looks like a television and consists of a display surface, called a screen, and a plastic or metal case to house the electrical components. A monitor often has a swivel base that allows the angle of the screen surface to be adjusted. The term **screen** is used to refer to both the surface of any display device and to any type of display device. A **video display terminal** (VDT) is a type of display device that also includes a keyboard. VDTs, also called dumb terminals, are usually connected to larger systems such as minicomputers or mainframes. An older term sometimes used to refer to monitor or VDT display devices is CRT. A **CRT**, which stands for **cathode ray tube**, is actually the large tube inside a monitor or VDT. The front part of the tube is the display surface or screen.

The most widely used monitors are equivalent in size to a 14- to 17-inch television screen. Monitors designed for use with desktop publishing, graphics, or engineering applications come in even larger sizes that can display full-size images of one or sometimes two 8 ¹/₂ by 11-inch pages of data. One company even makes a monitor that can be tilted 90 degrees to display either long or wide pages or two pages side by side *(Figure 5-32)*.

Resolution

The **resolution**, or clarity, of the image on the monitor depends on the number of individual dots displayed on the monitor and the distance between each dot. Each dot that can be illuminated is called a **picture element**, or **pixel**. The pixels are illuminated to form an image on the screen *(Figure 5-33)*. The distance between each pixel is called the **dot pitch**. The greater the number of pixels and the closer they are, the better the monitor resolution. The resolution of a monitor is important, especially when the monitor will be used to display graphics or other nontext information.

Figure 5-32
Portrait Display Labs manufactures a monitor that can be tilted 90 degrees to display long or wide pages or two pages side by side.

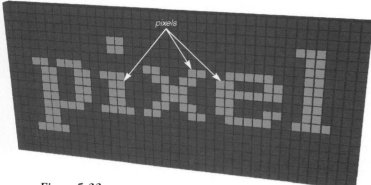

Figure 5-33
The word "pixel" shown here is made up of individual picture elements (pixels) as they would be displayed on a bit-mapped screen. Each pixel can be turned on or off to form an image on the screen.

Monitors used for graphics are called **dot-addressable displays** or **bit-mapped displays**. On these monitors, the number of addressable locations on the monitor corresponds to the number of pixels, or dots, that can be illuminated. The number of pixels that is actually displayed is determined by a combination of the software in the computer, the capability of the video adapter board in the computer, and the monitor itself. High-resolution display devices can produce an image that is almost equivalent to the quality of a photograph *(Figure 5-34)*.

Several video graphics standards have been developed, including CGA (Color Graphics Adapter), EGA (Enhanced Graphics Adapter), VGA (Video Graphics Array), and super VGA (SVGA). The term super VGA is often used for any resolution beyond 640 x 480. As shown in *Figure 5-35,* each standard provides for a different number of pixels and colors. Some manufacturers offer even higher resolution monitors. The resolution of most monitors sold for personal computer systems is SVGA.

Figure 5-34
High-resolution display devices can produce images that are equivalent to the quality of a photograph. These devices are often used in graphic arts, engineering, and scientific applications.

Standard	Year	Resolution (W xH)	Available Colors	Maximum Displayed Colors
CGA	1981	640 x 200	16	4
Hercules	1982	720 x 348	None	None
EGA	1984	640 x 480	64	16
VGA	1986	640 x 480	262,144	256
Super VGA	1988	800 x 600 to 1600 x 1200	16.7 million	16.7 million

Figure 5-35
A summary of the more widely used video graphics standards for display screens.

Each of the video graphics standards have a specific frequency or rate at which the video signals are sent to the monitor. Some monitors are designed to only work at a particular frequency and video standard. Other monitors, called **multiscanning** or **multisync monitors**, are designed to work within a range of frequencies and thus can work with different standards and video adapters.

Color Monitors

A **color monitor** can display text or graphics in color *(Figure 5-36)*. Color monitors are widely used with all types of computers because of reduced prices and because much of today's software is written to display information in color. Although some color monitors are capable of displaying millions of colors, the human eye cannot distinguish the differences. Most PC color monitors display up to 256 colors at one time.

Monochrome Monitors

Monochrome monitors display a single color such as white, green, or amber characters on a black background *(Figure 5-37)* or black characters on a white background. Monochrome monitors are less expensive than color monitors and are often used by businesses for word processing, order entry, and other applications that do not require color. Using a technique known as gray scaling, some monochrome monitors can display good-quality graphic images. **Gray scaling** involves converting an image into pixels that are different shades of gray like a black and white photograph.

Flat Panel Displays

A **flat panel display** is a thin display screen that does not use cathode ray tube (CRT) technology. Flat panel displays are most often used in portable computers but larger units that can mount on a wall or other structure are also available.

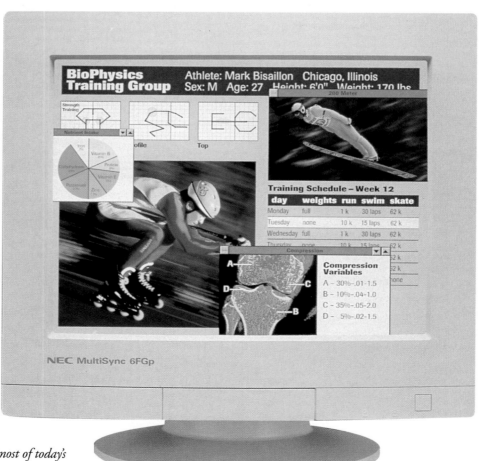

Figure 5-36
Color monitors are widely used because most of today's software is written to display information in color.

Two common types of technology used for flat panel displays are liquid crystal display (LCD) and gas plasma *(Figure 5-38)*.

In a **liquid crystal display** (LCD), a liquid crystal is deposited between two sheets of polarizing material. When an electrical current passes between crossing wires, the liquid crystals are aligned so light cannot shine through, producing an image on the screen. LCD technology is also commonly used in digital watches, clocks, and calculators. **Active matrix** LCD screens use individual transistors to control each crystal cell. **Passive matrix** LCD screens use fewer transistors; one for each row and column. Active matrix displays cost more but display a sharper, brighter picture (Figure 5-39).

Gas plasma screens substitute a neon gas for the liquid crystal material. Any locations on a grid of horizontal and vertical electrodes can be turned on to cause the neon gas to glow and produce the pixels that form an image. Gas plasma screens offer better resolution than LCD screens but are more expensive.

Figure 5-38
Flat panel displays are most often used on portable computers. The system on the left uses a liquid crystal display (LCD) and the system on the right uses a gas plasma display.

Figure 5-37
Monochrome monitors display a single color against a solid background.

Figure 5-39
Active matrix LCD screens produce the best color resolution by using individual transistors to control each crystal cell.

How Images Are Displayed on a Monitor

Most monitors used with personal computers and terminals use cathode ray tube (CRT) technology. When these monitors produce an image, the following steps occur *(Figure 5-40):*

1. The image to be displayed on the monitor is sent electronically from the CPU to the video circuits to the cathode ray tube.
2. An electron gun at the rear of the tube generates an electron beam towards the screen. The beam passes through holes in a metal screen called the *shadow mask.* The shadow mask helps align the beam so it hits the correct dot on the screen. The screen is coated with phosphor, a substance that glows when it is struck by the electron beam.
3. The yoke, which generates an electromagnetic field, moves the electron beam across and down the screen. **Interlaced monitors** illuminate every other line and then return to the top to illuminate the lines they skipped. **Noninterlaced monitors** illuminate the entire screen more quickly in a single pass. The speed at which the entire screen is redrawn is called the **refresh rate**.
4. The illuminated phosphors create an image on the screen.

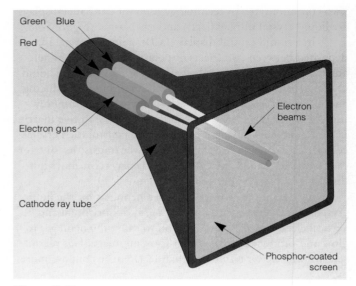

Figure 5-41
Each pixel on a color monitor screen is made up of three colored (red, green, and blue) phosphor dots. These dots can be turned on individually or in combinations to display a wide range of colors.

Figure 5-40
How an image is displayed on a monochrome cathode ray tube monitor.

Other Output Devices

Although printers and display devices provide the majority of computer output, other devices are available for particular uses and applications. These include data projectors, plotters, computer output microfilm devices, and voice output devices.

How Color Is Produced

To show color on a screen, each pixel must have three colored phosphor dots. These dots are the additive primary colors red, green, and blue *(Figure 5-41)*. A separate electron gun is used for each color. In the simplest combinations, eight colors can be generated – black (no color), red only, blue only, green only, magenta (red and blue), yellow (red and green), blue-green (blue and green), and white (red, blue, and green together). By varying the intensity of the electron beam striking the phosphors, and making some colored dots glow more than others, many more colors can be generated.

Data Projectors

A variety of devices are available to take the image that displays on a computer screen and project it so it can be clearly seen by a room full of people. Smaller, lower cost units, called **projection panels**, use liquid crystal display (LCD) technology and are designed to be placed on top of an overhead projector *(Figure 5-42)*.

Larger, more expensive units use technology similar to large-screen projection TV sets; separate red, green, and blue beams of light are focused onto the screen (*Figure 5-43* on the next page). The projection panels are easily portable and, depending on the overhead projector with which they are used, can be located at different distances from the projection screen. The three-beam projectors must be focused and aligned for a specific distance and thus once installed, are usually not moved.

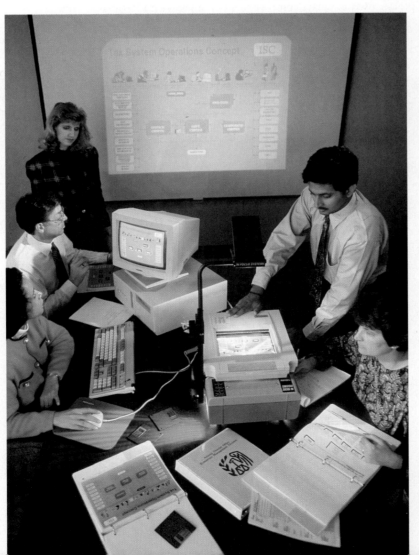

Figure 5-42
Projection panels are used together with overhead projectors to display computer screen images to a room full of people.

Plotters

A **plotter** is an output device used to produce high-quality line drawings such as building plans, charts, or circuit diagrams. These drawings can be quite large; some plotters are designed to handle paper up to 40 inches by 48 inches, much larger than would fit in a standard printer. Plotters can be classified by the way they create the drawing. The two types are pen plotters and electrostatic plotters.

As the name implies, **pen plotters** create images on a sheet of paper by moving one or more pens over the surface of the paper or by moving the paper under the tip of the pens.

Two different kinds of pen plotters are flatbed plotters and drum plotters. When a **flatbed plotter** is used to plot, or draw, the pen or pens are instructed by the software to move to the down position so the pen contacts the flat surface of the paper. Further instructions then direct the movement of the pens to create the image. Most flatbed plotters have one or more pens of varying colors or widths. The plotter shown in *Figure 5-44* is a flatbed plotter used to create color drawings.

A **drum plotter** uses a rotating drum, or cylinder, over which drawing pens are mounted. The pens can move to the left and right as the drum rotates, creating an image *(Figure 5-45)*. An advantage of the drum plotter is that the length of the plot is virtually unlimited because roll paper can be used. The width of the plot is limited by the width of the drum.

With an **electrostatic plotter,** the paper moves under a row of wires (called styli) that can be turned on to create an electrostatic charge on the paper. The paper then passes through a developer and the drawing emerges where the charged wires touched the paper. The electrostatic printer image is composed of a series of very small dots, resulting in relatively high-quality output. In addition, the speed of electrostatic plotting is faster than with pen plotters.

Computer Output Microfilm

Computer output microfilm (COM) is an output technique that records output from a computer as microscopic images on roll or sheet film *(Figure 5-46)*. The images stored on COM are the same as the images that would be printed on paper. The COM recording process reduces characters 24, 42,

Figure 5-43
The data projector uses three separate red, green, and blue beams to project data onto a screen. Single beam projectors are also available.

Figure 5-44
A color flatbed plotter.

or 48 times smaller than would be produced on a printer. The information is then recorded on sheet film called **microfiche** or on 16mm, 35mm, or 105mm roll film.

Microfilm has several advantages over printed reports or other storage media for certain applications. Some of these advantages are:

1. Data can be recorded on the film faster than printers; up to 30,000 lines per minute.
2. Costs for recording the data are lower. Studies have shown that microfilm can be as little as one-tenth the cost of printing a report.
3. Less space is required to store microfilm than printed materials. Microfilm that weighs one ounce can store the equivalent of 10 pounds of paper.
4. The cost to store a megabyte of information is less on microfilm than it is on disk.

To access data stored on microfilm, a variety of readers are available. They utilize indexing techniques to provide a quick reference to the data. Some microfilm readers can perform automatic data lookup, called **computer-assisted retrieval (CAR)**, under the control of an attached computer. With the indexing software and hardware now available for microfilm, a user can usually locate any piece of data in a database in less than 10 seconds, at a far lower cost per inquiry than using an online inquiry system consisting of a computer system that stores the data on a hard disk.

Voice Output

Another important means of generating output from a computer is voice output. **Voice output** consists of spoken words that are conveyed to the user from the computer. Thus, instead of reading words on a printed report or monitor, the user hears the words over earphones, the telephone, or other devices from which sound can be generated.

The data that produces voice output is usually created in one of two ways. First, a person can talk into a device that will encode the words in a digital pattern. For example, the words, *The number is,* can be spoken into a microphone, and the computer software can assign a digital pattern to the words. The digital data is then stored on a disk. At a later time, the data can be retrieved from the disk and translated back from digital data into voice, so the person listening will actually hear the words.

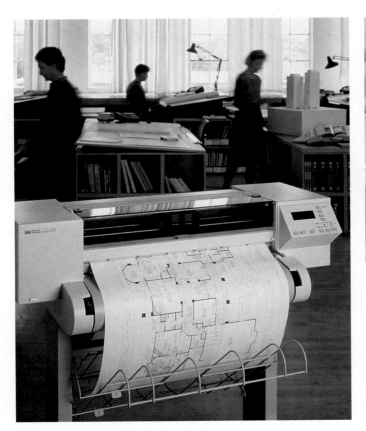

Figure 5-45
A drum plotter can handle larger paper sizes than a flatbed plotter.

Figure 5-46
Microfilm is often used for reports that must be kept on file but do not have to be referred to frequently.

Summary of Output from the Computer

A second type of voice generation is called voice synthesis. **Voice synthesis** can transform words stored in main memory into speech. The words are analyzed by a program that examines the letters stored in memory and generates sounds for the letter combinations. The software can apply rules of intonation and stress to make it sound as though a person were speaking. The speech is then projected over speakers attached to the computer.

You may have heard voice output used by the telephone company for giving number information. Automobile and vending machine manufacturers are also incorporating voice output into their products. The potential for this type of output is great and it will continue to be incorporated in products and services in the future.

The output step of the information processing cycle uses a variety of devices to provide users with information. The equipment discussed in this chapter, including printers, display devices, and other output devices are summarized in *Figure 5-47*.

OUTPUT DEVICE		DESCRIPTION
Speakers		Used for audio (sound) output.
Printers – Impact	Dot matrix	Prints text and graphics using small dots.
	Band	High-speed rotating band text-only printer.
	Chain	High-speed rotating chain text-only printer.
Printers – Nonimpact	Ink-jet	Sprays tiny drops of ink onto a page to form text and graphics. Prints quietly. Inexpensive color printer.
	Page (laser)	Works like a copying machine. Produces very high quality text and graphics.
	Thermal	Uses heat to produce high-quality color output.
Display Devices	Color monitors	Can display multiple colors to enhance information.
	Monochrome monitors	Displays one color on solid background. Less expensive than color.
	LCD	Flat panel liquid crystal display used for laptops. Available in color.
	Gas plasma	High-resolution flat panel display.
Data Projectors		Projects display screen image to a group.
Plotters		Produces hard-copy graphic output. Some can handle large paper sizes.
COM		Stores reduced-size image on sheet or roll film.
Voice		Communicates information to user in the form of speech.

Figure 5-47
A summary of the more common output devices.

COMPUTERS AT WORK

NoteStation – The Key to Getting the Right Music

Musicians and vocalists who purchase sheet music often have a problem finding music in the key that matches their instruments or vocal ranges. Traditionally printed sheet music usually comes in only one key. If the key is not right, the music must be transposed (converted) into another key. Transposing takes additional time and usually costs money if done by someone else. However, a company in California, using computers and multimedia software, appears to have solved the problem.

In combination with computer maker IBM, MusicWriter, Inc. of Los Gatos, California has developed NoteStation, a stand-alone multimedia kiosk that can generate sheet music in any key for more than 3,000 song titles. The potential sheet music buyer uses the NoteStation touch screen display to browse through the available songs by title, artist, style, or composer *(Figure 5-48)*. The system can even find songs if only a portion of the title is known. Once a song is selected, the sheet music is displayed on the screen. If desired, the customer can play a portion of the song. If the key is not right, it can be changed and the song played again. When the customer is happy with the music in his or her chosen key, the sheet music is printed on a laser printer or saved as a MIDI file on a diskette.

The advantages of NoteStation to musicians and vocalists are obvious. They can get their music in the key they want and listen to it before they buy it. If they are not exactly sure of what they want, using the computer to search through the song titles is much easier than leafing through pages of sheet music or a printed catalog. For the music stores where most NoteStations are installed, there are also numerous advantages. The music stores no longer have to order, stock, and inventory individual pieces of sheet music. Unless they run out of printer paper, they are never out of stock of any piece of music. The NoteStation kiosk takes a fraction of the space previously devoted to sheet music. The number of song titles available increases each month when the stores receive a new CD-ROM to load in the kiosk.

The NoteStation kiosk has significance beyond music publishing. The NoteStation is one of the first examples of what is called **point-of-sale manufacturing;** allowing the customer to design, manufacture, and purchase the product on the spot. The kiosk has become the showroom, warehouse, and manufacturing plant all rolled into a single unit that takes up fewer than 10 square feet of floor space. Eventually, this concept will be applied to many consumer products.

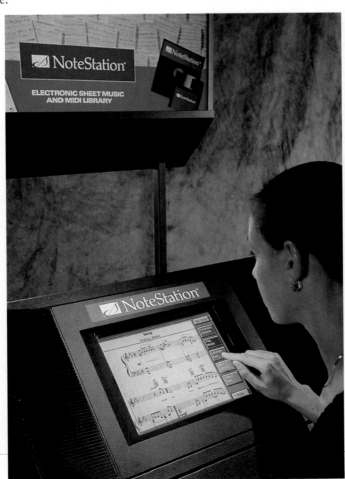

Figure 5-48

IN THE FUTURE

Virtual Reality   Beyond Entertainment

Most articles on virtual reality quickly move to discussions of games and rides designed to thrill the participants. Clearly, entertainment is the driving force behind most of today's VR applications. Many believe that VR will eventually have numerous practical applications that go beyond using a simulated laser gun to blast your opponent before he or she blasts you. The following discusses some of the probable future VR applications in training, medicine, and manufacturing.

Training

For some time, virtual reality like simulations have been used to train operators of expensive equipment such as airplanes and ships. In recent years, VR simulators have been developed for less expensive and complicated equipment such as trucks and construction equipment. The logical progression of this trend is that eventually, all products will come with VR training material that will help the user quickly and safely learn to use the equipment. For example, power tools such as a circular saw or electric drill could come with VR training materials that will enable the owner to saw or drill wood and build a project before attempting to use the real equipment.

Medicine

Medicine is another area where VR development work now being done may eventually be used on a widespread basis. To date, most of the VR work in medicine has involved learning systems. Different parts of the human anatomy have been digitized so students can use computer images to explore the body. Some work is already being done on using VR to simulate surgery. Portions of virtual bodies with internal organs and body fluids have been developed for these applications. Eventually, complete virtual patients will be developed to train medical personnel on all aspects of health care from initial consultation to post-operative recovery.

Manufacturing

Manufacturing companies are also experimenting with VR to improve design, production, and maintenance activities. VR prototypes will enable companies and prospective customers to evaluate designs before actual models are built. VR prototypes can also be used for repeated product testing. Manufacturing processes from welding to installing a nut and bolt can be tested for feasibility before production lines are built. Boeing is currently using a process closely related to VR called *augmented reality* to assist in manufacturing jumbo jets. Unlike VR, which creates a simulated scene, **augmented reality** superimposes information on a real scene. In Boeing's case, manufacturing procedures such as how to connect electrical wires in a plane are projected onto special glasses worn by the worker. The worker can see both the wiring diagram and the actual area of the plane where the wires are to be connected. Eventually, all equipment repair manuals might be available for such projected display as you work on the equipment.

All of the probable commercial applications of VR just discussed are either in limited use or under development. However, it may take years before they are widely used. In the meantime, there is this great VR game that you really should experience. Each player has a laser gun and the object of the game is . . .

Figure 5-49

What You Should Know

1. **Output** is data that has been processed into a useful form called information that can be used by a person or a machine. Output that is printed is called **hard copy**, and output that is displayed on a screen is called **soft copy**.

2. A **report** is information presented in an organized form. An **internal report** is used by individuals in the performance of their jobs. An **external report** is used outside the organization. The four common types of reports are: **narrative reports**, **detail reports**, **summary reports**, and **exception reports**. **Periodic reports**, also called **scheduled reports**, are produced on a regular basis. **On-demand reports** are created whenever they are needed for information that is not required on a scheduled basis.

3. **Computer graphics** are any non-text pictorial information. **Computer drawing programs** and **computer paint programs** allow an artistic user to create stunning looking works of art.

4. **Audio output**, sometimes called **audio response**, consists of sounds, including words and music, produced by the computer.

5. **Video output** consists of visual images that have been captured with a video input device, such as a VCR or camera, digitized, and directed to an output device such as a computer monitor. **High definition television** (HDTV) sets are designed for digital signals and may eventually replace computer monitors.

6. **Multimedia** is the combination of text, graphics, video, and sound. Most multimedia presentations use a technique called **hypermedia** that allows the user to quickly move to related subject areas. Because of the large amounts of data that multimedia applications require, most multimedia products available today are stored on CD-ROM disks.

7. **Virtual reality** (VR) refers to the use of a computer to create an artificial environment that can be experienced by the computer user. In its simplest form, VR software can display what appears to be a three-dimensional view of a place that can be explored by the user. In more advanced forms, VR software requires the user to wear specialized headgear, gloves, and body suits to enhance the experience of the artificial environment.

8. Generally, printers can be classified into two groups, impact or nonimpact, based on how they transfer characters to the paper.

9. **Impact printers** transfer the image onto paper by some type of printing mechanism striking the paper, ribbon, and character together. Most impact printers use **continuous-form paper**, which has pages that are connected together for a continuous flow through the printer.

10. A **dot matrix printer** produces printed images by striking wire pins against an inked ribbon. Most dot matrix printers used with personal computers have a single print head that moves across the page. Dot matrix printers used with larger computers have fixed print mechanisms at each print position and can print an entire line at a time.

11. The speed of impact printers with movable print heads is rated in **characters per second** (cps). The speed of impact printers that print one line at a time is rated in **lines per minute** (lpm). The speeds quoted by dot matrix printer manufacturers are usually for draft-quality printing. **Draft-quality** printing uses the minimum number of dots to form a character and achieve the fastest printing speed. To achieve a sharper, higher quality look, called **letter quality** (LQ) or **near letter quality** (NLQ), the printer overlaps printed dots.

12. Dot matrix printers with movable print heads are designed to print in a **bidirectional** manner; that is, the print head can print as it moves from left to right, and from right to left. Two types of paper feed mechanisms found on dot matrix printers are **tractor feed mechanisms** and **friction feed mechanisms**.

File   Edit   Section   Page   Tools   Options   Help

What You Should Know

13. Some dot matrix printers can print in multiple colors. Most dot matrix printers are available for less than $1,000.

14. Band and chain printers are impact printers used for high-volume output on large computer systems. **Band printers** use a horizontal, rotating band containing numbers, letters of the alphabet, and selected special characters. The **chain printer** is similar to a band printer and contains characters on a rotating chain.

15. **Nonimpact printing** means that printing occurs without having a mechanism striking against a sheet of paper.

16. An **ink-jet printer** sprays tiny drops of ink onto the paper. The **page printer** is a nonimpact printer that operates similar to a copying machine. Data is converted into light that is directed to a revolving drum. Each position on the drum touched by light attracts the toner (powdered ink) that is transferred onto the paper and then fused to the paper by heat and pressure. **Laser printers** use a laser beam aimed at the drum by a spinning mirror.

17. Page printers are rated by their speed and resolution. Speed is measured in **pages per minute (ppm)**. Page printer resolution is measured by the number of **dots per inch (dpi)** that can be printed.

18. **Thermal printers**, sometimes called **thermal transfer printers**, use heat to transfer colored inks from ink sheets onto the printing surface. A special type of thermal printer using a method called **dye diffusion** uses chemically treated paper to obtain color print quality equal to glossy magazines.

19. A number of printers have been developed for special purposes, including single label printers, bar code label printers, and portable printers.

20. A **display device** is the visual output device of a computer. A **monitor** looks like a television and consists of a display surface, called a screen, and a plastic or metal case to house the electrical components. The term **screen** is used to refer to both the surface of any display device and to any type of display device. A **video display terminal** (VDT) is a type of display device that also includes a keyboard. CRT, which stands for **cathode ray tube**, is an older term sometimes used to refer to monitor or VDT display devices. CRT is actually the large tube inside a monitor or VDT.

21. **The resolution**, or clarity, of the image on a monitor depends on the number of individual dots that are displayed on the monitor and the distance between each dot. Each dot that can be illuminated is called a **picture element,** or **pixel**. The distance between each pixel is called the **dot pitch**.

22. Monitors used for graphics are called **dot-addressable displays** or **bit-mapped displays**. Several video graphics standards have been developed, including CGA (Color Graphics Adapter), EGA (Enhanced Graphics Adapter), VGA (Video Graphics Array), and super VGA (SVGA). Some monitors are designed to only work with a particular frequency and video standard. Other monitors, called **multiscanning** or **multisync monitors**, are designed to work within a range of frequencies and thus can work with different standards and video adapters.

Start

23. A **color monitor** can display text or graphics in color. **Monochrome monitors** display a single color such as white, green, or amber characters on a black background, or black characters on a white background. Using a technique known as **gray scaling**, which involves converting an image into pixels that are different shades of gray like a black and white photograph, some monochrome monitors can display good quality graphic images.

24. A **flat panel display** is a thin display screen that does not use cathode ray tube (CRT) technology. In a **liquid crystal display** (LCD), a liquid crystal is deposited between two sheets of polarizing material. When an electrical current passes between crossing wires, the liquid crystals are aligned so light cannot shine through, producing an image on the screen. **Active matrix** LCD screens use individual transistors to control each crystal cell. **Passive matrix** LCD screens use fewer transistors; one for each row and column. **Gas plasma** screens substitute a neon gas for the liquid crystal material.

25. Most monitors used with personal computers and terminals use cathode ray tube (CRT) technology. An electron gun at the rear of the tube generates an electron beam toward the phosphor-coated screen, which glows when it is struck by the electron beam. **Interlaced monitors** illuminate every other line and then return to the top of the screen to illuminate the lines they skipped. **Noninterlaced monitors** illuminate the entire screen in a single pass. The speed at which the entire screen is redrawn is called the **refresh rate**. To show color on a screen, each pixel must have three colored phosphor dots (red, green, and blue). By varying the intensity of the electron beam striking the phosphors, many colors can be generated.

26. **Projection panels** use liquid crystal display (LCD) technology and are designed to be placed on top of an overhead projector.

27. A **plotter** is an output device used to produce high-quality line drawings such as building plans, charts, or circuit diagrams. **Pen plotters** create images on a sheet of paper by moving one or more pens over the surface of the paper or by moving the paper under the tip of the pens. When a **flatbed plotter** is used to plot, or draw, the pen or pens are instructed by the software to move to the down position so the pen contacts the flat surface of the paper. A **drum plotter** uses a rotating drum, or cylinder, over which drawing pens are mounted. With an **electrostatic plotter**, the paper moves under a row of wires (called styli) that can be turned on to create an electrostatic charge on the paper.

28. **Computer output microfilm** (COM) is an output technique that records output from a computer as microscopic images on sheet film, called **microfiche** or on rolls of film. Some microfilm readers can perform automatic data lookup, called **computer-assisted retrieval** (CAR).

29. **Voice output** consists of spoken words that are conveyed to the user from the computer. **Voice synthesis** can transform words stored in main memory into speech.

5:00 AM

File　　Edit　　Section　　Page　　Tools　　Options　　Help

Terms to Remember

active matrix (5.21)
audio output (5.4)
audio response (5.4)
augmented reality (5.28)

band printers (5.12)
bidirectional (5.11)
bit-mapped displays (5.19)

cathode ray tube (CRT) (5.18)
chain printers (5.13)
characters per second (cps) (5.10)
color monitor (5.20)
computer-assisted retrieval
　(CAR) (5.25)
computer drawing programs (5.4)
computer graphics (5.4)
computer output microfilm
　(COM) (5.24)
computer paint programs (5.4)
continuous-form paper (5.9)
CRT (5.18)

detail report (5.3)
display device (5.18)
dot matrix printer (5.10)
dot pitch (5.18)
dot-addressable displays (5.19)
dots per inch (dpi) (5.15)
draft quality (5.10)
drum plotter (5.24)
dye diffusion (5.15)

electronic plotter (5.24)
exception report (5.3)
external report (5.3)

flat panel display (5.20)
flatbed plotters (5.24)
friction feed mechanisms (5.12)

gas plasma (5.21)
gray scaling (5.20)

hard copy (5.2)
high definition television
　(HDTV) (5.5)
hypermedia (5.5)

impact printers (5.9)
ink-jet printer (5.13)
interlaced monitors (5.22)
internal report (5.2)

laser printers (5.14)
letter quality (5.11)
lines per minute (lpm) (5.10)
liquid crystal display (LCD) (5.21)

microfiche (5.25)
monitor (5.18)
monochrome monitors (5.20)
multimedia (5.5)
multiscanning (5.20)
multisync monitors (5.20)

narrative reports (5.3)
near letter quality (5.11)
nonimpact printing (5.13)
noninterlaced monitors (5.22)

on-demand reports (5.4)
output (5.2)

page printer (5.14)
pages per minute (ppm) (5.15)
passive matrix (5.21)
pen plotters (5.24)
periodic reports (5.4)
picture element (5.18)
pixel (5.18)
plotter (5.24)
point-of-sale manufacturing (5.27)
projection panels (5.23)

refresh rate (5.22)
report (5.2)
resolution (5.18)

scheduled reports (5.4)
screen (5.18)
soft copy (5.2)
summary report (5.3)

thermal printers (5.15)
thermal transfer printers (5.15)
tractor feed mechanisms (5.12)

video display terminal (VDT) (5.18)
video output (5.5)
virtual reality (VR) (5.7)
voice output (5.25)
voice synthesis (5.26)

File   Edit   Section   Page   Tools   Options   Help

Test Your Knowledge

Fill in the Blanks

1. _____ is data that has been processed into a useful form called information that can be used by a person or a machine.

2. Output that is printed is called _____, and output that is displayed on the screen is called _____.

3. _____ is the combination of text, graphics, video, and sound; most presentations of this type use a technique called _____ that allows the user to quickly move to related subject areas.

4. Generally, printers can be classified into two groups, _____ or _____, based on how they transfer characters to the paper.

5. Three different types of display devices are: _____, which display text and graphics in color; _____, which display a single color on a black or white background; and _____, which are thin display screens that do not use cathode ray tube (CRT) technology.

Short Answer

1. What is a report? How is an internal report different from an external report? How is a periodic report different from an on-demand report?

2. How is multimedia more than just a combination of traditional text-based computers and television? Why are most multimedia products available today stored on CD-ROM disks? In what four areas are multimedia applications primarily used?

3. How are impact printers different from nonimpact printers? Give at least two examples of each type of printer. What are the advantages and disadvantages of each printing method?

4. How are images displayed on a monitor that uses cathode ray tube (CRT) technology? How is color produced?

5. Although printers and display devices provide the majority of computer output, other devices are available for particular uses and applications. List at least three output devices other than printers or display devices. Briefly describe each.

Label the Figure

Instructions: Identify the parts of the monochrome cathode ray tube monitor shown in the figure below.

Start   5:02 AM

File   Edit   Section   Page   Tools   Options   Help

Points to Ponder

1

Reports can be classified by the way they present information. The four common types of reports are narrative reports, detail reports, summary reports, and exception reports. During your lifetime, you have probably given all of these reports, in either written or oral form. Describe a circumstance in which you offered each type of report.

2

Computer graphics and audio output are assuming increasingly important roles in art and music. Computer drawing programs and computer paint programs make it easy to draw perfect circles, three-dimensional figures, and arresting images. Electronic music technology enables a single person to produce sounds that once required a room full of musicians. What changes, if any, do you foresee in art or music as a result of these technologies? Do you think people who use computers to create graphic images or musical pieces should be called artists or musicians? Why or why not?

3

Some people believe that multimedia will revolutionize the way information is presented and the way people learn. It has even been predicted that eventually books will only be found in museums and antique stores. Do you think that multimedia will eventually replace all books, or certain types of books? Why or why not? What advantages, if any, do books have over multimedia?

4

Virtual reality (VR) software is currently being used to show clients proposed architectural changes, to allow customers to wander among available products in a virtual showroom or virtual office, and in three-dimensional electronic games. As computing power increases, and VR applications are able to run on lower cost computers, even more VR applications and VR technology will be available for a wider number of users. Think of at least three areas in which you think virtual reality software could be effectively employed. Describe how VR applications could be used in each.

5

When computers were first used in business, some people predicted the paperless office; a place where most documents would only exist electronically in the computer database. Many people now feel, however, that the widespread use of computers has actually elevated the quantity of paper used. Why do you think word processing software, spreadsheet programs, and low-cost printers might have increased the paperwork in the typical office? What steps could be taken to decrease the amount of paperwork?

6

Today, nearly all personal computers use two output devices – a monitor and a printer. Do you think these two output devices will still be the most popular twenty-five years from now? Why or why not? What other types of output devices do you think many personal computers will utilize? Why?

File   Edit   Section   Page   Tools   Options   Help

Out and About

1. Figure 5-31 on page 5.17 offers several questions to be considered when choosing a printer. List the questions posed in Figure 5-31 and answer each according to your current needs. Then, visit a computer store and find at least two printers that fit your requirements. Write down the name of each printer and note its advantages and disadvantages. If you were going to purchase one of these printers, which would you buy? Why?

2. Unlike ordinary television, which uses analog signals, high definition television (HDTV) sets are designed for digital signals. This results in clearer, sharper pictures and makes HDTV sets compatible with other digital technologies such as computers. Visit a library and research HDTV. How is analog technology different from digital technology? Will the development of HDTV be as significant as the introduction of color television approximately thirty years ago? What effect will the evolution of HDTV have on the computer industry?

3. Locate an organization that uses plotters. Possible users include architectural firms, electrical contractors, and a city planning department. Arrange to interview someone in the organization. Find out the purposes for which the plotter is used, what kind of plotter is used, and the advantages (or disadvantages) of using a plotter over creating a drawing by hand. If possible, ask to see a demonstration of the plotter's capabilities.

4. Examine the classified advertisement section of a newspaper or computer magazine. List all of the used computer output devices available. Which type of output device is most prevalent? Why? Choose two output devices in which you might be interested. Note the features and price of each. Would you consider purchasing either of these devices? Why or why not?

5. Contact a library or business that uses computer output microfilm (COM). Interview someone in the library or business to find out why COM is used. What advantages does computer output microfilm have over printed storage media? What are the disadvantages? How is the information accessed? Is the system capable of performing computer-assisted retrieval (CAR)?

6. Visit a computer vendor and obtain information about the highest and lowest priced monitors. Record the names of the monitors, their costs, and the features available with each. Do you think the more expensive monitor is worth the difference in price? Why or why not? Examine a portable computer that uses a flat panel display. What type of screen is it (LCD or gas plasma)? How does its image compare with the least expensive CRT monitor? How does it compare with the most expensive CRT monitor?

File   Edit   Section   Page   Tools   Options   Help

In the Lab with Windows 95

1 **Shelly Cashman Series Printer Lab**   Follow the instructions in Windows 95 Lab 1 on page 1.30 to display the Shelly Cashman Series Labs screen. Click Setting Up to Print. Click the Start Lab button. When the initial screen displays, carefully read the objectives. With your printer turned on, click the Print Questions button. Fill out the top of the Questions sheet and answer the questions as you step through the Printer Lab. Close the Shelly Cashman Series Labs.

2 **Shelly Cashman Series Monitor Lab**   Follow the instructions in Windows 95 Lab 1 on page 1.30 to display the Shelly Cashman Series Labs screen. Click Configuring Your Display. Click the Start Lab button. When the initial screen displays, carefully read the objectives. With your printer turned on, click the Print Questions button. Fill out the top of the Questions sheet and answer the questions as you step through the Monitor Lab. Close the Shelly Cashman Series Labs.

3 **Using a Screen Saver**   A screen saver, such as the one shown in *Figure 5-50,* displays when you are not actively using Windows. Later, when you press a key on the keyboard or move the mouse, the screen saver disappears from the screen. To activate or modify a screen saver, right-click an empty space on your desktop, and then click Properties on the shortcut menu. When the Display Properties dialog box displays, click the Screen Saver tab. Perform the following tasks: (1) Click the question mark button on the title bar and then click the edge of the picture of the monitor. When the pop-up window displays, right-click it. Click Print Topic on the shortcut menu and then click the OK button.

Click anywhere to remove the pop-up window. (2) Click the Screen Saver box arrow and then click Flying Windows. Click the Preview button to display the actual screen saver *(Figure 5-50).* Move the mouse. (3) Practice activating other screen savers. Close the Display Properties dialog box.

4 **Changing Desktop Colors**   Right-click an empty space on your desktop and then click Properties on the shortcut menu. When the Display Properties dialog box displays, click the Appearance tab. Perform the following tasks: (1) Click the question mark button on the title bar and then click the Scheme box. When the pop-up window displays, right-click it. Click Print Topic on the shortcut menu and then click the OK button. Click anywhere to remove the pop-up window. (2) Click the Scheme box arrow and then click Pumpkin (large). The sample displays as shown in *Figure 5-51.* (3) Practice clicking other color schemes. (4) Click the color scheme you want to use and then click the OK button.

5 **About Windows 95**   Double-click the My Computer icon on the desktop. Click Help on the menu bar of the My Computer window and then click About Windows 95. Answer the following questions: (1) To whom is Windows 95 licensed? (2) What percentage of system resources is free? Click the OK button. Close My Computer.

Figure 5-50

Figure 5-51

    5:05 AM

Where on the Web

1 **Tour Universal Studios**   Multimedia is the combination of text, graphics, video, and sound. Many Web sites present multimedia information. Complete the following steps to visit the MCA/Universal multimedia Web site *(Figure 5-52)* and see Universal Studios Backlot Tram Tour. If your PC has a QuickTime (.mov) player and sound card, you can add full- motion video and sound to your tour. With Netscape on the screen, type `http://www.mca.com/unicity/attractions/tram.html` in the Location text box and then press ENTER. Scroll down and read the page. Click Print on the File menu. Click OK. Hand in the printout.

2 **Stereos for Home and Car**   Most Web sites use a technique called hypermedia that allows the user to move quickly to related subject areas. Complete the following steps to become more familiar with hypermedia on the World Wide Web. With Netscape on the screen, type `http://www.crutchfield.com` in the Location text box and then press ENTER. Click What's In Our Catalog. Read and scroll down to the bottom of the page. Click a graphic for either Car Audio or Home Audio. Browse the information. Click Print on the File menu. Click Pages and then type 1 in the To text box. Click OK. Hand in the printout.

3 **Incredible Human Images**   Computer output includes computer graphics, which are any non-text pictorial information. Complete the following steps to see some amazing computer graphics of the human body. With Netscape

on the screen, type `http://www.nlm.nih.gov/research/research.html` in the Location text box and then press ENTER. Scroll down and click The Visible Human Project *(Figure 5-53)*. Scroll down and click images and animations. Click Color photographs of cryosections. Scroll down and view the images. Click Print on the File menu. Click Pages and then type 1 in the To text box. Click OK. Hand in the printout.

4 **VR Entertainment**   Virtual reality refers to the use of a computer to create an artificial environment that can be experienced by the user. Complete the following steps to learn more about virtual reality applications in entertainment. With Netscape on the screen, type `http://vr-atlantis.com` in the Location text box and then press ENTER. Scroll down the menu and click an area of information that seems interesting. Click Print on the File menu. Click Pages and then type 1 in the To text box. Click OK. Hand in the printout.

5 **Shelly Cashman Online**   Click Using Computers: A Gateway To Information, World Wide Web Edition on the Shelly Cashman Student Center Web page (`http://www.bf.com/scstudnt.html`). Scroll down and click Chapter 5. Complete the activities listed.

Figure 5-52

Figure 5-53

Secondary Storage

Objectives

After completing this chapter, you will be able to:

- Define secondary storage

- Identify the primary devices used for secondary storage

- Explain how data is stored on diskettes and hard disks

- Describe how data stored on diskettes can be protected

- Explain how magnetic tape storage is used with computers

- Describe four other forms of secondary storage: PC cards, optical disks, solid-state devices, and mass storage devices

- Describe how special-purpose storage devices such as smart cards are used

Storage is the fourth and final operation in the information processing cycle. Chapter 6 explains storage operations and the various types of secondary storage devices used with computers. Combining what you learn about storage with your knowledge of input, processing, and output will allow you to complete your understanding of the information processing cycle.

What Is Secondary Storage?

*I*t is important to understand the difference between how a computer uses main memory and how it uses secondary storage. As you have seen, main memory, also called primary storage or ram, temporarily stores programs and data that are being processed. **Secondary storage**, also called **auxiliary storage**, stores programs and data when they are not being processed, just as a filing cabinet is used in an office to store records. Records that are not being used are kept in the filing cabinet until they are needed. In the same way, data and programs that are not being used on a computer are kept in secondary storage until they are needed.

Most secondary storage devices provide a more permanent form of storage than main memory because they are nonvolatile, that is, data and programs stored on secondary storage devices are retained when the power is turned off. Main memory is volatile, which means that when power is turned off, whatever is stored in main memory is erased.

Secondary storage devices can be used as both input and output devices. When they are used to receive data processed by the computer, they are functioning as output devices. When some of their stored data is transferred to the computer for processing, they are functioning as input devices.

User secondary storage needs can vary greatly. Personal computer users may find the amount of data to be stored to be relatively small. For example, the names, addresses, and telephone numbers of several hundred friends or customers of a small business might require only 20,000 bytes of secondary storage (200 records x 100 characters per record). Users of large computers, such as banks or insurance companies, however, may need secondary storage devices that can store billions of characters. To meet the different needs of users, a variety of storage devices are available. *Figure 6-1* shows how different types of storage devices compare in terms of cost and speed. The secondary storage devices named in the pyramid are discussed in this chapter.

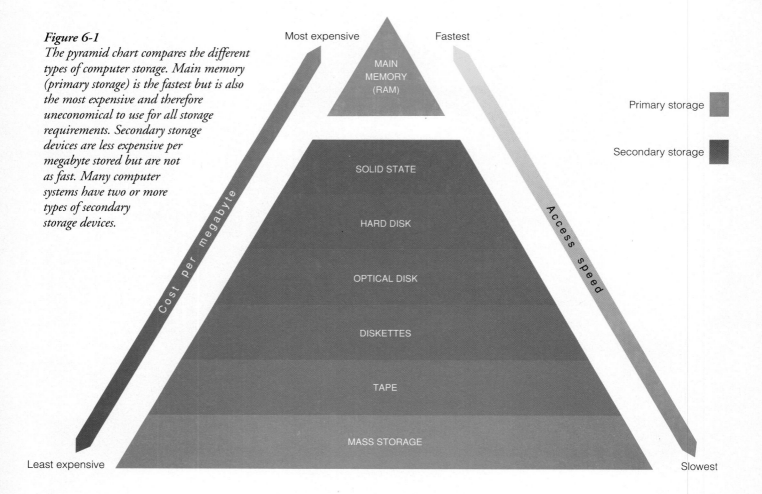

Figure 6-1
The pyramid chart compares the different types of computer storage. Main memory (primary storage) is the fastest but is also the most expensive and therefore uneconomical to use for all storage requirements. Secondary storage devices are less expensive per megabyte stored but are not as fast. Many computer systems have two or more types of secondary storage devices.

Magnetic Disk Storage

Magnetic disk is the most widely used storage medium for all types of computers. A **magnetic disk** consists of a round platter whose surface is covered with a magnetic material. Information can be recorded on or read from the magnetic surface. Magnetic disk offers high storage capacity, reliability, and the capability to directly access stored data. Magnetic disk types include diskettes, hard disks, and removable disk cartridges.

Diskettes

A **diskette** consists of a circular piece of thin mylar plastic (the actual disk), which is coated with an oxide material similar to that used on recording tape. In the early 1970s, IBM introduced the diskette as a new type of secondary storage. These diskettes were eight inches in diameter and were thin and flexible. Because they were flexible, they were often called **floppy disks**, or *floppies,* terms that are still used. Today, diskettes are used as a principal secondary storage medium for personal computers. This type of storage is convenient, reliable, and inexpensive.

Diskettes are available in two different sizes; $3^{1}/_{2}$ inch and $5^{1}/_{4}$ inch *(Figure 6-2)*. The size indicates the diameter (width) of the diskette.

Figure 6-2
The most commonly used diskettes are the $3 ^{1}/_{2}$" (above) and the $5 ^{1}/_{4}$" (left).

On a 3¹/₂-inch diskette, the circular piece of plastic is enclosed in a rigid plastic shell and a piece of metal called the shutter covers the reading and writing area. Paper liners help keep the recording surfaces clean *(Figure 6-3)*. When the 3¹/₂-inch diskette is inserted into a disk drive *(Figure 6-4)*, the drive slides the shutter to the side to expose a portion of both sides of the recording surface.

On a 5¹/₄-inch diskette, the circular piece of plastic is enclosed in a flexible, square protective jacket. The jacket has an opening on each side so that a portion of the diskette's surfaces are exposed for reading and writing as shown in *Figure 6-5*.

FORMATTING: PREPARING A DISKETTE FOR USE

Before a diskette can be used for secondary storage, it must be formatted. The **formatting** process prepares the diskette so it can store data and includes defining the tracks, cylinders, and sectors on the surfaces of a diskette *(Figure 6-6)*.

A **track** is a narrow recording band forming a full circle around the diskette. A **cylinder** is defined as all tracks of the same number. For example, track 0 on side 1 of the diskette and track 0 on side 2 of the diskette would be called cylinder 0. A **sector** is a pie-shaped section of the diskette. The term sector is more frequently used to refer to a track sector, a section of track within a sector. Each track sector holds 512 bytes. For reading and writing purposes, track sectors are grouped into clusters. A **cluster** consists of two to eight track sectors (the number varies depending on the operating system). A cluster is the smallest unit of diskette space used to store data. Even if a file consisted of only a few characters, one cluster would be used for storage. Each cluster can only hold data from one file, but a file can be made up of many clusters. The number of tracks and sectors created on a

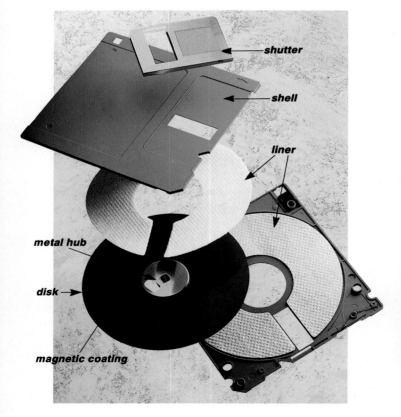

shutter

shell

liner

metal hub

disk

magnetic coating

Figure 6-3
In a 3 ¹/₂" diskette, the flexible plastic disk is enclosed between two liners that clean the disk surface of any microscopic debris and help to disperse static electricity. The outside cover is made of a rigid plastic material, and the recording window is covered by a metal shutter that slides to the side when the disk is inserted into the disk drive.

Figure 6-4
A user inserts a diskette into the disk drive of an IBM personal computer.

diskette when it is formatted varies based on the capacity of the diskette, the capabilities of the diskette drive being used, and the specifications in the operating system software that does the formatting. $5^1/_4$-inch diskettes are formatted with 40 or 80 tracks and 9 or 15 sectors on the surface of the diskette. $3^1/_2$-inch diskettes are usually formatted with 80 tracks and either 9, 18, or 36 sectors on each side.

In addition to defining the diskette surface, the formatting process erases any data that is on the diskette, analyzes the diskette surface for any defective spots, and establishes a directory that will be used to record information about files stored on the diskette. On personal computers using the DOS operating system, the directory is called the file allocation table. The **file allocation table (FAT)** file stores the filename, file size, the time and date the file was last changed,

and the cluster number where the file begins. The FAT file also keeps track of unused clusters and is used when the computer writes new files to the diskette. When you instruct the computer to list the files on a diskette, the information comes from the FAT file.

To protect data from being accidentally erased during formatting or other writing operations, diskettes have write-protection features. A $5^1/_4$-inch diskette has a write-protect notch. This notch is located on the side of the diskette. To prevent writing to a diskette, you cover this notch with a small piece of removable tape. Before writing data onto a diskette, the diskette drive checks the notch. If the notch is open, the drive will proceed to write on the diskette. If the

Figure 6-5
A 5 $^1/_4$" diskette consists of the disk itself enclosed within a protective jacket, usually made of vinyl material. The liner of the diskette is essentially friction-free so the disk can turn freely, but the liner does contact the disk and keep it clean. The magnetic surface of the diskette, which is exposed through the window in the jacket, allows data to be read and stored. The large hole (hub) in the diskette is used to mount the diskette in the disk drive. The small index hole is used by older disk drives as an indicator of where to store data.

Hub

Write-protect notch

Index hole

Liner   Disk   Alignment notches   Access window

Disk sector   Track sector

Tracks   Cluster (two track sectors)

This disk is divided into 9 sectors.

Figure 6-6
Each track on a diskette is a narrow, circular band separated from other tracks by a small gap. Diskettes typically have 40 to 80 tracks with the track closest to the outside edge numbered 0. The tracks are divided into sectors. Each sector of track holds 512 bytes of data. Two or more sectors form a cluster, the smallest amount of space used to record data.

notch is covered, the diskette drive will not write on the diskette *(Figure 6-7)*. On $3^1/2$-inch diskettes, the situation is reversed. Instead of a write-protect notch, there is a small window in the corner of the diskette. A piece of plastic in the window can be moved to open and close the window. If the write-protect window is closed, the drive can write on the diskette. If the window is open, the drive will not write on the diskette.

DISKETTE STORAGE CAPACITY

The amount of data you can store on a diskette depends on two factors: (1) the recording density; and (2) the number of tracks on the diskette.

The **recording density** is the number of bits that can be recorded on one inch of track on the diskette. This measurement is referred to as **bits per inch (bpi)**. The higher the recording density, the higher the storage capacity of the diskette. Most drives store the same amount of data on the longer outside tracks as they do on the shorter inside tracks. Thus, the bpi is measured on the innermost track where it is highest. Some newer drives use a different method. **Multiple zone recording (MZR)** records data at the same density on all

tracks. This means that the longer tracks closer to the outside edge of the disk can contain extra sectors. Each time a track becomes long enough to accept it, another sector is added.

The second factor that influences the amount of data that can be stored on a diskette is the number of tracks onto which data can be recorded. This measurement is referred to as **tracks per inch (tpi)**. As you learned earlier in this chapter, the number of tracks depends on the size of the diskette, the drive being used, and how the diskette was formatted.

The capacity of diskettes varies and increases every two or three years as manufacturers develop new ways of recording data more densely. Commonly used diskettes are referred to as either double-density or high-density. Older **single-density** diskettes that could only be written on one side are no longer used. **Double-density (DD) diskettes** can store 360K for a $5^1/4$-inch diskette and 720K for a $3^1/2$-inch diskette. **High-density (HD) diskettes** can store 1.2 megabytes (million characters) on a $5^1/4$-inch diskette and 1.44 megabytes on a $3^1/2$-inch diskette. **Extended-density (ED)** $3^1/2$-inch diskettes that can store 2.88 megabytes are also starting to be used. Even though it is smaller in size, a $3^1/2$-inch diskette can hold more data than a $5^1/4$-inch diskette because it has a higher recording density.

Figure 6-7
Data cannot be written on the 3 $^1/2$" diskette on the upper left because the window in the corner of the diskette is open. A small piece of plastic covers the window of the 3 $^1/2$" diskette on the upper right, so data can be written on this diskette. The reverse situation is true for the 5 $^1/4$" diskettes. The write-protect notch of the 5 $^1/4$" diskette on the lower left is covered and, therefore, data cannot be written to the diskette. The notch of the 5 $^1/4$" diskette on the lower right, however, is open. Data can be written to this diskette.

A special type of diskette, called a **floptical** diskette, combines optical and magnetic technology to achieve even higher storage rates (currently up to 21 megabytes) on what is basically a $3^1/_2$-inch diskette. A floptical disk drive uses a low-power laser to read grooves that have been permanently engraved in the diskette recording surface. The grooves allow closely spaced recording and higher bpi and tpi densities. Another advantage of a floptical drive is that it can also read double- and high-density $3^1/_2$-inch diskettes.

STORING DATA ON A DISKETTE

Regardless of the type of diskette or how it is formatted, the method of storing data on a diskette is essentially the same. When a $3^1/_2$-inch diskette is inserted into a diskette drive, the notches in the metal hub are engaged by a shaft connected to the drive motor *(Figure 6-8)*.

When you read from or write to a diskette, the motor spins the circular plastic recording surface at approximately 360 revolutions per minute. When you are not reading or writing, the disk does not spin. A lever opens the shutter to expose a portion of the plastic recording surface. Data is stored on tracks of the disk, using the same code, such as

ASCII, that is used to store the data in main memory. To do this, a recording mechanism in the drive called the **read/write head** rests on the top and bottom surface of the rotating diskette, generating electronic impulses. The electronic impulses change the magnetic polarity, or alignment, of magnetic areas along a track on the disk. The plus or minus polarity represents the 1 or 0 bits being recorded. To access different tracks on the diskette, the drive moves the read/write head from track to track. When reading data from the diskette, the read/write head senses the magnetic areas that are recorded on the diskette along the various tracks and transfers the data to main memory. When writing data to the diskette, the read/write head transfers data from main memory and stores it as magnetic areas on the tracks on the recording surface.

Data stored in sectors on a diskette must be retrieved and placed in main memory to be processed. The time required to access and retrieve the data is called the **access time**.

The access time for a diskette drive depends on three factors:

1. **Seek time**, the time it takes to position the read/write head over the proper track.

Read/write head

Shutter moves to one side exposing a portion of the disk surface

Drive moter engages hub and rotates disk surface

If light shines through write-protect window, diskette is write-protected and no data can be written to diskette.

Figure 6-8
When you insert a 3 ¹/₂" diskette in a drive, the notches in the metal hub are engaged by a drive motor shaft. A lever moves the shutter to one side so a portion of the disk surfaces are exposed. When you read from or write to a diskette, the shaft spins the disk at approximately 360 rpm. Read/write heads above and below the recording surface move in and out to read or write data.

2. **Rotational delay** (also called **latency**), the time it takes for the sector containing the data to rotate under the read/write head.
3. **Data transfer rate**, the time required to transfer the data from the disk to main memory.

The access time for diskettes varies from about 175 milliseconds (one millisecond equals $^1/_{1000}$ of one second) to approximately 300 milliseconds. What this means to the user is that, on the average, data stored in a single sector on a diskette can be retrieved in approximately $^1/_5$ to $^1/_3$ of one second.

THE CARE OF DISKETTES

With reasonable care, diskettes provide an inexpensive and reliable form of storage. In handling diskettes, you should take care to avoid exposing them to heat, cold, magnetic fields, and contaminated environments such as dust, smoke, or salt air. One advantage of the $3^1/_2$-inch diskette is that its rigid plastic cover provides more protection for the data stored on the plastic disk inside than the flexible cover on a $5^1/_4$-inch diskette. *Figure 6-9* shows you ways to properly care for your diskettes. Because the read/write head actually comes in contact with the diskette surface, wear takes place and the diskette will eventually become unreadable. To protect against loss, you should copy data onto other diskettes.

Hard Disks

Hard disks provide larger and faster secondary storage capabilities than diskettes. **Hard disks** consist of one or more rigid platters coated with an oxide material that allows data to be magnetically recorded on the surface of the platters *(Figure 6-10)*. The platters are usually made of aluminum but some newer disks use glass or ceramic materials. Most hard disks are permanently mounted inside the computer and are not removable like diskettes. On hard disks, the platters, the read/write heads, and the mechanism for moving the heads across the surface of the disk are enclosed in an airtight, sealed case. This helps to ensure a clean environment for the disk.

Figure 6-9
Guidelines for the proper care of diskettes.

Don't touch the disk surface. It is easily contaminated, which causes errors.

Don't use near magnetic fields including a telephone. Data can be lost if exposed.

Keep away from food and drinks.

Keep disks in a storage tray when not in use.

Don't place heavy objects on the disk

Keep away from smoke.

Don't expose the disk to excessive cold or heat or sunlight.

Insert disk carefully. Grasp upper edge and place it into the disk drive.

On minicomputers and mainframes, hard disks are sometimes called **fixed disks** because they cannot be removed like diskettes. They are also referred to as **direct-access storage devices (DASD)**. These hard disks are often larger versions of the hard disks used on personal computers and can be either mounted in the same cabinet as the computer or enclosed in their own stand-alone cabinet (*Figure 6-11*).

While most personal computers are limited to two to four disk drives, minicomputers can support 8 to 16 disk devices, and mainframe computers can support more than 100 high-speed disk devices.

HARD DISK STORAGE CAPACITY

Hard disks contain a spindle on which one or more disk platters are mounted (*Figure 6-12* on the next page). Each surface of a platter can be used to store data. Thus, if one platter is used in the drive, two surfaces are available for data. If two platters are used, four surfaces are available for data, and so on. Naturally, the more platters, the more data that can be stored on the drive. Like a diskette, hard disks must be formatted before they can be used to store data. Before a hard disk is formatted, it can be divided into separate areas called

partitions. Each partition can function as if it were a separate disk. Partitions are sometimes used to separate different types or classes of items such as programs and data or data from different organizations such as subsidiary companies. Separate partitions are also sometimes used for different operating systems. On personal computers, hard disk partitions are usually given letter identifiers, starting with the letter C. The letters A and B are reserved for diskette drives.

Access time for a hard disk is between ten and twenty milliseconds. This is significantly faster than for a diskette because of two reasons. First, a hard disk spins ten to twenty times faster than a diskette drive. Second, a hard disk is always spinning, whereas a diskette only starts spinning when a read or write command is received.

The storage capacity of hard drives is measured in megabytes or millions of bytes of storage. Common sizes for personal computers range from 100MB to 500MB of storage and even larger sizes are available. Each 10MB of storage is equivalent to approximately 5,000 printed pages, assuming approximately 2,000 characters per page.

Figure 6-10
A hard disk consists of one or more disk platters. Each side of the platter is coated with an oxide substance that allows data to be magnetically stored.

Figure 6-11
A high-speed, high-capacity fixed disk drive in a stand-alone cabinet.

Some disk devices used on large computers can store billions of bytes of information *(Figure 6-13)*. A billion bytes of information is called a **gigabyte**.

STORING DATA ON A HARD DISK

Storing data on hard disks is similar to storing data on diskettes. Hard disks rotate at a high rate of speed, usually 3,600 to 7,200 revolutions per minute. Hard disk read/write heads are attached to **access arms** that swing out over the disk surface to the correct track. The read/write heads float on a cushion of air and do not actually touch the surface of the disk. The distance between the head and the surface varies from approximately ten to twenty millionths of an inch. As shown in *Figure 6-14,* the close tolerance leaves no room for any type of contamination. If some form of contamination is introduced or if the alignment of the read/write heads is altered by something accidentally jarring the computer, the disk head can collide with and damage the disk surface, causing a loss of data. This event is known as a **head crash**. Because of the time needed to repair the disk and to reconstruct the data that was lost, head crashes can be extremely costly to users in terms of both time and money.

Depending on the type of disk drive, data is physically organized in one of two ways. One way is the sector method and the other is the cylinder method.

The **sector method** for physically organizing data on hard disks is similar to the method used for diskettes. Each track on the disk surface is divided into sectors. Each sector can contain a specified number of bytes. Data is referenced by indicating the surface, track, and sector where the data is stored.

With the **cylinder method**, all tracks of the same number on each recording surface are considered part of the same cylinder *(Figure 6-15)*. For example, the fifth track on all surfaces would be considered part of cylinder five. All twentieth tracks would be part of cylinder twenty, and so on. When the computer requests data from a disk using the cylinder method, it must specify the cylinder, recording surface, and record number. Because the access arms containing the read/write heads all move together, they are always over the same track on all surfaces. Thus, using the cylinder method to record data *down* the disk surfaces reduces the movement of the read/write head during both reading and writing of data.

Figure 6-13
The IBM 3390 disk drive is used on mainframe computer systems. Each drive, shown here being assembled during manufacturing, can hold 22.7 billion bytes of data.

Figure 6-12
A hard disk with its protective cover removed. The access arm and read/write head over the top platter can be clearly seen. Each platter surface, top and bottom, has an access arm and read/write head.

Some computers improve the apparent speed at which data is transferred to and from a disk by using disk cache. Similar in concept to the RAM cache memory described in Chapter 4, **disk cache** is an area of memory set aside for data most often read from the disk. Every time the computer requests data from the disk, disk cache software looks first for the data in the disk cache memory area. If the requested data is in disk cache, it is immediately transferred to the CPU and the slower disk read operation is avoided. Disk cache memory is updated every time a disk read takes place. In addition to the data requested from the disk, disk cache software also reads adjacent clusters on the assumption that they may be needed next. Disk cache software also makes disk write operations more efficient by temporarily holding data to be written until the CPU is not busy. Microsoft includes a disk cache program called SMARTDrive with the Windows and the DOS operating systems.

The flow of data to and from the hard disk is managed by electronic circuits called the hard disk controller. Sometimes the controller is a separate board in an expansion slot and sometimes the controller is part of the disk drive itself.

On personal computers, two types of controllers are most common, IDE and SCSI. **Integrated Drive Electronics** (IDE) controllers can operate one or two hard disk drives. Most motherboards have built-in IDE connectors that use a cable to attach directly to the disk drive. IDE controllers can transfer data to the disk at a rate of up to 8MB per second. **SCSI**, pronounced *scuzzy*, stands for **Small Computer System Interface**. SCSI controllers can support seven disk drives or any mix up to seven SCSI devices. SCSI devices are connected to each other in a chain with a cable between each device. SCSI controllers are faster than IDE controllers and can support up to 100MB per second transfer rates. SCSI controllers usually consist of a circuit board mounted in an expansion slot.

Data Compression

One way of storing more data on a disk is to use data compression. **Data compression** reduces the storage requirements of data by substituting codes for repeating patterns of data. For example, consider the familiar Ben Franklin saying, "Early to bed, early to rise, makes a man healthy, wealthy,

Figure 6-14 ▶
The clearance between a disk head and the disk surface is about 10 millionths of an inch. With this small difference, contamination such as a smoke particle, fingerprint, dust particle, or human hair could render the drive unusable. Hard disk drives are sealed to prevent contamination.

Cylinder 5 is comprised of all track 5s.

◀ *Figure 6-15*
The cylinder method reduces the movement of the read/write head (thereby saving time) by writing information down the disk on the same track of successive surfaces.

Human hair
3000 millionth
of an inch

Dust
particle
1550 millionth
of an inch

Fingerprint
600 millionth
of an inch

Smoke
particle
250 millionth
of an inch

Disk head
clearance
10 millionths
of an inch

Disk surface

and wise." Including punctuation, this phrase includes 56 characters. As shown in *Figure 6-16,* by substituting special characters for repeating patterns, the original phrase can be compressed to only 30 characters; a reduction of 46%. Compression is most often stated as a ratio of the size of the original uncompressed data divided by the size of the compressed data. In the *Figure 6-16* example, this would be a compression ratio of 1.9 to 1 (56 divided by 30). The codes substituted for the repeating patterns are filed in a table when the data is compressed. This substitution table is used to restore the compressed data to its original form when necessary.

The type of compression just described is called *lossless compression* because no data is lost in the process. Lossless compression works best for text and numeric data that cannot afford to lose any data. Compression ratios for lossless compression average 2 to 1 (the size of the data is reduced 50%). Other compression methods, called *lossy compression,* give up some accuracy for higher compression ratios (up to 200 to 1). Lossy compression methods are typically used to compress video images and sound. Video and sound can both have data removed without a noticeable reduction in the overall quality of the output. Lossy compression is usually accomplished with special hardware such as a video or sound expansion board.

Many manufacturers of complex software programs, such as word processing and spreadsheets, use compression methods to reduce the number of disks that are needed to distribute their products. Utility programs loaded with the software expand the software files as they are loaded on the user's system.

Some file compression programs, such as PKZIP, compress and uncompress data as directed by the user. Disk compression programs, such as Stacker, can be installed to automatically keep all files on a hard disk compressed until they are needed for processing.

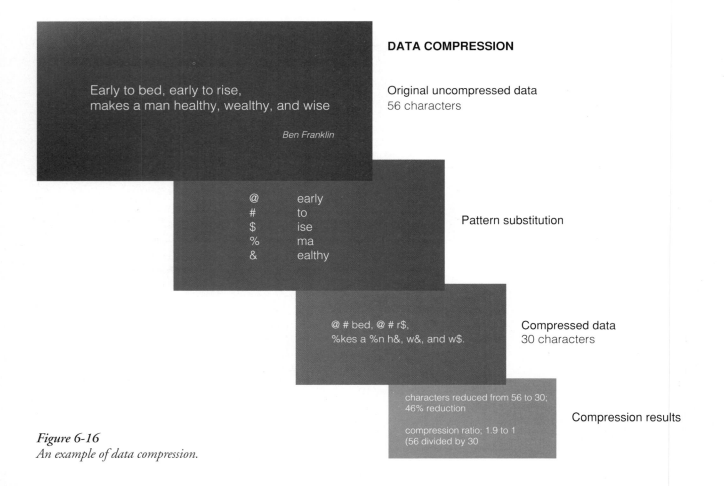

DATA COMPRESSION

Early to bed, early to rise,
makes a man healthy, wealthy, and wise

Ben Franklin

Original uncompressed data
56 characters

@   early
#   to
$ ise
%   ma
&   ealthy

Pattern substitution

@ # bed, @ # r$,
%kes a %n h&, w&, and w$.

Compressed data
30 characters

characters reduced from 56 to 30;
46% reduction

compression ratio; 1.9 to 1
(56 divided by 30

Compression results

Figure 6-16
An example of data compression.

RAID

As computers became faster, writing data to and reading data from increasingly larger disks became a bottleneck. Computers spent a large percentage of time waiting for data to go to or come from the disk drive. Rather than trying to build even larger and faster disk drives, some disk manufacturers began to connect multiple smaller disks into an integrated unit that acted like it was a single large disk drive. A group of integrated small disks is called a **RAID**, which stands for **redundant array of inexpensive disks**. RAID technology can be implemented in several ways called *RAID levels*.

In the simplest RAID method, called RAID level 1, one backup disk exists for each data disk *(Figure 6-17)*. Each backup disk contains the same information as its corresponding data disk. If the data disk fails, the backup disk becomes the data disk. Because the disks contain duplicate information, RAID level 1 is sometimes called **disk mirroring**.

RAID levels beyond level 1 all spread data across more than one drive. Dividing a logical piece of data, such as a record, word, or character, into smaller parts and writing those parts on multiple drives is called **striping** *(Figure 6-18)*. Some RAID levels call for a separate disk, called a parity or check disk, to keep track of information that can be used to recreate data if one of the data disks malfunctions. Other RAID levels store the parity information on the data disk. This parity information is an important part of RAID technology. It allows the system to rebuild, sometimes automatically, any information that is damaged on one of the data disks.

RAID disks offer a number of advantages over single large disks (called SLEDs for single large expensive disks). Because multiple read or write operations can take place at the same time, data can be read from or written to RAID disks faster. The biggest advantage, however, is the reduced risk of losing data. The capability to rebuild any damaged data is important to organizations that cannot afford to be without the information stored on their disks.

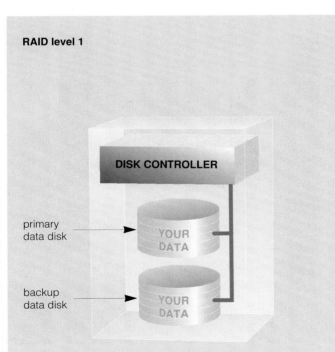

Figure 6-17
In RAID level 1, called disk mirroring, a backup disk exists for each data disk.

Figure 6-18
In RAID levels beyond level 1, data to be stored is divided into parts and written across several disks. This process is called striping. Some RAID levels call for additional parity disks that keep track of information to be used to recreate information if one of the data disks malfunctions.

Other Types of Hard Disks

Other devices that use hard disk technology are presented in this section. These include disk cartridges, hard cards, and removable disks.

DISK CARTRIDGES

Another variation of disk storage available for use with personal computers is the removable disk cartridge. **Disk cartridges**, which can be inserted and removed from a computer *(Figure 6-19)*, offer the storage and fast access features of hard disks and the portability of diskettes. Disk cartridges are often used when data security is an issue. At the end of a work session, the disk cartridge can be removed and locked up, leaving no data on the computer.

One unique type of disk cartridge is called a Bernoulli disk. The **Bernoulli disk cartridge** works with a special drive

Figure 6-19
A removable hard disk cartridge allows a user to remove and transport the entire hard disk from computer to computer or to lock it up in a safe.

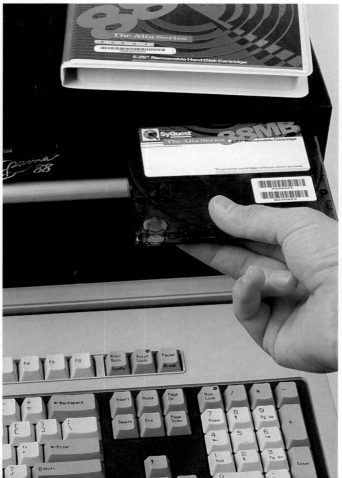

unit that uses a cushion of air to keep the flexible disk surface from touching the read/write head. The flexible disk surface reduces the chance of a head crash but does cause the cartridges to eventually wear out.

HARD CARDS

One option for installing a hard disk in a personal computer is a hard card. The **hard card** is a circuit board that has a hard disk built onto it. Hard cards provide an easy way to expand the storage capacity of a personal computer because the board can be installed into an expansion slot of the computer *(Figure 6-20)*. Because of lower prices on larger capacity disk drives, hard cards are not used as much as they once were.

REMOVABLE DISKS

Removable disk devices consist of the drive unit, which is usually in its own cabinet, and the removable recording media, called a **disk pack**. Removable disk packs consist of multiple metal platters that could record from 10 to 300 megabytes of data. Removable disk units were introduced in

Figure 6-20
A hard card is a hard disk drive on a circuit board that can be mounted in a computer's expansion slot.

the early 1960s and for nearly 20 years were the most prevalent type of disk storage on minicomputers and mainframes. During the 1980s, however, removable disks began to be replaced by hard fixed disks that offered larger storage capacities and higher reliability.

Maintaining Data Stored on a Disk

To prevent the loss of disk data, two procedures should be performed on a regular basis; backup and defragmentation.

BACKUP

Backup means creating a copy of important programs and data. To backup diskettes, simply copy the data on one diskette to another diskette. Diskettes are also commonly used to backup at least some of the data stored on a hard disk of a personal computer. Because hard disks can store large quantities of data (up to a gigabyte) diskettes are often used just to backup important files. Magnetic tape, another form of secondary storage, is commonly used to backup data stored on large-capacity hard disks.

DEFRAGMENTATION

When data is stored on a disk, it is placed in the first available clusters. The computer tries to place the data in clusters that are *contiguous* (all in a row), but contiguous clusters may not be available. When a file is stored in clusters that are not next to each other, the file is said to be **fragmented.** The term fragmented is also used to describe the condition of a disk drive that has many files stored in non-contiguous clusters *(Figure 6-21)*. Fragmentation causes the computer to run slower because reading data from the disk takes longer than if the data were all in one location. To solve this problem, the disk must be defragmented. **Defragmentation** reorganizes the data stored on the disk so files are located in contiguous clusters. Defragmentation programs are available as separate programs or as part of system utility packages. Some operating systems also contain defragmentation programs.

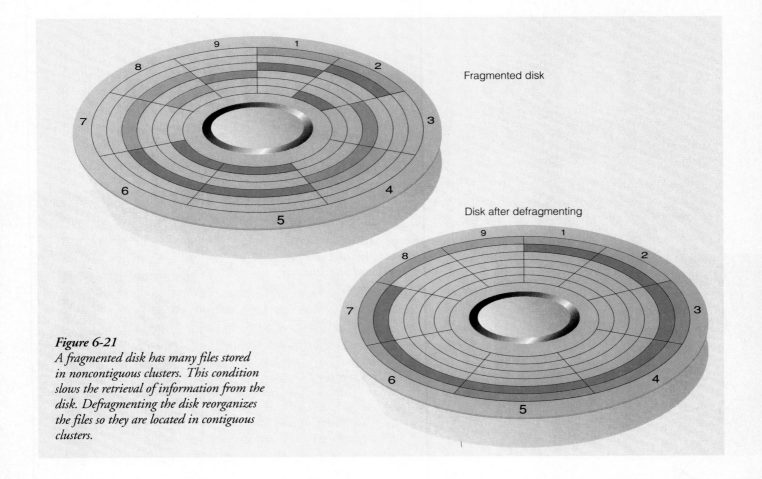

Fragmented disk

Disk after defragmenting

Figure 6-21
A fragmented disk has many files stored in noncontiguous clusters. This condition slows the retrieval of information from the disk. Defragmenting the disk reorganizes the files so they are located in contiguous clusters.

Magnetic Tape

During the 1950s and early 1960s, prior to the introduction of removable disk pack drives, magnetic tape was the primary method of storing large amounts of data. Today, even though tape is no longer used as the primary method of secondary storage, it still functions as a cost-effective way to store data that does not have to be accessed immediately. In addition, tape serves as the primary means of backup for most medium and large systems and is often used to transfer data from one system to another.

Magnetic tape consists of a thin ribbon of plastic. The tape is coated on one side with a material that can be magnetized to record the bit patterns that represent data. The most common types of magnetic tape devices are cartridge and reel-to-reel. Cartridge tape varies from $\frac{1}{4}$- or $\frac{1}{2}$-inch wide, and reel-to-reel tape is $\frac{1}{2}$-inch wide *(Figure 6-22)*.

Cartridge Tape Devices

A **cartridge tape** contains magnetic recording tape in a small rectangular plastic housing. One quarter-inch wide tape in cartridges slightly larger than audio tapes are frequently used for backup on personal computers. Faster and higher storage capacity $\frac{1}{2}$-inch cartridge tapes are increasingly replacing reel-to-reel tape devices on minicomputers and mainframes. For personal computers, cartridge tape units are designed to be internally mounted in a bay or in a separate external cabinet *(Figure 6-23)*.

Figure 6-22
One-half inch reel tape (top) and magnetic tape cartridge (bottom).

Figure 6-23
One-quarter inch cartridge tapes are often used to backup hard disks on personal computers. Drives can be either internal units mounted in a drive bay or external units.

Figure 6-24
Cartridge tape units used for larger systems have automatic loaders that allow multiple tapes to be recorded without the need of an operator.

For larger systems, cartridge tapes are usually mounted in their own cabinet. Cartridge tapes for larger systems are designed so multiple tapes can be automatically loaded and unloaded, allowing tape storage operations to take place unattended *(Figure 6-24)*.

Reel-to-Reel Tape Devices

Reel-to-reel tape devices use two reels: a supply reel to hold the tape that will be read from or written to, and the take-up reel to temporarily hold portions of the supply reel tape as it is being processed. As the tape moves from one reel to another, it passes over a read/write head, an electromagnetic device that can read or write data on the tape. At the completion of processing, tape on the take-up reel is wound back onto the supply reel.

Older style tape units used vertical cabinets with vacuum columns that held five or six feet of slack tape to prevent breaking during sudden start or stop operations.

Newer style tape units *(Figure 6-25)* allow a tape to be inserted through a slot opening similar to the way videotapes are loaded in a videocassette recorder. This front-loading tape drive takes less space and can be cabinet mounted. The drive automatically threads the end of the tape onto an internal take-up reel. Because of their size and cost, reel-to-reel tape drives are used almost exclusively on minicomputer and mainframe systems.

Reels of tape usually come in lengths of 300 to 3,600 feet and can store up to 200 megabytes of data.

Storing Data on Magnetic Tape

Tape is considered a **sequential storage** media because the computer must record and read tape records one after another. For example, to read the 1,000th record on a tape, the tape drive must first pass over the previous 999 records.

Figure 6-25
Newer style ¹/₂" inch tape drives allow the user to slide the tape into a slot at the front of the unit. The drive automatically threads the tape onto an internal take-up reel.

Binary codes, such as ASCII and EBCDIC, are used to represent data stored on magnetic tape. Within a code, each character is represented by a unique combination of bits. The bits are stored on tape in the form of magnetic areas *(Figure 6-26)*. The magnetic areas are organized into rows, called channels, that run the length of the tape. A combination of bits in a vertical column (one from each channel) is used to represent a character. An additional bit is used as a parity bit for error checking.

Tape density is the number of bits that can be stored on an inch of tape. As on disk drives, tape density is expressed in bits per inch, or bpi. Commonly used tape densities are 800, 1,600, 3,200 and 6,250 bpi. Some of the newer cartridge tape devices can record at densities higher than 60,000 bpi. The higher the density, the more data that can be stored on a tape.

Some tape drives can operate in a high-speed streaming mode used to backup and restore hard disk drives. In the **streaming mode**, the tape records data in exactly the same byte-by-byte order as it appears on the hard disk. When used to restore a hard disk, the data recorded on the tape in the streaming mode is used to recreate all the data on the hard disk. The advantage of streaming is that it is faster than normal tape operations and thus data can be recorded in less time. The disadvantage is that the streaming method cannot be used to selectively record or restore an individual file.

Another method of storing large amounts of data on tape is **digital audio tape** (DAT). DAT uses **helical scan technology** to write data at much higher densities across the tape at an angle instead of down the length of the tape *(Figure 6-27)*. Using this method, tape densities can be as high as 61,000 bpi.

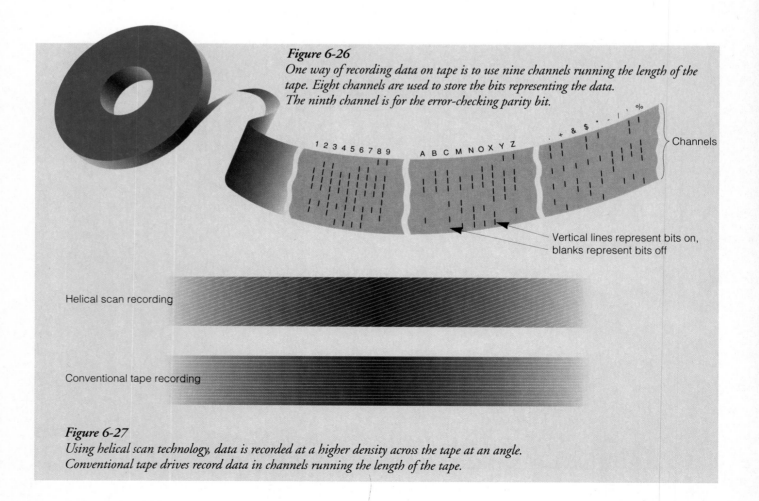

Figure 6-26
One way of recording data on tape is to use nine channels running the length of the tape. Eight channels are used to store the bits representing the data. The ninth channel is for the error-checking parity bit.

Channels

Vertical lines represent bits on, blanks represent bits off

Helical scan recording

Conventional tape recording

Figure 6-27
Using helical scan technology, data is recorded at a higher density across the tape at an angle. Conventional tape drives record data in channels running the length of the tape.

Other Forms of Secondary Storage

The conventional disk and tape devices just described comprise the majority of secondary storage devices and media, but other means for storing data are sometimes used. These include PC cards, optical disks, solid-state devices, and mass storage devices.

PC Cards

PC cards are small, credit card-sized cards that fit into PCMCIA expansion slots. You may recall from Chapter 4 that PCMCIA stands for the Personal Computer Memory Card International Association, the group that develops standards for the cards. Different versions and sizes of the cards are used for storage, communications, and additional memory.

Most often, PC cards are used on portable computers, but they can be incorporated into desktop systems as well. Although they are only 10.5mm thick (about .4 inch), PC cards used for storage contain small rotating disk drives 1.3 inches in diameter that can contain more than 200 megabytes of data *(Figure 6-28)*.

The storage cards can be useful for people who work with more than one computer or who have to share a computer with others. Their data can be maintained on a PC storage card and kept with them.

Optical Disks

Enormous quantities of information are stored on **optical disks** by using a laser to burn microscopic holes on the surface of a hard plastic disk.

A lower power laser reads the disk by reflecting light off the disk surface. The reflected light is converted into a series of bits that the computer can process *(Figure 6-29)*.

Figure 6-28
Type III PC cards are used for small removable disk drives that can hold over 200 megabytes of data.

Figure 6-29
To record data on an optical disk, a high-power laser heats the surface and makes a microscopic pit. To read data, a low-power laser light is reflected from the smooth unpitted areas and is interpreted as 1 bit. The pitted areas do not reflect the laser beam and are interpreted as 0 bits.

High-power laser beam   Low-power laser beam

Write   Read

A full-size, 14-inch optical disk can store 6.8 billion bytes of information. Up to 150 of these disks can be installed in automated disk library systems (called jukeboxes) that provide more than one trillion bytes (called a **terabyte**) of online storage. The smaller disks, just under five inches in diameter, can store more than 800 million bytes, or approximately 550 times the data that can be stored on a high-density 3¹/₂-inch diskette. That is enough space to store approximately 400,000 pages of typed data.

The smaller optical disk is called a **CD-ROM**, an acronym for compact disk read-only memory *(Figure 6-30)*. They use the same laser technology used for the CD-ROM disks that have become popular for recorded music. In fact, if a computer is equipped with a CD-ROM drive, a sound card, and speakers, audio CD-ROM disks can be played.

CD-ROM drives are often advertised as double-, triple-, or quadruple-speed drives. The ratings refer to how fast the drive can transfer data in relation to a standard established for CD-ROM drives used for multimedia applications. The original standard established a minimum transfer rate of 150 kilobytes per second (kbps). A double-speed drive can transfer data at 300 kbps, a triple-speed drive at 450 kbps, and a quadruple-speed drive at 600 kbps.

Most optical disks are prerecorded and cannot be modified by the user. These disks are used for applications such as an auto parts catalog where the information is changed only occasionally, such as once a month, and a new updated optical disk is created. Optical disk devices that provide for one-time recording are called **WORM** devices, an acronym for *write once, read many*. Erasable optical disk drives are just starting to be used. The most common erasable optical drives use **magneto-optical technology**, in which a magnetic field changes the polarity of a spot on the disk that has been heated by a laser.

Figure 6-30
A CD-ROM can store hundreds of times the information as can be stored on a diskette of similar size. Many reference materials, such as encyclopedias, catalogs, and even phone books, are now published on CD-ROM instead of paper.

Figure 6-31
Solid-state storage devices use rows of RAM chips to emulate a conventional rotating disk drive. This solid-state device can transfer data 15 to 20 times faster than a rotating disk system.

Because of their tremendous storage capacities, entire catalogs or reference materials can be stored on a single optical disk. Some people predict that optical disks will someday replace data now stored on film such as microfiche.

Solid-State Storage Devices

To the computer, solid-state storage devices act just like disk drives, only faster. As their name suggests, they contain no moving parts, only electronic circuits. **Solid-state storage devices** *(Figure 6-31)* use the latest in random access memory (RAM) technology to provide high-speed data access and retrieval. Rows of RAM chips provide megabytes of memory that can be accessed much faster than the fastest conventional disk drives. Solid-state storage devices are significantly more expensive than conventional disk drives offering the same

storage capacity. Unlike disk or tape systems, solid-state storage devices are volatile; if they lose power their contents are lost. For this reason, these devices are usually attached to emergency power backup systems.

Mass Storage Devices

Mass storage devices provide automated retrieval of data from a library of storage media such as tape or data cartridges. Mass storage is ideal for extremely large databases that require all information to be readily accessible even though any one portion of the database may be infrequently required. Mass storage systems take less room than conventional tape storage and can retrieve and begin accessing records within seconds. *Figure 6-32* shows a mass storage system that uses tape cartridges.

Figure 6-32
The inside of an automated mass storage system that uses tape cartridges. A robot arm with a camera mounted on top accesses and loads any one of thousands of tape cartridges in an average of 11 seconds. Each cartridge is a 4" x 4" square and about 1" thick and can hold up to 200 megabytes of data. The tapes are stored in a circular cabinet referred to as a silo.

Special-Purpose Storage Devices

Several devices have been developed for special-purpose storage applications. Three of these are memory buttons, smart cards, and optical memory cards.

Memory buttons are small storage devices about the size of a dime that look like watch batteries *(Figure 6-33)*. The buttons can currently hold up to 8,000 characters of information but storage capacities are increasing rapidly. To read or update information in the button, the user touches the button with a small, pen-like probe attached to a hand-held terminal. An audible sound is generated to indicate that the read or write operation has been completed. The buttons are used in applications where information about an item must travel with the item. Examples are laboratory samples, shipping containers, and rental equipment.

Figure 6-34
Smart cards are credit card-sized devices that contain a microprocessor in the left center of the card. The microprocessor can store up to 128,000 bits of information.

Figure 6-33
Memory buttons can hold up to 8,000 characters of information. The buttons are used in applications where information about an item must travel with the item. The buttons can be read or updated using a hand-held device.

Figure 6-35
The optical card can store up to 1,600 pages of information and images. It is the size and thickness of a credit card.

SUMMARY OF SECONDARY STORAGE

Smart cards are the same size and thickness of a credit card and contain a thin microprocessor capable of storing recorded information *(Figure 6-34)*. When it is inserted into compatible equipment, the information on the smart card can be read and, if necessary, updated. A current user of smart cards is the U. S. Marine Corps, who issues the cards to recruits instead of cash. Each time a recruit uses the card, the transaction amount is subtracted from the previous balance. Other uses of the card include employee time and attendance tracking (instead of time cards) and security applications where detailed information about the card holder is stored in the card.

Optical memory cards can store up to 1,600 pages of text or images on a device the size of a credit card *(Figure 6-35)*. Applications include automobile records and the recording of personal and health-care data.

Summary of Secondary Storage

Secondary storage is used to store programs and data that are not currently being processed by the computer. This chapter discussed the various types of secondary storage used with computers. The chart in *Figure 6-36* provides a summary of the secondary storage devices covered. What you have learned about these devices and storage operations in general can now be added to what you have learned about the input, processing, and output operations to complete your understanding of the information processing cycle.

TYPE	DEVICE	DESCRIPTION
Magnetic Disk	Diskette	Thin, portable plastic storage media that is reliable and low cost.
	Hard disk	Fixed platter storage media that provides large storage capacity and fast access.
	RAID	Multiple small disks integrated into a single unit.
	Disk cartridge	Portable disk unit that provides security.
	Hard card	Hard disk on expansion slot circuit board.
	Removable disk	Older style disk unit with removable disk packs.
Magnetic Tape	Cartridge tape	Tape enclosed in rectangular plastic housing.
	Reel tape	$1/2$-inch tape on 300 to 3,600 foot reel.
Other Storage Devices	PC card	Removable 1.3-inch disks used on portable computers.
	Optical disk	High capacity disks use laser to read and record data.
	Solid-state	Simulate disks using RAM chips to provide high-speed access.
	Mass storage	Automated retrieval of storage media such as tape or data cartridges.
Special-Purpose Devices	Memory button	Stores data on chip in small metal cannister.
	Smart card	Thin microprocessor stores data in credit card-sized holder.
	Optical card	Text and images stored in credit card-sized holder.

Figure 6-36
A summary of secondary storage devices.

COMPUTERS AT WORK

American Express Opts for Optical Storage

American Express' billing operation was once drowning in a sea of paperwork. The AMEX Travel Related Services Company (TRS) was one of the last large credit card operations that still included the actual charge receipts with the monthly statement sent to the cardholder. That meant that each day, several million charge documents had to be processed and temporarily stored until the card holder's bill was prepared. The paper system was prone to errors and at one time, nearly 200 people were assigned to tracking down missing receipts. TRS could have eliminated the receipts like most charge card processors, but they felt that including the receipts was a service to their cardholders.

TRS solved their paperwork problem by implementing the world's largest transaction processing system using optical storage. With the new system, paper charge slips are handled only once when an image of the receipt is captured and stored on a write-once read-many (WORM) optical disk.

After they are recorded, the paper receipts are destroyed. Each 12-inch disk can store 100,000 images; the equivalent of six filing cabinets of paper. In a typical year, more than 5,000 WORM disks are used. At the time the image is captured, billing information is also recorded. When it is time to prepare a cardholder's monthly billing statement, the images are electronically sorted and printed along with the statement giving the cardholder written proof of the charge.

Not only does the system offer a unique service to the cardholders, but it costs TRS less than their previous way of processing receipts; nearly 25% less, according to TRS estimates. As their slogan says about their card, "don't leave home without it;" but as far as charge receipts go, don't worry, they'll send them to you in the mail.

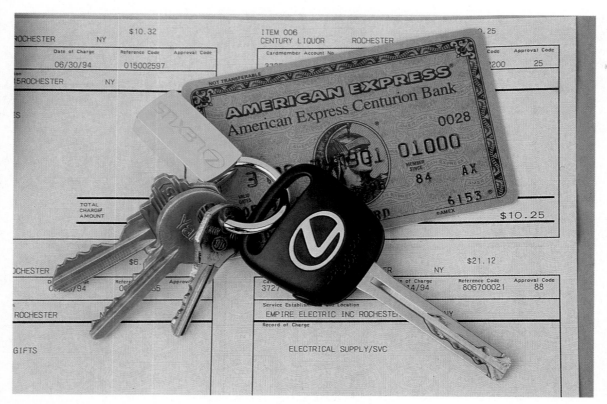

Figure 6-37

IN THE FUTURE

Memory Cubes

In the not-too-distant future, you may be able to fit the equivalent of a small library in the palm of your hand. Professor Peter Rentzepis at the University of California Irvine campus has patented a laser device capable of recording 6.5 trillion bits of information on a piece of plastic the size of a sugar cube. That is roughly equal to one million novels.

The plastic cube is made of commercially available polystyrene plastic that has been chemically treated *(Figure 6-38)*. To record data, a single laser beam is split in two and directed toward the cube at right angles. Where the laser beams meet, the plastic molecules are altered and the color changes from clear to blue. Blue molecules are considered 1 bit and the clear, unaltered plastic molecules are considered 0 bits. To read information, a different colored laser beam is used. The reading laser beam only interacts with the blue molecules making them briefly emit a red light. Sensors read the red light and transmit a 1 bit to the computer.

Several obstacles need to be overcome before the memory cubes become commercially feasible. The first challenge is the size of the equipment necessary to record and read the cubes.

The smallest size so far is approximately one foot square. This may not seem that big but it is still much too large for the fastest growing segment of the computer market; personal computers. The second challenge is even more formidable; heat. Currently, the cubes need to stay at very low temperatures to retain their stored information. If the cubes are left at room temperature, they lose their information in a few hours. Even when they are cooled with liquid nitrogen, they only retain their data for a few months. These challenges are worth pursuing however, because of the memory cube's potential. In addition to storing tremendous amounts of data in a small space, the cubes are inexpensive and, unlike disk drives, have no moving parts.

Figure 6-38

File   Edit   Section   Page   Tools   Options   Help

What You Should Know

1. Main memory, also called primary storage, temporarily stores programs and data that are being processed. **Secondary storage**, also called **auxiliary storage**, stores programs and data when they are not being processed.

2. Most secondary storage devices provide a more permanent form of storage than main memory because they are nonvolatile; that is, data and programs stored on secondary storage devices are retained when the power is turned off. Secondary storage devices are used as both input and output devices. To meet the different needs of users, a variety of secondary storage devices are available.

3. A **magnetic disk** consists of a round platter whose surface is covered with a magnetic material. Magnetic disk offers high storage capacity, reliability, and the capability to directly access stored data. Several types of magnetic disk include diskettes, hard disks, and removable disk cartridges.

4. A **diskette** consists of a circular piece of thin mylar plastic (the actual disk), which is coated with an oxide material similar to that used on recording tape. Because the original diskettes were flexible, they were often called **floppy disks**, or *floppies,* terms that are still used. Because they are convenient, reliable, and inexpensive, diskettes are used as a principal secondary storage medium for personal computers. Diskettes are available in two different sizes (diameters); 3 1/2 inches and 5 1/4 inches.

5. Before a diskette can be used for secondary storage, it must be formatted. The **formatting** process prepares the diskette so that it can store data and includes defining the tracks, cylinders, and sectors on the surfaces of a diskette. A **track** is a narrow recording band forming a full circle around the diskette. A **cylinder** is defined as all tracks of the same number. A **sector** is a pie-shaped section of the diskette. A **cluster**, the smallest unit of diskette space used to hold data, consists of two to eight

track sectors. The formatting process also erases any data on the diskette, analyzes the diskette surface for any defective spots, and establishes a directory that will be used to record information about files stored on the diskette. On personal computers using the DOS operating system, the directory is called the **file allocation table (FAT)**.

6. The amount of data you can store on a diskette depends on two factors: (1) the recording density; and (2) the number of tracks on the diskette.

7. The **recording density** is the number of bits that can be recorded on one inch of track on the diskette. This measurement is referred to as **bits per inch (bpi)**. Most drives store the same amount of data on the longer outside tracks as they do on the shorter inside tracks. Some newer drives, however, use **multiple zone recording (MZR)**, which records data at the same density on all tracks, so the longer tracks can contain extra sectors.

8. The measurement of the number of tracks onto which data can be recorded is referred to as **tracks per inch (tpi)**. This number depends on the size of the diskette, the drive being used, and how the diskette was formatted.

9. Older **single-density** diskettes that could only be written on one side are no longer used. **Double-density (DD) diskettes** can store 360K for a 5 1/4-inch diskette and 720K for a 3 1/2-inch diskette. **High-density (HD) diskettes** can store 1.2 megabytes (million characters) on a 5 1/4-inch diskette and 1.44 megabytes on a 3 1/2-inch diskette. **Extended-density (ED)** 3 1/2-inch diskettes that can store 2.88 megabytes are also starting to be used. A **floptical diskette** combines optical and magnetic technology to achieve even higher storage rates.

10. When you read from or write to a diskette, a motor spins the circular plastic recording surface at approximately 360 revolutions per minute. A recording mechanism in the drive called the **read/write head** rests on the top and bottom surface of the rotating diskette, generating electronic impulses. The electronic impulses change the polarity, or alignment, of magnetic areas along a track on the disk.

Start

11. When reading data from a diskette, the read/write head senses the magnetic areas that are recorded on the diskette along various tracks and transfers the data into main memory. The time required to access and retrieve data is called the access time. The access time for a diskette depends on three factors: **seek time**, **rotational delay** (also called **latency**), and **data transfer rate**.

12. With reasonable care, diskettes provide an inexpensive and reliable form of storage. Wear does take place, however, and a diskette will eventually become unreadable. To protect against loss, data should be copied onto other diskettes.

13. Hard disks provide larger and faster secondary storage capabilities than diskettes. **Hard disks** consist of rigid platters coated with an oxide material that allows data to be magnetically recorded on the surface of the platters. Most hard disks are permanently mounted inside the computer and are not removable like diskettes.

14. On minicomputers and mainframes, hard disks are sometimes called **fixed disks** because they cannot be removed like diskettes. They are also referred to as **direct-access storage devices (DASD)**.

15. Hard disks contain a spindle on which one or more disk platters are mounted. Like a diskette, hard disks must be formatted before they can be used to store data. Before a hard disk is formatted, it can be divided into separate areas called **partitions**, each of which can function as if it were a separate disk.

16. The storage capacity of hard drives is measured in megabytes, or millions of bytes, of storage. Some disk devices can store billions of bytes of information, called a **gigabyte**.

17. Storing data on hard disks is similar to storing data on diskettes. Hard disk read/write heads are attached to **access arms** that swing out over the disk surface to the correct track. The read/write heads float on a cushion of air and do not actually touch the surface of the disk. If some form of contamination is introduced or if the alignment of the read/write head is altered by something jarring the computer, the disk head can collide with and damage the surface of the disk. This event is known as a **head crash** and causes a loss of data.

18. Depending on the type of disk drive, data is physically organized in two ways. The **sector method** for physically organizing data on hard disks is similar to the method used for diskettes. With the **cylinder method**, all tracks of the same number on each recording surface are considered part of the same cylinder.

19. Some computers improve the apparent speed at which data is transferred to and from a disk by using a **disk cache**, an area of memory set aside for data most often read from the disk.

20. The flow of data to and from the hard disk is managed by electronic circuits called the hard disk controller. **Integrated Drive Electronics** (IDE) controllers can operate one or two disk drives. SCSI (**Small Computer System Interface**) controllers can support seven disk drives or any mix of up to seven SCSI devices.

21. **Data compression** reduces the storage requirements of data by substituting codes for repeating patterns of data. Compression ratios for *lossless compression,* in which no data is lost, average 2 to 1. *Lossy compression* gives up some accuracy for higher compression ratios (up to 200 to 1).

22. A group of integrated small disks is called a **RAID**, which stands for **redundant array of inexpensive disks**. In the simplest RAID method, called RAID level 1, one backup disk exists for each data disk. Because disks contain duplicate information, RAID level 1 is sometimes called **disk mirroring**. RAID levels beyond level 1 all spread data across more than one drive. Dividing a logical piece of data into smaller parts and writing those parts on multiple drives is called **striping**.

23. **Disk cartridges**, which can be inserted and removed from a computer, offer the storage and fast access features of hard disks and the portability of diskettes. The **Bernoulli disk cartridge** works with a special drive unit that uses a cushion of air to keep the flexible disk surface from touching the read/write head.

24. The **hard card** is a circuit board that has a hard disk built onto it. Hard cards provide an easy way to expand the storage capacity of a personal computer because the board can be installed into an expansion slot of the computer.

File   Edit   Section   Page   Tools   Options   Help

What You Should Know
(continued)

25. **Removable disk devices** consist of the drive unit, which is usually in its own cabinet, and the removable recording media, called a **disk pack**.

26. To prevent the loss of disk data, two procedures should be performed on a regular basis; backup and defragmentation. **Backup** means creating a copy of important programs and data. When a file is stored in clusters that are not next to each other, the file is said to be **fragmented**. **Defragmentation** reorganizes the data stored on the disk so files are located in contiguous clusters.

27. **Magnetic tape** consists of a thin ribbon of plastic coated on one side with a material that can be magnetized to record the bit patterns that represent data. At one time the primary method of storing large amounts of data, magnetic tape still functions as a cost-effective way to store data that does not have to be accessed immediately, serves as the primary means of backup for most medium and large systems, and is often used to transfer data from one system to another.

28. A **cartridge tape** contains magnetic recording tape in a small, rectangular plastic housing. **Reel-to-reel tape devices** use two reels: a supply reel to hold the tape that will be read from or written to, and the take-up reel to temporarily hold portions of the supply reel tape as it is being processed.

29. Tape is considered a **sequential storage** media because the computer must record and read tape records one after another. **Tape density** is the number of bits that can be stored on an inch of tape. Some tape drives can operate in a high-speed streaming mode used to backup and restore hard disk drives. In the **streaming mode**, the tape records data in exactly the same byte-by-byte order as it appears on the hard disk. Another method of storing large amounts of data on tape is **digital audio tape** (**DAT**). DAT uses **helical scan technology** to write data at much higher densities across the tape at an angle instead of down the length of the tape.

30. **PC cards** are small, credit card-sized cards that fit into PCMCIA expansion slots. Although they are only 10.5mm thick (about .4 inch), PC cards used for storage contain small rotating disk drives 1.3 inches in diameter that can contain over 200 megabytes of data.

31. Enormous quantities of information are stored on **optical disks** by using a laser to burn microscopic holes on the surface of a hard plastic disk. Up to 150 of these disks can be installed in automated disk libraries (called jukeboxes) that provide more than one trillion bytes (called a **terabyte**) of online storage. A smaller optical disk is called a **CD-ROM**, an acronym for compact disk-read only memory. Most optical disks are prerecorded and cannot be modified by the user. Optical disk devices that provide for one-time recording are called WORM devices, an acronym for write once, read many. The most common erasable optical devices use **magneto-optical technology**, in which a magnetic field changes the polarity of a spot on the disk that has been heated by a laser.

32. Solid-state storage devices contain no moving parts, only electronic circuits. **Solid-state storage devices** use the latest in random access memory (RAM) technology to provide high-speed data access and retrieval.

33. **Mass storage devices** provide automated retrieval of data from a library of storage media such as tape or data cartridges.

34. Several devices have been developed for special-purpose storage applications. **Memory buttons** are small storage devices about the size of a dime that look like watch batteries. The buttons are used in applications where information about an item must travel with the item. **Smart cards** are the same size and thickness of a credit card and contain a thin microprocessor capable of storing recorded information. Smart cards are used for employee time and attendance tracking and security applications where detailed information about the card holder is stored in the card. **Optical memory cards** can store up to 1,600 pages of text or images on a device the size of a credit card. Applications include automobile records and the recording of personal and health-care data.

Start   6:00 AM

File   Edit   Section   Page   Tools   Options   Help

Terms to Remember

access arms (6.10)
access time (6.7)
auxiliary storage (6.2)

backup (6.15)
Bernoulli disk cartridge (6.14)
bits per inch (bpi) (6.6)

cartridge tape (6.16)
CD-ROM (6.20)
cluster (6.4)
cylinder (6.4)
cylinder method (610)

data compression (6.11)
data transfer rate (6.8)
defragmentation (6.15)
digital audio tape (DAT) (6.18)
direct-access storage devices
    (DASD) (6.9)
disk cache (6.11)
disk cartridges (6.14)
disk mirroring (6.13)
disk pack (6.14)
diskette (6.3)
double-density (DD) diskettes (6.6)

extended-density (ED) diskettes (6.6)

file allocation table (FAT) (6.5)
fixed disks (6.9)
floppy disks (6.3)
floptical (6.7)
formatting (6.4)
fragmented (6.15)

gigabyte (6.10)

hard card (6.14)
hard disks (6.8)
head crash (6.10)
helical scan technology (6.18)
high-density (HD) diskettes (6.6)

Integrated Drive Electronics
    (IDE) (6.11)

latency (6.8)

magnetic disk (6.3)
magnetic tape (6.16)
magneto-optical technology (6.20)
mass storage devices (6.21)
memory buttons (6.21)
multiple zone recording (MZR) (6.6)

optical disks (6.19)
optical memory cards (6.22)

partitions (6.9)
PC cards (6.19)

RAID (6.13)
read/write head (6.7)
recording density (6.6)
redundant array of inexpensive disks
    (RAID) (6.13)
reel-to-reel tape devices (6.17)
removable disk (6.14)
rotational delay (6.8)

SCSI (6.11)
secondary storage (6.2)
sector (6.4)
sector method (6.10)
seek time (6.7)
sequential storage (6.17)
single-density (6.6)
Small Computer System Interface
    (SCSI) (6.11)
smart cards (6.22)
solid-state storage (6.21)
streaming mode (6.18)
striping (6.13)

tape density (6.18)
terabyte (6.20)
track (6.4)
tracks per inch (tpi) (6.6)

WORM (6.20)

Start   6:01 AM

Test Your Knowledge

Fill in the Blanks

1. ___Secondary Storage___ stores programs and data when they are not being processed.

2. A(n) ___Magnetic disk___ the most widely used storage medium for all types of computers, consists of a round platter whose surface is covered with a magnetic material.

3. ___Magnetic Tape___, which consists of a thin ribbon of plastic, functions as a cost-effective way to store data that does not have to be accessed immediately.

4. Enormous quantities of information are stored on ___Optical Disks___ by using a laser to burn microscopic holes on the surface of a hard plastic disk.

5. ___Solid-State Storage devices___ which contain only electronic circuits, use the latest in random access memory (RAM) technology to provide megabytes of memory that can be accessed much faster than conventional disk drives.

Short Answer

1. How is data written to and read from a diskette?

2. What is access time? On what three factors does access time depend? Briefly explain each. Why is access time significantly faster for a hard disk than for a diskette?

3. What is data compression? How is lossless compression different from lossy compression? For what kind of data is each type of compression used?

4. What two procedures should be performed on a regular basis to prevent the loss of disk data? Explain each.

5. What do memory buttons, smart cards, and optical memory cards have in common? How are they different? For what purpose is each used?

Label the Figure

Instructions: Write the appropriate secondary storage device in each level of the pyramid chart shown below.

Primary Storage

Most expensive   Fastest

MAIN MEMORY RAM

COST PER MEGABYTE   ACCESS SPEED

Least expensive   Slowest

Secondary Storage

File   Edit   Section   Page   Tools   Options   Help

Points to Ponder

1

Magnetic disks are called direct-access storage devices because a computer system can go directly to a desired piece of data. Magnetic tape, on the other hand, is called a sequential access storage device because data must be read in sequence, one piece of data after another. Although magnetic tape is slower than magnetic disks, it is less expensive and well-suited for certain applications such as providing a backup. Think of at least one other business application for which a sequential access storage device, such as magnetic tape, is ideal. Explain why magnetic tape is appropriate for the application. Think of at least one business application for which magnetic tape is unsuitable. Explain why.

2

Instead of supplying potential customers with printed brochures, a few companies now provide a marketing diskette or CD-ROM that can be used by customers with personal computers. Some automobile manufacturers provide a marketing diskette or CD-ROM that lets PC users "walk around and kick the tires" of a vehicle by furnishing photographs, statistics, option packages, and pricing information. A personal computer video game is even supplied that allows buyers to "test drive" a vehicle by participating in a wildlife photo safari. Think of another product that you could market. What kind of information would you provide? Do you think potential sales of the product would justify the cost of producing the diskette or CD-ROM? Why or why not?

3

Some CD-ROM disks contain interactive children's "books." Using these disks, a computer can read the story in several different languages, reread selected passages, show the book's illustrations, allow children to ask questions about what is on the screen, and even reveal surprises when children use a mouse to click some part of a picture. Discuss the advantages and disadvantages of these CD-ROM disks compared to watching a television program or hearing a story read by someone else.

4

The National Gallery of Art in Washington, D.C. has recorded its entire collection on an optical disk, including works that, because of space limitations, are not normally displayed. The images on the disk offer startling clarity – even brush strokes are visible. Users of the disk can almost instantaneously display any work in the collection, locate works based on a wide range of criteria (artist, nationality, period, and so on), and magnify portions of a work on the screen. The optical disk is being made available to schools around the country. Why do you think optical disk was chosen to store the gallery's collection instead of some other secondary storage medium such as magnetic disk or magnetic tape? In what school classes do you think the disk will be used? How? As more museums take advantage of optical disk technology, do you think museum attendance will decline? Why or why not?

5

Despite the risk of data loss, a study has shown that less than 35 percent of all companies, and less than 20 percent of small companies, have backup policies. Of companies that do have backup policies, more than one-quarter had experienced a computer crash in the past. It is estimated that data loss costs American companies approximately $4 billion each year. Why do you think so few companies backup their data? If you were the CEO of a large company, what backup policy would you establish? How would you make sure your policy was carried out?

6

Recently out of college, you have just been hired by Wiley's Widgets, LTD. Although Wiley's Widgets uses computers to produce letters, memorandums, and spreadsheets, much to your surprise, you find that all of the employee, customer, and inventory records are stored on paper in file cabinets. Your coworkers tell you that this is the way Wiley's Widgets has kept its records since the company was founded in 1865, and that old Mr. Wiley hates change. One day as you are riding the elevator up to your office, you bump into Mr. Wiley and mention the benefits of saving records using some form of computer secondary storage. Mr. Wiley is intrigued and wants to hear more. Write a memo to Mr. Wiley describing the advantages and, because Mr. Wiley is no fool, any disadvantages in using some type of secondary storage to store company records. What form of secondary storage would you recommend? Why?

File   Edit   Section   Page   Tools   Options   Help

Out and About

1. Some organizations, such as insurance companies, banks, libraries, and college registrars, are *information-intensive,* meaning that they must keep track of and manipulate large amounts of data. Visit an information-intensive organization and interview someone responsible for maintaining the organization's data. What are the organization's storage requirements? What type of secondary storage medium is used? Why? Have there ever been any problems with secondary storage? If so, how were the problems remedied? What type of backup procedures are employed?

2. The price of diskettes varies depending on such things as diskette size, recording density, the diskette manufacturer, and whether or not the diskette is already formatted for an Apple or IBM-compatible personal computer. Visit a store that sells computer supplies and compare the price of the least expensive diskettes to the price of the most expensive diskettes. What factors account for the difference in price? Which diskettes are recommended by the store's salesperson? Why? If you were buying diskettes for your own personal computer, which ones would you purchase? Why?

3. Because many companies store large amounts of information on hard disks that are permanently mounted inside the computer, the problem of data security has become an important issue. No companies can afford to have sensitive information on customers or product development stolen by industrial spies or dissatisfied employees. Visit a large firm and interview an employee on data security. How are records protected? Who has access to sensitive data? Have there ever been problems with data security? If so, what measures have been taken to make sure the problems do not recur?

4. As a result of the expanding storage requirements of some software and graphic files, new technologies are being developed that offer even greater secondary storage. These technologies include flash memory cards, glass disks, glass-ceramic disks, and "wet" hard drives. Using current computer magazines, prepare a report on one or more of these new technologies. What does the technology entail? What benefits does it offer? Why? When is the technology likely to be available for general use?

5. Visit a computer store and obtain information on the different types of hard disk drives available for personal computers. Summarize your findings and include data on price, storage capacity, and access speed. Calculate the cost per megabyte of storage for each drive. If you have a personal computer, which type of hard disk drive do you think is best suited for your current needs? Do you think the same disk drive will be adequate five years from now? Why or why not?

6. Many people feel that we have only begun to take advantage of smart card technology. In addition to the uses described in this chapter, smart cards that store the medical histories of the cardholders are being tested in New York, and smart cards have taken the place of food stamps for some residents of Dayton, Ohio. Visit a library and research smart cards. How much information can they contain? How do they work? In what applications have they been used? Why? How may smart cards be used in the future?

In the Lab with Windows 95

1 **Shelly Cashman Series Secondary Storage Lab**
Follow the instructions in Windows 95 Lab 1 on page 1.30 to display the Shelly Cashman Series Labs screen. Click Maintaining Your Hard Drive. Click the Start Lab button. When the initial screen displays, carefully read the objectives. With your printer turned on, click the Print Questions button. Fill out the top of the Questions sheet and answer the questions as you step through the Secondary Storage Lab. Close the Shelly Cashman Series Labs.

2 **Formatting a Floppy Disk**   Place an unformatted floppy disk in drive A and then double-click the My Computer icon on the desktop. When the My Computer window displays, click the 3¹/₂ Floppy [A:] icon. Click File on the menu bar and then click Format to display the Format dialog box. If necessary, change the displayed capacity of the floppy disk by clicking the Capacity box arrow and then clicking the appropriate capacity. In the Format type area, click Full. If it is not already selected, click Display summary when finished. Click the Start button. When the formatting is complete, a Format Results dialog box displays *(Figure 6-39)*. Click the Close button. Close the Format dialog box. Remove the floppy disk from drive A. Put your name on a label and place the label on the floppy disk. Close My Computer.

3 **Managing Files on a Disk**   Insert the floppy disk with your Windows Labs into drive A. Double-click the My Computer icon on the desktop. When the My Computer window displays, click View on the menu bar and then click Large Icons. Double-click the 3¹/₂ Floppy [A:] icon. If you do

not see your Windows 95 Labs in the 3¹/₂ Floppy [A:] window, double-click the folder name containing these files. Perform the following tasks: (1) Click the windows 95 lab 2-2 icon. If you do not have windows 95 lab 2-2, ask your instructor for a copy. (2) Click Edit on the menu bar and then click Copy. Click Edit on the menu bar and then click Paste. A new icon titled Copy of windows 95 lab 2-2 displays in the 3¹/₂ Floppy [A:] window *(Figure 6-40)*. (3) Click the Copy of windows 95 lab 2-2 icon. Click File on the menu bar and then click Rename. Type `windows 95 lab 6-3` and then press ENTER. (4) Click the windows 95 lab 6-3 icon. Click File on the menu bar and then click Print. (5) Click the windows 95 lab 6-3 icon. Click File on the menu bar and then click Delete. When the Confirm File Delete dialog box displays, click the Yes button. Notice that the windows 95 lab 6-3 icon no longer displays. Close the 3¹/₂ Floppy [A:] window. Close My Computer.

4 **Using Help**   Click the Start button on the taskbar, and then click Help on the Start menu. Click the Index tab, press TAB, type `Recycle Bin` and then press ENTER. Double-click Retrieving deleted files or shortcuts. When the Windows Help window displays, click the green dotted under-lined words, Recycle Bin. When the pop-up window displays, right-click it. Click Print Topic on the shortcut menu, and then click the OK button. Click anywhere. Close Help.

Figure 6-39

Figure 6-40

Where on the Web

1 **Viewing Movie Clips**   Complete the following steps to get an appreciation of the storage requirements for full-motion video. With Netscape on the screen, type `http://www.disney.com` in the Location text box and then press ENTER. Click Movies. Click Movie Clips. Click a movie of your choice. Approximately how many bytes of storage are required for the movie clips? Click Print on the File menu. Click OK. Hand in the printout.

2 **Your Favorite TV Music**   Complete the following steps to get an appreciation of the storage requirements for sound files (and to listen to your favorite TV theme music if you have a sound card). With Netscape on the screen, type `http://themes.parkhere.com/themes/index.html` in the Location text box and then press ENTER. Scroll down the TV Bytes page *(Figure 6-41)* to the heading New Themes For This Week. How much storage is required? Click Print on the File menu. Click Pages and then type 1 in the To text box. Click OK. Hand in the printout.

3 **Weather Maps**   Complete the following steps to get an appreciation of the storage requirements for graphics files (and to view a weather map such as that shown in *Figure 6-42*). With Netscape on the screen, type `http://www.accuwx.com` in the Location text box and then press ENTER. Scroll down and click Get Weather. Scroll down and click one of the map titles. Watch at the bottom of the Netscape window for the total size of the file. Click Print on the File menu. Click OK. Write the size of the file on the printout and hand it in.

4 **Infoseek Net Search**   Complete the following steps to use a Net Search utility to learn more about mass storage. With Netscape on the screen, click the Net Search button. Click Infoseek Guide. Type `mass storage` in the text box. Click the seek now button. Scroll down and click any one of the items. Read more about mass storage. Click Print on the File menu. Click Pages and then type 1 in the To text box. Click OK. Write a brief description of what you found on the printout and hand it in.

5 **Shelly Cashman Online**   Click Using Computers: A Gateway To Information, World Wide Web Edition on the Shelly Cashman Student Center Web page (`http://www.bf.com/scstudnt.html`). Scroll down and click Chapter 6. Complete the activities listed.

Figure 6-41

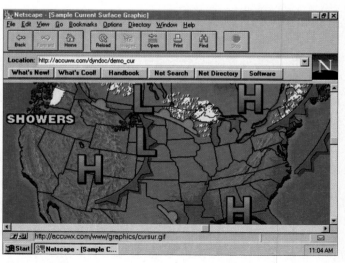

Figure 6-42

Communications and Networks

7

Computers are well recognized as important computing devices. They should also be recognized as important communications devices. It is now possible for a computer to communicate with other computers anywhere in the world. This capability, sometimes referred to as connectivity, allows users to quickly and directly access data and information that otherwise would have been unavailable or that probably would have taken considerable time to acquire. Banks, retail stores, airlines, hotels, and many other businesses use computers for communications purposes. Personal computer users communicate with other personal computer users. They can also access special databases available on larger computers to quickly and conveniently obtain information such as weather reports, stock market data, airline schedules, news stories, or even theater and movie reviews.

    This chapter provides an overview of communications with an emphasis on the communication of data and information. The chapter explains some of the terminology, equipment, procedures, and applications that relate to computers and their use as communications devices. How computers can be joined together into computer networks is discussed. Networks multiply the power of individual computers by allowing users to communicate and share hardware, software, and information.

Objectives

After completing this chapter, you will be able to:

- Describe several examples of how communications technology is used

- Define the term communications

- Describe the basic components of a communications system

- Describe the various transmission media used for communications channels

- Describe the different types of line configurations

- Describe how data is transmitted

- Identify and explain the communications equipment used in a communications system

- Describe the functions performed by communications software

- Explain the two major categories of networks, and describe three common network configurations

- Describe how bridges and gateways are used to connect networks

Examples of How Communications Is Used

*T*he ability to instantly and accurately communicate information is changing the way people do business and interact with each other. Advances in communications software and hardware now allow people to easily transmit voice and data communications around the world. The following applications rely on communications technology:

- Electronic mail
- Voice mail
- Teleconferencing
- FAX
- Groupware
- Telecommuting
- Electronic data interchange (EDI)
- Global positioning systems (GPS)
- Bulletin board systems (BBS)
- Online services

Electronic Mail

Electronic mail, also described in detail in Chapter 2, is the capability to use computers to transmit messages to and receive messages from other computer users. The other users may be on the same computer network or on a separate computer system reached through the use of communications equipment. Each E-mail user has an address to which mail can be sent. The address acts as a mailbox and accumulates messages. Most E-mail programs support distribution lists that send messages to several individuals at the same time.

Many organizations with internal computer networks provide E-mail for employees. Online service providers such as Prodigy and America Online also offer E-mail capabilities.

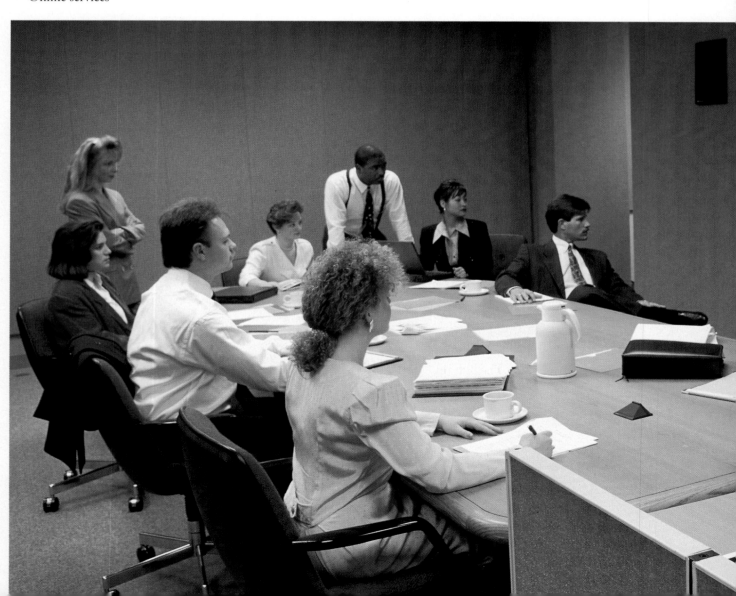

Voice Mail

Voice mail can be considered verbal electronic mail. Made possible by the latest computerized telephone systems, voice mail reduces the problem of telephone tag, where two people trying to reach each other wind up leaving a series of messages to please call back. With voice mail, the caller can leave a message, similar to leaving a message on an answering machine. The difference between voice mail and an answering machine is that with a voice mail system the caller's message is digitized so it can be stored on a disk like other computer data. This allows the party who was called to hear the message later (by converting it to an audio form) and also, if desired, add a reply or additional comments and forward the message to someone else who has access to the system.

Teleconferencing

Teleconferencing once meant three or more people sharing a phone conversation. Today, however, **teleconferencing** usually means video conferencing, the use of computers and television cameras to transmit video images and the sound of the participant(s) to a remote location that has compatible equipment *(Figure 7-1)*. Special software and equipment is used to digitize and compress the video image so it can be transmitted along with the audio over standard communications channels. Although the video image is not as clear for moving objects as commercial television, it does contribute to the discussion and is adequate for nonmoving objects such as charts and graphs. Video conferencing was originally developed for larger groups of people who had to use a room specially outfitted with video conferencing equipment. More recently, desktop video equipment has been developed to allow individual users to visually communicate with other people within their building or at remote locations *(Figure 7-2)*.

Figure 7-1
Video conferencing is used to transmit and receive video and audio signals over standard communications channels. This meeting is being transmitted to a video conference center at another location. The people at the other location are also being recorded and transmitted and can be seen on the TV monitor.

Figure 7-2
Desktop video conferencing equipment allows individual users to communicate with other employees on their computer network. Some systems can also connect to remote locations.

FAX

Facsimile, or FAX, equipment is used to transmit a reproduced image of a document over phone lines *(Figure 7-3)*. The document can contain text or graphics, can be hand-written, or be a photograph. FAX machines optically scan the document and convert the image into digitized data that is transmitted over a phone line. A FAX machine at the receiving end converts the digitized data back into its original image. FAX equipment is available as stand-alone machines or as part of data communications equipment called modems that are discussed later in this chapter. Using FAX software, the FAX modems can directly transmit computer-prepared documents or documents that have been digitized with the use of a scanner. FAX equipment is having an increasing impact on the way people transmit documents. Many documents that were previously sent through the mail are now sent by FAX. With the speed and convenience of a phone call, a document sent by FAX can be transmitted anywhere in the world.

Groupware

Groupware is a loosely defined term applied to software that helps multiple users work together by sharing information.

Groupware is part of a broad concept called **workgroup technology** that includes equipment and software that help group members communicate and manage their activities.

Some software applications discussed separately in this section, including E-mail and video conferencing, can also be considered groupware. Other groupware applications include:

- **Group Editing**   The capability for multiple users to revise a document with each set of revisions separately identified.
- **Group Scheduling**   A group calendar that tracks the time commitments of multiple users and helps schedule meetings when necessary.
- **Group Decision Support**   A decision support system that relies on the input of multiple users.
- **Workflow Software**   Software that automates repetitive processes such as processing an insurance claim, in which multiple persons must review and approve a document.

One of the more widely used groupware packages is Lotus Notes *(Figure 7-4)*. Notes uses a shared database approach to groupware. In addition, Notes offers E-mail and a programming language that can be used to develop customized groupware applications.

Figure 7-3
A facsimile (FAX) machine can send and receive copies of documents to and from any location where there is phone service and another FAX machine.

Figure 7-4
Notes from Lotus Corporation is one of the most widely used groupware packages. Notes allows users to share information and work together on documents. Notes also includes E-mail capabilities.

Groupware and workgroup technology are still relatively new ideas and, other than E-mail, are not yet widely used. The need for small staffs to work quickly and efficiently on changing job assignments will, however, increase the use of groupware.

Telecommuting

Telecommuting refers to the capability of individuals to work at home and communicate with their offices by using personal computers and communications channels. With a personal computer, an employee can access the main computer at the office. He or she can read and answer electronic mail. An employee can access databases and can transmit completed projects. Some predict that by the year 2000, ten percent of the work force will be telecommuters. Telecommuting provides flexibility, allowing companies and employees to increase productivity and, at the same time, meet the needs of individual employees. Some of the advantages of telecommuting include reducing the time used to commute to the office each week; eliminating the need to travel during poor weather conditions; providing a convenient and comfortable work environment for disabled employees or workers recovering from injuries or illnesses; and allowing employees to combine work with personal responsibilities such as child care.

Electronic Data Interchange (EDI)

Electronic data interchange (EDI) is the capability to electronically transfer documents from one business to another. EDI is frequently used by large companies for routine transactions such as purchase orders and billing. In some businesses, such as the automotive industry, EDI is the standard way of doing repeat business with suppliers. EDI offers a number of

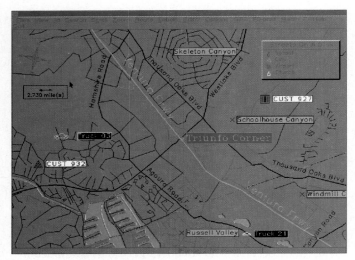

Figure 7-5
Satellite mapping software works with global positioning system
(GPS) equipment to help users locate their exact location on a
displayed map. Maps are available for most metropolitan areas.

advantages over paper documents, including the following:
- Lower transaction costs
- Reduced time to transmit documents
- Reduced data entry errors because data need not be reentered at the receiving end
- Reduced paper flow

Some companies have developed sophisticated EDI applications where orders from a customer are automatically created based on sales or inventory levels, transmitted to a vendor electronically, and shipped to the customer without any human intervention.

Global Positioning Systems (GPS)

A **global positioning system** (GPS) uses satellites to determine the geographic location of earth-based GPS equipment. Depending on the equipment used, a GPS system can be accurate up to 100 feet. GPS systems are often used for tracking and navigation of all types of vehicles; cars, trucks,

BBS	MODEM NUMBER	DESCRIPTION	LOCATION
America's Suggestion Box	516-471-8625	Collects and distributes consumer feedback	Ronkonkoma, NY
Automobile Consumer Services	513-624-0552	New and used car pricing reports	Cincinnati, OH
Boardwatch	303-973-4222	Lists of BBSs maintained by Boardwatch magazine	Denver, CO
BMUG BBS	510-849-2684	Macintosh support and information	Berkeley, CA
Exec PC	414-789-4210	Largest BBS in United States	Elm Grove, WI
FEDLINK ALIXII	202-707-4888	US government information	Washington, D.C.
NASA Spacelink	205-895-0028	NASA space information and history	Huntsville, AL
SBA Online	800-697-4636	Advice for small business owners	Washington, D.C.
The Well	415-332-6106	Whole Earth conferencing system	Sausalito, CA
WeatherBank	800-827-2727	Weather forecasts for any city	SaltLake City, UT

Figure 7-6
A partial list of the major bulletin boards in the United States.

Transmission Media

Transmission media are the materials or technologies that are used to establish the communications channel. Two types of transmission media include those that use some type of physical cabling and those that use wireless technology. Cabling media include twisted pair wire, coaxial cable, and fiber-optics cable. Wireless technology includes microwaves, radio waves, or light waves.

Twisted Pair Wire

Twisted pair wire *(Figure 7-10)* consists of pairs of copper wires that are twisted together. To insulate and identify the wires, each wire is covered with a thin layer of colored plastic. Twisted pair wire is commonly used for telephone lines and to connect personal computers with one another. It is an inexpensive transmission medium, and it can be easily strung from one location to another. A disadvantage of twisted pair wire is that it can be affected by outside electrical interference generated by machines such as fans or air conditioners. While this interference may be acceptable on a voice call, it can garble the data as it is sent over the line, causing transmission errors to occur.

Coaxial Cable

A **coaxial cable** is a high-quality communications line used in offices, and it can be laid underground or underwater. Coaxial cable consists of a copper wire conductor surrounded by a nonconducting insulator that is in turn surrounded by a woven metal outer conductor, and finally a plastic outer coating *(Figure 7-11)*. Because of its more heavily insulated construction, coaxial cable is not susceptible to electrical interference and can transmit data at higher data rates over longer distances than twisted pair wire.

The two types of coaxial cable, named for the transmission techniques they support, are baseband and broadband. **Baseband** coaxial cable carries one signal at a time. The signal, however, can travel very fast – in the area of ten million bits per second for the first 1,000 feet. The speed drops significantly as the length of the cable increases, and special equipment is needed to amplify (boost) the signal if it is transmitted more than approximately one mile.

mmunications equipment

Computer

Figure 7-10
Twisted pair wire is most commonly used for telephone lines and to connect personal computers with one another. It is inexpensive and can be easily strung from one location to another.

Nonconducting insulator

Plastic outer coating

Copper wire conductor

Outer conductor

Figure 7-11
On coaxial cable, data travels through the copper wire conductor. The outer conductor is made of woven metal mesh that acts as an electrical ground.

Broadband coaxial cable can carry multiple signals at one time. It is similar to cable TV where a single cable offers a number of channels to the user. A particular advantage of broadband channels is that data, audio, and video transmission can occur over the same line.

Figure 7-12
The fiber-optic cable (right) can transmit as much information as the 1,500-pair copper-wire cable (left).

Fiber Optics

Fiber-optics cable uses smooth, hair-thin strands of glass to conduct light with high efficiency *(Figure 7-12)*. The major advantages of fiber optics over wire cables include substantial weight and size savings and increased speed of transmission. Another advantage is that fiber-optic cable is not affected by electrical and magnetic fields. A single fiber-optic cable can carry several hundred thousand voice communications simultaneously. The disadvantages of fiber-optic cable are that it is more expensive than twisted pair or coaxial cable and it is more difficult to install and modify than metal wiring. Fiber optics is frequently being used in new voice and data installations.

Figure 7-13
The round antenna on this tower is used for microwave transmission. Microwave transmission is limited to line-of-sight. Antennas are usually placed 25 to 75 miles apart.

Microwave Transmission

Microwaves are radio waves that can be used to provide high-speed transmission of both voice and data. Data is transmitted through the air from one microwave station to another in a manner similar to the way radio signals are transmitted *(Figure 7-13)*. A disadvantage of microwaves is that they are limited to line-of-sight transmission. This means that microwaves must be transmitted in a straight line and that there can be no obstructions, such as buildings or mountains, between microwave stations. For this reason, microwave stations are characterized by antennas positioned on tops of buildings, towers, or mountains.

Satellite Transmission

Communications satellites receive microwave signals from earth, amplify the signals, and retransmit the signals back to earth. The microwave signals used by satellites are generally of a higher frequency than the signals used by terrestrial (earth-based) microwave equipment. **Earth stations** *(Figure 7-14)* are communications facilities that use large, dish-shaped antennas to transmit and receive data from satellites. The transmission *to* the satellite is called an **uplink** and the transmission *from* the satellite to a receiving earth station is called a **downlink**.

Many businesses with operations in multiple locations are now using private satellite systems to communicate information. If only a limited amount of information needs to be transmitted each day, such as daily sales results from a retail store, a small dish-shaped antenna can be used. **Very small aperture terminal** (VSAT) antenna measuring only one to three meters in size can transmit up to 19,200 bits per second. Higher speeds require larger antenna. The use of a private satellite using a VSAT antenna can be as low as $200 per month.

Communications satellites are usually placed about 22,300 miles above the earth in a **geosynchronous orbit** *(Figure 7-15)*. This means that the satellite is placed in an orbit where it rotates with the earth, so the same antennas on earth that are used to send and receive signals can remain fixed on the satellite at all times.

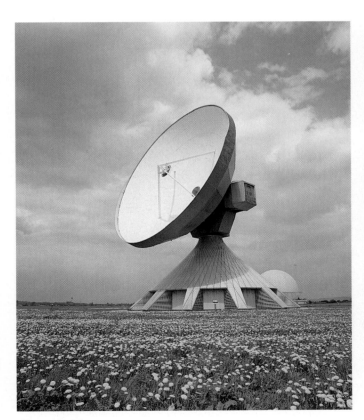

Figure 7-14
Earth stations use large, dish-shaped antennas to communicate with satellites.

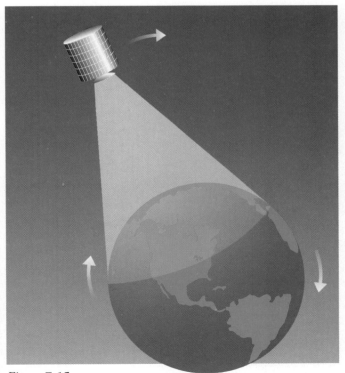

Figure 7-15
Communications satellites are placed in geosynchronous orbits approximately 22,300 miles above the earth. Geosynchronous means that the orbit of the satellite matches the rotation of the earth so the satellite is always above the same spot on the earth.

Several groups are planning on launching a series of low earth orbit (LEO) satellites between 1996 and 1998. For example, Motorola plans on launching 66 satellites as part of their Iridium system that will offer inexpensive, two-way voice and data communications from any spot on the globe. Because they will orbit only 400 to 500 miles above the earth, the LEO satellites will not be as expensive to build or launch as geosynchronous satellites. The closer distance will also mean that earth-based phones and other satellite communications equipment will not have to be as powerful.

Wireless Transmission

Wireless transmission uses one of three techniques to transmit data: light beams, radio waves, or carrier-connect radio, which uses the existing electrical wiring of a building to act as an antenna. These methods are sometimes used by companies to connect devices that are in the same general area such as an office or business park. For example, the unit shown in *Figure 7-16* uses light beams to transmit or receive data over a distance up to 70 feet. Local wireless systems offer design flexibility and portability but provide slower transmission speed than wired connections.

For longer distances, radio-wave wireless systems are becoming widely used. Motorola sells time on its ARDIS network that contains more than 1,100 base radio stations serving more than 8,000 cities in 50 states. Potential users include companies with large numbers of service personnel who need access to their company's computer data when they are at a customer site. For example, a repair technician may need to know the nearest location of a particular part. Using a portable radio data terminal *(Figure 7-17)* the technician could access the company's inventory database and obtain information about the availability of the required part.

A wireless device available to the general public that offers many of the same advantages as private radio networks is a cellular telephone. A **cellular telephone** uses radio waves to communicate with a local antenna assigned to a specific geographic area called a cell *(Figure 7-18)*. Cellular phones are often used in automobiles. As a cellular telephone user travels

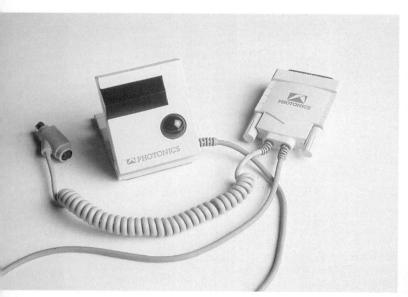

Figure 7-16
This wireless communication device from Photonics Corp. transmits data by bouncing infrared light beams off reflective surfaces such as a ceiling or a wall. The unit can also receive reflected light signals and convert them back to data. The device can transmit one million bits of data per second and has a range of thirty feet.

Figure 7-17
The portable terminal uses radio waves to communicate with a base radio station that is connected to a host computer. Using such a terminal, service technicians can instantly inquire as to the availability of repair parts.

from one cell to another, a computer that monitors the activity in each cell switches the conversation from one radio channel to another. By switching channels in this manner, the same channel can be used by another caller in a nonadjacent cell. Individual cells range from one to ten miles in width and use between 50 and 75 radio channels. Cellular telephone channels can be used for both voice and data transmission.

An Example of a Communications Channel

When data is transmitted over long distances, several different transmission media are generally used to make a complete communications channel. *Figure 7-19* on the next page illustrates how some of the various transmission media could be used to transmit data from a personal computer on the West Coast of the United States to a large computer on the East Coast. An example of the steps that could occur are as follows:

1. An entry is made on the personal computer. The data is sent over telephone lines from the computer to a microwave station.

2. The data is then transmitted from one microwave station to another.
3. The data is transmitted from the last microwave station to an earth station.
4. The earth station transmits the data to the communications satellite.
5. The satellite relays the data to another earth station on the other side of the country.
6. The data received at the earth station is transmitted to microwave stations.
7. The data is sent by telephone lines to the large computer.

This entire transmission process would take less than one second. Not all data transmission is as complex as this example, but such sophisticated communications systems do exist to meet the needs of some users.

Figure 7-18
When you place a call from a cellular phone, the signal is picked up by the nearest cellular antenna. The antennas are located in cells positioned one to ten miles wide. The cellular antenna relays the signal to the mobil telephone switching office (MTSO). If the call is being made to a conventional telephone, the signal enters the regular phone system lines. If the cellular phone is being used in a moving vehicle, the MTSO can automatically switch the signal to the closest cellular antenna. Receiving a call on a cellular phone reverses the process.

Line Configurations

Two major **line configurations** (types of line connections) commonly used in communications are point-to-point lines and multidrop, or multipoint, lines.

Point-to-Point Lines

A **point-to-point line** is a direct line between a sending and a receiving device. It may be one of two types: a switched line or a dedicated line *(Figure 7-20)*.

SWITCHED LINE

A **switched line** uses a regular telephone line to establish a communications connection. Each time a connection is made, the line to be used for the call is selected by the telephone company switching stations (hence the name switched line). Using a switched line for communicating data is the same process as one person using a telephone to call another person. The communications equipment at the sending end dials the telephone number of the communications equipment at the receiving end. When the communications equipment at the receiving end answers the call, a connection is established and data can be transmitted. The process of establishing the communications connection is sometimes referred to as the handshake. When the transmission of data is complete, the communications equipment at either end terminates the call by hanging up and the line is disconnected.

An advantage of using switched lines is that a connection can be made between any two locations that have telephone service and communications equipment. For example, a personal computer could dial one computer to get information about the weather and then hang up and place a second call to another computer to get information about the stock market. A disadvantage of a switched line is that the quality of the line cannot be controlled because the line is chosen at random by the telephone company switching equipment. The cost of a switched line is the same for data communications as for a regular telephone call.

DEDICATED LINE

A **dedicated line** is a line connection that is always established (unlike the switched line where the line connection is reestablished each time it is used). The communications device at one end is always connected to the device at the other end. A user can create his or her own dedicated line connection by running a wire or cable between two points, such as between two offices or buildings, or the dedicated line can be provided

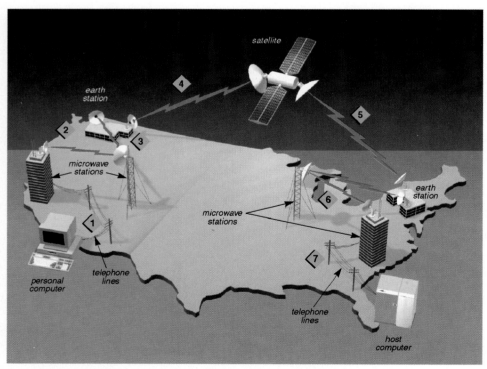

Figure 7-19
The use of telephone wires, microwave transmission, and a communications satellite allows a personal computer to communicate with a large host computer.

by an outside organization such as a telephone company or some other communications service company. If the dedicated line is provided by an outside organization, it is sometimes called a **leased line,** or a **private line.** The quality and consistency of the connection is better than on a switched line because a dedicated line is always established. Use of dedicated lines provided by outside organizations are usually charged on a flat-fee basis, which is a fixed amount each month regardless of how much time the line is actually used to transmit data. The cost of dedicated lines varies based on the distance between the two connected points and, sometimes, the speed at which data will be transmitted.

Multidrop Lines

The second major line configuration is called a **multidrop line,** or **multipoint line.** This type of line configuration is commonly used to connect multiple devices, such as terminals or personal computers, on a single line to a main computer, sometimes called a **host computer** *(Figure 7-21).*

For example, a ticket agent could use a terminal to enter an inquiry requesting flight information from a database stored on a main computer. While the request is being transmitted to the main computer, other terminals on the line are not able to transmit data. The time required for the data to be transmitted to the main computer, however, is short – most likely less than one second. As soon as the inquiry is received by the computer, a second terminal can send an inquiry. With such short delays, it appears to the users that no other terminals are using the line, even though multiple terminals may be sharing the same line.

The number of terminals to be placed on one line is a decision made by the designer of the system based on the anticipated amount of traffic on the line. For example, 100 or more terminals could be contained on a single line, provided each one would send only short messages, such as inquiries, and each terminal would use the communications line only a few hours per day. But if longer messages, such as reports, were required and if the terminals were to be used almost continuously, the number of terminals on one line would have to be smaller.

A leased line is almost always used for multidrop line configurations. The use of multidrop lines can decrease line costs considerably because one line is used by many terminals.

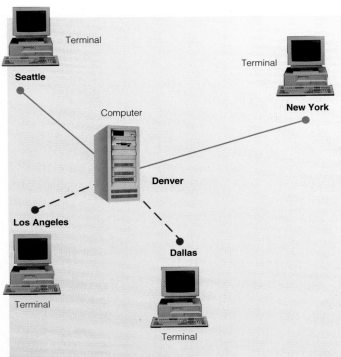

Figure 7-20
A point-to-point line configuration using both switched telephone (dial-up) lines (– – – –) and dedicated lines (——) are connected to a computer in Denver. The dedicated lines are always connected, whereas the switched lines have to be connected each time they are used.

Figure 7-21
Two multidrop lines connect several cities with a computer in Denver. Each line is shared by terminals at several locations. Multidrop line configurations are less expensive than individual lines to each remote location.

Characteristics of Communications Channels

The communications channels just described can be categorized by a number of characteristics including the type of signal, transmission mode, transmission direction, and transmission rate.

Types of Signals: Digital and Analog

Computer equipment is designed to process data as **digital signals**, which are individual electrical pulses that represent the bits that are grouped together to form characters. Telephone equipment was originally designed to carry only voice transmission, which is comprised of a continuous electrical wave called an **analog signal** *(Figure 7-22)*. Thus, a special piece of equipment called a *modem* is required to convert the digital signals to analog signals so telephone lines can carry data. Modems are discussed in more detail later in this chapter.

To provide better communications services, telephone companies are now offering **digital data service**, communications channels specifically designed to carry digital instead of voice signals. Digital data service is available within and between all major metropolitan areas and provides higher speed and lower error rates than voice lines. Modems are not needed with digital data service; instead, users connect to the communications line through a device called a **digital service unit** (DSU).

Transmission Modes: Asynchronous and Synchronous

In **asynchronous transmission mode** *(Figure 7-23)*, individual bytes (made up of bits) are transmitted at irregular intervals, such as when a user enters data. To distinguish where one byte stops and another starts, the asynchronous transmission mode uses a start and a stop bit. An additional bit, called a *parity bit*, is sometimes included at the end of each byte. As you learned in the discussion of memory in Chapter 4, parity bits are used for error checking and they detect if one of the data bits has been changed during transmission. The asynchronous transmission mode is used for lower speed data transmission and is used with most communications equipment designed for personal computers.

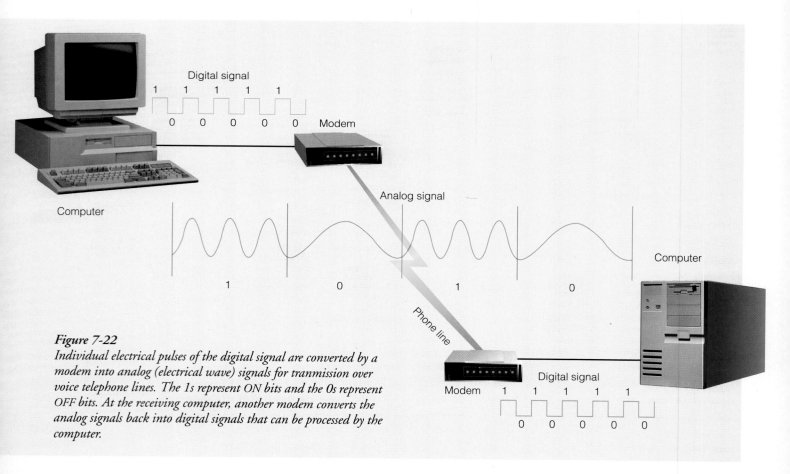

Figure 7-22
Individual electrical pulses of the digital signal are converted by a modem into analog (electrical wave) signals for tranmission over voice telephone lines. The 1s represent ON bits and the 0s represent OFF bits. At the receiving computer, another modem converts the analog signals back into digital signals that can be processed by the computer.

In the **synchronous transmission mode** *(Figure 7-23)*, large blocks of data are transmitted at regular intervals. Timing signals synchronize the communications equipment at both the sending and receiving ends and eliminate the need for start and stop bits for each byte. Error-check bits and start and stop bytes, called sync bytes, are also transmitted. Synchronous transmission requires more sophisticated and expensive equipment but it does give much higher speeds and accuracy than asynchronous transmission.

Direction of Transmission: Simplex, Half-Duplex, and Full-Duplex

The direction of data transmission is classified as either simplex, half-duplex, or full-duplex *(Figure 7-24)*. In **simplex transmission**, data flows in one direction only. Simplex is used only when the sending device, such as a temperature sensor, never requires a response from the computer. For example, if a computer is used to control the temperature of a building, numerous sensors are placed throughout it. Each sensor is connected to the computer with a simplex transmission line because the computer only needs to receive data from the

temperature sensors and does not need to send data back to the sensors.

In **half-duplex transmission**, data can flow in both directions but in only one direction at a time. An example is a citizens band radio. The user can talk or listen but not do both at the same time.

In **full-duplex transmission**, data can be sent in both directions at the same time. A normal telephone line is an example of full-duplex transmission. Both parties can talk at the same time. Full-duplex transmission is used for most interactive computer applications and for computer-to-computer data transmission.

Transmission Rate

The transmission rate of a communications channel is determined by its bandwidth and its speed. The **bandwidth** is the range of frequencies that a channel can carry. Because transmitted data can be assigned to different frequencies, the wider the bandwidth, the more frequencies. Thus, more data can be transmitted at the same time.

Figure 7-23
In asynchronous transmission mode, individual bytes are transmitted. Each byte has start, stop, and error-check bits.
In synchronous transmission mode, multiple bytes are sent in a block with start bytes at the beginning of the block and error-check bits and stop bytes at the end of the block. Synchronous transmission is faster and more accurate.

Figure 7-24
Simplex transmission allows data to flow in one direction only. Half-duplex transmission allows data to flow in both directions but not at the same time. Full-duplex transmission allows data to flow in both directions simultaneously.

The speed at which data is transmitted is usually expressed as bits per second or as a baud rate. **Bits per second (bps)** is the number of bits that can be transmitted in one second. Using a 10-bit byte to represent a character (7 data bits, 1 start, 1 stop, and 1 parity bit), a 9,600 bps transmission would transmit 960 characters per second. At this rate, a 20-page, single-spaced report that has an average of 3,000 characters per page would be transmitted in a little more than one minute. The **baud rate** is the number of times per second that the signal being transmitted changes. With each change, one or more bits can be transmitted. At speeds up to 2,400 bps, usually only one bit is transmitted per signal change and, thus, the bits per second and the baud rate are the same. To achieve speeds in excess of 2,400 bps, more than one bit is transmitted with each signal change and, thus, the bps will exceed the baud rate. *Figure 7-25* shows the range of transmission rates that can be achieved with different media. Each year, communications companies invent ways to increase these rates.

Communications Equipment

If a terminal or a personal computer is within approximately 1,000 feet of another computer, the two devices can usually be directly connected by a cable. At distances of more than 1,000 feet, however, the electrical signal weakens to the point that some type of special communications equipment is required to increase or change the signal to transmit it farther. A variety of communications equipment exists to perform this task, but the equipment that a user is most likely to encounter is a modem, a multiplexor, and a front-end processor. Computers that are connected to a network, which are discussed later in this chapter, usually require a network interface card.

Modems

A **modem** converts the digital signals of a terminal or computer to analog signals that are transmitted over a communications channel. It also converts analog signals it receives into digital signals that are used by a terminal or computer. The word modem comes from a combination of the words *mo*dulate, which means to change into a sound or analog signal, and *dem*odulate, which means to convert an analog signal into a digital signal. A modem is needed at both the sending and receiving ends of a communications channel.

MEDIA	RATE*
Twisted pair wire (voice-grade phone line)	300 bps to 28.8 Kbps
Twisted pair wire (direct connection)	1 to 10 Mbps
Coaxial cable	1 to 20 Mbps
Fiber-optic cable	up to 200 Mbps
Terrestial microwave	1.544 Mbps
Satellite microwave	64 to 512 Kbps
Wireless (radio wave)	4.8 to 19.2 Kbps

*RATE:	bps	bits per second
	Kbps	kilo (thousand) bits per second
	Mbps	mega (million) bits per second

Figure 7-25
Transmission rates of different media.

Figure 7-26
An external modem is connected to a terminal or computer and to a telephone outlet.

Figure 7-27
An internal modem is mounted inside a personal computer.

An **external modem** *(Figure 7-26)* is a separate, or stand-alone, device that is attached to the computer or terminal by a cable and to the telephone outlet by a standard telephone cord. An advantage of an external modem is that it can be easily moved from one terminal or computer to another.

An **internal modem** *(Figure 7-27)* is a circuit board installed inside a computer or terminal. Internal modems are generally less expensive than comparable external modems but once installed, they are not as easy to move.

Modems can transmit data at rates from 300 to 38,400 bits per second (bps). Most personal computers would use a modem between 2,400 and 14,400 bps. Business or heavier volume users would use faster and more expensive modems.

Multiplexors

A **multiplexor,** sometimes referred to as a MUX, combines more than one input signal into a single stream of data that can be transmitted over a communications channel *(Figure 7-28).* The multiplexor at the sending end codes each character it receives with an identifier that is used by the multiplexor at the receiving end to separate the combined data stream into its original parts. A multiplexor may be connected to a separate

modem or may have a modem built in. By combining the individual data streams into one, a multiplexor increases the efficiency of communications and saves the cost of individual communications channels.

Front-End Processors

A **front-end processor** is a computer that is dedicated to handling the communications requirements of a larger computer. Relieved of these tasks, the larger computer is then dedicated to processing data, while the front-end processor communicates the data. Tasks that the front-end processor would handle include **polling** (checking the connected terminals or computers to see if they have data to send), error checking and correction, and access security to make sure that a connected device or the user of the connected device is authorized to access the computer.

Network Interface Cards

A **network interface card** (NIC) fits in an expansion slot of a computer and attaches to the cable or wireless technology used to connect the devices in the network. The NIC has circuits that coordinate the transmission, receipt, and error checking of transmitted data.

Figure 7-28
At the sending end, a multiplexor (MUX) combines separate data transmissions into a single data stream. At the receiving end, the multiplexor separates the single stream into its original parts.

Communications Software

Sometimes communications equipment is preprogrammed to accomplish its designed communications tasks. Other times, the user must load a program before transmitting data. These programs, referred to as **communications software,** can perform a number of tasks including dialing (if a switched telephone line is used), file transfer, terminal emulation, and data encryption.

Dialing software allows you to store, review, select, and dial telephone numbers of computers that can be called. The software provides a variety of meaningful messages to assist you in establishing a connection before transmitting data. For example, a person using a personal computer and a modem at home to communicate with a computer at the office could use dialing software to establish the communications connection. The software would display the office computer's telephone number on the user's personal computer screen. The user would enter the appropriate command for the dialing software to begin dialing the office computer and to establish a connection. During the 10 or 15 seconds of this process, the software would display messages to indicate specifically what was happening, such as "DIALING," "CARRIER DETECT" (which means that the office computer has

answered), and "CONNECTED" (to indicate that the communications connection has been established and data transmission can begin).

File transfer software allows you to move one or more files from one system to another. Generally, you have to load the file transfer software on both the sending and receiving computers.

Terminal emulation software allows a personal computer to imitate or appear to be a specific type of terminal, so the personal computer can connect to another, usually larger, computer *(Figure 7-29)*. Most minicomputers and mainframes are designed to work with terminals that have specific characteristics such as speed and parity. Terminal emulation software performs the necessary speed and parity conversion.

Data encryption protects confidential data during transmission. **Data encryption** is the conversion of data at the sending end into an unrecognizable string of characters or bits and the reconversion of the data at the receiving end. Without knowing how the data was encrypted, someone who intercepted the transmitted data would have a difficult time determining what the data meant.

Figure 7-29
Terminal emulation software makes a personal computer function as if it were a particular type of terminal. Terminal emulation software is often used to allow PCs to communicate with larger systems such as minicomputers or mainframes. This screen, from Crosstalk for Windows, shows how a personal computer is set up to emulate a Hewlett-Packard (HP) model 700/94 terminal.

Communications Protocols

Communications software is written to work with one or more protocols. A **protocol** is a set of rules and procedures for exchanging information between computers. Protocols define how the communications link is established, how information is transmitted, and how errors are detected and corrected. Using the same protocol, different types and makes of computers can communicate with each other. Over the years, numerous protocols have been developed. The table shown in *Figure 7-30* lists some of the more widely used protocols. Today, however, there are strong efforts to establish standards that all computer and communications equipment manufacturers will follow. The International Standards Organization (ISO) based in Geneva, Switzerland has defined a set of communications protocols called the **Open Systems Interconnection** (OSI) model. The OSI model has been endorsed by the United Nations.

Communications Networks

A communications **network** is a collection of terminals, computers, and other equipment that uses communications channels to share data, information, hardware, and software. Networks can be classified as either local area networks or wide area networks.

Local Area Networks (LANs)

A **local area network**, or LAN, is a privately owned communications network that covers a limited geographic area such as a school computer laboratory, an office, a building, or a group of buildings.

The LAN consists of a communications channel that connects either a series of computer terminals together with a minicomputer or, more commonly, a group of personal computers to one another. Very sophisticated LANs can connect a variety of office devices such as word processing equipment, computer terminals, video equipment, and personal computers.

Three common applications of local area networks are hardware, software, and information resource sharing. **Hardware resource sharing** allows each personal computer in the network to access and use devices that would be too expensive to provide for each user or would not be justified for each

PROTOCOL	DESCRIPTION
Ethernet	One of the most widely used protocols for LANS
Token ring	Uses an electronic token to avoid transmission conflict by only allowing one device to transmit at at time
PowerTalk	Links Apple Macintosh computers
FDDI	Fiber Distributed Data Interface; high-speed fiber-optic protocol
SNA	System Network Architecture; primarily used to link large systems
TCP/IP	Transmission Control Protocol/Internet Protocol; used on the Internet
X.25	International standard for packet switching
ATM	Asynchronous Transfer Mode; recently developed protocol for transmitting voice, data, and video over any type of media
IPX	Used on Novell Netware networks
Xmodem	PC protocol that uses 128-byte blocks
Ymodem	PC protocol that uses 1,024-byte blocks
Zmodem	PC protocol that uses 512-byte blocks
Kermit	PC protocol that uses variable-length blocks

Figure 7-30
Some of the more commonly used communications protocols. Protocols specify the procedures that are used during transmission.

user because of only occasional use. For example, when a number of personal computers are used on the network, each may need to use a laser printer. Using a LAN, a laser printer could be purchased and made a part of the network. Whenever a user of a personal computer on the network needed the laser printer, it could be accessed over the network. *Figure 7-31* depicts a simple local area network consisting of four personal computers linked together by a cable. Three of the personal computers (computer 1 in the sales and marketing department, computer 2 in the accounting department, and computer 3 in the personnel department) are available for use at all times. Computer 4 is used as a **server**, a computer dedicated to handling the communications needs of the other computers in the network. The users of this LAN have connected the laser printer to the server. Using the LAN, all computers and the server can use the printer. In small networks, the server computer can also be used to run applications, along with the other computers on the network. In large networks, the server is usually dedicated to providing network services such as hardware, software, and information resource sharing.

Software resource sharing consists of storing frequently used software on the hard disk of the server so the software can be accessed by multiple users. Sharing software is a common practice for both in-house and commercial software. Many software vendors now sell a network version of their software. When a commercial software package is accessed by many users, it is sometimes necessary to obtain a special agreement from the software vendor called a **site license**. The site license fee is usually based on the number of computers on the network and is less than if individual copies of the software package were purchased for each computer.

Information resource sharing allows anyone using a personal computer on the local area network to access data stored on any other computer in the network. In actual practice, hardware resource sharing and information resource sharing are often combined. For example, in *Figure 7-31,* the daily sales records could be stored on the hard disk associated with the server unit personal computer. Anyone needing access to the sales records could use this information resource. The capability to access and store data on common secondary storage is an important feature of many local area networks.

Information resource sharing is usually provided by using either the file-server or client-server method. Using the

computer 1
sales and
marketing

computer 2
accounting

computer 3
personnel

computer 4
service

hard disk
(daily sales
records)

laser printer

LOCAL AREA NETWORK

Figure 7-31
A local area network (LAN) consists of multiple personal computers or terminals connected to one another. The LAN allows users to share hardware and information.

file-server method, the server sends an entire file at a time. The requesting computer then performs the processing. With the **client-server** method, as much processing as possible is done on the server system before data is transmitted.

Figure 7-32 illustrates how the two methods would process a request for information stored on the server system for customers with balances over $1,000. With the file-server method, the user transmits a request for the customer file to the server unit (1). The server unit locates the customer file (2) and transmits the entire file to the requesting computer (3). The requesting computer selects customers with balances over $1,000 and prepares the report (4).

With the client-server method, the user transmits a request for customers with a balance over $1,000 to the server unit (1). The server unit selects the customer records that meet the criteria (2) and transmits the selected records to the requesting computer (3). The requesting computer prepares the report (4). The client-server method greatly reduces the amount of data sent over a network but requires a more powerful server system.

A local area network does not have to use a single server computer. A **peer-to-peer network** allows any computer to share the software, data, or hardware (such as a printer) located on any other computer in the network. Peer-to-peer networks are appropriate for a small number of users who primarily work on their own computers and only occasionally need to use the resources of other computers.

Simple peer-to-peer networks need a minimum amount of software to manage their activities. Often the necessary software is provided by the manufacturer of the network interface cards or other hardware used to link the networked systems. Artisoft's LANtastic, Microsoft's Windows for Workgroups, and Apple's AppleTalk are examples of peer-to-peer network software. Client-server networks, however, need more sophisticated software, called a network operating system, to keep them running efficiently. A **network operating system** (**NOS**) is software that allows a user to manage the resources of a computer network. The NOS runs on the server computer in addition to the client operating systems, such as DOS, Windows, or OS/2, that run on the individual computers that make up the network. A NOS usually provides the following capabilities:

• **Administration** Adding, deleting, and organizing client users and performing maintenance tasks such as backup.

FILE-SERVER

1 Request for customer file

1
3

3 Entire customer file transmitted

4 Requesting computer selects customers with balances over $1,000 and prepares report

2 Server locates and transmits entire customer file

CLIENT-SERVER

1 Request for balances over $1,000

1
3

3 Records of customers with balances over $1,000 transmitted

4 Requesting computer prepares report

2 Server selects customers with balances over $1,000

Figure 7-32
A request for information about customers with balances over $1,000 would be processed differently by file-server and client-server networks.

- **File Management**   The capability to quickly locate and transfer files from the server to the client computers.
- **Printer Management**   The capability to prioritize print jobs and direct reports to specific printers on the network.
- **Security**   The capability to restrict access to network resources. Novell's Netware, Microsoft's Advanced NT Server, and IBM's LAN Server are examples of network operating systems.

Wide Area Networks (WANs)

A **wide area network**, or WAN, is geographic in scope (as opposed to local) and uses telephone lines, microwaves, satellites, or a combination of communications channels. A wide area network limited to the area surrounding a city is sometimes referred to as a **metropolitan area network**, or MAN. Public wide area network companies include so-called **common carriers** such as the telephone companies. Telephone company deregulation has encouraged a number of companies to build their own wide area networks. For example, EDS has built one of the larger private communications networks *(Figure 7-33)* to handle the needs of its computer services business and the needs of its parent company, General Motors.

Communications companies, such as MCI, have built WANs to compete with other communications companies. Companies called **value-added carriers** lease channels from the common carriers to provide specialized communications services referred to as **value-added networks** (VANs). For example, Tymnet, Inc. operates a VAN that provides packet-switching services. **Packet-switching** combines individual packets of information from various users and transmits them together over a high-speed channel. The messages are separated and distributed over lower speed channels at the receiving end. Sharing the high-speed channel is more economical than each user having their own high-speed channel. Most common carriers are now offering **Integrated Services Digital Network** (ISDN) services. ISDN is an international standard for the digital transmission of both voice and data using different channels and communications companies. Using ISDN lines, data can be transmitted over one or more separate channels at 64,000 bits per second. Future plans for ISDN include the use of fiber-optic cable that will allow transmission rates up to 2.2 billion bits per second. These higher speeds will allow full-motion video images to be transmitted.

Figure 7-33
The control room for EDSNET, the private communications network of Electronic Data Systems Corporation (EDS). The network was built by EDS spanning a three-year period and with a cost of more than $1 billion. The network provides communications for EDS, its computer services customers, and its parent company, General Motors.

The Internet

The largest and best known wide area network is the Internet. The **Internet** is a worldwide network of computer networks. It is difficult to give numbers for the size of the Internet because of its rapid growth. In late 1994, it was estimated that the Internet consisted of the following:

- 30 million users worldwide
- Users located in 100 countries
- 20,000 member organizations
- 21,000 connected networks
- 2 million connected computers

Because of its tremendous size and number of users, some have called the Internet a "virtual community." The Internet was originally started in 1969 as a way of linking government researchers at four universities. Other university and private research sites were added over the years. The Internet really started to grow in the late 1980s when a number of public and private networks were joined together with the National Science Foundation network. Since 1988, the Internet has doubled in size every year. Some of the services and resources available on the Internet include the following:

- **Electronic mail**   E-mail can be sent anywhere in the world to users with an Internet address. Addresses can be obtained free of charge.
- **File transfer**   Thousands of files on countless subjects are available for transfer.
- **Database search**   More than 200 universities and several public libraries have their databases online and available for review. Internet offers several tools for finding information on a particular subject.
- **Remote logon**   The capability to run a program located on another computer.
- **Discussion and news groups**   Thousands of discussion topics currently exist, or you can start your own on a subject of interest.
- **Games**   A variety of single and multiple player games.

Students can usually gain access to the Internet through one of their school's computer systems. Most colleges and universities have access. Individuals can gain access through many of the online service providers. Businesses or other organizations that want to regularly use the Internet can obtain direct connection rights. For further examples of using the Internet, see page 7.43.

Network Configurations

The configuration, or physical layout, of the equipment in a communications network is called **topology**. Communications networks are usually configured in one or a combination of three patterns. These configurations are star, bus, and ring networks. Although these configurations can be used with wide area networks, they are illustrated here with local area networks. Devices connected to a network, such as terminals, printers, or other computers, are referred to as **nodes**.

Star Network

A **star network** contains a central computer and one or more terminals or personal computers connected to it, forming a star. A pure star network consists of only point-to-point lines between the terminals and the computer, but most star networks, such as the one shown on the next page in *Figure 7-34,* include both point-to-point lines and multidrop lines. A star network configuration is often used when the central computer contains all the data required to process the input from the terminals, such as an airline reservation system. For example, if inquiries are being processed in the star network, all the data to answer the inquiry would be contained in the database stored on the central computer.

A star network can be relatively efficient and close control can be kept over the data processed on the network. Its major disadvantage is that the entire network is dependent on the central computer and the associated hardware and software. If any of these elements fail, the entire network is disabled. Therefore, in most large star networks, backup computer systems are available in case the primary system fails.

Bus Network

When a **bus network** is used, all the devices in the network are connected to and share a single cable. Information is transmitted in either direction from any one personal computer to another. Any message can be directed to a specific device. An advantage of the bus network is that devices can be attached or detached from the network at any point without disturbing the rest of the network. In addition, if one computer on the network fails, this does not affect the other users of the network. *Figure 7-31* on page 7.22 illustrates a simple bus network.

Ring Network

A **ring network** does not use a centralized host computer. Instead, a circle of computers communicate with one another *(Figure 7-35)*. A ring network can be useful when the processing is not done at a central site, but at local sites. For example, computers could be located in three departments: accounting, personnel, and shipping and receiving. The computers in each of these departments could perform the processing required for each of the departments. On occasion, however, the computer in the shipping and receiving department could communicate with the computer in the accounting department to update certain data stored on the accounting department computer. Data travels around a ring network in one direction

Laser printer

Host computer

Figure 7-34
A star network contains a single, centralized host computer with which all the terminals or personal computers in the network communicate. Both point-to-point and multidrop lines can be used in a star network.

only and passes through each node. Thus, one disadvantage of a ring network is that if one node fails, the entire network fails because the data does not get past the failed node. An advantage of a ring network is that less cable is usually needed than for a star network and therefore network cabling costs are lower.

A common type of ring network is called a token ring network. A **token ring network** constantly circulates an electronic signal, called a token, around the network. Devices on the network that want to send a message take the token and attach it to their data. When it is attached to data, the token is not available for other devices to use. When data is delivered to its destination, the data is replaced with an acknowledgment that the data was received. When the original sending device receives the token and the acknowledgment, the token is again made available for other devices to use.

Connecting Networks

Certain circumstances require you to connect separate networks. You do this by using gateways, bridges, and routers. A **gateway** is a combination of hardware and software that allows users on one network to access the resources on a *different* type of network. For example, a gateway could be used to connect a local area network of personal computers to a mainframe computer network. A **bridge** is a combination of hardware and software used to connect *similar* networks. For example, if a company had similar but separate local area networks of personal computers in its accounting and marketing departments, the networks could be connected with a bridge. In this example, using a bridge makes more sense than joining all the personal computers together in one large network because the individual departments only occasionally need to access information on the other network. A router is used when several networks are connected together. A **router** is an intelligent network-connecting device that can route communications traffic directly to the appropriate network. In the case of a partial network failure, routers are smart enough to determine alternate routes.

Figure 7-35
In a ring network, all computers are connected in a continous loop. Data flows around the ring in one direction only.

An Example of a Communications Network

The diagram in *Figure 7-36* illustrates how two personal computer networks and a mainframe computer can be connected to share information with each other and with outside sources.

The marketing department operates a bus network of four personal computers (1). Frequently used marketing data and programs are stored in the server unit (2). The personal computers in the marketing department share a laser printer (3). A modem (4) is attached to the marketing server unit so outside sales representatives can use a dial telephone line (5) to call the marketing system and obtain product price information.

The administration department operates a bus network of three personal computers (6). As with the marketing network, common data and programs are stored on a server unit (7) and the administration personal computers share a laser printer (8). Because the administration department sometimes needs information from the marketing system, the two similar networks are connected with a LAN bridge (9). The bridge allows users on either network to access data or programs on the other network.

Administration department users sometimes need information from the company's mainframe computer system (10). They can access the mainframe through the use of a gateway (11) that allows different types of network systems to be connected. All communications with the mainframe computer are controlled by a front-end processor (12). A dial telephone line (13) connected to a modem (14) allows remote users to call the mainframe and allows mainframe users to call other computers. A leased telephone line (15) and a modem (16) are used for a permanent connection to

1   **MARKETING PC NETWORK**

5 — Dial telephone line

4 — Modem

2 — Server unit

9 — Bridge

3 — Shared laser printer

11 — Gateway

MAINFRAME COMPUTER NETWORK

13 — Dial telephone line

14 — Modem

15 — Leased telephone line to corporate HQs

16 — Modem

Front-end processor

12

MUX

17

19 — Microwave antenna

18 — Gateway

Mainframe computer

10

Summary of Communications and Networks

the computer at the corporate headquarters, several hundred miles away. The leased line can carry the signals of up to four different users. The signals are separated by the use of a multiplexor (MUX) (17). A gateway (18) connects the front-end processor and mainframe system to a microwave antenna (19) on the roof of the building. The microwave antenna sends and receives data from a computer at the manufacturing plant located two miles away. The front-end processor also controls mainframe computer terminals located throughout the company (20).

Communications will continue to affect how people work and how they use computers. Individuals and organizations are no longer limited to local data resources but instead, with communications capabilities, they can obtain information from anywhere in the world at electronic speed. With communications technology rapidly changing, today's businesses are challenged to find ways to adapt the technology to provide better products and services for their customers and make their operations more efficient. Networks are one way that organizations are making individual computers more powerful. By joining individual computers into networks, computing resources are expanded and the ability of individuals to communicate with each other is increased. For individuals, the new technology offers increased access to worldwide information and services and provides new opportunities in business and education.

6   **ADMINISTRATION PC NETWORK**

7   Server unit   **8**

Shared laser printer

20

Terminals

• • •

Figure 7-36
The two personal computer networks are connected together with a bridge. A gateway is used to connect the administration personal computer network with the mainframe. All communications with the mainframe are controlled by a separate computer called a front-end processor. Modems are used to connect the networks to leased and dial telephone lines.

COMPUTERS AT WORK

Satellites Help Track Moving Vans

Have you ever stayed around the house or apartment all day waiting for an item to be delivered by truck? When you call the trucking company, all they can tell you is, "the truck is on the way!" This is not the case with North American Van Lines. If you ship your items with North American, they can tell you the exact location of their trucks within 1,000 feet. North American, the fifth largest trucking company in the United States, has outfitted its trucks with a two-way satellite communications system manufactured by Qualcomm of San Diego, California. Besides being able to pinpoint the location of its trucks, North American can instantly communicate with the drivers. There is no longer a wait until the driver pulls off the road to call in. The two-way communication feature allows North American to direct its drivers to pick up additional cargo as they pass through an area. Before they had the systems, drivers might have driven through an area not knowing that a load was waiting. The system offers benefits to the drivers, as well. If a driver runs into trouble because of bad weather or a mechanical breakdown, he or she can send a message to the home office in Indiana *(Figure 7-36)*. Even if the truck is in the middle of a snow storm on a stretch of deserted highway, the message will get through instantly. The system has even been used to dispatch emergency help to the scenes of accidents. Like many other business systems that have been computerized, the benefits of the North American Van Lines system may one day be made directly available to North American customers. North American is considering allowing its regular customers who frequently ship high-tech cargo such as computers and medical equipment to directly access the tracking system.

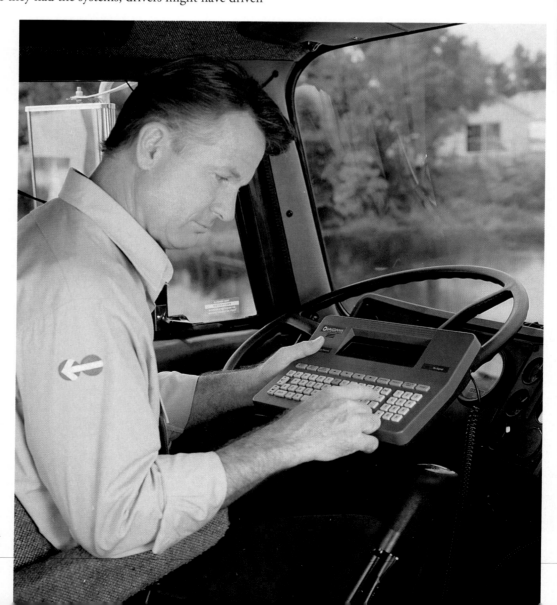

Figure 7-36

IN THE FUTURE

The Information Superhighway

Many believe that the path to the future may be along what has been called the **Information Superhighway**; a nationwide and eventually worldwide network of information and services. Originally proposed as part of the 1991 High Performance Computing and Communications (HPCC) initiative, the scope of the U.S. network was expanded in 1993 as part of the **National Information Infrastructure** (NII). The NII is envisioned as a high-speed digital network that will make information services, training, education, medical services, and government data available to everyone, including individuals as well as businesses and larger organizations. Universal access is one of the key principles of NII.

Some of the preliminary work on a nationwide network is already being accomplished by private organizations such as cable TV and telephone companies. This is consistent with the NII plan to allow private companies to construct and operate much of the network. The U.S. government's challenge is to provide guidelines, standards, and incentives to make sure that separately constructed parts of the network can communicate with each other and that all individuals have access to the network at a reasonable price. Several other countries have similar nationwide networks planned or under development. Eventually, all these networks could be linked together using software that automatically translates one language into another.

Figure 7-37

What You Should Know

1. The capability of a computer to communicate with other computers, sometimes called connectivity, allows users to quickly and directly access data and information that otherwise would have been unavailable or that probably would have taken considerable time to acquire.

2. **Electronic mail** is the capability to use computers to transmit messages and receive messages from other computer users.

3. **Voice mail,** which can be considered verbal electronic mail, digitizes a caller's message so it can be stored on disk like other computer data.

4. Today, **teleconferencing** usually means video conferencing, the use of computers and television cameras to transmit video images and the sound of the participant(s) to a remote location that has compatible equipment.

5. **Facsimile,** or FAX, equipment is used to transmit a reproduced image of a document over phone lines. FAX machines convert the image into digitized data that is transmitted and then convert the digitized data back into its original image at the receiving end.

6. **Groupware** is a loosely defined term applied to software that helps multiple users work together by sharing information. Groupware is part of a broad concept called **workgroup technology** that includes equipment and software that help group members communicate and manage their activities.

7. **Telecommuting** refers to the ability of individuals to work at home and communicate with their offices by using personal computers and communications channels.

8. **Electronic data interchange** (**EDI**) is the capability to electronically transfer documents from one business to another. EDI is frequently used by large companies for routine transactions such as purchase orders and billing.

9. A **global positioning system** (**GPS**) uses satellites to determine the geographic location of earthbased GPS equipment. GPS systems are often used for tracking and navigation of all types of vehicles.

10. A **bulletin board system** (**BBS**) allows users to communicate with one another and share information.

11. **Online services,** sometimes called **information services,** include information and services provided to users who subscribe to the service for a fee.

12. **Communications,** sometimes called **data communications,** refers to the transmission of data and information over a communications channel between one computer or terminal and another computer. **Telecommunications** describes any type of long-distance communications including television signals. **Teleprocessing** refers to the use of computers and communications equipment to access computers and computer files located elsewhere.

13. A **communications channel,** also called a **communications line, communications link,** or **data link,** is the path the data follows as it is transmitted from the sending equipment to the receiving equipment in a communications system.

14. **Transmission media** are the materials or technologies that are used to establish the communications channel. Two types of transmission media are those that use some type of physical cabling (including twisted pair wire, coaxial cable, and fiber-optics cable) and those that use wireless technology (including microwaves, radio waves, or light waves).

15. **Twisted pair wire** consists of pairs of copper wires that are twisted together. Twisted pair wire is commonly used for telephone lines and to connect personal computers with one another.

16. A **coaxial cable** is a high-quality, heavily insulated communications line that is used in offices and can be laid underground or underwater. **Baseband** coaxial cable carries one signal at a time. **Broadband** coaxial cable can carry multiple signals at one time.

17. **Fiber-optic** cable uses smooth, hair-thin strands of glass to conduct light with high efficiency. Fiber optics is frequently being used in new voice and data installations.

18. **Microwaves** are radio waves that can be used to provide high-speed transmission of both voice and data. Data is transmitted through the air from one microwave station to another in a manner similar to the way radio signals are transmitted.

19. **Communications satellites** receive microwave signals from earth, amplify the signals, and retransmit the signals back to earth. **Earth stations** are communications facilities that use large, dish-shaped antennas to transmit and receive data from satellites. The transmission *to* the satellite is called an **uplink** and the transmission *from* the satellite to a receiving earth station is called a **down-link**. To transmit a limited amount of information, a small satellite dish can be used. **Very small aperture terminal** (VSAT) antenna measuring only one to three meters in size can transmit up to 19,200 bits per second. Communications satellites are usually positioned about 22,300 miles above the earth in a **geosynchonous orbit**, meaning that the satellite is placed in an orbit where it rotates with the earth.

20. **Wireless transmission** uses one of three techniques to transmit data: light beams, radio waves, or carrier-connect radio. A **cellular telephone** uses radio waves to communicate with a local antenna assigned to a specific geographic area called a cell.

21. Two major **line configurations** (types of line connections) commonly used in communications are point-to-point lines and multidrop, or multipoint, lines.

22. A **point-to-point** line is a direct line between a sending and a receiving device. A **switched line** uses a regular telephone line to establish a communications connection. The process of establishing the communications connection is sometimes referred to as the **handshake**. A **dedicated line** is a line connection that is always established (unlike the switched line where the line connection is reestablished each time it is used). If the dedicated line is provided by an outside organization, it is sometimes called a **leased line**, or a **private line**.

23. The second major line configuration is called a **multidrop**, or **multipoint**, **line**. This type of line configuration is commonly used to connect multiple devices on a single line to a main computer, sometimes called a **host computer**.

24. Communications channels can be categorized by a number of characteristics including the type of signal, transmission mode, transmission direction, and transmission rate.

25. Computer equipment is designed to process data as **digital signals**, which are individual electrical pulses that represent the bits that are grouped together to form characters. Telephone equipment was originally designed to carry only voice transmission, which is comprised of a continuous electrical wave called an **analog signal**. A special piece of equipment called a modem is used to convert between the digital signals and analog signals so that telephone lines can carry data. To provide better communication services, telephone companies are now offering **digital data service**, communications channels, which are specifically designed to carry digital instead of voice signals. Modems are not needed with digital data service; instead, users connect to the communications line through a device called a **digital service unit** (DSU).

26. In **asynchronous transmission mode**, individual bytes (made up of bits) are transmitted at irregular intervals, such as when a user enters data. In the **synchronous transmission mode**, large blocks of data are transmitted at regular intervals.

File　　Edit　　Section　　Page　　Tools　　Options　　Help

What You Should Know
(continued)

27. In **simplex transmission**, data flows in one direction only. In **half-duplex transmission**, data can flow in both directions but in only one direction at a time. In **full-duplex transmission**, data can be sent in both directions at the same time.

28. The transmission rate of a communications channel is determined by its bandwidth and its speed. The **band-width** is the range of frequencies that a channel can carry. The speed at which data is transmitted is usually expressed as **bits per second (bps)**, the number of bits that can be transmitted in one second, or as **baud rate**, the number of times per second the signal being transmitted changes.

29. A variety of communications equipment exists to increase or change a signal to transmit it farther, but the equipment a user is most likely to encounter is a modem, a multiplexor, and a front-end processor. Computers that are connected to a network usually require a network interface card.

30. A **modem** converts the digital signals of a terminal or computer to analog signals that are transmitted over a communications channel. An **external modem** is a separate, or stand-alone, device that is attached to the computer or terminal by a cable and to the telephone outlet by a standard telephone cord. An **internal modem** is a circuit board that is installed inside a computer or terminal.

31. A **multiplexor**, sometimes referred to as a MUX, combines more than one input signal into a single stream of data that can be transmitted over a communications channel, thus increasing the efficiency of communications and saving on the cost of individual communications channels.

32. A **front-end processor** is a computer that is dedicated to handling the communications requirements of a larger computer. Tasks that the front-end processor would handle include **polling** (checking the connected terminals or computers to see if they have data to send), error checking and correction, and access security.

33. A **network interface card** (NIC) fits in an expansion slot of a computer and attaches to the cable or wireless technology used to connect the devices in the network.

34. Programs that a user must load before transmitting data, referred to as **communications software**, can perform a number of tasks. **Dialing software** allows you to store, review, select, and dial telephone numbers of computers that can be called. **File transfer software** allows you to move one or more files from one system to another. **Terminal emulation software** allows a personal computer to imitate or appear to be a specific type of terminal so the personal computer can connect to another usually larger computer. **Data encryption** protects confidential data through the conversion of data at the sending end into an unrecognizable string of characters or bits and the reconversion of the data at the receiving end.

35. A **protocol** is a set of rules and procedures for exchanging information between computers. The International Standards Organization (ISO) based in Geneva, Switzerland has defined a set of communications proto-cols, called the **Open Systems Interconnection** (OSI) model, which has been endorsed by the United Nations.

36. A communications **network** is a collection of terminals, computers, and other equipment that uses communica-tions channels to share data, information, hardware, and software.

37. A **local area network,** or LAN, is a privately owned com-munications network that covers a limited geographic area. Three common applications of local area networks are hardware, software, and information resource sharing.

Start

38. **Hardware resource sharing** allows each personal computer in the network to access and use devices that would be too expensive to provide for each user or would not be justified for each user because of only occasional use. A **server** is a computer dedicated to handling the communications needs of the other computers in a network.

39. **Software resource sharing** consists of storing frequently used software on the hard disk of the server so the software can be accessed by multiple users. When a commercial software package is accessed by many users, it is sometimes necessary to obtain a special agreement from the software vendor called a **site license**.

40. **Information resource sharing** allows anyone using a personal computer on the local area network to access data stored on any other computer in the network. Using the **file-server** method, the server sends an entire file at a time and the requesting computer then performs the processing. With the **client-server** method, as much processing as possible is done on the server system before the data is transmitted.

41. A **peer-to-peer network** allows any computer to share software, data, or hardware located on any other computer in the network. A **network operating system** (NOS) is software that allows a user to manage the resources of a computer network.

42. A **wide area network**, or WAN, is geographic in scope (as opposed to local) and uses telephone lines, microwaves, satellites, or a combination of communications channels. A wide area network limited to the area surrounding a city is sometimes referred to as a **metropolitan area network**, or MAN. Public wide area network companies include so-called **common carriers** such as the telephone companies. Companies called **value-added carriers** lease channels from the common carriers to provide specialized communications services referred to as **value-added networks** (VANs). **Packet-switching** combines individual packets of information from various users and transmits them together over a high-speed channel. Most common carriers are now offering **Integrated Services Digital Network** (ISDN) services. ISDN is an international standard for the digital transmission of both voice and data using different channels and communications companies.

43. The largest and best known wide area network is the Internet. The **Internet** is a worldwide network of computer networks.

44. The configuration, or physical layout, of the equipment in a communications network is called **topology**. Devices connected to a network, such as terminals, printers, or other computers, are referred to as **nodes**.

45. A **star network** contains a central computer and one or more terminals or personal computers connected to it, forming a star. A star network configuration is often used when the central computer contains all the data required to process the input from the terminals.

46. When a **bus network** is used, all the devices in the network are connected to and share a single cable. Information is transmitted in either direction from any one personal computer to another.

47. A **ring network** does not use a centralized host computer. Data travels around a ring network in one direction only and passes through each node. A **token ring network** constantly circulates an electronic signal, called a token, around the network. If a device has the token, a message can be sent.

48. A **gateway** is a combination of hardware and software that allows users on one network access to the resources on a *different* type of network. A **bridge** is a combination of hardware and software that is used to connect *similar* networks. A **router** is an intelligent network connecting device that can route communications traffic directly to the appropriate network.

Terms to Remember

analog signal (7.16)
asynchronous transmission mode
   (7.16)

bandwidth (7.17)
baseband (7.9)
baud rate (7.18)
bits per second (bps) (7.18)
bridge (7.27)
broadband (7.10)
bulletin board system (BBS) (7.7)
bus network (7.26)

cellular telephone (7.12)
client-server (7.23)
coaxial cable (7.9)
common carriers (7.24)
communications (7.8)
communications channel (7.8)
communications line (7.8)
communications link (7.8)
communications satellites (7.11)
communications software (7.20)

data communications (7.8)
data encryption (7.20)
data link (7.8)
dedicated line (7.14)
dialing software (7.20)
digital data service (7.16)
digital service unit (DSU) (7.16)
digital signals (7.16)
downlink (7.11)

earth stations (7.11)
electronic data interchange (EDI) (7.5)
electronic mail (7.2)
external modem (7.19)

facsimile (7.4)
FAX (7.4)
fiber optics (7.10)

file-server (7.23)
file transfer software (7.20)
front-end processor (7.19)
full-duplex transmission (7.17)

gateway (7.27)
geosynchronous orbit (7.11)
global positioning system (GPS) (7.6)
groupware (7.4)

half-duplex transmission (7.17)
handshake (7.14)
hardware resource sharing (7.21)
host computer (7.15)

information resource sharing (7.22)
information services (7.7)
information superhighway (7.31)
Integrated Services Digital Network
   (ISDN) (7.24)
internal modem (7.19)
Internet (7.25)

LAN (7.21)
leased line (7.15)
line configurations (7.14)
local area network (LAN) (7.21)

MAN (7.24)
metropolitan area network
   (MAN) (7.24)
microwaves (7.11)
modem (7.18)
multidrop line (7.15)
multiplexor (7.19)
multipoint line (7.15)

National Information Infrastructure
   (NII) (7.31)
network (7.21)
network interface card (NIC) (7.19)
network operating system
   (NOS) (7.23)
nodes (7.26)

online services (7.7)
Open Systems Interconnection
   (OSI) (7.21)

packet-switching (7.24)
peer-to-peer network (7.23)
point-to-point line (7.14)
polling (7.19)
private line (7.15)
protocol (7.21)

ring network (7.27)
router (7.27)

server (7.22)
simplex transmission (7.17)
site license (7.22)
software resource sharing (7.22)
star network (7.26)
switched line (7.14)
synchronous transmission mode (7.17)

telecommunications (7.8)
telecommuting (7.5)
teleconferencing (7.3)
teleprocessing (7.8)
terminal emulation software (7.20)
token ring network (7.27)
topology (7.26)
transmission media (7.9)
twisted pair wire (7.9)

uplink (7.11)

value-added carriers (7.24)
value-added networks (VANs) (7.24)
very small aperture terminal
   (VSAT) (7.11)
voice mail (7.3)

WAN (7.24)
wide area network (WAN) (7.24)
wireless transmission (7.12)
workgroup technology (7.4)

Test Your Knowledge

Fill in the Blanks

1. _____refers to the transmission of data and information over a channel such as a telephone line, between one computer and another computer.

2. In _____ transmission mode, individual bytes (made up of bits) are transmitted at irregular intervals, while in _____ transmission mode, large blocks of data are transmitted at regular intervals.

3. The direction of data transmission is classified as either _____ (data flows in one direction only), _____ (data can flow in both directions but in only one direction at a time), or _____ (data can be sent in both directions at the same time).

4. Communications equipment includes a(n) _____, which converts the digital signals of a terminal or computer to analog signals, a(n) _____, which combines more than one input signal into a single stream of data, a(n) _____, which is a computer dedicated to handling the communications requirements of a larger computer, and a(n) _____ that fits in an expansion slot of a computer and attaches to the cable or wireless technology used to connect the devices in a network.

5. A(n) _____ is a combination of hardware and software that allows users on one network to access the resources on a different network, while a(n) _____ is a combination of hardware and software that is used to connect similar networks.

Short Answer

1. List seven examples of how communications technology is used. Briefly describe each.

2. Name three transmission media that use some type of physical cabling. How are they different? Name three transmission media that use wireless technology. How are they different?

3. Two major line configurations commonly used in communications are point-to-point lines and multidrop lines. What are point-to-point lines? How is a switched line different from a dedicated line? What are multidrop lines?

4. What is communications software? Describe four tasks that can be performed by communications software.

5. What is a network? How is a local area network (LAN) different from a wide area network (WAN)? Briefly describe three common network topologies.

Label the Figure

Instructions: Identify the basic components of a communications system shown in the figure below.

File   Edit   Section   Page   Tools   Options   Help

Points to Ponder

1

This chapter describes several applications that rely on communications technology. Which of these applications would you be most likely to use as a college student? Which application do you think you would use in your career? Which application would you be most likely to use for social reasons? Which application do you think will have the greatest impact on society over the next twenty-five years? Explain why you answered each part of this question as you did.

2

Plagiarism is the act of stealing someone else's ideas or words and passing them off as one's own. In ancient Greece, however, "plagiarism" often worked in reverse; in an effort to give his thoughts a wider audience, an unknown author would pass off his own ideas or words as the work of someone famous. Some people feel that the anonymity provided by electronic mail and computerized bulletin board systems will also lead to a wider dissemination of ideas by eliminating biases based on age, gender, race, social class, or cultural origin. Others believe, however, that the high cost of the necessary computer equipment will continue to keep a large percentage of the

population silent. What do you think? Will these applications give more people the opportunity to express their views? Why or why not?

3

Computer bulletin board systems (BBSs) have led to some controversies related to the issue of free speech. Police have closed bulletin board systems providing information that could be used to commit crimes, such as telephone codes that can be employed to make free long-distance telephone calls. It is more difficult, however, to control the posting of confidential material, hate messages, and discriminatory correspondence. Bulletin board systems are often available to a large geographic area, and statutes and standards vary from state to state and community to community. Some BBS operators have pulled communications they considered objectionable, but many feel this amounts to censorship. Do you think a bulletin board system operator has the right to control what information is presented? Why or why not? What regulations, if any, do you think should be passed to control the type of material that can be posted on a bulletin board system? Why?

4

The number of employees telecommuting either full or part time in the United States more than doubled from 1988 to 1991 and is expected to double again by 1996. Studies have shown that telecommuting workers are 10 to 20 percent more productive than their office-bound brethren. There are disadvantages to telecommuting, however, including the inability of office managers to oversee workers, the difficulty in conducting spontaneous staff meetings, and a potential loss of "team spirit." Whether or not telecommuting is a success seems to depend primarily on the employee's personality and the employer's ability to make adjustments. What type of personality do you think is necessary for someone to telecommute successfully? What types of adjustments must be made by employers? Given your personality and the career you intend to pursue, do you think you would be a successful telecommuter? Why or why not?

5

During a typical day, you probably encounter communication situations that have distinct directions of transmission. Describe three circumstances you have experienced with different directions of transmission; one in which the direction of communication was comparable to simplex transmission, another in which the direction

Windows 95

Start

Out and About

of communication was comparable to half-duplex transmission, and a third in which the direction of communication was comparable to full-duplex transmission. Why did you classify each situation as you did? Do you think communication would have been improved if the direction of transmission had been different? Why or why not?

6

Although analog telephone transmissions can be tapped fairly easily, data encryption can make digital telephone transmissions very difficult to tap. So that police can gather the evidence necessary to convict some criminals, the FBI has proposed legislation that would require all providers of electronic communications to use equipment capable of being wiretapped. An encryption standard, the details of which would be available only to law enforcement agencies, has also been presented that would eventually eliminate all other standards. Some businesses and civil liberties groups have objected to the proposals, insisting that wiretapping would become too easy, and there is no guarantee unauthorized government eavesdropping would not take place. What do you think? Should government be allowed to regulate data communications? Why or why not?

1. Many experts feel that online information services will eventually be as much a part of our lives as newspapers, radio, and television are today. Figure 7-8 on page 7.7 furnishes the names of major online information service providers and offers a brief description of each. Call the phone numbers for at least three of the services listed to obtain additional information. What services are offered? Does the service require a particular type of user interface? What is the membership fee? Are there other fees (such as a minimum monthly charge, hourly access fee, or added cost for certain services)? From the information supplied, in which online information service are you most interested? Why?

2. Questions have been raised regarding concerns that cellular telephones cause brain tumors or other health problems. A Florida man has filed a lawsuit, claiming that his wife's death resulted from a brain tumor induced by radiation from her cellular telephone. Although the Cellular Telecommunications Industry Association maintains thousands of studies have been done showing the phones are not hazardous, an advisory group that has reviewed the studies feels they contain data gaps and insufficient evidence. Visit a library and, using current newspapers and periodicals, prepare a report on the health issues related to cellular telephone use. On the basis of your findings, do you think the use of cellular telephones is safe? Why or why not? What additional studies, if any, do you think should be done?

Out and About

3. Many schools and offices have a network connecting their computers. Locate a school or office that uses a network and talk to someone connected to it about how the network works. What are the advantages of having a network? What are the disadvantages? Find out what type of network (star, bus, ring, or token ring) it is and draw a simple diagram of the network. Why is that network topology used? Have there ever been any problems with the network? If so, would the problems have been avoided with a different network configuration? Is the network connected to another network? If so, how?

4. To take advantage of computerized telecommunications over analog phone lines, a modem is an essential piece of equipment. Visit a computer vendor and compare several modems. List the characteristics of each, including such items as the transmission rate, the cost, and whether it is an internal or external modem. If you have a personal computer, or know what type of personal computer you would like to have, ask a salesperson to recommend a modem for your personal computer. On the basis of the information you have gathered, which modem would you be most likely to purchase? Why?

5. Regardless of your interests, a computer bulletin board system (BBS) probably exists that is tailor-made for you. Currently, there are more than 50,000 public-access bulletin boards in the United States dealing with a wide range of topics, including politics, the environment, sports, religion, alternative lifestyles, music, and business opportunities. Make a list of at least three areas of interest to you. Then, by using a personal computer magazine, contacting a local computer users' group, or telephoning an online information service that offers a BBS, discover the name of a bulletin board system that fits each of your interests. If possible, find out the answers to such questions as: How do you connect to the BBS? Are any fees required? Are electronic mail services offered? Are public domain software and shareware provided that can be downloaded (copied from the BBS) to a personal computer system?

6. Facsimile equipment has become incredibly popular. FAX machines are now an essential piece of equipment for even small businesses, and many people have FAX machines in their homes. As a result, FAX machines are now available at a variety of stores including computer stores, office supply stores, discount stores, electronics stores, and catalog stores. Visit three different types of stores and find FAX machines that offer similar features. Write down the brand name of each machine, the available features, in what store the machine was found, and the cost of each. Ask a salesperson to explain the machine's warranty and the store's service policy. From what you have learned, in which store would you be most likely to purchase a FAX machine? Why?

In the Lab with Windows 95

1 **Shelly Cashman Series Communications Lab**   Follow the instructions in Windows 95 Lab 1 on page 1.30 to display the Shelly Cashman Series Labs screen. Click Connecting to the Internet. Click the Start Lab button. When the initial screen displays, carefully read the objectives. With your printer turned on, click the Print Questions button. Fill out the top of the Questions sheet and answer the questions as you step through the Communications Lab. Close the Shelly Cashman Series Labs.

2 **Understanding the Modems Properties Dialog Box**   Click the Start button on the taskbar, point to Settings on the Start menu, and then click Control Panel on the submenu. Double-click the Modems icon in the Control Panel window. When the Modems Properties dialog box displays, click the General tab *(Figure 7-39)*. Click the first modem in the list, and then click the Properties button. When the modem's dialog box displays, click the General tab and then answer the following questions: (1) To which port is the modem connected? (2) Approximately where is the speaker volume set? (3) What is the maximum speed for the modem? Click the Connection tab and then answer the following questions: (4) What is the number of Data bits? (5) What is the Parity? (6) What is the number of Stop bits? Close the modem's dialog box. Close the Modems Properties dialog box. Close Control Panel.

3 **Creating a Text File for File Transfer**   Text files (also called ASCII files) are often used in online file transfer operations because they can be read by any word processing package or editor. Many Windows 95 users use Notepad to create files to upload to a bulletin board or a friend's computer.

Click the Start button on the taskbar, point to Programs on the Start menu, point to Accessories on the Programs submenu, and then click Notepad on the Accessories submenu. Maximize the Notepad window. Type the first paragraph on page 7.8 under the heading, What Is Communications?, as shown in *Figure 7-40*. To indent the first line of the paragraph, press the SPACEBAR five times. Press ENTER at the end of each line on page 7.8. Use the same error-correction techniques in Notepad as you used in WordPad (see Windows 95 Lab 1 on page 2.36). When your document is correct, click File on the menu bar, and then click Save. Type `a:windows 95 lab 7-3` and then click the Save button. With your printer turned on, click Print on the File menu. Close Notepad.

4 **Using Help to Understand Phone Dialer**   Click the Start button on the taskbar, point to Programs on the Start menu, point to Accessories on the Programs submenu, and then click Phone Dialer on the Accessories submenu. When Phone Dialer displays, click Help on its menu bar, and then click What's This. Using the question mark pointer, click the Number to dial text box. Read the information in the pop-up window and then click anywhere to remove it from your screen. Repeat this process for the other areas of the window. Answer the following questions: (1) What techniques can use to enter the number you want to dial? (2) How do you dial an entered number? Close Phone Dialer.

Figure 7-39

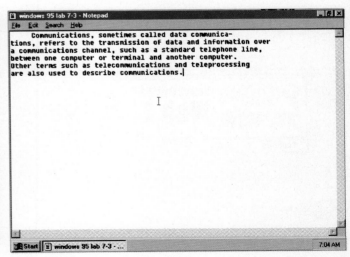

Figure 7-40

File   Edit   Section   Page   Tools   Options   Help

Where on the Web

1 **TalkBack Live**   To visit the CNN Web site *(Figure 7-41)* and learn about how the latest communications technology is being used in an audience-interactive TV program, complete the following steps. With Netscape on the screen, type `http://www.cnn.com/CNN/Programs` in the Location text box and press ENTER. Scroll down and click TalkBack Live. Scroll down and read the page. What interactive audience response elements are used? Click Print on the File menu. Click OK. Write your answer on the printout and hand it in.

2 **Chat on the Web**   WebChat is a form of "live" e-mail on the World Wide Web. Complete the following activities to learn more about WebChat. With Netscape on the screen, type `http://www.irsociety.com/wbs/about.html` in the Location text box and press ENTER. Scroll down and read the page. Click Surf on top of the WBS page. Click the link to listen in. Scroll down and click a station that interests you. Click the Enter Channel button. Click Print on the File menu. Click OK. Hand in the printout.

3 **E-mail the President**   Electronic mail (e-mail) is the capability to use computers to transmit messages and receive messages from other computer users. Complete the following steps to tour the White House *(Figure 7-42)* and use e-mail to place a message in the guest book. With Netscape on the screen, type `http://www.whitehouse.gov` in the Location text box and press ENTER. Scroll down and click Tours. Take one of the tours. Return to the bottom of the White House home page and click Electronic Guest Book.

Scroll down and type the requested information. Click Print on the File menu. Click OK. Scroll down and click the Send button. If the Security Information dialog box opens, click the Continue button. Hand in the printout.

4 **Yahoo Directory**   A global positioning system (GPS) uses satellites to determine the geographic location of earth-based GPS equipment. Complete the following steps to use the Yahoo Directory to learn more about GPS. With Netscape on the screen, click the Net Search button. Click Yahoo. Click Science. Click Geography. Click Navigation. Click GPS-Global Positioning System. Scroll down and click a topic that sounds interesting. Scroll down and read the page. Click Print on the File menu. Click Pages and then type 1 in the To text box. Click OK. Hand in the printout.

5 **Shelly Cashman Online**   Click Using Computers: A Gateway To Information, World Wide Web Edition on the Shelly Cashman Student Center Web page (`http://www.bf.com/scstudnt.html`). Scroll down and click Chapter 7. Complete the activities listed.

Figure 7-41

Figure 7-42

The Internet

The Internet is a network of networks. It links approximately 30 million people and thousands of organizations worldwide. The number of people using the Internet is growing 5% each month. The Internet is a vast resource of information and services. Some of the things you can do on the Internet are listed on the right.

- Send and receive electronic mail
- Transfer files
- Search databases
- Participate in discussions on particular subjects
- Play games
- Run programs on remote computers
- Order products and services

Figure 1
Many local, regional, national, and international networks are connected together to form the Internet. This is a diagram of the National Science Foundation network (NSFNET), which is one of the larger national networks.

- **30 million users**
- **Users located in more than 100 countries**
- **20,000 member organizations**
- **21,000 connected networks**
- **2 million networked computers**
- **Number of users growing at 5% per month**

INTERNET TERMS

ARCHIE	A method of locating files on the Net.
FAQ	Frequently Asked Question. Lists of FAQs help users learn about a particular topic on the Net.
FLAME	Slang term for an aggressive or rude message.
FTP	File Transfer Protocol. Method of transferring files from one computer to another.
GOPHER	A menu-based system for exploring the Net.
IRC	Internet Relay Chat. Interactive discussion among multiple users.
MOSAIC	Graphical user interface that uses hypertext links.
NET	Abbreviation for the Internet.
NEWSGROUPS	Discussion groups on various topics.
PPP	Point-to-Point Protocol. A type of Internet connection.
SLIP	Serial Line Internet Protocol. A type of Internet connection.
SURFING	Slang term for browsing the Net.
TCP/IP	Transmission Control Protocol/Internet Protocol. Primary communications protocol used on the Net.
TELNET	A terminal emulation communications protocol that allows users to login to other computer systems.
URL	Uniform Resource Locator. The Internet address where a document can be found.
USENET	An informal group of systems that exchange news on a variety of topics.
VERONICA	A search tool used with Gopher.
WAIS	Wide Area Information Service. A system for finding information in Net databases.
WWW	World Wide Web. A linked hypertext system used for accessing Net resources.

Figure 2
Common Internet terms.

Figure 3
A quick and easy way to get connected to the Internet is to buy a starter kit such as Netscape Navigator Personal Edition. This kit provides the necessary communications and utility software and a choice of Internet service providers.

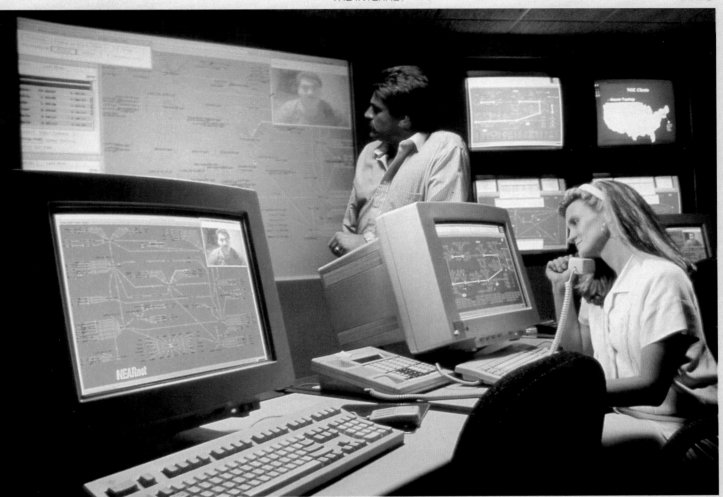

Figure 4
Some portions of the Internet are administered by private companies that provide Internet access and services. This photograph shows the control center of Nearnet, an Internet access provider that serves the northeastern United States.

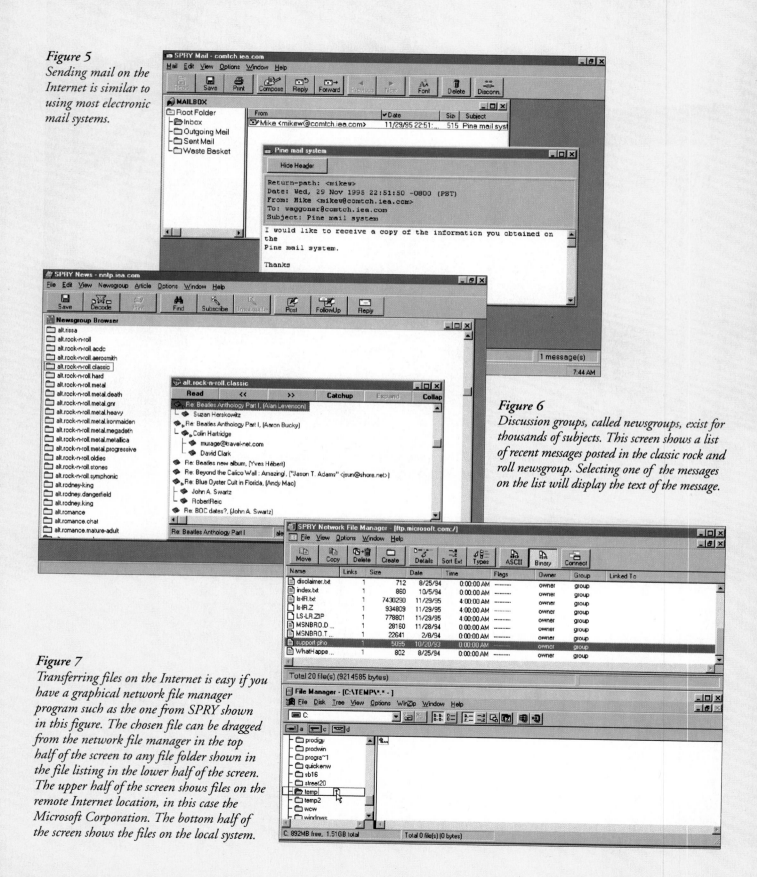

Figure 5
Sending mail on the Internet is similar to using most electronic mail systems.

Figure 6
Discussion groups, called newsgroups, exist for thousands of subjects. This screen shows a list of recent messages posted in the classic rock and roll newsgroup. Selecting one of the messages on the list will display the text of the message.

Figure 7
Transferring files on the Internet is easy if you have a graphical network file manager program such as the one from SPRY shown in this figure. The chosen file can be dragged from the network file manager in the top half of the screen to any file folder shown in the file listing in the lower half of the screen. The upper half of the screen shows files on the remote Internet location, in this case the Microsoft Corporation. The bottom half of the screen shows the files on the local system.

Figure 8
A wide variey of information is available on the Internet from government and educational organizations. This screen shows population estimates that are updated monthly by the U.S. Census Bureau.

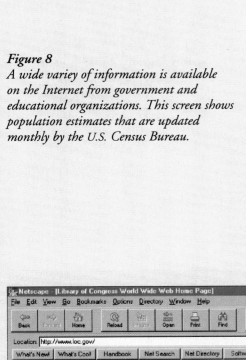

Figure 9
The Library of Congress is another source of research information on many subjects.

Figure 10
A number of employers are now listing job openings and information about their companies on the Internet.

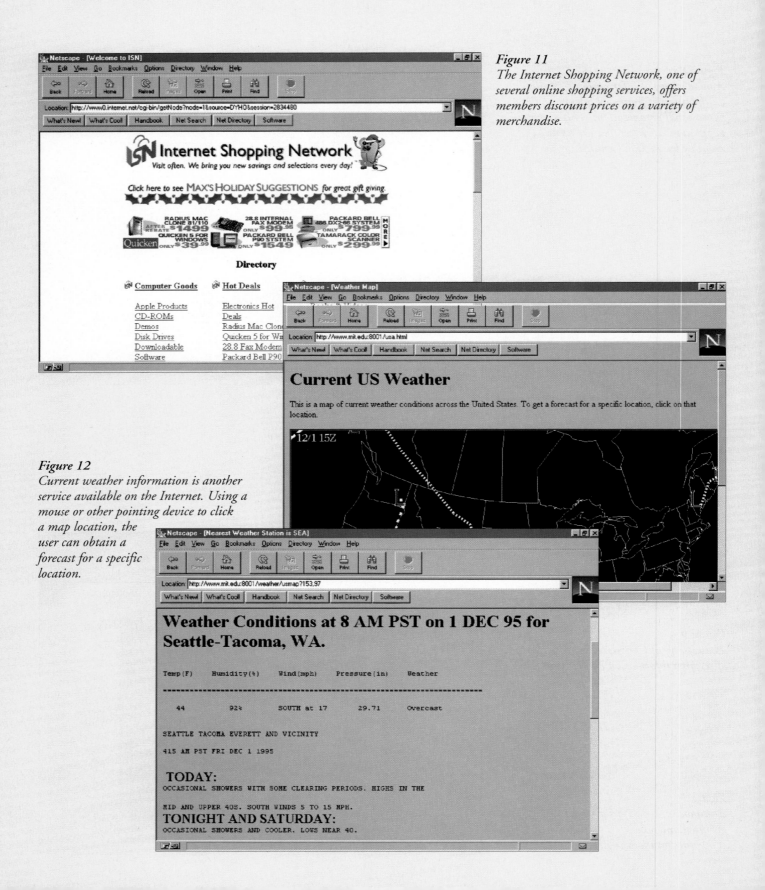

Figure 11
The Internet Shopping Network, one of several online shopping services, offers members discount prices on a variety of merchandise.

Figure 12
Current weather information is another service available on the Internet. Using a mouse or other pointing device to click a map location, the user can obtain a forecast for a specific location.

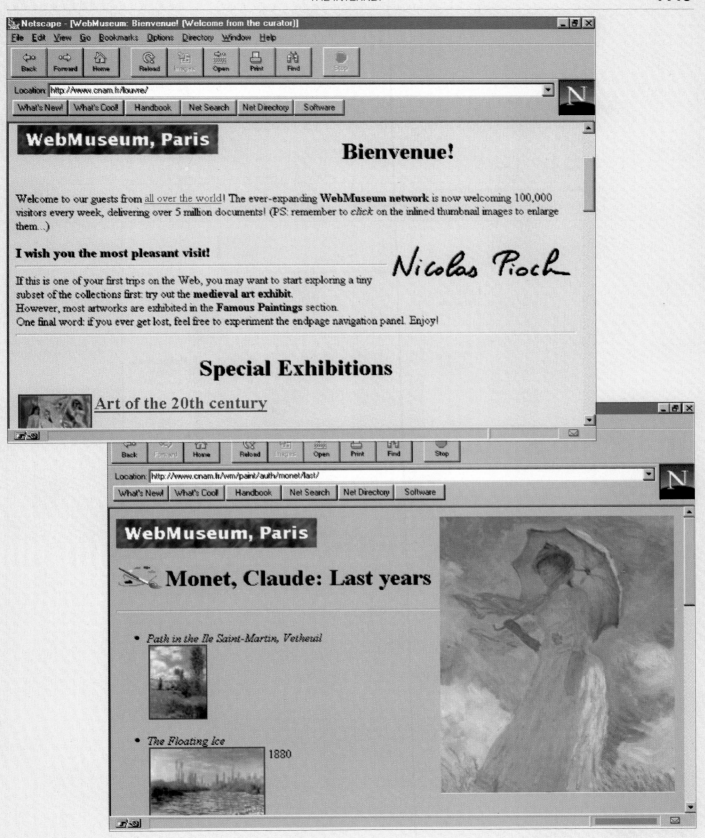

Figure 13
A number of international locations have English language services. These screens above show information on the Louve Museum in Paris, France. This service resides on a computer in Paris connected to the Internet. The information includes details on current exhibits and information on famous painters. Digital images of many of the paintings can be displayed and downloaded.

Figure 15
The White House, home of the United States President, is also connected to the Internet. Electronic visitors can sign the guest book, listen to messages from the President and Vice President, and take a tour.

The White House -- A Living Museum

The White House has been the scene of many events in the history of our nation. Here the President holds meetings that decide national and international policy, signs new legislation, and carries out the many duties of the office. Here, too, the President and First Family entertain guests and live their private lives, as every President except George Washington has done. Designed by Irish born architect, James Hoban, the White House contains numerous artworks and fine crafts from every era of American history.

Operating Systems and System Software

8

Objectives

After completing this chapter, you will be able to:

- Describe the three major categories of system software

- Define the term operating system

- Describe the various types of operating systems and explain the differences in their capabilities

- Describe the functions of an operating system, including allocating system resources, monitoring system activities, and disk and file management

- Explain the difference between proprietary and portable operating systems

- Name and briefly describe the major operating systems that are being used today

- Discuss utilities and language translators

When most people think of software they think of application software such as word processing, spreadsheet, and database software. For application software to run on a computer, however, another type of software is needed to interface between the user, the application software, and the equipment. This software consists of programs referred to as the operating system. The operating system is part of what is called system software.

This chapter discusses operating system features of both large and small computer systems. It is important to understand the features of large computer operating systems because these features are steadily being implemented on small systems such as personal computers.

What Is System Software?

System software consists of all the programs including the operating system that are related to controlling the operations of the computer equipment. Some of the functions that system software perform include: starting up the computer; loading, executing, and storing application programs; storing and retrieving files; and performing a variety of functions such as formatting disks, sorting data files, and translating program instructions into machine language. System software can be classified into three major categories; operating systems, utilities, and language translators.

What Is an Operating System?

An **operating system** (OS) consists of one or more programs that control the allocation and usage of hardware resources such as memory, CPU time, disk space, and peripheral devices. These programs function as an interface between the user, the application programs, and the computer equipment *(Figure 8-1)*.

The operating system is usually stored on disk. For a computer to operate, the essential and most frequently used instructions in the operating system must be copied from the disk and stored in the main memory of the computer. This *resident* portion of the operating system is called by many different names: the **supervisor**, **monitor**, **executive**, **master program**, **control program**, or **kernel**. Commands that are included in the resident portion of the operating system are called **internal commands**. The *nonresident* portions of the operating system are called **external commands**. The nonresident portions of the operating system remain on the disk and are available to be loaded into main memory whenever they are needed.

Most operating systems allow the user to give specific instructions to the computer, such as to list all the files on a diskette or to copy a file from one diskette to another. These instructions are called the **command language**. The portion of the operating system that carries out the command language instructions is called the **command language interpreter**.

Figure 8-1
The operating system and other system software programs act as an interface between the user, the application software, and the computer.

System Software

Operating system
System programs

Application Software

User

Loading an Operating System

The process of loading an operating system into main memory is called **booting** the system. *Figure 8-2* shows information that is displayed during this process. The actual information displayed will vary depending on the make of the computer and the equipment installed. For larger systems, the boot process is similar. The following steps explain what happens during the boot process on an IBM compatible personal computer using the Windows 95 operating system.

1. When you turn on your computer, the power supply distributes current to the motherboard and the other devices located in the system unit case.
2. The surge of electricity causes the CPU chip to reset itself and look to the BIOS chip for instructions on how to proceed. **BIOS** stands for **Basic Input/Output System**. The BIOS is a set of instructions that provide the interface between the operating system and the hardware devices. The BIOS is stored in a read-only memory (ROM) chip.
3. The BIOS chip begins a set of tests to make sure the equipment is working correctly. The tests, called the **POST** for **Power On Self Test**, check the memory, keyboard, buses, and expansion cards. After some of the early tests are completed, the BIOS instructions are copied into memory where they can be executed faster than in ROM.
4. After the POST tests are successfully completed, the BIOS begins looking for the boot program that will load the operating system. Usually it first looks in floppy disk drive A. If an operating system disk is not loaded in drive A, the BIOS looks in drive C, the drive letter usually given to the first hard drive.
5. The boot program is loaded into memory and executed. The boot program then begins loading the *resident* portion of the operating system into memory. This resident portion is called the *kernel*.
6. The operating system then loads system configuration information. System configuration information is contained in several files called the registry. The **registry** files contain information on what hardware and software is installed and individual user preferences for mouse speed, wallpaper, passwords, and other user-specific information. In earlier versions of the Windows operating system, hardware and software configuration information was contained in the **CONFIG.SYS** and **AUTOEXEC.BAT** files and other files ending in the letters *ini*.
7. For each hardware device identified in the registry, such as mouse, CD-ROM drive, or a scanner, the operating system loads a device driver program. A **device driver** program tells the computer how to communicate with a device.
8. The remainder of the operating system is loaded and the desktop and icons appear on the screen. Programs that are in the Start Up group are executed.

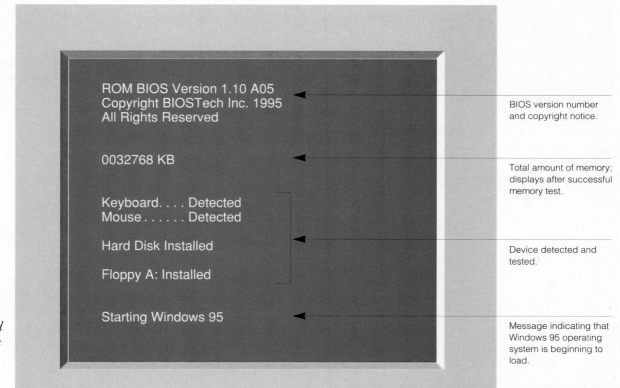

Figure 8-2
An example of information that is displayed during the boot process.

Types of Operating Systems

The types of operating systems include single program, multitasking, multiprocessing, and virtual machine operating systems. These operating systems can be classified by two criteria: (1) whether they allow more than one user to use the computer at the same time and (2) whether they allow more than one program to run at the same time *(Figure 8-3)*.

Single Program

Single program operating systems allow only a single user to run a single program at one time. This was the first type of operating system developed. Older personal computers used this type of operating system. For example, a single program operating system allowed you to load only one application, such as a spreadsheet, into main memory. To work on another application, such as word processing, you would exit the spreadsheet application and load the word processing program into memory.

Multitasking

Multitasking operating systems allow more than one program to run at the same time on one computer. Even though the CPU is only capable of working on one program instruction at a time, its capability to switch back and forth between programs makes it appear as though all programs are running at the same time. For example, with a multitasking operating system, the computer could be performing a complex spreadsheet calculation and at the same time be downloading a file from another computer while the user is writing a memo with the word processing program.

Multitasking operating systems on personal computers can usually support a single user running multiple programs. Multitasking operating systems on some personal computers and most minicomputers and mainframes can support more than one user running more than one program. This version of a multitasking operating system is sometimes called a **timesharing** or **multiuser** operating system. These operating systems also allow more than one user to run the same program. For example, a wholesale distributor may have dozens of terminal operators entering sales orders using the same order entry program on the same computer.

	SINGLE PROGRAM	MULTITASKING	MULTIPROCESSING	VIRTUAL MACHINE
NUMBER OF PROGRAMS RUNNING	One program	More than one program	More than one program each CPU	More than one program on each operating system
NUMBER OF USERS	One user	One or more than one user (timesharing)	More than one user each CPU	More than one user on each operating system

Figure 8-3
Operating systems can be classified by whether they allow more than one user and whether they allow more than one program to be operating at the same time.

Multiprocessing

Computers that have more than one CPU are called **multiprocessors**. A **multiprocessing** operating system coordinates the operations of computers with more than one CPU. Because each CPU in a multiprocessor computer can be executing one program instruction, more than one instruction can be executed simultaneously. Besides providing an increase in performance, most multiprocessors offer another advantage. If one CPU fails, work can be shifted to the remaining CPUs. There are two ways to implement multiprocessing *(Figure 8-4)*. In **asymmetric multiprocessing**, application tasks are assigned to a specific CPU. Each CPU has its own amount of memory. In **symmetric multiprocessing**, application tasks may be assigned to whatever CPU is available. Memory, as needed, is shared among the CPUs. Symmetric multiprocessing is more complex but achieves a higher processing rate because the operating system has more flexibility in assigning tasks to available CPUs.

As mentioned in Chapter 4, some microprocessors have multiple CPUs designed into a single chip. Other multiprocessor systems use physically separate CPUs. Some of the systems with separate CPUs are designed to keep operating even if one of the CPUs fails. **Fault-tolerant computers** are built with redundant components such as memory, input and output controllers, and disk drives. If any one of the components fail, the system can continue to operate with the duplicate component. Fault-tolerant systems are used for airline reservation systems, communications networks, bank teller machines, and other applications where it is important to keep the computer operating at all times.

Virtual Machine

A **virtual machine** (VM) operating system allows a single computer to run two or more different operating systems. The VM operating system allocates system resources such as memory and processing time to each operating system. To users, it appears that they are working on separate systems, hence the term virtual machine. The advantage of this approach is that an organization can run different operating systems (at the same time) that are best suited to different tasks. For example, some operating systems are best for interactive processing and others are best for batch processing. With a VM operating system, both types of operating systems can be run concurrently.

Figure 8-4
In asymmetric multiprocessing, application tasks are assigned to a specific CPU that has its own memory.
In symmetric multiprocessing, application tasks are assigned to any available CPU that shares memory with the other CPUs.

Functions of Operating Systems

The operating system performs a number of functions that allow the user and the application software to interact with the computer. These functions apply to all operating systems but become more complex for operating systems that allow more than one program to run at a time. The functions can be grouped into three types: allocating system resources, monitoring system activities, and disk and file management *(Figure 8-5)*.

Allocating System Resources

The primary function of the operating system is to allocate, or assign, the resources of the computer system. That is, just as a police officer directs traffic, the operating system decides what resource will currently be used and for how long. These resources include the CPU, main memory, and the input and output devices such as disk and tape drives and printers.

CPU MANAGEMENT

Because a CPU can only work on one program instruction at a time, a multitasking operating system must keep switching the CPU among the different instructions of the programs that are waiting to be performed. A common way of allocating CPU processing is time slicing. A **time slice** is a fixed amount of CPU processing time, usually measured in milliseconds (thousandths of a second). With this technique, each user in turn receives a time slice. Because some instructions take less time to execute than others, some users may have more instructions completed in their time slice than other users. When a user's time slice has expired, the operating system directs the CPU to work on another user's program instructions, and the most recent user moves to the end of the line to await the next time slice *(Figure 8-6)*. Unless the system has a heavy work load, however, users may not even be aware that their program has been temporarily set aside. Before they notice a delay, the operating system has allocated them another time slice and their processing continues.

Because some work has a higher priority or is more important than other work, most operating systems have ways to adjust the amount of time slices a user receives, either automatically or based on user-specified criteria. One technique for modifying the number of time slices is to have different priorities assigned to each user. For each time slice received by the lowest priority, the highest priority would receive several consecutive time slices. For example, it would be logical to assign a higher priority to a program that processes

ALLOCATING RESOURCES	MONITORING ACTIVITIES	DISK AND FILE MANAGEMENT
CPU management	System performance	Formatting
Memory management	System security	Copying
Input/output management		Deleting

Figure 8-5
Operating system functions.

Figure 8-6
With the time slice method of CPU management, each application is allocated one or more fixed amounts of time called slices. Higher priority (more important) applications receive more consecutive slices than lower priority applications. When its processing time has expired, an application goes to the end of the line until all other applications have received at least one time slice. Here, application 2 is the lowest priority and so receives only one time slice. Application 1 is the highest priority and receives three time slices.

orders and records sales than to an accounting program that could be run at a later time. Another way to allocate time slices is based on the type of work being performed. For example, some operating systems automatically allocate more time slices to interactive processes such as keyboard entry than they do to CPU-only processes such as calculations. This gives a higher priority to users entering data than to a report being printed.

Another way of assigning processing priorities is to designate each job as either foreground or background. **Foreground** jobs receive a higher processing priority and more CPU time. Data entry would be an example of a job that would be classified as a foreground job. **Background** jobs receive a lower processing priority and less CPU time. Printing a report or calculating payroll are examples of jobs that could be classified as background jobs.

MEMORY MANAGEMENT

During processing, items such as the operating system, application program instructions, data waiting to be processed, and work space used for calculations, sorting, and other temporary tasks are stored in main memory. It is the operating system's job to allocate, or assign, each of these items to areas of main memory. Data that has just been read into main memory from an input device or is waiting to be sent to an output device is stored in areas of main memory called **buffers.** The operating system assigns the location of the buffers in main memory and manages the data that is stored in them.

Operating systems allocate at least some portion of memory into fixed areas called **partitions** *(Figure 8-7).* Some operating systems allocate all memory on this basis while others use partitions only for the operating system instructions and buffers.

Another way of allocating memory is called virtual memory management, or virtual storage. **Virtual memory management** increases the effective (or *virtual*) limits of memory by expanding the amount of main memory to include disk space. Without virtual memory management, an entire program must be loaded into main memory during execution. With virtual memory management, only the portion of the program that is currently being used is required to be in main memory. Virtual memory management is used with multitasking operating systems to maximize the number of programs using memory at the same time. The operating system performs

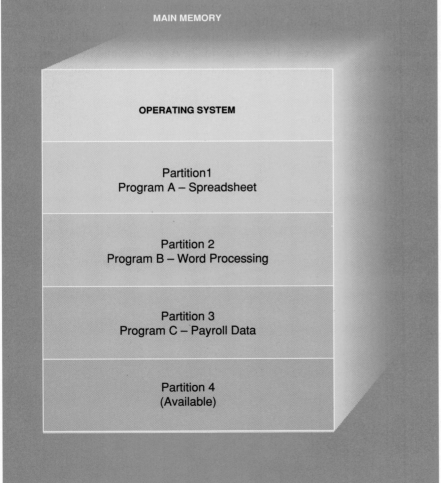

MAIN MEMORY

OPERATING SYSTEM

Partition1
Program A – Spreadsheet

Partition 2
Program B – Word Processing

Partition 3
Program C – Payroll Data

Partition 4
(Available)

Figure 8-7
Some computer systems allocate memory into fixed blocks called partitions. The CPU then keeps track of programs and data by assigning them to a specific partition.

virtual memory management by transferring data and instructions to and from memory and the disk by using one or both of the two methods, segmentation and paging.

In **segmentation**, programs are divided into logical portions called **segments**. For example, one segment of a program may edit data and another segment may perform a calculation. Because the segments are based on logical portions of a program, some segments are larger than others. When a particular program instruction is required, the segment containing that instruction is transferred from the disk into main memory.

In **paging**, a fixed number of bytes is transferred from the disk each time data or program instructions are required. This fixed amount of data is called a **page**, or a **frame**. The size of a page, generally from 512 to 4,000 bytes, is determined by the operating system. Because a page is a fixed number of bytes, it may not correspond to a logical division of a program like a segment.

In both segmentation and paging, a time comes when memory is full but another page or segment needs to be read into memory. When this occurs, the operating system makes room for the new data or instructions by writing back to disk one or more of the pages or segments currently in memory. This process is referred to as **swapping** *(Figure 8-8)*. The operating system usually chooses the least recently used page or segment to transfer back to disk.

INPUT AND OUTPUT MANAGEMENT

At any given time, more than one input device can be sending data to the computer. At the same time, the CPU could be ready to send data to an output device such as a terminal or printer or a storage device such as a disk. The operating system is responsible for managing these input and output processes.

Some devices, such as a tape drive, are usually allocated to a specific user or application program. This is because tape is a sequential storage medium, and generally it would not make sense to have more than one application writing records to a single tape. Disk drives are usually allocated to all users because the programs and data files that users need are stored on these devices. The operating system keeps track of disk read and write requests, stores these requests in buffers along with the associated data for write requests, and usually processes them sequentially. A printer could be allocated to all users or restricted to a specific user. For example, a printer

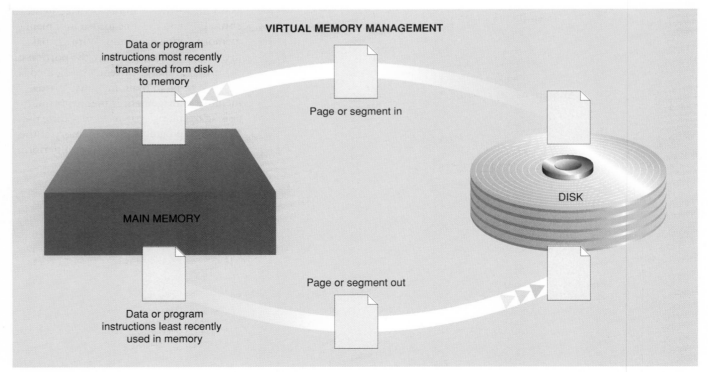

Figure 8-8
With virtual memory management, the operating system expands the amount of main memory to include available disk space. Data and program instructions are transferred to and from memory and disk as required. The segmentation technique transfers logical portions of programs that may be different sizes. The paging technique transfers pages of the same size. To make room for the new page or segment, the least recently used page or segment is swapped, or written back to the disk.

would be restricted to a specific user if the printer was going to be used with preprinted forms such as payroll checks.

Because the printer is a relatively slow device compared to other computer system devices, the technique of spooling is used to increase printer efficiency and reduce the number of printers required. With **spooling** *(Figure 8-9),* a report is first written (saved) to the disk before it is printed. Writing to the disk is much faster than writing to the printer. For example, a report that may take one-half hour to print (depending on the speed of the printer) may take only one minute to write to the disk. After the report is written to the disk, the CPU is available to process other programs. The report saved on the disk can be printed at a later time or, in a multitasking operating system, a print program can be run (at the same time other programs are running) to process the **print spool** (the reports on the disk waiting to be printed).

Because many input and output devices use different commands and control codes to transmit and receive data, programs called **device drivers** are used by the operating system to control these devices. For example, a different device driver would be required for a high-resolution color monitor than for a standard-resolution monochrome monitor. Device drivers are usually supplied with the operating system or by the device manufacturers.

Monitoring System Activities

Another function of the operating system is monitoring the system activity. This includes monitoring system performance and system security.

SYSTEM PERFORMANCE

System performance can be measured in a number of ways but is usually gauged by the user in terms of response time. **Response time** is the amount of time from the moment a user enters data until the computer responds.

Response time can vary based on what the user has entered. If the user is simply entering data into a file, the response time is usually within a second or two. However, if the user has just completed a request for a display of sorted data from several files, the response time could be minutes.

A more precise way of measuring performance is to run a program that is designed to record and report system activity.

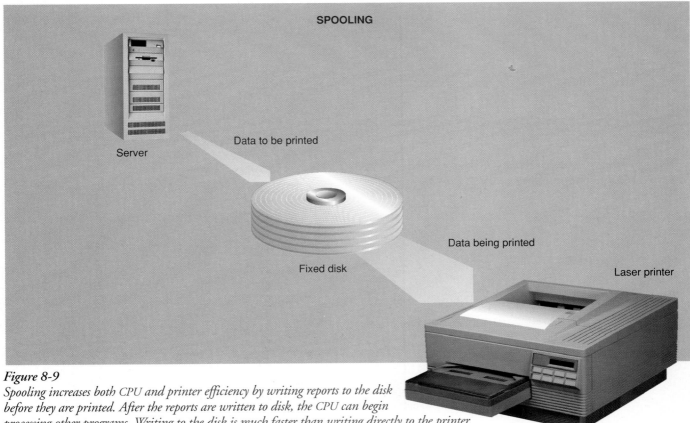

SPOOLING

Server

Data to be printed

Fixed disk

Data being printed

Laser printer

Figure 8-9
Spooling increases both CPU and printer efficiency by writing reports to the disk before they are printed. After the reports are written to disk, the CPU can begin processing other programs. Writing to the disk is much faster than writing directly to the printer.

Among other information, these programs usually report CPU **utilization,** the amount of time that the CPU is working and not idle, waiting for data to process. *Figure 8-10* shows a CPU performance measurement report.

Another measure of performance is to compare the CPU utilization with the disk input and output rate, referred to as disk I/O. How a virtual memory management operating system swaps pages or segments from disk to memory as they are needed was previously discussed. Systems with heavy work loads and insufficient memory or CPU power can get into a situation called **thrashing,** where the system is spending more time moving pages to and from the disk than processing the data. System performance reporting can alert the computer user to this problem.

System Security

Most multiuser operating systems provide for a logon code, a user ID, and a password that must all be entered correctly before a user is allowed to use an application program *(Figure 8-11)*. Each is a word or series of characters. A **logon code** usually identifies the application that will be used, such as accounting, sales, or manufacturing. A **user ID** identifies the user, such as Jeffrey Ryan or Mary Gonzales. The **password** is usually confidential; often it is known only to the user and the computer system administrator. The logon code, user ID, and password must match entries in an authorization file. If they do not match, the user is denied access to the system. Both successful and unsuccessful logon attempts are often recorded in a file so management can review who is using or attempting to use the system. These logs can also be used to allocate computing expenses based on the percentage of system use by an organization's various departments.

Disk and File Management

In addition to allocating system resources and monitoring system activities, most operating systems contain programs that can perform functions related to disk and file management. Some of these functions include formatting disks and diskettes, deleting files from a disk, copying files from one secondary storage device to another, and renaming stored files.

Figure 8-10
System performance measurement programs report the amount of time the CPU is actually working and not waiting to process data.

Figure 8-11
The logon code, user ID, and password must all be entered correctly before the user is allowed to use the computer. Because the password is confidential, it is usually not displayed on the screen when the user enters it.

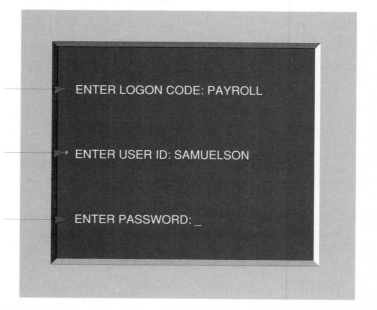

Logon code; usually specifies application to be used

User ID; usually name of user

Password; unique word or combination of characters known only to user

ENTER LOGON CODE: PAYROLL

ENTER USER ID: SAMUELSON

ENTER PASSWORD: _

Popular Operating Systems

The first operating systems were developed by manufacturers for the computers in their product line. When the manufacturers came out with another computer or model, they often produced an improved and different operating system. Because programs are designed to be used with a particular operating system, this meant that users who wanted to switch computers, either from one vendor to another or to a different model from the same vendor, would have to convert their existing programs to run under the new operating system. Today, however, the trend is away from operating systems limited to a specific model and toward operating systems that will run on any model by a particular manufacturer.

Going even further, many computer users are supporting the move away from **proprietary operating systems** (meaning privately owned) and toward **portable operating systems** that will run on many manufacturers' computers. The advantage of portable operating systems is that the user is not tied to a particular manufacturer. Using a portable operating system, a user could change computer systems, yet retain existing software and data files, which usually represent a sizable investment in time and money. For example, consider a small business that purchases a computer system to handle their immediate needs and to provide for several years of anticipated growth. Five years later, the business has reached the capacity of the computer; no more memory or terminals can be added. In addition, the manufacturer of the five-year-old computer does not make a larger or more powerful model. Because the business originally chose a computer that used a portable operating system, it can purchase a more powerful computer from another manufacturer that offers the same portable operating system and continue to use the existing software and data files.

One of the most popular portable operating systems is DOS, which is discussed along with the several other computer operating systems in this section.

DOS

DOS stands for **Disk Operating System,** the most widely used operating system on personal computers. Several slightly different but compatible versions of DOS exist. The two most widely used, MS-DOS and PC-DOS, were both originally developed by Microsoft Corporation in 1981.

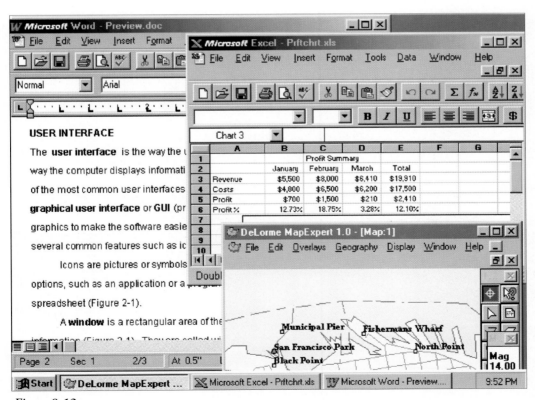

Figure 8-12
The Microsoft Windows 95 operating system provides a graphical user interface that makes computers easy to use. This screen shows three different applications; word processing, spreadsheet, and a map program. Each application is displayed in a window.

MS-DOS is marketed directly by Microsoft and is installed on most IBM-compatible personal computer systems. **PC-DOS** was developed by Microsoft for IBM and is installed by IBM on systems that IBM sells. Through the years, DOS has been improved many times. Each new version, called a *release,* has added new features and capabilities. However, DOS remains primarily a single user, single program operating system. Most importantly, DOS is unable to take full advantage of the newer 32-bit microprocessors, but DOS does have a large installed base, estimated at more than 100 million users.

The DOS operating system often operates with a shell program. A **shell** program usually provides a limited graphic interface and certain utility functions such as file maintenance.

Windows

Microsoft Windows is the most widely used graphical user interface operating system for personal computers. The most recent version of Windows, called **Windows 95** (*Figure 8-12* on the previous page), is a true multitasking operating system designed to take advantage of 32-bit microprocessors.

Previous versions of Windows, identified by version numbers 3.1 or below, required a version of the DOS operating system on the same computer. These earlier versions of Windows were sometimes referred to as a graphical user interface **operating environment** because they acted as an interface between the user and the DOS operating system.

Common features of all Windows operating systems include support for the use of a mouse, icons, menus, the capability to have several applications open at the same time, and the capability to easily move data from one application to another.

Windows NT

Microsoft Windows NT is a sophisticated version of Windows that is designed for use on client-server computer systems. Like the latest version of Windows, Windows NT is a complete operating system that does not require DOS. Unique features of Windows NT include the following:

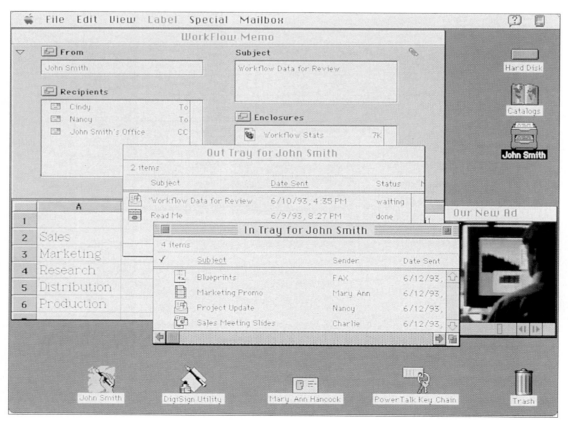

Figure 8-13
Apple's Macintosh operating system offers a graphical user interface and the capability to display information in separate windows.

- Support for most major networking communications protocols
- The capability to run 32-bit application programs
- *User Manager,* a program that creates user accounts and manages system security
- *Performance Monitor,* a program that measures network performance

Because it is more complex than Windows, Windows NT requires significant system resources including 12 to 16 MB of memory and 75 to 100 MB of disk space.

Macintosh

The Apple **Macintosh** multitasking operating system used the first commercially successful graphical user interface when it was released with Macintosh computers in 1984 *(Figure 8-13).* Since then, it has set the standard for operating system ease of use and has been the model for most of the new graphical user interfaces developed for non-Macintosh systems. Distinctive features of the latest version of the operating system, called System 7.5, include built-in networking support, electronic mail, and an extensive step-by-step help system called Apple Guide.

OS/2

OS/2 is IBM's operating system designed to work with 32-bit microprocessors *(Figure 8-14).* Besides being able to run programs written specifically for OS/2, the operating system can also run programs written for DOS or Windows. Like Windows, OS/2 has a graphical user interface. OS/2 is popular with businesses that need a sophisticated operating system to use for day-to-day operations. Several different versions of OS/2 exist, including an entry-level version designed to work on systems with only 4 MB of memory and a more complex version designed to work on servers with multiple processors. The latest version of OS/2 is called OS/2 Warp, version 3.

UNIX

The **UNIX** operating system was developed in the early 1970s by scientists at Bell Laboratories. It was specifically designed to provide a way to manage a variety of scientific and specialized computer applications. Because of federal regulations, Bell Labs (a subsidiary of AT&T) was prohibited from actively promoting UNIX in the commercial marketplace.

Figure 8-14
IBM's OS/2 operating system takes advantage of the increased processing power of the latest 32-bit microprocessors.

Instead, for a low fee, Bell Labs licensed UNIX to numerous colleges and universities where it obtained a wide following. With the deregulation of the telephone companies in the 1980s, AT&T was allowed to enter the computer system marketplace. With increased promotion and the trend toward portable operating systems, UNIX has aroused tremendous interest. One of the advantages of UNIX is its extensive library of more than 400 instruction modules that can be linked together to perform almost any programming task. Today, most major computer manufacturers offer a multiuser version of the UNIX operating system to run on their computers.

With all its strengths, however, UNIX has not yet obtained success in the commercial business systems marketplace. Some people attribute this to the fact that UNIX has never been considered user friendly. For example, most of the UNIX program modules are identified by obscure names such as MAUS, SHMOP, and BRK. Other critics contend that UNIX lacks the file management capabilities to support the online interactive databases that increasingly more businesses are implementing. With the support of most major computer manufacturers, however, these problems are being worked on, and UNIX may become one of the major operating systems of the coming years.

Figure 8-15
The NextStep operating system from NeXT Computer is designed to help software developers create new applications in significantly less time than using traditional methods and operating systems.

NextStep

The NextStep operating system from NeXT Computer was originally written to operate on the computers they manufactured. In recent years, NeXT has rewritten the operating system to run on Intel and other microprocessors and has stopped manufacturing computers to concentrate on NextStep development and marketing. NextStep is fundamentally different because it is the only object-oriented operating system *(Figure 8-15)*. Objects are a combination of the separate procedures and data that are used by most programs and operating systems. The main impact of object-oriented technology is that programs can be developed in much less time; some say in as little as one-tenth the time of traditional methods. NeXT hopes that NextStep, which has been designed to support object-oriented programming, will appeal to businesses that must develop new applications quickly.

Other Operating Systems

Other popular operating systems exist in addition to those just discussed. Most mainframe operating systems are unique to a particular make of computer or are designed to be compatible with one of IBM's operating systems such as DOS/VS, MVS, or VM, IBM's virtual machine operating system.

Although not yet widely used, the MACH operating system has been called a possible replacement for the increasingly popular UNIX operating system and possibly the standard operating system of the future. Considered a stream-lined version of UNIX, MACH has the support of several large governmental and educational organizations. Currently being developed by Carnegie Mellon University, MACH has also been chosen by the Open Software Foundation (OSF), a 170-member organization that is trying to establish an industry-wide operating system standard.

Utilities

Utility programs perform specific tasks related to managing computer resources or files. Many utility programs are included with the operating system. These utility programs usually handle frequently performed tasks such as copying and moving files and formatting disks. Other utility programs are sold separately or in a group with other utility programs that are designed to work together. A brief description of some of the tasks addressed by utility programs follows:

- **File Management**   Listing, editing, copying, moving, and deleting files and directories.
- **Disk Management**   Formatting and defragmenting disks.
- **Memory Management**   Configuring a system to make the most memory available for running application programs. Memory managers do this by moving certain programs, such as device drivers, to other areas of RAM.
- **Backup and Restore**   Backup software allows the user to select one or more files for copying to diskettes or tape. The backup software monitors the copying process and alerts the user if an additional diskette or tape is needed. Restore software reverses the process and allows the user to reinstate files that have been previously copied to disk or tape.
- **Data Recovery**   Data recovery software assists the user in rebuilding files that have been deleted or files that have been damaged.
- **Data Compression**   Reduces the amount of space that a file requires. See Chapter 6 for a discussion on how data compression works.
- **Virus Protection**   A virus is a computer program that is designed to copy itself into other programs and spread through multiple computer systems. Most virus programs cause damage to files on the system where the virus is present. Virus protection programs use a number of methods to prevent virus programs from being loaded on a computer.

Another type of utility program is a screen saver. If the same image is displayed on a monitor for long periods of time, a very dim version of the image can be permanently etched on the monitor screen. A **screen saver** program prevents this problem, called *ghosting,* by dimming the brightness of the screen or displays moving images on the screen. The screen saver program automatically starts if the image on a screen does not change for a certain period of time that can be set by the user. The moving image screen savers are often quite entertaining and allow the user to choose from a variety of images. *Figure 8-16* is an example of a screen saver display.

Language Translators

Special-purpose system software programs called **language translators** are used to convert the programming instructions written by programmers into the machine instructions that a computer can understand. Language translators are written for specific programming languages and computer systems.

Summary of Operating Systems and System Software

System software, including the operating system, utilities, and language translators, are essential parts of a computer system and should be understood by users who want to obtain the maximum benefits from their computers. This is especially true for the latest personal computer operating systems that include features such as virtual memory management and multitasking. Understanding and being able to use these and other features will give users more control over their computer resources.

Figure 8-16
The After Dark screen saver utility program from Berkeley Systems prevents an image from being permanently etched on a monitor screen by displaying entertaining images that move across the screen.

COMPUTERS AT WORK

NextStep: Objects May Be Closer Than They Appear

NeXT Computer believes that its NextStep operating system has a significant advantage that business users will want. So far, the businesses that have tried NextStep think that NeXT is right. NextStep is the only operating system designed to support object-oriented computing. Objects are combinations of data and procedures that are treated separately by traditional operating systems. One advantage of objects is that they are *smart*. Because they contain procedures that specify how they behave in certain situations, much less programming code is required and applications can be developed in a fraction of the time. An example of an object would be an invoice that knows how to print itself. Instead of using a program to specify exactly how to print the invoice data, an invoice object merely has to be sent a message saying, print. Another advantage of objects is that they are reusable. Over time, the user builds a library of objects that can be used to quickly create applications. NeXT claims that with NextStep, applications can be developed in one-fifth to one-tenth the time. Many of their customers have found this to be true.

Chrysler Financial, the financing subsidiary of the Chrysler automobile company, used NextStep to create a system for processing all car loans. They developed their first five applications in four months, less time than it takes to even design most programs. In the next four months, Chrysler Financial developed nineteen more applications. These applications are being used by approximately 3,000 people at 100 financial centers. Another NextStep user, Swiss Bank Corporation, developed a sophisticated options trading system in only two and one-half months.

NeXT believes that three trends will help NextStep become successful in the corporate market:
- The move to client/server computing
- The move to object-oriented computing
- The continued reengineering of major businesses that requires them to develop new ways of processing information

If NeXT is correct, the widespread use of objects may be closer that some people think.

Figure 8-17

IN THE FUTURE

Is There a Future for Utility Software?

Some utility software developers worry about the future of their type of software. Recently, it seems that every time a good utility program is developed, it is not long before a similar utility program shows up as part of one of the major operating systems. When users upgrade to the new version of an operating system and obtain the additional utility programs, they have little, if any, incentive to pay for the utilities separately. Examples of utilities that started out as separate programs but have wound up as part of the operating system include the following:

- Communications
- Memory management
- File management
- Backup and restore
- Disk compression
- Virus protection
- Performance monitoring

To better support the increased use of computer networks, several developers have plans to include features such as network configuration management, network security, and electronic mail in future versions of their operating systems.

As with the consolidation in the application software industry, some worry that the trend of moving utilities into the operating system will lead to less competition and less innovation. Optimistic and confident developers point out that good utility programs will always find a market. Still others suggest that moving utilities into the operating system is a natural evolution with several advantages. They claim that users want to minimize the number of companies they buy products from and, perhaps more importantly, want to minimize the number of companies they have to talk with if something goes wrong.

Figure 8-18

What You Should Know

1. **System software** consists of all the programs, including the operating system, that are related to controlling the operations of the computer equipment. System software can be classified into three major categories; operating systems, utilities, and language translators.

2. An **operating system** (OS) consists of one or more programs that control the allocation of hardware resources such as memory, CPU time, disk space, and peripheral devices. These programs function as an interface between the user, the application programs, and the computer equipment.

3. For a computer to operate, the essential and most frequently used instructions in the operating system must be copied from disk and stored in the main memory of the computer. This *resident* portion of the operating system is called by many different names: the **supervisor**, **monitor**, **executive**, **master program**, **control program**, or **kernel**. Commands that are included in the resident portion of the operating system are called **internal commands**. The *nonresident* portions of the operating system are called **external commands** that remain on disk and are available to be loaded into main memory when needed.

4. Most operating systems allow the user to give specific instructions to the computer. These instructions are called the **command language**. The **command language interpreter** is the portion of the operating system that carries out the command language instructions.

5. The process of loading an operating system into main memory is called **booting** the system. When the computer is turned on, the power supply distributes current to the motherboard and the other devices located in the system unit case. The CPU chip is reset and looks to the BIOS chip for instructions on how to proceed. The **BIOS**, which stands for **Basic Input/Output System**, is as set of instructions that provides the interface between the operating system and the hardware devices. The BIOS

chip runs a series of tests, called the POST, for **Power On Self Test**, to make sure the equipment is working correctly. Aficer the POST tests are completed, the BIOS loads the boot program that loads the *resident* portion of the operating system, called the *kernel,* into memory. The operating system then loads system configuration information contained in several files called the registry. The registry files contain information on what hardware and software is installed and individual user preferences. In earlier versions of the Windows operating system, hardware and software configuration information was contained in the **CONFIG.SYS** and **AUTOEXEC.BAT** files and other files ending in the letters *ini.* For hardware devices, the operating system loads device driver programs that tell the computer how to communicate with the devices. The remainder of the operating system is loaded and the desktop and icons appear on the screen. Programs that are in the Start Up group are executed.

6. Operating systems can be classified by two criteria: (1) whether they allow more than one user to use the computer at the same time; and (2) whether they allow more than one program to run at the same time.

7. **Single program** operating systems allow only a single user to run a single program at one time.

8. **Multitasking** operating systems allow more than one program to be run at the same time on one computer. Multitasking operating systems on some personal computers and most minicomputers and mainframes that can support more than one user running multiple programs, are called **timesharing** or **multiuser** operating systems.

9. Computers that have more than one CPU are called **multiprocessors**. A multiprocessing operating system coordinates the operations of computers with more than one CPU. In **asymmetric multiprocessing**, application tasks are assigned to a specific CPU. In **symmetric multiprocessing**, application tasks may be assigned to whatever CPU is available. **Fault-tolerant computers** are built with redundant components and can continue to operate with duplicate components if one of the components fails.

10. A **virtual machine** (VM) operating system allows a single computer to run two or more different operating systems.

File   Edit   Section   Page   Tools   Options   Help

What You Should Know
(continued)

11. The primary function of the operating system is to allocate, or assign, the resources of the computer system. These resources include the CPU, main memory, and the input and output devices.

12. A common way a multitasking operating system allocates CPU processing time is time slicing. A **time slice** is a fixed amount of CPU processing time, usually measured in milliseconds (thousandths of a second). Processing priorities can be assigned by designating each job as either a **foreground** job, which receives a higher priority and more CPU time, or a **background** job, which receives a lower priority and less processing time.

13. It is the operating system's job to allocate, or assign, items to areas of main memory. Data that has just been read into main memory from an input device or is waiting to be sent to an output device is stored in areas of main memory called **buffers**. Operating systems allocate at least some portion of main memory into fixed areas called **partitions**. The effective (or virtual) limits of memory can be increased by **virtual memory management**, which expands the amount of main memory to include disk space. With virtual memory management, only the portion of the program currently being used is required in main memory. In **segmentation**, the operating system performs virtual memory management by dividing programs into logical portions called **segments**. In **paging**, virtual memory management is performed by transferring a fixed number of bytes, called a **page** or a **frame**, from the disk each time data or program instructions are required. The process of making room for new data or instructions by writing back to disk one or more of the segments or pages currently in memory is referred to as **swapping**.

14. The operating system is responsible for managing input and output processes. The technique of spooling is used to increase printer efficiency and reduce the number of printers required. With **spooling**, a report is first written to disk (saved) before it is printed. The report saved on disk can be printed at a later time or, on a multitasking operating system, a print program can be run at the same time other programs are running to process the **print spool** (the reports on the disk waiting to be printed). Because many input and output devices use different commands and control codes to transmit and receive data, programs called **device drivers** are used by the operating system to control these devices.

15. Another function of the operating system is monitoring system activity. This includes monitoring system performance and system security.

16. System performance is usually gauged by the user in terms of **response time**, the amount of time from the moment a user enters data until the computer responds. **CPU utilization** is the amount of time that the CPU is working and not idle, waiting for data to process. Systems with heavy work loads and insufficient memory or CPU power can get into a situation called **thrashing**, where the system is spending more time moving pages to and from the disk than processing data.

17. Most multiuser operating systems monitor system security by providing for a logon code, a user ID, and a password that must all be entered correctly before a user is allowed to use the application program. A **logon code** usually identifies the application that will be used. A **user ID** identifies the user. The **password** is usually confidential; often it is known only to the user and the computer system administrator.

18. In addition to allocating system resources and monitoring system activities, most operating systems contain programs that can perform functions related to disk and file management.

19. Although the first operating systems were developed by manufacturers for computers in their product lines, today the trend is away from operating systems limited to a specific model and toward operating systems that will run on any model by a particular manufacturer. Going even further, many computer users are supporting the move away from **proprietary operating systems** (meaning privately owned) and toward **portable operating systems** that will run on many manufacturers' computers.

20. **DOS** stands for **Disk Operating System**, the most widely used operating system on personal computers. **MS-DOS** is marketed by Microsoft and is installed on most IBM-compatible personal computer systems. **PC-DOS** was developed by Microsoft for IBM and is installed by IBM on systems that IBM sells. Each new version of DOS, called a *release*, has added new features and capabilities.

21. Microsoft Windows is the most widely used graphical user interface for personal computers. Prior versions of Windows (version numbers 3.1 and below) were not technically an operating system, but were actually an **operating environment**, a graphical user interface designed to work in combination with an operating system. Like an operating environment, a **shell** program acts as an interface between the user and the operating system.

22. **Microsoft Windows NT** is a sophisticated version of Windows that is designed for use on client-server computer systems. Like the latest version of Windows (Windows 95), Windows NT is a complete operating system that does not require DOS.

23. The Apple **Macintosh** multitasking operating system used the first commercially successful graphical user interface. It has set the standard for operating system ease of use and has been the model for most of the new graphical user interfaces designed for non-Macintosh systems.

24. **OS/2** is IBM's operating system designed to work with 32-bit microprocessors. The operating system can run programs written for OS/2, DOS, or Windows. OS/2 has a graphical user interface (like Windows).

25. The **UNIX** operating system was developed in the early 1970s by scientists at Bell Laboratories to provide a way to manage a variety of scientific and specialized computer applications. Today, most major computer manufacturers offer a multiuser version of the UNIX operating system to run on their computers.

26. The NextStep operating system, from NeXT Computer, is the only object-oriented operating system. The main impact of object-oriented technology is that programs can be developed in much less time.

27. Other operating systems include mainframe operating systems (unique to a particular machine or designed to be compatible with one of IBM's operating systems) and MACH (considered a streamlined version of UNIX).

28. **Utility programs** perform specific tasks related to managing computer resources or files. These tasks include: file management, disk management, memory management, backup and restore, data recovery, data compression, and virus protection. A **screen saver** program prevents a problem called *ghosting* (having a dim version of a long-displayed image etched on the monitor screen) by dimming the brightness of the screen or displays moving images on the screen.

29. Special-purpose system software programs called **language translators** are used to convert the programming instructions written by programmers into the machine language instructions that a computer can understand.

Terms to Remember

asymmetric multiprocessing (8.5)
AUTOEXEC.BAT (8.3)

background (8.7)
Basic Input/Output System (BIOS) (8.3)
BIOS (8.3)
booting (8.3)
buffers (8.7)

command language (8.2)
command language interpreter (8.2)
CONFIG.SYS (8.3)
control program (8.2)
CPU utilization (8.10)

device driver (8.9)
Disk Operating System (DOS) (8.11)
DOS (8.11)

executive (8.2)
external commands (8.2)

fault-tolerant computers (8.5)
foreground (8.7)
frame (8.8)

internal commands (8.2)

kernel (8.2)

language translators (8.16)
logon code (8.10)

Macintosh (8.13)
master program (8.2)
Microsoft Windows NT (8.12)
monitor (8.2)
MS-DOS (8.12)
multiprocessing (8.5)
multiprocessors (8.5)
multitasking (8.4)
multiuser (8.4)

operating environment (8.12)
operating system (8.2)
OS/2 (8.13)

page (8.8)
paging (8.8)
partitions (8.7)
password (8.10)
PC-DOS (8.12)
portable operating systems (8.11)
POST (8.3)
Power On Self Test (POST) (8.3)
print spool (8.9)
proprietary operating systems (8.11)

registry (8.3)
response time (8.9)

screen saver (8.16)
segmentation (8.8)
segments (8.8)
shell (8.12)
single program (8.4)
spooling (8.9)
supervisor (8.2)
swapping (8.8)
symmetric multiprocessing (8.5)
system software (8.2)

thrashing (8.10)
time slice (8.6)
timesharing (8.4)

UNIX (8.13)
user ID (8.10)
utility programs (8.15)

virtual machine (VM) (8.5)
virtual memory management (8.7)

Windows 95 (8.12)

File   Edit   Section   Page   Tools   Options   Help

Test Your Knowledge

Fill in the Blanks

1. System software can be classified into three major categories; _____, _____, and _____.

2. A(n) _____ consists of one or more programs that manage the operations of a computer.

3. _____ is the most widely used operating system on personal computers.

4. The _____ operating system, developed by scientists at Bell Laboratories, was specifically designed to provide a way to manage a variety of scientific and specialized computer applications.

5. Special-purpose system software programs called _____ are used to convert the programming instructions written by programmers into machine instructions that a computer can understand.

Short Answer

1. What is a single program operating system? How is a multitasking operating system different from a multi-processing operation system? What is a virtual machine OS?

2. What is virtual memory management? With what types of operating systems is virtual memory management used? Why? How is segmentation different from paging? What is thrashing?

3. How are proprietary operating systems different from portable operating systems? What is the advantage of portable operating systems?

4. What do Microsoft Windows, Windows NT, Macintosh, and OS/2 have in common? How are they different? Why are earlier versions of Windows called operating environments?

5. What are utility programs? What are some of the tasks addressed by utility programs? What is the purpose of a screen saver?

Label the Figure

Instructions: Complete the diagrams to show the two ways in which multiprocessing is implemented.

_____ **Multiprocessing**   _____ **Multiprocessing**

Points to Ponder

1

In its role as an interface between application programs and computer hardware, one of the things an operating system does is provide a common set of computer functions. Some basic tasks need to be accomplished by almost all application programs, such as getting input from the keyboard. The operating system converts an application program's simple instruction to perform a task to the more complex set of instructions the hardware needs to complete the task. Make a list of at least six functions you think must be performed by almost all application programs. Rank your list from the function that you believe is performed most to the function that you believe is performed least. Briefly explain why you ranked the functions as you did.

2

You are the team leader of a group developing a new operating system. As team leader, you are responsible for providing a "vision" of the ideal operating system. Write a description of the perfect operating system. Answer such questions as: What type of operating system (single program, multitasking, multiprocessing, or virtual machine) is it? How does the operating system allocate system resources, monitor system activities, and manage disks and files? What kind of interface does the operating system use? Explain why you think each of the features of your ideal operating system is important.

3

You are the CEO of Computers and Advanced Technology (CAT), a company that specializes in the manufacture of laptop computers (company slogan: "Life is better with a CAT on your lap"). Your research department has just developed a new operating system, the features of which promise to make most other operating systems seem antiquated. Although the operating system was designed specifically to work with CAT laptop computers, your programmers assure you that it can be adapted to work with other personal computers. As CEO, you now have a decision to make. Should the new operating system remain proprietary, possibly enhancing the sale of CAT computers, or should you instruct your programmers to make it portable, thus making it marketable to a wider spectrum of users? Explain your decision.

4

You have been hired as a consultant by a small, family-run printing business that wants to purchase its first personal computers. The company intends to buy twelve PCs and does not plan to obtain any more computers for about five years. Your job is to make a recommendation regarding the type of personal computers the company should purchase and the operating system (DOS, Windows, Windows NT, Macintosh, OS/2, UNIX, or NextStep) it should buy to work with the computers. Write a report to the company giving your recommendations and explaining the reasons behind them.

5

Some of the tasks described in this chapter that are addressed by utility programs include file management, disk management, memory management, backup and restore, data recovery, data compression, virus protection, and screen saver. If you could afford to purchase only four of these utility programs for your personal computer, which would you buy? Why? If you were purchasing utility programs for an entire company, which four do you think are most important? Why? If the utility programs you would buy for your personal computer are not the same as the utility programs you think are most important for a company, briefly explain why the lists are different.

6

The latest in utility programs are intelligent utilities. These utility programs can be customized to fit your needs and will perform a task until you tell it to stop. For example, intelligent utilities can be programmed to turn on your computer at a certain time, automatically backup files you've changed, examine the latest stock prices and advise you when to buy or sell, or even check your calendar and remind you to buy a birthday or anniversary gift for your spouse! If you had an intelligent utility, what types of tasks would you program it to do? What tasks could you program it to do in your chosen career field? As intelligent utilities continue to develop, what effect do you think they will have on an individual's personal and professional life in the future?

File   Edit   Section   Page   Tools   Options   Help

Out and About

1. Using current computer magazines and business publications, research the ways in which one of the operating systems described in this chapter is being used today. What kinds of businesses are using the operating system? Why? How much is the operating system being used by individuals on personal computers? What are the advantages of the operating system? What are the disadvantages? What are the system requirements and price of the operating system? From your research, what do you think is the future of the operating system?

2. Find out the operating system that is used on your, or a friend's, personal computer. What company manufactures the operating system? What type of interface does the operating system use? Does the operating system support multitasking? Refer to the documentation that accompanied the computer or operating system to determine the operating system's version and release number, and the year it was produced. Try to find out when the first version of the operating system was introduced, when the next version is expected, and how much the company charges for upgrades.

3. Locate a department in your school or a local company that uses a mainframe computer. Interview an administrator in charge of the mainframe about the computer's operating system. What operating system is used? How was the operating system chosen? What are the advantages of the operating system? What are the disadvantages? Have there ever been any problems with the operating system? Has the operating system been changed to meet specific needs of the department or company? If so, how? Does the administrator anticipate using the same operating system five years from now? Why or why not?

4. Bill Gates, the founder of Microsoft Corporation, is a modern legend. Gates is one of the wealthiest men in America, and Microsoft is one of the most influential companies in the computer industry. The fascinating story of Bill Gates and Microsoft is told in several books, including: *Hard Drive: Bill Gates and the Making of the Microsoft Empire* (by James Wallace), *Gates* (by Stephen Manes), and *Accidental Empires: How the Boys of Silicon Valley Make Their Millions, Battle Foreign Competition, and Still Can't Get a Date* (by Robert X. Cringely). Read one of these books, or another book on Gates and Microsoft, and write a report on the qualities you think led to the success of Bill Gates and Microsoft.

Start   8:04 AM

File   Edit   Section   Page   Tools   Options   Help

Out and About
(continued)

5. Application programs are designed to be used with specific operating systems. When you purchase software, it is important to read the program's packaging to determine if it is compatible with the operating system on your personal computer. Operating systems undergo frequent revisions, each of which is designated by a version number. A higher version number means a more recent revision (DOS 6.0 is a newer version than DOS 5.0). Usually, operating systems are downwardly compatible, meaning that an application program written for an earlier version of an operating system will work with a later version of the same operating system. Often, however, an application program written for a later version of an operating system will not work correctly with an earlier version. Visit a computer software vendor and find four application programs in which you are interested that require the DOS operating system. Which of the programs could you run on your personal computer if you had DOS 3.3? DOS 5.0? DOS 6.0?

6. Many utility programs are available for users of personal computers. Visit a computer store, or read a computer magazine, and choose two utility programs in which you are interested. Write a review of the two programs. What is the function of each? What are the system requirements? How easy is the program to use? How much does the program cost? In your opinion, is the utility worth the price? Why or why not? If you could buy only one of the utility programs, which would you purchase? Why?

Windows 95

Start   8:04 AM

File   Edit   Section   Page   Tools   Options   Help

In the Lab with Windows 95

1 Shelly Cashman Series System Software Lab   Follow the instructions in Windows 95 Lab 1 on page 1.30 to display the Shelly Cashman Series Labs screen. Click Evaluating Operating Systems. Click the Start Lab button. When the initial screen displays, carefully read the objectives. With your printer turned on, click the Print Questions button. Fill out the top of the Questions sheet and answer the questions as you step through the System Software Lab. Close the Shelly Cashman Series Labs.

2 Shelly Cashman Series Ergonomics Lab   Follow the instructions in Windows 95 Lab 1 on page 1.30 to display the Shelly Cashman Series Labs screen. Click Working at Your Computer. Click the Start Lab button. When the initial screen displays, carefully read the objectives. With your printer turned on, click the Print Questions button. Fill out the top of the Questions sheet and answer the questions as you step through the Ergonomics Lab. Close the Shelly Cashman Series Labs.

3 Displaying Your System Configuration   Click the Start button on the taskbar, point to Settings on the Start menu, and then click Control Panel on the Settings submenu. Double-click the System icon in the Control Panel window. When the System Properties dialog box displays, click the Device Manager tab *(Figure 8-19)*. One at time, double-click CDROM, Keyboard, Modem, Monitor, and Mouse in the list. Write down, in order, the types of devices on your system. Close the System Properties dialog box. Close Control Panel.

4 Performing Calculations   Click the Start button on the taskbar, point to Programs on the Start menu, point to Accessories on the Programs submenu, and then click Calculator on the Accessories submenu. Click View on the menu bar and then click Standard to display the standard calculator. If it is not already activated, press NUM LOCK. Enter 23.65+98.4 and then press ENTER. The result displays in the Calculator window *(Figure 8-20)*. Press ESC to clear the calculation. Type 4624 and then click the sqrt button. Write down the result. Press ESC. Write down the results of each of these calculations: (1) 2489 divided by 8; (2) 54 multiplied by 78; and (3) 65 minus 423.5. Close Calculator.

5 Switching Between Open Applications   Click the Start button on the taskbar and then click Help on the Start menu. Click the Find tab, press TAB, type switching between running programs and then press ENTER. Read and print the topic. Follow the instructions in Windows 95 Lab 1 on page 2.36 to start WordPad. Follow the instructions in Windows 95 Lab 3 on page 3.30 to start Paint. How many program buttons are on the taskbar? Which one is recessed? Click the Document - WordPad button on the taskbar. What happens? Click the untitled - Paint button on the taskbar. What happens? Click the Windows Help button on the taskbar. What happens? Right-click the Help window and then point to Keep Help on Top on the shortcut menu. Is your default to keep the Help window on top of open applications or not? Close Help. Close Paint. Close WordPad.

Figure 8-19

Figure 8-20

8:05 AM

Where on the Web

1 **Operating Systems**   System software can be classified into three major categories: operating systems, utilities, and language translators. Complete the following steps to use the Yahoo Directory to learn more about operating systems. With Netscape on the screen, click the Net Search button. Click Yahoo. Scroll down and click Computers. Scroll down and click Operating Systems. Scroll down and click one of the operating systems. Scroll down and click a topic that sounds interesting. Scroll down and read the page. Click Print on the File menu. Click Pages and then type 1 in the To text box. Click OK. Write a brief description of what you found on the printout and hand it in.

2 **CBS Eye Screensaver**   The After Dark screen saver utility program prevents an image from being permanently etched on a monitor screen by displaying entertaining images that move across the screen. Complete the following steps to download an After Dark compatible screen saver of the CBS Eye. With Netscape on the screen, type `http://www.cbs.com/scrnsvr` in the Location text box and press ENTER. Scroll down and click the type of system you have. Click Print on the File menu. Click OK. Click Download. Click the Save To Disk button in the Unknown File Type dialog box. Specify an appropriate destination in the Save As dialog box and then click OK. Hand in the printout.

3 **The Power of Objects**   NextStep is the only operating system designed to support object-oriented computing. Complete the following steps to learn about NeXT's efforts to "Bring the power of objects to the Web." With Netscape on the screen, type `http://next.com` in the Location text box and press ENTER. Scroll down and click WebObjects. Scroll down and read the page. What is WebObjects? Click Print on the File menu. Click OK. Write your answer on the printout and hand it in.

4 **Virus Protection**   Utility programs include virus-protection programs that use a number of methods to prevent virus programs from being loaded on a computer. Complete the following steps to learn more about virus protection from the McAfee Web site. With Netscape on the screen, type `http://www.mcafee.com` in the Location text box and press ENTER. Scroll down the page and click VIRUS INFO LIBRARY. Scroll down and click one of the topics. Scroll down and read about the topic. Click Print on the File menu. Click Pages and then type 1 in the To text box. Click OK. Hand in the printout.

5 **Shelly Cashman Online**   Click Using Computers: A Gateway To Information, World Wide Web Edition on the Shelly Cashman Student Center Web page (`http://www.bf.com/scstudnt.html`). Scroll down and click Chapter 8. Complete the activities listed.

Figure 8-21

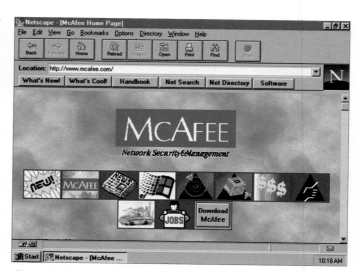

Figure 8-22

How to Purchase, Install, and Maintain a Personal Computer

*A*t some point in time, perhaps during this course, you may decide to buy a computer system. It could be your first system or a replacement system. The decision is an important one and will require an investment of both time and money. The following guidelines are presented to help you purchase, install, and maintain your system. The guidelines assume you are purchasing a desktop personal computer, often referred to as a PC. It is further assumed that the computer will be used for home or small business use. Because it is the most widely purchased type of system, some of the guidelines assume an IBM-compatible computer is being purchased. Most of the guidelines however, may be applied to the purchase of any personal computer, including a Macintosh or other non-DOS or non-Windows system. The type of system you purchase should be determined by your software requirements and the need to be compatible with other systems with which you work. Many of the guidelines can also be applied to purchasing a portable computer such as a laptop. A laptop computer may be an appropriate choice if you need computing capability when you travel. Keep in mind, though, that many laptop computer users also have larger capacity desktop systems at home and/or at work. The laptop systems are commonly used for applications such as word processing and electronic mail that the user needs when he or she is traveling.

How to Purchase a Computer System

1 **Determine what applications you will use on your computer.** This decision will guide you as to the type and size of computer. Artists and others who work with graphics will need a larger, better quality monitor and additional disk space.

2 **Choose your software first.** Some packages only run on Macintosh computers, others only on a PC. Certain packages only run under the Windows operating system. In addition, some software requires more memory and disk space than other packages. Most users will want at least word processing and spreadsheet packages. For the most software for the money, consider purchasing an integrated package or a software suite that offers reduced pricing on several applications purchased at the same time. Be sure the software contains the features that are necessary for the work you will be performing.

3 **Be aware of *hidden costs*.** Realize there will be additional costs associated with buying a computer. Such costs may include the following: an additional phone line or outlet to use a modem; computer furniture; consumable supplies such as diskettes and paper; diskette holders; reference manuals on specific software packages; and special training classes you may want to take. Depending on where you buy your computer, the seller may be willing to include some or all of these in the system purchase price.

4 **Buy equipment that meets the *Energy Star* power consumption guidelines.** These guidelines require that computer systems, monitors, and printers reduce electrical consumption if they have not been used for some period of time, usually several minutes. Equipment meeting the guidelines can display the *Energy Star* logo.

5 **Consider buying from local computer dealers, retail stores, or direct mail companies.** Each has certain advantages. The local dealer or retail store can more easily provide hands-on support, if necessary. With a mail-order company, you are usually limited to speaking to someone over the phone. Mail-order companies usually, but not always, offer the lowest prices. The important thing to do when you are shopping for a system is to make sure you are comparing identical or similar configurations. Local companies can be found in the phone book. Call first to see if they sell to individual customers; some sell only or primarily sell to businesses. Phone numbers for mail-order companies can be found in their advertisements that run in PC periodicals. Most libraries subscribe to several of the major PC magazines. If you call a mail-order firm, ask if it has a catalog that can be sent to you. If you do not buy a system right away, call for another catalog; prices and configurations change frequently.

6 **Use a spreadsheet, like the one shown in Figure 1, to compare purchase alternatives.** Use a separate sheet of paper to take notes on each vendor's system and then summarize the information on the spreadsheet.

Figure 1

A spreadsheet is an effective way to summarize and compare the prices and equipment offered by different system vendors. List your desired system in the column labeled Desired. Place descriptions on the lines and enter prices in the boxes.

SYSTEM COST COMPARISON WORKSHEET

		Desired	#1	#2	#3	#4
Base	Mfr	–				
System	Model					
	Processor	Pentium				
	Speed	100MHz				
	Power supply	150watts				
	Expansion slots	5				
	Local bus video	yes				
	Operating System	Windows				
	Price					
Memory	RAM	16MB				
	L2 Cache	256K				
	Price					
Disk	Mfr					
	Size	1.0GB				
	Price					
Video	Mfr/Model					
Graphics	Memory	2MB				
	Price					
Diskette	3.5 inch	3.5 inch				
	Combo 3.5/5.25					
Color	Mfr/Model					
Monitor	Size	15 inch				
	Dot Pitch	0.28mm				
	Price					
Sound	Mfr/Model					
Card	Price					
Speakers	Mfr/Model					
	Watts					
	Size	2 inch				
	Price					
CD-ROM	Mfr/Model					
	Speed	Quad				
	Price					
Mouse	Mfr					
	Price					
Fax	Mfr/Model					
Modem	Speed	28.8kbps				
	Price					
Printer	Mfr/Model					
	Type	ink jet				
	Speed	6ppm				
	Price					
Surge	Mfr/Model					
Protector	Price					
Tape	Mfr/Model					
Backup	Price					
UPS	Mfr/Model					
	Price					
Other	Sales Tax					
	Shipping					
	1 YR Warranty	standard				
	1 YR On-Site Svc					
	3 YR On-Site Svc					
	TOTAL					
Software	List free software					

7 Consider more than just price. Do not necessarily buy the lowest priced system. Consider intangibles such as how long the vendor has been in business, its reputation for quality, and reputation for support.

8 Do some research. Talk to friends, coworkers, and teachers. Ask what type of system and software they bought and why. Would they recommend their systems and the companies they bought from? Are they satisfied with their software? Spend some time at the library reviewing computer periodicals. Most have frequent articles that rate systems and software on cost, performance, and support issues.

9 Look for free software. Many system vendors now include free software with their systems. Some even let you choose which software you want. Free software only has value, however, if you would have purchased it if it had not come with the computer.

10 Buy a system compatible with the one you use elsewhere. If you use a personal computer at work or at some other organization, make sure the computer you buy is compatible. That way, if you need or want to, you can work on projects at home.

11 **Consider purchasing an on-site service agreement.** If you use your system for business or otherwise cannot afford to be without your computer, consider purchasing an on-site service agreement. Many of the mail-order vendors offer such support through third-party companies. Agreements usually state that a technician will be on-site within 24 hours. Some systems include on-site service for only the first year. It is usually less expensive to extend the service for two or three years when you buy the computer instead of waiting to buy the service agreement later.

12 **Use a credit card to purchase your system, if possible.** Many credit cards now have purchase-protection benefits that cover you in case of loss or damage to purchased goods. Some also extend the warranty of any products purchased with the card. Paying by credit card also gives you time to install and use the system before you have to pay for it. Finally, if you're dissatisfied with the system and cannot reach an agreement with the seller, paying by credit card gives you certain rights regarding withholding payment until the dispute is resolved. Check your credit card agreement for specific details.

13 **Avoid buying the smallest system available.** Studies show that many users become dissatisfied because they did not buy a powerful enough system. Plan on buying a system that will last you for at least three years. If you have to buy a smaller system, be sure it can be upgraded with additional memory and devices as your system requirements grow. Consider the entries in the box below as a minimum recommended system. Each of the components are discussed separately in the box to the right.

Base System Components

Pentium Processor, 100 megahertz
150 watt power supply
1.0 GB hard disk drive
16 MB of RAM
3 open expansion slots
1 open expansion bay
local bus
video card with 2 MB of RAM
1 parallel and 2 serial ports
3.5" diskette drive
15" or 17" SVGA color monitor
mouse or other pointing device
enhanced keyboard
inkjet or personal laser printer
surge protector
latest version of operating system
FCC Class B approved

Optional Components

28.8 Kbps fax modem
sound card and speakers
4X CD-ROM drive
color ink jet printer
tape backup
uninterruptable power supply

Processor:
A Pentium processor with a speed rating of 100 megahertz is needed for today's more sophisticated software, even word processing software. Buy a system that can be upgraded to the next generation processor.

Power Supply:
150 watts. If the power supply is too small, it will not be capable of supporting additional expansion cards you may want to add in the future. The power supply should be UL (Underwriters Laboratory) approved.

Hard Disk:
1 gigabyte (GB). Each new release of software requires more hard disk space. Even with disk compression programs, disk space is used up fast. Start with more disk than you ever think you will need.

Memory (RAM):
16 megabytes (MB). Like disk space, the new applications are demanding more memory. It is easier and less expensive to obtain the memory when you buy the system than if you wait until later.

Expansion Slots:
At least three open slots. Expansion slots are needed for scanners, tape drives, video capture boards, and other equipment you may want to add in the future as your needs change and the price of this equipment becomes lower.

Expansion Bay:
At least one open bay. An expansion (drive) bay will let you add another disk or diskette drive, a tape drive, or a CD-ROM drive.

Local Bus Video Card:
Local bus video cards provide faster video performance than video cards that use the slower expansion bus. Make sure the video card has at least 2 MB of memory.

Ports:
At least one parallel and two serial ports. The parallel port will be used for your printer. The serial ports can be used for additional printers, external modems, joysticks, a mouse, and some network connections.

Diskette Drives:
Most software is now distributed on 3.5-inch disks or CD-ROMs. If you need to

read the older 5.25-inch disks, consider buying a combination, which is only slightly more expensive than a single 3.5-inch diskette drive. The combination device has both 3.5-inch and 5.25-inch disk drives in a single unit.

Color Monitor:
15 or 17 inch. This is one device where it pays to spend a little more money. A 17-inch super VGA (SVGA) monitor with a dot pitch of 0.28 mm or less will display graphics better than a 15-inch model. For health reasons, make sure you pick a low- radiation model. Also, look for a monitor with an antiglare coating on the screen or consider buying an antiglare filter that mounts on the front of the screen.

Pointing Device:
Most systems include a mouse as part of the base package. Some people prefer to use a trackball.

Enhanced Keyboard:
Almost always included with the system. Check to make sure the keyboard is the *enhanced* and not the older *standard* model. The enhanced keyboard also is sometimes called the *101 keyboard* because it has 101 keys (some enhanced keyboards have even more keys). If you are concerned about possible wrist injuries, get one of the ergonomically designed keyboards.

Printer:
Ink-jet and personal laser printers produce excellent graphic output and now are only slightly more expensive than dot matrix printers, which now are used primarily for multipart form printing applications. Inexpensive color ink jet printers are also available.

Surge Protector
A voltage spike can literally destroy your system. It is low cost insurance to protect

yourself with a surge protector. Do not merely buy a fused multiple plug outlet from the local hardware store. Buy a surge protector designed for computers with a separate protected jack for your phone (modem) line.

Operating System:
Almost all new systems come with an operating system, but it is not always the most current version. Make sure the operating system is the one you want and is the latest version.

FCC Class B approved
The Federal Communications Commission (FCC) provides radio frequency emission standards that computer manufacturers must meet. If a computer does not meet the FCC standards, it could cause interference with radio and television reception. Class B standards apply to computers used in a home. Class A standards apply to a business installation.

Fax Modem:
28.8Kbps speed for both the modem and FAX. Volumes of information are available via online databases. In addition, many software vendors provide assistance and free software upgrades via bulletin boards. For the speed they provide. 28.8Kbps modems are worth the extra money. Facsimile (fax) capability costs only a few dollars more and gives you additional communication options.

Sound Card and Speakers:
Increasingly more software and support materials are incorporating sound. For the best quality sound, buy amplified speakers with their own powered amplifier and a separate subwoofer.

CD-ROM Drive:
Multimedia requires a CD-ROM drive. Also, many large software programs are now available on CD-ROM, which greatly reduces installation time. Get at least a quad speed model (transfer rate of 600 Kbps).

Tape Backup
Larger hard disks make backing up data on diskettes impractical. Internal or external tape backup systems are the most common solution. Some portable units, great if you have more than one system, are designed to connect to your printer port. The small tapes can store the equivalent of hundreds of diskettes.

Uninterruptable Power Supply (UPS):
A UPS uses batteries to start or keep your system running if the main electrical power is turned off. The length of time they provide depends on the size of the batteries and the electrical requirements of your system but is usually at least 10 minutes. The idea of a UPS is to give you enough time to save your work. Get a UPS that is rated for your size system.

Remember that the types of applications you want to use on your system will guide you as to the type and size of computer that is right for you. The ideal computer system you choose may differ from the general recommendation presented here. Determine your needs and buy the best system your budget will allow.

How to Install a Computer System

1. Read the installation manuals *before* you start to install your equipment. Many manufacturers include separate installation instructions with their equipment that contain important information. Take the time to read them.

2. Allow for adequate workspace around the computer. A work space of at least two feet by four feet is recommended.

3. Install bookshelves. Bookshelves above and/or to the side of the computer area are useful for keeping manuals and other reference materials handy.

4. Install your computer in a well-designed work area. An applied science called **ergonomics** is devoted to making the equipment people use and the surrounding work area safer and more efficient. Ergonomic studies have shown that the height of your chair, keyboard, monitor, and work surface is important and can affect your health. See *Figure 2* for specific work area guidelines.

5. Use a document holder. To minimize neck and eye strain, obtain a document holder that holds documents at the same height and distance as your computer screen.

Figure 2
More than anything else, a well-designed work area should be flexible to allow adjustment to the height and build of different individuals. Good lighting and air quality should also be considered

6. Provide adequate lighting. Use nonglare bulbs that illuminate your entire work area.

7. While working at your computer, be aware of health issues. See *Figure 3* for a list of computer user health guidelines.

8. Have a phone nearby that can be used while you are sitting at the computer. Having a phone near the computer really helps if you need to call a vendor about a hardware or software problem. Often the vendor support person can talk you through the correction while you are on the phone. To avoid data loss, however, do not place diskettes on the phone or near any other electrical or electronic equipment.

9. Obtain a computer tool set. Computer tool sets are available from computer dealers, office supply stores, and mail-order companies. These sets will have the right size screwdrivers and other tools to work on your system. Get one that comes in a zippered carrying case to keep all the tools together.

10. Save all the paperwork that comes with your system. Keep it in an accessible place with the paperwork from your other computer-related purchases. To keep different-sized documents together, consider putting them in a sealable plastic bag.

11. Record the serial numbers of all your equipment and software. Write the serial numbers on the outside of the manuals that came with the equipment as well as in a single list that contains the serial numbers of all your equipment and software.

12. Keep the shipping containers and packing materials for all your equipment. This material will come in handy if you have to return your equipment for servicing or have to move it to another location.

Figure 3
All computer users should follow the guidelines below to maintain their health.

Computer User Health Guidelines

1. Work in a well-designed work area. See Figure 2 for guidelines.
2. Alternate work activities to prevent physical and mental fatigue. If possible, change the order of your work to provide some variety.
3. Take frequent breaks. Every 15 minutes look away from the screen to give your eyes a break. At least once per hour, get out of your chair and move around. Every two hours, take at least a 15 minute break.
4. Incorporate hand, arm, and body stretching exercises into your breaks. At lunch, try to get outside and walk.
5. Make sure your computer monitor is designed to minimize electromagnetic radiation (EMR). If it is an older model, consider adding EMR reducing accessories.
6. Try to eliminate or minimize surrounding noise. Noisy environments contribute to stress and tension.
7. If you frequently have to use the phone and the computer at the same time, consider using a telephone headset. Cradling the phone between your head and shoulder can cause muscle strain.
8. Be aware of symptoms of repetitive strain injuries; soreness, pain, numbness, or weakness in neck, shoulders, arms, wrists, and hands. Do not ignore early signs; seek medical advice.

Static electricity can permanently damage the microprocessor chips on the circuit boards. Before you replace the cover, take several photographs of the computer showing the location of the circuit boards. These photos may save you from taking the cover off in the future if you or a vendor has a question about which equipment controller card is installed in which expansion slot. If you don't feel comfortable performing this step by yourself, ask a more experienced computer user to help. If you buy your system from a local dealer, have the dealer perform this step with you.

14. **Identify device connectors.** At the back of your system there are a number of connectors for the printer, the monitor, the mouse, a phone line, and so on. If they are not already identified by the manufacturer, use a marking pen to write the purpose of each connector on the back of the computer case.

15. **Complete and send in your equipment and software registration cards right away.** If you are already entered in the vendors user database, it can save you time when you call in with a support question. Being a registered user also makes you eligible for special pricing on software upgrades.

16. **Install your system in an area where the temperature and humidity can be maintained.** Try to maintain a constant temperature between 60 and 80 degrees Fahrenheit when the computer is operating. High temperatures and humidity can damage electronic components. Be careful when using space heaters; their hot, dry air has been known to cause disk problems.

17. **Keep your computer area clean.** Avoid eating and drinking around the computer. Smoking should be avoided also. Cigarette smoke can quickly cause damage to the diskette drives and diskette surfaces.

18. **Check your home or renters insurance policy.** Some policies have limits on the amount of computer equipment they cover. Other policies do not cover computer equipment at all if it is used for a business (a separate policy is required).

13. **Look at the inside of your computer.** Before you connect power to your system, remove the computer case cover and visually inspect the internal components. The user manual usually identifies what each component does. Look for any disconnected wires, loose screws or washers, or any other obvious signs of trouble. Be careful not to touch anything inside the case unless you are grounded.

How to Maintain a Computer System

1. **Start a notebook that includes information on your system.** This notebook should be a single source of information about your entire system, both hardware and software. Each time you make a change to your system, adding or removing hardware or software, or when you change system parameters, record the change. Include the following items:

- Serial numbers of all equipment and software.
- Vendor support phone numbers. These numbers are often buried in user manuals. Look up these numbers once and record all of them on a single sheet of paper at the front of your notebook.
- Date and vendor for each equipment and software purchase.
- Software log; date and version number for each piece of software installed or uninstalled.
- Trouble log; a chronological history of any equipment or software problems. This history can be helpful if the problem persists and you have to call for support.
- Notes on discussions with vendor support personnel (can be combined with trouble log). *(Figure 4.)*

2. **Periodically review disk directories and delete unneeded files.** Files have a way of building up and can quickly use up your disk space. If you think you may need a file in the future, back it up to a diskette.

3. **Any time you work inside your computer turn off the power and disconnect the equipment from the power source.** In addition, before you touch anything inside the computer, touch an unpainted metal surface such as the power supply. This will help to discharge any static electricity that could damage internal components.

4. **Reduce the need to clean the inside of your system by keeping the surrounding area dirt and dust free.** Diskette cleaners are available but should be used sparingly (some owners never use them unless they experience diskette problems). If dust builds up inside the computer it should be carefully removed with compressed air and a small vacuum. Don't touch the components with the vacuum.

5. **Back up key files and data.** Use the operating system or a utility program to create an emergency disk to help you restart your computer if it crashes. Important data files should be regularly copied to diskettes, tape, or another computer.

6. **Periodically, defragment your hard disk.** Defragmenting your hard disk reorganizes files so they are in contiguous (adjacent) clusters and makes disk operations faster. Defragmentation programs have been known to damage files so make sure your disk is backed up first.

7. **Protect your system from computer viruses.** Computer viruses are programs designed to *infect* computer systems by copying themselves into other computer files. The virus program spreads when the infected files are used by or copied to another system. Virus programs are dangerous because they are often designed to damage the files of the infected system. You can protect yourself from viruses by installing an anti-virus program.

8. **Learn to use system diagnostic programs.** If they did not come with your system, obtain a set. These programs help you identify and possibly solve problems before you call for technical assistance. Some system manufacturers now include diagnostic programs with their systems and ask that you run the programs before you call for help.

PC OWNER'S NOTEBOOK OUTLINE

1. Vendor phone numbers
   Vendor
   City/State
   Product
   Phone #

2. Serial numbers
   Product
   Manufacturer
   Serial #

3. Purchase history
   Date
   Product
   Manufacturer
   Vendor
   Cost

4. Software log
   date installed/uninstalled
   password list

5. Trouble log
   Date
   Time
   Problem
   Resolution

6. Support calls
   Date
   Time
   Company
   Contact
   Problem
   Comments

7. Vendor paperwork

Figure 4
This suggested notebook outline to organize important information about your computer should be kept on hand.

Information Management: Files and Databases

9

Objectives

After completing this chapter, you will be able to:

- Discuss data management and explain why it is needed

- Describe sequential files, indexed files, and direct files

- Explain the difference between sequential retrieval and random retrieval of records from a file

- Describe the data maintenance procedures for updating data including adding, changing and deleting

- Discuss the advantages of a database management system (DBMS)

- Describe hierarchical, network, and relational database systems

- Explain the use of query language

- Describe the responsibilities of a database administrator (DBA)

- Explain several guidelines for creating database files

- Discuss personal computer database systems

To provide maximum benefit to a company, data must be carefully managed, organized, and used. The purpose of this chapter is to explain the need for data management, how files on secondary storage are organized and maintained (kept current), and the advantages, organization, and use of databases. Learning this information will help you better understand how data and information is stored and managed on a computer.

Data Management

For data to be useful, it must be accurate and timely. **Data management** refers to procedures that are used to keep data accurate and timely and provide for the security and maintenance of data. The purpose of data management is to ensure that data required for an application will be available in the correct form and at the proper time for processing. Both data processing professionals and users share the responsibility for data management.

To illustrate the need for data management, *Figure 9-1* uses an example of a credit bureau. A summary of the application follows.

- Data entered into the database of the credit bureau is acquired from numerous sources such as banks and stores. The data includes facts such as income, history of paying debts, bankruptcies, and certain personal information.
- When the data is entered into the computer, it becomes a part of the database. The database is stored on a secondary storage device such as a hard disk.
- Customers of the credit bureau can call and request information about an individual. The credit bureau employee uses a terminal to retrieve information from the database and gives the caller a brief credit history of the person in question. The system also generates a record that causes a complete credit history to be printed that is mailed to the credit bureau customer.

Data Accuracy

For a user, such as a credit bureau customer, to have confidence in the information provided by a computer system, he or she first must be confident that the data used to create the information is accurate. **Data accuracy**, sometimes called **data integrity**, means that the source of the data is reliable and the data is correctly reported and entered. For example, if someone incorrectly reports to the credit bureau that an individual did not pay a bill and this information becomes part of the database, a customer could be denied credit unjustly. Users must be confident that the people and organizations providing data to the credit bureau provide accurate data. In addition, the data they obtain must be entered into the computer correctly. This is called reliable data entry. In the credit bureau example, if a bank reports that the balance on a credit card account is $200, but the balance is incorrectly entered as $2,000, the information passed on to a credit bureau customer would be invalid.

Credit bureau sources

Terminal

Credit data

Credit bureau database

Phone reports

Printed reports

Credit bureau customers

Figure 9-1
A credit bureau must carefully manage the data in its database because the data is what the credit bureau sells to its customers. Data management procedures must be in place to make sure the data is accurate and timely and to provide for the proper security and maintenance of the data.

Accurate data must also be timely. Timely data means-the data has not lost its usefulness because time has passed. For example, assume that five years ago a salary of $20,000 was entered for an individual. Today, that data is not timely because five years have passed and the person may be earning either less or more.

Data Security

Data management also includes managing data security. **Data security** refers to protecting data to keep it from being misused or lost. This is important because misuse or loss of data can have serious consequences. In the credit bureau example, a person's credit rating and history of financial transactions are confidential. People do not want their credit information made available to unauthorized persons. Therefore, the credit bureau must develop systems and procedures that allow only authorized personnel to access the data stored in the database. In addition, if the data in the database should be lost or destroyed, the credit bureau must have a way to recover the correct data. Therefore, data in an information system is periodically copied, or backed up. **Backup** refers to making copies of data files so if data is lost or destroyed, a timely recovery can be made and processing can continue. Backup

copies are normally kept in fireproof safes or in a separate building to ensure that a single disaster, such as a fire, will not destroy both the primary and the backup copy of the data.

Data Maintenance

Data maintenance, another aspect of data management, refers to the procedures used to keep data current. When data is maintained it is called **updating** and includes procedures for **adding** new data, such as creating a record for a new person to include in the credit bureau database; **changing** existing data, such as posting a change of address to an existing record; and **deleting** obsolete data, such as removing inactive records.

Summary of Data Management

Data management includes managing data accuracy, data security, and data maintenance *(Figure 9-2)*. If data management procedures are inadequate, the information processing system will not perform as intended and the output will have little value.

The data accumulated by organizations is stored in files. The next section discusses files and how they are organized and maintained.

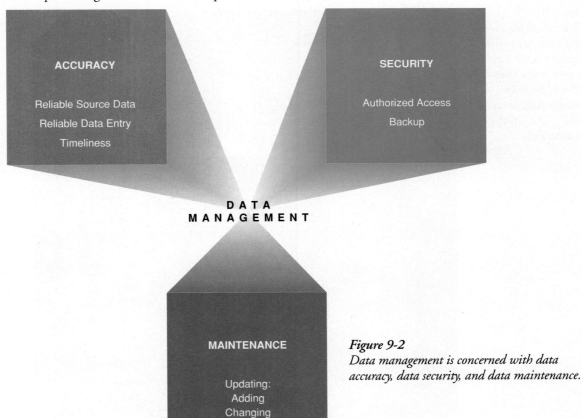

Figure 9-2
Data management is concerned with data accuracy, data security, and data maintenance.

What Is a File?

A **file** is a collection of related data or information stored under a single name. For many types of files, such as text, graphics, or sound, the data is relatively unstructured. For example, a word processing text file consists of variable-length words, sentences, and paragraphs. For database applications, however, files are made up of structured groups of related facts called **records**. The same type of facts recorded for one record are also recorded for all other records in the same file. The individual facts that make up the records are called **fields**. *Figure 9-3* shows an example of a payroll file. Individual records exist for each employee. Each record contains fields for Social Security number, employee name, and paycheck amount. Files contain data that relates to one subject. For example, a business can have separate files that contain data related to payroll, personnel, inventory, customers, vendors, and so forth. Most companies have hundreds, sometimes thousands, of files that store the data pertaining to their business. Files that are stored on secondary storage devices can be organized in several different ways, and there are advantages and disadvantages to each of these types of file organization.

Types of File Organization

Three types of file organization are used on secondary storage devices. These are sequential, indexed, and direct or relative, file organization. Files stored on tape are processed as sequential files. Files on disk are usually indexed or direct.

Sequential File Organization

Sequential file organization means that records are stored one after the other, normally in ascending or descending order, based on a value in each record called the key. The **key**, also called the key field, is a field that contains unique data, such as a Social Security number, part number, or customer number that is used to identify the records in a file *(Figure 9-4)*. The key is a different value for each record.

Records stored using sequential file organization are also retrieved sequentially. **Sequential retrieval**, also called **sequential access**, means the records in a file are retrieved one record after another in the same order as the records are stored. For example, in *Figure 9-4*, the file contains student records stored in sequence by student identification number. The data in the file is retrieved one record after another in the same sequence as it is stored in the file.

Figure 9-3
This payroll file stored on a diskette contains payroll records. Each payroll record contains a Social Security number field, a name field, and a paycheck amount field.

Sequential retrieval has a major disadvantage – because records must be retrieved one after another in the same sequence as they are stored, the only way to retrieve a record is to read all preceding records first. Therefore, in *Figure 9-4*, if the record for Joan Schwartz must be retrieved, the records for Tom Lee and Ray Ochoa must be read before retrieving the Joan Schwartz record. Because of this, sequential retrieval is not used when fast access to a particular record is required. However, sequential retrieval is appropriate when records are processed one after another. An example is a weekly payroll application where employee records are processed sequentially one after another.

A common use of sequential files is as backup files, where data from a disk is copied onto a tape or another disk so that if the original data becomes unusable, the original file can be restored from the backup file.

Indexed File Organization

A second type of file organization is called **indexed file organization**. Just as in a sequential file, records are stored in an indexed file in an ascending or descending sequence based on the value in the key field of the record.

An indexed file, however, also has an index that itself is a file. An **index** consists of a list containing the values of a key field and the corresponding disk address for each record in a file (*Figure 9-5* on the next page). In the same way that an index for a book points to the page where a particular topic is covered, the index for a file points to the place on a disk where a particular record is located. The index is updated each time a record is added to or deleted from the file. The index is retrieved from the disk and placed in main memory when the file is to be processed.

Records can be accessed in an indexed file both sequentially and randomly. As previously discussed, sequential retrieval means that the records in a file are retrieved one record after another in the same order as the records are stored. **Random access**, also called **direct access**, means the

Figure 9-4
The student records in this file are stored sequentially in ascending order using the student identification number as the key field. The records in this file will be retrieved sequentially.

Student identification number (key field)

Student name

227395TOM LEE

294671RAY OCHOA

295433JOAN SCHWARTZ

system can go directly to a record without having to read the preceding records. For example, with sequential retrieval, to read the fiftieth record in a file, records 1 through 49 would be read first. With random access, the system can go directly to the fiftieth record. To directly access a record in an indexed file, the index is searched until the key of the record to be retrieved is found. The address of the record (also stored in the index) is then used to retrieve the record directly from the file without reading any other records. An advantage of indexed files is that usually more than one index can be maintained. Each index can be used to access records in a particular order. For example, an employee file might have three separate indexes; one for employee number, a second for employee name, and a third for Social Security number. A disadvantage of indexed files is that searching an index for a record in a large file can take a long time. In addition, maintaining one or more indexes adds to the processing time whenever a record is added or deleted.

Direct File Organization

A **direct file** (sometimes called a relative or random file) uses the key value of a record to determine the location on the disk where the record is or will be stored. For example, a program could establish a file that has nine locations where records can be stored. These locations are sometimes called **buckets**. If the key in the record is a one-digit value (1-9), then the value in the key would specify the relative location within the file where the record was stored. For example, the record with key 3 would be placed in relative location, or bucket, 3, the record with key 6 would be placed in relative location 6, and so on. A bucket can also contain multiple records.

Usually, the storage of records in a file is not so simple. For instance, what if the maximum number of records to be stored in a direct file is 100 and the key for the record is a four-digit number? In this case, the key of the record could not be

Figure 9-5
The index in an indexed file contains the key field and the corresponding disk address for each record in the file. Here, the index contains the employee number, which is the key for the employee file, and the disk address for the corresponding employee record.

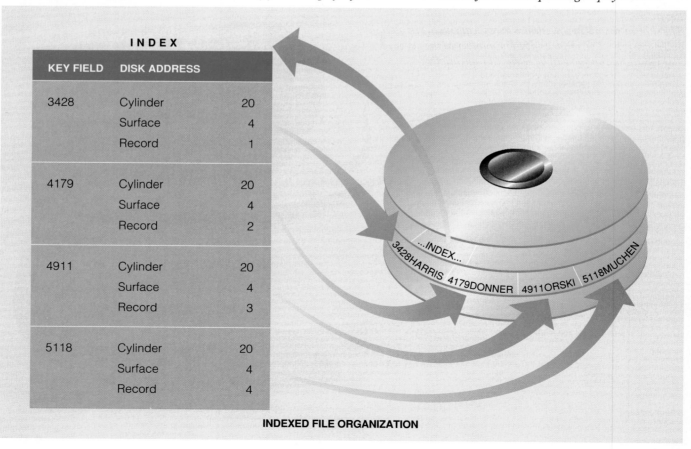

INDEXED FILE ORGANIZATION

used to specify the relative or actual location of the record because the four-digit key could result in up to 9,999 records. In cases such as these, an arithmetic formula is used to calculate the relative or actual location in the file where the record is stored. The process of using a formula and performing the calculation to determine the location of a record is called **hashing**.

One hashing method is the division/remainder method. With this method, the computer uses a prime number close to but not greater than the number of records to be stored in the file. A **prime number** is a number divisible by only itself and 1. For example, suppose you have 100 records. The number 97 is the closest prime number to 100 without being greater than 100. The key of the record is then divided by 97 and the remainder from the division operation is the relative location where the record is stored. For example, if the record key is 3428, the relative location where the record will be stored in the file is location 33 *(Figure 9-6)*.

Direct files present one problem you do not encounter with sequential or indexed files. In all three file organization methods, the key in the record must be unique so it can uniquely identify the record. For example, the employee number, when acting as the key in an employee file, must be unique. No two employees can have the same number. When a hashing technique is used to calculate a disk address, however, it is possible that two different keys could identify the same location on disk. For example, employee number 3331 generates the same relative location (33) as employee number 3428. When the locations generated from the different keys are the same, they are called **synonyms**. The occurrence of this event is called a **collision**. A method that is often used to resolve collisions is to place the record that caused the collision in the next available storage location. This location may be in the same bucket (if multiple records are stored in a bucket) or in the next bucket *(Figure 9-7)*.

Figure 9-6
When the value 3428 is divided by the prime number 97, the remainder is 33. This remainder is used as the bucket where the record with key 3428 is stored in the direct file.

Figure 9-7
Sometimes the hashing computation produces synonyms, or records that have the same relative address. In this example, both records have a relative address of 33. When the computer tries to store the second record and finds that location 33 is already full, it stores the second record at the next available location. Here, record 3331 is stored in location 34.

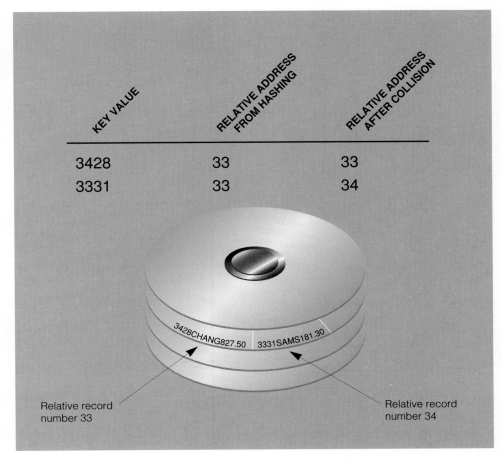

KEY VALUE	RELATIVE ADDRESS FROM HASHING	RELATIVE ADDRESS AFTER COLLISION
3428	33	33
3331	33	34

Relative record number 33

Relative record number 34

Once a record is stored in its relative location within a direct file, it can be retrieved either randomly or sequentially. The method normally used with direct files is random retrieval. A record is retrieved from a direct file by performing three steps.

1. The program obtains the key of the record to be retrieved. The value of the key, such as an employee number, is entered by the user or is read from another file.
2. The program determines the location of the record to be retrieved by performing the same hashing process as when the record was initially stored. Thus, to retrieve the record with key 3428, the key value would be divided by the prime number 97. The remainder, 33, specifies the location of the bucket where the record is stored.
3. The software directs the computer to bucket 33 to retrieve the record.

Sequential retrieval from a direct file can be accomplished by indicating that the record from the first relative location is to be retrieved, followed by the record from the second relative location, and so on. All the records in the file are retrieved based on their relative location in the file.

Summary of File Organization Concepts

Files are organized as either sequential, indexed, or direct files. Sequential file organization is used on tape and requires that the records in the file be retrieved sequentially. Indexed and direct files are stored on disk and the records are accessed either sequentially or randomly.

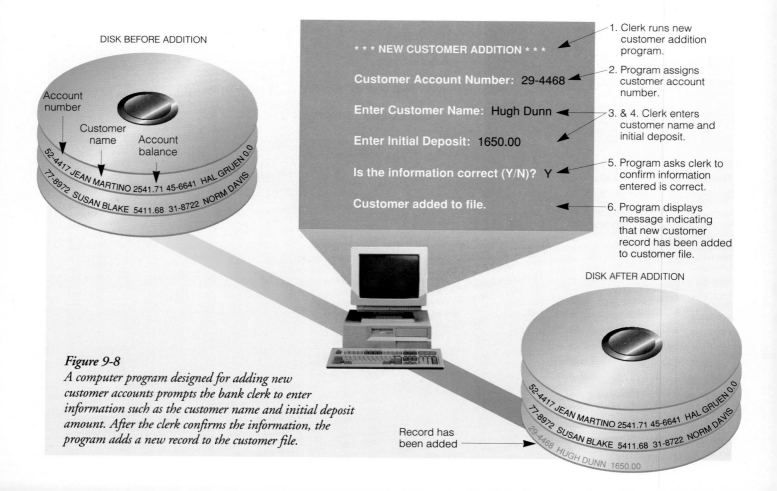

Figure 9-8
A computer program designed for adding new customer accounts prompts the bank clerk to enter information such as the customer name and initial deposit amount. After the clerk confirms the information, the program adds a new record to the customer file.

How Is Data in Files Maintained?

Data stored on secondary storage must be kept current to ensure it will produce accurate results when it is processed. To keep the data current, the records in the files must be updated. Updating records within a file means adding records to the file, changing records within the file, and deleting records from the file.

Adding Records

Records are added to a file when additional data is needed to make the file current. For example, if a customer opens a new account at a bank, a record containing the data for the new account must be added to the bank's account file. The process that would take place to add this record to the file is detailed in the steps below and shown in *Figure 9-8*.

1. The bank clerk runs a program designed for adding new customer accounts.
2. The computer program assigns a new customer number.
3. The clerk enters personal information about the customer. For purposes of this example, the only personal information entered is the customer name.

4. The clerk enters the initial deposit amount.
5. The program asks the clerk to confirm that the information entered is correct.
6. The update program writes the new customer record to the file. The location on the disk where the record is written will be determined by the program that manages the disk. In some cases, a new record will be written between other records in the file. In other cases, such as illustrated in *Figure 9-8*, the new record will be added to the end of the file.

Whenever data is stored on secondary storage for later use, the capability to add records must be present to keep the data current.

Changing Records

Changing data takes place for two primary reasons: (1) to correct data that is known to be incorrect, and (2) to update data when new data becomes available *(Figure 9-8)*.

Figure 9-9
After the customer account number is entered, the program displays the customer name and the current balance. The clerk uses this information to verify that the correct account number has been entered and that there are sufficient funds in the account to cover the requested withdrawal. After the clerk enters the withdrawal amount, the program asks the clerk if the information is correct. After the clerk confirms that the information is correct, the customer record is changed.

As an example of the first type of change, assume in *Figure 9-8* that instead of entering Hugh Dunn as the name for the customer, the bank clerk enters Hugh Done. The error is not noticed and the customer leaves the bank. When the customer receives his statement, he notices the error and contacts the bank to request that the spelling of his name be corrected. To do this, the bank clerk would enter Hugh Dunn as a change to the name field in the record. This change replaces data known to be incorrect with data known to be correct.

A bank account example can also be used to illustrate the second reason for change – to update data when new data becomes available. This type of change is made when a customer deposits or withdraws money. In *Figure 9-9* on the prevous page, Jean Martino withdraws $500. The following steps occur when the record for Jean Martino must be changed to reflect her withdrawal.

1. The bank clerk enters Jean Martino's account number, 52-4417.
2. The program displays Ms. Martino's name and account balance. This information allows the clerk to verify that the correct account number was entered and that the account contains sufficient funds to cover the withdrawal.
3. The clerk enters the withdrawal amount of $500.
4. The program asks the clerk to confirm the transaction.
5. After the transaction is confirmed, the customer record on the disk is changed. After the change, the record stored on the disk contains the new account balance.

Changing data stored on secondary storage to reflect the correct and current data is an important part of the updating process required for data.

Deleting Records

Records are deleted when they are no longer needed as data. *Figure 9-10* shows the updating procedures to delete a record for Hal Gruen, who has closed his account. The following steps occur to delete the record.

DISK BEFORE DELETION

Figure 9-10

To close an account, the clerk enters a customer account number. The program displays the customer name and account balance so the clerk can verify that the correct account number was entered and there is no money in the account. When the clerk confirms that the correct account is displayed, the program writes an asterisk in the first position of the customer account record. Other programs are designed to not process records with asterisks in the first position.

1. The bank clerk enters Hal Gruen's account number, 45-6641.
2. The program displays Hal Gruen's name and account balance.
3. The program asks the clerk to confirm that the correct account is displayed.
4. The actual processing that occurs to delete a record from a file depends on the type of file organization being used and the processing requirements of the application. Sometimes, the record is removed from the file. Other times, as in this example, the record is not removed from the file. Instead, the record is *flagged,* or marked in some manner, so it will not be processed again. In this example, an asterisk (*) is added at the beginning of the record.
5. The program displays a message indicating that the account has been closed.

Application programs for bank transactions such as deposits and withdrawals are designed to not process records that begin with an asterisk. Even though the record is still physically stored on the disk, it is effectively deleted because it will not be retrieved for processing.

Flagged records are used in applications where data should no longer be processed but must be maintained for some period of time, such as until the end of the year. Periodically, the user can run a utility program that reorganizes the current records and removes the flagged records. Deleting records that are no longer necessary reduces the size of files and makes additional disk space available for other applications.

Summary of How Data Is Maintained

Data maintenance is updating, or adding, changing, and deleting data stored on secondary storage. The maintenance of data is essential for information derived from the processing of that data to be reliable. When updating data, it does not matter if the data is stored as a single file or if it is part of a series of files organized into a database. The concept of adding, changing, and deleting data to keep it current remains the same.

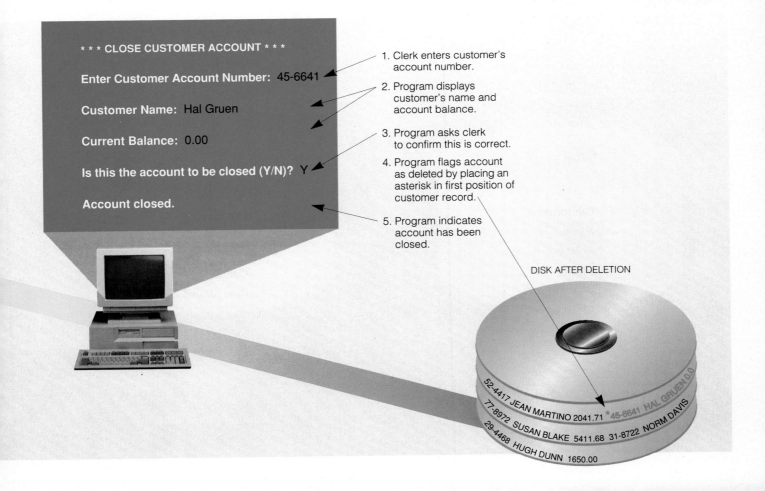

* * * CLOSE CUSTOMER ACCOUNT * * *

Enter Customer Account Number: 45-6641

Customer Name: Hal Gruen

Current Balance: 0.00

Is this the account to be closed (Y/N)? Y

Account closed.

1. Clerk enters customer's account number.

2. Program displays customer's name and account balance.

3. Program asks clerk to confirm this is correct.

4. Program flags account as deleted by placing an asterisk in first position of customer record.

5. Program indicates account has been closed.

DISK AFTER DELETION

52-4417 JEAN MARTINO 2041.71 *45-6641 HAL GRUEN 0.0

77-8972 SUSAN BLAKE 5411.68 31-8722 NORM DAVIS

29-4468 HUGH DUNN 1650.00

Databases: A Better Way to Manage and Organize Data

Most business people realize that next to the skills of their employees, data (and the information it represents) is one of a company's more valuable assets. They recognize that the information accumulated on sales trends, competitors' products and services, employee skills, and production processes is a valuable resource that would be difficult, if not impossible, to replace.

Unfortunately, in many cases, this resource is located in different files in different departments throughout the organization, often known only to the individuals who work with their specific portion of the total information. In these cases, the potential value of the information goes unrealized because it is not known to people in other departments who may need it or because it cannot be accessed efficiently. In an attempt to organize their information resources and provide for timely and efficient access, many companies have implemented databases.

What Is a Database?

This chapter has previously presented how data elements (characters, fields, and records) can be organized in files. In file-oriented systems, a **flat file** is independent and contains all the information necessary to process the records in that file. Although technically a flat file can be considered a database because it is a collection of data, the term **database** usually means multiple related files. Because these files are related, users can access data in multiple files at one time. A **database management system** (DBMS) is the software that allows the user to create, maintain, and report the data and file relationships. By contrast, a **file management system**, sometimes called a flat-file management system, is software that allows the user to create, maintain, and access one file at a time.

Figure 9-11
In a file-oriented system, each file contains the customer name and address. In the database system, only the customer file contains the name and address. Other files, such as the catalog file, use the customer number to retrieve the customer name and address when it is needed for processing.

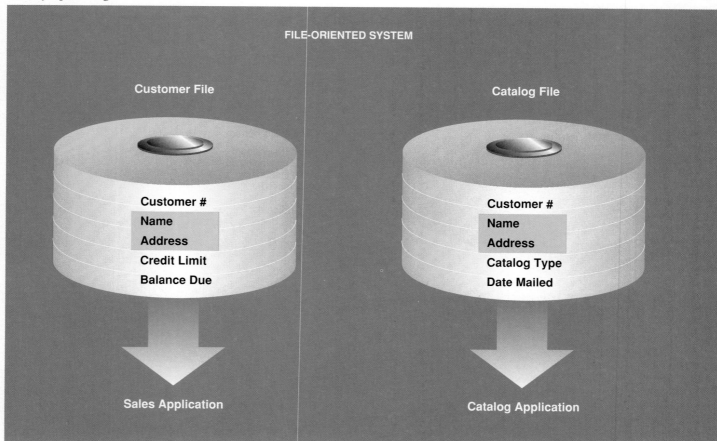

Why Use a Database?

The following example *(Figure 9-11)* illustrates some of the advantages of a database system as compared to a file-oriented system. Assume that a business periodically mails catalogs to its customers. If the business is using a file-oriented system, it would probably have a file used for the catalog mailing application that contains information about the catalog plus customer information such as customer account number, name, and address. Files that are used in a file-oriented system are independent of one another. Therefore, other applications, such as the sales application, which also need customer information would each have files that contain the same customer information that is stored in the catalog mailing file. Thus, in a file-oriented system, the customer data would be duplicated several times in different files. This duplication of data wastes secondary storage space. In addition, it makes maintaining the data difficult because when a customer record must be updated, all files containing that data must be individually updated.

In a database system, however, only one of the applications would have a file containing the customer name and address data. That is because in a database system, files are integrated; that is, related files are linked together by the database management system either through predefined

relationships or through common data fields. In this example, the link could be the customer account number. If the sales file contained the customer account number, name, and address, the catalog mailing file would only need to contain the customer's account number plus the other catalog information. When the catalog application program is executed, the customer's name and address would be obtained from the sales file. The advantage of the database is that because the files are integrated, the customer name and address would only be stored once. This saves secondary storage space. It also allows data to be maintained more easily because update information need only be entered once.

As the previous example illustrates, a database system offers a number of advantages over a file-oriented system. These advantages and several others are summarized as follows:

- **Reduced data redundancy**   Redundant, or duplicate, data is greatly reduced in a database system. Frequently used data elements such as names, addresses, and descriptions are stored in one location. Having such items in one instead of many locations lowers the cost of maintaining the data.
- **Improved data integrity**   Closely related to reduced data redundancy is the database advantage of improved data integrity. Because data is only stored in one place, it is more

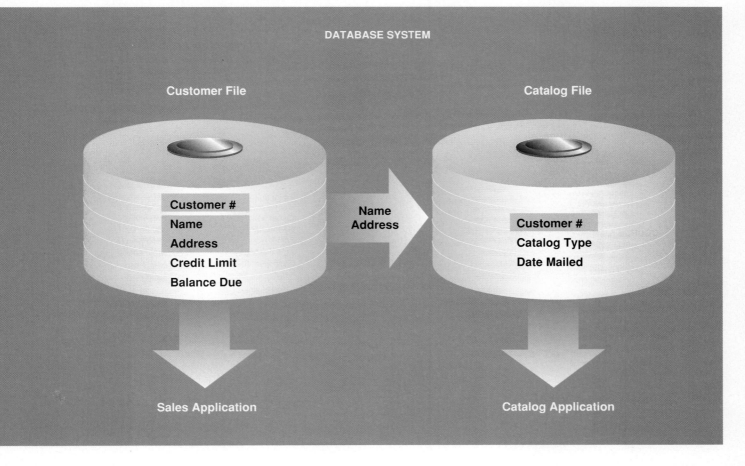

likely to be accurate. When it is updated, all applications that use the data will be using the most current version.

- **Easier reporting**   The capability to extract data from multiple files at one time makes it easier to produce meaningful inquiries and reports.
- **Improved data security**   Most database management systems allow the user to establish different levels of security over information in the database. For example, a department manager may have *read only* privileges on certain payroll data, which means the manager could inquire about the data but not change it. The payroll supervisor would have *full update* privileges, meaning the supervisor not only could inquire about the data but also could make changes. A nonmanagement employee would probably have no access privileges to the payroll data and could neither inquire about nor change the data.
- **Reduced development time**   Because data is better organized in a database, development of programs that use this data is more efficient and takes less time. The need to create new files is reduced. Instead, new attributes are added to existing files.

The following section discusses the ways databases can be organized.

Types of Database Organization

The four types of database organization are: hierarchical, network, relational, and object-oriented.

Hierarchical Database

In a **hierarchical database** *(Figure 9-12)*, data is organized in a series like a family tree or organization chart (the term hierarchy means an organized series). Like a family tree, the hierarchical database has branches made up of parent and child records. Each **parent record** can have multiple child records. However, each **child record** can have only one parent. The parent record at the top of the database is referred to as the **root record**.

Hierarchical databases are the oldest form of database organization and reflect the fact that they were developed when the disk and memory capacity of computers was limited and most processing was done in batches of transactions. Data access is sequential in the sense that an inquiry begins at the root record and proceeds down the branch until the requested data is found. All parent-child relationships are

HIERARCHICAL DATABASE

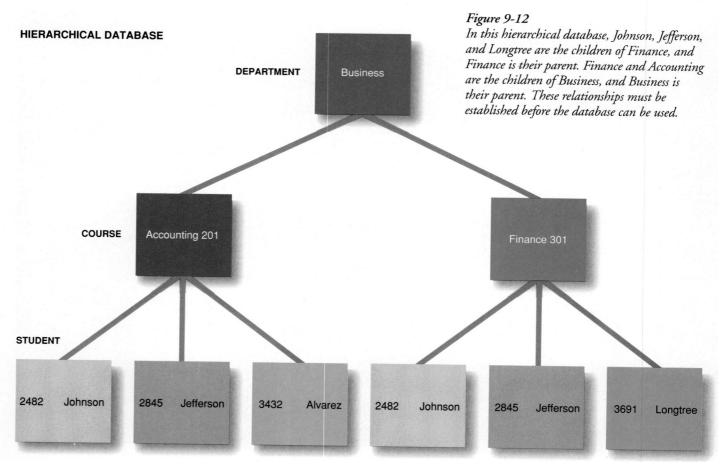

Figure 9-12
In this hierarchical database, Johnson, Jefferson, and Longtree are the children of Finance, and Finance is their parent. Finance and Accounting are the children of Business, and Business is their parent. These relationships must be established before the database can be used.

established when the database is created in a separate process that is sometimes called *generating* the database.

After the database is created, access must be made through the established relationships. This points out two disadvantages of hierarchical databases. First, records located in separate branches of the database cannot be accessed easily at the same time. Second, adding new fields to database records or modifying existing fields, such as adding the four-digit ZIP code extension, requires the redefinition of the entire database. Depending on the size of the database, this redefinition process can take a considerable amount of time. The advantage of a hierarchical database is that because the data relationships are predefined, access to and updating of data is very fast.

Network Database

A **network database** *(Figure 9-13)* is similar to a hierarchical database except that each child record can have more than one parent. In network database terminology, a child record is referred to as a **member** and a parent record is referred to as an **owner**. Unlike the hierarchical database, the network database is able to establish relationships between different branches of the data and thus offers increased access capability for the user. However, like the hierarchical database, these data relationships must be established prior to the use of the database and must be redefined if fields are added or modified.

Relational Database

The relational database structure takes advantage of large-capacity, direct-access storage devices that were not available when the hierarchical and network methods were developed. In a **relational database**, data is organized in tables that in database terminology are called **relations**. The tables are further divided into rows (called **tuples**) and fields (called **attributes**). The tables can be thought of as files and the rows as records. The range of values that an attribute can have is called a **domain**.

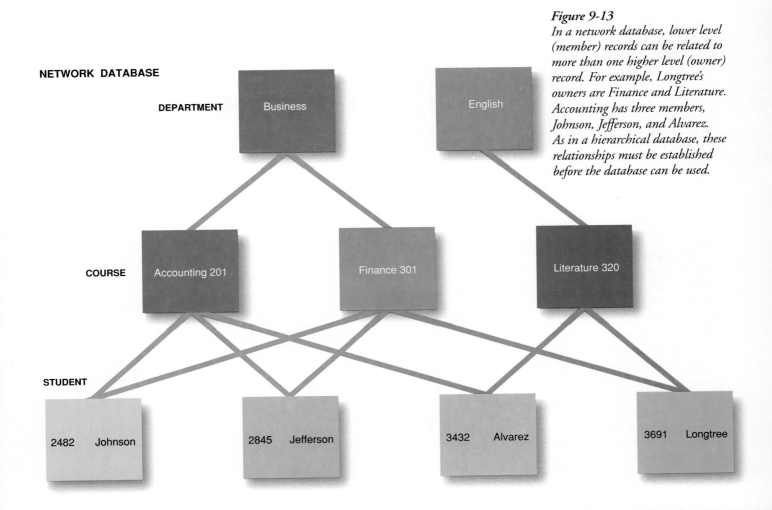

Figure 9-13
In a network database, lower level (member) records can be related to more than one higher level (owner) record. For example, Longtree's owners are Finance and Literature. Accounting has three members, Johnson, Jefferson, and Alvarez. As in a hierarchical database, these relationships must be established before the database can be used.

NETWORK DATABASE

DEPARTMENT — Business — English

COURSE — Accounting 201 — Finance 301 — Literature 320

STUDENT — 2482 Johnson — 2845 Jefferson — 3432 Alvarez — 3691 Longtree

These terms with a Student Master Table are illustrated in *Figure 9-14.*

Recall that a key advantage of a database is its capability to link multiple files together. A relational database accomplishes this by using a common field that exists in each file. For example, in a database for a college, the link between files containing student information could be the student identification number. Hierarchical and network databases can also extract data from multiple files, but in these database structures, the data relationships that will enable the multiple file combination must be defined when the database is created. The advantage of a relational database is that the data relationships do not have to be predefined. The relational database needs only a common field in both data files to make a relationship between them *(Figure 9-15)*. Because it is sometimes difficult to know ahead of time how data will be used, the flexibility provided by a relational database is an important advantage.

Another advantage of a relational database is its capability to add new fields. All that need be done is to define the fields in the appropriate table. With hierarchical and network database systems, the entire database has to be *redefined*:

existing relationships have to be reestablished to include the new fields. A disadvantage of a relational database is that its more complex software requires more powerful computers to provide acceptable performance.

Object-Oriented Database

In recent years, another type of database structure has been developed based on object-oriented technology. An **object-oriented database** keeps track of objects, entities that contain both data and the action that can be taken on the data. For example, a nonobject-oriented database employee record would contain only data about the employee; information such as employee number, name, address, department, pay rate, and so on. An object-oriented database employee record would contain the same data but would also include information on how to display or print the employee record and how to calculate the employee's pay. Object-oriented databases are also designed to contain nontext data such as photographs, graphics, and sound. Some relational databases can also contain nontext data. Object-oriented technology is discussed in more detail in Chapter 12.

RELATIONAL DATABASE STRUCTURE

Figure 9-14
This example shows the terms used with relational databases.

Figure 9-15
In a relational database, files (called tables) do not require predefined relationships as they do with hierarchical or network databases. Instead, common fields are used to link one table to another. For example, Student ID# could be used to link the Student Master Table in Figure 9-14 with the Course-Student Table (a). Department ID could be used to link the Department Table (b) with the Course-Master Table (c).

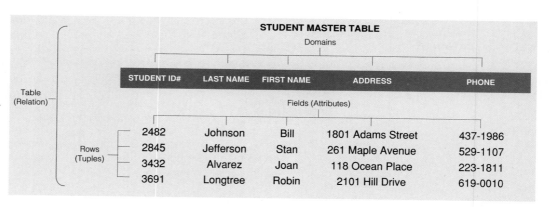

STUDENT MASTER TABLE
Domains

STUDENT ID#	LAST NAME	FIRST NAME	ADDRESS	PHONE
2482	Johnson	Bill	1801 Adams Street	437-1986
2845	Jefferson	Stan	261 Maple Avenue	529-1107
3432	Alvarez	Joan	118 Ocean Place	223-1811
3691	Longtree	Robin	2101 Hill Drive	619-0010

Table (Relation) — Fields (Attributes) — Rows (Tuples)

a COURSE-STUDENT TABLE

COURSE	STUDENT ID#
ACC201	2482
ACC201	2845
ACC201	3432
FIN301	2492
FIN301	2845
FIN301	3691
LIT320	3691

b DEPARTMENT TABLE

DEPARTMENT ID	DEPARTMENT NAME
BUS	Business
ENG	English

Database Management Systems

A number of common database management system features are available, including the following described in *Figure 9-16*.

- **Data dictionary** The data dictionary defines each data field that will be contained in the database files. Information stored in the dictionary includes field name, field size, description, type of data (e. g., text, numeric, or date), default value, validation rules, and the relationship to other data elements.
- **Utilities** Database management system utility programs provide for a number of maintenance tasks including creating files and dictionaries, monitoring performance, copying data, and deleting unwanted records.
- **Security** Most database management systems allow the user to specify different levels of user access privileges. The privileges can be established for each user for each type of access (retrieve, update, and delete) to each data field.

Be aware that without some type of access security, the data in a database is more subject to unauthorized access than in a decentralized system of individual files.

- **Query language** The query language is one of the most valuable features of a database management system. It allows the user to retrieve information from the database based on the criteria and in the format specified.
- **Recovery** More sophisticated database management systems keep a log that records what the record looked like before and after a change is made (called the before and after *image*). This log is used to restore the database in the event of a hardware or software malfunction. Using **forward recovery**, also called **rollforward**, the log is used to automatically reenter transactions from the last time the system was backed up. Using **backward recovery**, also called **rollback**, the log is used to reverse transactions that took place during a certain period of time, such as an hour. The transactions for this period of time then have to be reentered.

Figure 9-16
A summary of common database management system features.

FEATURE	DESCRIPTION
Data Dictionary	Defines data files and fields
Utility Program	Creates files and dictionaries, monitors performance, copies data and deletes unwanted records
Security	Controls different levels of access to a database
Query Language	Allows user to specify report content and format
Recovery	Helps restore database after an equipment or software malfunction

C COURSE-MASTER TABLE

COURSE	COURSE NAME	DEPARTMENT ID	UNITS	MAX ENROLLMENT
ACC201	Advanced Accounting	BUS	4	50
FIN301	Investments	BUS	2	30
LIT320	Modern Literature	ENG	3	20

Query Languages: Access to the Database

A **query language** is a simple English-like language that allows users to specify what data they want to see on a report or screen display. Although each query language has its own grammar, syntax, and vocabulary, these languages can generally be learned in a short time by persons without a programming background.

Most database management systems include a feature called query by example. **Query by example** (QBE) helps the user construct a query by displaying a list of fields that are available in the files from which the query will be made. In addition, the user can specify selection criteria to limit the number of records displayed. *Figure 9-17* shows a query by example screen from the Microsoft Access for Windows database.

A Query Example

Figure 9-18 shows how a user might query a relational database. This example illustrates the relational operations that might be performed when a relational database inquiry is made. These three **relational operations** are select, project, and join. They allow the user to manipulate the data from one or more files to create a unique **view**, or subset, of the total data.

The **select relational operation** selects certain records (rows or tuples) based on user-supplied criteria. In the example, the user queries the database to select records from the sales order file that contain part number C-143. Selection criteria can be applied to more than one field and can include tests to determine if a field is greater than, less than, equal to, or not equal to a value specified by the user. Connectors such as AND and OR can also be used.

The **project relational operation** specifies the fields (attributes) that appear on the query output. In the example, the user wants to see the names of the customers who placed orders for part number C-143.

The **join relational operation** is used to combine two files (relations or tables). In the example, the customer number, a field contained in each file, is used to join the two files. After the query is executed, most query languages allow the user to give the query a unique name and save it for future use.

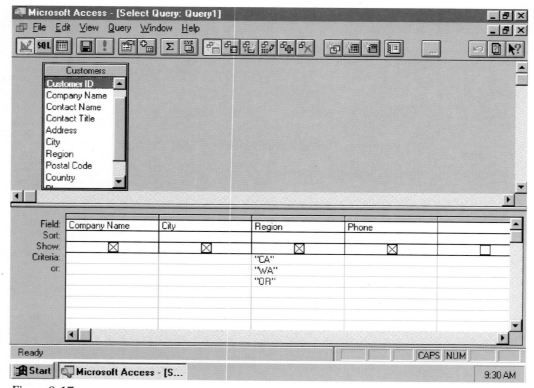

Figure 9-17
Query by example (QBE) helps a user construct a query. In this example from Microsoft Access for Windows 95, four fields have been chosen from the list of fields in the Customers file. Selection criteria under the Region field will limit the query to customers from California, Washington, or Oregon.

Structured Query Language

One of the most widely used query languages is **Structured Query Language**, often referred to as **SQL** (sometimes pronounced *sequel*). SQL received increased support as the emerging relational database management system query language when, in 1985, the American National Standards Institute formed a committee to develop industry standards for SQL. The standards were issued in 1987. Today, most database software vendors have incorporated SQL into their products. The standardization of SQL will further accelerate its implementation on a wide range of computer systems from personal computers to supercomputers. This action, coupled with the increasing dominance of relational databases, will mean that SQL will be available to many computer users. *Figure 9-19* shows an example of the SQL statements that would be used to create the response (view) shown in *Figure 9-18.*

SELECT ORDNO, CUSTNO, CUSTNAME, PARTNO, QTYORD

FROM SALESORDERS, CUSTOMERS

WHERE SALESORDERS.PARTNO = "C-143" AND

      SALESORDERS.CUSTNO = CUSTOMERS.CUSTNO

ORDER BY ORDNO

Figure 9-19 ▲
These Structured Query Language (SQL) statements will generate the response (view) shown in Figure 9-18. The statements specify that the sales order number (ORDNO), customer number (CUSTNO), part number (PARTNO), and quantity ordered (QTYORD) appear on the report. The report information will be taken from records in the SALESORDERS file where the part number is C-143 and from records in the CUSTOMERS file where the customer number matches the customer number in the records selected from the SALESORDERS file (the records with a C-143 part number). Information on the report will be listed in sales order number (ORDNO) sequence.

Figure 9-18 ▼
The three relational operations (select, project, and join) are used to produce a response to the query. The query response is referred to as a view.

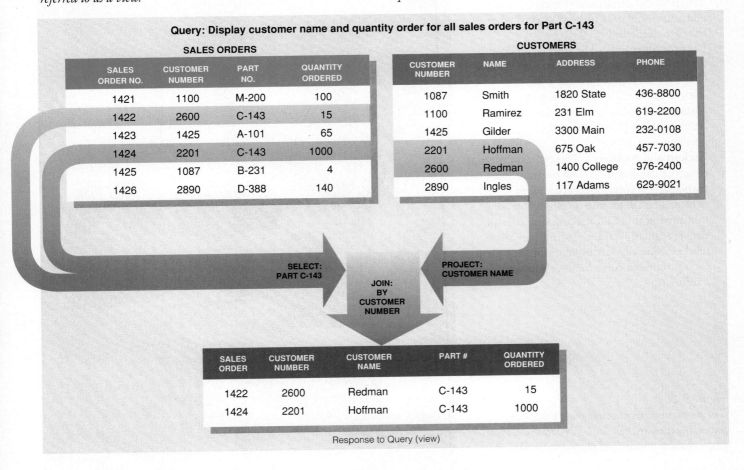

Database Administration

The centralization of an organization's data into a database requires much cooperation and coordination on the part of the database users. In file-oriented systems, if a user wanted to keep track of some data, he or she would just create another file, often duplicating some data that was already being tracked by someone else. In a database system, the user must first check to see if some or all of the data is already on file and if not, how it can be added to the system. The role of coordinating the use of the database belongs to the database administrator.

The Database Administrator

The **database administrator,** or **DBA,** is the person responsible for managing all database activities *(Figure 9-20).* In small organizations, this person usually has other responsibilities such as the overall management of the computer resources. In medium and large organizations, the role of the DBA is a full-time job for one or more people. The job of the DBA usually includes the following responsibilities:

- **Database design** The DBA determines the design of the database and specifies where to add additional data file and records when they are needed.
- **User coordination** The DBA is responsible for letting users know what data is available in the database and how the users can retrieve it. The DBA also reviews user requests for additions to the database and helps establish priorities for their implementation.
- **Backup and recovery** The centralization of data in a database makes an organization particularly vulnerable to a computer system failure. The DBA is often responsible for minimizing this risk, making sure that all data is regularly backed up and preparing (and periodically testing) contingency plans for a prolonged equipment or software malfunction.

- **System security** The DBA is responsible for establishing and monitoring system access privileges to prevent the unauthorized use of an organization's data.
- **Performance monitoring** The performance of the database, usually measured in terms of response time to a user request, can be affected by a number of factors such as file sizes and the types and frequency of inquiries during the day. Most database management systems have utility programs that enable the DBA to monitor these factors and make adjustments to provide for more efficient database use.

In addition to the DBA, the user also has a role in a database management system.

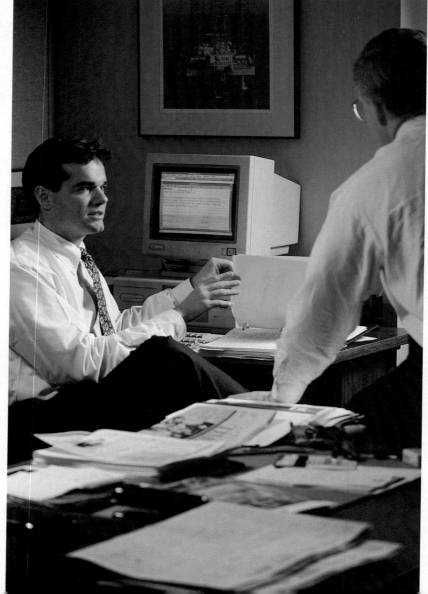

Figure 9-20
The database administrator plays a key role in managing a company's data. The DBA should possess good technical and management skills.

The Responsibility of the User in a Database Management System

One of the user's first responsibilities is to become familiar with the data in the existing database. First time database users are often amazed at the wealth of information available to help them perform their jobs more effectively.

Another responsibility of the user, in organizations of any size, is to play an active part in the specification of additions to the database. The maintenance of an organization's database is an ongoing task that must be constantly measured against the overall goals of the organization. Therefore, users must participate in designing the database that will be used to help them achieve those goals and measure their progress.

Guidelines for Designing Database Files

Carefully designed database files can make it easy for a user to query and report on database information. For relational database files a process called **normalization** is used to organize data into the most efficient and logical file relationships. For flat files, formal rules do not exist but the common sense guidelines shown in *Figure 9-21* can be applied to both relational and flat files.

Personal Computer Database Systems

A variety of software packages are available for personal computers, ranging from simple file management programs to full relational database management systems. Some of the popular database packages designed for personal computers include Microsoft Access, dBASE 5, Paradox, and FoxPro.

As with large system packages, many personal computer software vendors have developed or modified existing packages to support Structured Query Language (SQL). The advantage of SQL packages for personal computers is that they can directly query mainframe databases that support SQL.

With so many software packages available (a recent survey included 43), it is difficult to decide which one to choose. If you have simple requirements, a file management package is probably all you need. If you need the capability of a database, one of the more popular database management systems will offer you increased capability and growth potential.

Summary of File and Database Management

Understanding the data management, file, and database concepts presented in this chapter gives you a knowledge of how data is stored and managed on a computer. This information will be useful to you, whether you are a home computer user who wants to store personal data or a computer user accessing the database of a company.

DATABASE FILE GUIDELINES

Design your file on paper first.
Write down everything you want to keep track of in the database. Organize the data into logical groups. Large groups of data should probably be separate files.

Include a unique key field.
Database systems need a unique field to identify each record. If one is not specified, database systems usually assign a sequential number to each record. That may be fine for a list of personal friends, but it is not efficient for large files or files that are frequently accessed. For some data, the choice is obvious such as the Social Security number for an employee file. If a unique field has to be established, avoid creating one that has built-in *significance* such as a combination of customer's address and name (e.g., 1813WILL). Significant key fields make sense at first but eventually break down when duplicates are encountered.

Use separate fields for logically distinct items.
If an item will ever need to be referred to separately, it should be stored in a separate field. A person's name is a good example. To be thorough, you need at least six fields: Salutation (Mr., Mrs., Ms.), First Name, Middle Name or Initial, Last Name, Suffix (Jr.), and Nickname.

Do not create fields for information that can be derived from entries in other fields.
For example, in an employee file, do not include a field for age. Instead, store the employee's birth date. That way, the employee's age can always be accurately calculated.

Allow enough space for each field.
Think about the type of data that will be stored and allow sufficient but not unnecessary space. If foreign names and addresses are going to be stored, allow extra room. Numeric fields should be equal to the largest total that may be displayed or printed from the data.

Set default values for frequently entered data.
Some database programs let you set a field value for use during data entry. Unless you override it, the value is entered as part of the record. An example would be a state code in a name and address file. If most of the entries in a name and address file will be from the same state, say Oregon, a default value of OR can be assigned to the state code. The value OR will be automatically displayed during data entry. If the new entry is from Oregon, the state code does not have to be entered. If the new entry is not from Oregon, the user enters the correct two-letter state code.

Figure 9-21
Guidelines for creating database files.

COMPUTERS AT WORK

Finding Information Among the Data

Relational database software is helping many organizations find information among the millions of facts that they process each day. Once the information is found, database software keeps the information readily available for future use.

For example, Whirlpool Corporation, a manufacturer of home appliances, uses data on 15 million customers and 20 million installed appliances as a source of information for marketing, sales, product design, and customer service. Recently, database access to information on installed products allowed Whirlpool to replace a defective part on hundreds of washers *before* they broke and caused damage to customer's homes and Whirlpool's reputation. Database information on the frequency of repairs has also helped Whirlpool lower spare parts inventories.

Viewlogic, a developer of sophisticated circuit design software, is another company that is using relational database software to manage a critical customer-related operation. Viewlogic customer service representatives use database software to search for answers to questions from an average of 200 customers per day. An exact match of the reported problem and the answers on file is not necessary. Using a relevance scoring system based on key words, the search process looks for answers that are related to the problem. Whenever a new problem is encountered, its solution is added to the database.

Database applications like the ones used at Whirlpool and Viewlogic have not been used in the past because the data was unorganized or too voluminous to access efficiently. But relational database software, larger capacity hard disk drives, and faster computers have overcome these obstacles for many organizations.

Figure 9-22

IN THE FUTURE

Nontext Databases

As shown by the tremendous interest in multimedia, computers are being used for much more than traditional text processing. Database applications are moving in a similar direction. Sounds, graphics, and video are more frequently being incorporated into stand-alone documents and will soon be part of database files as well. Although not yet widely used, some database developers have already added capabilities for keeping track of nontext data. Several of the leading database packages can incorporate graphic images including photographs into the actual database files.

One of the most promising nontext database applications is geographic information systems (GIS). GIS systems take traditional data and merge it with geographic information to produce a map that graphically displays the data. The maps are used to show existing or potential customers and the location of particular types of businesses or services. Any information that can be tied to a geographic reference such as a street address, ZIP code, or county name can be converted to a graphical map display. One early use of GIS is in site selection for retail stores. Western Auto, an auto parts retailer, uses GIS software not only to help select the locations for its stores but also to determine what inventory items should be stocked. Using census and market research data, Western Auto creates a detailed demographic profile of a potential store site. The information helps them decide if the area is likely to have do-it-yourselfers who need a selection of repair parts or mechanically challenged individuals who are more likely to buy polishes and accessories.

Nontext databases will grow rapidly but probably not as stand-alone products. Instead, nontext information will just be one more option that you can process on your computer. Visual and audio data items are being incorporated now. How long will it be before taste, touch, and smell elements can be added to a database?

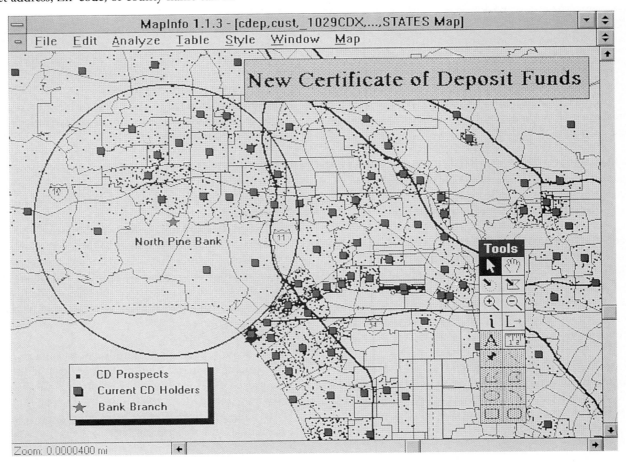

Figure 9-23

File   Edit   Section   Page   Tools   Options   Help

What You Should Know

1. **Data management** refers to procedures that are used to keep data accurate and timely and provide for the security and maintenance of data.

2. **Data accuracy**, sometimes called **data integrity**, means that the source of the data is reliable and the data is correctly reported and entered. Accurate data must also be timely.

3. **Data security** refers to protecting data to keep it from being misused or lost. **Backup** refers to making copies of data files so if data is lost or destroyed, a timely recovery can be made and processing can continue.

4. **Data maintenance**, another aspect of data management, refers to the procedures used to keep data current. When data is maintained it is called **updating** and includes procedures for **adding** new data, **changing** existing data, and **deleting** obsolete data.

5. A **file** is a collection of related data or information stored under a single name. Files are made up of structured groups of related facts called **records**. The individual facts that make up the records are called **fields**.

6. **Sequential file organization** means that records are stored one after the other, normally in ascending or descending order, based on a value in each record called the key. The **key**, also called the **key field**, is a field that contains unique data. **Sequential retrieval**, also called **sequential access**, means the records in a file are retrieved one record after another in the same order as the records are stored.

7. A second type of file organization is called **indexed file organization**. An indexed file has an index that itself is a file. An **index** consists of a list containing the value of a key field and the corresponding disk address for each record in a file. Records can be accessed both sequentially and randomly. **Random access**, also called **direct access**, means the system can go directly to a record without having to read the preceding records.

8. A **direct file** (sometimes called a relative or random file) uses the key value of a record to determine the location on the disk where the record is stored. These locations are sometimes called **buckets**. The process of using a formula and performing the calculation to determine the location of a record is called **hashing**. One hashing method is the division/remainder method, in which the computer uses a **prime number** (a number divisible by only itself and 1) to determine the relative location where the record is stored. When locations generated from different keys are the same, they are called **synonyms**. The occurrence of this event is called a **collision**.

9. Data stored on secondary storage must be kept current to ensure it will produce accurate results when processed. Records are added to a file when additional data is needed to make the file current. Changing data takes place for two primary reasons: (1) to correct data that is known to be incorrect, and (2) to update data when new data becomes available. Records are deleted when they are no longer needed as data.

10. In file-oriented systems, a **flat file** is independent and contains all the information necessary to process the records in that file. Although technically a flat file can be considered a database because it is a collection of data, the term **database** usually means multiple related files. A **database management system** (DBMS) is the software that allows the user to create, maintain, and report the data and file relationships. By contrast, a **file management system**, sometimes called a flat-file management system, is software that allows the user to create, maintain, and access one file at a time.

11. A database system offers a number of advantages over a file-oriented system including: reduced data redundancy, improved data integrity, easier reporting, improved data security, and reduced development time. The four types of database organization are hierarchical, network, relational, and object-oriented.

Windows 95

Start

12. In a **hierarchical database**, data is organized in a series like a family tree or organization chart (the term hierarchy means an organized series). Each **parent record** can have multiple child records. However, each **child record** can have only one parent. The parent record at the top of the database is referred to as the **root record**. Because data relationships are predefined, access to and updating of data is very fast.

13. A **network database** is similar to a hierarchical database except that each child record can have more than one parent. In network database terminology, a child record is referred to as a **member** and a parent record is referred to as an **owner**. The network database is able to establish relationships between different branches of data and thus offers increased access capability.

14. In a **relational database**, data is organized in tables that in database terminology are called **relations**. The tables are further divided into rows (called **tuples**) and fields (called **attributes**). The range of values that an attribute can have is called a **domain**. Data relationships do not have to be predefined.

15. An **object-oriented database** keeps track of objects, which are entities that contain both data and the action that can be taken on the data. Object-oriented databases are also designed to contain nontext data.

16. Common database management system features include: a data dictionary, utilities, security, query language, and recovery. Using **forward recovery**, also called **rollforward**, a log that records what the record looked like before and after a change is made is used to automatically reenter transactions from the last time the system was backed up. Using **backward recovery**, also called **rollback**, the log is used to reverse transactions that took place during a certain period of time.

17. A **query language** is a simple, English-like language that allows users to specify what data they want to see on a report or screen display. **Query by example** (QBE) helps the user construct a query by displaying a list of fields that are available in the file from which the query will be made.

18. Three **relational operations** that might be performed when a user queries a relational database are select, project, and join. They allow the user to create a unique **view**, or subset, of the total data. The **select relational operation** selects certain records (rows or tuples) based on user-supplied criteria. The **project relational operation** specifies the fields (attributes) that appear on the query output. The **join relational operation** is used to combine two or more files (relations or tables).

19. One of the most widely used query languages is **Structured Query Language**, often referred to as SQL (sometimes pronounced sequel).

20. The centralization of an organization's data into a database requires much cooperation and organization on the part of the database users. The **database administrator**, or **DBA**, is the person responsible for managing all database activities. The job usually includes the following responsibilities: database design, user coordination, backup and recovery, system security, and performance monitoring. The user is responsible for becoming familiar with the data in the existing database and playing an active part in the specification of additions to the database.

21. For relational database files, a process called **normalization** is used to organize data into the most efficient and logical file relationships.

22. A variety of software packages are available for personal computers, ranging from simple file management programs to full relational database management systems.

Terms to Remember

adding (9.3)
attributes (9.15)

backup (9.3)
backward recovery (9.17)
buckets (9.6)

changing (9.3)
child record (9.14)
collision (9.7)

data accuracy (9.2)
data integrity (9.2)
data maintenance (9.3)
data management (9.2)
data security (9.3)
database (9.12)
database administrator (DBA) (9.20)
database management system
   (DBMS) (9.12)
DBA (9.20)
deleting (9.3)
direct access (9.5)
direct file (9.6)
domain (9.15)

fields (9.4)
file (9.4)
file management system (9.12)
flat file (9.12)
forward recovery (9.17)

hashing (9.7)
hierarchical database (9.14)

index (9.5)
indexed file organization (9.5)

join relational operation (9.18)

key (9.4)
key field (9.4)

member (9.15)

network database (9.15)
normalization (9.21)

object-oriented database (9.16)
owner (9.15)

parent record (9.14)
prime number (9.7)
project relational operation (9.18)

query by example (QBE) (9.18)
query language (9.18)

random access (9.5)
records (9.4)
relational database (9.15)
relational operations (9.18)
relations (9.15)
rollback (9.17)
rollforward (9.17)
root record (9.14)

select relational operation (9.18)
sequential access (9.4)
sequential file organization (9.4)
sequential retrieval (9.4)
SQL (9.19)
Structured Query Language
   (SQL) (9.19)
synonyms (9.7)

tuples (9.15)

updating (9.3)

view (9.18)

File   Edit   Section   Page   Tools   Options   Help

Test Your Knowledge

Fill in the Blanks

1. _____ refers to procedures that are used to keep data accurate and timely and provide for the security and maintenance of data.

2. _____ means the records in a file are retrieved one record after another in the same order as the records are stored, while _____ means the system can go directly to a record without having to read the preceding records.

3. Updating records within a file means _____ records to the file, _____ records within the file, and _____ records from the file.

4. A(n)_____ is a simple, English like language that allows users to specify what data they want to see on a report or screen display.

5. The responsibilities of a database administrator (DBA) include: _____, _____, _____, _____, and _____.

Short Answer

1. How are sequential file organization, indexed file organization, and direct file organization different? What storage medium is used with each type of file organization?

2. What advantages does a database management system (DBMS) offer over a file-oriented system? Briefly explain each.

3. How are hierarchical database, network database, and relational database systems different? What are the advantages of each system?

4. Why is it important that database files be carefully designed? What are some guidelines for creating database files?

5. List some popular database packages designed for personal computers. What is the advantage of SQL packages for personal computers? How should you choose a database software package?

Label the Figure

Instructions: Complete the following table to show the concerns of data management.

DATA MANAGEMENT		
ACCURACY	**SECURITY**	**MAINTENANCE**
		Updating:

9:02 AM

Points to Ponder

1

Data management includes managing data security. One of the ways in which this is done is to restrict access and update privileges for different levels of data to certain groups of individuals. Consider your student file. In addition to your name, address, and grades, this file may contain information on your ethnicity, gender, family, financial status, health, extra-curricular activities, disciplinary record, and so on. Using this file as an example, list what data, if any, each of the following groups should be able to access: you, other students, faculty, administrators, and outside organizations. Which groups, if any, should have update privileges, and what data should they be able to update? Explain your answers.

2

Imagine if, instead of using a central database, your school used a file-oriented system to handle student records. Basic data (such as your name, address, and telephone number) might be kept in a central office file; financial data might be kept in the school business office file; and data concerning your grades and the credits you have earned might be kept in a file by each individual instructor or department from which you have taken a class. How would such a system affect your life as a student? What would be the disadvantages of a file-oriented system for student records? Can you think of any advantages a file-oriented system would have over a database system? If so, what?

3

Every week you probably have contact with a database. This contact may be direct, such as the query of a library database for a specific book, or indirect, such as the purchase of a scanned item whose price is determined from a database. Make a list of all your database contacts during the past two weeks, either direct or indirect. If databases did not exist, how would the two weeks have been different? Overall, do you think your life is easier or more difficult because of databases? Why?

4

Many companies now have computerized personnel databases. These databases generally contain data on employment status, salary, employment history, attendance, and job performance. They may also contain personal information (health, age, family, interests, and so on), opinion ("Mary tends to be overly aggressive"), rumors ("John seems to be romantically involved with a coworker"), and even a picture. Personnel records have always been a key factor in deciding job promotion or termination, and they have sometimes been misused. Some people feel, however, that the information in a personnel record is given additional merit when part of a computer file or printout. What information do you think should be in a personnel file? Why? What information do you think should not be included in a personnel file? Why?

5

The type of database organization employed depends on such factors as the kind of data in the database, how frequently the data needs to be updated, and how the data is used. Consider some information that you would want to store in a database on your personal computer. On the basis of the factors mentioned, what type of database organization (hierarchical, network, or relational) would you use? Why? What type of database organization would be least appropriate for your data? Why?

6

This chapter outlines some of the job responsibilities of a database administrator (DBA). Starting salaries of $50,000 for database administrators are common, and senior DBAs can earn as much as $100,000. Database administrators typically have taken courses in computer science, programming or systems analysis, and business. In addition, classes that deal with problem solving (such as mathematics, philosophy, or related subjects) are suggested. Database administrators must be aware of new technologies, able to resolve conflicts, curious and tenacious, and have a wide range of interests. Create a resume that you could use in applying for a position as database administrator. Include courses you have taken and, using your college catalog, courses you may take. Describe any work experiences in which you had responsibilities similar to those of a DBA. Give examples of situations in which you demonstrated some of the qualities required of a database administrator.

File　Edit　Section　Page　Tools　Options　Help

Out and About

1. Visit a computer store and obtain information on a file management system and a database management system. Compare the features, processing requirements, and prices of the two packages. On the basis of your comparison, which system of managing data files is more appropriate for your current needs? Why? Do you think the same system would still be best five years from now? If you were choosing a system of managing data files for a small business, would your decision be different? Why or why not?

2. Automobile dealers frequently use databases that contain information about both cars in their own inventories and cars in the inventories of other dealers who sell the same make. Salespeople use these databases to find a car that meets a customer's requirements and then, if the car is in another dealer's inventory, they "dealer trade" for the desired car. Visit an automobile dealership that uses a computerized database and ask a salesperson for a demonstration. How many dealers are represented in the database? How is the database used? What criteria can be employed when querying the database? How often is the database updated? What are the advantages and disadvantages offered by using the database?

3. In 1991, the U.S. Supreme Court decision in *Feist v. Rural Telephone* removed much of the protection corporate databases had previously enjoyed. This decision held that, despite the effort involved in creating a database, publishers did not deserve copyright protection and the facts compiled could be copied, even by competitors. Visit a library and, using law books and periodicals, find out more about the *Feist v. Rural Telephone* decision and the protection of corporate databases. Why did the court decide as it did? Can some databases, especially those dealing with proprietary data, be protected in other ways (such as with trade-secrets law or by arranging data in a creative manner)? What effect has the Supreme Court's decision had on American business?

4. Most libraries use computerized databases to keep track of their collections. A library database often contains not only titles on its own shelves, but also titles in other libraries where an individual has borrowing privileges. Visit a public or school library that uses a database. Interview the person in charge or a librarian. How often is the database updated? What are the benefits of using a database? What are the drawbacks?

Start　　　　9:04 AM

File   Edit   Section   Page   Tools   Options   Help

Out and About
(continued)

5. One of the most interesting applications of computerized databases is in the sports arena. Some database programs help individual athletes, such as the Sport Sight program that studies pitchers' motions and the Sport Technology program that analyzes golf swings. Other programs, such as one from Sports-Tech International, are used by several college and professional teams to compare game tapes and   determine how opponents tend to handle particular situations. The Indiana Pacers credit their database program in the draft selection of basketball star Kenny Williams and their defeat of Michael Jordan and the Chicago Bulls in the first six games the   teams played after starting the system. Using current computer magazines, research the relationship between computerized databases and sports. How are databases currently being used? How could they be used in the future? What impact will computerized databases have on individual and team sports?

6. Law enforcement agencies are some of the most extensive users of databases. Visit your local police department to find out about the role computerized databases play in law enforcement. Does the department maintain its own database? To what other databases does the department have access? How are databases used? Do any problems ever result from the use of databases (for example, what happens if an individual pulled over for a traffic violation has the same name as a wanted felon)? What are the advantages and disadvantages of police use of computerized databases for law-abiding citizens?

In the Lab with Windows 95

1 **Shelly Cashman Series Database Lab**   Follow the instructions in Windows 95 Lab 1 on page 1.30 to display the Shelly Cashman Series Labs screen. Click Designing a Database. Click the Start Lab button. When the initial screen displays, carefully read the objectives. With your printer turned on, click the Print Questions button. Fill out the top of the Questions sheet and answer the questions as you step through the Database Lab. Close the Shelly Cashman Series Labs.

2 **Working with Folders**   Click the Start button on the taskbar, point to Programs on the Start menu, and then click Windows Explorer on the Programs submenu. Maximize Windows Explorer. Click View on the menu bar and then click Large Icons.

Insert the floppy disk with your Windows Labs into drive A. If necessary, drag the vertical scroll box to the top of the scroll bar in the All Folders window. Click the My Computer icon in the All Folders window, double-click the 3¹/₂ Floppy [A:] icon in the Contents of 'My Computer' window, and then click the 3¹/₂ Floppy [A:] icon in the All Folders window. Click File on the menu bar, point to New, and then click Folder on the submenu. Type windows labs and then press ENTER. Double-click the 3¹/₂ Floppy [A:] icon in the All Folders window. Click View on the menu bar, point to Arrange Icons, and then click by Name *(Figure 9-24)*. Follow the same procedure to create a folder with your first name as its name. Click the windows labs folder in the All Folders window. How many files are in this folder? Right-click the folder of your first name and then click Rename on the shortcut menu. Type your last name and then press ENTER. Right-click the folder of your last name and then click Delete on the shortcut menu. When the Confirm Folder Delete dialog box displays, click the Yes button. Close Windows Explorer.

3 **Working with Files in Folders**   Open Windows Explorer as discussed in Windows Lab 2. Maximize Windows Explorer. With your Windows Labs floppy disk in drive A, click the My Computer icon in the All Folders window, double-click the 3¹/₂ Floppy [A:] icon in the Contents of 'My Computer' window, and then double-click the 3¹/₂ Floppy [A:] icon in the All Folders window.

With the 3¹/₂ Floppy [A:] icon selected in the All Folders window, click the first file in the list (windows 95 lab 2-1) in the Contents window. While holding down the CTRL key, click each of the remaining files in the Contents window (do not select the folder); and then release the CTRL key. All files to be moved are highlighted *(Figure 9-25)*. Click Edit on the menu bar and then click Cut. Double-click the windows labs folder in the Contents window. How many files are in the windows labs folder? Click Edit on the menu bar and then click Paste. How many files are in the windows labs folder now?

Click and then right-click the windows 95 lab 2-2 icon. Click Copy on the shortcut menu. Click Edit on the menu bar and then click Paste. How many files are in the windows labs folder now? Right-click the Copy of windows 95 lab 2-2 icon and then click Delete on the shortcut menu. When the Confirm File Delete dialog box displays, click Yes. Close Windows Explorer.

Figure 9-24

Figure 9-25

File Edit Section Page Tools Options Help

Where on the Web

1 **House Hunting on the Web** Several of the leading database packages can incorporate graphic images including photographs into the actual database files. Complete the following steps to see how this technology is being used in real estate applications similar to the one shown in *Figure 9-26*. With Netscape on the screen, type `http://www.infi.net/REWeb` in the Location text box and press ENTER. Click Search Listings. Click the Search button. Click one of the Area buttons. Click one of the listings. If the listing has No Photo Available, click the Back button on the Netscape toolbar and then click another listing. Click Print on the File menu. Click OK. Hand in the printout.

2 **Search for Search Engines** Search engines are software programs that allow you to search huge databases of information on the World Wide Web. Complete the following steps to learn more about these search engines. With Netscape on the screen, click the Net Search button. Scroll down and read the descriptions of some different search engines. Are they all the same? Click Print on the File menu. Click OK. Click one of the search engines. Type some text in the Search text box and submit the query. Write the search engine, what you searched for, and a brief description of what you found on the printout and hand it in.

3 **Call Toll Free** Relational database software is helping many organizations find information among the millions of facts that they process each day. Complete the following steps to become your own toll-free directory assistance operator *(Figure 9-27)*. With Netscape on the screen, type `http://www.tollfree.att.net` in the Location text box

and press ENTER. Scroll down and type `Boyd & Fraser` in the Search field text box. Click Submit. If the Security Information dialog box displays, click Continue. Click Print on the File menu. Click OK. Hand in the printout.

4 **More on SQL** One of the more widely used query languages is Structured Query Language (SQL). Complete the following steps to use a Web search engine to find more information about SQL. With Netscape on the screen, click the Net Search button. Click Infoseek Guide. Type `sql` in the text box. Click the seek now button. Click one of the matches to your query. Scroll down and read the page. Click Print on the File menu. Click Pages and then type 1 in the To text box. Click OK. Write a brief description of what you found on the printout and hand it in.

5 **Shelly Cashman Online** Click Using Computers: A Gateway To Information, World Wide Web Edition on the Shelly Cashman Student Center Web page (`http://www.bf.com/scstudnt.html`). Scroll down and click Chapter 9. Complete the activities listed.

Figure 9-26

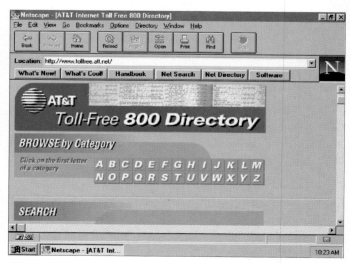

Figure 9-27

Windows 95

Start   9:06 AM

Information Systems

10

Objectives

After completing this chapter, you will be able to:

- Define the term information system and identify the six elements of an information system

- Describe why information is important to an organization

- Explain how managers use information by describing the four managerial tasks

- Discuss the different levels in an organization and how the information requirements differ for each level

- Explain the qualities of information

- Describe the different types of information systems and the trend toward integration

- Explain how personal computers are used in information systems

An **information system** is a collection of elements that provides accurate, timely, and useful information. As discussed in Chapter 1, all information systems that are implemented on a computer are comprised of the six elements: equipment, software, accurate data, trained information systems personnel, knowledgeable users, and documented procedures (Figure 10-1 on the next page). Each element contributes to a successful information system, and conversely, a weakness in any of these elements can cause an information system to fail. People who create, use, or change any type of information system should consider all six elements to ensure success.

Why Is Information Important to an Organization?

Increasingly more organizations are realizing that the information in their databases is an important asset that must be protected. Like more tangible assets such as buildings and equipment, an organization's information assets have a present and future value and have costs associated with their acquisition, maintenance, and storage. Information is no longer thought of as a by-product of doing business, but rather as a key ingredient in both short- and long-range decision making. Just as many companies have consistently utilized product strategies, some companies are now developing *information strategies* that specify the types of information they want available for decision making *(Figure 10-2)*.

Several factors have contributed to the increased need for timely and accurate information. Among these factors are expanded markets, increased competition, shorter product life cycles, and government regulation.

Expanded markets means that to be successful today, businesses must sell their products in as many markets as possible. Often this means national as well as international distribution of a product. Companies that produce a product for local or regional use are at a disadvantage against companies that produce larger volumes of products for a wider distribution. When companies expand their markets, they must have more information about a larger number of potential selling areas (markets) and the different ways of getting their products to those markets. Automobiles are an example of this trend. The number of automobile producers has decreased, and the surviving companies have moved to worldwide distribution of their products.

Increased competition means that competing companies are financially stronger and better organized. To compete successfully, it is important for an organization to have current information on how competitors are selling their products. Many companies now maintain large databases that include information on competitive product features, prices, and methods of distribution. For consumer product companies, this information often includes sales and the percent of the total market. This information is important in measuring the impact of advertising campaigns. For example, many companies will measure the impact of a new advertising campaign

Figure 10-1
The six elements of an information system.

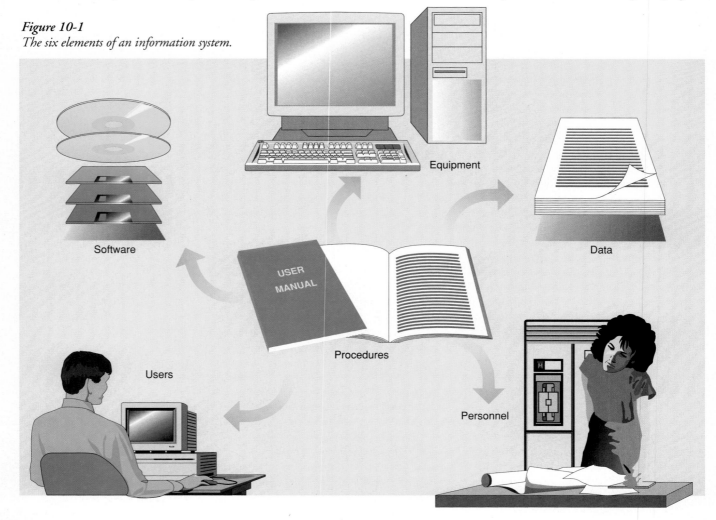

Software

Equipment

USER MANUAL

Procedures

Data

Users

Personnel

in a limited geographic area such as a large metropolitan city before they use the advertising nationwide.

Shorter product life cycles mean that companies have less time to perfect a product. More often than not, the product has to be successful when it is first introduced because companies have less time to make corrections after a product is introduced. This means that before they introduce products, they must have accurate information about what potential customers want. Shorter product life cycles have led to the increased use of test marketing. Company managers use the results of tests to decide advertising, packaging, and product features. Shorter product life cycles have also required companies to begin work earlier on next-generation products. To do this, managers must have information about existing product features that customers want changed and new features they want added.

Government regulation has also contributed to the need for more information. One good example of this is in human resource management. To comply with equal employment opportunity (EEO) guidelines and laws, organizations must keep detailed records on employee testing, hiring, and promotion practices. The employee database, once used almost exclusively for payroll purposes, has now been expanded to include valuable information on employee skill and education levels as well as the results of performance reviews. With this information, companies can document their compliance with government regulations and guidelines.

How Do Managers Use Information?

All employees in an organization need information to effectively perform their jobs, but the primary users of information are managers. **Managers** of an organization are the men and women responsible for directing the use of resources such as people, money, materials, and information so the organization can operate efficiently and prosper. Managers work toward this goal by performing the four management tasks of planning, organizing, leading, and controlling.

1. *Planning* involves establishing goals and objectives. Upper-level management plans by establishing the strategies of the organization to help meet these goals and objectives. For example, upper-level management often prepares a three- to five-year plan that includes strategies on how to enter new markets or increase existing market share. Lower-level management plans by establishing specific policies and procedures to implement the strategies. A lower-level management plan might include a specific inventory quantity to be maintained for a part.

INFORMATION STRATEGY:

1. What internal and external factors will affect the future sucess of the organization?

   Examples: interest rates, labor costs, raw material prices, government regulation, consumer trends, competive products.

2. What sources of information are available to monitor these factors?

   Examples: Newspapers, trade journals, government studies, private research.

3. How often should each of these factors be monitored? Daily, weekly, monthly, quarterly, annually?

4. What form should reports on these factors take? Written, oral, statistical, graphic, on-site visits?

5. Who should receive these reports?

Figure 10-2
Questions organizations must address when developing an information strategy.

2. *Organizing* includes identifying and bringing together the resources necessary to achieve the plans of an organization. Resources include people, money, materials (facilities, equipment, raw materials), and information. Organizing also involves establishing the management structure of an organization such as the departments and reporting relationships. For example, to introduce a new product, a company can assign responsibility to an existing department or form a new team whose sole responsibility is the new product.

3. *Leading,* sometimes referred to as *directing,* involves instructing and authorizing individuals to perform the necessary work. To lead effectively, managers must be able to communicate what needs to be done and motivate people to do the work. Leadership often takes place at daily or weekly meetings where managers meet with their employees to discuss job priorities.

4. *Controlling* involves measuring performance and, if necessary, taking corrective action. Daily production reports are a control device that give managers the information they need to make any necessary adjustments in production rate or product mix.

The four management tasks shown in *Figure 10-3* are usually performed in a sequence that becomes a recurring cycle. Actual performance is measured against a previously established plan as part of the control task; this often results in a revised plan. The revised plan may result in additional organizational and leadership activities, and so the cycle repeats itself. The four tasks are related and a change in one task usually affects one or more of the other tasks.

All managers perform these management tasks, but their area of focus, such as finance or production, and the information they need to perform the tasks is influenced by their level in the organization.

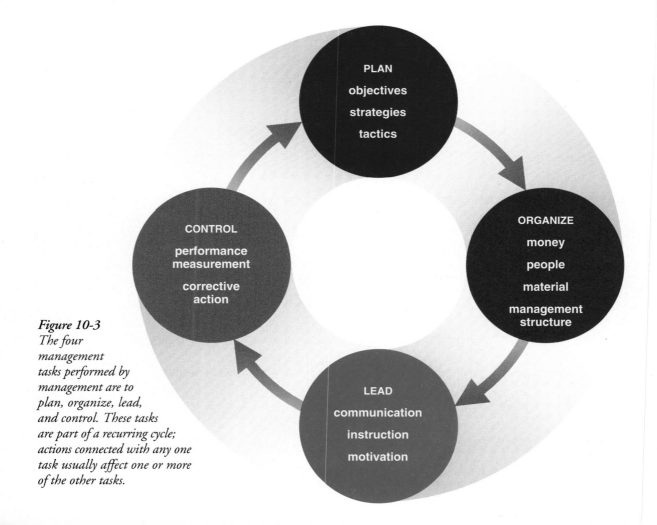

Figure 10-3
The four management tasks performed by management are to plan, organize, lead, and control. These tasks are part of a recurring cycle; actions connected with any one task usually affect one or more of the other tasks.

Management Levels in an Organization

Management is usually classified into three levels; senior management, middle management, and operational management. The names for these levels can vary. As shown in *Figure 10-4,* these three levels of management are above a fourth level of the organization consisting of the production, clerical, and nonmanagement staff. Together, these four levels make up the entire organization. The following sections discuss these levels and their different informational requirements.

Senior Management – Strategic Decisions

Senior management, also referred to as executive or top management, includes the highest management positions in an organization. Senior management is concerned with the long-range direction of the organization. Senior managers are primarily responsible for **strategic decisions** that deal with the overall goals and objectives of an organization. Examples of strategic decisions are whether to add or discontinue a product line or whether to diversify into a new business. The time frame for such decisions is usually long range, starting one or more years in the future and continuing for several years or indefinitely. Senior management decisions often involve factors that cannot be directly controlled by the organization such as the changing trends of society. An example of such a trend is the increasing average age of the population. Senior management decisions often require information from outside the company such as industry statistics, consumer surveys, or broad economic indicators, such as the change in personal income or the number of new houses being built.

Senior management is also responsible for monitoring how current operations are meeting the objectives of previously made strategic decisions. For example, are sales of a new product meeting previously forecasted levels? Because senior management is concerned with all areas of an organization, it must rely on summarized information to review all operations in a timely manner. Often information on current operations is presented only if it is significantly above or below what was planned. This helps senior management to focus on only the variations that require its involvement.

Another senior management responsibility is to supervise middle management personnel.

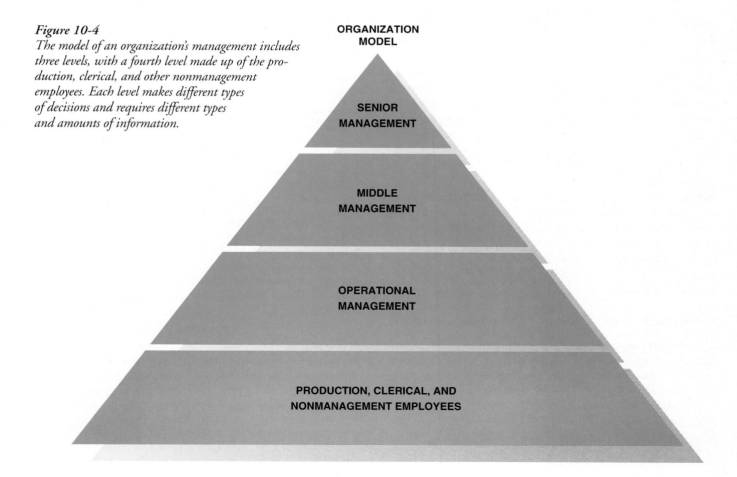

Figure 10-4
The model of an organization's management includes three levels, with a fourth level made up of the production, clerical, and other nonmanagement employees. Each level makes different types of decisions and requires different types and amounts of information.

ORGANIZATION MODEL

SENIOR MANAGEMENT

MIDDLE MANAGEMENT

OPERATIONAL MANAGEMENT

PRODUCTION, CLERICAL, AND NONMANAGEMENT EMPLOYEES

Middle Management – Tactical Decisions

Middle management is responsible for implementing the strategic decisions of senior management. To do this, middle managers make **tactical decisions** that implement specific programs and plans necessary to accomplish the stated objectives. Tactical decisions could include how to best advertise and promote a company's products. Such decisions usually involve a shorter time frame than strategic decisions but often cover an entire year. Although they are interested in external events that may influence their work, middle managers are more concerned with the internal operations of the organization and, therefore, rely on information generated by the organization. Middle management also uses summarized and exception-oriented reports although not to the extent of senior management. Middle management sometimes must review detailed information to understand performance variances.

Middle management is also responsible for supervising operational management.

Operational Management – Operational Decisions

Operational management supervises the production, clerical, and nonmanagement staff of an organization. In performing their duties, operational managers make **operational decisions** that usually involve an immediate action such as accepting or rejecting an inventory delivery or approving a purchase order. The operational decisions should be consistent with and support the tactical decisions made by middle management. The decision time frame of operational managers tasks is usually very short, such as a day, a week, or a month. Operational managers directly supervise the production and support of an organization's product or service; thus, they need detailed information telling them what was produced. Summary and exception reporting, always an important tool for senior- and middle-level managers, is increasingly being used by operational managers. There are two reasons for this change. First, upper levels of management are allowing lower levels of management to make more decisions. Second, because of computerized systems, the information necessary to make decisions at lower levels is more readily available.

Nonmanagement Employees – On-the-Job Decisions

Nonmanagement employees, which include production, clerical, and staff personnel, also need frequent information to perform their jobs. The trend toward flexible manufacturing systems has increased the need for information to be available to the production worker. Instead of working at the same task repeatedly, production workers often work as a team on related tasks. Some manufacturing plants allow a team of workers to move with the product from the beginning of production to the end. Such changes require production workers to understand more about the production process than ever before. Often, this information is made available to the workers through the use of production-floor terminals that can be used to inquire on the next production process or tool required. Some systems tell the workers which job they should work on next.

Today, clerical and nonproduction workers also have more information available to them than in the past. For example, more documentation of administrative systems is being placed online for immediate access. As previously mentioned, this is part of a trend toward giving lower level, nonmanagement employees the information they need to make decisions made formerly by managers.

Other Approaches to Management Organization

Most organizations are structured into levels as shown in *Figure 10-4* on page 10.5. Across these four levels, management and employees are usually divided into *functional* groups such as finance, manufacturing, marketing, and so on. Each functional group usually includes employees from each level; senior, middle, and operational management, and nonmanagement employees *(Figure 10-5)*. Within each level there may be several layers of management.

Sometimes a functional organization can prove to be a barrier to employee communication and getting work done efficiently. For example, before a middle manager in marketing can ask an operational manager in finance to perform a task, a finance middle manager must first approve the request. Sometimes the marketing middle manager might even have to ask his or her top management marketing person to ask his or her counter-part in finance (meaning the corresponding top management person in finance) to first approve the request and then pass the request *down the line* to the finance person who is being requested to do the work. This process is called following the *chain of command,* which means that employees only perform work approved by their immediate supervisors. As you can imagine, this formal request and approval process can significantly delay action being taken.

To improve intercompany communication, increase productivity, and decrease the amount of time it takes to respond to problems, many companies have adopted or are experimenting with management structures different from the traditional functional organization. Some of these new approaches to management and organization structure include reengineering, cross-functional organization, core competencies, organizational architecture, and horizontal organization. Although each of these approaches is slightly different, they all include the following common features:

- **Fewer levels of management.** Older established companies sometimes have as many as ten to fifteen layers of management between a nonmanagement employee and the top executive. Progressive companies are eliminating as many layers of management as possible so remaining managers can work more closely with nonmanagement employees and customers. All layers of management have been affected by this trend, but middle managers have lost the most jobs.

- **Employees are organized by process not function.** A process, such as order fulfillment or product development, typically involves several functional areas such as sales, manufacturing, engineering, and finance. Some companies are now placing all employees involved with a process into a single group dedicated to efficiently carrying out the process tasks. The person responsible for managing the process group is sometimes called the *process owner.*

- **Self-managed teams are used wherever possible.** Although they have long been used for one-time projects, teams of employees with different functional backgrounds are now being given ongoing responsibilities and being told to manage themselves. An important requirement for this approach is to give the team a well-defined purpose and measurable performance goals.

The impact of these new management methods and structures on information systems has been significant. Task and process teams often require information that was previously prepared by separate functional departments. With fewer levels of management, managers are required to rely more on exception reports to help them allocate their limited time to the most important areas. With the increasing pressure to reduce costs, information system managers have been encouraged to **downsize** operations by moving applications from mainframe and minicomputer systems to networks of personal computers. Some companies have eliminated their in-house information system departments altogether. In a process called **outsourcing**, companies hire outside firms to provide information systems support for a contracted fee.

Whatever form of organization companies adopt, they realize that they must develop an *information architecture* that matches their *organization architecture.*

With the importance of information to an organization and how it is used by various levels clearly outlined, the characteristics, or qualities, that all information should have will be explained.

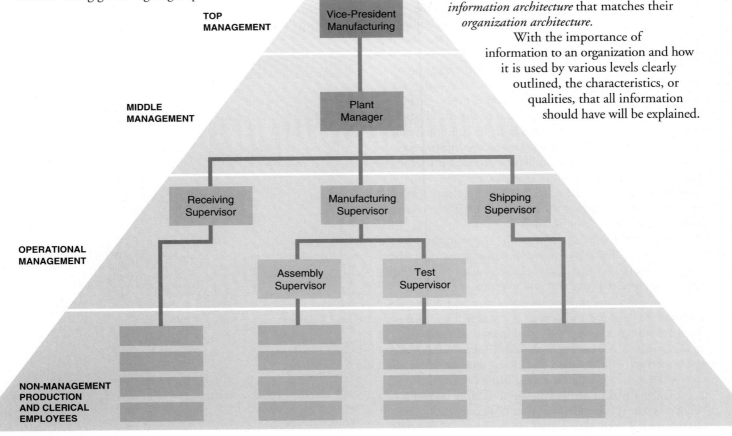

Figure 10-5
Most organizations are divided into functional groups such as finance, manufacturing, marketing, and administration. As shown in this organization chart, functional groups usually have employees at each level of the organization. Within a level, there are sometimes two or more layers of management as shown in the operational management level.

Qualities of Information

As previously mentioned, the purpose of processing data is to create information. Just as data should have certain characteristics, so too should information. These characteristics are often called the qualities of information *(Figure 10-6)*. Terms used to describe these qualities include: accurate, verifiable, timely, organized, meaningful, useful, and cost effective.

Although it may seem obvious, the first quality of information is that it should be *accurate*. Inaccurate information is often worse than no information at all. Accuracy is also a characteristic of data. Although accurate data does not guarantee accurate information, it is impossible to produce accurate information from erroneous data. Remember the term GIGO introduced earlier; it stands for *Garbage In, Garbage Out.*

Closely related to accuracy is that information be *verifiable*. This means that if necessary, the user can confirm the information. For example, before relying on the amounts in a summary report, an accountant would want to know that the totals could be supported by details of the transactions. The accountant could verify the accuracy of the report totals by testing some or all of the totals by adding up the supporting detail records and comparing the results to the report.

Another quality of information is that it must be *timely*. Although most information loses its value with time, some information, such as trends, becomes more valuable as time passes and more information is obtained. The point to remember is that the timeliness must be appropriate for any decisions that will be made based on the information. Up-to-the-minute information may be required for some decisions such as the inventory level of a key part, while older information may be satisfactory or more appropriate for other decisions such as the number of employees planning vacations in the coming month.

To be most valuable, information should be *organized* to suit users' requirements. For example, a sales manager who assigns territories on a geographic basis would need prospect lists sorted by postal code and not by prospect name.

Meaningful information indicates that the information is relevant to the person who receives it. Certain information is only meaningful to specific individuals or groups within an organization. Management should eliminate extraneous and unnecessary information and always consider the audience when it is accumulating or reporting information.

To be *useful*, information should result in an action being taken or specifically not being taken, depending on the situation. Often, this quality can be improved through exception reporting, which focuses only on the information that exceeds certain limits. An example of exception reporting is an inventory report showing items whose balance on hand is less than a predetermined minimum quantity. Instead of the manager having to look through an entire inventory report to find such items, the exception report would quickly bring these items to the attention of the managers responsible for maintaining the inventory.

Last, but not least, information must be *cost effective*. That is, the cost to produce the information must be less than the value of the information. This can sometimes be hard to determine. If the value of the information cannot be determined, perhaps the information should be produced only as managers require it, instead of on a regular basis. Many organizations periodically review the information they produce in reports to determine if the reports maintain the qualities of information just described. The cost of producing these reports can, therefore, still be justified or possibly reduced.

Although the qualities of information have been discussed in combination with computer systems, these qualities apply to all information regardless of how it is produced. Being knowledgeable of these qualities will help you evaluate the information you receive and provide every day, whether or not it is generated by a computer.

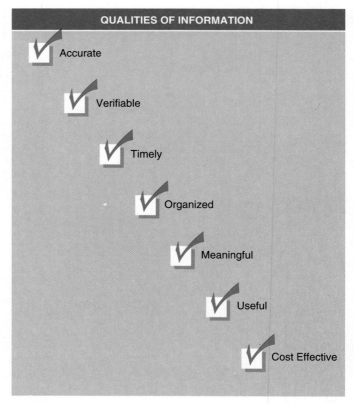

Figure 10-6
The qualities of information are characteristics that all information should have, whether or not it is produced by a computer.

Types of Information Systems

Information systems that are implemented on a computer are generally classified into four categories: (1) transaction processing systems; (2) management information systems; (3) decision support systems; and (4) expert systems.

Transaction Processing Systems

A **transaction processing system** (TPS) processes data generated by the day-to-day transactions of an organization *(Figure 10-7)*. Some examples of a TPS are billing systems, inventory control systems, accounts payable systems, and order entry systems.

When computers were first used for processing business applications, the information systems developed were primarily TPSs. Usually, the purpose was to computerize an existing manual system. This approach often resulted in faster processing, reduced clerical costs, and improved customer service. The first TPSs were usually batch processing systems. In **batch processing**, transaction data is collected and, at a later time, all transactions are processed as a *batch*. As computers became more powerful, online transaction processing systems were developed. With **online transaction processing** (OLTP), transactions are processed as they are entered. All related records are updated at the same time. Today, most TPSs use online transaction processing. However, some processing tasks, such as calculating payroll checks or printing invoices, are most efficiently performed on a batch basis.

Although the TPS was originally designed to process daily transactions, it was modified over time to provide summaries, trends, and exception data useful to management. Today, TPSs are often a part of management information systems, which are discussed in the next section.

Management Information Systems

The concept of management information systems evolved as managers realized that computer processing could be used for more than just day-to-day transaction processing and that the computer's capability to perform rapid calculations and compare data could be used to produce meaningful information for management. A **management information system** (MIS) refers to a computer-based system that generates timely and accurate information for managing an organization. Frequently, a management information system is integrated with a transaction processing system. For example, to process

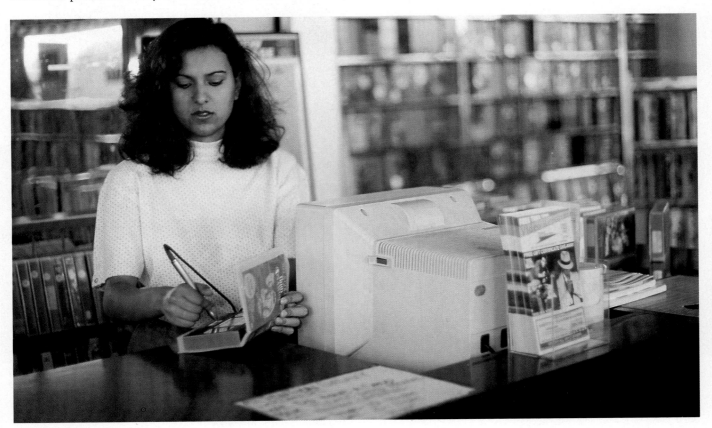

Figure 10-7
Transaction processing systems (TPSs) process the day-to-day transactions of an organization.

a sales order, the transaction processing system would record the sale, update the customer's accounts receivable balance, and make a deduction from the inventory. In the related management information system, reports would be produced that show slow- or fast-selling products, customers with past due accounts receivable balances, and inventory items that need reordering. In the management information system, the focus is on the information that management needs to do its job *(Figure 10-8)*.

A special type of management information system is the executive information system. **Executive information systems** (EIS) are management information systems that have been designed for the information needs of senior management. Company-wide management information systems usually address the information needs of all levels of management. Because senior managers may not be familiar with (or comfortable with) computer systems, the EIS features make them easier for executives to use. The EIS user interface often uses a mouse or a touch screen to help executives unfamiliar with using a keyboard. One leading system uses a remote control device similar to those used to control a television set.

Another aspect of the EIS user interface is the graphic presentation of information. The EIS relies heavily on graphic presentation of both the processing options *(Figure 10-9)* and data. Again, this is designed to make the system easier to use.

Because executives focus on strategic issues, the EIS often has access to external databases such as the Dow Jones News/Retrieval service. Such external sources of information can provide current information on interest rates, commodity prices, and other leading economic indicators.

Although they offer great promise, many EISs have not been successfully implemented and many executives have stopped using them. A common reason cited in several failed attempts is the mistake of not modifying the system to the specific needs of the individual executives who will use the system. For example, many executives prefer to have information presented in a particular sequence with the option of seeing different levels of supporting detail information such as cost data on a spreadsheet. The desired sequence and level of detail varies for each executive. It appears that an EIS must

Figure 10-8
Management information systems (MIS) focus on the summary information and exceptions that managers use to perform their jobs.

Figure 10-9
Executive information systems (EIS) often use graphics and touch screens to make the systems easier to use by executives who may not be familiar with computers.

be tailored to the executives' requirements or the executives will continue to manage with information they have obtained through previously established methods.

Decision Support Systems

Frequently, management needs information that is not routinely provided by transaction processing systems and management information systems. For example, a vice president of finance may want to know the net effect on company profits if interest rates on borrowed money increase and raw material prices decrease. Transaction processing systems and management information systems do not usually provide this type of information. Decision support systems have been developed to provide this information.

A **decision support system** (DSS) is a system designed to help someone reach a decision by summarizing or comparing data from either or both internal and external sources. Internal sources include data from an organization's database such as sales, manufacturing, or financial data. Data from external sources could include information on interest rates,

population trends, new housing construction, or raw material pricing. Frito Lay, for example, collects and reports sales data on its own and competitors' products every day *(Figure 10-10)*. The information is part of a decision support system that allows Frito Lay to analyze important trends in days or weeks instead of the months that it used to take.

Decision support systems often include query languages, statistical analysis capabilities, spreadsheets, and graphics to help the user evaluate the decision data. More advanced decision support systems also include capabilities that allow users to create a model of the variables affecting a decision. With a **model**, users can ask *what-if* questions by changing one or more of the variables and seeing what the projected results would be. A simple model for determining the best product price would include factors for the expected sales volume at each price level. Many people use electronic spreadsheets for simple modeling tasks. A decision support system is sometimes combined with executive information systems (EIS).

Figure 10-10
Frito Lay, a major producer of snack foods, has developed a decision support system that uses sales information collected daily on hand-held terminals by more than 10,000 sales-people. The system helps Frito Lay spot sales trends in days or weeks instead of the months it used to take.

Generally speaking, a decision support system is more analytical and is designed to work on unstructured problems that do not have a predefined number of variables. For example, a problem involving how to finance a company's growth would involve estimates of sales, income, depreciation, interest rates, and other variables that would best be handled by a decision support system. An executive information system is primarily oriented toward collecting and presenting meaningful information from a variety of sources.

Figure 10-11
Nexpert Object is a powerful expert system that provides a highly visual presentation of its data, rules, and conclusions.

Expert Systems

Expert systems, sometimes called **knowledge systems**, combine the knowledge on a given subject of one or more human experts into a computerized system that simulates the human experts' reasoning and decision-making processes (Figure 10-11). Thus, the computer also becomes an *expert* on the subject.

Expert systems are made up of the combined subject knowledge of the human experts, called the **knowledge base**, and the **inference rules** that determine how the knowledge is used to reach decisions. Although they may appear to *think*, the current expert systems actually operate within narrow preprogrammed limits and cannot make decisions based on common sense or on information outside their knowledge base. An example of how a simple expert system uses rules to identify an animal is shown in *Figure 10-12*.

A more practical application of an expert system has been implemented by Ford Motor Company to help its

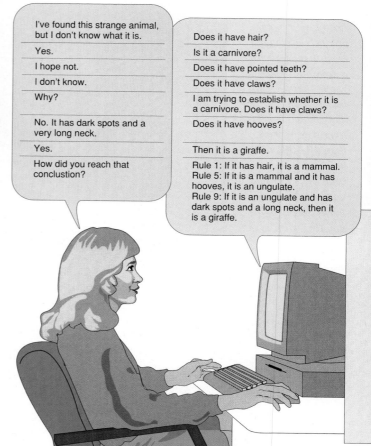

dealers diagnose engine repair problems. Previously, when they encountered an engine problem they could not solve, dealers would call Dearborn, Michigan to talk with a Ford engine expert. Now dealers can access a nationwide computer system that Ford has developed to duplicate the reasoning that Kujawski uses when trouble-shooting a problem (*Figure 10-13* on the next page).

Although expert systems can be used at any level in an organization, to date they have been primarily used by non-management employees for job-related decisions. Expert systems have also been successfully applied to problems as diverse as diagnosing illnesses, searching for oil, and making soup. These systems are part of an exciting branch of computer science called **artificial intelligence**, the application of human intelligence to computer systems. Artificial intelligence is discussed further in Chapter 14.

Integrated Information Systems

With today's sophisticated software, it can be difficult to classify a system as belonging uniquely to one of the four types of information systems previously discussed. For example, much of today's application software provides both transaction and MIS information, and some of the more advanced software even includes some decision support capabilities. Although expert systems still operate primarily as separate systems, the trend is clear: combine all of an organization's information needs into a single, integrated information system.

Figure 10-12
A simulated dialog between a user and a simple expert system is designed to identify an animal based on observations about the animal provided by the user. Notice how answers to certain questions result in other questions that narrow the possible conclusions. Once a conclusion is reached, the expert system can display or print the rules upon which the conclusion was based.

The Role of Personal Computers in Information Systems

The personal computer is playing an increasingly significant role in modern information systems. As organizations have moved toward decentralizing decision making, personal computers have given managers access to the information they need to make their decisions. Nonmanagement employees also benefit from having information available through networked personal computers on their desk or in the production area. For many applications, personal computers are more cost effective than larger systems.

One study estimated that the cost to process a million transactions on a mainframe is fifty times more expensive than on a personal computer. Flexibility is another advantage of personal computers. Individual or networks of personal computers can often be added more quickly than the corresponding amount of equipment that would be needed with minicomputer or mainframe systems. Many professionals believe the ideal information system involves a network of personal computers attached to a server, minicomputer, or mainframe that stores the common information that many users can access. This centralized data and decentralized computing arrangement allows users and organizations the most flexibility over controlling their information resources.

Summary of Information Systems

Numerous factors have combined to make information an increasingly important asset for most organizations. Organizations manage this asset using information systems, computer-based systems that provide the information necessary to manage the activities of the organization. Information systems provide different types of information based on the users' needs, which is often related to the users' level in the organization. New approaches to management organization are requiring corresponding changes in information systems.

The trend of information systems is to combine and integrate transaction, MIS, decision support, and expert systems that previously operated independently.

Figure 10-13
Ford Motor Company has developed an expert system that incorporates the knowledge of engine repair expert Gordy Kujawski. Instead of calling Kujawski, Ford dealers can now access the expert system when they are trying to diagnose engine problems.

COMPUTERS AT WORK

Computers at Work: Expert Systems Capture and Apply Knowledge

Many organizations now use the power of the computer to make decisions based on complex rules and the intuition, judgment, and experience of veteran workers. Expert systems, also called knowledge systems, combine these elements into a set of computer-based rules used to make a decision. Thus, the computer becomes the expert. The following are several examples of expert systems in use.

Lockheed Missile & Space Co. uses an expert system to help speed the purchase of materials ranging from industrial coolant to satellite and rocket parts. The problem with the old system was a complicated purchasing request form that required the user to answer 104 questions. Less than one-quarter of the old forms were properly completed, causing them to be returned, sometimes several times, for corrections. The expert system now in place leads the user through the purchase request form. Based on the type and cost of the material being purchased, the expert system asks relevant questions and skips sections of the purchasing request that do not apply. With the old system, completing a purchasing request could take up to six weeks. With the expert system, most requests are completed in two days.

British Columbia Telephone (BCTel), Canada's second largest telephone company, uses expert systems in several applications. In its Business division, the company uses an expert system to suggest the type of phone service for business customers. The expert system evaluates calling patterns and the amount of voice and data communications to recommend a specific mix of phone services. The expert system even estimates the expected costs of the service. BCTel uses another expert system to reroute calls during peak periods such as holidays. The expert system analyzes the telephone network traffic every five minutes and suggests alternate routes if the main lines become overloaded.

Successful applications such as the ones just described encourage other organizations to apply expert systems software to a wide variety of decision-making problems. Knowledge is perhaps the most underused asset organizations have. Expert systems help capture that knowledge and make it available to the entire organization.

Figure 10-14

IN THE FUTURE

The Virtual Corporation

In discussing how companies will function in the future, many management theorists describe what has been termed the **virtual corporation**, which is a temporary network of companies that join together to provide goods and services. Virtual corporations form quickly and stay together only as long as the opportunity remains profitable.

The term virtual corporation comes from the concept of virtual memory, not virtual reality. As discussed in Chapter 4, with virtual memory management, computers can increase the amount of memory by temporarily using available disk space. In a virtual corporation, the capabilities of one company are increased by adding the capabilities of one or more other companies. In a virtual corporation, each partner contributes it **core competencies**; what it does best. One company may be responsible for product design, another for manufacturing, and a third for sales. The initial idea for a product may have come from another company. This partnering approach has been used in the past for one-time projects such as motion pictures and construction projects but now is being applied to consumer products and services as well.

For example, because they lacked manufacturing capacity, Apple Computer, Inc. asked Sony Corporation to produce one model of its PowerBook line of computers. The arrangement allowed Apple to get the PowerBook model to market faster than if Apple tried to make the unit itself.

As the virtual corporation extends its boundaries to include separate businesses, its information systems must expand also. *Interenterprise information systems* will have to be developed. Each virtual corporation partner must be part of a network that allows them to efficiently communicate a wide variety of information such as designs, costs, and plans. The networks and software applications necessary to handle this information flow must be established quickly with the thought that they may exist for only as long as the joint product or service is in demand.

Many legal and organizational problems will have to be worked out before virtual corporations can operate as well as described by management theorists. When they are in operation, it will be the information systems that hold them together. In fact, it may be that information will be the only inventory that a virtual corporation owns.

Figure 10-15

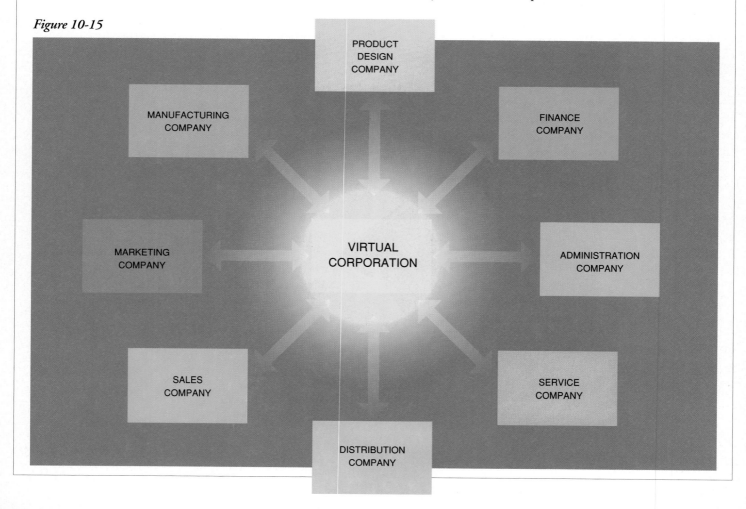

File   Edit   Section   Page   Tools   Options   Help

What You Should Know

1. An **information system** is a collection of elements that provides accurate, timely, and useful information. All information systems that are implemented on a computer are comprised of six elements: equipment, software, accurate data, trained information systems personnel, knowledgeable users, and documented procedures.

2. Several factors have contributed to the increased need for timely and accurate information. Among these factors are expanded markets, increased competition, shorter product life cycles, and government regulations.

3. **Managers** of an organization are the men and women responsible for directing the use of resources such as people, materials, and information so the organization can operate efficiently and prosper. Managers work toward this goal by performing the four management tasks of planning, organizing, leading, and controlling.

4. **Senior management**, also referred to as executive or top management, includes the highest management positions in an organization. Senior managers are primarily responsible for **strategic decisions** that deal with the overall goals and objectives of an organization.

5. **Middle management** is responsible for implementing the strategic decisions of senior management. To do this, middle managers make **tactical decisions** that implement specific programs and plans necessary to accomplish the stated objectives.

6. **Operational management** supervises the production, clerical, and nonmanagement staff of an organization. In performing their duties, operational managers make **operational decisions** that usually involve an immediate action.

7. **Nonmanagement employees**, which include production, clerical, and staff personnel, also need frequent information to perform their jobs.

8. Across the four levels of an organization, management and employees are usually divided into *functional groups*. Because a functional organization can prove to be a barrier to employee communication and getting work done efficiently, many companies have adopted or are experimenting with other management structures. Although each of these approaches is slightly different, they all include some common features: fewer levels of management, employees organized by process not function, and the use of self-managed teams wherever possible.

9. With the increasing pressure to reduce costs, information systems managers have been encouraged to **downsize** operations by moving applications from mainframe and minicomputer systems to networks of personal computers. In a process called **outsourcing**, companies hire outside firms for a contracted fee to provide information systems support.

Start   10:00 AM

File   Edit   Section   Page   Tools   Options   Help

What You Should Know

(continued)

10. Characteristics that information should have are often called the qualities of information. Terms used to describe these qualities include: accurate, verifiable, timely, organized, meaningful, useful, and cost effective.

11. Information systems that are implemented on a computer are generally classified into four categories: (1) transaction processing systems; (2) management information systems; (3) decision support systems; and (4) expert systems.

12. A **transaction processing system** (TPS) processes data generated by the day-to-day transactions of an organization. In **batch processing**, transaction data is collected and, at a later time, all transactions are processed as a *batch*. With **online transaction processing** (OLTP), transactions are processed as they are entered.

13. A **management information system** (MIS) refers to a computer-based system that generates timely and accurate information for managing an organization. An **executive information system** (EIS) is a management information system designed for the information needs of senior management.

14. A **decision support system** (DSS) is a system designed to help the user reach a decision by summarizing or comparing data from either or both internal and external sources. More advanced decision support systems also include capabilities that allow users to create a model of the variables affecting a decision. With a **model**, users can ask what-if questions by changing one or more of the variables and seeing what the projected results would be.

15. **Expert systems**, sometimes called **knowledge systems**, combine knowledge on a given subject of one or more human experts into a computer system that simulates human experts' reasoning and decision making processes. Expert systems are made up of the combined subject knowledge of the human experts, called the **knowledge base**, and the **inference rules** that determine how the knowledge is used to reach decisions. An exciting branch of computer science called **artificial intelligence** is the application of human intelligence to computer systems.

16. With today's sophisticated software, it can be difficult to classify a system as belonging uniquely to one of the four types of information systems. Although expert systems still operate primarily as separate systems, the trend is clear: combine all of an organization's informational needs into a single, integrated information system.

17. The personal computer is playing an increasing role in modern information systems. Personal computers give managers and nonmanagement employees access to information, are more cost effective than larger systems, and provide increased flexibility.

Start   10:00 AM

File   Edit   Section   Page   Tools   Options   Help

Terms to Remember

artificial intelligence (10.13)

batch processing (10.9)

core competencies (10.16)

decision support system
   (DSS) (10.11)
downsize (10.7)

executive information systems
   (EIS) (10.10)
expert systems (10.12)

inference rules (10.12)
information system (10.1)

knowledge base (10.12)
knowledge systems (10.12)

management information system
   (MIS) (10.9)
managers (10.3)
middle management (10.6)
model (10.11)

nonmanagement employees (10.6)

online transaction processing
   (OLTP) (10.9)
operational decisions (10.6)
operational management (10.6)
outsourcing (10.7)

senior management (10.5)
strategic decisions (10.5)

tactical decisions (10.6)
transaction processing system
   (TPS) (10.9)

virtual corporation (10.16)

10:01 AM

File   Edit   Section   Page   Tools   Options   Help

Test Your Knowledge

Fill in the Blanks

1. A(n) _____ is a collection of elements that provides accurate, timely, and useful information.

2. All information systems that are implemented on a computer are comprised of six elements: _____, _____, _____, _____, _____, and _____.

3. The managerial task of _____ involves establishing goals and objectives, while the task of _____ includes identifying and bringing together the resources necessary to achieve these goals and objectives.

4. _____, which include production, clerical, and staff personnel, need frequent information to perform their jobs.

5. Today, _____, which process data generated by an organization's day-to-day transactions, are often a part of _____, which generate timely and accurate information for managing an organization.

Short Answer

1. Why is information important to an organization? List some factors that have contributed to the increased need for timely and accurate information.

2. How are the information requirements of senior management, middle management, and operational management different?

3. What are the qualities that all information should have? Briefly explain each.

4. What are the four categories into which information systems are generally classified? Briefly explain each. Why is there a trend toward integrated information systems?

5. Why are personal computers playing an increasing role in information systems? What do many professionals believe is the ideal information system? Why?

Label the Figure

ORGANIZATION MODEL

Instructions:
Complete the following model to show the levels in an organization.

File   Edit   Section   Page   Tools   Options   Help

Points to Ponder

1

It is difficult to deny the importance of information to a business. Ironically, however, some people believe that while 50 years ago managers had too little information, now they may have too much. Managers can be overwhelmed by the information available through increasingly effective information systems, online public databases used by business (currently there are more than 5,000), expanding media coverage, and improved communications. Some business consultants feel the flood of information has added to managerial stress and forced managers to spend more time sifting information than making crucial business decisions. To address this dilemma, software products have been developed to sort through information sources on the basis of a manager's criteria, and a few businesses are turning to outside firms to preprocess information, checking it for relevance. Can an individual ever have too much information? Why or why not? If so, what do you think can be done about this problem?

2

This chapter describes two kinds of processing used by transaction processing systems: batch processing and online transaction processing. Consider the student records at your school. Identify three types of information that could be updated (or processed) using batch processing. Identify three types of information that could be updated (or processed) using online transaction processing. Explain why each form of processing would be appropriate. Is there any type of information that you feel must be dealt with using a specific kind of processing? Why or why not?

3

Health care in the United States has been an important topic during the past few years. The cost of health care is more than $800 billion and is growing at about 13 percent per year, more than twice the rate of economic growth. Some people believe information technology could reduce health care costs. One of the country's largest health maintenance organizations uses a computerized system that maintains medical records, orders and reports the results of lab tests, sends prescriptions to the center's pharmacy, and even helps doctors make a diagnosis on the basis of reported symptoms. A similar system guides doctors toward more cost-effective decisions when ordering medicines and tests. How could these systems lower the cost of health care? What effect would they have on the quality of health care? What could be some disadvantages of applying information technology to health care?

4

According to this chapter, information should be accurate, verifiable, timely, organized, meaningful, useful, and cost effective. Think of some information you acquired that had a significant impact on your life. What was the information and how did it affect you? Which of the qualities of information did it have? Why? Would the information have been as important if it lacked any of these qualities? Why or why not?

5

Information systems are intended to help businesses be more productive. Yet, some studies indicate that computers have resulted in only a marginal increase in productivity. According to one study of companies that introduced new office systems, approximately 40 percent failed to achieve their intended goals. Several reasons have been suggested for this failure. Some feel workers are spending too much time on relatively unimportant tasks (such as sorting through irrelevant information, polishing memos on a word processor, or adding unnecessary graphics to a spreadsheet). Others think rapid developments in software mean workers must be frequently retrained, preventing them from pursuing more productive activities. Still others maintain that the power of computers has raised people's goals, making it appear as though productivity has suffered when the new goals are not met. What do you think? If you were a manager, what steps would you take to ensure that information systems and computers enhanced your company's productivity?

6

This chapter outlines four levels in an organization. At each level, a different type of decision is made and different information is required. Using your school as a sample organization, identify what school personnel you would categorize at each level. Justify your classification on the basis of the kind of decisions made by the personnel and/or the information each requires.

Out and About

1. As pointed out in this chapter, information systems are used not only by managers but by nonmanagement employees as well. Interview a nonmanagement employee who uses an information system, or consider a nonmanagement job you have held that uses an information system. What type of information system is it? How is the system used? What information does it provide? How does the organization benefit from the information? In what ways was the job different before the system was used? Is the job easier or more difficult as a result of the information system? Why?

2. Expert systems have occasionally been a source of controversy. Recently, a British doctor created a medical uproar with a computer program that determines whether a patient is likely to live or die. The program assesses a patient's chances based on his or her medical condition and history. If the patient is unlikely to survive ninety days of treatment, a black coffin with a white cross lights up on the screen. The doctor maintains a lot of money can be saved by withdrawing treatment earlier from patients who are hopelessly ill. Using library resources, prepare a report on this or another controversial expert system. For what purpose is the expert system used? What advantages does it offer? Why is the system controversial? Is your overall reaction to the expert system positive or negative? Why?

3. Most organizations are divided into functional groups, perhaps even your school. Visit an organization that uses functional groups and interview someone about the organization's structure. Draw a detailed diagram (similar to *Figure 10-5* on page 10.7) showing the specific job titles at various levels within each functional group. What are the advantages and disadvantages of a functional grouping? What steps could be taken to overcome the disadvantages? Has any other approach to management and organization structure ever been considered? If so, what?

4. Interview a manager at a local company. Find out the level of management at which the individual serves by determining the kinds of decisions he or she makes and what information is used to reach those decisions. What type of information system does the manager use? How does the information system influence the manager's decisions? Is any information necessary that is not provided by the system? What? Could the information by provided by an information system?

5. Visit a large supermarket or department store and speak to a manager about how transaction processing systems are used. How does the system help in processing orders, authorizing credit, recording sales data, or performing market analysis? What advantages does a transaction processing system provide for the retailer? What advantages does the system provide for the consumer? Are there any disadvantages to using a transaction processing system? If so, what?

6. A recent development in information systems is communication and data sharing among different organizations. An interorganizational information system (IOIS) is a technological or social system used to help in the collection, analysis, and relay of information among organizations. Some companies, such as Wal-Mart, are already using electronic data interchange, a procedure that facilitates the exchange of data from one organization's computer to the computer system of another organization. Using recent computer magazines, prepare a report on interorganizational information systems. How can these systems be used? What tools will be needed to manage these systems? What are the possible benefits of interorganizational systems? What are the potential disadvantages?

Windows 95

Start   10:04 AM

In the Lab with Windows 95

1 **Movie Box Office Simulation**   Obtain information from your instructor on the location (path) of the file MOVIES.EXE. Click the Start button on the taskbar, and then click Run on the Start menu. In the Open text box, type the path and filename movies. For example, type c:\sclabs\movies and then press ENTER to display the Movie Box Office window *(Figure 10-16)*. Use the options to simulate a ticket vending operation at a movie theater. Enter the following data and determine the amount due for all transactions: (1) Psycho, matinee, 3 tickets; (2) Jaws, no matinee, 1 ticket; (3) Gone With The Wind, matinee, 3 tickets; (4) North By Northwest, matinee, 4 tickets; (5) Jaws, no matinee, 2 tickets.

Write down the summary lines that display in the Transaction Record list box. Close Movie Box Office.

2 **Changing Desktop Patterns and Wallpaper**   Right-click an empty space on your desktop, and then click Properties on the shortcut menu. When the Display Properties dialog box displays, click the Background tab. Scroll through the files in the Pattern area, click Triangle, and then click the OK button. Notice the desktop now displays the triangles pattern.

Display the Display Properties dialog box again. In the Wallpaper area, click Tile. Scroll through the files in the Wallpaper area, click Clouds, and then click the OK button. Notice the desktop now displays clouds *(Figure 10-17)*. If you select Wallpaper, it overrides any patterns or colors you have selected. To turn off the Pattern and/or Wallpaper, select [None] in each list in the Display Properties dialog box. Then, click the OK button.

3 **Capturing Screen Images**   Click the Start button on the taskbar, point to Programs on the Start menu, and then point to Accessories on the submenu. Press PRINT SCREEN. Click WordPad on the Accessories submenu. In WordPad, type `Below is a Windows 95 Screen Shot`: and press ENTER twice. Click Edit on the menu bar and then click Paste. Practice using the scroll bars to scroll through the document. Insert the floppy disk with your Windows Labs into drive A. Click the Save button on the toolbar. When the Save As dialog box displays, type `a:\windows labs\windows 95 lab 10-3` and then click the Save button. Click the Print button on the toolbar to print the file. Close WordPad.

4 **More About Using Help**   Click the Start button on the taskbar, and then click Help on the Start menu. When the Help Topics: Windows Help window displays, click the Find tab. Press TAB, type `copy help` and then double-click Copying information from a Help topic. When the Help window displays, click the Options button, click Print Topic, and then click the OK button to print its contents.

Click the Options button, point to Font, and then click Large on the submenu. Click the Options button, point to Font, and then click Small on the submenu. Click the Options button, point to Font, and then click Normal on the submenu. What is the purpose of the Font command on the Options menu? Close the Help window.

Figure 10-16

Figure 10-17

File   Edit   Section   Page   Tools   Options   Help

Where on the Web

1 **Check Your Stocks** A branch of computer science called artificial intelligence is the application of human intelligence to computer systems. Complete the following steps to test a stock market data server created by the Artificial Intelligence Laboratory at M.I.T. *(Figure 10-18)*. With Netscape on the screen, type http://stockmaster.com in the Location text box and press ENTER. Read about StockMaster. Click Print on the File menu. Click OK. Write a brief description of StockMaster on the printout and hand it in.

2 **Expert Systems** Expert systems are computer systems that simulate human experts' reasoning and decision-making processes. Complete the following steps to use the Yahoo Directory to learn more about expert systems. With Netscape on the screen, click the Net Search button. Click Yahoo. Click Science. Scroll down and click Computer Science. Click Artificial Intelligence. Click Expert Systems. Scroll down and click a topic that sounds interesting. Scroll down and read the page. Click Print on the File menu. Click Pages and then type 1 in the To text box. Click OK. Write a brief description of what you found on the printout and hand it in.

3 **Paint Your Room** Complete the following steps to visit a home improvement Web site *(Figure 10-19)*, and check out a program that estimates how much paint is needed for your remodeling project. With Netscape on the screen, type http://www.btw.com in the Location text box and press ENTER. Scroll down and click Home Improvement. Scroll down and click Paint Estimator. Scroll down and type

the requested information in the appropriate text boxes. Click the Calculate button. If the Security Information dialog box displays, click the Continue button. Based on the textbook discussion of Types of Information Systems, what type of system is the Paint Estimator? Click Print on the File menu. Click OK. Write your answer on the printout and hand it in.

4 **Search the Net** Complete the following steps to use a Net Search utility to learn more about information systems. With Netscape on the screen, click the Net Search button. Click Infoseek Guide. Type one of the Terms to Remember from the end of the chapter in the text box. Click the seek now button. If no items are found that match your search, click the Search Again button and try another. Scroll down and click any one of the items. Read more about that topic. Click Print on the File menu. Click Pages and then type 1 in the To text box. Click OK. Write a brief description of what you found on the printout and hand it in.

5 **Shelly Cashman Online** Click Using Computers: A Gateway To Information, World Wide Web Edition on the Shelly Cashman Student Center Web page (http://www.bf.com/scstudnt.html). Scroll down and click Chapter 10. Complete the activities listed.

Figure 10-18

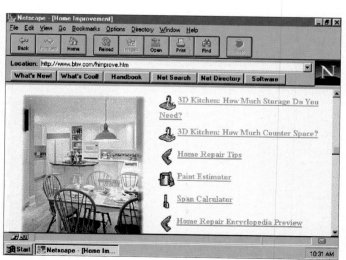

Figure 10-19

Information System Development

11

After completing this chapter, you will be able to:

- Explain the phases and paths of the system development life cycle

- Explain the importance of project management and documentation

- Define commercial application software and describe the difference between horizontal and vertical applications

- Discuss each of the steps of acquiring commercial application software

- Discuss the reasons for developing custom software

- Describe how various analysis and design tools, such as data flow diagrams, are used

- Explain how program development is part of the system development life cycle

- Explain several methods used for conversion to a new system

- Discuss the installation and maintenance of an information system

Every day, competition, government regulations, and other such influences cause people to face new challenges as they try to obtain the information they need to perform their jobs. A new product, a new sales commission plan, or a change in tax rates are just three examples of why an organization must change the way it processes information. Sometimes, these challenges can be met by existing methods but other times, meeting the challenge requires an entirely new way of processing data. In these cases, a new or modified information system is needed. As a computer user, either as an individual or within your organization, it is possible you will someday participate in acquiring, developing, or modifying a system. Creating an information system can be described by phases known as the system development life cycle. This chapter illustrates each phase of this process by using a case study about the wholesale auto parts division of the Sutherland Company.

What Is the System Development Life Cycle?

The **system development life cycle** (SDLC) is an organized approach for obtaining an information system. Regardless of the type or complexity of an information system, the structured process of the SDLC should be followed whenever an information system is acquired or developed. The activities of the SDLC can be grouped into distinct phases.

The Phases of the System Development Life Cycle

As shown in *Figure 11-1,* the phases of the system development life cycle are:
- Analysis
- Acquisition or Design
- Customizing or Development
- Implementation
- Maintenance

Each of the phases includes important activities relating to the acquisition or development of an information system.

As *Figure 11-1* also shows, there is an *acquisition path* and a *development path* in the system development life cycle. After the analysis phase, an organization can either choose to acquire a system by purchasing software or develop one by writing its own software. If an organization does not find a suitable system during the acquisition phase, it will move to

the design phase of the development path. All system projects have analysis, implementation, and maintenance phases.

Before explaining each of the phases, project management and documentation will be discussed because these two activities are ongoing processes performed throughout the cycle. The information system specialists and users who participate in the various phases of the SDLC will also be identified.

Project Management

Project management involves planning, scheduling, reporting, and controlling the individual activities that make up the system development life cycle. These activities are usually recorded in a **project plan** on a week-by-week basis that includes an estimate of the time to complete the activity and the start and finish dates. As you might expect, the start of many activities depends on the successful completion of other activities. For example, implementation activities cannot begin until you have completed at least some, if not all, of the development activities. An effective way of showing the relationship of project activities is with a graphic display called a Gantt chart *(Figure 11-2).* A Gantt chart, named after the developer, shows time across the top of the chart and a list of activities to be completed down the left side. Marks on the

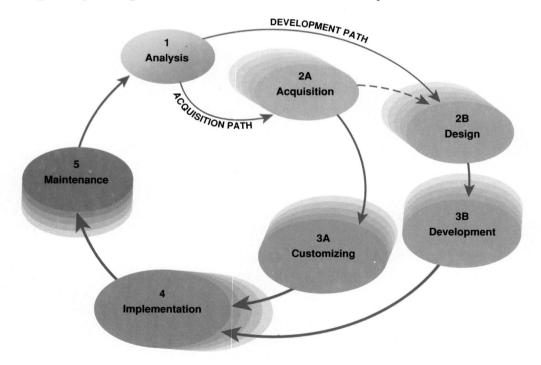

Figure 11-1
The system development life cycle consists of five phases along one of two paths that depend on whether software is acquired or developed.

chart indicate when an activity begins and is completed. Lines or bars between the marks indicate progress toward completing the task.

The importance of maintaining a realistic schedule for project management cannot be overstated. Without a realistic schedule, the success of a project is in jeopardy from the start. If project members do not believe the schedule is realistic, they may not participate to the full extent of their abilities. Project management is a place for realistic, not wishful, thinking.

Project management should be practiced throughout the development process. In most projects, activities need frequent rescheduling. Some activities will take less time than originally planned and others will take longer. To measure the impact of the actual results and revised estimates, they should be recorded regularly and a revised project plan issued. Project management software provides an efficient method of recording results and revising project plans.

Documentation

Documentation refers to written materials produced as part of the system development life cycle such as a report describing the overall purpose of the system or layout forms used to design reports and screens. Documentation should be identified and agreed on prior to beginning the project. Well-written, thorough documentation makes it easier for users and others to understand why particular decisions are made. Too often, documentation is put off until the completion of a project and is never adequately finished. Documentation should be an ongoing part of the entire development process and should not be thought of as a separate phase. Well-written, thorough documentation can also extend the useful life of a system. Unfortunately, systems are sometimes replaced simply because no one understands how they work.

Who Participates in the System Development Life Cycle?

Every person who will be affected by the new system should have the opportunity to participate in its development. The participants fall into two categories: users and information system personnel such as systems analysts and computer programmers. Systems analysts work closely both with the users and the programmers to define the system. The systems analyst's job is challenging, requiring good communication, analytical, and leadership skills to keep the development process on track and on schedule. Good communication skills are especially important during analysis, the first phase of the system development life cycle.

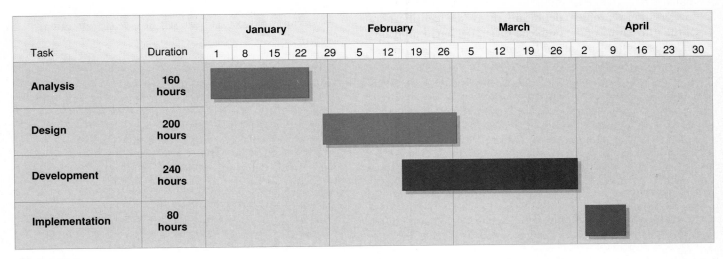

Figure 11-2
A Gantt chart is an effective way of showing the time relationships of the project activities.

Analysis Phase

Analysis is the separation of a system into its parts to determine how the system works. In addition, the analysis phase of a project also includes the identification of a proposed solution to the problems identified in the current system. A system project can originate in several ways, but a common way is for the manager of a user department, such as accounting or personnel, to contact the information systems department with a request for assistance. The initial request may be verbal, but it is eventually written on a standard form that becomes the first item of documentation *(Figure 11-3)*. In most organizations, requests for new system projects exceed the capacity of the information systems department to implement them. Therefore, the manager of the information systems department must review each request and make a preliminary determination as to the potential benefit for the company. Requests for large development projects, such as an entirely new system, are often reviewed by committees made up of users, information systems department personnel, and representatives of top management. When the managers of the user and information systems departments determine a request warrants further review, one or more systems analysts will be assigned to begin a preliminary investigation, which is the first step in the analysis phase.

The Preliminary Investigation

The purpose of the **preliminary investigation** is to determine if a request justifies further detailed investigation and analysis. The most important aspect of the preliminary investigation is **problem definition**, that is the identification of the true nature of the problem. Often the stated problem and the real problem are not the same. For example, suppose the manager of the accounting department requests a new accounts receivable report showing recent customer payments. An investigation might reveal the existing accounts receivable reports would be acceptable if the customer payments were recorded daily instead of once a week.

The real problem is customer payments are being recorded too late to be included in the existing reports. Thus, the preliminary investigation determines the real source of the problem.

The preliminary investigation begins with an interview of the manager who submitted the request. Depending on the request, other users can be interviewed as well. For example, a request might involve data or a process affecting morethan one department, or clerical workers may have to be interviewed to obtain detail information.

The preliminary investigation is usually quite short when compared to the remainder of the project. At the end of the investigation, the systems analyst presents the findings to management of both the user department and information systems department and recommends the next action. Sometimes the results of a preliminary investigation indicate an obvious solution that can be implemented at minimal cost. Other times, however, the only thing the preliminary investigation does is confirm there is a problem needing further study. In these cases, detailed system analysis is recommended. Managers of the user department, the information systems department, and the systems analyst work together to decide how to proceed.

Detailed System Analysis

Detailed system analysis involves both a thorough study of the current system and at least one proposed solution to the problems found.

SUTHERLAND COMPANY
REQUEST FOR SYSTEM SERVICES

ISD CONTROL #: **2143**

I. To Be Completed By Person Requesting Services
SUBMITTED BY: **MIKE CHARLES** DEPT: **AUTO PARTS SALES** DATE: **1/23/95**

REQUEST TYPE: ☐ MODIFICATION   ☑ NEW SYSTEM

NEED: ☐ ASAP   ☑ IMMEDIATE   ☐ LONG RANGE

BRIEF STATEMENT OF REQUEST (attach additional material, if necessary)
**NEED ORDER ENTRY AND INVOICING CAPABILITY.
EXISTING SYSTEM CAN NO LONGER KEEP UP WITH INCREASED
SALES VOLUME.**

☐ ADDITIONAL MATERIAL ATTACHED

II. To Be Completed By Information Systems Department
REQUEST INVESTIGATED BY: **FRANK PEACOCK**   DATE: **2/3/95**
COMMENTS: **INVOICING RUNNING 3 DAYS BEHIND SHIPMENTS.
RECOMMEND DETAILED SYSTEM ANALYSIS**

III. Disposition
☑ REQUEST APPROVED FOR IMMEDIATE IMPLEMENTATION
☑ ANALYST ASSIGNED: **MARY RUIZ**
☐ REQUEST APPROVED FOR IMPLEMENTATION AS SOON AS POSSIBLE
☐ REQUEST REJECTED
COMMENTS: _____

SIGNED: *George Lucey*   DATE: **2/15/95**

Figure 11-3
The system development project usually starts with a request from a user. The request should be documented on a form such as this one to provide a record of the action taken.

The study of the current system is important for two reasons. First, it helps increase the systems analyst's understanding of the activities a new system would perform. Second, and perhaps most important, studying the current system builds a relationship between the systems analyst and the user. The systems analyst will have much more credibility with users if he or she understands how the users currently perform their job responsibilities. This may seem an obvious point, but surprisingly, many systems are created or modified without studying the current system or without adequately involving the users.

The basic fact-gathering techniques used during the detailed system analysis are: (1) interviews, (2) questionnaires, (3) reviewing current system documentation, and (4) observing current procedures. During this phase of the system study, the systems analyst must develop a critical, questioning approach to each procedure within the current system to determine what is actually taking place. Often systems analysts find operations are being performed not because they are efficient or effective, but because they have always been done that way.

Information gathered during this phase includes: (1) the output of the current system, (2) the input to the current system, and (3) the procedures used to produce the output.

An effective method for documenting this information is called structured analysis. **Structured analysis** is the use of analysis and design tools such as data flow diagrams, data dictionaries, process specifications, structured English, decision tables, and decision trees to document the specifications of an information system.

DATA FLOW DIAGRAMS

One of the difficulties in analyzing any system is how to document the findings in a way that can be understood by users, programmers, and other systems analysts. Structured analysis addresses this problem by using graphics to represent the flow of data. These graphics are called data flow diagrams.

A **data flow diagram** (DFD) graphically shows the flow of data through a system. The key elements of a DFD *(Figure 11-4)* are arrows, or vectors, called data flows that represent data; circles (also called bubbles) that represent processes such

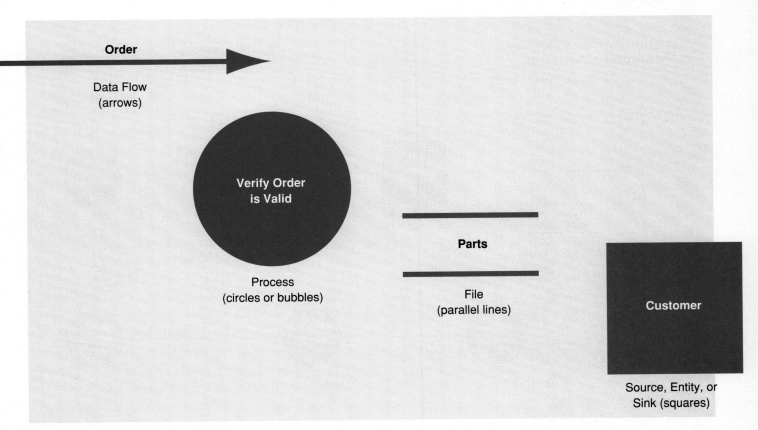

Figure 11-4
The symbols used to create data flow diagrams.

as verifying an order or creating an invoice; parallel lines that represent data files; and squares, called entities, sources, or sinks, that represent either or both an originator or a receiver of data such as a customer.

Because they are visual, DFDs are particularly useful for reviewing the existing or proposed system with the user *(Figure 11-5)*. DFDs are prepared on a level-by-level basis. The top level only identifies major processes. Lower levels further define the higher levels. For example, in *Figure 11-5,* the Apply Invoice Payment process in the lower left corner could have its own separate DFD to define subprocesses that take place.

DATA DICTIONARIES

The **data dictionary** describes the elements making up the data flow. Each element can be thought of as equivalent to a field in a record. The data dictionary also includes information about the attributes of each element such as length, where the element is used (which files and data flows include the element), and any values or ranges the element might have, such as the value 002 in *Figure 11-6* for a credit limit code to indicate a $5,000 credit line. The data dictionary is created by the systems analyst in the analysis phase and is used in all subsequent phases of the system development life cycle.

STRUCTURED ENGLISH

Process specifications describe and document what happens to a data flow when it reaches a process circle. For example in *Figure 11-5,* process specifications describe what happens in each of the circles. One way of writing process specifications is to use **structured English**, a style of writing and presentation that describes the alternatives and actions that are part of the process. *Figure 11-7* shows an example of a structured English process specification describing a policy for order processing.

DECISION TABLES AND DECISION TREES

Another way of documenting the system during the analysis phase is with a decision table or decision tree. A **decision table** or a **decision tree** identifies the actions that should be taken under different conditions. *Figures 11-8* and *11-9* show a decision table and decision tree for the order processing policy described with structured English in *Figure 11-7.* Decision tables and trees are an excellent way of showing the desired action when the action depends on multiple conditions.

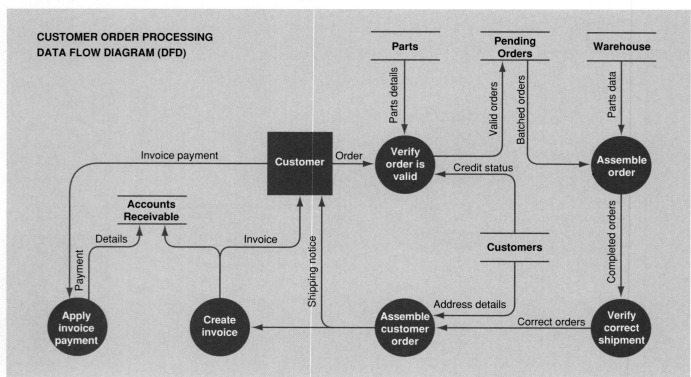

Figure 11-5
Data flow diagrams (DFDs) are used to graphically illustrate the flow of data through a system. The customer (box in diagram) both originates and receives data (represented by arrows). The circles indicate where actions take place on the data. Files are shown as parallel lines.

DATA DICTIONARY - DATA ELEMENT	
Data Element Name:	limit
Aliases:	credit-code, limit-code, credit-limit
Description:	Code indicating customer's credit limit used in order processing and credit management
Length:	3 characters
Type:	alphanumeric
Values and Meanings:	CSH cash or check in advance COD collect on delivery 001 $1 to $1,000 credit line 002 $1,001 to $5,000 credit line 003 $5,001 to $10,000 credit line 004 $10,001 to $20,000 credit line
Credit Limit Code →	
Default Value:	COD - collect on delivery
Validation Rules	1. Must be one of established values 2. Null value not allowed
Files Containing Element:	Customer-Master, Credit-Limits

Figure 11-6
A data dictionary records information about each of the data elements that make up a data flow.

		Rules			
		1	2	3	4
Conditions					
1.	Order > 1,000	Y	Y	N	N
2	Unpaid invoice over 90 days old	Y	N	Y	N
Actions					
1.	Issue order confirmation	N	Y	Y	Y
2.	Reject order	Y	N	N	N
3.	Credit follow-up	N	N	Y	N

Figure 11-8
Decision tables help a user quickly determine the course of action based on two or more conditions. This decision table is based on the order processing policy described in Figure 11-7. For example, if an order is $1,000 or less and the customer has an unpaid invoice over 90 days old, the policy (Rule 3) is to issue an order confirmation and perform a credit follow-up on the past due invoice.

STRUCTURED ENGLISH

If order amount exceeds $1,000
     If customer has an unpaid invoice over 90 days old
          Do not issue order confimation
          Write message on order reject report
     Otherwise (account is in good standing)
          Issue order confirmation
Otherwise (order is $1,000 or less)
     If customer has an unpaid invoice over 90 days old
          Issue order confirmation
          Write message on credit follow-up report
     Otherwise (account is in good standing)
          Issue order confirmation

Figure 11-7
Structured English is an organized way of describing what actions are taken on data. This structured English example describes an order processing policy.

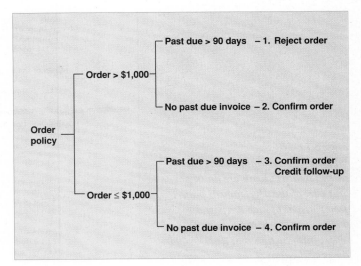

Figure 11-9
Like a decision table, a decision tree illustrates the action to be taken based on the given conditions but presents it graphically. This decision tree is based on the order processing policy described in Figure 11-7.

Making the Decision on How to Proceed

Just as at the completion of the preliminary investigation, at the completion of the analysis phase, the user, systems analyst, and management face another decision on how to proceed. At this point the systems analyst should have completed a study of the current system and, using the same tools and methods, developed one or more proposed solutions to the current system's identified problems. Sometimes, the systems analyst is asked to prepare a feasibility study and a cost/benefit analysis. These two reports are often combined.

The **feasibility study** discusses whether the proposed solution is practical and capable of being accomplished. The **cost/ benefit analysis** identifies the estimated costs of the proposed solution and the benefits (including potential cost savings) expected. If there are strong indications at the beginning of the project that some type of new system will likely be developed, the feasibility study and cost/benefit analysis are sometimes performed as part of the preliminary investigation.

The systems analyst presents the results of his or her work in a written report *(Figure 11-10)* to both user and information systems department management who consider the alternatives and the resources, such as time, people, and money of the organization. The end of the analysis phase is usually when the organization faces a **make-or-buy decision** and has to decide to either acquire a commercial software package from an outside source, develop the software themselves, or have a third party develop the software. If a decision is made to proceed, the project enters the acquisition phase if a software package is going to be obtained or the design phase if software is going to be developed. If a suitable software package cannot be found, an organization will shift to the design phase of the development path.

Figure 11-10
Written reports summarizing the systems analyst's work are an important part of the development project. Two portions of such a report are shown. The top portion shows the report introduction that describes why the investigation of the order entry system was performed. The middle portion of the report (not shown) describes the problems that were found during the investigation. The bottom portion shows three possible solutions and the action recommended by the information systems manager.

SUTHERLAND COMPANY

MEMORANDUM

TO: Management Review Committee
FROM: George Lacey, Information Systems Manager
DATE: April 3, 1995
SUBJECT: Detailed Investigation and Analysis of Order Entry System

Introduction

A detailed system investigation and analysis of the order entry system was conducted as a result of approval given by the management review committee on March 1. The findings of the investigation are presented below.

Objectives of Detailed Investigation and Analysis

The study investigated reported problems of the wholesale auto parts order entry system. We have received complaints that orders were not being shipped promptly and that customers were not notified about out-of-stock parts when they placed their orders. In addition, invoices are not sent to customers until twelve to sixteen days after orders are shipped. The objective of this study was to determine where the problems existed and to develop alternative solutions.

Findings of the Detailed Investigation and Analysis

The following problems appear to exist within the order entry system:

Possible Solutions:

1.   Acquire a separate personal computer LAN system and order entry software. Estimated costs: LAN server, $50,000. Software license, $50,000. Training, $12,000. Annual maintenance, $20,000.

2.   Obtain commercial application software for auto parts order entry and invoicing that would run on the main computer. Estimated costs: Software license, $50,000 to $100,000. Annual software maintenance, 10% of license fee. Training, $10,000.

3.   Internally develop necessary order entry software to run on main computer. Estimated costs:
     (1) System analysis and design, $26,000; (2) Programming and implementation, $40,000;
     (3) Training, $7,000; (4) Terminal emulation software (ten users), $2,000.

Recommended Action

The information systems department recommends alternative 2, the investigation of existing commercial application software that could run on the main computer. If suitable software cannot be found, we recommend the design of a computerized order entry and invoicing system utilizing alternative 3.

George Lacey

Analysis at Sutherland

The Sutherland Company is a large corporation with three separate divisions selling tools, electric motors, and auto parts. Although the tool and electric motor divisions have been computerized for some time, the auto parts division, started just a year ago, has been small enough that it has relied on personal computers with spreadsheet, word processing, and database packages. In the last six months, however, auto parts sales doubled and the order entry and invoicing systems are now incapable of keeping up with the increased work load.

Mike Charles, the auto parts sales manager, decides to submit a request for system services to the information systems department that provides computer services for the other Sutherland divisions. George Lacey, the head of the information systems department, assigns Frank Peacock, a senior systems analyst, to investigate Mike's request.

As part of the preliminary investigation, Frank interviews Mike to try to determine the problem. During his interview with Mike and a subsequent tour of the auto parts sales department, Frank discovers invoices are not being sent to customers until twelve to sixteen days after their parts orders have shipped. In addition, Frank discovers customers complain about shipments being late and about not being notified when parts they ordered are not available. To quantify the expected increases in sales volume, Frank has Mike prepare the transaction volume summary shown in *Figure 11-11*. As a result of his preliminary investigation, Frank recommends a detailed system analysis. George Lacey agrees with Frank's recommendation and assigns systems analyst Mary Ruiz to perform a detailed analysis.

Mary reviews Frank's notes and begins to perform a detailed analysis of the auto parts order entry and invoicing systems. As part of her study, Mary interviews several people in the auto parts division and prepares several documents including a data flow diagram (see *Figure 11-5* on page 11.6), a data dictionary definition for the different credit limits assigned to customers (see *Figure 11-6* on page 11.7), and a structured English statement of the order processing policy (see *Figure 11-7* on page 11.7).

After studying the manual procedures for a week, Mary discusses her findings with George Lacey. Based on Mary's work, George writes a report to the management review committee recommending the order entry and invoicing systems be computerized *(Figure 11-10)*. The report contains three possible solutions: (1) obtain a separate PC LAN using a server, (2) obtain a commercial application software package to run on the main computer, and (3) internally develop the necessary software for the main computer.

Before proceeding to develop the necessary software internally, George recommends Sutherland try to find a suitable commercial software package that can run on Sutherland's main computer. The management review committee meets every month to review requests for additional computer equipment and software. The committee is made up of top management representatives from each division, the finance department, and the information systems department. Based on George's report, the management review committee authorizes the information systems department to find a commercial package to satisfy the auto parts division's order entry and invoicing requirements.

TRANSACTION VOLUME SUMMARY

	LAST YEAR	CURRENT	1 YEAR ESTIMATE	3 YEAR ESTIMATE
Number of Customers	175	300	400	600
Orders per Month	525	950	1250	1900
Invoices per Month	600	1100	1375	2100

Figure 11-11
A transaction volume summary was prepared to estimate the projected growth at Sutherland Company. Systems should be designed to handle the projected volume of transactions, not just the current volume.

Acquisition Phase

Once the analysis phase has been completed, the **acquisition** phase begins. It has four steps: (1) summarizing the application requirements, (2) identifying potential software vendors, (3) evaluating software alternatives, and (4) making the purchase. Before describing these steps, commercial application software will be discussed.

What Is Commercial Application Software?

Commercial application software is already-developed software available for purchase. Prewritten software is available for computers of all sizes. Most users know about the numerous application packages available for personal computers. In addition, users should be aware that numerous packages are available for larger computers. This section discusses the categories of commercial application software available, how to determine software requirements, and how to acquire the software. This information is important to know because it is possible you will someday either acquire application software for yourself or participate in software selection for your organization.

It's probably safe to say at least some part of every type of business, government branch, or recreational pastime has been computerized. *Figure 11-12* is an excerpt from a category listing from an application software catalog. Within each category, numerous programs are available to perform different types of tasks. This catalog contains listings for more than 20,000 individual software packages. Notice this list is divided into two parts: nonindustry specific and industry specific. The more commonly used terms are horizontal and vertical applications.

Horizontal application software is software used by many different types of organizations. Accounting packages are a good example of horizontal applications because they apply to most organizations. If, however, an organization has a unique way of doing business, then it requires a package developed specifically for that job. Software developed for a unique way of doing business, usually within a specific industry, is called **vertical application software**. Examples of specific industries using vertical software include food service, construction, and real estate. Each of these industries has unique information processing requirements.

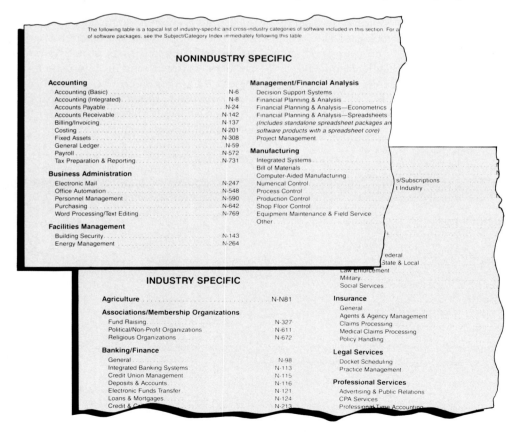

Figure 11-12
An excerpt from a category listing in an application software catalog that contains information on more than 20,000 individual software packages.

The difference between horizontal and vertical application software is important to understand. If you become involved in selecting software, one of the first things you will have to decide is how unique is the task for which you are trying to obtain software. If the task is not unique to your business, you will probably be able to use a horizontal application package. Horizontal application packages tend to be widely available (because they can be used by a greater number of organizations) and less expensive. If your task is unique to your type of organization, you will probably have to search for a vertical software solution. Often an organization's total software requirements are made up of a combination of unique and common requirements.

Now that you understand what commercial application software is, the steps used to acquire it will be discussed.

Summarizing the Application Requirements

One way organizations summarize their software requirements is in a request for proposal. A **request for proposal**, or RFP, is a written list of an organization's software requirements. This list is given to prospective software vendors to help the vendors determine if they have a product that is a possible software solution. Just as the depth of application evaluations varies, so do RFPs. RFPs for simple applications may be only a single page consisting of the key features and a transaction volume summary. Other RFPs for large systems could consist of more than a hundred pages that identify desired key and secondary features. An example of a page from an RFP is shown in *Figure 11-13*.

If an organization wants to acquire a specific piece of software (or hardware) that is available from several vendors, an RFQ can be used. **A request for quotation** (**RFQ**) is a request for a written price quotation on an item to be purchased. A RFQ is an organized way to compare price, delivery, and other purchasing terms offered by different vendors.

Identifying Potential Software Vendors

After you have an idea of the software features you want, your next step is to locate potential vendors selling the type of software you are interested in buying. If the software will be implemented on a personal computer, a good place to start looking for software is a local computer store. Most computer stores have a wide selection of application software.

SUTHERLAND COMPANY
REQUEST FOR PROPOSAL
ACCOUNTS PAYABLE

Features	Standard Feature	Comments
1. Interface to general ledger	✔	
2. Matching to receiving documents	✔	
3. Matching to purchasing documents	✔	
4. Automatic check printing	✔	
5. Recurring payments		PLANNED FOR NEXT RELEASE
6. Flexible payment selection	✔	
7. Checking statement reconciliation		WILL DO ON CUSTOM BASIS
8. Consolidated check preparation	✔	
9. Duplicate invoice check		NO PLANS FOR THIS FEATURE
10. Manual check processing	✔	

Reports		
1. Vendor listing	✔	BY NAME, BUYER
2. Invoice register	✔	
3. Check register	✔	
4. Cash requirements	✔	WEEKLY & MONTHLY
5. Detail aging	✔	30, 60, 90, 120 + DAYS
6. Form 1099 reports		PLANNED FOR NEXT RELEASE
7. Account distribution	✔	
8. Bank statement reconciliation		WILL DO ON CUSTOM BASIS

Figure 11-13
A request for proposal (RFP) documents the features users want in a software package.

and can suggest several packages for you to consider. If you have prepared an RFP, even a simple one, it will help the store representative to narrow the choices. If you require software for a minicomputer or mainframe, you won't find it at the local personal computer store. For this type of software, which can cost tens to hundreds of thousands of dollars, the best place to start is the computer manufacturer. In addition to having some software themselves, most manufacturers have a list of software companies with which they work – companies specializing in developing software for the manufacturer's equipment. **Software houses** are businesses specializing in developing software for sale. **Value-added resellers** (VARs), also called **system houses**, not only sell software but also sell the computer equipment. VARs have resale agreements with one or more computer manufacturers and take full responsibility for equipment, software, installation, and training. Sometimes, they even provide equipment maintenance, although this is usually left to the equipment manufacturer or a separate service organization. The advantage of dealing with a VAR is the user deals with only a single company for the entire system. VARs often specialize in a particular application area such as law offices, manufacturing, or hotel systems.

System integrators are similar to VARs in that they can offer a total system solution but they generally do not limit themselves to one or two types of computers as VARs do.

Another place to find software suppliers, especially for vertical applications, is to look in trade publications, which are magazines written for specific businesses or industries. Companies and individuals who have written software for these industries often advertise in the trade publications. Some industry trade groups also maintain lists of companies providing specific software solutions.

For horizontal applications, many computer magazines publish regular reviews of individual packages and often have annual reviews of several packages of the same type. *Figure 11-14* shows a software review of an accounting package.

Another way to identify software suppliers is to hire a knowledgeable consultant. Although the fee paid to a consultant increases your software costs, it may be worth it, considering the real cost of making a bad decision. Many consultants specialize in assisting organizations of all sizes to identify and implement software packages. A good place to start looking for a consultant would be to contact professional organizations in your industry. Your accountant may also be able to recommend a possible software solution or a consultant.

FACT FILE

Macola Progression, Version 6.0

Macola Inc., 333 East Center St., Marion, OH 43301-0485; 800-468-0834; fax, 614-382-0239.

List price: $995 per module; 5-user system manager, $995; $995 for each additional 5 users.

Requires: Server: 8MB RAM, 300MB hard disk space, NetWare 3.1 or later. DOS workstation: 640K RAM, 1MB hard disk space, DOS 3.1. Windows workstation: 4MB RAM, 1MB hard disk space, Windows 3.1

In short: Macola's distribution modules (Inventory Management, Customer Order Processing, Purchase Order and Receiving, and Bill of Materials) are the heart of its accounting software library. They are well complemented by Macola's financial and manufacturing modules and a host of third-party applications.

497 ON READER SERVICE CARD

SUITABILITY TO TASK

Macola Progression

	POOR	FAIR	GOOD	EXCELLENT
Financial accounting	●	●	●	○
Managing orders and inventory	●	●	●	●
Reporting	●	●	●	○
Customization and implementation	●	●	●	●
Auditing and securing data	●	●	●	●

Figure 11-14
Many publications regularly evaluate applications software.
This review also included a narrative discussion of the package.

Evaluating Software Alternatives

After you have identified several possible software solutions, you must evaluate them and choose one. First, match each choice against your original requirements list. Be as objective as possible–try not to be influenced by the salesperson or representative demonstrating the software or the appeal of the marketing literature. Match each package against your list or RFP and give each package a score. Take into consideration that some features are probably more important than others. Try to complete this rating in writing either during or immediately after a demonstration of the package while the features are still fresh in your mind *(Figure 11-15).*

The next step is to talk to existing users of the software. For vertical application software packages, software vendors routinely provide user references. User references are important because if a software package does (or does not) work for an organization like yours, it probably will (or will not) work for you.

Finally, try the software yourself. For a small application, this may be as simple as entering a few sample transactions using a demonstration copy of the software at the computer store. For large applications, it may require one or more days of testing at the vendor's office or on your existing computer to be sure the software meets your needs.

If you are concerned about whether the software can handle a certain transaction volume efficiently, you may want to perform a benchmark test. A **benchmark test** measures the time it takes to process a set number of transactions. For example, a benchmark test could consist of measuring the time it takes a particular software package to produce a sales summary report using 1,000 sales transactions. Comparing the time it takes different packages to perform the same task using the same data and the same equipment is one way of measuring the packages' relative performance.

Figure 11-15
You should ask to see a demonstration of any program you are considering purchasing. During or after the demonstration, you should rate how well the package meets your requirements.

Making the Purchase

When you purchase software, you usually do not own it. What you are actually purchasing is a **software license** *(Figure 11-16),* which is the right to use the software under certain terms and conditions. One of the usual terms and conditions of a software license is that you can use the software on a single computer only. In fact, some software is licensed to a specific computer and the serial number of the computer is recorded in the license agreement. Other license restrictions include prohibitions against making the software available to others (for example, renting it or leasing it) and modifying or translating the software into another language. These restrictions are designed to protect the rights of the software developer, who does not want someone else to benefit unfairly from the developer's work.

For personal computer users, software license terms and conditions usually cannot be modified. But for larger computer users, terms of the license agreements can sometimes be modified and, therefore, should be carefully reviewed and considered a part of the overall software selection process. Modifications to the software license are generally easier to obtain before the sale is made than after.

Acquisition at Sutherland

Based on the directions of the management review committee, a software selection committee is formed with Mike Charles as the chairperson. Mary Ruiz and Frank Peacock from the information systems department are also members, as are the order entry and billing supervisors from the auto parts division. Also asked to participate is Bill Comer, computer systems specialist with Sutherland's CPA firm. Mary and Frank take the information developed during the analysis phase and summarize it into a request for proposal (RFP). The RFP is sent to ten software vendors that Bill Comer has identified. Eight of the ten vendors send a response to the RFP within the one month deadline set by Sutherland. Most of the vendors had contacted and visited the auto parts operation to gather information necessary for their responses.

Of the eight replies, Sutherland chooses three vendors for further discussions. The committee eliminates five of the vendors because they believe these systems do not meet the requirements of an auto parts distributor. The software selection committee visits the offices of all three remaining software vendors for a thorough demonstration of their respective packages. In addition, the committee visits a customer of each of the three vendors. The vendor and customer site visits are conducted during a one-month period.

At this point, Sutherland faces a difficult choice. None of the commercial software packages is significantly better than the other and all three have areas needing substantial modifications to meet Sutherland's way of doing business. The software selection committee summarizes its findings in a report to the management review committee. After discussing the report, the management review committee authorizes the information services department to begin development of an order entry and invoicing system to run on Sutherland's existing computer system.

Figure 11-16
A software license grants the purchaser the right to use the software but does not include ownership rights.

Commercial Applications Versus Custom Software

Each year, the number of application software packages increases. With so much software available, why would an organization choose to develop its own applications?

There could be several reasons. The most common reason is the organization's software requirements are so unique it is unable to find a package meeting its needs. In such a case, the organization would choose to develop the software itself or have it developed specifically for them. Application software developed by the user or at the user's request is called **custom software**. An example of a requirement for custom software might be a government agency implementing a new health care service. If the service has new forms and procedures and is different from previous services, it is unlikely any appropriate software exists.

Another reason to develop rather than buy software is that new software must work with existing custom software. This is an important point to keep in mind; once an organization chooses to use custom software, it will usually choose custom software for future applications as well. This is because it is often difficult to make custom software work with purchased software. The following example illustrates this point.

Suppose a company has previously developed a custom inventory control software system and now wants to computerize its order entry function. Order entry software packages allow the user to sell merchandise from stock and, therefore, must work closely with the inventory files. In fact, many order entry systems are sold together with inventory control systems. If the company wants to retain its existing inventory

control application, it would probably have a hard time finding a commercial order entry package capable of working with its custom inventory files. This is because the software and the database structures used in the commercial package will not be the same as the existing software. For this reason, the company would probably decide to develop a custom order entry application.

Both custom and commercial software have their advantages and disadvantages. The advantage of custom software is if it is correctly developed, it will match an organization's exact requirements. The disadvantages of custom software are it is one of a kind, difficult to change, often poorly documented, and usually more expensive than commercial software. In addition, custom software projects are often difficult to manage and complete on time.

The advantage of commercial software is that it is ready to install immediately. After sufficient training, usually provided by the vendor who developed or sold the software, people can begin using the software for productive work. The disadvantage of commercial software is that an organization will probably have to change some of its methods and procedures to adapt to the way the commercial software functions.

A good guideline for evaluating an organization's need for custom or commercial software is to look for a package with an 80% or better fit with the requirements. If there is less than an 80% fit, an organization should either consider custom software or reevaluate its requirements. *Figure 11-17* shows the most likely software solutions for different application requirements.

APPLICATION CHARACTERISTICS	APPLICATION EXAMPLE	MOST LIKELY SOFTWARE SOLUTION
Applicable to many different types or organizations	Accounts receivable	Horizontal application package
Specific to a particular type of business or organization	Hotel room reservations	Vertical application package
Unique to a specific organization or business	Space shuttle launch program	Custom software

Figure 11-17
Software guidelines for different types of applications.

Customizing Phase

Ideally, acquired commercial application software will meet 80% or more of an organization's requirements. But what about the other 20% or so? For these requirements, the organization has two choices: change its way of doing business to match the way the software works, or modify the way the software works to match its organization. Usually, it will choose a combination of the two alternatives.

Modifying a commercial application package is usually referred to as **customizing**, or **tailoring**. The process of customizing a commercial package involves the following four steps:

1. Identify potential modifications.
2. Determine the impact of changing current operations to match the software and thus avoid making a modification.
3. Specify the amount of work required to make the modifications and the corresponding cost.
4. Choose which modifications will be made. If possible, the modifications should be made prior to the system being implemented. This avoids users having to relearn how the system works.

Some software vendors do not recommend or support modifications to their packages. Other vendors facilitate modifications by providing copies of the programs or by doing the modifications themselves, usually for a fee. Generally speaking, the larger and more expensive the application package, the more likely modifications will be required and will be permitted.

Customizing at Sutherland

Because the software selection committee does not choose a commercial application software package, the customizing phase does not take place at Sutherland.

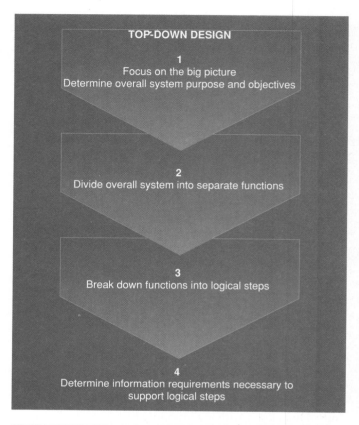

Figure 11-18
Top-down design is appropriate for large projects and the design of entire systems. Bottom-up design is used when a specific output must be produced, such as a new report, from an existing system.

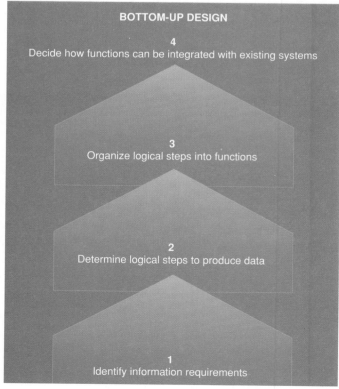

Design Phase

The proposed solution developed as part of the analysis phase usually consists of what is called a **logical design**, which means the design was deliberately developed without regard to a specific computer or programming language and no attempt was made to identify which procedures should be automated and which procedures should be manual. This approach avoids early assumptions that may limit the possible solutions.

During the **design** phase the logical design will be transformed into a **physical design** that identifies the procedures to be automated. The physical design also specifies the programming language that will be used and the equipment needed for the system.

Structured Design Methods

The system design usually follows one of two methods, top-down design or bottom-up design *(Figure 11-18)*.

TOP-DOWN DESIGN

Top-down design, also called **structured design**, focuses on the major functions of the system, such as recording a sale or generating an invoice, and keeps breaking down those functions into smaller and smaller activities, sometimes called modules, that can eventually be programmed. Top-down design is a popular method because it focuses on the total requirements and helps users and systems analysts reach an early agreement on what the major functions of the new system are.

BOTTOM-UP DESIGN

Bottom-up design focuses on the required information. The approach used determines what output is needed and moves up to the processes needed to produce the output.

In practice, most systems analysts use a combination of the top-down and bottom-up designs. Some information requirements, such as payroll checks, for example, have required data elements that correspond to bottom-up design. Other requirements, such as management-oriented exception reports based on the needs of a particular user, are better suited to a top-down design. Regardless of the design method used, the systems analyst will eventually need to complete the design activities.

Design Activities

Design activities include individual tasks a systems analyst performs to design an information system. These include designs for the output, input, database, processes, system controls, and testing.

OUTPUT DESIGN

The design of the output is critical to the successful implementation of the system. Output provides information to the users, and information is the basis for the justification of most computerized systems. For example, most users do not know (or necessarily care) how the data will be processed, but they usually do have clear ideas on how they want the information output to look. Often, requests for new or modified systems begin with a user-prepared draft of a report the current system does not produce. During **output design**, the systems analyst and the user document specific screen and report layouts to display or report information from the new system.

INPUT DESIGN

During **input design**, the systems analyst and the user identify what data needs to be entered into the system to produce the desired output and where and how the data will be entered. The systems analyst and the user determine the sequence of inputs and computer responses, called a **dialogue**, the user will encounter when he or she enters data.

DATABASE DESIGN

During **database design**, the systems analyst uses the data dictionary information developed during the analysis phase and merges it into new or existing system files. During this phase of the design, the systems analyst works closely with the database administrator to identify existing database elements that can be used to satisfy design requirements.

Efficient file design can be a challenging task, especially with relational database systems that stress minimum data redundancy (duplicate data). The systems analyst must also consider the volume of database activity. For example, large, frequently accessed files may need a separate index file to allow inquiries to be processed in an amount of time acceptable to the user.

PROCESS DESIGN

During **process design**, the systems analyst specifies exactly what actions will be taken on the input data to create output information. Decisions on the timing of actions are added to the logical processes the systems analyst identified in the analysis phase. For example, the systems analyst might have found in the analysis phase that an exception report should be produced if inventory balances fall below a certain level. During the process design phase, the frequency of the report will be determined.

One way to document the relationship of different processes is with a **system flowchart** *(Figure 11-19)*. The system flowchart shows the major processes (each of which may require one or more programs), reports (including their distribution), data files, and the types of input devices, such as terminals, that will provide data to the system.

Some of the special symbols used in a system flowchart are shown in *Figure 11-20*.

During process design the systems analyst, the user, and the other members of the development project sometimes meet to conduct a **structured walkthrough**, a step-by-step review of the process design. The purpose of these sessions is to identify any design logic errors and to continue the communication between the systems analyst and the user. Structured walk-throughs are also used to review work during other phases of the system development life cycle.

SYSTEM CONTROLS

An important aspect of the design phase is the establishment of a comprehensive set of system controls. **System controls** ensure only valid data is accepted and processed by authorized users. Adequate controls must be established for two reasons: (1) to ensure the accuracy of the processing and the information generated from the system, and (2) to prevent computer-related fraud.

There are five types of controls considered by the systems analyst. These controls are: (1) source document controls, (2) input controls, (3) processing controls, (4) accounting controls, and (5) access controls.

1. **Source document controls** include serial numbering of certain input documents such as invoices, credit memos, and paychecks.
2. **Input controls** are established to assure the complete and accurate conversion of data from the source documents or other sources to a machine-processable form. Editing data as it enters the system is the most important form of input controls.
3. **Processing controls** refer to procedures established to determine the accuracy of data after it has been input to the system. For example, the accuracy of the total accounts receivable could be verified by taking the prior day's total, adding the current day's sales invoices, and subtracting the current day's payments.

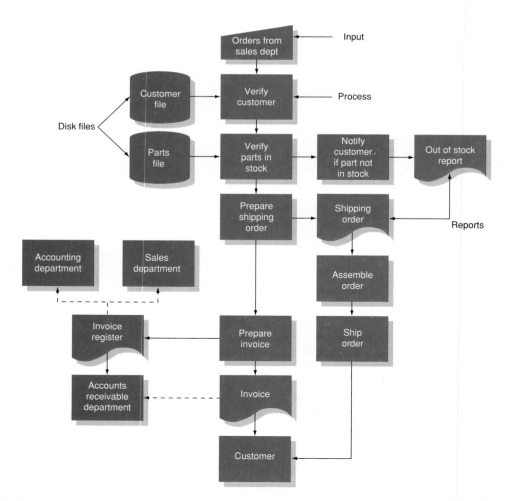

Figure 11-19

The system flowchart documents the equipment used to enter data, such as the terminals for the salespeople and the order department, the processes that will take place, such as the Verify Customer process, the files that will be used, such as the Parts and Customer files, and the reports that will be produced, such as the Shipping Order. Dotted lines indicate additional copies of reports, such as the copy of the Invoice that is sent to the Accounts Receivable Department.

4. **Accounting controls** provide assurance that dollar amounts recorded in the accounting records are correct. One type of accounting control is making sure detail reports are created to support the summary reports used to make entries in an organization's financial system. For example, many companies record sales by product line based on a summary report showing product line totals. In addition to this summary report, a detail report showing individual product sales should also be prepared and agreed to the summary report.

5. **Access controls** specify what levels of security are required for different processes. For example, in a payroll system, the capability to change pay rates would have a more restricted level of security than the capability to make changes to an employee's address.

TESTING DESIGN

During the design phase, test specifications are developed. The exact tests to be performed should be specified by someone other than the user or the systems analyst, although both should be consulted. Users and systems analysts have a tendency to test only what has been designed. An impartial third party, who has not been actively involved in the design, is more likely to design a test for, and therefore discover, a procedure or type of data overlooked in the design. Sometimes organizations avoid test design and test their systems with actual transactions. While such *live testing* is valuable, it may not test all conditions the system is designed to process. This is especially true of error or exception conditions that do not occur regularly. For example, payroll systems are usually designed to reject input for hours worked over some limit, say 60 hours in a week. If only actual data is used to test the system, this limit may not be tested. Thus, it is important to design testing specifications that test each system control by using both valid and invalid data. Types of tests include the following:

- **Unit testing**   Tests individual programs.
- **System testing**   Tests all programs in an application.
- **Integration testing**   Tests a new application to make sure it works with other applications.
- **Acceptance testing**   Demonstrates to the users that the system can meet user-designed test criteria.

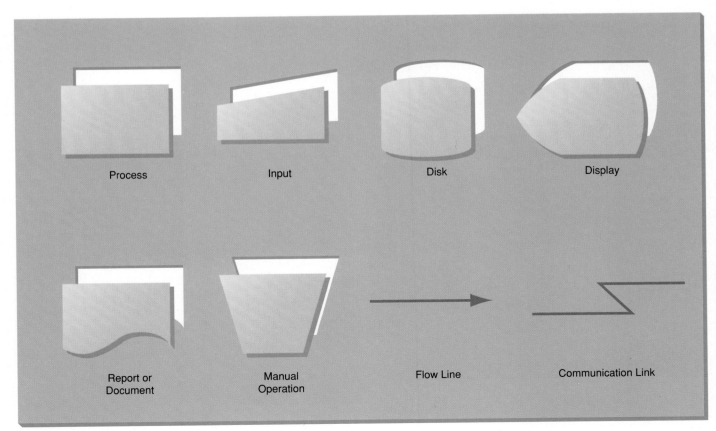

Figure 11-20
Symbols used for preparing a system flowchart.

Process   Input   Disk   Display

Report or Document   Manual Operation   Flow Line   Communication Link

Design Review

At the end of the design phase, management performs a **design review** and evaluates the work completed so far to determine whether to proceed *(Figure 11-21)*. This is a critical point in any development project, and all parties must take equal responsibility for the decision.

Usually, the design review will only result in requests for clarification of a few items. But sometimes an entire project will be terminated. Although canceling or restarting a project from the beginning is a difficult decision, in the long run it is less costly than implementing an inadequate or wrong solution. If management decides to proceed, the project enters the development phase.

Before discussing the development phase, prototyping and computer-aided software engineering are discussed. Prototyping is a development method that can be used in several phases of system development. Computer-aided software engineering is an automated approach to system design.

Prototyping

Prototyping is building a working model of the new system. The advantage of prototyping is it lets the user actually experience the system before it is completed. Some organizations use prototyping during the analysis phase, while others use it during the design phase. Still other companies use prototyping to go directly from the preliminary investigation to an implemented system. These companies continue refining the prototype until the user says it is acceptable. Another advantage of prototyping is that because the system is built in small steps, it requires end users and developers to have frequent meetings to discuss how the system should operate.

A disadvantage of such an accelerated approach is that key features of a new system, especially exception conditions, may be overlooked. Another disadvantage is that documentation, an important part of any system development effort, is usually not as well or as thoroughly prepared. Used as a tool to show the user how the system will operate, prototyping can be an important system development tool.

Computer-Aided Software Engineering (CASE)

Many organizations are now using computer software specifically developed to aid the system development life cycle

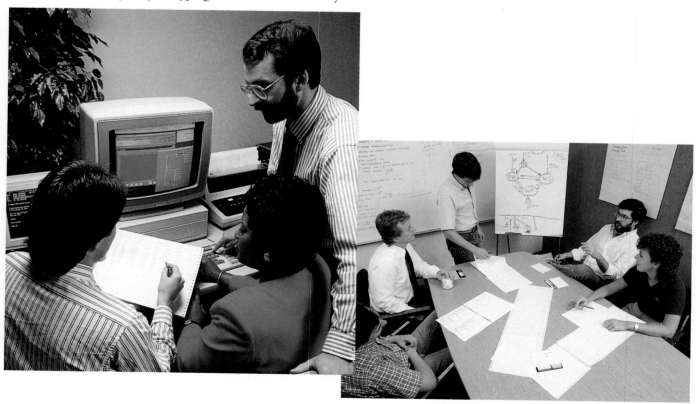

Figure 11-21
The design review is a critical point in the development process. Representatives from the user information systems departments and top management meet to determine if the system should be developed as designed or if additional design work is necessary.

process. **Computer-aided software engineering** (CASE) refers to the use of automated computer-based tools to design and manage a software system *(Figure 11-22)*. Sometimes these tools, such as a data dictionary, exist separately. Other CASE vendors have combined several tools into an integrated package referred to as a **CASE workbench**. CASE workbench tools might include:

- *Analysis and design tools* such as data dictionaries, decision tables, or data flow diagram builders
- *Prototyping tools* used to create models of the proposed system
- *Code generators* that create actual computer programs
- An *information repository* that cross references and organizes all information about a system
- *Management tools* that assist in the management of a systems project

In addition to the benefits of increased productivity, CASE tools promote the completion of the design work before development begins. Starting the development work before the design is completed often results in work that has to be redone. A disadvantage of CASE tools is that it can take a long time to learn how to use them.

Design at Sutherland

Upon approval by the management review committee, Mary Ruiz begins designing the order entry and invoicing system. After she studies existing documents and talks to users, Mary designs printed reports and screen displays. Mary reviews the sample output and screen displays with Mike Charles and the employees who will be doing the order entry. To graphically show how the overall system will work, Mary prepares a system flowchart (see *Figure 11-19* on page 11.18). The system flowchart shows that auto parts orders will be entered on terminals in the sales department and will use data in the Parts and Customer files to verify the orders are valid. Shipping orders and invoices are two of the reports produced. An important part of Mary's design time involves specifying the system controls to be used during processing. These controls include verifying the customer number before processing the order and checking to see if the ordered part is in stock. If the ordered part is not in stock, the customer is notified immediately.

After completing her design work, Mary meets with representatives from the user and information systems departments and top management to review her design. After Mary explains the design, the committee agrees to develop the system.

Figure 11-22
Computer-aided software engineering (CASE) packages help users design complex systems. Excelerator by Intersolv allows users to create and revise data flow diagrams, data dictionary elements, screens, reports, and process specifications.

Development Phase

Once the system design phase has been completed, the project enters the system development phase. There are two parts to the **development phase**: program development and equipment acquisition.

Program Development

The process of developing the software, or programs, required for a system is called **program development** and includes the following steps: (1) reviewing the program specifications, (2) designing the program, (3) coding the program, (4) testing the program, and (5) finalizing the program documentation. The primary responsibility for completing these tasks is assumed by computer programmers who work closely with the systems analyst who designed the system. Chapter 12 explains program development in depth. The important concepts to understand now are that this process is a part of the development phase of the system development life cycle and its purpose is to develop the software required by the system.

Equipment Acquisition

During the development phase, final decisions will be made on what additional equipment, if any, will be required for the new system. A preliminary review of the equipment requirements would have been done during the analysis phase and included in the written report prepared by the systems analyst. Making the equipment acquisition prior to the development phase would be premature because any equipment selected should be based on the requirements specified in the design phase. Equipment selection is affected by factors such as the number of users who will require personal computers or terminals and the disk storage required for new files and data elements. In some cases, a new or upgraded computer is required. If an organization chose to acquire a commercial software package instead of developing software, the equipment acquisition would take place during the acquisition phase.

Development at Sutherland

During the development phase, Mary works closely with the two programmers who are assigned to the project. She regularly meets with the programmers to answer questions about the design and to check on the progress of their work. Prior to starting the programming, Mary arranges for the programmers to meet with the auto parts sales employees so the programmers will have a better understanding of the purpose of the new system.

Because the sales department already has personal computers, no additional input devices are required. Terminal emulation software is installed on the PCs to enable them to communicate with Sutherland's central computer.

Figure 11-23
All users should be trained on the system before they use it to process actual transactions. Training should include both classroom and hands-on sessions.

Implementation Phase

Implementation is the phase of the system development life cycle when people actually begin using the new system. This critical phase of the project usually requires careful timing and the coordination of all the project participants. Important parts of this phase contributing to the success of the new system are training and education, conversion, and post-implementation evaluation.

Training and Education

Someone once said, "If you think education is expensive, you should consider the cost without it." The point is that untrained users can prevent the estimated benefits of a new system from ever being obtained or, worse, contribute to less efficiency and more costs than when the old system was operational. *Training* consists of showing people exactly how they will use the new system *(Figure 11-23)*. This training can include classroom-style lectures and should include hands-on sessions using realistic sample data on the equipment the individuals will be using. *Education* consists of learning new principles or theories that help people understand and use the system. For example, before implementing a manufacturing system, many companies require their manufacturing personnel to attend classes on material requirements planning (MRP), shop floor control, and other essential manufacturing topics.

Conversion

Conversion refers to the process of changing from the old system to the new system. A number of different methods of conversion can be used including direct, parallel, phased, and pilot *(Figure 11-24* on the next page).

With **direct conversion**, the user stops using the old system one day and begins using the new system the next. The advantage of this approach is it is fast and efficient. The disadvantage is it is risky and can seriously disrupt operations if the new system does not work correctly the first time.

Parallel conversion consists of continuing to process data on the old system while some or all of the data is also processed on the new system. Results from both systems are compared, and if they agree, all data is switched to the new system. Parallel conversion requires the most effort because two systems are operating simultaneously.

Phased conversion is used with larger systems that can be broken down into individual modules that can be implemented separately at different times. An example would be a complete business system that could have the accounts receivable, inventory, and accounts payable modules implemented separately in phases. Phased conversions can be direct, parallel, or a combination of both.

Pilot conversion means the new system will be used first by only a portion of the organization, often at a separate location such as a plant or an office.

At the beginning of conversion, existing data must be made ready for the new system. Converting existing manual and computer-based files so they can be used by a new system is called **data conversion**.

Post-Implementation Evaluation

After a system is implemented, it is important to conduct a **post-implementation evaluation** to determine if the system is performing as designed, if operating costs are as anticipated, and if any modifications are necessary to make the system operate more effectively.

Implementation at Sutherland

Before they begin to use the new system to enter real transactions, the users participate in several training sessions. Because this is the first application in the auto parts division to use the main system, Mary begins the training sessions with an overview of how the main computer system processes data.

Before the system can be used, the Parts and Customer files have to be converted from the files on the PCs. Separate conversion programs are written for each file. After the files are converted, they are carefully reviewed by Mike Charles and other department employees.

Although he knows it means extra work, Mike decides a parallel conversion is the safest way to implement the new system. Using this method, Mike verifies the results of the new system with those of the existing system. Actual use of the system begins on the first business day of the month so transaction totals can be balanced to accounting reports.

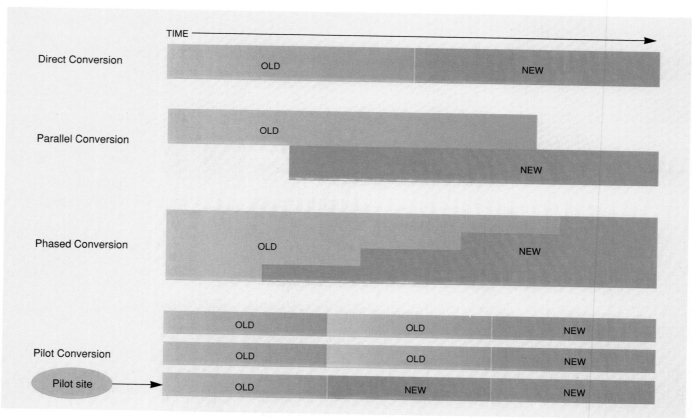

Figure 11-24
Different methods of converting from an old to a new system

Because they are thoroughly trained, the order clerks feel comfortable when they begin entering real orders. They encounter a few minor problems, such as orders for special parts not in the parts file. These problems become less frequent and at the end of the month, after Mike compares the old system and the new system report totals, he decides to discontinue the use of the old system.

During the post-implementation review, Mike and Mary discover nine out of ten customer orders are now shipped the same day as the order is received. Before the new system was implemented, less than half the orders were shipped within two days of receipt. Invoices, which once lagged twelve to sixteen days behind shipments, are now mailed on the same day. Perhaps the most positive benefit of the new system is that customer complaints about order processing are practically eliminated.

Maintenance Phase

Maintenance is the process of supporting the system after it is implemented. Maintenance consists of three activities: performance monitoring, change management, and error correction.

Performance Monitoring

Performance monitoring is the ongoing process of comparing response times, file sizes, and other system performance measures against the estimates prepared during the analysis, design, and implementation phases. Variances from these estimates may indicate the system requires additional equipment resources, such as more memory or faster disk drives.

Change Management

Change is an inevitable part of any system; thus, all users of the system should be familiar with methods and procedures that provide for change. Sometimes, changes are required because existing requirements were overlooked. Other times, new information requirements caused by external sources such as government regulations will force change. Or perhaps someone has an idea for improving the system.

A key part of change management is documentation. The same documentation standards that were followed during the analysis and design phases should also be used to record changes. In fact, in many organizations, the same document used to request new systems (see *Figure 11-3* on page 11.4) is used to request changes to an existing system. Thus, the system development life cycle continues as the analysis phase begins on the change request.

Error Correction

Error correction deals with problems caused by programming and design errors discovered after the system is implemented. Often these errors are minor problems, such as the ZIP code not appearing on a name and address report, and can be quickly fixed by a programmer. Other times, however, the error requires more serious investigation by the systems analyst before a correction can be determined. Design errors not found until after a system is implemented are much more expensive to correct than had they been found earlier.

Maintenance at Sutherland

During the months following the system implementation, users discover a number of minor errors in the system. The programming staff quickly corrects most of these errors, but in one case involving special credit terms for a large customer, Mary Ruiz becomes involved and prepares specifications for the necessary program changes.

Approximately one year after Mike Charles submits his original request for a computerized order entry and invoicing system, he submits another request *(Figure 11-25)* for a change to the system to provide for a new county sales tax. This type of request does not require a preliminary investigation and is assigned to Mary Ruiz as soon as she is available. Mike submits his request five months before the tax is scheduled to go into effect, which allows ample time for the necessary program changes to be implemented.

Summary of the System Development Life Cycle

Although the system development life cycle may appear to be a straightforward series of steps, in practice it is a challenging activity calling for the skills and cooperation of all involved. New development tools have made the process more efficient but the success of any project always depends on the commitment of the project participants. The understanding you have gained from this chapter will help you participate in information system development projects and give you an appreciation for the importance of each phase.

SUTHERLAND COMPANY

REQUEST FOR SYSTEM SERVICES

ISD CONTROL #: **4703**

I. To Be Completed By Person Requesting Services
SUBMITTED BY: **MIKE CHARLES**   DEPT: **AUTO PARTS SALES**   DATE: **2/1/96**

REQUEST TYPE: ☑ MODIFICATION   ☐ NEW SYSTEM

NEED: ☑ ASAP   ☐ IMMEDIATE   ☐ LONG RANGE

BRIEF STATEMENT OF REQUEST (attach additional material, if necessary)
  SALES INVOICE PROGRAM NEEDS TO PROVIDE FOR
  1% COUNTY TAX THAT WILL GO INTO EFFECT JULY 1, 1996

☑ ADDITIONAL MATERIAL ATTACHED   **COUNTY TAX RATE SCHEDULE**

- -

II. To Be Completed By Information Systems Department
REQUEST INVESTIGATED BY: _____ DATE: _____
COMMENTS: _____

- -

III. Disposition
  ☐ REQUEST APPROVED FOR IMMEDIATE IMPLEMENTATION
  ☐ ANALYST ASSIGNED: _____
  ☐ REQUEST APPROVED FOR IMPLEMENTATION AS SOON AS POSSIBLE
  ☐ REQUEST REJECTED
COMMENTS: _____

SIGNED: _____ DATE: _____

Figure 11-25
The same form used to request a new system (see Figure 11-3) is also used to request a modification to an existing system.

COMPUTERS AT WORK

The Case for CASE

Like many new technologies, when Computer-Aided Software Engineering (CASE) was first promoted, its backers claimed it was the *silver bullet* that would kill the monster backlog of applications waiting to be developed. And, like most technologies, the actual results did not live up to the early claims.

The move from mainframes to client/server LANs has also slowed the use of CASE because CASE software vendors have had to scramble to adapt their products that were originally developed for use on and development of larger systems. But CASE has adapted to the new system architectures and many organizations now use it to speed development of new applications.

The City of Phoenix, Arizona Police Department used CASE tools from Unisys Corporation to develop a system that has helped solve several crimes. The system, called PACE, which stands for Police Automated Computer Entry, keeps track of information recorded by field officers, even when someone is not arrested. The information results in a database of activity that took place at a particular time and location.

The database has proved helpful in identifying both witnesses and suspects for crimes that were later reported.

Federated Department Stores has chosen CASE tools from Seer Technologies to move mainframe applications to client/server networks. Before choosing a totally integrated CASE approach, Federated experimented with PC-based application development tools. Federated found that the application development tools were great for building stand-alone desktop applications but did not work well with their overall plans to reengineer most of the company's business processes. They decided they needed a more comprehensive set of tools that addressed the entire system development life cycle and not just the development phase. The CASE software met those needs.

Despite these and other notable successes, many users are still hesitant to implement CASE software. For some, the view of CASE has changed from an easy-to-use wonder tool to a hard-to-learn, hard-to-use tool. But for others who have invested the time and effort, CASE has more than proved its value as an organized and efficient way of developing applications.

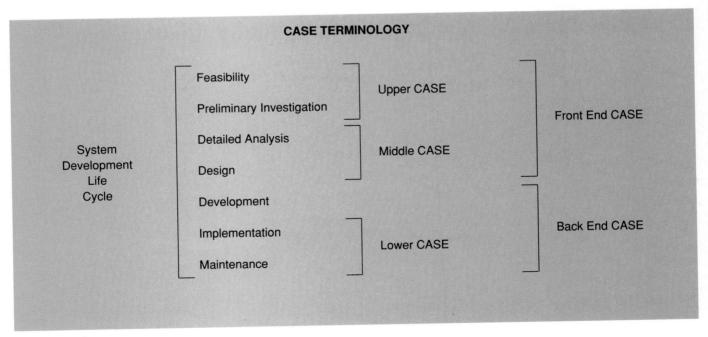

Figure 11-26

IN THE FUTURE

A RADical New Way to Develop Applications

In an attempt to decrease the amount of time it takes to develop a new application, some companies are trying a new approach called rapid application development (RAD).

With RAD, less time is spent on the traditionally separate phases of analysis and design. Using a RAD approach, analysis, design, and development are combined into a single process. Users work closely with developers using prototyping tools to create portions of the new application. Frequent user feedback helps refine the prototype until it becomes a usable system.

Instead of delivering an entire system at one time, RAD applications are usually delivered in modules as they are completed. The average development time for a module is three to four months and no module should take longer than six months. This is considerably less time than the 18 to 36 month development times that are common for business applications.

In order for a RAD approach to be successful, its supporters recommend the following:

- Both user and developer must have a firm understanding of the system's purpose and how it fits into the overall organization.
- The contents of key files should be determined before the RAD project begins. Other file contents can wait because they will become apparent as the system is developed.
- The overall project should be divided into manageable modules that can be developed in several months.
- Upon completion, individual modules should be implemented as soon as possible.
- Teamwork is critical. Teams must include people who will eventually use the system.

Ultimately, the success of RAD will depend less on state-of-the-art software tools and more on the ability of the user and the developer to efficiently cooperate and work together. And when that happens, it really will be RAD.

Figure 11-27

What You Should Know

1. The **system development life cycle** (SDLC) is an organized approach for obtaining an information system. The activities of the SDLC can be grouped into distinct phases: analysis, acquisition or design, customizing or development, implementation, and maintenance.

2. Project management and documentation are ongoing processes performed throughout the system development life cycle. **Project management** involves planning, scheduling, reporting, and controlling the individual activities that make up the SDLC. These activities are usually recorded in a project plan on a week-by-week basis that includes an estimate of the time to complete the activity and start and finish dates. **Documentation** refers to written materials produced as part of the system development life cycle.

3. Every person who will be affected by the new system should have the opportunity to participate in its development. The participants fall into two categories: users and information systems personnel.

4. **Analysis** is the separation of a system into its parts to determine how the system works. The analysis phase of a project also includes the identification of a proposed solution to the problems identified in the current system.

5. The purpose of the **preliminary investigation** is to determine if a request for a new system project justifies further detailed investigation and analysis. The most important aspect of the preliminary investigation is problem definition, which is the identification of the true nature of the problem.

6. **Detailed system analysis** involves both a thorough study of the current system and at least one proposed solution to the problems found. **Structured analysis** is the use of analysis and design tools such as **data flow diagrams, data dictionaries, process specification, structured English, decision tables,** and **decision trees** to document specifications of an information system.

7. Sometimes the systems analyst is asked to prepare a feasibility study and a cost/benefit analysis. The **feasibility study** discusses whether the proposed solution is practical and capable of being accomplished. The **cost/benefit analysis** identifies the estimated costs of the proposed solution and the benefits expected.

8. The end of the analysis phase is usually when organizations face a **make or buy decision** and have to decide either to acquire a commercial software package from an outside vendor, develop software themselves, or contract with a third party to develop software.

9. Once the analysis phase has been completed, the **acquisition** phase begins. It has four steps: (1) summarizing the application requirements, (2) identifying potential software vendors, (3) evaluating software alternatives, and (4) making the purchase.

10. **Commercial application software** is already developed software available for purchase. **Horizontal application software** is software used by many different types of organizations. Software developed for a unique way of doing business, usually within a specific industry, is called **vertical application software**.

11. A **request for proposal**, or RFP, is a written list of an organization's software requirements. A **request for quotation** (RFQ) is a request for a written price quotation on an item to be purchased.

11:00 AM

**What You
Should Know**

(continued)

12. Most computer stores have a wide selection of application software for personal computers. **Software houses** are businesses specializing in developing software for sale. **Value added resellers** (VARs), also called **system houses**, not only sell software but also sell computer equipment. **System integrators** are similar to VARs in that they can offer a total system solution, but they generally do not limit themselves to one or two types of omputers as do VARs.

13. Evaluating software alternatives involves matching each choice against the requirements list, talking to other users of the software, and trying the software. A **benchmark test** measures the time it takes to process a set number of transactions.

14. When software is purchased, it is not usually owned. What is actually purchased is a **software license**, which is the right to use the software under certain terms and conditions.

15. Application software developed by the user or at the user's request is called **custom software**. Modifying a commercial application package is usually referred to as **customizing**, or **tailoring**.

16. The proposed solution developed as part of the analysis phase usually consists of what is called a **logical design**. During the **design** phase, the logical design will be transformed into a **physical design** that identifies the procedures to be automated.

17. The system design usually follows one of two methods: top-down design or bottom-up design. **Top-down design**, also called **structured design**, focuses on the major functions of the system and keeps breaking those functions down into smaller and smaller activities. **Bottom-up design** focuses on the required information.

18. During **output design**, the systems analyst and the user document specific screen and report layouts to display or report information from the new system.

19. During **input design**, the systems analyst and the user identify what data needs to be entered into the system to produce the desired output. The systems analyst and the user determine the sequence of inputs and computer responses, called a **dialogue**, the user will encounter when he or she enters data.

20. During **database design**, the systems analyst uses the data dictionary information developed during the analysis phase and merges it into the new or existing system files.

21. During **process design**, the systems analyst specifies exactly what actions will be taken on the input data to create output information. One way to document the relationship of different processes is with a **system flowchart**. During process design, the systems analyst, the user, and other members of the development project sometimes meet to conduct **structured walk-throughs**, a step-by-step review of the process design.

22. **System controls** ensure only valid data is accepted and processed. The five types of controls considered by the systems analyst are: (1) **source document controls**, (2) **input controls**, (3) **processing controls**, (4) **accounting controls**, and (5) **access controls**.

23. Types of tests include the following: **unit testing** (testing individual programs), **system testing** (testing all programs in an application), **integration testing** (testing a new application) to make sure it works with other applications, and **acceptance testing** (demonstrating to the users that the system can meet user designed test criteria).

Start

24. At the end of the design phase, management performs a **design review** and evaluates the work completed so far to determine whether to proceed.

25. **Prototyping** is building a working model of the new system. **Computer-aided software engineering** (CASE) refers to the use of automated computer-based tools to design and manage a software system. A CASE **workbench** is an integrated package that combines several tools, which may include: *analysis and design tools, prototyping tools, code generators, an information repository, and management tools.*

26. The two parts to the **development phase** are: program development and equipment acquisition. The process of developing the software, or programs, required for a system is called **program development**. During the development phase, final decisions are made on what additional equipment, if any, must be acquired for the new system.

27. **Implementation** is the phase of the system development life cycle when people actually begin using the new system. Training and education is an important part of this phase.

28. **Conversion** refers to the process of changing from the old system to the new system. With **direct conversion**, the user stops using the old system one day and begins using the new system the next. **Parallel conversion** consists of continuing to process data on the old system while some or all of the data is also processed on the new system. **Phased conversion**, used with larger systems, can be broken down into individual modules that can be implemented separately at different times. **Pilot conversion** means the new system will be used first by only a portion of the organization. Converting existing manual and computer-based files so they can be used by a new system is called **data conversion**.

29. After a system is implemented, it is important to conduct a **post-implementation evaluation** to determine if the system is performing as designed.

30. **Maintenance** is the process of supporting the system after it is implemented. Maintenance consists of three activities: performance monitoring, change management, and error correction.

31. **Performance monitoring** is the ongoing process of comparing system performance measures against the estimates prepared during the analysis, design, and implementation phases. Change is an inevitable part of any system. A key part of change management is documentation. Error correction deals with problems caused by programming and design errors after the system is implemented.

File   Edit   Section   Page   Tools   Options   Help

Terms to Remember

acceptance testing (11.19)
access controls (11.19)
accounting controls (11.19)
acquisition (11.10)
analysis (11.4)

benchmark test (11.13)
bottom-up design (11.17)

CASE workbench (11.21)
commercial application software
     (11.10)
computer-aided software engineering
     (CASE) (11.21)
conversion (11.23)
cost/benefit analysis (11.8)
custom software (11.15)
customizing (11.16)

database design (11.17)
data conversion (11.24)
data dictionary (11.6)
data flow diagram (DFD) (11.15)
decision table (11.6)
decision tree (11.6)
design (11.17)
design review (11.20)
detailed system analysis (11.4)
development phase (11.22)
dialogue (11.17)
direct conversion (11.23)
documentation (11.3)

feasibility study (11.8)

horizontal application software
     (11.10)

implementation (11.23)
input controls (11.18)
input design (11.17)
integration testing (11.19)

logical design (11.17)

maintenance (11.25)
make-or-buy decision (11.8)

output design (11.17)

parallel conversion (11.23)
performance monitoring (11.25)
phased conversion (11.24)
physical design (11.17)
pilot conversion (11.24)
post-implementation evaluation
     (11.24)
preliminary investigation (11.4)
problem definition (11.4)
process design (11.17)
processing controls (11.18)
process specifications (11.16)
program development (11.22)
project management (11.2)
project plan (11.2)
prototyping (11.20)

request for proposal (RFP) (11.11)
request for quotation (RFQ) (11.11)
RFP (11.11)
RFQ (11.11)

software houses (11.12)
software license (11.14)
source document controls (11.18)
structured analysis (11.5)
structured design (11.17)
structured English (11.6)
structured walkthrough (11.18)
system controls (11.18)
system development life cycle
     (SDLC) (11.2)
system flowchart (11.18)
system houses (11.12)
system integrators (11.12)
system testing (11.19)

tailoring (11.16)
top-down design (11.17)

unit testing (11.19)

value-added resellers (VARs) (11.12)
vertical application software (11.10)

Start   11:01 AM

Test Your Knowledge

Fill in the Blanks

1. The _____ is an organized approach to obtaining an information system.

2. _____ involves planning, scheduling, reporting, and controlling the individual activities that make up the system development life cycle; while _____ refers to written materials produced as part of the system development life cycle describing the overall purpose of the system.

3. _____ is already developed software available for purchase.

4. Three analysis and design tools are: a(n) _____, which graphically shows the flow of data through a system; the_____, which describes the elements making up the data flow; and a(n) _____, which identifies the actions that should be taken under different conditions.

5. Unlike _____ conversion, in which the user stops using the old system one day and begins using the new system the next, _____ conversion consists of continuing to process data on the old system while some or all of the data is also processed on the new system.

Short Answer

1. How is horizontal application software different from vertical application software? Why is it important to understand the difference between the two types of application software?

2. What are the four steps in the acquisition phase? Briefly explain each.

3. Why would an organization choose to develop custom software? What guidelines can be used for evaluating the need for custom software versus commercial application software?

4. What is program development? List the five steps in program development. Who is responsible for program development?

5. What is maintenance? What three activities are part of maintenance? Briefly describe each.

Label the Figure

Instructions: Identify the phases in the system development life cycle.

Points to Ponder

1

The system development life cycle may be undertaken in response to a problem, or problems, that an organization is experiencing. Think of a difficult problem you had and were able to solve. List, in the order in which they were taken, all of the steps you followed to solve the problem. Using the system development life cycle as a guide, in which phase (analysis, acquisition or design, customizing or development, implementation, or maintenance) would you place each step in your solution to the problem? Why? Which phase do you think was most crucial in solving your problem? Why? Which phase do you think was least important? Why?

2

Upon completion of the analysis phase of the SDLC, a written report is submitted by the systems analyst. This report explains why an investigation of the current system was performed, describes the problems that were found, and outlines possible solutions and the action recommended. Some authorities have found that in most instances, any changes suggested by the user after this report is completed are resisted. Why do you think this is true? Under what circumstances should user changes be considered? Why? Should suggested changes ever be ignored? Why or why not?

3

Prepare one of the following:

a. A data flow diagram illustrating the flow of information through your school's computer system during class registration.

b. A decision table or decision tree showing whether or not you will register for a class given at least two conditions.

c. A system flowchart documenting the data you enter, processes you perform, files you use, and reports you produce in registering for a specific class.

4

Occasionally organizations hire an outside consultant to identify software suppliers. Although some organizations feel these consultants have saved them considerable sums of money, others insist they would have been better off not hiring a consultant. Under what circumstances do you think a company would hire a consultant? What advantages, if any, could a consultant have in locating software suppliers, choosing appropriate software packages, and helping to implement those packages? What problems, if any, could an outside consultant encounter? To be most effective, what sort of cooperation would a consultant need from the organization?

5

Imagine you are the head of the information systems department for a small manufacturing firm. Several department managers have contacted your office complaining that the current information system is outdated (it is almost eight years old) and is no longer meeting their needs, so you have organized a committee to investigate the problem. At your first meeting, George, a department manager, suggests a representative from Colonial Computing, the vendor that supplied the current computer system, be made a part of the system development team. Martha, another department manager, strongly disagrees. In fact, she maintains that if it is necessary to acquire a new system, the firm should consider using several different vendors instead of a single supplier. What are the strengths and weaknesses of the suggestions made by each department manager? As head of the committee, how would you resolve the conflict?

6

Problems encountered during system development are easier and less expensive to remedy at some phases in the system development life cycle than at others. At what phase of the system development life cycle would it be easiest to identify problems? At what phase would it be most difficult? At what phase would it be easiest and least expensive to solve problems? At what phase would it be most difficult and most expensive? Explain your answers.

File   Edit   Section   Page   Tools   Options   Help

Out and About

1. Is the system development life cycle always the best method of creating solutions to information systems problems? Some systems analysts feel that prototyping, used from preliminary investigation to system implementation, results in greater user satisfaction and increased likelihood that users will be able to work with the final system. Interview a systems analyst at a company, or from the computer department or information systems department in your school, about his or her opinion of the system development life cycle versus prototyping. What does he or she feel is the best approach to developing information systems? What are the advantages and disadvantages of the SDLC? What are the advantages and disadvantages of prototyping? Under what circumstances would he or she choose to use each approach? Can either the system development life cycle or prototyping be used when solving noncomputer related problems? Why or why not?

2. Identify a problem on campus, or a problem you have, that could be solved using a personal computer and application software. Write a request for proposal (RFP), similar to that shown in *Figure 11-13* on page 11.11, documenting the features you think would be necessary in the application software. Visit a software vendor and, using your RFP, attempt to find at least two software packages that meet most of your requirements. Evaluate the software by scoring each package against your list of requirements, talking to people who use the software (if possible), and trying the software yourself. On the basis of your evaluation, which software package, if any, would you choose? Why?

3. Using trade publications or computer magazines, find advertisements for or articles on at least three examples of vertical application software. Who makes each software package? For what industry is the software designed? What is its function? What capabilities does it have that cannot be found in horizontal application software? How much does the software cost?

4. Locate a computer consultant by using the yellow pages, newspapers, or computer store references. Arrange to interview the consultant about his or her job. What services does the consultant provide? What advantages does the consultant offer a company? What tools does he or she use? What kind of education, experience, and personality is required to be an effective computer consultant? What is the most difficult part of a consultant's job? What is the most rewarding aspect of being a consultant?

5. Occasionally we hear stories about computer errors that cost individuals or organizations a great deal of money and trouble. Locate a newspaper or magazine article on such an error. Describe the error. After reading the article, do you think it was really a computer error or was it a mistake made in some phase of the system development life cycle? Why? If you believe a mistake was made in a phase of the SDLC, in which phase was it made? How? What could have been done to prevent the "computer error?"

6. In 1994, the median salary for systems analysts was $45,000, and top systems analysts were making as much as $75,000. Some authorities believe that soon all types of businesses, including software companies, manufacturing firms, and brokerage houses, will need systems analysts to monitor the information systems essential to modern companies. It is expected that more than 20,000 systems analyst positions will be added by the year 2000. Using want ads from newspapers, computer publications, or trade journals, and possibly calling some prospective employers, find out what qualities employers are looking for in a systems analyst. Describe the type of education, experience, achievements, and personality that make an individual a successful candidate for a systems analyst position.

File   Edit   Section   Page   Tools   Options   Help

In the Lab with Windows 95

1 **Traffic Sign Tutorial**   Obtain information from your instructor on the location (path) of the file TRAFFIC.EXE. Click the Start button on the taskbar and then click Run on the Start menu. In the Open text box, type the path and file-name traffic. For example, type c:\sclabs\traffic and then press ENTER to display the Traffic Sign Tutorial window *(Figure 11-28)*. Drag the signs to their correct containers. If you drag a sign to the wrong container, it will snap back to its original location.

Click Options on the menu bar and then click Clear to initialize the tutorial. Click Options on the menu bar and then click Show to display the correct answers. Click Options on the menu bar and then click Clear. Click Options on the menu bar and then click Quiz. Answer the quiz questions. Close Traffic Sign Tutorial.

2 **Arranging Windows on Your Desktop**   Click the Start button on the taskbar, point to Programs on the Start menu, point to Accessories on the Programs submenu, and then click Paint on the Accessories submenu. Click the Start button on the taskbar, point to Programs on the Start menu, point to Accessories on the Programs submenu, and then click Notepad on the Accessories submenu.

Right-click an empty area on your taskbar, and then click Tile Vertically on the shortcut menu *(Figure 11-29)*. What do vertically tiled windows look like? Right-click an empty area on your taskbar, and then click Tile Horizontally on the shortcut menu. What do horizontally tiled windows look like? Right-click an empty area on your taskbar, and then click Cascade on the shortcut menu. What do cascaded windows look like? Right-click an empty area on your taskbar, and then click Minimize All Windows on the shortcut menu.

Right-click untitled - Paint on the taskbar, and then click Close on the shortcut menu. Click Untitled - Notepad on the taskbar. Close Notepad.

3 **Creating a Drawing**   Click the Start button on the taskbar, point to Programs on the Start menu, point to Accessories on the Programs submenu, and then click Paint on the Accessories submenu. Maximize Paint.

Change the background color to royal blue by right-clicking the color royal blue in the color box at the bottom of the Paint window, click File on the menu bar, and then click New. Click the Brush tool in the tool box at the left edge of the Paint window. Change the foreground color to yellow by clicking the color yellow in the color box.

Move the mouse pointer into the blue window. Use the mouse to write your name in cursive. Drag the mouse through your entire name, or release the mouse between each character. If you make a mistake, click Edit on the menu bar and then click Undo to erase your last draw.

Click File on the menu bar and then click Print Preview. With your printer turned on, click the Print button on the Print Preview toolbar, and then click the OK button. Close Paint.

Figure 11-28

Figure 11-29

Windows 95

Start   11:05 AM

File   Edit   Section   Page   Tools   Options   Help

Where on the Web

1 **Visit Silicon Studio**   Complete the following steps to visit Silicon Studio's Web site *(Figure 11-30)* and learn more about system integrators and VARs. With Netscape on the screen, type `http://www.studio.sgi.com/StudioInfo` in the Location text box and press ENTER. Click Studio History. Read and scroll down the page. Is Silicon Studio a system integrator or a VAR? Click Print on the File menu. Click Pages and then type 1 in the To text box. Click OK. Write your answer on the printout and hand it in.

2 **Computer-Based Design Tools**   Computer-aided software engineering (CASE) refers to the use of automated computer-based tools to design and manage a software system. Complete the following steps to use the Yahoo Directory to learn more about CASE. With Netscape on the screen, click the Net Search button. Click Yahoo. Click Business. Click Companies. Click Computers. Click Software. Click Programming Tools. Click CASE. Scroll down and click a company. What CASE product /service does the company offer? Click Print on the File menu. Click Pages and then type 1 in the To text box. Click OK. Write your answer on the printout and hand it in.

3 **Tour the Smithsonian**   To visit the Smithsonian Institute's Web site *(Figure 11-31)* and learn more about information system development, complete the following steps. With Netscape on the screen, type `http://www.si.edu` in the Location text box and press ENTER. Scroll down and click Welcome. Read and scroll down the page. Click Navigating The Electronic Smithsonian. Scroll down and read the page. What do you think are some of

the special problems associated with developing World Wide Web information systems such as the Smithsonian? Click Print on the File menu. Click Pages and then type 1 in the To text box to print just the first page. Click OK. Write your answer on the printout and hand it in.

4 **Rapid Application Development**   In an attempt to decrease the amount of time it takes to develop a new application, some companies are trying a new approach called rapid application development (RAD). Complete the following steps to use a Net Search utility to learn more about RAD. With Netscape on the screen, click the Net Search button. Click Infoseek Guide. Type `rapid application development` in the text box. Click the seek now button. Scroll down and click any one of the items. Read more about that topic. Click Print on the File menu. Click Pages and then type 1 in the To text box. Click OK. Write a brief description of what you found on the printout and hand it in.

5 **Shelly Cashman Online**   Click Using Computers: A Gateway To Information, World Wide Web Edition on the Shelly Cashman Student Center Web page (`http://www.bf.com/scstudnt.html`). Scroll down and click Chapter 11. Complete the activities listed.

Figure 11-30

Figure 11-31

Program Development and Programming Languages

12

Objectives

After completing this chapter, you will be able to:

- Define the term computer program

- Describe the five steps in program development

- Explain the concepts of structured program design

- Explain and illustrate the sequence, selection, and iteration control structures used in structured programming

- Define the term programming language and discuss the various categories of programming languages

- Explain and discuss application generators

- Explain and discuss object-oriented programming

- Discuss the programming languages that are commonly used today

- Explain the factors that should be considered when choosing a programming language

The system development life cycle covers the entire process of taking a plan for processing data through various phases until it becomes a functioning information system. During the development phase of this cycle, computer programs are written. The purpose of these programs is to process data and produce information as specified in the information system design. This chapter focuses on the steps taken to write a program and the available tools that make the program development process more efficient. This chapter also discusses the different languages used to write programs.

Although you may never write a program yourself, you may someday request information that will require a program to be written or modified; thus, you should understand how a computer program is developed.

What Is a Computer Program?

A **computer program** is a detailed set of instructions that directs a computer to perform the tasks necessary to process data into information. These instructions, usually written by a computer programmer, can be coded (written) in a variety of programming languages discussed later in this chapter. To create programs that are correct (produce accurate information) and maintainable (easy to modify), programmers follow a process called program development.

What Is Program Development?

Program development is the process of producing one or more programs to perform specific tasks on a computer. The process of program development has evolved into a series of five steps most experts agree should take place when any program is developed *(Figure 12-1)*.

1. *Review specifications.* The programmer reviews the specifications created by the systems analyst during the system design phase.
2. *Design.* The programmer determines and documents the specific actions the computer will take to accomplish the desired tasks.
3. *Code.* The programmer writes the actual program instructions.
4. *Test.* The written programs are tested to make sure they perform as intended.
5. *Finalize documentation.* Throughout the program development process, the programmer documents, or writes, explanatory information about the program. In this final step, the documentation produced during steps 1 through 4 is brought together and organized.

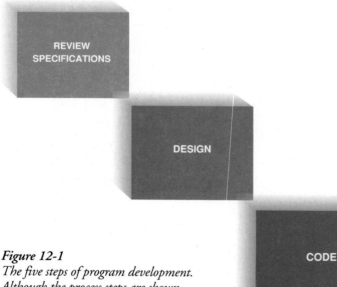

Figure 12-1
The five steps of program development. Although the process steps are shown sequentially, program development usually requires returning to previous steps to correct errors.

Step 1 – Reviewing the Program Specifications

Although these five steps are listed sequentially, the program development process usually requires returning to previous steps to correct errors that are discovered.

To better understand how the steps in the program development process relate to the overall development of an information system, the phases of the system development life cycle are shown in *Figure 12-2*. Program development is a phase on the development path of the system development life cycle. If, after the analysis phase, an organization is unable to acquire commercial software that meets its needs, it shifts to the design phase. The development phase, which includes program development, follows the design phase and is made up of the five steps shown in *Figure 12-1* on the previous page.

The first step in the program development process is a review of the program specifications. **Program specifications** can consist of data flow diagrams, system flowcharts, process specifications that indicate the action to be taken on the data, a data dictionary identifying the data elements that will be used, screen formats, report layouts, and actual documents such as invoices or checks. These documents help the programmer understand the work that needs to be done by the program. Also, the programmer meets with the user and the systems analyst who designed the system to understand the purpose of the program from the user's point of view.

If the programmer believes some aspect of the design should be changed, such as a screen layout, he or she discusses it with the systems analyst and the user. If the change is agreed on, the written design specification is changed. The programmer, however, should not change the specified system without the agreement of the systems analyst and the user. If a change is authorized, it should be recorded in the system design. The systems analyst and the user, through the system design, have specified what is to be done. It is the programmer's job to determine *how* to do it.

Large programming jobs are usually assigned to more than one programmer. In these situations, a good system design is essential so each programmer can be given a logical portion of the system to be programmed.

Figure 12-2
Program development occurs during the development phase of the system development life cycle.

Step 2 – Designing the Program

After the programmer has carefully reviewed the specifications, program design begins. During **program design**, a logical solution to the programming task is developed and documented. The solution is broken down into a step-by-step procedure called an **algorithm**. Determining the logic for a computer program can be an extremely complex task. To aid in program design and development, a method called structured program design is commonly used.

Structured Program Design

Structured program design is a methodology emphasizing three main program design concepts: modules, control structures, and single entry/single exit. Use of these concepts helps create programs that are easy to write, read, understand, check for errors, and modify.

MODULES

With structured design, programming problems are *decomposed* (separated) into smaller parts called modules.

Each **module**, sometimes referred to as a **subroutine**, performs a given task within the program. The major benefit of this technique is it simplifies program development because each module of a program can be developed individually. When the modules are combined, they form a complete program that accomplishes the desired result.

Structure charts, also called **hierarchy charts**, are often used to decompose and represent the modules of a program. When the program decomposition is completed, the entire structure of a program is illustrated by the hierarchy chart *(Figure 12-3),* which shows the relationship of the modules within the program.

CONTROL STRUCTURES

In structured program design, three basic **control structures** are used to form the logic of a program. All logic problems can be solved by a combination of these structures. The three basic control structures are: sequence, selection, and iteration.

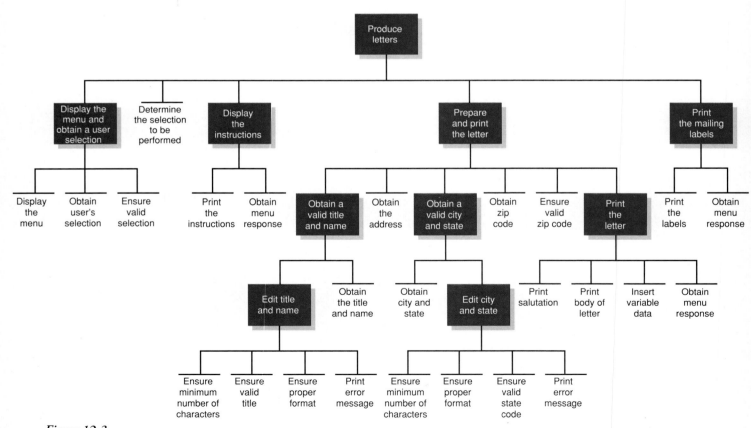

Figure 12-3

In this structure chart, the relationship of individual program modules is graphically shown as boxes. The text below each box indicates the processing steps that would be performed.

1. In the **sequence structure**, one process occurs immediately after another. In *Figure 12-4*, each rectangular box represents a particular process that is to occur. For example, a process could be a computer instruction to multiply two numbers. Each process occurs in the exact sequence specified, one process followed by the next.

2. The second control structure, called the **selection structure**, or **if-then-else structure**, gives programmers a way to represent conditional program logic *(Figure 12-5)*. Conditional program logic can be expressed in the following way: *If* the condition is true, *then* perform the true condition processing, *else* perform the false condition processing. When the if-then-else structure is used, the *if* portion of the structure tests a given condition. The true portion of the statement is executed if the condition tested is true, and the false portion of the statement is executed if the condition is false. An if-then-else structure might be used to determine if an employee is hourly or salaried and then process the employee accordingly. To do this, an employee code might be tested to determine if an employee is hourly. If the employee is hourly, the true portion of the structure would be executed and hourly pay would be calculated. If the employee is not hourly, the false portion of the structure would be executed and salary pay would be calculated. The selection, or if-then-else, structure is used by programmers to represent conditional logic problems.

    A variation of the selection structure is the case structure. The **case structure** is used when a condition being tested can lead to more than two alternatives *(Figure 12-6)*. In a program, a menu is an example of a case structure because it provides multiple processing options.

3. The third control structure, called the **iteration structure**, or **looping structure**, means one or more processes continue to occur as long as a given condition remains true. There are two forms of this control structure: the **do-while structure** and the **do-until structure** *(Figure 12-7* on the next page). In the do-while structure, a condition is tested.

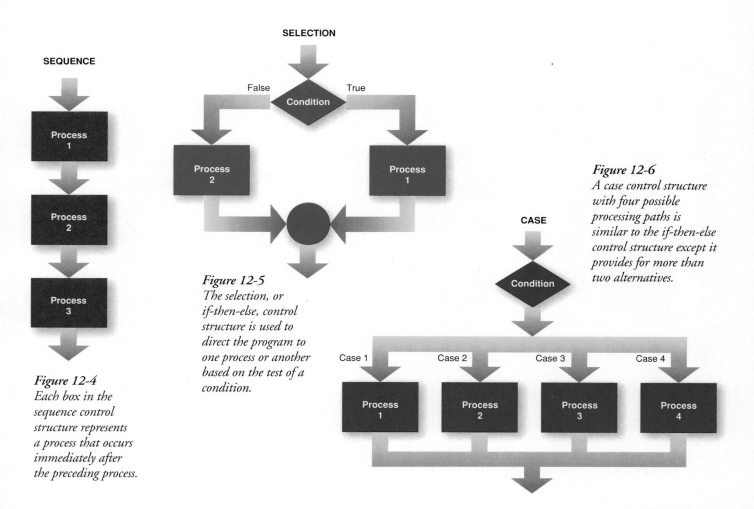

SEQUENCE

SELECTION

CASE

Figure 12-4
Each box in the sequence control structure represents a process that occurs immediately after the preceding process.

Figure 12-5
The selection, or if-then-else, control structure is used to direct the program to one process or another based on the test of a condition.

Figure 12-6
A case control structure with four possible processing paths is similar to the if-then-else control structure except it provides for more than two alternatives.

If the condition is true, the process is performed. The program then *loops* back and tests the condition again. If the condition is still true, the process is performed again. This looping continues until the condition being tested is false. At that time, the program exits the loop, moves to another section of the program, and performs some other processing. An example of this type of testing would be a check to see if all records have been processed.

The do-until control structure is similar to the do-while except the condition tested is at the end instead of the beginning of the loop. Processing continues *until* the condition is met.

Programmers combine these three control structures–sequence, selection, and iteration–to create program logic solutions. A structured program design rule that applies to these control structures and how they are combined is the single entry/single exit rule.

SINGLE ENTRY/SINGLE EXIT

An important concept in structured programming is **single entry/single exit**, meaning there is only one entry point and one exit point for each of the three control structures. An **entry point** is the point where a control structure is entered. An **exit point** is the point where the control structure is exited. For example, in *Figure 12-8*, when the if-then-else structure is used, the control structure is entered at the point where the condition is tested. When the condition is tested, one set of instructions will be executed if the condition is true and another set will be executed if the condition is false. Regardless of the result of the test, however, the structure is exited at the single exit point.

This feature substantially improves the logic of a program because, when reading the program, the programmer can be assured that whatever happens within the if-then-else structure, the control structure will always be exited at a common point. Prior to the use of structured programming, many programmers would transfer control to other parts of

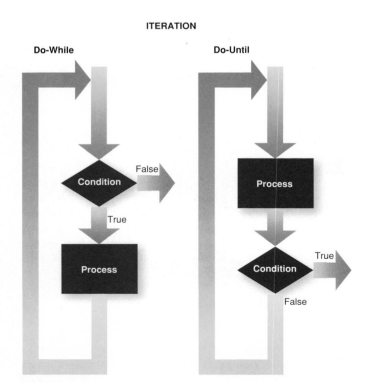

Figure 12-7
The iteration control structure has two forms, do-while and do-until. In the do-while structure, the condition is tested before the process. In the do-until structure, the condition is tested after the process.

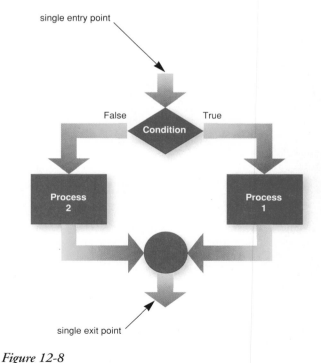

Figure 12-8
Structured programming concepts require all control structures to have a single entry point and a single exit point. This contributes to programs that are easier to understand and maintain.

a program without following the single entry/single exit rule. This practice led to poorly designed programs that were extremely difficult to read, check for errors, and modify. Because the logic path of such programs jumps from one section of the program to another, the programs are sometimes referred to as *spaghetti code*.

Program Design Tools

Programmers use several popular program design tools to develop and document the logical solutions to the problems they are programming. Two commonly used design tools are program flowcharts and pseudocode.

PROGRAM FLOWCHARTS

Program flowcharts were one of the first program design tools. *Figure 12-9* shows a flowchart drawn in the late 1940s by Dr. John von Neumann, a computer scientist and one of the first computer programmers. In a **program flowchart**, all the logical steps of a program are represented by a combination of symbols and text.

A set of standards for program flowcharts was published in the early 1960s by the American National Standards Institute (ANSI). These standards, which are still used today, specify symbols, such as rectangles and diamonds, used to represent the various operations performed on a computer *(Figure 12-10)*. Program flowcharts were used as the primary means of program design for many years prior to the introduction of structured program design. During these years, programmers designed programs by focusing on the detailed steps required for a program and creating logical solutions for each new combination of conditions as it was encountered. Developing programs in this manner led to poorly designed programs.

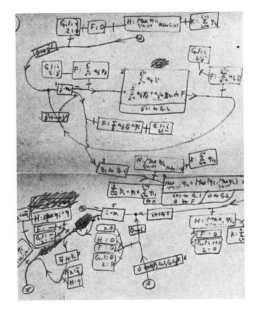

Figure 12-9
An example of an early flowchart developed by computer scientist Dr. John von Neumann in the 1940s to solve a problem involving game theory. This flowchart was drawn prior to the standardization of flowchart symbols and the development of structured design techniques.

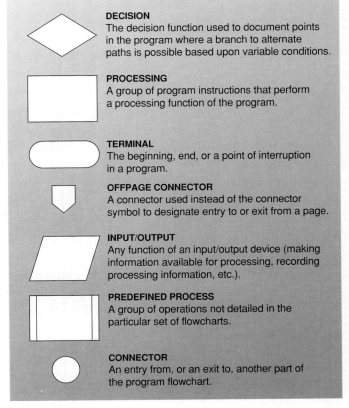

DECISION
The decision function used to document points in the program where a branch to alternate paths is possible based upon variable conditions.

PROCESSING
A group of program instructions that perform a processing function of the program.

TERMINAL
The beginning, end, or a point of interruption in a program.

OFFPAGE CONNECTOR
A connector used instead of the connector symbol to designate entry to or exit from a page.

INPUT/OUTPUT
Any function of an input/output device (making information available for processing, recording processing information, etc.).

PREDEFINED PROCESS
A group of operations not detailed in the particular set of flowcharts.

CONNECTOR
An entry from, or an exit to, another part of the program flowchart.

Figure 12-10
Standard symbols used to create program flowcharts.

Today, programmers are taught to apply the structured design concepts when they create program flowcharts *(Figure 12-11)*. When they use basic control structures, program flowcharts are a valuable program design tool.

PSEUDOCODE

Some experts in program design advocate the use of pseudocode when designing the logic for a program. In **pseudocode**, the logical steps in the solution of a problem are written as English statements and indentations are used to represent the control structures *(Figure 12-12)*. An advantage of pseudocode is it eliminates the time spent with flowcharting

to draw and arrange symbols while attempting to determine the program logic. The major disadvantage is that, unlike flowcharting, pseudocode does not provide a graphic representation, which some people find easier to interpret when they examine programming logic.

To ensure that the program design is efficient and correct, many development teams use structured walkthroughs.

Structured Walkthrough

After a program has been designed, the programmer schedules a structured walkthrough of the program. The **structured walkthrough** is a review of the program logic by

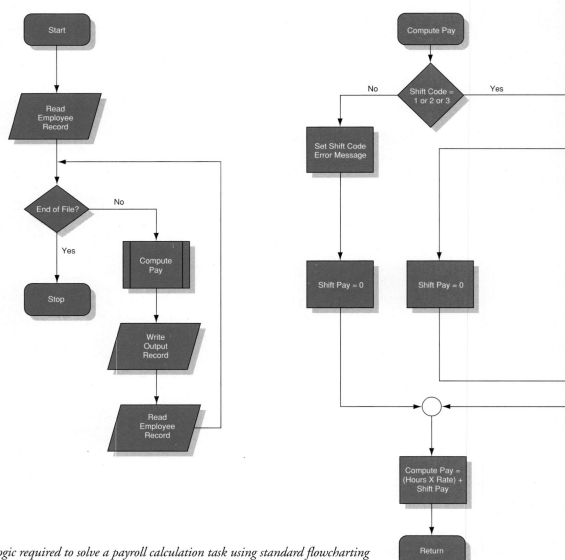

Figure 12-11
This flowchart displays the logic required to solve a payroll calculation task using standard flowcharting symbols and the three control structures of structured programming.

other members of the development team. During the walkthrough, the person who designed the program explains the program logic. The purpose of the design walkthrough is to review the logic of the program for errors, and if possible, improve program design. Early detection of errors and approval of program design improvements reduces the overall development time and therefore the cost of the program. It is much better to find errors and make needed changes to the program during the design step than to make them later in the program development process. Structured walkthroughs are also used to review work in other phases of the system development life cycle.

Once the program design is complete, the programmer can begin to code the program.

Step 3 – Coding the Program

Coding the program refers to the process of writing the program instructions that process the data and produce the output specified in the program design. As previously mentioned, programs are written in different languages, each of which has particular rules on how to instruct the computer to perform specific tasks such as read a record or multiply two numbers. Fortunately, most of the commonly used languages adhere to code standards established by the American National Standards Institute (ANSI). **Code standards** enable the same program to work on different types of computers.

If the program design is thorough, logical, and well structured, the coding process is greatly simplified and can sometimes be a one-for-one translation of a design step into a program step. Coding language is explained in detail later in this chapter. The amount of time it takes to code a program can be shortened if an organization maintains a code library. A **code library** stores partial or complete programs written to solve a particular problem such as calculating city, county, and state sales taxes. Before starting a new program, a programmer checks the code library to see if any existing code can be reused.

```
MAIN PROCESSING MODULE:

Read employee record
DO WHILE not end of file
    Compute pay
    Write output record
    Read employee record
ENDDO
Stop

COMPUTE PAY MODULE:

IF shift code = 1 or 2 or 3
    IF shift code = 1
        Set shift pay = 0
    ELSE
        IF shift code = 2
            Set shift pay = $10.00
        ELSE
            Set shift pay = $20.00
        ENDIF
    ENDIF
ELSE
    Set shift code error message
    Set shift pay = 0
ENDIF
Compute pay = (hours X rate) + shift pay
RETURN
```

Figure 12-12
This pseudocode is another way of documenting the logic shown in the flowchart in Figure 12-11.

Step 4 – Testing the Program

Before a program is used to process real data and produce information people rely on, it should be thoroughly tested to make sure it is functioning correctly. A programmer can perform several different types of tests.

Desk checking is the process of reading the program and mentally reviewing its logic. This is a simple process performed by the programmer who wrote the program or by another programmer. This process can be compared to proof-reading a letter before you mail it. Desk checking can also uncover **syntax errors**, which are violations of the grammar rules of the language in which the program was written. An example of a syntax error would be the program command READ being misspelled REED. Syntax errors missed by the programmer during desk checking are identified by the computer when it decodes the program instructions.

Logic testing is what most programmers think of when the term testing is used. During **logic testing**, the sequence of program instructions is tested to make sure it provides the correct result. Logic errors may be the result of a programming oversight such as using the wrong data to perform a calculation or a design error such as forgetting to specify that some customers do not have to pay sales tax when they purchase merchandise.

Logic testing is performed with **test data**, which is data that simulates real data the program will process when it is implemented. To obtain an independent and unbiased test of the program, test data and the review of test results should be the responsibility of someone other than the programmer who wrote the program. The test data should be developed by referring to the system design, but it should also try to *break* or *crash* the program by including data outside the range of data found during normal operations. For example, if the specifications of a payroll program stated that an employee should never work in excess of 60 hours per week, the program should be designed, coded, and tested to display an error message if the hours exceed 60. If such an error is found, the program should display an error message or in some other way indicate an invalid number of hours has been entered.

One of the more colorful terms of the computer industry is **debugging**, which refers to the process of locating and correcting program errors, called **bugs**, found during testing. A popular story is that the term bug was first used when the failure of one of the first computers was traced to a moth lodged in the electronic components *(Figure 12-13)*. Most programming languages include a **debugger** program that identifies syntax errors and allows the programmer to stop the program while it is running to examine program values such as the result of a calculation.

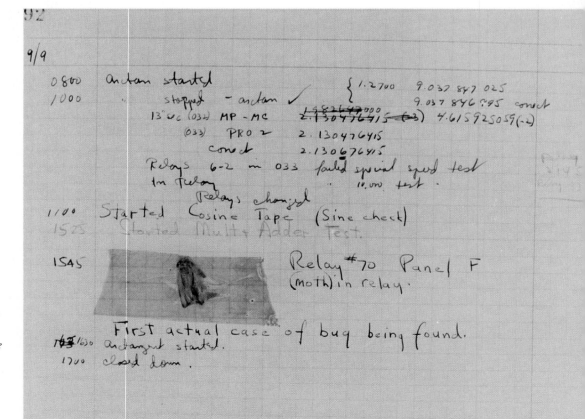

Figure 12-13
In 1945, the cause of the temporary failure of the world's first electro-mechanical computer, the Mark 1, was traced to a dead moth (shown taped to the log book) caught in the electrical components. Some say this event is the origin of the term bug, meaning a computer error.

Step 5 – Finalizing Program Documentation

Documentation, which is the preparation of documents explaining the program, is an essential but sometimes neglected part of the programming process. Documentation should be an ongoing part of developing a program and should only be finalized, meaning organized and brought together, after the program is successfully tested and ready for implementation. Documentation developed during the programming process should include a narrative description of the program, program design documents such as flowcharts or pseudocode, program listings, and test results. Comments in the program itself are also an important part of program documentation *(Figure 12-14)*. Data entry and computer operations procedures should also be documented prior to implementation.

In addition to helping programmers develop programs, documentation is valuable because it helps the next programmer who is asked, six months or one year later, to make a change to the program. Proper documentation can substantially reduce the amount of time the new programmer will have to spend learning enough about the program to know how best to make the change.

```
REM Program 12-14
REM Determining a Salesperson's Commission
REM Dave Brame, CIS 204, Div. 01
REM September 30, 1996
REM **************************************
REM Clear Screen
CLS
REM Request Data from Operator
INPUT "Commission rate =====> ", Rate
INPUT "Week 1 sales =========> ", Week1
INPUT "Week 2 sales =========> ", Week2
INPUT "Return sales =========> ", Returns
```

Figure 12-14
Most programming languages allow programmers to place explanatory comments directly in the program. This is an effective way of documenting the program. In this QuickBASIC program, comment lines are identified by the letters REM, which is an abbreviation for REMARK.

Program Maintenance

Program maintenance includes all changes to a program once it is implemented and processing real transactions. Sometimes, maintenance is required to correct errors not found during the testing step. Other times, maintenance is required to make changes resulting from new information requirements. It may surprise you to learn that the majority of all business programming today consists of maintaining existing programs, not writing new programs.

Because so much time is spent on maintenance programming, it should be subject to the same policies and procedures, such as design, testing, and documentation, required for new programs. Unfortunately, this is not always the case. Because maintenance tasks are usually shorter than new programming efforts, they often are not held to the same standards. The result is that over time, programs can become unrecognizable when compared with their original documentation. Maintaining high standards for program maintenance not only can lower overall programming costs, but also lengthen the useful life of a program.

Summary of Program Development

The key to developing quality programs for an information system is to follow the steps of the program development process. Program specifications must be carefully reviewed and understood. Programmers should use structured concepts to design programs that are modular, use the three control structures, and follow the single entry/single exit rule. Programmers should carefully code and test the program and finalize documentation. If each of these steps is followed, programmers will create quality programs that are correct and can be easily read, understood, and maintained.

What Is a Programming Language?

As mentioned at the beginning of this chapter, computer programs can be written in a variety of programming languages. People communicate with one another through language, established patterns of words and sounds. A similar definition can also be applied to a **programming language**, which is a set of written words and symbols that allow the programmer or user to communicate with the computer. As with English, Spanish, Chinese, or other spoken languages, programming languages have rules, called syntax, that govern their use.

Categories of Programming Languages

Hundreds of programming languages are available, each with its own syntax. Some languages were developed for specific computers and others, because of their success, have been standardized and adapted to a wide range of computers. Programming languages can be classified into one of four categories: machine language, assembly language, high-level languages, and fourth-generation languages.

Machine Language

Machine language is the fundamental language of the computer's processor. Programs written in all other categories of languages are eventually translated into machine language before they are executed. Individual machine language instructions exist for each of the commands in the computer's instruction set (the operations such as add, move, or read that are specific to each computer). Because the instruction set is unique for a particular processor, machine languages are different for computers that have different processors.

(a) MACHINE LANGUAGE
9b df 46 0c 9b d9 c0 9b db 7e f2 9b d9 46 04 9b d8 c9 9b d9 5e fc
9b d9 c0 9b dc 16 ac 00 9b dd d8 9b dd 7e f0 90 9b 8a 66 f1 9e 9b dd c0 76 19
9b d9 46 fc 9b dc 0e b4 00 9b de e9 9b d9 5e 08 90 9b
eb 0d 90
8b 46 fc 8b 56 fe 89 46 08 89 56 0a

Figure 12-15
Program instruction chart for: (a) machine language (printed in a hexadecimal form), (b) assembly language, and (c) a high-level language called C. The machine language and assembly language instructions correspond to the high-level instructions and were generated when the high-level language statements were translated into machine language. As you can see, the high-level language requires fewer program instructions and is easier to read.

Most microprocessor manufacturers, however, design their new microprocessors so they will run programs written for earlier generations within the same *family* (product line) of microprocessors.

The advantage of writing a program in machine language is the programmer can control the computer directly and accomplish exactly what needs to be done. Therefore, well-written machine language programs are very efficient. The disadvantages of machine language programs are they take a long time to write and they are difficult to review if the programmer is trying to find an error. In addition, because they are written using the instruction set of a particular processor, the programs will only run on computers with the same type of processor. Because they are written for specific processors, machine languages are also called **low-level languages**. *Figure 12-15(a)* shows an example of machine language instructions.

Assembly Language

To make it easier for programmers to remember the specific machine instruction codes, assembly languages were developed. An **assembly language** is similar to a machine language, but uses abbreviations called **mnemonics** or **symbolic operation codes** to represent the machine operation code. Another difference is assembly languages usually allow **symbolic addressing**, which means a specific computer memory location can be referenced by a name or symbol, such as TOTAL, instead of by its actual address as it would have to be referenced in machine language. Assembly language programs can also include **macroinstructions** that generate more than one machine language instruction.

Assembly language programs are converted into machine language instructions by a special program called an **assembler**. Even though assembly languages are easier to use than machine languages, they are still considered a low-level language because they are so closely related to the specific design of the computer. *Figure 12-15(b)* shows an example of assembly language instructions.

(b) ASSEMBLY LANGUAGE	(c) HIGH-LEVEL LANGUAGE
| ```
      fld WORD PTR [bp+12];qty
fld   ST(0)
      fstp TBYTE PTR [bp-14]
      fld  DWORD PTR [bp+4];price
fmul ST(0),ST(1)
      fstp DWORD PTR [bp-4];gross
``` | `gross = qty * price;` |
| ```
fld   ST(0)
         fcom QWORD PTR $T20002
fstp ST(0)
      fstsw      WORD PTR [bp-16]
      fwait
mov   ah,BYTE PTR [bp-15]
      sahf
ffreeST(0)
      jbe $I193
``` | `if (qty > ceiling)` |
| ```
      fld DWORD PTR [bp-4];gross
      fmul QWORD PTR $T20003
fsub
      fstp DWORD PTR [bp+8];net
      fwait
``` | `net = gross - (gross * discount_rate);` |
| ```
      jmp SHORT $I194
      nop
``` | `else` |
| ```
      $I193:
mov   ax,WORD PTR [bp-4];gross
mov   dx,WORD PTR [bp-2]
mov   WORD PTR [bp+8],ax ;net
mov   WORD PTR [bp+10],dx
      $I194:
``` | `net = gross;` |
```

High-Level Languages

High-level languages were developed in the late 1950s and 1960s. **High-level languages** more closely resemble what most people would think of as a language because they contain nouns, verbs, and mathematical, relational, and logical operators that can be grouped together to form what appear to be sentences (*Figure 12-15(c)* on the previous page). These sentences are called **program statements**. Because of these characteristics, high-level languages can be read by programmers and are thus easier to learn and use than machine or assembly languages. Another important advantage over low-level languages is high-level languages are usually machine independent, which means they can run on different types of computers.

As mentioned previously, all languages must be translated into machine language before they can be executed. High-level languages are translated in one of two ways: with a compiler or an interpreter.

A **compiler** converts an entire program into machine language that is usually stored on a disk for later execution. The program to be converted is called the **source program** and the machine language produced is called the **object program** or **object code**. Compilers check the program syntax, perform limited logic checking, and make sure that data to be used in comparisons or calculations, such as a discount rate, is properly defined somewhere in the program. An important feature of compilers is they produce an error listing of all program statements not meeting the program language rules. This listing helps the programmer make the necessary changes to debug or correct the program. *Figure 12-16* illustrates the process of compiling a program.

Because machine language is unique to each processor, different computers require different compilers for the same language. For example, a mainframe, minicomputer, and personal computer would each have different compilers that would translate the same source language program into the specific machine language for each computer.

While a compiler translates an entire program, an **interpreter** translates one program statement at a time and

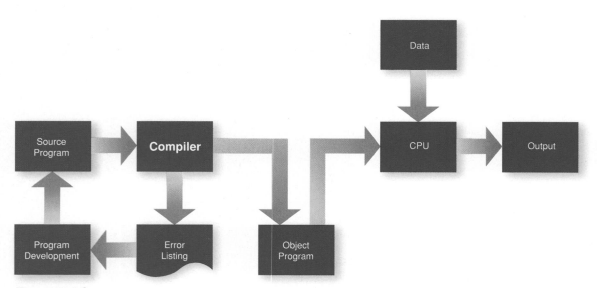

Figure 12-16
When a compiler is used, a source language program is compiled into a machine language object program. When the user wants to run the program, the object program is loaded into the main memory of the CPU and the program instructions begin executing. As instructed by the program, the CPU processes data and creates output. Errors in the source program identified during compilation are shown on an error listing that is used to make the necessary corrections during program development.

then executes the resulting machine language before translating the next program statement. When using an interpreter, each time the program is run, the source program is interpreted into machine language and executed. No object program is produced. *Figure 12-17* illustrates this process.

The advantage of interpreters is the compiling process is not necessary before program changes can be tested. The disadvantage of interpreters is interpreted programs do not run as fast as compiled programs because the translation to machine language occurs each time the program is run. Interpreted languages were once common on personal computers because early PCs did not have the memory or computing power required by compilers. Compilers for most high-level languages are now available for the newer and more powerful personal computers.

Fourth-Generation Languages

The evolution of computer languages is sometimes described in terms of generations with machine, assembly, and high-level languages considered the first, second, and third generations, respectively. Each generation offered significant improvements in ease of use and programming flexibility over the previous generation. Although a clear definition does not yet exist, **fourth-generation languages** (4GLs), sometimes called **very high level languages**, continue the programming language evolution by being even easier to use than high-level languages for both the programmer and the nonprogramming user.

A term commonly used to describe fourth-generation languages is **nonprocedural**, which means the programmer does not specify the procedures to be used to accomplish a task as is done with lower procedural language generations. Instead of telling the computer how to do the task, the programmer tells the computer *what* is to be done, usually by describing the desired output. A database query language *(Figure 12-18)* is an example of a nonprocedural fourth-generation language.

The advantage of fourth-generation languages is they are *results* oriented (*what* is to be done, not *how*), and they

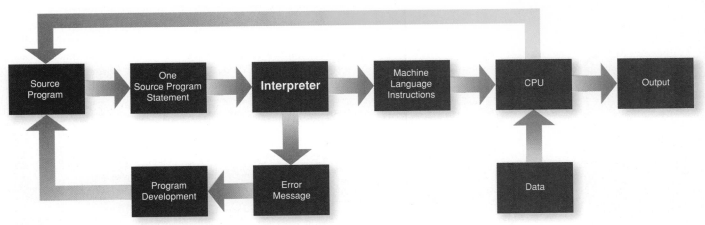

Figure 12-17
When an interpreter is used, one source language statement at a time is interpreted into machine language instructions that are executed immediately by the CPU. As instructed by the machine language instructions, the CPU processes data and creates output. Error messages indicating an invalid source language statement are produced as each source program statement is interpreted and are used to make the necessary corrections during program development.

LIST CUSTOMERS CUSTOMER.NAME WITH BALANCE.DUE>1000

Figure 12-18
This database query is considered an example of a fourth-generation language because it tells the computer what the user wants, not how to perform the processing. The query will produce a list of customers with balances greater than $1,000.

can be used by nonprogramming personnel. The disadvantage of fourth-generation languages is they do not provide as many processing options to the programmer as other language generations and they require more computer processing power than other language generations. Most experts, however, believe their ease of use far outweighs these disadvantages and they predict fourth-generation languages will continue to be more widely used.

An extension of fourth-generation languages is a natural language. A **natural language**, sometimes called a **fifth generation language**, is a type of query language that allows the user to enter a question as if he or she were speaking to another person. For example, a fourth-generation query might be stated as LIST SALESPERSON TOTAL-SALES BY REGION. A natural language version of that same query might be TELL ME THE NAME OF EACH SALESPERSON AND THE TOTAL SALES FOR EACH REGION. The natural language allows the user more flexibility in the structure of the query and can even ask the user a question if it does not understand what is meant by the initial query statement. A few natural languages are available today but they are not yet widely used.

Application Generators

Application generators, also called **program generators**, are programs that produce source-language programs, such as BASIC or COBOL, based on input, output, and processing specifications entered by the user. Application generators are available as stand-alone programs or as part of other software such as CASE and database packages. Application generators can greatly reduce the amount of time required to develop a program. They are designed on the basis that most programs are comprised of standard processing modules, such as routines to read, write, or compare records, that can be combined together to create unique programs. These standard processing modules are stored in a library and are selected and grouped together based on user specifications. Application generators often use menu and screen generators to assist in developing an application.

A **menu generator** lets the user specify a menu (list) of processing options that can be selected. The resulting menu is automatically formatted with heading, footing, and prompt line text.

A **screen generator**, sometimes called a **screen painter**, allows the user to design an input or output screen by entering the names and descriptions of the input and output data directly on the screen. The advantage is the user enters the data exactly as it will appear after the program is created. As each data name, such as Order No., is entered, the screen generator asks the user to specify the length and type of data that will be entered and what processing, if any, should take place before or after the data is entered. As shown in *Figure 12-19,* screen generators can create both GUI and character-based screens.

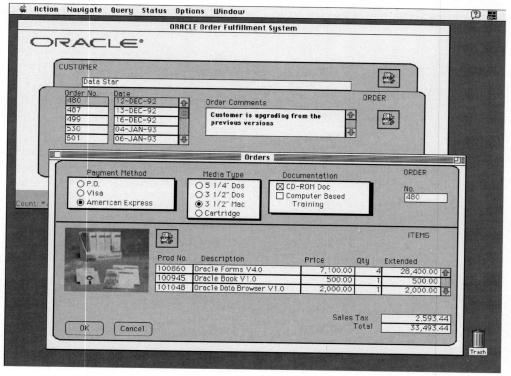

Object-oriented Programming

Object-oriented programming (OOP) is a new approach to developing software that allows programmers to create **objects**, a combination of data and program instructions. Traditional programming methods keep data, such as files, independent of the programs that work with the data. Each traditional program, therefore, must define how the data will be used for that particular program. This often results in redundant programming code that must be changed every time the structure of the data is changed, such as when a new field is added to a file. With OOP, the program instructions and data are combined into objects that can be used repeatedly by programmers whenever they need them. Specific instructions, called **methods**, define how the object acts when it is used by a program. The capability to combine methods (instructions) with objects (data) is called **encapsulation**. The following example, illustrated in *Figure 12-20* on the next page, describes how OOP minimizes the number of instructions that must be defined.

With OOP, programmers define classes of objects. Each **class** contains the methods unique to that class. As shown in *Figure 12-20*, the class of animals could contain methods on how animals eat, sleep, and breathe. Each class can have one or more subclasses. Each subclass contains the methods of its higher level classes plus whatever methods are unique to the subclass. For example, the subclass Humans contains the method Talk. The subclass Dogs contains the method Bark. Both subclasses, Humans and Dogs, also contain the Eat, Sleep, and Breathe methods of the higher class, Animals. The OOP capability to pass methods to lower levels is called **inheritance**. A specific **instance** of an object contains all methods from its higher level classes plus any methods unique to the object. For example, the object Anne contains a method on how to play the violin. The object Anne also inherits the Eat, Sleep, Breathe, and Talk methods from the higher levels. The object Bowser contains methods on how Bowser bites and chases cars. Although these methods may be shared by other humans and dogs, respectively, they cannot be placed at higher levels because they are not shared by all humans or dogs. When an OOP object is sent an instruction to do something, called a **message**, unlike a traditional program, the message does not have to tell the OOP object exactly what to do. *What to do* is defined by the methods the OOP object

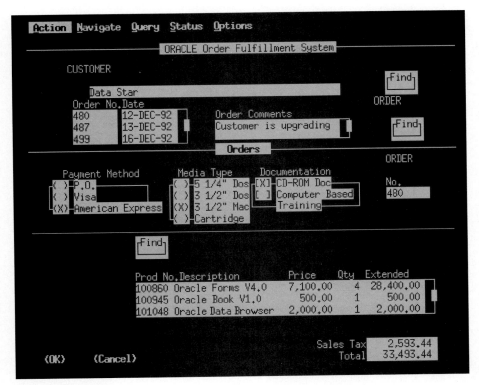

Figure 12-19
Oracle Forms from Oracle Corporation can generate either graphical user interface (GUI) screens such as the one on the left or character-based screens such as the one on the right.

contains or has inherited. For example, in *Figure 12-20,* if the object Bowser was sent a message to bark, the method of barking would be defined by the bark method in the subclass Dogs. However, if the object Butch was sent the same message to bark, its actions would be defined by the bark (perhaps a growl) associated with Butch. This illustrates that higher level methods can be overridden to define actions unique to a particular object or class.

A business example of an object might include a class called Invoices. With traditional programming, each time an invoice is displayed on a screen, specific programming instructions are included in the program. With OOP, a method called Display could be part of the object Invoice. An OOP program would only have to send a message identifying the object (Invoice) and stating the desired method (Display). How to display the invoice would be defined as part of the Invoice object.

As OOP is used by an organization, the organization builds a library of OOP objects and classes that can be reused. The more extensive the library, the more powerful and efficient

OOP becomes. OOP development systems allow programmers to access such libraries and link objects to quickly build programs. Popular OOP languages include C++, Visual Basic, Turbo Pascal, SmallTalk, and HyperTalk (used on Apple Macintosh computers).

OOP languages are often described as being event-driven instead of procedural. **Event-driven** means that the program is designed to respond to events that take place when an application is run. An event can be pressing a particular key, using the mouse, or entering a particular value in response to a prompt. Events can take place at any time or in any sequence. Procedural programs, on the other hand, usually assume that processing continues from beginning to end in a linear manner.

Closely related to OOP are object-oriented software and object-oriented operating systems. **Object-oriented software** means applications developed using OOP programming techniques. **Object-oriented operating systems** are operating systems specifically designed to run OOP applications.

Figure 12-20
Object-oriented programming (OOP) allows procedures (called methods) to be combined with data to form objects. In traditional programming, procedures are defined by the program instructions that are separate from the data. In OOP, the methods define how the object will act when it is referenced and how it can be inherited from higher levels, called classes. For example, the method BARK can be inherited by BOWSER from the class DOGS. Objects can also have unique methods that differ from higher level methods. Thus, BUTCH can have a different BARK than BOWSER. The capability to inherit methods from higher levels makes programming more efficient because only methods unique to the specific object need to be defined. A specific occurrence of an object is called an instance.

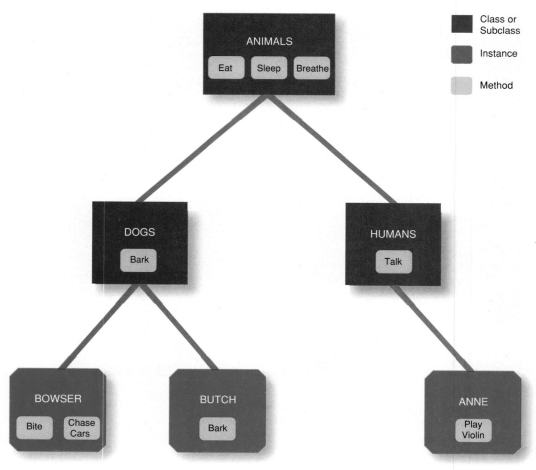

Programming Languages Used Today

Although hundreds of programming languages have been developed, only a few are used extensively enough to be recognized as industry standards. Most of these are high-level programming languages that can be used on a variety of computers. This section discusses commonly used programming languages, their origins, and their primary purpose.

To help illustrate the differences, program code for the languages is shown. Except for the code shown for the Visual Basic language, the programming code solves the problem of computing the net sale of a transaction by multiplying the quantity sold times the sales price. A discount of 5% is calculated if the gross sale is more than $100.00.

BASIC

BASIC, which stands for **B**eginner's **A**ll-purpose **S**ymbolic **I**nstruction **C**ode, was developed by John Kemeny and Thomas Kurtz in 1964 at Dartmouth College *(Figure 12-21)*. They originally designed BASIC to be a simple, interactive programming language for college students to learn and use. Since then, other versions of BASIC have been developed including Microsoft **QuickBASIC** (also referred to as **QBASIC**). BASIC is widely used on both PCs and minicomputers to develop business applications. Versions of BASIC are also used as macro languages in some application software.

```
5010 REM *****************P R O C E S S   A N D   D I S P L A Y********
5040 GROSS = QTY * SLSPR
5050 IF GROSS > CEILING THEN NET = GROSS - (GROSS * DISC) ELSE NET = GROSS
5070 PRINT "THE NET SALES IS ";
5080 PRINT USING "$$#,###.##"; NET
5090 RETURN
```

Figure 12-21
An excerpt from a BASIC program.

Visual Basic

Visual Basic, developed by Microsoft Corporation in the early 1990s, is an object-oriented extension of the BASIC programming language. Visual Basic has a number of features that assist the user in designing a Windows-compatible graphical user interface (GUI). Once the GUI is designed, programming code is written to specify what happens when GUI features are used, such as selecting a button, or when data is entered. *Figure 12-22* shows a simple currency conversion program developed with Visual Basic. The first screen shows the design of the graphical user interface. The second screen shows the program code that will execute when the Command1 (CONVERT) button is chosen. The third screen shows the finished application.

Figure 12-22
This figure shows how the Microsoft Visual Basic programming language is used to develop an application to convert dollars to French francs. The first screen shows how the programmer builds the user interface. Text1 will be entered by the user. Text2 will display the result after the user chooses the Command1 button. The second screen shows the program code that is associated with the screen. When the user chooses the Command1 button (shown as Command1_Click in the program code), the value in Text1 is multiplied by 5.7345 (the francs to dollars exchange rate) and displayed in the Text2 box. The third screen shows the finished application.

COBOL

COBOL (COmmon Business Oriented Language) was introduced in 1960. Backed by the U. S. Department of Defense, COBOL was developed by a committee of representatives from both government and industry. Rear Admiral Grace M. Hopper was a key person on the committee and is recognized as a prime developer of the COBOL language. COBOL is one of the more widely used programming languages for business applications *(Figure 12-23)*. Using an English-like format, COBOL instructions are arranged in sentences and grouped into paragraphs. The English format makes COBOL easy to write and read, but also makes it a wordy language that produces lengthy program code. COBOL is very good for processing large files and performing relatively simple business calculations. Other languages are better suited to performing complex mathematical formulas and functions.

C

The **C** programming language *(Figure 12-24)* was developed at Bell Laboratories in 1972 by Dennis Ritchie. It was originally designed as a programming language for writing systems software, but is now considered a general-purpose programming language and is widely used on personal computers. C is a powerful programming language that requires professional programming skills to be used effectively. The C programming language is used to develop a wide variety of software, including operating systems, application programs such as word processors and spreadsheets, and business applications. C programs are often used with the UNIX operating system (most of the UNIX operating system is written in C).

```
00100    016200 CO10-PROCESS-AND-DISPLAY.
00101    016400***************************************************
00102    016600* FUNCTION:              CALCULATE NET SALES AMOUNT   *
00103    016700*                        AND DISPLAY RESULTS          *
00104    016800* ENTRY/EXIT:            B000-LOOP-CONTROL            *
00105    016900* CALLS:                 NONE                        *
00106    017100***************************************************
00107    017300        COMPUTE GROSS-SALES-WRK = QUANTITY-SOLD-WRK * SALES-PRICE-WRK.
00108    017500        IF GROSS-SALES-WRK IS GREATER THAN CEILING
00109    017600            COMPUTE NET-SALES-WRK = GROSS-SALES-WRK -
00110    017700                (GROSS-SALES-WRK * DISCOUNT-RATE)
00111    017800        ELSE
00112    017900            MOVE GROSS-SALES-WRK TO NET-SALES-WRK.
00113    018100        MOVE NET-SALES-WRK TO NET-SALES-OUTPUT.
00114    018300        DISPLAY CLEAR-SCREEN.
00115    018500        WRITE PRINT-LINE FROM DETAIL-LINE
00116    018600            AFTER ADVANCING 2.
```

Figure 12-23

An excerpt from a COBOL program. Notice the additional words in the COBOL program compared to the BASIC program in Figure 12-21 on page 12.19. Although the extra words increase the time it takes to write a COBOL program, they also make the program easier to read and understand.

```
float gross;
gross = qty * price;
if (gross > ceiling)
    net = gross - (gross * discount_rate);
else
    net = gross;
return(net);
```

Figure 12-24
An excerpt from a C program.

C++

C++ (pronounced C plus plus) is an object-oriented extension of the C programming language. Developed by Bjarne Stroustrup at Bell Laboratories in the 1980s, C++ includes all of the standard C language plus additional features for working with objects, classes, and other object-oriented programming concepts. Like C, C++ is a powerful and efficient language but can be difficult to learn. C++ is frequently used to develop application software.

FORTRAN

FORTRAN (**FOR**mula **TRAN**slator) was developed by a team of IBM programmers led by John Backus. Released in 1957, FORTRAN was designed as a programming language to be used by scientists, engineers, and mathematicians *(Figure 12-25)*. FORTRAN is considered the first high-level language developed and is noted for its capability to easily express and efficiently calculate mathematical equations.

```
  1    67.000          SUBROUTINE CALC(QTY,SALES,DISC,MAX,GROSS,NET)
  2    68.000          REAL SALES, DISC, MAX, GROSS, NET
  3    69.000          INTEGER QTY
  4    70.000          GROSS = QTY * SALES
  5    71.000          IF(GROSS .GT. MAX) THEN
  6    72.000   1         NET = GROSS - (GROSS * DISC)
  7    73.000   1      ELSE
  8    74.000   1         NET = GROSS
  9    75.000   1      ENDIF
 10    76.000          PRINT *, "   "
 11    77.000          RETURN
```

Figure 12-25
An excerpt from a FORTRAN program.

```
BEGIN                                  (* Begin procedure *)
   GROSS := SALES * QTY;
   IF GROSS > CEILING
      THEN NET := GROSS - (GROSS * DISCOUNT_RATE)
      ELSE NET := GROSS;
   WRITELN('THE NET SALES IS $',NET:6:2);
END;                                   (* End of procedure *)
```

Figure 12-26
An excerpt from a Pascal program.

Pascal

The **Pascal** language was developed in 1968 by Niklaus Wirth, a computer scientist at the Institut für Informatik in Zurich, Switzerland. It was developed for teaching programming. The name Pascal is not an abbreviation or acronym, but rather the name of a mathematician, Blaise Pascal (1623-1662), who developed one of the earliest calculating machines. Pascal is available for use on both personal and large computers and was one of the first programming languages developed where the instructions in the language were designed and written so programmers would be encouraged to develop programs that follow structured program design principles *(Figure 12-26)*. An object-oriented version of Pascal called Turbo Pascal has been developed by Borland Corporation.

Ada

The programming language **Ada** is named for Augusta Ada Byron, Countess of Lovelace, a mathematician in the 1800s, who is thought to have written the first computer program. The development of Ada, which is based on Pascal, was supported by the U. S. Department of Defense, which requires its use on all U. S. government military projects. Ada was introduced in 1980 and designed to facilitate the writing and maintenance of large programs used over a long period of time. The language encourages coding of readable programs that are also portable, allowing them to be transferred from computer to computer *(Figure 12-27)*.

```
31     GROSS_SALES_PRICE := FLOAT(QUANTITY * SALES_PRICE);
32     if GROSS_SALES_PRICE > 100.0 then
33        NET_SALES_PRICE := GROSS_SALES_PRICE - (GROSS_SALES_PRICE * 0.05)
34     else
35        NET_SALES_PRICE := GROSS_SALES_PRICE
36     end if;
```

Figure 12-27
An excerpt from an Ada program.

Other Programming Languages

In addition to the commonly used programming languages just discussed, a number of other languages are sometimes used. *Figure 12-28* lists some of these languages and their primary uses.

ALGOL	**ALGO**rithmic **L**anguage – The first structured procedural language
APL	**A P**rograming **L**anguage – Uses special symbols to manipulate tables of numbers
FORTH	Similar to C – Creates fast and efficient program code; originally developed to control astronomical telescopes
HYPERTALK	Object-oriented language – Developed by Apple to manipulate cards that can contain text, graphics, and sound
LISP	**LIS**t **P**rocessing – Used for artificial intelligence applications
LOGO	Primarily known as an educational tool – Used to teach programming and problem-solving to children
MODULA-2	A successor to Pascal – Used for developing systems software
PILOT	**P**rogrammed **I**nquiry **L**earning **O**r **T**eaching – Used to write computer-aided instruction programs
PL/1	**P**rogramming **L**anguage One – Business and scientific language that combines many of the features of FORTRAN and COBOL
PROLOG	**PRO**gramming **LOG**ic – Used for artificial intelligence applications
RPG	**R**eport **P**rogram **G**enerator – Uses special forms to help user specify input, output, and calculation requirements of a program
SMALLTALK	Considered the first of the object-oriented programming languages

Figure 12-28
Other computer languages.

How to Choose a Programming Language

Although each programming language has its own unique characteristics, selecting a language for a programming task can be a difficult decision. Factors to be considered include the following:

1. *The programming standards of the organization.* Many organizations have programming standards specifying that a particular language is used for all applications.
2. *The need to interface with other programs.* If a program is going to work with other existing or future programs, ideally it should be written in the same language as the other programs.
3. *The suitability of a language to the application to be programmed.* As discussed, most languages are best suited to a particular type of application. For example, FORTRAN works well with applications requiring many complex calculations.
4. *The expertise of the available programmers.* Unless another language is far superior, you should choose the language used by the existing programmers.
5. *The need for the application to be portable.* If the application will run on different systems, a language common to the different systems should be chosen.

Summary of Program Development and Programming Languages

Because of their large installed base, procedural languages such as COBOL and BASIC will continue to be used for many years. A clear trend exists toward the creation of programs using nonprocedural tools, such as object-oriented, fourth-generation, and natural languages. These tools allow developers and users to concentrate more on *what* they want done than *how* they want it done. Your knowledge of the program development process and programming languages will help you to understand how the computer converts data into information and help you to obtain better results if you directly participate in the programming process.

COMPUTERS AT WORK

COBOL: The Language That Keeps Marching On

Starting in the 1970s, the BASIC programming language was being widely used on minicomputers, and many predicted the demise of COBOL. In the 1980s, the most talked about language was C and again, many predicted that COBOL's days were over. Now in the 1990s, object-oriented languages such as Visual Basic and C++ are the hot topic and people are still predicting the end of COBOL. How is it that COBOL, after 35 years, is still being used by thousands of organizations around the world and new COBOL applications are being developed every day?

For one reason, it is because of the tremendous number of COBOL programs that were written in the past. One study estimated more than 70 *billion lines* of COBOL code are in existence. COBOL was used almost exclusively for business system development in the 1960s and early 1970s when many businesses first installed computers. The self-documenting nature of COBOL has also contributed to its continued use. Because COBOL code is easy to read, it is not

difficult for maintenance programmers to figure out how a program works and make necessary changes. Some believe that other languages, such as C++, are not only more difficult to learn but are also more difficult to maintain because of their more concise and sometimes cryptic coding structure.

One company that decided to stick with COBOL was NCH Chemical of Irving, Texas. When NCH decided to replace their mainframe and minicomputers with a PC LAN, they did not want to rewrite more than 500 existing COBOL applications that were essential to their business. Instead of converting to another language, they chose a version of COBOL specifically developed for PCs called Micro Focus COBOL from Micro Focus Inc. Using Micro Focus COBOL, most of NCH's programs were directly converted to the LAN. Some programs that had been extensively modified over the years were rewritten using Micro Focus development tools.

The advantages of modern programming languages have not been overlooked by Micro Focus and existing COBOL users. Micro Focus COBOL includes some object-oriented features, and specifications for a standardized version of object-oriented COBOL are under development by the American National Standards Institute (ANSI).

Object-oriented COBOL! Who would have thought that after 35 years COBOL would still be around and would be borrowing the latest concepts from other languages?

Figure 12-29

IN THE FUTURE

Computing Naturally

Although query languages, such as SQL, have made accessing information much easier than in the past, many users, especially those who only make an occasional query, still find them difficult to use. The problem is that most query languages require the user to know the name of the file they want to access and the name of the data fields they want to display or print.

The solution to this problem is the use of a **natural language** that translates the user's plain English statements into file and field names and logical operators the computer can understand and process. With a natural language, questions like "What projects are over budget?" or "What's up in sales?" can be converted into standard SQL commands. Users do not need to know how to form a SQL statement or what the database structure looks like. All they need to know is how to ask a question in English. It sounds simple enough, but the actual process that takes place is quite complex. Here is what happens when using Natural Language, from Natural Language, Inc., a software product that interprets whole English sentences into SQL statements.

1. The user enters a request for information in the form of a question.
2. The software identifies the individual words in the request. Each word is matched against a 100,000-word dictionary and, if necessary, spelling is corrected. Words are identified by type, such as verbs and nouns.
3. The request is rebuilt in the best grammatical structure.
4. A first attempt is made to interpret the sentence into a database query.

5. Ambiguous references (what the software does not understand) are resolved by comparing the references with three sources; previous questions from the user, a library of concepts, and a library of rules that are specific to the user's organization. Previous questions can help identify pronouns such as who, or they, or it. For example, if two questions were asked, "Who are the top three salespersons?" and "What are they paid?", the *they* in the second sentence would be identified with the *salespersons* in the first sentence. The concepts library enables the system to understand a statement such as, "Turn the stew down", because its common-sense knowledge base tells it that things that are turned down are burners on stoves, and stew goes on a stove burner. The rules library contains a knowledge base that is specific to the user's organization.
6. The question is echoed back to the user in English.
7. A SQL statement is built and sent to the database manager.
8. The answer to the SQL statement is presented as a table, graph, or English sentence.

Although not yet widely used, natural language interfaces are estimated to become part of approximately 25% of all relational database management systems by 1996. Eventually, they will be part of all database systems and most, if not all, application packages as well. A logical evolution of the natural language interface is its integration with voice recognition. Already under development, a voice recognition natural language interface would be ideal for information inquiry applications such as airline reservations and hotel availability.

Figure 12-30

What You Should Know

1. A **computer program** is a detailed set of instructions that directs a computer to perform the tasks necessary to process data into information. **Program development** is the process of producing one or more programs to perform specific tasks on a computer. The process of program development has evolved into a series of five steps most experts agree should take place when any program is developed: (1) review of program specifications, (2) program design, (3) coding, (4) testing, and (5) finalizing documentation.

2. **Program specifications** can consist of data flow diagrams, system flowcharts, process specifications that indicate the action to be taken on the data, a data dictionary identifying the data elements that will be used, screen formats, report layouts, and actual documents. These documents help the programmer understand the work that needs to be done by the program.

3. During **program design**, a logical solution to the programming task is developed and documented. The solution is broken down into a step-by-step procedure called an **algorithm**. A methodology called **structured program design** emphasizes three main program concepts: modules, control structures, and single entry/single exit.

4. Each **module**, sometimes referred to as a **subroutine** in programming, performs a given task within the program. **Structure charts**, also called hierarchy charts, are often used to decompose and represent the modules of a program.

5. In structured program design, three basic **control structures** are used to form the logic of a program. In the **sequence structure**, one process occurs immediately after another. The **selection structure**, or **if-then-else structure**, gives programmers a way to represent conditional program logic. A variation of the selection structure, the **case structure**, is used when a condition being tested

can lead to more than two alternatives. The **iteration structure**, or **looping structure**, means one or more processes continue to occur as long as a given condition remains true. There are two forms of this control structure: the **do-while structure** and the **do-until structure**.

6. An important concept in structured programming is **single entry/single exit**, meaning there is only one entry point and one exit point for each of the three control structures. An **entry point** is the point where a control structure is entered. An **exit point** is the point where the control structure is exited.

7. Two commonly used design tools are program flowcharts and pseudocode. In a **program flowchart**, all the logical steps of a program are represented by a combination of symbols and text. In **pseudocode**, the logical steps in the solution of a problem are written as English statements, and indentations are used to represent the control structures. To ensure that the program design is efficient and correct, many organizations use a **structured walkthrough**, which is a review of the program logic by other members of the development team.

8. **Coding** the program refers to the process of writing the program instructions that process data and produce the output specified in the program design. **Code standards** enable the same program to work on different types of computers. A **code library** stores partial or complete programs written to solve a particular problem.

9. Before a program is used to process real data and produce information, it should be thoroughly tested. **Desk checking** is the process of reading the program and mentally reviewing its logic. Desk checking can also uncover **syntax errors**, which are violations of the grammar rules of the language in which the program is written. During **logic testing**, the sequence of program instructions is tested to make sure it provides the correct result. Logic testing is done with **test data**, which is data that simulates the type of input the program will process when it is implemented. **Debugging** refers to the process of locating and correcting program errors, called **bugs**, found during testing. Most programming languages include a **debugger**, a program that identifies syntax errors and allows the programmer to stop the program while it is running to examine values.

File   Edit   Section   Page   Tools   Options   Help

What You Should Know
(continued)

10. Documentation, the preparation of documents explaining the program, should be an ongoing part of developing a program and should only be finalized (organized and brought together) after the program is successfully tested and ready for implementation. **Program maintenance** includes all changes to a program once it is implemented and processing real transactions.

11. A **programming language** is a set of written words and symbols that allows the programmer or user to communicate with the computer. Programming languages can be classified into one of four categories: machine language, assembly language, high-level languages, and fourth-generation languages.

12. **Machine language** is the fundamental language of the computer's processor. Programs written in all other categories of languages are eventually converted into machine language before they are executed. Because they are written for specific processors, machine languages are also called **low-level languages**.

13. An **assembly language** is similar to a machine language, but uses abbreviations called **mnemonics** or **symbolic operation codes** to represent the machine operation code. Assembly languages usually allow **symbolic addressing**, which means a specific computer memory location can be referenced by a name or symbol instead of its actual address. Assembly language programs can also include **macroinstructions** that generate more than one machine instruction. Assembly language programs are converted into machine language instructions by a special program called an **assembler**.

14. **High-level languages** more closely resemble what most people would think of as a language because they contain nouns, verbs, and mathematical, relational, and logical operators that can be grouped together to form what appear to be sentences. These sentences are called **program statements**.

15. A **compiler** converts an entire high-level language program into machine language that is usually stored on a disk for later execution. The program to be converted is called the **source program** and the machine language produced is called the **object program** or **object code**. While a compiler translates an entire program, an **interpreter** translates one program statement at a time and then executes the resulting machine language before translating the next program statement.

16. Although a clear definition does not yet exist, **fourth-generation languages** (4GLs), sometimes called very high level languages, continue the programming language development by being even easier to use than high-level languages for both the programmer and nonprogramming user. A term commonly used to describe fourth-generation languages is **nonprocedural**, which means the programmer does not specify the procedures to be used to accomplish a task as is done with lower procedural language generations.

17. An extension of fourth-generation languages is a natural language. A **natural language**, sometimes called a **fifth generation language**, is a type of query language that allows the user to enter a question as if he or she were speaking directly to another person.

18. **Application generators**, also called **program generators**, are programs that produce source-language programs. A **menu generator** lets the user specify a menu (list) of processing options that can be selected. A **screen generator**, sometimes called a **screen painter**, allows the user to design an input or output screen by entering the names and descriptions of the input and output data directly on the screen.

19. **Object-oriented programming** (OOP) is a new approach to developing software that allows programmers to create **objects**, a combination of data and program instructions. Specific instructions, called **methods**, define how the object acts when it is used by a program. The capability to combine methods (instructions) with objects (data) is called **encapsulation**.

20. With OOP, programmers define classes of objects. Each **class** contains the methods unique to that class. The OOP capability to pass methods to lower levels is called **inheritance**. A specific **instance** of an object contains all methods from its higher level classes plus any methods unique to the object. When an OOP object is sent an instruction to do something, called a **message**, the message does not have to tell the OOP object exactly what to do, because *what to do* is defined by the methods the OOP object contains or has inherited.

21. OOP languages are often described as being event-driven instead of procedural. **Event-driven** means the program is designed to respond to events that can take place when an application is run. Closely related to OOP are **object-oriented software**, applications that are developed using OOP programming techniques, and **object-oriented operating systems**, which are operating systems specifically designed to run OOP applications.

22. Although hundreds of programming languages have been developed, only a few are used extensively enough to be recognized as industry standards.

23. **BASIC**, which stands for **B**eginner's **A**ll-purpose **S**ymbolic **I**nstruction **C**ode, was originally designed to be a simple, interactive programming language and is widely used on both PCs and minicomputers to develop business applications. Other versions of BASIC have been developed including Microsoft **QuickBASIC** (also referred to as **QBASIC**). Microsoft **Visual Basic** is an object-oriented extension of the BASIC programming language.

24. **COBOL** (**CO**mmon **B**usiness **O**riented **L**anguage), developed by a committee of representatives from both government and industry, is one of the most widely used programming languages for business applications.

25. The C programming language was originally designed for writing systems software, but is now considered a general-purpose programming language and is widely used on PCs. **C++** is an object-oriented extension of the C programming language.

26. FORTRAN (**FOR**mula **TRAN**slator) is considered the first high-level language developed and is noted for its capability to easily express and efficiently calculate mathematical equations. The **Pascal** language, available for use on both personal and large computers, was developed for teaching programming and fosters the development of programs that follow structured program design. The programming language **Ada**, designed to facilitate the writing and maintenance of large programs used over a long period of time, encourages coding of readable programs that are also portable.

27. Factors to be considered when choosing a programming language include: (1) the programming standards of the organization, (2) the need to interface with other programs, (3) the suitability of a language to the application to be programmed, (4) the expertise of the available programmers, and (5) the need for the application to be portable.

Terms to Remember

Ada (12.23)
algorithm (12.4)
application generators (12.16)
assembler (12.14)
assembly language (12.13)

BASIC (12.19)
bugs (12.10)

C (12.21)
C++ (12.22)
case structure (12.5)
class (12.17)
COBOL (12.21)
code library (12.9)
code standards (12.9)
coding (12.9)
compiler (12.14)
computer program (12.2)
control structures (12.4)

debugger (12.10)
debugging (12.10)
desk checking (12.10)
do-until structure (12.5)
do-while structure (12.5)

encapsulation (12.17)
entry point (12.6)
event-driven (12.18)
exit point (12.6)

fifth-generation language (12.16)
FORTRAN (12.22)
fourth-generation languages
   (4GLs) (12.15)

hierarchy charts (12.4)
high-level languages (12.14)

if-then-else structure (12.5)
inheritance (12.17)
instance (12.17)
interpreter (12.15)
iteration structure (12.5)

logic testing (12.10)
looping structure (12.5)
low-level languages (12.13)

machine language (12.13)
macroinstructions (12.14)
menu generator (12.16)
message (12.17)
methods (12.17)
mnemonics (12.13)
module (12.4)

natural language (12.16)
nonprocedural (12.15)

object code (12.14)
object program (12.14)
object-oriented operating systems
   (12.18)
object-oriented programming
   (OOP) (12.17)
object-oriented software (12.18)
objects (12.17)

Pascal (12.23)
program design (12.4)
program development (12.2)
program flowchart (12.7)
program generators (12.16)
program maintenance (12.11)
program specifications (12.3)
program statements (12.14)
programming language (12.12)
pseudocode (12.8)

QBASIC (12.19)
QuickBASIC (12.19)

screen generator (12.16)
screen painter (12.16)
selection structure (12.5)
sequence structure (12.5)
single entry/single exit (12.6)
source program (12.14)
structure charts (12.4)
structured program design (12.4)
structured walkthrough (12.8)
subroutine (12.4)
symbolic addressing (12.13)
symbolic operation code (12.13)
syntax errors (12.10)

test data (12.10)

very high level languages (12.15)
Visual Basic (12.20)

Start   12:01 PM

File   Edit   Section   Page   Tools   Options   Help

Test Your Knowledge

Fill in the Blanks

1. A(n) _____ is a detailed set of instructions that directs a computer to perform the tasks necessary to process data into information.

2. Structured program design is a methodology emphasizing three main program design concepts: _____, which perform a given task within the program; _____, which form the logic of the program; and _____, meaning there is only one entry point and one exit point for each control structure.

3. A(n) _____ is a set of written words and symbols that allows the programmer or user to communicate with the computer.

4. _____ are programs that produce source-oriented programs based on input, output, and processing specifications entered by the user.

5. _____, an interactive programming language originally designed for college students, is widely used on both PCs and minicomputers to develop business applications; while _____, one of the more widely used programming languages for business applications, is very good for processing large files and performing relatively simple calculations.

Short Answer

1. What are the five steps in program development? Briefly describe each.

2. What do the sequence structure, selection structure, and iteration structure have in common? How are they different?

3. How are machine languages and assembly languages different? Why are they both considered low-level languages? In what way are low-level languages different from high-level languages?

4. What is object-oriented programming (OOP)? How are traditional programming methods different from object-oriented programming? Why are OOP languages often described as being event-driven, instead of procedural?

5. What factors should be considered when choosing a programming language? Briefly explain the importance of each.

Label the Figure

Instructions: In the following figure, identify each of the standard symbols used to create program flowcharts.

Points to Ponder

1

When computers were first introduced in schools, computer programming was routinely taught to students at the college, high school, and even elementary school levels. As time passed, however, the emphasis turned toward learning to use productivity software. Some educators feel programming should still be an integral part of computer education. They point out that many new applications include a programming language with which users can write programs to work in the application. They also maintain that knowledge of programming helps people recognize the kinds of problems that computers can, and cannot, be used to solve. Teachers also point out that programming improves logical and critical thinking skills. How important do you think it is to learn programming? Why? Who should be taught computer programming? Should programming in some form be a part of computer education at every level? Why or why not?

2

Using structured program design concepts and the flowchart symbols shown in *Figure 12-10* on page 12.7, prepare a program flowchart showing the logical steps in performing a common task such as balancing a checkbook or changing the oil in a car. Be as detailed and accurate as possible. When you are finished, ask a classmate to check the logic of your flowchart by performing a structured walk-through.

3

One programmer describes his job as being a combination of engineer and artist. What do you think he meant by this? Is computer programming a science, a skill, a craft, or an art? Why? Computer programmers in small organizations are generally responsible for all five steps in program development, while programmers in large organizations often divide up program development and take part in only one or two steps. If you were a programmer, would you prefer to work in a small or a large organization? Why? If you did work in a large company, in what step of program development would you be most interested? Why?

4

One day in 1990, a software bug prevented the AT&T Long Distance Network from completing almost one-third of the long distance calls attempted, and it lost half of its 800-number service. The telephone system depends on more than two million lines of code. Given these numbers, do you think it is possible to remove all bugs from software programs? Why or why not? What can be done to reduce the number of software bugs? If software bugs are inevitable, or at least to be expected, what steps can people relying on computer programs take to deal with them?

5

Machine language programs tend to be lengthy, difficult to code, and time-consuming to write. Despite this, some U.S. Department of Defense programming is done in machine language because of the speed with which these programs can be executed. Using the four categories into which programming languages can be classified, describe an application you feel would be ideal for a language in each category. Tell why a language in that category would be an appropriate choice for the applications you describe.

6

Because each programming language has its strengths and weaknesses, different languages are used for different applications. Some authorities believe, however, it would be best to develop a single programming language that could be used for all applications. What would be the advantages of writing all applications using the same programming language? What would be the disadvantages? Do you think such a "generic" programming language will ever be developed? Why or why not?

File   Edit   Section   Page   Tools   Options   Help

Out and About

1. Some sophisticated application packages come with programming languages (sometimes called macro languages) that can be used to write programs within the application. For example, Microsoft Excel, a spreadsheet program, includes Visual Basic, and Microsoft Word, a word processing program, includes WordBasic. Visit a software vendor and find an application package that contains a programming language. What is the name of the application? What is the name of the programming language? For what purpose is the programming language used? If possible, ask to see a demonstration of the programming language. Does the language appear difficult to use? Why or why not? Would the inclusion of a programming language in the application package be a significant factor in your decision whether or not to purchase the package? Why or why not?

2. Just a few decades ago, computer programs consisting of 3,000 lines of code were thought to be long. Current word processing programs, however, might be as many as several hundred thousand lines long! What will computer programming be like in the future? Some experts see such trends as continued movement toward natural languages, greater participation in programming by computer users, and computers taking a more active part in their own programming. Using computer magazines and library resources, prepare a report on what programming will be like in ten years. How will programming be different from what it is today? Who will be doing the programming? How will they be doing it? What effect could developments in computer hardware have on programming?

3. Some organizations are forced to spend a great deal of time maintaining old, poorly written, badly documented programs that are nevertheless essential to the organization's business. Special software tools, such as Renaissance from Viasoft, have been developed to handle this problem. These software tools can convert cumbersome, disorganized programs into structured code. Using current computer magazines, research this or another software programming tool. How does it work? How much can it do? What does it not do? What are the advantages of using this tool? What are the disadvantages?

4. Visit the computer center at your school and talk to one of the individuals in charge about the most widely used applications. Choose at least two applications and find out the programming language in which they are written. Why do you think that language was chosen? Can you think of any other languages that might have been appropriate? Ask for a partial print out of each program. Circle and identify any program code related to the material in this chapter. If you think you can figure out the purpose of any program statements, underline the statement and explain it.

5. Programming languages can be classified as procedural (concerned with *how* something is done) or nonprocedural (concerned with *what* is to be done), business-oriented (capable of handling large data files and executing basic computations) or scientific-oriented (capable of performing sophisticated calculations), and general-purpose (designed to solve different types of problems) or special-purpose (designed to deal with one specific type of problem or application). Visit a library and prepare a report on one of the languages listed in *Figure 12-28* on page 12.24. Describe the history, intent, and use of the language. Then, categorize the language according to the classifications suggested above. Explain why you classified the language as you did.

6. While enrollment in computer science programs has dropped, estimates anticipate an almost 50 percent increase in the number of new programmer positions between 1988 and the year 2000. What knowledge and skills are required to land one of these jobs? Using classified ads from newspapers, computer magazines, and trade journals, try to determine what employers are looking for in prospective programmers. What programming languages are most in demand? What other course work is required? What kind of experience is helpful? What are the programmer's responsibilities? What salary can be expected? What are the opportunities for advancement?

Start   12:04 PM

File Edit Section Page Tools Options Help

In the Lab with Windows 95

1 Shelly Cashman Series Programming Language Lab
Follow the instructions in Windows 95 Lab 1 on page 1.30 to display the Shelly Cashman Series Labs screen. Click Designing a Database. Click the Start Lab button. When the initial screen displays, carefully read the objectives. With your printer turned on, click the Print Questions button. Fill out the top of the Questions sheet and answer the questions as you step through the Programming Language Lab. Close the Shelly Cashman Series Labs.

2 **Adjusting Keyboard Speed** Click the Start button on the taskbar, point to Settings on the Start menu, and then click Control Panel on the Settings submenu. Double-click the Keyboard icon in the Control Panel window. When the Keyboard Properties dialog box displays, click the Speed tab *(Figure 12-31)*. Use the question mark button to answer the following two questions: (1) What is repeat delay? (2) What is repeat rate?

Drag the Cursor blink rate slider to Fast. Drag the Cursor blink rate slider to Slow. Which setting do you prefer? Click the General tab. What type of keyboard is connected to your system? Close the Keyboard Properties dialog box. Close Control Panel.

3 **Searching for Executable Files** Click the Start button on the taskbar, click Find on the Start menu, and then click Files or Folders. When the Find dialog box displays, click the Name & Location tab, click View on the menu bar and then click Details. Click the Named text box, and then type *.exe in the text box. Press TAB, and then type c:\ in the Look in text box. If it is not already selected, click Include subfolders. Click the Find Now button to display the results of the search. Sort the list of files by name by clicking the Name column heading *(Figure 12-32)*. Scroll through the list of files and find the filename, Explorer. In what folder is Explorer located? How large is the file, in bytes?

To sort the list of files by In Folder, Size, Type, or Modified, click the respective column heading. Practice sorting the list of files by clicking the column headings.

Click the New Search button and then click the OK button. Use the same procedure to search for the filename, command.com, and then write down the name of the folder where this file is located. Close the Find dialog box.

4 **Accessing the MS-DOS Prompt** Click the Start button on the taskbar, point to Programs on the Start menu, and then click MS-DOS prompt on the Programs submenu. When the MS-DOS Prompt window displays, type ver and press ENTER. Write down the operating system installed on your computer. Press ALT+ENTER; that is, hold down the ALT key and while holding down the ALT key, press ENTER, and then release both keys. Press ALT+ENTER again. What is the purpose of ALT+ENTER? Type exit and press ENTER.

5 **Using Help** Click the Start button on the taskbar and then click Help on the Start menu. When the Help Topics: Windows Help window displays, click the Find tab. Press TAB, type programs menu and then double-click Adding a program to the Start or Programs menu. Read and print the topic. Close Help.

Figure 12-31

Figure 12-32

File   Edit   Section   Page   Tools   Options   Help

Where on the Web

1 **QuickTime Viewer**   One difficulty in using Web browser programs is that many different file formats exist for the graphics, video, and sound files on the Web. Complete the following steps to download a viewer program for video files in the QuickTime format. With Netscape on the screen, type `http://popularmechanics.com` in the Location text box and press ENTER. Click Owners Manual *(Figure 12-33)*. Scroll down and click QuickTime Viewers. Click Print on the File menu. Click Pages and then type 1 in the To text box. Click the OK button. Follow the directions to download the QuickTime MoviePlayer. Click the Save To Disk button in the Unknown File Type dialog box. Specify an appropriate destination in the Save As dialog box and then click OK. Hand in the printout.

2 **The Yahoo Directory**   Complete the following steps to use the Yahoo Directory to learn more about programming languages. With Netscape on the screen, click the Net Search button. Click Yahoo. Scroll down and click Computers. Scroll down and click Programming Languages. How many languages are listed? Click a language. Scroll down and click a topic that sounds interesting. Scroll down and read the page. Click Print on the File menu. Click Pages and then type 1 in the To text box. Click OK. Write your answer on the printout and hand it in.

3 **Discovery Channel Online**   Complete the following steps to learn more about program development and computer languages. With Netscape on the screen, type `http://www.discovery.com` in the Location text box and press ENTER. Scroll down *(Figure 12-34)* and click Tools.

Scroll down and click Search. Click the Search text box and then type `computer languages`. Click the Submit Search button. If the Security Information dialog box displays, click the Continue button. Scroll down and click one of the topics listed. Click Print on the File menu. Click Pages and then type 1 in the To text box. Click OK. Write a brief description of what you found on the printout and hand it in.

4 **Visual Basic Web Site**   To see a home page developed exclusively for the Visual Basic programming language, complete the following steps. With Netscape on the screen, type `http://www.apexsc.com/vb` in the Location text box and press ENTER. Scroll down and read the list of different areas. Click About Carl & Gary's. Scroll down and read the page. How are the costs of operating this Web site paid for? Click Print on the File menu. Click Pages and then type 1 in the To text box. Click OK. Write your answer on the printout and hand it in.

5 **Shelly Cashman Online**   Click Using Computers: A Gateway To Information, World Wide Web Edition on the Shelly Cashman Student Center Web page (`http://www.bf.com/scstudnt.html`). Scroll down and click Chapter 12. Complete the activities listed.

Figure 12-33

Figure 12-34

    12:06 PM

Multimedia

Multimedia is the combination of sound, images, graphics, and text. These elements are controlled by a computer system that allows a user to interact with the multimedia presentation. This interaction is one of the key features of multimedia. Unlike television, which can also combine the same elements, multimedia allows the user to choose what material will be presented and in what sequence. The following figures illustrate just some of the thousands of multimedia applications.

Figure 1   *MULTIMEDIA PC*

To run multimedia applications on your PC, it should be equipped with a sound card, a color monitor, and speakers. Because most multimedia applications are available on a CD-ROM, you should also have a CD-ROM drive. To record sounds, you need a microphone. Many PCs now come equipped with these components. Multimedia upgrade kits that contain these items can also be purchased.

Figure 2   *INFORMATION*

Multimedia is often used to provide information in hotels, airports, and other places where infrequent visitors have common questions.
The touch screen on the left is available in many locations in Atlanta, Georgia to help visitors find their way around the city. The touch screen on the right is used to help visitors to Stonybrook Laboratories find the name and phone number of the person they have come to see.

Adventures - [Bloomington Bicycle Club]

File   Options   Main Category   Sub Category   State/Prov   Country   Custom   Help

Main | Bicycling | A Riding Tour in Rural Indiana | Next | #9 of 163

A Riding Tour in Rural Indiana   Indiana

Cycling through southwestern Indiana. Courtesy Bloomington Bicycle Club.

- Push your body and legs to the limit as you pedal through rural Indiana.

- Share this cycling adventure with hundreds of other riders.

- See beautiful countryside and enjoy musical entertainment at night.

Figure 3   *TRAVEL*

Travel destination is a popular multimedia subject. Some focus on specific locations, such as Hawaii, and others include information on multiple sites. The Complete Adventures CD-ROM from Deep River Publishing includes information on hundreds of travel activities around the world. Besides photos and video segments, the package provides specific information on costs, the best time to visit, and whether or not the activity is suitable for children.

***Figure 5* TRAINING**
Many organizations use multimedia for employee training. The interactive nature of multimedia lets employees proceed at their own pace and review material in the sequence they determine.

***Figure 4* DO-IT-YOURSELF**
This multimedia software from Books That Work helps users plan and build a deck. The software includes actual deck photographs and standard designs that can be modified. Construction notes include animations that show how to cut, nail, and install various deck components. After the deck is designed, the package creates a detailed shopping list that includes estimated prices for each item.

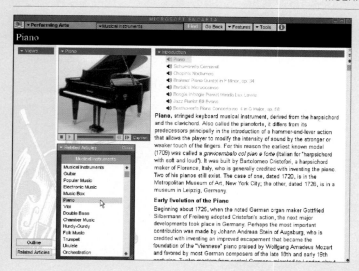

Figure 6 REFERENCE
Encyclopedias are one of the more widely used multimedia reference materials. This screen shows information from the Microsoft Encarta interactive multimedia encyclopedia. The speaker-shaped icons at the top of the text indicate that audio segments can be listened to.

Figure 7 REFERENCE
Video segments are often included in multimedia packages. This figure shows a video clip of an eagle catching a fish that can be viewed in the Microsoft Encarta multimedia encyclopedia.

Figure 8 MAGAZINES
Several multimedia magazines are now available and more are planned. Medio Magazine includes regular sections on entertainment, living, news, finance, sports, kidstuff, and technology. Audio and video clips are included for recent movies, TV shows, and recordings.

Figure 9 HEALTH and MEDICINE
The Mayo Clinic helped develop the multimedia family health reference shown on the left. Illustrations, animations, and actual photographs are included on hundreds of health and first aid topics. The A.D.A.M. (Animated Dissection of Anatomy for Medicine) multimedia software, shown on the right, is used by medical students to learn about the body and by practicing physicians to communicate information to their patients.

Figure 10 MUSIC
Multimedia software has been specifically developed to aid musicians in recording. Software exists that will automatically translate input from an instrument into sheet music. Once the music is recorded, it can be edited in a manner similar to editing a word processing document; sections of the music can be cut, copied, or changed to a different instrument. The tempo can be changed and special effects, such as fade and echo, can be added. After each change, the user can play back all or a part of the piece.

Figure 11 MORPHING

Morphing is an animation technique sometimes seen in multimedia presentations. It involves blending two images together. In the first screen, the image of the man on the left will be combined with the woman on the right. The lines and dots shown in the second screen help the software align the images. The morphed image is shown at the bottom of the second screen.

Security, Ethics, and Privacy

13

Objectives

After completing this chapter, you will be able to:

- Understand the different types of security risks that can threaten computer systems

- Describe different ways computer systems can be safeguarded

- Describe how a computer virus works and steps that can be taken to prevent viruses

- Explain why computer backup is important and how it is accomplished

- Discuss the steps in a disaster recovery plan

- Discuss ethical issues with respect to the information age

- Discuss issues relating to information privacy

The more people depend on computers in their work and daily lives, the more important it is to make sure the systems they use are protected from damage and misuse. People and organizations have come to rely on computers and some require their systems to be available 24 hours a day. For this reason, this chapter identifies the risks to a computer system and the safeguards that can be taken to minimize these risks.

In addition, society is becoming more concerned about the ethical use of computer systems and the difference between what is right, what is wrong, and what is criminal. Finally, the issue of information privacy is discussed including the current laws that are designed to keep certain data confidential.

Computer Security: Risks and Safeguards

A computer **security risk** is defined as any event or action that could cause a loss to computer equipment, software, information, or processing capability. The following section describes some of the more common computer security risks and what can be done to minimize or prevent their consequences. This section concludes with a discussion on how to develop an overall computer security plan.

Computer Viruses

A computer **virus** is an illegal and potentially damaging computer program designed to *infect* other software by attaching itself to the software with which it comes in contact. Usually, virus programs are designed to maliciously damage computer systems by destroying or corrupting data. If infected software is transferred to or accessed by another computer system, the virus will spread to the other system. *Figure 13-1* shows how a virus can spread from one system to another. Viruses have become a serious problem in recent years and currently there are thousands of known virus programs.

Three main types of viruses exist: a boot sector virus, a file virus, and a Trojan horse virus. A **boot sector virus** replaces the program that is used to start the system (the boot program) with a modified version of the program. When the infected boot program is run, it loads the virus into the computer's memory. Once a virus is in memory, it can spread to any diskette inserted into the computer. A **file virus** inserts virus code into program files. The virus then spreads to any program that accesses the infected file. A **Trojan horse virus** (named after the Greek myth) is a virus that hides within or is designed to look like a legitimate program.

Some viruses interrupt processing by freezing a computer system temporarily and displaying sounds or messages. For example, when the Stoned boot sector virus is triggered, it causes the infected computer to display a message saying "Your computer is now stoned" *(Figure 13-2)*. Other viruses contain time bombs or logic bombs. A **time bomb** is a program that performs an activity on a particular date. A well-known time bomb is the Michelangelo virus, which destroys data on a user's hard disk on March 6, Michelangelo's birthday. A logic

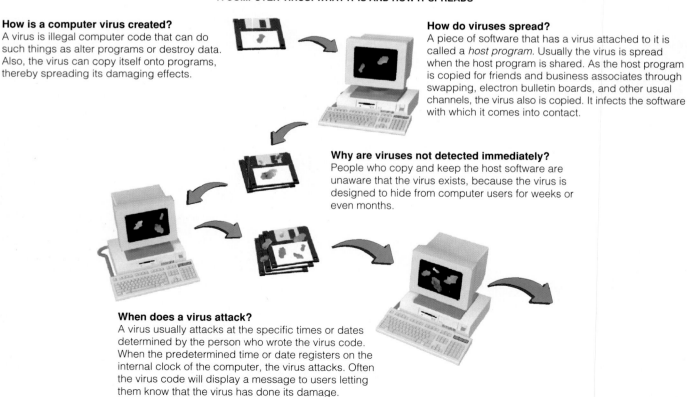

A COMPUTER VIRUS: WHAT IT IS AND HOW IT SPREADS

How is a computer virus created?
A virus is illegal computer code that can do such things as alter programs or destroy data. Also, the virus can copy itself onto programs, thereby spreading its damaging effects.

How do viruses spread?
A piece of software that has a virus attached to it is called a *host program*. Usually the virus is spread when the host program is shared. As the host program is copied for friends and business associates through swapping, electron bulletin boards, and other usual channels, the virus also is copied. It infects the software with which it comes into contact.

Why are viruses not detected immediately?
People who copy and keep the host software are unaware that the virus exists, because the virus is designed to hide from computer users for weeks or even months.

When does a virus attack?
A virus usually attacks at the specific times or dates determined by the person who wrote the virus code. When the predetermined time or date registers on the internal clock of the computer, the virus attacks. Often the virus code will display a message to users letting them know that the virus has done its damage.

Figure 13-1
This figure shows how a virus can spread from one computer system to another.

bomb is a program that performs an activity when a certain action has occurred, such as an employee being terminated.

Another type of malicious program is a worm. Although it is often called a virus, a worm, unlike a virus, does not attach itself to another program. Instead, a **worm** program is designed to repeatedly copy itself in memory or on a disk drive until no memory or disk space remains. When no memory or disk space remains, the computer stops working.

Virus Detection and Removal

To protect against computer viruses, **anti-virus programs**, called **vaccines**, have been developed. Most anti-virus programs, however, only protect against viruses written before the vaccine was released. Anti-virus programs work by looking for viruses that attempt to modify the boot program, the operating system, and other programs that are normally read from but not written to (*Figure 13-3* on the next page). Anti-virus programs also look for specific patterns of known virus code called a **virus signature**. Virus signature files need to be frequently updated to include newly discovered viruses.

One type of virus that is extremely difficult to detect is called a polymorphic virus. A **polymorphic virus** is designed to modify its program code each time it attaches itself to another program or file. Because it never looks the same, a polymorphic virus cannot be detected with a virus signature.

Another way vaccine programs prevent viruses is by *inoculating* existing program files. When a program file is **inoculated**, information such as the file size and file creation date is recorded in a separate inoculation file. Using this information, the vaccine program can tell if a virus program has tampered with the program file.

Besides detecting viruses, anti-virus programs also have utilities to remove or repair infected programs and files. Before attempting to remove or repair files, however, the anti-virus programs usually require the user to restart the computer using a rescue disk (actually a diskette). The **rescue disk** contains an uninfected copy of certain operating system commands and essential information about the computer that enables the computer to restart correctly. Once the computer has been *cleanly* restarted, the repair and removal programs can be run.

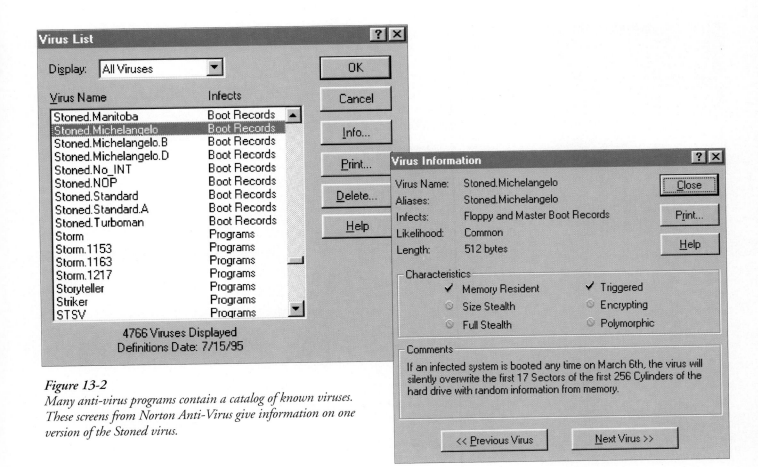

Figure 13-2
Many anti-virus programs contain a catalog of known viruses. These screens from Norton Anti-Virus give information on one version of the Stoned virus.

To protect against being infected by a computer virus, experts recommend the following:

- Install virus protection software *(Figure 13-3)* on every system you work on. Most businesses and large organizations have adopted this policy. The cost of anti-virus software is much less than the cost of rebuilding damaged files.
- Before using any diskette, use a virus scan program to check for viruses. This is true even for shrink-wrapped software from major developers. Even commercial software has been infected and distributed to unsuspecting users.
- Check all programs downloaded from bulletin boards. Viruses are often first placed in seemingly innocent programs on bulletin boards so they will affect a large number of users.

Sometimes damaged files cannot be repaired and must be replaced with uninfected backup copies. The process of making backup copies of programs and files is discussed later in this chapter.

Companies and individuals that need help with virus-infected PCs can contact The National Computer Security Association (NCSA) at 900-555-NCSA for low-cost assistance.

Unauthorized Access and Use

Unauthorized access can be defined as computer trespassing or using a computer system without permission. Persons who deliberately try to illegally access computer systems, usually by using a modem, are called **crackers**. The term **hacker**, although originally a positive term, also has become associated with persons who try to break into computer systems. Some intruders do not do any damage; they merely wander around the accessed system before logging off. Other intruders leave some evidence of their presence by either leaving a message or deliberately altering data.

Unauthorized use is the use of a computer system or computer data for unapproved or possibly illegal activities. Unauthorized use may range from an employee using a computer for keeping his or her child's soccer league scores to someone gaining access to a bank funds system and creating an unauthorized transfer.

The key to preventing both unauthorized access and unauthorized use is computer security that controls who can access the computer, when they can access it, and what actions they can perform while accessing the computer. Many commercial software packages are designed to implement

Figure 13-3
Anti-virus programs check disk drives and memory for computer viruses. The top screen allows the user to select the drives to be scanned. The middle screen displays the status during the scan, and the bottom screen shows the results.

these types of **access controls** through a process called identification and authentication. **Identification** verifies that the user is a valid user, and **authentication** verifies that the user is who he or she claims to be. The authentication technique used should match the degree of risk associated with the unauthorized access. An organization should regularly review the levels of authorization for users to determine if the levels are still appropriate. Three methods of authentication exist: remembered information, possessed objects, and biometric devices.

With **remembered information** authentication, a user is required to enter a word or series of characters that matches an entry in a security file in the computer. Most multi-user operating systems provide for a logon code, a user ID, and a password (all forms of remembered information) that must all be entered correctly before a user is allowed to use an application program. A **logon code** usually identifies the application that will be used, such as accounting, sales, or manufacturing. A **user ID** is a code that identifies the user. User ID's are usually assigned by the organization and are often a version of the user's name or initials. For example, a user ID for employee Mary Beth Gonzales may be

GONZALMB; that is, the first six letters of her last name followed by her first and middle initials.

A **password** is usually confidential; often it is known only by the user and the computer system administrator. The logon code, user ID, and password must match entries in an authorization file. If they don't match, the user is denied access to the system.

Users usually select their own passwords. Often, they try to choose a word or series of characters that will be easy to remember. The problem is that if it is too simple, such as a persons initials or birthday, it can be easily guessed. As shown in *Figure 13-4,* each character added to a password significantly increases the number of possible combinations and the length of time it would take for someone to guess the password. Some techniques users can follow to create passwords are:
- Choose names of obscure places in other countries
- Join two words together
- Mix initials and dates together
- Choose words from other languages
- Choose family names far back in your family tree
- Add letters to or subtract letters from an existing word

PASSWORD PROTECTION

Number of Characters	Possible Combinations	Average Time to Discover	
		Human	Computer
1	36	3 minutes	.000018 seconds
2	1,300	2 hours	.00065 seconds
3	47,000	3 days	.02 second
4	1,700,000	3 months	1 second
5	60,000,000	10 years	30 seconds
10	3,700,000,000,000,000	580 million years	59 years

- Possible characters include the letters A-Z and numbers 0-9
- Human discovery assumes one try every 10 seconds
- Computer discovery assumes one million tries per second
- Average time assumes password would be discovered in approximately half the time it would take to try all possible combinations

Figure 13-4
This table shows the effect of increasing the length of a password made up of letters and numbers. The longer the password, the more difficult it is to discover. Long passwords, however, are more difficult for users to remember. Even long passwords do not provide complete protection against unauthorized access. So called "sniffer" programs have been used to copy passwords as they are entered by authorized users. The copied passwords are later retrieved and used to logon to the computer. Because the password used is valid, the unauthorized access is difficult to discover.

The more creative a user is when assigning a password, the more difficult it is for someone to discover. Many software programs now incorporate rules when users create their passwords. For example, a minimum length of 6 characters is common, and a mixture of numbers and letters is often required. One software package requires between 6 and 10 characters, 2 of which must be numeric. Following these guidelines, the password SUE04 is invalid because it is too short, but SUE0412 is valid. This password is also easy for the user to remember because SUE is her daughter's name and April 12 is her son's birthday (04/12).

A variation of remembered information authentication is called dialog. With **dialog** authentication, one of several possible items of personal information, such as a spouse's first name, a birth date, or a mother's maiden name, is randomly chosen from information on file and asked of the user. Like a password, the dialog response must match information already on file or access is denied.

A **possessed object** is any item that a user must carry to gain access to the computer facility. Examples of possessed objects are badges, cards, and keys. Possessed objects are often used in conjunction with personal identification numbers. A **personal identification number** (**PIN**) is a numeric password, either assigned by the issuing organization or selected by a user. An example of a PIN is the number that must be entered when using an automated teller machine (ATM) card.

A **biometric device** is one that verifies personal characteristics to authenticate a user. Examples of personal characteristics are fingerprints, voice pattern, signature, hand size, and retinal (eye) patterns.

A biometric device translates a user's personal characteristic into a digital code that is compared to a digital code stored in the computer. If the digital code in the computer does not match the user's code, access is denied.

Biometric security is gaining in popularity because it is a virtually foolproof method of authentication. Passwords can be copied and possessed objects can be duplicated, but personal characteristics like fingerprints cannot be lost; they

Figure 13-5
This retinal scanner identifies a user by reading the tiny blood vessel patterns in the back of the eye.

Figure 13-6
A user's identity can be verified by a scanner that reads a finger or thumb print.

are always with the user. Because they can be expensive, biometric devices are most often used with highly sensitive data by government security organizations, the military, and financial institutions.

Many types of biometric security devices are currently in use. Retinal scanners *(Figure 13-5)* read the tiny blood vessels in the back of the eye. These blood vessel patterns are as unique as a fingerprint, which also can be tested by a finger or thumb print scanner *(Figure 13-6)*. A biometric pen measures the pressure a person exerts and the motion used to write a signature *(Figure 13-7)*. Typing patterns and rhythms can be measured with keystroke analysis devices. The shape, size, and other characteristics of a person's hand can be measured using hand geometry systems. Finally, biometric devices can verify a person's speaking voice.

Although the advantages of biometric devices are clear, they do have some disadvantages. For example, if someone cuts his or her thumb, a finger or thumb print scanner may reject a valid user. If a user is nervous, a voice, signature, or typing pattern may not match. Some people also question the health safety of retinal scanners. However, because access security is becoming more important, these problems will be addressed and the use of biometric security devices is likely to increase.

An access control method sometimes used to authenticate remote users is the callback system. With a **callback system**, remote users can only be connected to the computer system after the computer calls them back at a previously established telephone number. To initiate the callback system, the user calls the computer and enters a logon code, user ID, and password. If these entries are valid, the computer instructs the user to hang up the telephone connection. The computer then calls the user back at the previously established number. This prevents access to the computer by a person who has stolen or guessed the logon code, user ID, and password. Unless that person is also at the authorized phone number, they will not get on the system.

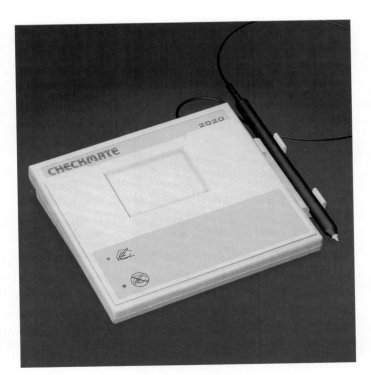

Figure 13-7
A biometric pen device can measure the characteristics of a person's signature.

The callback system only works for users who regularly work away from the computer at the same location, such as from home or a remote office. The callback system does not work for employees who travel and need to access the computer from different locations and therefore different phone numbers.

No matter what type of identification and authentication is used, the computer system should record both successful and unsuccessful access attempts. Unsuccessful access attempts should be investigated immediately. Successful access should be reviewed for irregularities such as use of the system after normal working hours or by remote terminals. Records of system usage also can be used to allocate information processing expenses based on the percentage of system use by various departments. In addition, organizations should have written policies regarding the personal use of computers by employees. Some organizations prohibit such use entirely. Others permit personal use on the employee's own time, before or after work. Most organizations have informal policies decided on a case-by-case basis. Whatever the policy, it should be made clear to employees and any personal use should be approved in advance.

Hardware Theft

Hardware theft of most desktop and larger computer systems is generally not a problem. Physical access controls such as locked doors and windows are usually adequate to protect the equipment in a home or office. Most offices and some homes also install alarm systems. School computer labs and other similar areas that have a large number of irregular users often install additional physical security such as cables or other devices that lock the equipment to a desk or floor *(Figure 13-8)*.

Portable equipment such as notebook computers or personal digital assistants (PDAs) do pose serious theft risks. A fully configured high-end notebook computer may cost $6,000 or more and yet weigh less than seven pounds. Such a device can be a tempting target to a thief who can sell the stolen computer for a fraction of its cost and still make thousands of dollars.

Common sense and a constant awareness of the risk are the best preventive measures against portable computer theft. Physical devices, such as cables that can temporarily lock a portable to a desk or table, also can be used. Portable

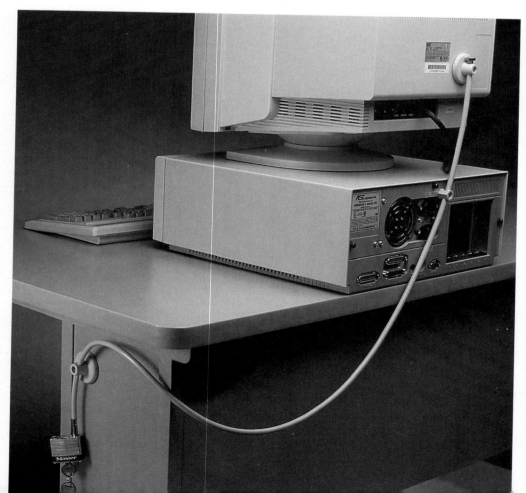

Figure 13-8
Cable locking devices can be used to prevent the theft of desktop and portable computer equipment.

computing devices should not be left out in the open, such as on the seat of a car, or be left unattended in a public place, such as in an airport or a restaurant. All information on portable computers should be regularly backed up.

Software Theft

With the increased use of personal computers, software theft, often called **software piracy**, has become a major problem. Some people have difficulty understanding why they should pay hundreds, perhaps thousands, of dollars for what appears to be an inexpensive diskette or tape. Perhaps they don't understand that ownership rights are not acquired when software is purchased. Users generally do not have the right to copy, loan, rent, or in any way, distribute the software. Estimates are that for every authorized copy of a commercial program, there is at least one illegal copy. One study reported that software piracy resulted in worldwide losses of more than $12 billion per year. Software piracy is a violation of copyright law and is a federal crime. Software companies take illegal copying seriously, and in some cases offenders who have been caught have been vigorously prosecuted. Penalties can include fines up to $250,000 and up to five years in jail. Many organizations and businesses have written policies prohibiting the copying and use of copyrighted software. Some of these organizations enforce the policy by periodically checking to make sure that all software is properly licensed. In order to promote a better understanding of piracy problems and, if necessary, to take legal action, a number of major U.S. software companies formed the Business Software Alliance (BSA). BSA operates anti-piracy hotlines in the United States and 24 countries *(Figure 13-9)*.

To reduce the cost for organizations with large numbers of users, software vendors often offer special discount pricing. The more copies of a program an organization purchases, the greater the discount. Network versions of many software packages also are available. These packages allow network users to share a single copy of the software that resides on the network server computer. Network software can be priced based on a fixed fee for an unlimited number of users, a maximum

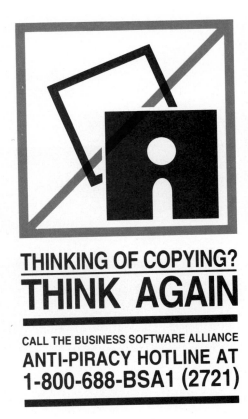

THINKING OF COPYING?
THINK AGAIN

CALL THE BUSINESS SOFTWARE ALLIANCE
ANTI-PIRACY HOTLINE AT
1-800-688-BSA1 (2721)

Figure 13-9
The Business Software Alliance fights against software piracy by operating anti-piracy hotlines in the United States and 24 other countries.

number of users, or on a per user basis. Sometimes organizations will purchase a software site license. A **site license** gives an organization the right to install the software on multiple computers at a single site. The site license fee is less than if individual copies of the software package were purchased for each computer.

In addition to purchasing commercial software, an organization or individual also can consider acquiring shareware and public domain software. **Shareware** is software that users may try out on their own systems before paying a fee. If the users decide to keep and use the software, they send in a registration fee to the software publisher *(Figure 13-10)*. **Public domain software** is free software that is not copyrighted and can therefore be distributed among users. The quality of shareware and public domain software varies greatly. Both shareware and public domain software can be obtained from BBSs and also from public domain software libraries.

Information Theft

There can be several reasons for the deliberate theft of information from a computer system. Organizations may steal or buy stolen information to learn about a competitor. Other information that has value includes credit card and telephone charge card numbers. Both types of numbers are frequently stored in an accounting or administrative department file on the computer.

Most organizations prevent information theft by implementing the user identification and authentication controls discussed in the previous section of this chapter on Unauthorized Access and Use. These controls work well to prevent the theft of information that resides on computers located on an organization's premises. Information transmitted over communications channels, however, offers a higher degree of risk because it can be intercepted. Portable computers that may contain sensitive company information generally do not have the same level of access controls and therefore also carry a higher risk of information theft.

Figure 13-10
PC-Write is a shareware word processing program for the DOS operating system. Users can try the program for free. If they want to continue using the program, and receive a reference manual and support, they are given instructions on how to register the program. The registration form is included in the program as a document.

One way to protect sensitive data is to use encryption. **Encryption** is the process of converting readable data, called **plaintext**, into unreadable characters, called **ciphertext**. The conversion is accomplished with a formula that uses a code, called an **encryption key**, to modify the plaintext. The encryption key also is used by the person who receives the ciphertext message to **decrypt** (or **decipher**) the data back into the original plaintext.

Many methods exist for encrypting data. *Figure 13-11* shows examples of some simple encryption methods. Often, an encryption formula will use more than one technique, such as a combination of transposition and substitution. Some organizations develop their own encryption methods but most use available software packages. An encryption method widely used by the U.S. government is the **data encryption standard** (DES). *Figure 13-12* on the next page illustrates the Gettysburg Address encrypted with the DES.

Most data encryption is accomplished using software. In a controversial announcement made in 1993, the U.S. government proposed establishing a federal standard for voice and data encryption that would use a hardware approach.

The proposed standard called for the use of an encryption formula called **Skipjack** implemented in a tamper-resistant microprocessor called the **Clipper chip**. The idea was to have the Clipper chip built into voice, data, and fax communication devices. Since many computers now offer all three communications capabilities, Clipper chips also would be directly installed in PCs. Government security agencies such as the National Security Agency and the Federal Bureau of Investigation have stated they want a single hardware-based encryption method like the Clipper chip so they can, if necessary and, if authorized, monitor private communications. Because of widespread opposition to the government's proposal, plans to implement the Clipper chip have been put on indefinite hold.

System Failure

A **system failure** is defined as a prolonged malfunction of a computer system. System failures are caused by natural disasters such as fires, floods, storms, or by events such as

ENCRYPTION METHODS

NAME	METHOD	PLAINTEXT	CIPHERTEXT	EXPLANATION
Transposition	Switch the order of characters	COMPUTER	OCPMTURE	Adjacent characters swapped
Substitution	Replace characters with others	PRINTER	EOJLZRO	Each letter replaced with another
Expansion	Insert characters between existing characters	TAPE	TYAYPYEY	Letter Y inserted after each character
Compaction	Characters removed and stored elseware	HARDWARE	HADWRE	Every third letter removed (R and A)

Figure 13-11
This table shows four methods of encryption; or translating plaintext into ciphertext. Most encryption programs use a combination of methods.

electrical power problems that are discussed in this section. Two ways of minimizing the impact of a system failure, back-up and disaster recovery planning, also are discussed.

One of the most common causes of system failures is electrical power variations. Electrical power variations can cause loss of data or loss of equipment. If the computer equipment is connected to a network, multiple systems can be damaged with a single power disturbance. Electrical disturbances include undervoltages, overvoltages, and noise.

An **undervoltage** occurs when there is a drop in the electrical supply. In North America, electricity normally flows at approximately 120 volts through the wall plug. Any significant drop below 120 volts is considered an undervoltage. A **brownout** is a prolonged drop in power and a **blackout** is a complete power failure. Undervoltages can cause a loss of data but generally do not damage equipment. An **overvoltage** occurs when the incoming electrical power increases significantly above the normal 120 volts. Overvoltages, or **power surges**, can cause immediate and permanent damage to hard-

ware. A momentary overvoltage, called a **spike**, occurs when the power increase lasts for less than one millisecond (one thousandth of a second). Spikes are caused by uncontrollable disturbances, such as lightning bolts, or controllable disturbances, such as turning on a piece of equipment that is on the same electrical circuit. **Noise** is any unwanted signal, usually varying quickly, that is mixed with the normal voltage entering the computer. Noise is caused from external devices such as fluorescent lighting, radios, and televisions, as well as from components within the computer itself. Computer power supplies are designed to filter out noise and noise is generally not a risk to hardware or data.

To protect against overvoltages, surge protectors are used. A **surge protector**, also called a **surge suppressor**, uses special electrical components to keep an overvoltage from reaching the computer equipment *(Figure 13-13)*. Small overvoltages are absorbed by the surge protector without damage. Large overvoltages, such as those caused by a lightning strike, will cause the surge protector to fail in order to

Four score and seven years ago our fathers brought forth on this continent, a new nation, conceived in liberty, and dedicated to the proposition that all men are created equal.

Now we are engaged in a great civil war, testing whether that nation or any nation so conceived and so dedicated, can long endure. We are met on a great battle field of that war. We have come to dedicate a portion of that field as a final resting place for those who here gave their lives that the nation might live. It is altogether fitting and proper that we should do this.

Figure 13-12
This figure shows the first two paragraphs of the Gettysburg Address in plaintext and ciphertext. It was encrypted using a software package that employs the DES encryption formula.

protect the computer equipment. Surge protectors are not 100% effective; large power surges can bypass the protector and repeated small overvoltages can permanently weaken a surge protector. Some experts recommend replacing surge protectors every two to three years.

For additional electrical protection, many users connect an uninterruptable power supply to the computer. An **uninterruptable power supply** (UPS) is a device that contains surge protection circuits and one or more batteries that can provide power during a temporary or permanent loss of power. The amount of time a UPS allows a user to continue working depends on the electrical requirements of the computer system and the size of the batteries in the UPS. A UPS for a PC should provide from ten to thirty minutes of use in the case of a total power loss. This should be enough time to save work currently being worked on and to properly shut down the computer.

Backup Procedures

To prevent against data loss caused by a system failure, computer users should have backup procedures. A **backup** is a copy of information stored on a computer. Used as a verb, to *back up* a file means to make a copy. **Backup procedures** specify a regular plan of copying and storing key data and program files. In the case of a system failure or the discovery of corrupted files, backup copies can be used to **restore** the files (reload the files on the computer). Backup copies are normally kept in fireproof safes or vaults or **offsite**, in a building different from the computer site. Offsite storage is used so a single disaster, such as a fire, will not destroy both the primary and the backup copy of the data.

An installation can perform three types of backup: full, differential, or incremental. A **full backup** includes all files in the computer. A full backup provides the best protection because all program and data files are copied. Because a full backup can take a long time, however, it is often used in conjunction with differential and incremental backups. A **differential backup** duplicates only the files that have changed *since the last full backup*. An **incremental backup** duplicates

Figure 13-13
Circuits inside a surge protector protect against overvoltages.

only the files that have changed since the last full *or incremental backup*. The following will clarify the difference between a differential backup and an incremental backup. With a differential backup, you always have two backups; the full backup and the differential backup of all changes since the last full backup. With incremental backups, you may have several incremental backup copies. The first incremental backup copies all changes since the last full backup. Subsequent incremental backups only copy changes since the last incremental backup. Differential backups may be appropriate if there are relatively few changes in relation to the total amount of data to be backed up. If there are many changes, incremental backups will take less time. *Figure 13-14* outlines the advantages and disadvantages of each type of backup.

Generally, an organization develops a policy where a full backup is performed at regular intervals, such as at the end of each week and at the end of the month. Between full backups, differential or incremental backups are performed. *Figure 13-15* shows an approach for backing up a system for one month. This mixture of full and incremental backups provides an efficient way of protecting data and provides several restore starting points if a problem is found with incorrect data. Whatever backup procedures an organization adopts, they should be clearly stated, in writing, and be consistently followed.

Sometimes important individual files are backed up separately and a *three generation backup* policy is often used. The oldest copy of the file is called the **grandfather**. The second oldest copy of the file is called the **father**. The most recent copy of the file is called the **son**.

Backup and restore programs are available from many sources including most developers of anti-virus programs and developers of utility software. Backup and restore programs also are included with most operating systems and with backup devices such as cartridge tape drives.

Disaster Recovery Plan

Because the prolonged loss of computing capability could seriously damage an organization's ability to function, a disaster recovery plan should be developed. A **disaster recovery**

TYPE OF BACKUP	ADVANTAGES	DISADVANTAGES
Full	Fastest recovery method. All files are saved.	Longest backup time.
Differential	Fast backup method. Requires minimal space to backup.	Recovery is time consuming because need last full backup plus the differential backup.
Incremental	Fastest backup method. Requires minimal space to backup. Only most recent changes saved.	Recovery is most time consuming because need last full backup and all incremental backups since last full backup.

Figure 13-14
The advantages and disadvantages of different backup methods.

plan is a written plan describing the steps an organization would take to restore computer operations in the event of a disaster. A disaster recovery plan contains four major components: the emergency plan, the backup plan, the recovery plan, and the test plan *(Figure 13-16)*.

THE EMERGENCY PLAN

An **emergency plan** specifies the steps to be taken immediately after a disaster strikes. The emergency plan is usually organized by type of disaster, such as fire, flood, or earthquake. Depending on the nature and extent of the disaster, some emergency procedures will differ. All emergency plans should contain the following information:

- Names and phone numbers of people and organizations to be notified (e.g., management, fire department, police department)
- Procedures to be followed with the computer equipment (e.g., equipment shutdown, power shutoff, file removal)
- Employee evacuation procedures
- Return procedures; that is, who can reenter the facility and what actions are they to perform

THE BACKUP PLAN

Once the procedures in the emergency plan have been followed, the next step is to follow the backup plan. The **backup plan** specifies how an organization will use backup files and equipment to resume information processing. Because an organization's normal location may be destroyed or unusable, the backup plan should include an alternate computer facility. The backup plan identifies these items:

- The location of backup data, supplies, and equipment
- The personnel responsible for gathering backup resources and transporting them to the alternate computer facility
- A schedule indicating the order and approximate time each application should be up and running

For a backup plan to be successful, it is crucial that an installation back up all critical resources; that is, hardware, software, data, facilities, supplies, and documentation. Because personnel could be injured in a disaster, it is also crucial that multiple people, including possibly non-employees, are trained in the backup and recovery procedures.

The location of the alternate computer facility is also important. It should be close enough to be convenient, yet

DAY	TYPE OF BACKUP
Each Monday	Incremental or Differential
Each Tuesday	Incremental or Differential
Each Wednesday	Incremental or Differential
Each Thursday	Incremental or Differential
1st Friday	Full
2nd Friday	Full
3rd Friday	Full
End of Month	Full

Figure 13-15
This table shows a backup strategy that can be used each month. The tapes used for Monday, Tuesday, Wednesday, and Thursday backups would be the same each week. The tapes used for Friday backups would be used again the following month. A new tape would be used each month for the end of month backup. End of month backup tapes are usually kept for at least one year.

PARTS OF A DISASTER RECOVERY PLAN

Emergency Plan
Evacuation plans and list
of people to notify

Backup Plan
Identity and location of backup resources

Recovery Plan
Specific steps and timeplan to resume
computer operations

Test Plan
Simulates diasters to find
weaknesses in overall plan

Figure 13-16
A summary of the four parts of a disaster recovery plan.

not too close that a single disaster, such as an earthquake, could destroy both the main and alternate computer facility. Two types of alternate computer facilities exist: a hot site and a cold site. A **hot site** is an alternate computer facility that has compatible computer resources; that is, it already has installed the necessary hardware, software, and communications equipment. Because installing and maintaining a hot site is quite expensive, many organizations instead use a cold site as their alternate computer facility. A **cold site** is an empty facility that can accommodate the necessary computer resources. A cold site requires immediate installation of computer equipment and software in case of disaster. Instead of using a hot or cold site as the alternate computer facility, some organizations enter into **reciprocal backup relationships** with other firms; that is, in case of disaster, one firm provides space, and sometimes equipment, to the other.

THE RECOVERY PLAN

The **recovery plan** specifies the actions to be taken to restore full information processing operations. Like the emergency plan, the recovery plan will differ for each type of disaster. To plan for disaster recovery, committees should be established, with each responsible for different forms of recovery. For example, one committee may be designated in charge of hardware replacement and another responsible for software replacement.

THE TEST PLAN

To provide assurance that the disaster plan is complete, it should be tested. A **disaster recovery test plan** contains information for simulating different levels of disasters and recording an organization's ability to recover. In a simulation, all personnel would be required to follow the steps outlined in the disaster recovery plan. Any recovery actions that are required but are not in the plan should be added to the plan. Although simulations can be scheduled, the best test of the plan is to simulate a disaster without advance notice.

Developing a Computer Security Plan

The individual risks and safeguards previously mentioned and the disaster recovery plan should all be incorporated into an overall computer security plan. A **computer security plan** summarizes in writing the safeguards that are in place to protect an organization's information assets. A computer security plan should do the following:

- Identify all information assets of an organization, including equipment, software, documentation, procedures, people, data, facilities, and supplies.
- Identify all security risks that may cause an information asset loss. Risks should be ranked from most likely to occur to least likely. An estimated value should be placed on each risk, including the value of lost business. For example, what is the estimated loss if customers cannot place orders for one hour, one day, or one week.
- For each risk, identify the safeguards that exist to detect, prevent, and recover from a loss.

The computer security plan should be updated annually or more frequently for major changes in information assets, such as the addition of a new computer or the implementation of a new application. In developing the plan, it should be kept in mind that some degree of risk is unavoidable. The more secure a system is, the more difficult it is for everyone to use. The goal of a computer security plan is to match an appropriate level of safeguards against the identified risks. Fortunately, most organizations will never experience a major information system disaster. Because many organizations and individuals rely heavily on computers, however, disaster recovery must be planned for.

Ethics and the Information Age

Like any powerful technology, computers can be used for both good and bad actions. The standards that determine whether an action is good or bad are called ethics. **Computer ethics** are the moral guidelines that govern the use of computers and information systems. Five areas of computer ethics that are frequently discussed are software theft (piracy), unauthorized use of computer systems, the accuracy of computer information, codes of conduct, and the privacy of computerized information. Software piracy and unauthorized use were covered earlier in this chapter during the discussion of computer risks and safeguards. Privacy of computerized information is discussed in a separate section at the end of this chapter. The following sections deal with the accuracy of computer information and codes of conduct.

Information Accuracy

Organizations have long been concerned about the accuracy of computer input. Inaccurate input can result in erroneous information and incorrect decisions based on that information. Information accuracy is even more of an issue today because many users access information maintained by other organizations, such as online service providers. Often, the organization providing access to the information did not create the information. An example is the airline flight schedules available from several online service providers. The question that arises is "Who is responsible for the accuracy of the information?" Does the responsibility rest solely with the original creator of the information or does the service that passes along the information also have some responsibility to verify its accuracy? Legally, these questions have not been resolved.

In addition to concerns about the accuracy of computer input, some people have raised questions about the ethics of using computers to alter output, primarily graphic output such as retouched photographs. Using graphics equipment and software, photographs can be digitized and edited to add, change, or remove images *(Figure 13-17)*. One group who is opposed to any manipulation of an image is the National Press Photographers Association. They believe that allowing even the slightest alteration could eventually lead to deliberately misleading photographs. Others believe that digital photo retouching is acceptable as long as the significant

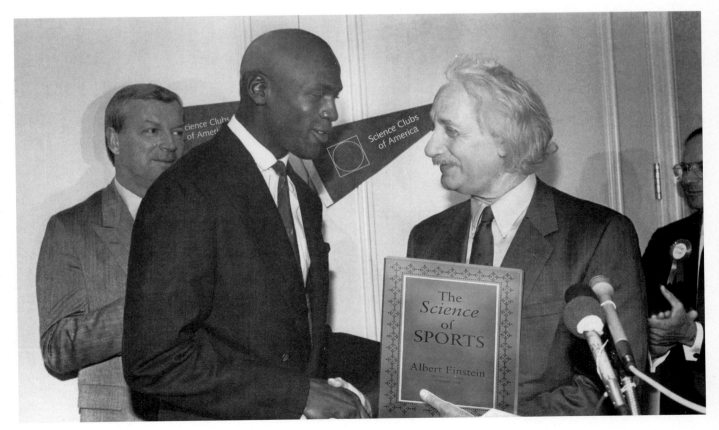

Figure 13-17
This digitally altered photograph shows sports star Michael Jordan (born 1963) meeting famous scientist Albert Einstein (deceased since 1955).

content or meaning of the photograph is not changed. Digital retouching is another area where legal precedents have not yet been established.

Codes of Conduct

Recognizing that individuals and organizations need specific standards for the ethical use of computers and information systems, a number of computer related organizations have established **codes of conduct**, which are written guidelines that help determine whether a specific computer action is ethical or unethical *(Figure 13-18)*. Many businesses have adopted similar codes of conduct and made them known to their employees.

One of the problems with ethical issues in business is that some people believe ethical decisions are the responsibility of management, not employees. This is often true in service departments, such as information processing or accounting, whose organization function is sometimes interpreted to be providing whatever information upper-level management wants. Codes of conduct that apply to an entire organization can help in this area by giving all employees, management included, a standard against which they can measure their actions.

Information Privacy

Information privacy has to do with the rights of individuals and organizations to deny or restrict the collection and use of information about them. In the past, it was easier to maintain privacy because information tended to be kept in separate locations; individual stores had their own credit files, government agencies had separate records, doctors had separate files, and so on. It is now technically and economically feasible, however, to store large amounts of related data about individuals in one database. Some people believe this increases the possibility for unauthorized use. Many people also are concerned that their privacy is violated when computers are used to monitor their activities. Both of these issues, unauthorized collection and use of information and employee monitoring, are discussed in the following sections.

Unauthorized Collection and Use of Information

Many individuals are surprised to learn that information provided for magazine subscriptions, product warranty registration cards, contest entry forms, and other separate

CODE OF CONDUCT

1. Computers may not be used to harm other people.

2. Employees may not interfere with other's computer work.

3. Employees may not snoop in other's computer files.

4. Computers may not be used to steal.

5. Computers may not be used to bear false witness.

6. Employees may not use other's computer resources without authorization.

7. Employees may not illegally copy or use software.

8. Employees may not use other's output.

Figure 13-18
An example of a code of conduct that an employer may distribute to employees.

documents is often sold to national marketing organizations. The national marketing organizations combine this acquired data with other information obtained from public sources, such as driver license and vehicle registration information, to create an electronic profile of an individual. The combined information is then sold to organizations who want to send information on their product, service, or cause to a specific group of individuals, such as all sports car owners, over 40 years of age, living in the southeastern United States. Direct marketing supporters say that the use of information in this way lowers overall selling costs and therefore product prices as well. Critics of the electronic profiles contend that the combined information may reveal more about individuals than anyone has a right to know. Critics contend that, at a minimum, individuals should be informed the information they furnish may be provided to others and have the right to deny the transfer.

The concern about privacy has led to federal and state laws regarding the storage and disclosure of personal data *(Figure 13-19)*. Common points in some of these laws include the following:

1. Information collected and stored about individuals should be limited to what is necessary to carry out the function of the business or government agency collecting the data.
2. Once collected, provisions should be made to restrict access to the data to those employees within the organization who need access to it to perform their job duties.
3. Personal information should be released outside the organization collecting the data only when the person has agreed to its disclosure.
4. When information is collected about an individual, the individual should know that the data is being collected and have the opportunity to determine the accuracy of the data.

DATE	LAW NAME	PURPOSE
1994	**Computer Abuse Amendments Act**	Amends 1984 act to outlaw transmission of harmful computer code such as viruses.
1992	**Cable Act**	Extends privacy of Cable Communications Policy Act of 1984 to include cellular and other wireless services.
1991	**Telephone Consumer Protection Act**	Restricts activities of telemarketers.
1988	**Computer Matching and Privacy Protection Act**	Regulates the use of government data to determine the eligibility of persons for federal benefits.
1988	**Video Privacy Protection Act**	Forbids retailers from releasing or selling video-rental records without customer consent or a court order.
1986	**Electronic Communications Privacy Act (ECPA)**	Provides the same right of privacy protection for the postal delivery service and telephone companies to the new forms of electronic communications, such as voice mail, E-mail, and cellular telephones.
1984	**Cable Communications Policy Act**	Regulates disclosure of cable TV subscriber records.
1984	**Computer Fraud and Abuse Act**	Outlaws unauthorized access of federal government computers.
1978	**Right to Financial Privacy Act**	Strictly outlines procedures federal agencies must follow when looking at customer records in banks.
1974	**Privacy Act**	Forbids federal agencies from allowing information to be used for a reason other than which it was collected.
1974	**Family Educational Rights and Privacy Act**	Gives students and parents access to school records and limits disclosure of records to unauthorized parties.
1970	**Fair Credit Reporting Act**	Prohibts credit reporting agencies from releasing credit information to unauthorized people and allows consumers to review their credit records.

Figure 13-19
A summary of the major U.S. government laws concerning privacy.

Several federal laws deal specifically with computers. The 1986 Electronic Communications Privacy Act (ECPA) provides the same protection that covers mail and telephone communications to new forms of electronic communications such as voice mail. The 1988 Computer Matching and Privacy Protection Act regulates the use of government data to determine the eligibility of persons for federal benefits. The 1984 and 1994 Computer Fraud and Abuse Acts outlaw unauthorized access to federal government computers and the transmission of harmful computer code such as viruses.

One law with an apparent legal loophole is in the Fair Credit Reporting Act. Although the act limits the rights of others viewing a credit report to those with a *legitimate business need*, a legitimate business need is not defined. The result is that just about anyone can say they have a legitimate business need and gain access to someone's credit report.

Credit reports contain much more than just balance and payment information on mortgages and credit cards. The largest credit bureaus maintain information on family income, number of dependents, employment history, bank balances, driving records, and social security numbers. In total, these credit bureaus have more than 400 million records on more than 160 million people. Some credit bureaus sell combinations of the data they have stored in their database to direct marketing organizations. Because of continuing complaints about credit report errors and the invasion of privacy, the U.S. Congress is considering a major revision of the Fair Credit Reporting Act.

Employee Monitoring

Employee monitoring involves the use of computers to observe, record, and review employee communications and keyboard activity. The most frequently discussed issue is whether or not an employer has the right to read employee E-mail messages. Actual policies vary widely, with some organizations declaring E-mail messages will be regularly reviewed and others stating E-mail is considered private. Most organizations, estimated in one study to be approximately 75%, do not have formal E-mail policies, which, in effect, means that E-mail could be read without notifying employees.

At present, no laws exist relating to E-mail. The 1986 Electronic Communications Privacy Act does not cover communications within an organization. Because many believe that such internal communications should be private, several lawsuits have been filed against employers. In response to the issue of workplace privacy, the U.S. Congress proposed the Privacy for Consumers and Workers Act, which entitles employees to be notified if their employer is monitoring electronic communications. Supporters of the legislation hope that it will also restrict the types and amount of monitoring that employers can legally conduct.

Summary of Security, Ethics, and Privacy

Increased reliance on computer systems and computerized information makes it essential that steps are taken to protect the systems and information from known risks. The livelihood of many organizations and individuals depends on the computer systems they use every day. Both society and individuals, however, have an obligation to use computer systems responsibly and not abuse the power they provide. This presents constant challenges that sometimes weigh the rights of the individual against increased efficiency and productivity. The computer must be thought of as a tool whose effectiveness is determined by the skill and experience of the user. With the computer knowledge you have acquired you will be better able to participate in decisions on how to ethically and efficiently use computerized information systems. To measure your ethical views, answer the ethics questionnaire in *Figure 13-20*.

COMPUTER ETHICS

	Ethical	Unethical	Crime
1. An employee installs a new upgraded version of a word processing program on his office computer. Because no one will be using the old version of the program, the employee takes it home to use on his personal computer so his children can use it to write school papers.	☐	☐	☐
2. While reviewing her employee's E-mail messages, a department manager discovers that one of her employees is using the E-mail system to operate a weekly football betting pool. employee	☐	☐	☐
manager	☐	☐	☐
3. A company hires a consultant to develop a custom program. After completing the program, the consultant tries to license the program to other companies.	☐	☐	☐
4. An employee learns the password to the personnel system and uses it to review the salaries of the corporate officers. No use is made of the information. "I was just curious" is the individual's response when caught.	☐	☐	☐
5. A bank employee electronically transfers money from an inactive customer account to his own personal account. After pay day, the employee transfers the money plus interest back to the inactive account.	☐	☐	☐
6. While reviewing a list of available programs on a bulletin board, a user notices the name of a program that is similar to a popular spreadsheet package. After downloading the program, the user discovers that the program appears to be a test version of the popular spreadsheet program that sells for $200 in computer stores. The user keeps and uses the program.	☐	☐	☐
7. A programmer is asked to write a program that she knows will generate inaccurate financial information. When she questions her manager about the program, she is told to write the program or risk losing her job. She writes the program. programmer	☐	☐	☐
manager	☐	☐	☐
8. As a practical joke, an employee enters a program on the company computer. Each time an employee uses a diskette on the company network, the program is copied to the diskette. The first time the diskette is used after January 1, a "Happy New Year" message is displayed.	☐	☐	☐
9. A newspaper uses photo retouching software to remove a billboard advertisement for a competitive newspaper from the background of a front-page photo.	☐	☐	☐
10. A company occasionally uses software to monitor the productivity of its staff. It only uses the software to monitor an employee thought to be repeatedly goofing off.	☐	☐	☐

Figure 13-20
Indicate whether you think the described situation is ethical, unethical, or a crime. Discuss your answers with your instructor and other students.

COMPUTERS AT WORK

Active Badges Help Locate Users

Tired of missing phone calls because you were away from your desk? Frustrated by not being able to find a co-worker you know is in the building? These and similar employee location problems are being solved by **active badge systems** developed by Olivetti Research Limited of Cambridge, England.

The active badge contains a small transmitter and is worn on the outside of clothing. Every fifteen seconds the badge emits an infrared signal that is picked up by sensors in offices and hallways. Infrared signals are used because they do not penetrate walls and therefore can be traced to a specific location. The sensors are connected to a computer that updates a database of locations and users. The computer used for the sensors is connected to an organization's main computer or computer network so users can display location information.

If a user is in a meeting or otherwise does not want to be disturbed, he or she can press a button on the badge twice.

This results in a busy message on the location display. The busy status remains until the user changes locations. If a user does not want to be located at all, they can place their badge in a pocket, purse, or drawer. The badges have a light sensor that shuts them off in the dark.

Advanced versions of the devices called Authentication Badges are currently under development. Authentication badges contain small microprocessors that can be programmed. One anticipated use of authentication badges is as security devices that will let authorized users enter restricted areas.

Active Badges are just one type of device called a Portable Interactive Computing Object (PiCO). Olivetti has plans for an entire family of smart PiCO devices that can be attached to persons or things. Olivetti believes the increased productivity achieved from the use of the devices will more than offset any concerns about worker privacy.

Figure 13-21

IN THE FUTURE

Who Will Set The Standards and Methods of Information Privacy?

One positive result of the U.S. government's Clipper chip proposal was that it stimulated a lot of debate over how information should be protected and who should set the standards. Although the proposed plan was voluntary, many objected to the government's plan to have encryption chips imbedded in voice, data, and fax machines, including computers. Opponents of the plan were worried that the government-controlled encryption standard would make it easier for government agencies to eavesdrop on electronic communications. It should be noted that numerous laws and procedures currently in effect supposedly prevent this type of abuse.

Opponents also complained that the encryption formula would be kept by the National Security Agency (NSA), the highly secret international intelligence organization. In the past, NSA has been criticized for operating independently with little government supervision. Other arguments against the Clipper chip were that foreign companies and governments would not use an encryption device controlled by the U.S. government and that serious criminals could easily bypass the chip by using a different software-based encryption method.

Judging by the number of articles that dealt with the government's proposal, many people apparently believe the government should stay out of the electronic privacy standards and methods business. Part of this opinion is undoubtedly just a conservative view that the government should involve itself as little as possible in the activities of businesses and individuals. Others firmly believe that the use of many different encryption methods, instead of just one government-approved method, provides the best protection against widespread information theft and the invasion of electronic privacy.

Figure 13-22

What You Should Know

1. A **computer security risk** is defined as any event or action that could cause a loss to computer equipment, software, information, or processing capability.

2. A computer **virus** is an illegal and potentially damaging computer program designed to *infect* other software by attaching itself to the software with which it comes in contact. A **boot sector virus** replaces the program that is used to start the system with a modified version of the program. A **file virus** inserts virus code into program files. A **Trojan horse virus** is a virus that hides within or is designed to look like a traditional program.

3. Some viruses contain time bombs or logic bombs. A **time bomb** is a program that performs an activity on a particular date. A **logic bomb** is a program that performs an activity when a certain action has occurred. A **worm**, unlike a virus, does not attach itself to a program, but instead is designed to repeatedly copy itself in memory or on a disk drive until there is no memory or disk space remaining.

4. To protect against viruses, **anti-virus programs**, called **vaccines**, have been developed. Anti-virus programs look for viruses that attempt to modify the boot program, the operating system, and other programs that are normally read from but not written to. Anti-virus programs also look for specific patterns of known virus code called a **virus signature**. A **polymorphic virus**, which is designed to modify its program code each time it attaches itself to another program or file, is extremely difficult to detect.

5. When a program file is **inoculated**, information such as the file size and file creation date is recorded in a separate inoculation file. Using this information, a vaccine program can tell if a virus program has tampered with the program file. A **rescue disk** contains an uninfected copy of certain operating system commands and essential information about the computer that enables the computer to restart correctly.

6. **Unauthorized access** can be defined as computer trespassing; in other words, using a computer system without permission. Persons who deliberately try to illegally access computer systems, usually by using a modem, are called **crackers**. The term **hacker**, although originally a positive term, also has become associated with persons who try to break into computer systems. **Unauthorized use** is the use of a computer system or computer data for unapproved or possibly illegal activities.

7. Many commercial software packages are designed to implement **access controls** through a process called identification and authentication. **Identification** verifies that the user is a valid user, and **authentication** verifies that the user is who he or she claims to be. Three methods of authentication exist: remembered information, possessed objects, and biometric devices.

8. With **remembered information** authentication, a user is required to enter a word or series of characters that matches an entry in a security file in the computer. Most multiuser operating systems provide for a **logon code**, a **user ID**, and a **password** (all forms of remembered information) that must be entered correctly before a user is allowed to use an application program. With **dialog** authentication, which is a variation of remembered information authentication, one of several possible items of personal information is randomly chosen from information on file and asked of the user.

9. A **possessed object** is any item that a user must carry to gain access to the computer facility. A possessed object is often used in combination with a **personal identification number** (PIN), which is a numeric password either assigned by the issuing organization or selected by a user.

10. A **biometric device** is one that verifies personal characteristics to authenticate a user. Examples of personal characteristics are fingerprints, voice pattern, signature, hand size, and retinal (eye) patterns.

11. A **callback system**, which is an access control method sometimes used to authenticate remote users, connects users to the computer system only after the computer calls them back at a previously established telephone number.

12. Hardware theft of most desktop and larger computer systems is generally not a problem. Portable equipment, however, such as notebook computers or personal digital assistants (PDAs), do pose serious theft risks. Common sense and a constant awareness of the risk are the best preventive measures.

13. With the increased use of personal computers, software theft, often called **software piracy**, has become a major problem. Users generally do not have the right to copy, loan, rent, or in any way distribute software when it is purchased. A **site license** gives an organization the right to install software on multiple computers at a single site. **Shareware** is software that users may try out on their own systems before paying a fee. **Public domain software** is free software that is not copyrighted and can therefore be distributed among users.

14. Most organizations prevent information theft by implementing user identification and authentication controls. One way to protect sensitive data is to use encryption.

15. **Encryption** is the process of converting readable data, called **plaintext**, into unreadable characters, called **ciphertext**. The conversion is accomplished with a formula that uses a code, called an **encryption key**, to modify the plaintext. The encryption key is also used by the person who receives the ciphertext message to **decrypt** (or **decipher**) the data back into the original plaintext. An encryption method widely used by the U.S. government is the **data encryption standard** (DES). A proposed federal standard for voice and data encryption requires the use of an encryption formula named **Skipjack** implemented in a tamper-resistant microprocessor called the **Clipper chip**.

16. A **system failure** is defined as a prolonged malfunction of a computer system. System failures are caused by natural disasters or events such as electrical power problems. An **undervoltage** occurs when there is a drop in the electrical supply. A **brownout** is a prolonged drop in power and a **blackout** is a complete power failure. An **overvoltage**, or **power surge**, occurs when the incoming electrical power increases above the normal 120 volts. A momentary overvoltage, called a **spike**, occurs when the power increase lasts for less than one millisecond. **Noise** is any unwanted signal that is mixed with the normal voltage entering the computer.

17. A **surge protector**, also called a **surge suppressor**, uses special electrical components to keep an overvoltage from reaching the computer equipment. An **uninterruptable power supply** (UPS) is a device that contains surge protection circuits and one or more batteries that can provide power during a temporary or permanent loss of power.

18. A **backup** is a copy of information stored on a computer. **Backup procedures** specify a regular plan of copying and storing key data and program files. In the case of a system failure or the discovery of corrupted files, backup copies can be used to **restore** the files (reload the files on the computer). Backup copies are normally kept in fireproof safes or vaults or **offsite**, in a building different from the computer site. An installation can perform three types of backup: **full backup**, **differential backup**, or **incremental backup**.

19. Sometimes important individual files are backed up separately, and a *three-generation* backup policy is often used. The oldest copy of the file is called the **grandfather**, the second oldest copy is called the **father**, and the most recent copy is called the **son**.

20. A **disaster recovery plan** is a written plan describing the steps an organization would take to restore computer operation in the event of a disaster. A disaster recovery plan contains four major components: the emergency plan, the backup plan, the recovery plan, and the test plan.

13:00

**What You
Should Know**
(continued)

21. The **emergency plan** specifies the steps to be taken immediately after a disaster strikes. The **backup plan** specifies how an organization will use backup files and equipment to resume information processing. Two types of alternate computer facilities exist: a **hot site** and a **cold site**. Some organizations enter into **reciprocal backup relationships** with other firms; that is, in case of disaster one firm provides space, and sometimes equipment, to the other.

22. The **recovery plan** specifies the actions to be taken to restore full information processing operations. The **disaster recovery test plan** contains information for simulating different levels of disasters and recording an organization's capability to recover.

23. A **computer security plan** summarizes in writing the safeguards that are in place to protect an organization's information assets.

24. **Computer ethics** are the moral guidelines that govern the use of computers and information systems. In addition to software theft (piracy) and unauthorized use of computer systems, other areas of computer ethics frequently discussed are the accuracy of information, codes of conduct, and the privacy of computerized information.

25. Inaccurate input can result in erroneous information and incorrect decisions based on the information. Information accuracy is even more of an issue today because many users access information maintained by other organizations. Some people also have raised questions about the ethics of using computers to alter output.

26. Recognizing that individuals and organizations need specific standards for the ethical use of computers and information systems, a number of computer-related organizations have established **codes of conduct**, which are written guidelines that help determine whether a specific computer action is ethical or unethical.

27. **Information privacy** has to do with the rights of individuals and organizations to deny or restrict the collection and use of information about them. Concern with the unauthorized collection and use of information has led to federal and state laws regarding the storage and disclosure of personal data. A second information privacy issue is **employee monitoring**, which involves the use of computers to observe, record, and review employee communications and keyboard activity.

Terms to Remember

access controls (13.5)
active badge systems (13.22)
anti-virus programs (13.3)
authentication (13.5)

backup (13.13)
backup plan (13.15)
backup procedures (13.13)
biometric device (13.6)
blackout (13.12)
boot sector virus (13.2)
brownout (13.12)

callback system (13.7)
ciphertext (13.11)
Clipper chip (13.11)
codes of conduct (13.18)
cold site (13.16)
computer ethics (13.17)
computer security plan (13.16)
computer security risk (13.2)
crackers (13.4)

data encryption standard (13.11)
decipher (13.11)
decrypt (13.11)
dialog (13.6)
differential backup (13.13)
disaster recovery plan (13.14)
disaster recovery test plan (13.16)

emergency plan (13.15)
employee monitoring (xx)
encryption (13.11)
encryption key (13.11)

father (13.14)
file virus (13.2)
full backup (13.13)

grandfather (13.14)

hacker (13.4)
hot site (13.16)

identification (13.5)
incremental backup (13.13)
information privacy (13.8)
inoculated (13.3)

logic bomb (13.2)
logon code (13.5)

noise (13.12)

offsite (13.13)
overvoltage (13.12)

password (13.5)
personal identification number
     (PIN) (13.6)
plaintext (13.1)
polymorphic virus (13.3)
possessed object (13.6)
power surges (13.2)
public domain software (13.10)

reciprocal backup relationships (13.16)
recovery plan (13.16)
remembered information (13.5)
rescue disk (13.3)
restore (13.13)

shareware (13.10)
site license (13.10)
Skipjack (13.11)
software piracy (13.9)
son (13.14)
spike (13.12)
surge protector (13.12)
system failure (13.11)

time bomb (13.2)
Trojan horse (13.2)

unauthorized access (13.4)
unauthorized use (13.4)
under voltage (13.12)
uninterruptable power supply
     (UPS) (13.13)
user ID (13.5)

vaccines (13.3)
virus (13.2)
virus signature (13.3)

File   Edit   Section   Page   Tools   Options   Help

Test Your Knowledge

Fill in the Blanks

1. A(n) _____ is defined as any event or action that could cause a loss to computer equipment, software, information, or processing capability.

2. A(n) _____ is an illegal and potentially damaging computer program designed to *infect* other software by attaching itself to the software with which it comes in contact.

3. In the case of a system failure or the discovery of corrupted files, _____ copies of information stored on a computer can be used to _____ files (reload the files on the computer).

4. A(n) _____ is a written scheme describing the steps an organization would take to restore computer operations in the event of a catastrophe.

5. _____ has to do with the rights of individuals and organizations to deny or restrict the collection and use of knowledge about them.

Short Answer

1. What is a computer security plan? What should a computer security plan do? How often should a computer security plan be updated?

2. How are a boot sector virus, a file virus, and a Trojan horse virus different? What is the purpose of an anti-virus program? What do experts recommend to protect against being infected by a computer virus?

3. What is software piracy? Why is software piracy a crime? In addition to purchasing commercial software, in what other ways can an individual legally acquire software?

4. How are a full backup, differential backup, and incremental backup different? Where are backup copies normally kept? Why?

5. What are computer ethics? What five areas of computer ethics are frequently discussed? Briefly explain each.

Label the Figure

Instructions: Identify the four parts of a disaster recovery plan in the following figure.

PARTS OF A DISASTER RECOVERY PLAN

_____	Evacuation plans and list of people to notify
_____	Identity and location of backup resources
_____	Specific steps and timeplan to resume computer operations
_____	Simulates disasters to find weaknesses in overall plan

Start   13:02

Points to Ponder

1

In a famous case, Robert Morris was found guilty of infecting a computer network with a virus that damaged data and files for more than 6,000 users. Morris's sentence was 400 hours of community service, a three-year probation, and a $10,000 fine. Some people feel this sentence was too lenient, given the extent of harm the virus caused. Others believe Morris actually did the network a favor by demonstrating the limitations of its security system. Was the punishment appropriate? Why or why not? Would this punishment serve as a deterrent to other potential computer criminals?

2

Some companies are unwilling to prosecute hackers after they are caught. This decision is usually a result of the youth of most hackers and the organization's reluctance to publicize its vulnerability. Many authorities argue that hackers will not stop until they are brought to trial and their crimes are made public. What are the advantages and disadvantages of publicizing the misdeeds of known hackers? Should all hackers be openly prosecuted? Why or why not?

3

In 1990, Lotus Development Corporation created a database of consumer information called

Marketplace that it intended to sell to small and medium businesses. After thousands of consumers asked that their names be removed from the database, Lotus withdrew the product. Nevertheless, other databases are routinely bought and sold. Although there are certain benefits to shared databases, such as faster decisions on credit applications and access to products which would otherwise be unfamiliar, the problem with selling databases is twofold: accuracy and privacy. A study of 1,500 reports from three large credit bureaus discovered mistakes in 43 percent of the files, and it is generally agreed that some personal information should not be made public. What measures can be taken to solve these problems? What restrictions, if any, should be placed on selling or sharing databases? Should some databases not be shared under any circumstances?

4

As databases become more complete and widely accessed, it has become possible to learn about almost any individual. Information garnered from credit card purchases, warranty cards, voting records, opinion polls, telephone records, and so on can be used to form a picture of a person's habits, likes, and interests. Make a list of information you have supplied over the past year that might be recorded in a database. If someone was able to combine all of this information, how do you think you would be described? Is the description accurate? Why or why not?

5

Recently, a photograph of a public figure accused of murder was run on the cover of a national news magazine. Using a computer, the photograph had been retouched to give the person a more sinister appearance. Many people objected to the photograph, arguing that it distorted the facts and could lead people to believe in the individual's guilt before being tried. Other people claimed the photograph was not offered as an exact representation and was only enhanced to graphically point out the seriousness of the crime. What do you think? Under what circumstances, if any, is it all right to enhance a photograph using a computer? Should any, or all, retouched photographs include a written disclaimer indicating the photograph has been modified?

6

Using computerized employee monitoring systems, employers can keep track of every keystroke an employee makes, determine the efficiency with which an employee works, record the files an employee has accessed, and note how many breaks an employee takes. Some managers keep copies of E-mail sent between employees. Employers insist these systems protect the security and enhance the productivity of the organization. Many employees, however, find these practices dehumanizing and an invasion of privacy. Who is right? Do these systems place undo stress on employees? What limits, if any, should be placed on employee monitoring?

Out and About

1. What motivates hackers? Are they simply intellectual adventurers, thrilled by the challenge of entering other computer systems, or are they selfish, sometimes malicious, busybodies intent on accessing information to which they have no right? Are their motivations different from those who create computer viruses? What, if anything, should be done to deter hackers? Prepare a report on a hacker-related book to answer these and some of your own questions about hackers. Suggested titles include: *Cyberpunk–Outlaws and Hackers on the Computer Frontier* (Katie Hafner and John Markoff), *Hackers: Heroes of the Computer Revolution* (Steven Levy), and *The Hacker Crackdown: Law and Disorder on the Electronic Frontier* (Bruce Sterling).

2. An issue related to computer ethics is the effect of computers on the environment, particularly in terms of the power they deplete. An Environmental Protection Agency survey indicates that 30 to 40 percent of personal computer users leave their personal computer systems running all the time. The EPA estimates that personal computers and computer peripherals squander about two billion dollars worth of electricity annually! To combat this, the EPA has initiated the Energy Star program. Computer system components that use less than 30 watts when idle are awarded an "Energy Star" label. Visit a computer vendor and make a list of computer components that have the Energy Star designation. Which components are most likely to meet the Energy Star requirements? Which components are least likely to meet the requirements? Is there a significant difference in price between components with an Energy Star and those without an Energy Star?

3. With today's global markets, privacy and computer security have become international issues. The International Association of Computer Crime Investigators has been formed to look into computer-related crimes worldwide. Several countries, including France, Spain, and Sweden, have laws concerning the transmission of data across their borders, and trans-border data flow is becoming an increasingly complex issue. Visit a library and prepare a report on the international transmission of data. What are some of the laws with which organizations should be familiar when doing business in the world market?

4. Visit a local business, or the computer center at your school, and interview the individual in charge of computer security. What does he or she perceive as the gravest security threats? What security measures are in place to handle these threats? Are these measures adequate? Is there a code of conduct or policy regarding computer use? If so, to whom does it apply? What activities are prohibited? How does the organization deal with violators?

5. Find out as much information as you can about your student file. What type of information is stored in the file? Who has access to the file? What information in the file are you allowed to see? What information are others (students or faculty) allowed to see? How is the accuracy of the information in the file verified? Who can change information in the file? What information security measures are in force? Can you get a list of the individuals who see your file? How long is the file retained after you graduate?

6. Computer software can be protected through a patent or a copyright. A patent provides an owner, under certain conditions, with a monopoly on the ideas behind the software for 17 years. A copyright protects the expression of an idea, but not the idea itself. The Software Protection Law, enacted by Congress in 1980, prohibits the literal copying of a program or its component parts, but does not prevent copying the ideas behind the software. Each of these measures involves subtle distinctions that have resulted in several lawsuits. Some software creators, such as Lotus Development Corporation, have been successful in their litigation, while others, such as Apple, have not. Using law books or current periodicals, prepare a report on at least two court cases, one in which the software developer won and one in which the software developer lost. Describe each case and explain how they were different. Do you think the decision was correct in each case? Why or why not?

File   Edit   Section   Page   Tools   Options   Help

In the Lab with Windows 95

1 **Shelly Cashman Series Anti-Virus Lab**   Follow the instructions in Windows 95 Lab 1 on page 1.30 to display the Shelly Cashman Series Labs screen. Click Keeping Your Computer Virus Free. Click the Start Lab button. When the initial screen displays, carefully read the objectives. With your printer turned on, click the Print Questions button. Fill out the top of the Questions sheet and answer the questions as you step through the Anti-Virus Lab. Close the Shelly Cashman Series Labs.

2 **Understanding Backup**   Click the Start button on the taskbar, point to Programs on the Start menu, point to Accessories on the Programs submenu, point to System Tools on the Accessories submenu, and then click Backup on the System Tools submenu. If a Welcome screen displays, click the OK button. If a Microsoft Backup screen displays, click the OK button. When the Untitled - Microsoft Backup window displays, maximize it and then click the Backup tab *(Figure 13-23)*. Click Help on the menu bar and then click Help Topics. Double-click Backing Up, Restoring, and Comparing Files; and then double-click Backing up your entire system. Read and print the Help topic. Close Help.

Insert the floppy disk with your Windows Labs into drive A. Click the box to the left of the 3¹/₂ Floppy [A:] icon in the Select files to backup area. Look at the bottom of the Untitled - Microsoft Backup window. How many files will be backed up? How many kilobytes are in these files? Click Help on the menu bar and then click About Backup. Who developed Microsoft Backup? Click the OK button. Close Microsoft Backup.

3 **Scanning a Disk**   Click the Start button on the taskbar, point to Programs on the Start menu, point to Accessories on the Programs submenu, point to System Tools

on the Accessories submenu, and then click ScanDisk on the System Tools submenu. When the ScanDisk window displays, click the Advanced button. When the ScanDisk Advanced Options dialog box displays, click Always in the Display summary area and then click the OK button.

Insert the floppy disk with your Windows Labs into drive A. Click the 3¹/₂ Floppy [A:] icon in the Select the drive(s) you want to check for errors area and then click Standard in the Type of test area *(Figure 13-24)*. Click the Start button. When the ScanDisk Results dialog box displays, answer these questions: (1) What errors, if any, were detected? (2) In bytes, what is your total disk space? (3) How many folders are on the floppy disk? (4) How many user files are on the floppy disk? (5) How many bytes are available on the disk? Click the Close button. Close ScanDisk.

4 **Checking System Resources**   Click the Start button on the taskbar, point to Programs on the Start menu, point to Accessories on the Programs submenu, point to System Tools on the Accessories submenu, and then click Resource Meter on the System Tools submenu. If a Resource Meter dialog box displays, click the OK button. Right-click the resource meter icon that displays to the left of the time on the taskbar and then click Details on the shortcut menu. What percentage of system resources are free? Click the OK button. Right-click the recourse meter icon on the taskbar and then click Exit on the shortcut menu.

Figure 13-23   *Figure 13-24*

13:05

File   Edit   Section   Page   Tools   Options   Help

Where on the Web

1 **The FBI**   The FBI's National Computer Crime Squad investigates violations of the Federal Computer Fraud and Abuse Act of 1986. Complete the following steps to visit the FBI's Web site *(Figure 13-25)* and learn more about the computer crimes the FBI investigates. With Netscape on the screen, type `http://www.fbi.gov` in the Location text box and press ENTER. Click Print on the File menu. Click Pages and then type 1 in the To text box. Click the OK button. Scroll down and click Computer Crime Investigations. Scroll down and read the page. List five computer crimes the FBI investigates on the printout and hand it in.

2 **Internet Security**   A computer security risk is defined as any event or action that could cause a loss to computer equipment, software, information, or processing capability. Complete the following steps to read about Fraud Protection at the Sprint Web site. With Netscape on the screen, type `http://www.sprintbiz.com/jproducts/jfraudpro.html` in the Location text box and press ENTER. Scroll down and read the page. Click Print on the File menu. Click the OK button. Hand in the printout.

3 **Cyberbanking**   Cyberbanking is the offering of a number of banking services through electronic means to both individuals and businesses. Complete the following steps to learn more about cyberbanking from First Union Corporation *(Figure 13-26)*. With Netscape on the screen, type `http://www.firstunion.com` in the Location text box and press ENTER. Click Search. Type `electronic funds`

`transfer` in the Search text box and click Search. Scroll down the page and click one of the topics. Click Print on the File menu. Click Pages and then type 1 in the To text box. Click the OK button. Write a brief summary of what you found on the printout and hand it in.

4 **Encryption**   The U.S. government's Clipper chip proposal has stimulated a lot of debate. Complete the following steps to learn more about the Clipper chip. With Netscape on the screen, click the Net Search button. Click Yahoo. Type `clipper chip` in the Search text box and click the Search button. Click one of the topics. Click Print on the File menu. Click Pages and then type 1 in the To text box. Click the OK button. Write a brief summary of what you found on the printout and hand it in.

5 **Shelly Cashman Online**   Click Using Computers: A Gateway To Information, World Wide Web Edition on the Shelly Cashman Student Center Web page (`http://www.bf.com/scstudnt.html`). Scroll down and click Chapter 13. Complete the activities listed.

Figure 13-25

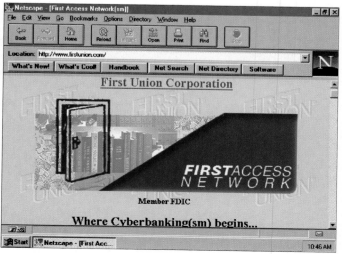

Figure 13-26

Windows 95

Start   Netscape - [Federal ...   10:45 AM

Start   Netscape - [First Acc...   10:46 AM

Start   13:06

Your Future in the Information Age

14

After reading the preceding chapters, you may be interested enough in computers to consider a career in the information processing industry. The information processing industry is growing rapidly and offers many rewarding jobs. The first part of this chapter discusses the types of positions available, how much they currently pay, and how to prepare for a job.

Even if you do not work in the information processing industry, computers will undoubtedly affect your work and leisure activities. The second half of this chapter discusses trends in information processing that will affect these areas.

The Information Processing Industry

The information processing industry is one of the largest industries in the world with annual sales close to $200 billion. Approximately two-thirds of this total is related to equipment sales and the remainder comes from software and services sales. Job opportunities in the industry come primarily from three areas: the companies that manufacture computer-related equipment; the companies that develop software; and the companies that hire information processing professionals to work with these products. As in any major industry, many service companies support each of these three areas. Examples are companies that sell computer supplies and companies that consult on communication networks.

The Computer Equipment Industry

The computer equipment, or hardware, industry includes all manufacturers and distributors of computers *(Figure 14-1)* and computer-related equipment such as disk and tape drives, monitors, printers, and communications equipment.

The five largest minicomputer and mainframe manufacturers in the United States – IBM, Digital Equipment Corporation, UNISYS, Hewlett-Packard, and AT&T GIS – are large organizations with tens of thousands of employees worldwide. Major personal computer manufacturers include Compaq, Apple, Packard Bell, IBM, and Gateway. The largest computer company, IBM, has annual sales of over $60 billion. In addition to the major companies, the computer equipment industry also is known for the many new start-up companies that appear each year. These new companies take advantage of rapid changes in equipment technology, such as wireless communications, networking, multimedia, and fiber optics, to create new products and new job opportunities.

Besides the companies that make end user equipment, thousands of companies make components that most users never see. These companies manufacture chips (CPU, memory, and special purpose), power supplies, wiring, and the hundreds of other parts that go into computer equipment.

Figure 14-1
Personal computers are assembled and tested on production lines.

What Are the Career Opportunities in Information Processing?

The use of computers in so many aspects of life has created thousands of new jobs. Because of rapid changes in technology, many of the current jobs did not even exist ten years ago. The following section describes some of the current career opportunities.

The Computer Software Industry

The computer software industry includes all the developers and distributors of applications and system software. Thousands of companies provide a wide range of software from operating systems to complete business systems. Software is a huge industry with annual sales exceeding $50 billion. Leading companies include Microsoft, Oracle, Computer Associates, Novell, and Lotus. Most software companies specialize in one particular type of software product, such as business application software, or productivity tools, such as word processing or spreadsheets. The largest companies, however, have multiple products.

Information Processing Professionals

Information processing professionals are the people who put the equipment and software to work to produce information for the end user *(Figure 14-2)*. This includes people such as programmers and systems analysts who are hired by companies to work in an information systems department.

Working in an Information Systems Department

The people in the information systems department work together as a team to meet the information demands of their organizations. Several job positions already have been discussed, including database administrator (Chapter 9), systems analysts (Chapter 11), and programmers (Chapter 12). In addition to these jobs, many other positions exist. These positions can be divided into four main groups:
1. Operations
2. System Development
3. Technical Services
4. End User Computing

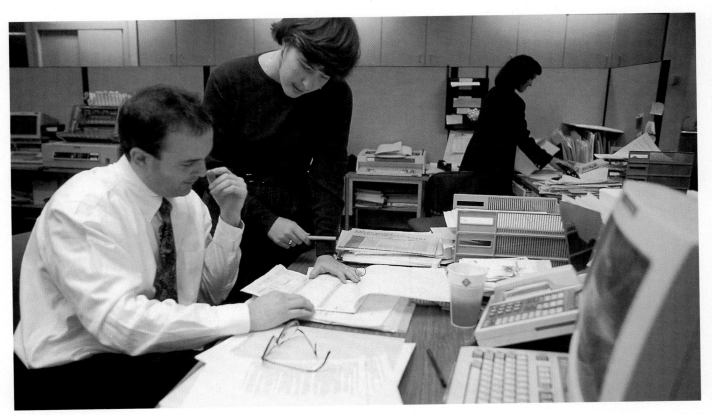

Figure 14-2
Computer professionals must be able to understand the end user's point of view and often meet with the user to review his or her information processing requirements.

The chart in *Figure 14-3* shows some of the management and nonmanagement positions in each of these groups that are described in the following section.

OPERATIONS

The **operations group** is responsible for operating the centralized (computer center) equipment and network administration including both data and voice communications. The **computer operator** performs equipment related activities such as monitoring performance, running jobs, and backup and restore. A **communications specialist** evaluates, installs, and monitors data and/or voice communications equipment and software. A **PC network specialist** installs and maintains local area networks. A **control clerk** accounts for all input and output processed by the computer center. A **data entry operator** uses a data entry device, such as a terminal or PC, to transcribe data from source documents into a computer. The **data librarian** maintains the collection of production and backup tapes and disks.

SYSTEM DEVELOPMENT

The **system development group** is responsible for analyzing, designing, developing, and implementing new information systems and maintaining and improving existing systems. The **systems analyst** works closely with users to analyze their requirements and design an information system solution. The **application programmer** converts the system design into the appropriate computer language. The **technical writer** works with the analyst, programmer, and user to create program and system documentation, and user manuals.

TECNICAL SERVICES

The **technical services group** is responsible for the evaluation and integration of new technologies, the administration of the organization's data resources, and support of the central computer operating system. A **technical evaluator** researches new technologies, such as wireless communications, and recommends how such technologies can be used by the organization. The **database analyst** is familiar with the organization's database structure and assists systems analysts and programmers in developing or modifying applications that use the database. The **system programmer** installs and maintains operating system software and provides technical support to other staff. The **quality assurance specialist** reviews programs and documentation to make sure they meet the organization's standards.

GROUP	MANAGEMENT	NONMANAGEMENT
Operations	Computer Operations Manager	Computer Operator
	Network Administration Manager	Communications Specialist
	Voice Communications Manager	PC Network Specialist
		Control Clerk
		Data Entry Operator
		Data Librarian
System Development	System Development Manager	Systems Analyst
	Programming Manager	Application Programmer
	Project Manager	Technical Writer
Technical Services	Technical Support Manager	Technical Evaluator
	Database Administrator	Database Analyst
	Systems Software Manager	System Programmer
	Quality Assurance Manager	Quality Assurance Specialist
End User Computing	End User Computing Manager	PC Support Specialist
	Information Center Manager	Information Center Specialist
	Office Automation Manager	Office Automation Specialist
	Training Manager	Trainer
		EIS Specialist

Figure 14-3
This table shows some of the management and nonmanagement jobs available within an information systems department.

END USER COMPUTING

The **end user computing group** is responsible for assisting end users in working with existing systems and in using productivity software and query languages to obtain the information necessary to perform their jobs. The **PC support specialist** installs and supports personal computer equipment and software. The **information center specialist** assists users in obtaining information from an organization's existing database and putting it in a form that they can use, such as presentation graphics. The **office automation specialist** assists users in implementing both computerized and noncomputerized office automation technologies. A **trainer** develops education and training materials to teach users how to use existing and new applications. The **executive information system (EIS) specialist** works with senior management to develop reports and systems to meet their information requirements.

As you can see, an information systems department provides career opportunities for people with a variety of skills and talents. Other information industry jobs are found in the areas of sales, service and repair, education and training, and consulting.

Sales

Sales representatives must have a general understanding of computers and a specific knowledge of the product they are selling. Strong interpersonal, or people, skills are important, including listening ability and strong oral and written communication skills. Sales representatives are usually paid based on the amount of product they sell, and top sales representatives are often the most highly compensated employees in a computer company.

Some sales representatives work directly for equipment and software manufacturers and others work for resellers. Many personal computer products are sold through dealers *(Figure 14-4)*. Some dealers, such as Egghead Discount Software, specialize in selling popular software products.

Service and Repair

Being a **service and repair technician** is a challenging job for individuals who like to troubleshoot and solve problems and who have a strong background in electronics *(Figure 14-5)*. In the early days of computers, repairs were often made

Figure 14-4
Computer retailers need sales people who understand personal computers and have good people skills.

Figure 14-5
Computer service and repair requires a knowledge of electronics.

at the site of the computer equipment. Today, however, malfunctioning components, such as circuit boards, are usually replaced and taken back to the service technician's office or sent to a special facility for repair. Many equipment manufacturers include special diagnostic software with their computer equipment that helps the service technician identify the problem. Using a modem, some computer systems can automatically telephone another computer at the service technician's office and leave a message that a malfunction has been detected.

Education and Training

The increased sophistication and complexity of today's computer products has opened wide opportunities in computer education and training *(Figure 14-6)*. Qualified instructors are needed in schools, colleges, universities, and in private industry. In fact, the high demand for teachers has created a shortage at the university level, where many instructors have been lured into private industry because of higher pay. This shortage probably will not be filled in the near future; the supply of Ph.D.s, usually required at the university level, is not keeping up with the demand.

Consulting

After building experience in one or more areas, some individuals become **consultants**, who are people that draw upon their experience to give advice to others. Consultants must have not only strong technical skills in their area of expertise, but also must have the people skills to effectively communicate their suggestions to their clients. Qualified consultants are in high demand for such tasks as computer system selection, system design, and communications network design and installation.

Figure 14-6
A high demand in schools and industry exists for qualified instructors who can teach information processing subjects.

Compensation and Growth Trends for Information Processing Careers

Compensation is a function of experience and demand for a particular skill. Demand is influenced by geographic location, with metropolitan areas usually having higher pay than rural areas. *Figure 14-7* shows the result of a salary survey of over 85,000 computer professionals across the United States and Canada.

As shown in *Figure 14-8,* some industries pay higher than others for the same job. According to the survey, financial services companies pay the highest salaries. These companies have many challenging applications and pay the highest rate to obtain the best qualified employees.

According to the U. S. Bureau of Labor Statistics, the fastest growing computer career positions through the year 2005 will be systems analyst, programmer, and computer repair technician *(Figure 14-9)*.

PROGRAMMING (Commercial):	Median Salary ($000)
Mainframe	
Junior Programmer	32
Programmer/Analyst	37
Senior Programmer/Analyst	42
Midrange	
Junior Programmer	30
Programmer/Analyst	35
Senior Programmer/Analyst	40
Microcomputer	
Junior Programmer	32
Programmer/Analyst	40
Senior Programmer/Analyst	45
Software Engineer	
Junior Software Engineer	35
Software Engineer	45
Senior Software Engineer	50
BUSINESS SYSTEMS:	
Systems Analyst	45
Consultant	46
EIS Analyst	46

Figure 14-7
Salary levels (in thousands of dollars) for different computer industry positions. (Source: Source EDP, 1994 Computer Salary Survey)

SPECIALISTS:	Median Salary ($000)
Data Base Management	
Data Base Analyst	45
Data Base Administrator	50
LAN Administrator	40
End User Support	
PC Support Specialist	35
PC Analyst	41
System Administrator/Mgr.	42
Telecommunications	
Voice Analyst	37
Data Communications Analyst	45
System Programmer	46
EDP Auditing	
EDP Auditor	37
Senior EDP Auditor	45
Technical Writing	
Writer	30
Editor	38
System Integrator	46
MANAGEMENT:	
MIS Director/CIO	
Small/Medium Shop	58
Large Shop	70
Applications Development	61
Technical Services	59
Project Manager	58
Project Leader	50
SALES:	
Account Representative	57
Pre/Post Sales Support Rep.	41
Management	74
DATA CENTER:	
Data Center Manager	46
Computer Operations	
Operator	22
Senior Operator	27
Operations Support	
Technician	30
Senior Technician	33
Communications/Network	
Operator	32
Senior Operator	38

PROGRAMMER COMPENSATION BY INDUSTRY

	Salary	% of Average
Financial Services	$38,913	115.6%
Other Services	37,715	112.0%
Manufacturing	36,431	108.2%
Government	36,108	107.2%
Information Services	34,865	103.5%
Transportation /Utilities	33,806	100.4%
Retail	32,744	97.2%
Education	30,926	91.8%
Medical/Legal Services	30,457	90.5%
Construction/Mining/ Agriculture	30,000	89.1%
Average	$33,672	100.0%

Figure 14-8
Some industries tend to pay more for the same job position.
This table shows the average 1994 salary for a programmer.

(Source: *Datamation Magazine 1994 Salary Survey*)

PROJECTED GROWTH
1992 - 2005
(thousands of jobs)

	1992	2005	Change	% Change
Systems Analysts	455	956	501	110%
Programmers	555	723	168	30%
Computer Repair	83	120	37	45%

Figure 14-9
The table above shows the projected growth rates for computer-related careers as compiled by the U. S. Bureau of Labor Statistics.

Preparing for a Career in Information Processing

To prepare for a career in the information processing industry, individuals must decide what computer field they are interested in and obtain education in the field they choose. The three major computer fields and some of the opportunities for obtaining education in those fields are described below.

What Are the Fields in the Information Processing Industry?

While this book has focused primarily on the use of computers in business, three broad fields actually exist in the information processing industry: computer information systems; computer science; and computer engineering. **Computer information systems** (CIS) refers to the use of computers to provide the information needed to operate businesses and other organizations. The field of **computer science** includes the technical and theoretical aspects of computers and system software. **Computer engineering** deals with the design and manufacturing of electronic computer components and computer hardware. Each field provides unique career opportunities and has specialized requirements.

Obtaining Education for Information Processing Careers

Trade schools, technical schools, community colleges, colleges, and universities all offer formal education and certification or degree programs in computer information systems, computer science, and computer engineering. Usually, schools have separate programs for each area.

With the wide variety of career opportunities that exist in information processing, it is difficult to make anything other than broad general statements when it comes to discussing degree requirements for employment in the industry. As in most other industries, the more advanced degree an individual has in a chosen field, the better that individual's chances are for success. While not having a degree may limit a person's opportunities for securing a top position, it will neither prevent entry nor preclude success in an information processing career.

Career Development in the Information Processing Industry

People employed in the information processing industry have several ways to develop their skills and increase recognition among their peers. These include professional organizations, certification, and professional growth and continuing education activities. Numerous publications also can help an individual keep up with changes in the information processing industry.

Professional Organizations

Computer-related organizations have been formed by people who have common interests and a desire to share their knowledge. Two of the organizations that have been influential in the industry are the Association for Computing Machinery (ACM) and the Data Processing Management Association (DPMA). The **Association for Computing Machinery** (ACM) is composed of persons interested in computer science and computer science education. A large number of college and university computer educators are members. The **Data Processing Management Association** (DPMA) is a professional association of programmers, systems analysts, and information processing managers. Both ACM and DPMA offer the following benefits:

- chapters throughout the United States and in several foreign countries
- monthly meetings
- workshops, seminars, and conventions
- journals and articles
- special interest groups (SIGs)
- continuing education material
- student chapters

Attending professional meetings provides an excellent opportunity for students to learn about the information processing industry and to meet and talk with professionals in the field.

In addition to these and other professional organizations, user groups exist for most makes of computers. A **user group** is a group of people with common computer equipment or software interests that meet regularly to share information. Most metropolitan areas have one or more local computer societies that meet monthly to discuss topics of common interest about personal computers. For anyone employed or interested in the computer industry, these groups can be an effective and rewarding way to learn and continue career development.

Certification

Many professions offer certification programs to encourage and recognize the efforts of their members to attain a level of knowledge about their professions. Some computer industry companies, such as Novell, Microsoft, and IBM, offer certification programs on their hardware and software products. Although no states require that computer professionals be certified or licensed, it has been proposed by some groups.

The most widely recognized certification program in the information processing industry is administered by the **Institute for the Certification of Computer Professionals**

(ICCP). The Institute is sponsored and supported by several professional organizations including ACM and DPMA. Prior to 1994, the ICCP offered four different certification designations. The best known of these was the Certified Data Processor (CDP). Other designations were Certified Computer Programmer (CCP), Certified Systems Professional (CSP), and Associate Computer Professional (ACP). Starting in 1994, the first three designations were combined under one standard title: **Certified Computing Professional (CCP)**. The **Associate Computing Professional (ACP)** still exists for entry level personnel. To become certified, a CCP candidate must pass a core examination and any two specialty examinations. ACP candidates must pass the core examination and at least one computer language test. *Figure 14-10* summarizes the requirements for the certifications.

Professional Growth and Continuing Education

Because of rapid changes in technology, staying aware of new products and services in the information processing industry can be a challenging task. One way of keeping up is by participating in professional growth and continuing education activities. This broad category includes events such as

CERTIFIED COMPUTING PROFESSIONAL (CCP)		ASSOCIATE COMPUTING PROFESSIONAL (ACP)

CORE EXAMINATION

Human and Organization Framework	Data and Information	Technology
Systems Concepts	System Development	Associated Disciplines

any two of the following
CCP EXAMINATIONS

Management	Office Information Systems
Procedural Programming	Systems Security
Systems Development	Software Engineering
Business Information Systems	Systems Programming
Communications	Data Resource Management

any one of the following
ACP EXAMINATIONS

FORTRAN	RPG/400
Pascal	COBOL
BASIC	C
RPG II	Ada

CCP CERTIFICATION

ACP CERTIFICATION

Figure 14-10
The Institute for the Certification of Computer Professionals (ICCP) offers two certification programs. This chart summarizes the examination requirements for each program.

workshops, seminars, conferences, conventions, and trade shows that provide both general and specific information on equipment, software, services, and issues affecting the industry. Workshops and seminars usually last a day or two, while conferences, conventions, and trade shows often last a week. The largest trade show in the United States, **COMDEX**, brings together over 2,000 vendors to display their newest products and services to 200,000 attendees *(Figure 14-11)*.

Computer Publications

Another way of keeping informed about what is going on in the computer industry is to regularly read one or more computer industry publications *(Figure 14-12)*. You can choose from hundreds of publications. Some publications, such as *Computerworld, InfoWorld,* and *PC Week,* are like newspapers and cover a wide range of issues. Other publications are oriented toward a particular topic area such as communications, personal computers, or a specific equipment manufacturer. Many of the more popular publications can be found in public or school libraries.

Summary of Computer Career Opportunities

With the increased use of computers, the prospects for computer-related career opportunities are excellent. Not only are the numbers of traditional information processing jobs, such as programmer and systems analyst, expected to increase, but the application of the computer to existing occupations will create additional job opportunities. Regardless of an individual's career choice, a basic understanding of computers should be an essential part of any employee's job skills.

As discussed in the remainder of this chapter, computers will continue to have an important impact on work and leisure activities.

Figure 14-11
COMDEX is one of the largest computer product trade shows in the world. More than 2,000 vendors display their newest products and services to 200,000 attendees.

Trends in Computers and Information Processing

The features titled In the Future at the end of each chapter highlight computer-related developments that may take place in the near future. The following section discusses additional changes that are likely to happen in the workplace and at home based on current trends. Before discussing these changes, however, two trends that will have a widespread influence will be reviewed; digital convergence and the application of artificial intelligence.

Digital Convergence

Digital convergence describes the merging of technologies and products from the communications, entertainment, publishing, and computing industries. What is making this merger possible is the conversion of the information transmitted by each of these industries into a digital form that can be processed, stored, and distributed by computers. The conversion of non-computer information into a digital form has been going on for some time but has been limited by hardware and software. For example, digital phone service has been available for a number of years but digitized video, which requires tremendous amounts of data, has not been widely implemented. Recent advances in both hardware and software, however, make it clear that high-quality digitized video and audio will eventually be widely available. The following section will discuss some of the changes that will take place in the areas of communications, entertainment, and publishing.

In the area of communications, wider use of fiber optic cabling will allow data to be transmitted at higher speeds. The higher volume transmission will enable data-intensive

Figure 14-12
Numerous computer industry publications are available at bookstores, libraries, or by subscription.

applications such as video and graphics to be transmitted over phone equipment. Video will become a more common component of transmitted information such as electronic mail. Another probable application of video will allow customer service representatives to show customers how to use or repair their products while they are talking to them.

Wireless communications will also become more common. Personal digital assistants (PDAs), the small hand-held computing devices that are used by mobile workers, usually have a wireless capability to send and receive data.

In the entertainment area, the digitization will mean that entertainment products such as movies and television programming can be distributed in ways not previously possible. For example, in the future, a user could choose a personalized selection of previously recorded shows, movies, or events and have them down loaded into their digital entertainment system to be viewed at the user's convenience. It will certainly be more convenient than trying to program a VCR to record multiple events!

In the area of publishing, significant changes already are underway. For example, every picture and every drawing in this book is digitized. These digitized images are placed into position on each page by a designer using a computer application called QuarkXpress. Then, through the use of specialized equipment, the digitized book is transformed to film from which printing plates are made.

Several major newspapers and magazines now offer online versions of their publications.

Another available service allows a user to choose any number of topics on which they want to receive information. The service company, which reviews and classifies articles from numerous sources, provides the user with a summary of the articles that meet the user's area of interest. Full versions of the articles also can be provided. Digitized electronic versions of traditional books also are becoming increasingly available.

Eventually, all forms of communications (written, visual, and audio) will be digitized and will be able to be stored, modified, and communicated by computers.

Figure 14-13
Robots are often used in situations requiring
repetitive actions and where it would be unsafe or
unhealthy for a human to perform the same task.

Artificial Intelligence

Artificial intelligence (AI) is the application of human intelligence to computers. Stated another way, it is the attempt to make computers imitate human actions and thinking. Experts predict that eventually some form of AI will be incorporated into most products and services. Several AI applications have been previously discussed; voice input and speech recognition (Chapter 3), expert systems (Chapter 10), and a natural language interface (Chapter 12). The following sections discuss four other applications of AI: robotics, vision systems, fuzzy logic, and agent software.

Robotics

Robotics deals with the development of **robots**, which are devices that mimic human actions and appear to function with some degree of intelligence. Robots are commonly used in manufacturing and in other situations where it would be unsafe or unhealthy for a human to perform the same task *(Figure 14-13)*.

Vision Systems

A **vision system** uses a camera and a computer to identify objects by digitizing their image and then comparing the image against a database of known shapes. Based on the identity of the object, the computer can be programmed to take a specific action. Vision systems are currently used to inspect products for manufacturing errors such as missing or broken parts. The U.S. Army has an experimental driver-less vehicle that uses a vision system to avoid obstacles such as boulders or ditches while driving over rough terrain.

Fuzzy Logic

Fuzzy logic, a type of mathematics, deals with values that are not precise and values that have a degree of uncertainty. For example, consider the following simplified situation. A production manager is trying to estimate the number of products a new assembly line will be able to produce. His best guess is 60 units per hour. Under the worst conditions, he believes the assembly line can produce at least 40 units per hour and under the best conditions perhaps as many as 100 units per hour. Assigning a weight of 1.0 to his most likely guess and zero to his best and worst case estimates, a diagram like the one shown in *Figure 14-14* is produced. This fuzzy logic diagram graphically represents the degree of certainty associated with the estimated range of assembly line

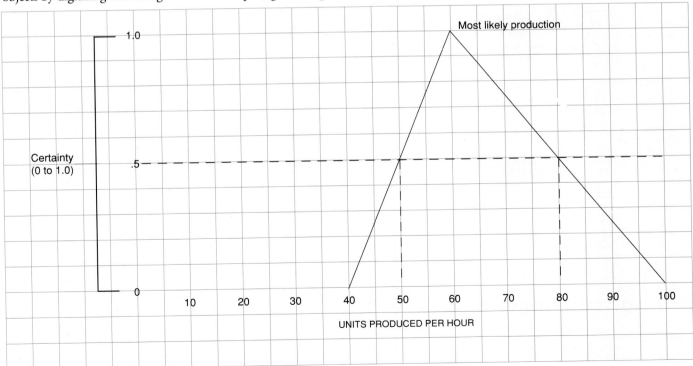

Figure 14-14
Fuzzy logic deals with imprecise numbers and degrees of certainty and uncertainty. This fuzzy logic diagram represents the number of units a production manager thinks a new assembly line will produce each hour. The production manager's confidence level, from a low of zero to a high of 1.0, is shown on the left side of the chart. The chart shows the production manager is 50% certain that production will be between 50 and 80 units per hour.

output. For example, the diagram shows there is a 50% certainty the output will be between 50 and 80 units per hour.

To date, applications of fuzzy logic primarily have been in controllers for consumer products such as video cameras, air conditioners, and washing machines. In these products, fuzzy logic is used to make continuous small adjustments instead of merely switching a feature on or off. Wider use of fuzzy logic is expected as fuzzy logic software tools are developed.

Agent Software

For more than 40 years, AI experts have talked about the advantages of *smart software;* that is, software with built-in intelligence. In recent years, this concept has become known as agent software. Although not precisely defined, the term **agent** has come to mean a software program that can independently carry out tasks on behalf of a user. Some agents perform work within a single program and other agents, sometimes called *network agents,* perform tasks on remote computers before bringing the results back to the user.

An example of agents that work within single programs are the *wizards* included with Microsoft Corporation's productivity software applications, such as Word and Excel. Wizards take you step-by-step through a process such as creating a document. Wizards prompt the user to answer questions and then use the answers to complete the task. *Figure 14-15* shows a wizard screen used to create a memorandum. Other software developers have incorporated smart software similar to wizards.

Network agents are generally more intelligent than wizards because they perform their work on remote computers and cannot prompt the user for information on how to continue. A common use of a network agent is gathering information on a particular subject. For example, a network agent might be directed to research all references to Civil War battles in the state of Virginia. Some network agents require specific instructions but others can be given general instructions such as "book a flight from New York to Boston on the morning of June 20." The agent software would then choose which airline and a specific flight from the flights available. Agent software already has been incorporated into several E-mail packages that allow the user to filter incoming messages and be immediately notified of messages from specific individuals or on specific subjects.

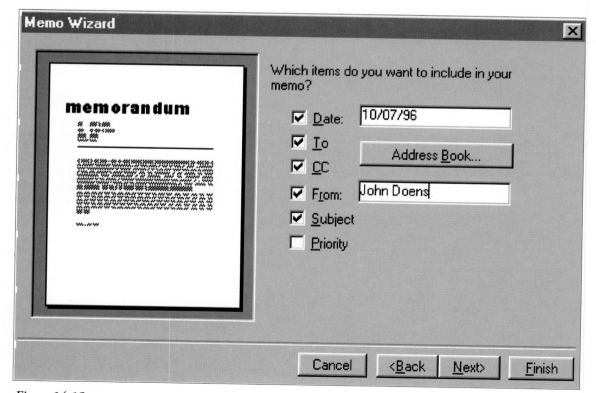

Figure 14-15
Microsoft Word word processing software includes wizards, which are software agents that help a user complete tasks. The wizards ask the user to fill in information or accept the default values. The answers are then used to automatically complete the task, in this case, creating a memorandum document.

Information Systems in Business

The largest use of computers is in business. Millions of systems ranging from mainframes to personal computers are installed and used for applications such as inventory control, billing, and accounting. This section discusses how these traditional applications will be affected by changes in technology and methods.

How Will Existing Information Systems Change?

Existing business information systems will continue to undergo profound changes as new technology, software, and methods are applied to the huge installed base of traditional business system users. The expansion of networks and the increased use of digitized information means that users will have a wider variety of data and information available for decision making, and more flexibility presenting information on reports and displays. The increased number of people using computers will make the computer-user interface even more important. These and other trends that will affect the information systems of tomorrow are shown in *Figure 14-16* on this and the next page.

SOFTWARE
- Fourth-generation and natural languages will enable the user to communicate with the computer in a more conversational manner
- Object orientation will combine processes and methods with data
- Computer aided software engineering (CASE) and rapid application development (RAD) will shorten the system development time frame
- Increased use of decision support and artificial intelligence systems will help users make decisions
- Easier access to networks such as the Internet
- Operating systems available for multiplatform use
- Integrated applications will eliminate the need for separate programs for word processing, spreadsheets, graphics, telecommunications, and other applications
- Virtual reality will be common for training and recreation

EQUIPMENT
- Increased use of personal computers networked to other PCs and to server computers
- World-wide communication networks will allow users to access data or send messages from any location
- Larger systems will be used as central storehouses of data with processing done on a decentralized basis by powerful personal computers
- Increased use of page printers that can print high quality graphics and text
- Reduced instruction set computers (RISC) and parallel processing that will greatly increase the number of instructions that can be processed at one time
- Increased use of portable computing equipment such as notebook computers and personal digital assistants
- Increased competition among processor manufacturers will lead to much faster and less expensive computers
- Plug and play components will enable additional features to be easily added to systems

Figure 14-16
Trends affecting information systems of tomorrow.

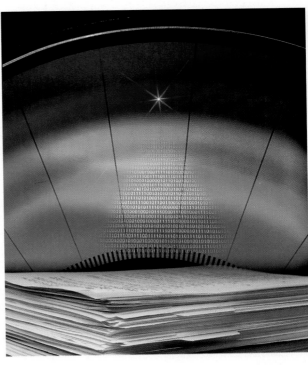

DATA
- Automatic input of data at the source where it is created
- Compound documents that combine text, numbers, and non-text data such as voice, image, and full motion video
- Digital cash will facilitate online commercial transactions

Figure 14-16 (continued)

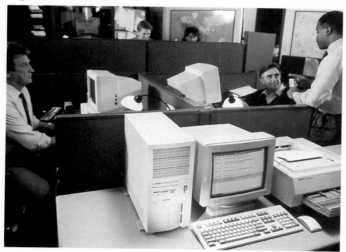

USERS
- Most people will be "computer literate," with a basic understanding of how computers work, and how to use them in their jobs
- Increased responsibility for design, operation, and maintenance of information processing systems
- Users will increasingly rely on computers to manage the continuing proliferation of information (the worldwide volume of printed information doubles every eight years)
- Will use computers to collaborate with other workers
- Will use computers and online databases to obtain information and update skills and knowledge

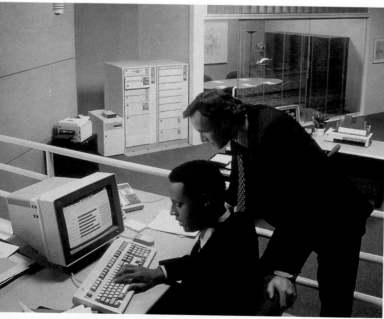

INFORMATION SYSTEMS PERSONNEL
- Increased interface with users
- Shift from machine and software orientation to user application orientation
- Emphasis will change from how to capture and process data to how to more effectively use the data available and create information
- Reduced staff levels will have to handle increased processing workloads
- Some processing operations will be "outsourced" to independent contractors
- Continuous need for retraining and education to keep up with new technology

The Automated Office

The **automated office**, sometimes referred to as the **electronic office**, makes use of electronic devices such as computers, facsimile machines, and computerized telephone systems to make office work more productive. Automated office applications, such as word processing, electronic mail, voice mail, desktop publishing, facsimile, image processing, and teleconferencing, started out as separate, stand-alone applications. In recent years, however, the trend has been to integrate these applications into a network of devices and services that can share information. According to surveys, over one-half of the U.S. workforce has access to a PC and half of the PCs used in business are connected to some type of network. Eventually all applications will be integrated and users will be able to combine tasks that are now performed separately.

Stand-alone office machines also will become part of the same networks used to link computers *(Figure 14-17)*. In

Figure 14-17
Eventually, most office machines will be connected to computer networks and share information with other devices.

a concept called **Microsoft At Work**, Microsoft Corporation has proposed a standardized intelligent graphical user interface that will be built into all office machines such as copiers, printers, and fax machines. The interface will allow data to be sent to or received from any device on the network. The office phone system also will become part of an organization's network. Microphones and speakers will be incorporated into desktop computer systems and automatic dialing will be a utility program that can be accessed from any application. Incoming calls, including the name and photo of the caller (if on file), will be displayed on a user's screen.

Another condition that will be affected by technology improvements is the amount of paper used in the office. A goal of having a *paperless* office may not be realistic but the increasing use of electronic documents will result in the *less-paper* office. One advantage of electronic documents is that they can incorporate video and sound data elements.

In the future, office equipment and tasks will be automated and *smart*.

The Digital Factory

As with automated office applications, the goal of the **digital factory** is to increase productivity through the use of networked, computer-controlled equipment. Technologies used in the digital factory include computer-aided design, computer-aided engineering, and computer-aided manufacturing. Once thought of as stand-alone processes, these technologies now are being linked together into what is called computer-integrated manufacturing. A brief review of these technologies follows.

COMPUTER-AIDED DESIGN (CAD)

Computer-aided design (CAD) uses a computer and special graphics software to aid in product design (*Figure 14-18*). The CAD software eliminates the laborious drafting that used to be required and allows the designer to dynamically change the size of some or all of the product and view the design from different angles. The capability to store the design electronically offers several advantages over traditional manual methods. One advantage is that the designs can be changed more easily than before. Another is that the design database can be reviewed more easily by other design engineers.

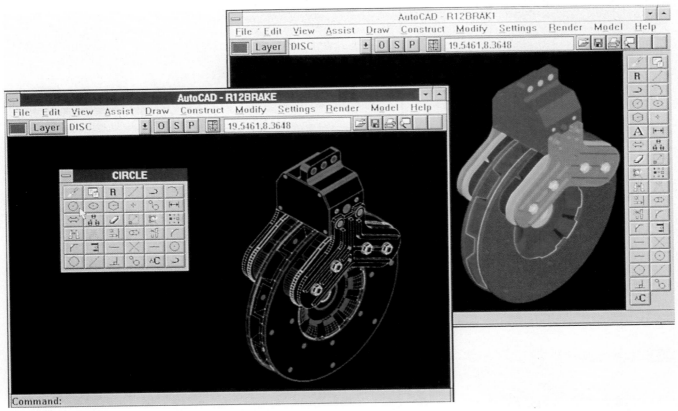

Figure 14-18
Computer-aided design (CAD) is an efficient way to develop plans for new products.

This increases the likelihood that an existing part will be used in a product instead of a new part designed. For example, if a support bracket was required for a new product, the design engineer could review the design database to see if any existing products used a support bracket that would be appropriate for the new product. This not only decreases the overall design time but increases the reliability of the new product by using proven parts.

COMPUTER-AIDED ENGINEERING (CAE)

Computer-aided engineering (CAE) is the use of computers to test product designs. Using CAE, engineers can test the design of a car or a bridge before it is built *(Figure 14-19)*. Sophisticated programs simulate the effects of wind, temperature, weight, and stress on product shapes and materials. Before the use of CAE, prototypes of products had to be built and subjected to testing that often destroyed the prototype. CAE allows engineers to create a computer prototype that can be tested under a variety of conditions. CAE allows products to be tested in some conditions, such as earthquakes, that could not previously be simulated.

COMPUTER-AIDED MANUFACTURING (CAM)

Computer-aided manufacturing (CAM) is the use of computers to control production equipment. CAM production equipment includes software-controlled drilling, lathe, welding, and milling machines.

COMPUTER-INTEGRATED MANUFACTURING (CIM)

Computer-integrated manufacturing (CIM) is the total integration of the manufacturing process using computers *(Figure 14-20)*. Using CIM concepts, individual production processes are linked so that the production flow is balanced and optimized and products flow at an even rate through the factory. In a CIM factory, automated design processes are linked to automated machining processes that are linked to automated assembly processes that are linked to automated testing and packaging. Under ideal CIM conditions, a product will move through the entire production process under computer control. Many companies may never fully implement CIM because it is so complex. But CIM's related concepts of minimum inventory and efficient demand-driven production are valid and will be incorporated into many manufacturers' business plans.

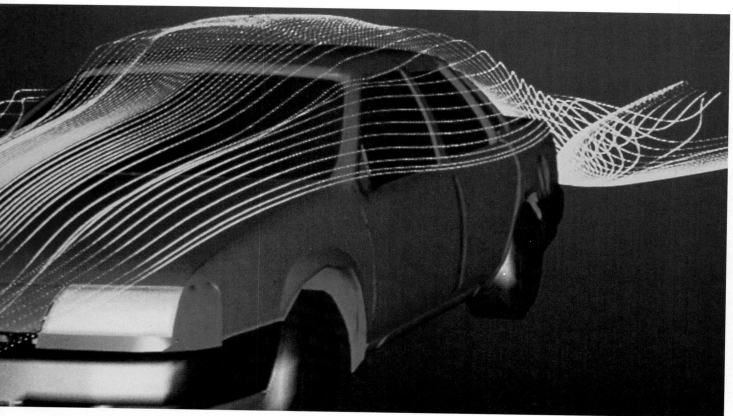

Figure 14-19
Computer-aided engineering (CAE) allows the user to test a product design before the product is built.

The Computer-Integrated Enterprise

Although in the previous sections we discuss the office and factory separately, the trend is the **computer-integrated enterprise** – an organization in which all information storage and processing is performed by a network of computers and intelligent devices. In a computer-integrated enterprise, all office, factory, warehouse, and communications systems are linked using a common interface allowing authorized users in any functional area of the organization to access and use data stored anywhere in the organization. Instead of being machine- or software-oriented as today's systems, future systems will be document- or information-oriented. The user will not need to separately start a word processing, spreadsheet, or communications program. Instead, users will be able to create and distribute compound documents that contain text, graphics, numbers, and full-motion video. They will be able to record, in their own voice, comments or questions about the document before it is stored or routed to someone else in the organization. For example, a new product marketing plan could contain a text description of the product, a spreadsheet showing projected sales, and a narrated video showing the product in use. If the president of a company had questions about the plan, he or she could add questions to the plan in his or her own voice, and route the plan to the appropriate person for a response.

Bringing the Information Age Home

Millions of personal computers have been purchased for home use, and the use of personal computers in the home is expected to increase. Currently, approximately one in three homes have at least one personal computer. In 1994, for the first time, the sales of PCs for home use equaled the purchases of PCs for business use. Just as the use of computers in the workplace has changed how people work, the use of computers in homes is changing family life.

The Use of Personal Computers in the Home

People use personal computers in their homes in a variety of ways. These ways usually fall into five general categories: (1) personal services, (2) control of home systems, (3) telecommuting, (4) education, and (5) entertainment.

PERSONAL SERVICES

In many ways, running a home is similar to running a small business. The productivity tools you use in the office, such as word processing, spreadsheet, and database, also can be used in the home to help you with creating documents,

Figure 14-20
The concept of computer-integrated manufacturing (CIM) is to use computers to integrate all phases of the manufacturing process from planning and design to manufacturing and distribution.

with financial planning and analysis, and with filing and organizing data. Personal computer software also is available to assist you with home accounting applications such as balancing checkbooks, making household budgets, and preparing tax returns *(Figure 14-21)*. In addition, using a personal com-puter to transmit and receive data over telephone lines allows home users to access a wealth of information and services from online service providers such as America Online and Prodigy. Stock brokerage firms such as Charles Schwab & Co. have developed software that allows users to buy and sell stock online and manage their investments. Eventually, most if not all financial services will be able to be performed from home using a computer.

CONTROL OF HOME SYSTEMS

Another use of computers in the home is to control home systems such as security, environment, lighting, and landscape sprinkler systems. Personal computers used in this manner are usually linked to special devices such as alarms for security; thermostats for temperature control; and timing devices for lighting and sprinkler systems. For example, if the personal computer system has communications capabilities, a homeowner who is away can use a telephone or another computer to call home and change the operation of one of the control systems. Suppose a homeowner is on vacation in Texas and learns that heavy rains have been falling at home in Pennsylvania. He or she could call the computer and use the keys of a touch-tone telephone to instruct the computer to turn off the garden sprinkler system.

Most existing home control systems were installed after the home was built and often consist of separate systems to control each set of devices. This will change in the future. The Electronic Industries Association has issued a wiring standard called the Consumer Electronics Bus (CEBus). The CEBus sets standards for sending information throughout a home using existing electrical wiring, phone lines, TV cable, and nonwired techniques such as radio waves. In a related effort, Echelon Corporation is designing chips to be used in consumer electronics and building products. The chips will allow appliances, lighting systems, and other home products to be networked together and controlled by a single system using a consistent set of commands *(Figure 14-22)*. Although they are not yet widely implemented, these changes will result in what many refer to as the intelligent

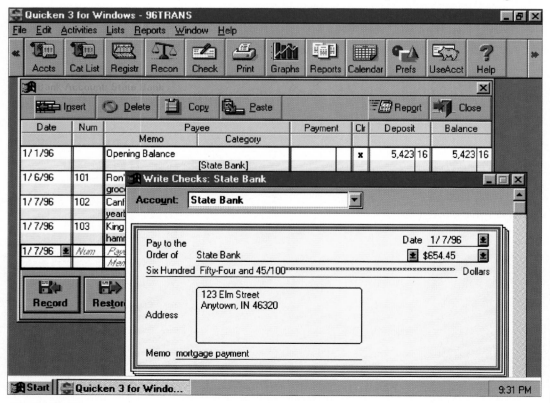

Figure 14-21
A number of personal finance programs, such as Quicken for Windows shown here, help keep track of personal expenditures and allow you to produce computer-prepared checks.

home or smart house. Smart home products are expected to be a $2 billion a year business by the year 2000.

TELECOMMUTING

Telecommuting refers to the ability of individuals to work away from the office, often at home and communicate by using personal computers and communications lines. Many companies have found that employees can do their jobs just as well on the road or at home. According to one survey, nearly 10 million people telecommute to work at least two times a week. Some cities such as Telluride, Colorado and Pullman, Washington have implemented programs to upgrade local communications capabilities in order to attract telecommuters. The number of telecommuters increases about 20% each year and is expected to include as many as 20 million workers by the year 2000.

EDUCATION

The use of personal computers for education, called **computer-aided instruction** (CAI), is another rapidly growing area. Whereas CAI is frequently used to describe software that is developed and used in schools, much of the same software is available for home users. CAI software can be classified into three types: drill and practice, tutorials, and simulations.

Drill and practice software uses a flash-card approach to teaching by allowing users to practice skills in subjects such as math and language. A problem or word appears on the computer screen and the user enters the answer. The computer accepts the answer and responds by telling the student whether the answer is correct or incorrect. Sometimes the user gets second and third chances to select the correct answer before the computer software reveals the correct answer.

With **tutorial software**, the computer software uses text, graphics, and sometimes sound to teach a user concepts about subjects such as chemistry, music theory, or computer literacy. Following the instruction, tutorial software might present true/false or multiple choice questions to help the user ensure that he or she understands the concepts.

The third type of CAI, **simulation software**, is designed to teach a user by creating a model of a real-life situation. For example, many simulation packages are available to teach business concepts.

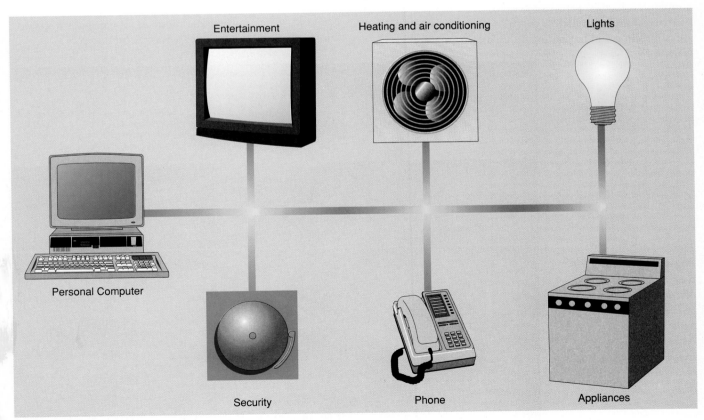

Figure 14-22
Eventually, many homes will contain networks that will enable household devices to be connected to a central computer.

In an approach that is sometimes called **remote learning**, some trade schools, colleges and universities now offer students with personal computers the opportunity to take electronic correspondence courses in their homes. Lessons and assignments for classes are transmitted between the student and the school over communications lines.

Education in the home through CAI or electronic correspondence courses allows home users to learn at their own pace, in the convenience of their home, and at a time that fits into their personal schedule. Well-written educational software can be so entertaining that it is sometimes difficult to distinguish between it and entertainment software.

ENTERTAINMENT

Entertainment software, or game playing, on home computers always has had a large following among the younger members of the family. Many adults, however, are surprised to find that entertainment software also can provide them with hours of enjoyment. Popular types of entertainment software include arcade games, board games, simulations, and interactive graphics programs. Most people are familiar with the arcade-type games (similar to video games) that are available for computers. A popular board game is computer chess. Simulations include games such as baseball and football and a variety of flight simulators that allow users to pretend they are controlling and navigating different types of aircraft *(Figure 14-23)*.

Also available are a wide variety of interactive graphic adventure games that range from rescuing a princess from a castle's dungeon to solving a murder mystery. Some games can be played in groups using a network. The software usually allows players to adjust the level of play to match their abilities, that is, beginner through advanced. With entertainment software, the computer becomes a fun, skillful, and challenging game partner.

In addition to playing games, some personal computer users use their home computer as a tool for personal hobbies. Computers are used by hobbyists to design quilt and stained glass patterns, run model trains, organize stamp, doll, and photography collections, and write, transpose, play, and print musical scores.

Summary of Your Future in the Information Age

Based on current and planned developments, the impact of computers and the information age will be even greater in the future than it has been to date. Individual PCs, in the workplace and the home, will increasingly be connected to networks that will provide access to information and services. Few tasks will exist where the computer or computer accessed information will not be able to provide assistance.

Figure 14-23
Flight simulators, such as the one shown here from Microsoft Corporation, can be both fun and educational. Some simulators offer realistic instrument consoles and regional flight patterns that help teach the user about flying.

COMPUTERS AT WORK

Rapid Prototyping Using Stereolithography

Using a process called stereolithography, manufacturers can now produce prototype parts directly from engineering drawings. **Stereolithography** (SL) uses a computer, a laser, and photochemistry to build a three dimensional model of a part one thin layer at a time.

The process starts with special software that converts a computer-aided design (CAD) drawing into horizontal slices 0.0025 inches thick. This information is used to direct an ultraviolet laser beam towards a vat of a liquid plastic called photopolymer. Wherever the liquid plastic is exposed to the laser, it hardens. After each pass of the laser, a platform in the liquid is lowered, submerging the hardened material just under the surface of the liquid plastic. Each pass of the laser adds another layer of hardened plastic that bonds with the previously created material. Layer by layer, the part is formed. After the part is completely formed, it is removed from the vat and exposed to ultraviolet radiation to finish hardening. The finished part can then be sanded, painted, or sprayed with a metal coating.

Because three dimensional prototypes are a common requirement for most industrial and consumer products, stereolithography has a large potential marketplace. More than 80% of the world's auto manufacturers and 75% of the major aerospace and aircraft manufacturers use stereolithography in their engineering and manufacturing operations. Without using stereolithography or some other rapid prototyping technology, prototypes have to be made the traditional way; by hand or by using machine tools to cut, grind, and drill a part into shape. Stereolithography is a much faster and more precise process and can be used several times in the same amount of time it would take with traditional methods. Users of stereolithography systems have reported cost and time savings of approximately 50%. Although full stereolithography systems can cost up to $500,000, 3D Systems of California, the leading stereolithography system supplier, is developing a desktop system that could eventually sell for as little as $5,000.

Figure 14-24

IN THE FUTURE

Human Computer Integration

Microprocessors have rapidly spread from the desktop PC to many, if not most of the appliances people use everyday. Televisions, VCRs, stereos, phones, copiers, fax machines, microwaves, refrigerators, coffee makers, bread machines, alarm clocks, bathroom scales, and automobiles all contain one or more chips that monitor their operations and enable people to control some of the device's functions. Some believe that eventually the microprocessor will become an integral part of the most complex device known–the human body.

An early phase of this process will involve implanting chips to assist the body in performing its functions. For example, a microprocessor could be used to regulate the release of hormones in the same way that microprocessors regulate the fuel mixture in modern autos. An even more futuristic use of embedded microprocessors is called CyberSight, an application conceived by Canadian futurist Frank Ogden. With CyberSight, a microprocessor would interface with a person's optic nerve and allow him or her to see information transmitted over a wireless link. A firefighter, for example, could have the floor plans of a burning building transmitted from a computer database and displayed in his or her mind before deciding to enter. Or a police officer could download mug shots of suspected criminals from a criminal database without arousing suspicion or returning to the police car.

A further phase of human computer integration could involve downloading a person's intelligence into a microprocessor. The best estimates are that the human brain stores about 10^{18} bits of information, or a billion billion bits. The brain processes those bits at 10^{16} bits per second. Based on current chip densities, it would take a chip the size of a large house to store the amount of information the brain keeps track of. But if chip densities keep doubling every two years, as they have for the last twenty years, a chip that could fit in your hand (or your head) could hold 10^{18} bits by the year 2020. This potential technical possibility raises all sorts of challenging ethical questions. For example, if memories were recorded in a chip could they or should they be edited? Could they be used to prove or disprove someone's innocence or guilt? Could someone's silicon consciousness make legally binding decisions? These are just some of the questions that will have to be answered.

Figure 14-25

File   Edit   Section   Page   Tools   Options   Help

What You Should Know

1. The information processing industry is one of the largest industries in the world with annual sales of close to $200 billion. Job opportunities in the industry come primarily from three areas: the companies that manufacture computer-related equipment; the companies that develop software; and the companies that hire information processing professionals to work with these products.

2. The people in the information systems department work together as a team to meet the information demands of their organizations. Positions in an information systems department can be divided into four main groups.

3. The **operations group** is responsible for operating the centralized (computer center) equipment and network administration including both data and voice communications. Positions in the operations group include **computer operator**, **communications specialist**, **PC network specialist**, **control clerk**, **data entry operator**, and **data librarian**.

4. The **system development group** is responsible for analyzing, designing, developing, and implementing information systems and maintaining and improving existing systems. Positions in the system development group include **systems analyst**, **application programmer**, and **technical writer**.

5. The **technical services group** is responsible for the evaluation and integration of new technologies, the administration of the organization's data resources, and support of the central computer operating system. Positions in the technical services group include **technical evaluator**, **database analyst**, **system programmer**, and **quality assurance specialist**.

6. The **end user computing group** is responsible for assisting end users in working with existing systems and in using productivity software and query languages to obtain the information necessary to perform their jobs. Positions in the end user computing group include **PC support specialist**, **information center specialist**, **office automation specialist**, **trainer**, and **executive information system (EIS) specialist**.

7. Other information industry jobs are found in the areas of sales, service and repair, education and training, and consulting. **Sales representatives** must have a general understanding of computers and a specific knowledge of the product they are selling. Being a **service and repair technician** is a challenging job for individuals who like to troubleshoot and solve problems and have a strong background in electronics. The increased sophistication and complexity of today's computer products has opened wide opportunities in computer education and training. After building experience in one or more areas, some individuals become **consultants**, who are people that draw upon their experience to give advice to others.

8. Compensation is a function of experience and demand for a particular skill. To prepare for a skill in the information processing industry, individuals must decide what computer field they are interested in and obtain education in the field they choose.

9. Three broad fields exist in the information processing industry. **Computer information systems** (CIS) refers to the use of computers to provide the information needed to operate businesses and other organizations. The field of **computer science** includes the technical and theoretical aspects of computers and system software. **Computer engineering** deals with the design and manufacturing of electronic computer components and computer hardware.

10. Trade schools, technical schools, community colleges, colleges, and universities all offer formal education and certification or degree programs in computer information systems, computer science, and computer engineering.

Start   14:00

File   Edit   Section   Page   Tools   Options   Help

What You Should Know (continued)

11. Persons employed in the information processing industry can develop their skills through professional organizations, certification, and professional growth and continuing education activities.

12. The **Association for Computing Machinery** (ACM) is composed of persons interested in computer science and computer science education. The **Data Processing Management Association** (DPMA) is a professional association of programmers, systems analysts, and information processing managers. A **user group** is a group of people with common computer equipment or software interests who meets regularly to share information.

13. The most widely recognized certification program in the information processing industry is administered by the **Institute for the Certification of Computer Professionals** (ICCP). Two certification designations are **Certified Computing Professional** (CCP) and **Associate Computing Professional** (ACP).

14. One way of keeping up with new products and services in the information processing industry is by participating in professional growth and continuing education activities. The largest trade show in the United States, **COMDEX**, brings together more than 2,000 vendors to display their newest products and services to 200,000 attendees. Hundreds of computer industry publications also are available.

15. Two trends that will have a widespread influence are digital convergence and the application of artificial intelligence. **Digital convergence** describes the merging of technologies and products from the communications, entertainment, publishing, and computing industries. **Artificial intelligence** (AI) is the application of human intelligence to computers. Voice input and speech recognition, expert systems, and natural language interfaces are all applications of AI. Other AI applications include robotics, vision systems, fuzzy logic, and agent software.

16. **Robotics** deals with the development of **robots**, which are devices that mimic human actions and appear to function with some degree of intelligence. A **vision system** uses a camera and a computer to identify objects by digitizing their images and then comparing the images against a database of known shapes. **Fuzzy logic**, a type of mathematics, deals with values that are not precise and values that have a degree of uncertainty. Although not precisely defined, the term **agent** has come to mean a software program that can independently carry out tasks on behalf of a user.

17. The largest use of computers is in business. Existing business information systems will continue to undergo profound changes as new technology, software, and methods are applied to the huge installed base of computer users.

18. The **automated office**, sometimes referred to as the **electronic office**, makes use of electronic devices such as computers, facsimile machines, and computerized telephone systems to make work more productive. In a concept called **Microsoft At Work**, Microsoft Corporation has proposed a standardized intelligent graphical user interface that will be built into all office machines allowing data to be sent to or received from any device on the network.

19. As with automated office applications, the goal of the **digital factory** is to increase productivity through the use of networked, computer-controlled equipment. Technologies used in the digital factory include **computer-aided design** (CAD), **computer-aided engineering** (CAE), and **computer-aided manufacturing** (CAM).

20. **Computer-integrated manufacturing** (CIM) is the total integration of the manufacturing process using computers. The current trend is toward the **computer-integrated enterprise** – an organization in which all information storage and processing is performed by a network of computers and intelligent devices – allowing authorized users in any functional area of the organization to access and use data stored anywhere in the organization.

21. Millions of personal computers have been purchased for home use, and the use of personal computers in the home is expected to increase. The ways people use personal computers in their homes usually fall into five general categories: (1) personal services, (2) control of home systems, (3) telecommuting, (4) education, and (5) entertainment.

22. Personal services includes the use of computers in the home for creating documents, financial planning and analysis, and filing and organizing data. Personal computer software also is available to assist with home accounting applications and to transmit and receive data over telephone lines, allowing home users to access a wealth of information and services.

23. Another use of computers in the home is to control home systems such as security, environment, lighting, and landscape sprinkler systems. Telecommuting refers to the ability of individuals to work at home and communicate with their offices by using personal computers and communications lines.

24. The use of personal computers for education, called **computer-aided instruction** (CAI), is another rapidly growing area. CAI software can be classified into three types: **drill and practice software**, **tutorial software**, and **simulation software**. In an approach that is sometimes called **remote learning**, some trade schools, colleges, and universities now offer students with personal computers the opportunity to take electronic correspondence courses in their homes.

25. Entertainment software, or game playing, on home computers always has had a large following among the younger members of the family, but it also can provide adults with hours of enjoyment. Popular types of entertainment software include arcade games, board games, simulations, and interactive graphics programs.

Terms to Remember

agent (14.14)
application programmer (14.14)
artificial intelligence (AI) (14.13)
Associate Computing Professional
   (ACP) (14.9)
Association for Computing
   Machinery (ACM) (14.8)
automated office (14.16)

Certified Computing Professional
   (CCP) (14.9)
COMDEX (14.10)
communications specialist (14.4)
computer engineering (14.8)
computer information systems
   (CIS) (14.8)
computer operator (14.4)
computer science (14.8)
computer-aided design (CAD) (14.17)
computer-aided engineering
   (CAE) (14.18)
computer-aided instruction
   (CAI) (14.21)
computer-aided manufacturing
   (CAM) (14.18)
computer-integrated enterprise
   (14.19)
computer-integrated manufacturing
   (CIM) (14.18)
consultants (14.6)
control clerk (14.4)

data entry operator (14.4)
data librarian (14.4)
Data Processing Management
   Association (DPMA) (14.8)
database analyst (14.4)
digital convergence (14.11)
digital factory (14.17)
drill and practice software (14.21)

electronic office (14.16)
end user computing group (14.5)
executive information system (EIS)
   specialist (14.5)

fuzzy logic (14.13)

information center specialist (14.5)
Institute for the Certification of
   Computer Professionals
   (ICCP) (14.9)

Microsoft At Work (14.17)

office automation specialist (14.5)
operations group (14.4)

PC network specialist (14.4)
PC support specialist (14.5)

quality assurance specialist (14.4)

remote learning (14.21)
robotics (14.13)
robots (14.13)

sales representatives (14.5)
service and repair technician (14.5)
simulation software (14.21)
stereolithography (SL) (14.23)
system development group (14.4)
system programmer (14.4)
systems analyst (14.4)

technical evaluator (14.4)
technical services group (14.4)
technical writer (14.4)
trainer (14.5)
tutorial software (14.21)

user group (14.9)

vision system (14.13)

Test Your Knowledge

Fill in the Blanks

1. Job opportunities in the information processing industry come primarily from three areas: _____, _____, and _____.

2. Two positions in the systems development group of an information systems department are the _____, who works closely with users to analyze their requirements and design an information systems solution, and the _____, who converts the system design into the appropriate computer language.

3. The most widely recognized certification program in the information processing industry is administered by the _____, which is sponsored and supported by several professional organizations including the ACM and DPMA.

4. _____ describes the merging of technologies and products from the communications, entertainment, publishing, and computing industries.

5. Although the use of computers in the office and the factory can be discussed separately, the trend is the _____ – an organization in which all information storage and processing is performed by a network of computers and intelligent devices.

Short Answer

1. What are the four groups into which positions in an information systems department can be divided? What are the responsibilities of each group?

2. Upon what factors does compensation for information processing careers depend? What industries pay the highest salaries? Why? According to the U.S. Bureau of Labor Statistics, what will be the fastest growing computer career positions through the year 2005?

3. How is the Association for Computing Machinery (ACM) different from the Data Processing Management Association (DPMA)? What benefits are offered by both associations? What is a user group?

4. What is the goal of the digital factory? What are some of the technologies used in the digital factory? Briefly describe each.

5. What is computer-aided instruction (CAI)? How are drill and practice software, tutorial software, and simulation software different? What advantages does education in the home through CAI or electronic correspondence courses offer?

Points to Ponder

1

A researcher from International Resource Development, Inc. reported that about one-fourth of the work force may have emotional problems related to the use of computers. Many established workers expressed feelings of incompetence, loss of control, job insecurity, and anticipated demotion with the introduction of personal computers in the workplace. Some experts believe these feelings, which are occasionally called compuphobia, could lead frustrated workers to sabotage computer systems and equipment. Why are established workers more apt to experience compuphobia than new employees? Are the fears of these workers justified? Why or why not? If you were the manager of a department in which computers were being introduced, what would you do to prevent compuphobia?

2

This chapter describes many current career opportunities in information processing. Choose the four positions in which you are most interested and explain why. What do the four positions you have chosen have in common? What personal qualities and experiences do you have that would help you be successful in any of the four positions? What types of classes do you think you should take to prepare for a career in these positions? Why?

3

With the introduction of information technology, a group of life insurance companies was able to reduce their administrative staff by 45 percent and at the same time expand their business by 25 percent. While experts feel information technology will result in a net increase in the number of available jobs, most admit that many people without computer skills will be displaced. What responsibilities, if any, does an organization have to displaced workers? Why? What steps, if any, should government take to prepare displaced workers for a changing workplace?

4

Some companies offer employees discount programs on purchasing personal computers. Although this may simply seem to be a generous perk, a few people wonder if it is really intended as a means of getting additional work out of employees. It was once thought that computers would shorten the length of the work day, but the introduction of such items as portable computers, facsimile machines, modems, cellular telephones, and paging devices, along with increasingly global markets that know no time zones, has blurred the boundary between office and home. While some individuals applaud the added flexibility, others regret the loss of "personal" time. How do you feel? Under what circumstances would you be willing to work beyond normal office hours? Why? What effects do you think extended working hours will have on society as a whole? Does all work and no play truly make Jack a dull boy?

5

Imagine you have been given fifteen days to write a ten-page paper. Your teacher has promised to give extra credit for each day the paper is turned in early and to deduct credit for each day the paper is submitted after the deadline. On graph paper, construct a fuzzy logic diagram similar to that shown in *Figure 14-14* on page 14.13, illustrating your degree of certainty regarding the completion date. Indicate the days on the horizontal axis and the certainty (0, 0.5, 1.0) on the vertical axis. Mark the number of days it will take you to complete the paper under the best conditions (the topic is familiar, the library has the necessary resources, your other course work is light, and so on), your most likely guess of the number of days it will take you to complete the paper, and the number of days it will take you to complete the paper under the worst conditions (the demands on your time are heavy, the materials you need are unavailable, your word processor breaks down, and so on), and then connect the marks.

Windows 95

Out and About

6

It has been argued that American education lags far behind technological developments. Children still spend years learning skills such as long division, an operation that can be performed in seconds on a five-dollar calculator. Many urge that curriculums be totally reexamined; teaching procedures that are performed more efficiently using a computer can be abandoned, and instead students could be taught to take advantage of a computer's capabilities. Others insist, however, that unless people are familiar with skills like long division they will not know when, perhaps because of an input error, the information supplied by a computer or calculator is incorrect. Some teachers also feel that these computational skills help to develop the rigorous thought processes necessary in the information age. Consider your own education. In terms of technology, do you think that education was adequate? What skills or concepts, if any, did you spend time learning that now, because of computers, you feel are unnecessary? At what age should students be introduced to computers? What computer-related topics should students be taught in elementary school and secondary school? Explain your answers.

1. How would you like to work in an information systems department? Choose a position in *Figure 14-3* on page 14.4 in which you are interested, contact an individual who works in that position in a local organization, and arrange to interview that individual about his or her job. What are the individual's responsibilities? What are the most difficult aspects of the job? To what professional organizations does he or she belong? What certification, if any, is required? What type of educational background does the individual have? Approximately how much does the position pay? What are the opportunities for advancement? After receiving answers to these and other questions, is this a career into which you would like to enter? Why or why not?

2. Digital convergence is expected to have an impact in several areas, including communications, entertainment, and publishing. Choose an area in which you are interested and, using library resources and current computer magazines, prepare a report on the anticipated effect of digital convergence. What changes will probably result in the area? What types of hardware and software will be necessary? How is the area likely to look when digital convergence is realized? Will anything that you think is valuable be lost? How will people's lives be different? When is it expected that the effects of digital convergence will be realized?

Out and About
(continued)

3. Try out a software application that includes an agent, or wizard, such as Microsoft Word or Microsoft Excel. For what purpose is the wizard used? What are the advantages of using a wizard to complete the task over simply performing the task on your own? What are the disadvantages? Is the final result created by the wizard more or less attractive, creative, or distinctive than what you could have done on your own? Why? Would you be more likely to purchase an application with an agent than one that did not have one? Why or why not?

4. Arrange for a tour of a factory. What digital technologies are used in the factory? How are they used? What advantages are offered by these technologies? Does the factory use robots? If so, how and why? How have the factory's workers been affected by the new technologies? What kind of training did they undergo? Where any positions lost as a result of the technologies introduced? Where any new positions created?

5. Visit a software vendor and locate at least two different packages that can be used to assist with home accounting, such as balancing checkbooks, making household budgets, or preparing tax returns. What is the name of each package? What is the cost? What are the hardware requirements? If possible, test the packages and perform the same task with each. Is one package easier to use? If so, why? Does either package provide more capabilities than the other? What? On the basis of your examination, which package, if any, would you be most inclined to purchase? Why?

6. Volunteer to help out in a primary or secondary school class while it is using computer-aided instruction (CAI). What type of software is being used? Is it effective? Do you think the same topic could be taught more effectively using a different type of software? Why or why not? Could the topic be taught better by a teacher? Why? How do the students respond to CAI? From your observation, what do you think are the advantages of CAI? What are the disadvantages? In general, are your feelings about computer-aided instruction positive or negative? Why?

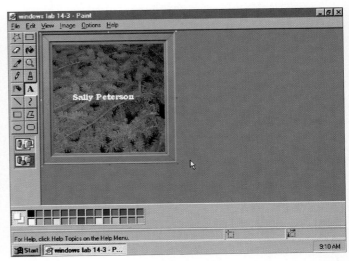

In the Lab with Windows 95

1 Shelly Cashman Series Computers of the Future Lab
Follow the instructions in Windows 95 Lab 1 on page 1.30 to display the Shelly Cashman Series Labs screen. Click Exploring the Computers of the Future. Click the Start Lab button. When the initial screen displays, carefully read the objectives. With your printer turned on, click the Print Questions button. Fill out the top of the Questions sheet and answer the questions as you step through the Computers of the Future Lab. Close the Shelly Cashman Series Labs.

2 Transferring Information Between Applications
Click the Start button on the taskbar, point to Programs on the Start menu, point to Accessories on the Programs submenu, and then click Paint on the Accessories submenu. Maximize Paint. Click File on the menu bar and then click Open. Scroll through the bitmap files, click Gold Weave, and then click the Open button to display the bitmap file on the screen *(Figure 14-26)*. If the bitmap files do not appear, ask your instructor where they are located. Click Edit on the menu bar and then click Select All. Right-click the Gold Weave graphic and then click Copy on the shortcut menu. Close Paint.

Click the Start button on the taskbar, point to Programs on the Start menu, point to Accessories on the Programs submenu, and then click WordPad on the Accessories submenu. Type `Below is a graphic opened in Paint and copied to WordPad:` and then press ENTER twice. Click Edit on the menu bar and then click Paste. Press ENTER twice and then type your name. Click the Save button on the toolbar. Type `a:\windows labs\windows 95 lab 14-2` and then click the Save button. Click the Print button on the toolbar. Close WordPad.

3 Modifying a Graphic Image   Start Paint as described in Windows 95 Lab 2. Click File on the menu bar and then click Open. Scroll through the bitmap files, click Forest, and then click the Open button. Click Help on the menu bar and then click Help topics. Click the Contents tab, double-click Putting Text in Pictures and then double-click Typing and formatting text. Read and print the topic. Close Help.

Click the Text tool in the tool box. Move the mouse pointer into the graphic and then drag a rectangle in the middle of the Forest graphic. The rectangle in the graphic is called a text frame. Notice that a text toolbar now appears on the screen; you may move the text toolbar anywhere on the window. If your text toolbar does not appear, right-click the rectangular text frame you just drew and then click Text Toolbar.

Click the color white in the color box at the bottom of the Paint window. Click the Font box arrow on the text toolbar and then click Bookman Old Style. Click the Font Size box arrow on the text toolbar and then click 12. Click the Bold button on the text toolbar. Close the text toolbar. Click inside the text frame and type your name *(Figure 14-27)*. When finished, click File on the menu bar and then click Save As. Type `a:\windows labs\windows 95 lab 14-3` and then click the Save button. Click File on the menu bar, click Print, and then click the OK button. Close Paint.

Figure 14-26

Figure 14-27

Where on the Web

1 Job Hunting on the Web The information processing industry is one of the largest industries in the world with annual sales close to $200 billion. Complete the following steps to learn more about career opportunities within this industry. With Netscape on the screen, type `http://espan.iquest.net/cgi-bin/gate2?espan~simple/search.html` in the Location text box and press ENTER. Type `systems analyst` in the Searchwords text box. Click the Search button. If the Security Information dialog box displays, click the Continue button. Scroll down and click one of the listings. Click Print on the File menu. Click the OK button. Hand in the printout.

2 World Wide Web Careers To visit the Pathfinder Web site *(Figure 14-28)* and learn about the types of careers that support a Web site of this size and quality, complete the following steps. With Netscape on the screen, type `http://www.pathfinder.com` in the Location text box and press ENTER. Scroll down the home page to get an appreciation of the size of this Web site. Click About Pathfinder (near the top of the home page). Click content partners. Click Print on the File menu. Click Pages and then type 1 in the To text box. Click the OK button. Scroll down and count how many persons are involved in this Web site. Write your answer on the printout and hand it in.

3 Telecommuting Telecommuting refers to the ability of individuals to work away from the office, often at home, and communicate by personal computers and communications lines. Complete the following steps to learn more about telecommuting. With Netscape on the screen, click the

Net Search button. Click Infoseek Guide and type `telecommuting` in the text box. Click the seek now button. Scroll down and click one of the topics. Click Print on the File menu. Click Pages and then type 1 in the To text box. Click the OK button. Write a brief summary of what you found on the printout and hand it in to your instructor.

4 Shopping for CDs The term, agent, means a software program that can independently carry out tasks on behalf of its user. Andersen Consulting's BargainFinder Agent *(Figure 14-29)* will search stores on the World Wide Web to find the best price for a CD or album. Complete the following steps to test out its shopping agent. With Netscape on the screen, type `http://bf.cstar.ac.com/bf` in the Location text box and press ENTER. Scroll down and click Top 40 List. Scroll down and click an album in the list. Read about BargainFinder. Scroll down and see the results of its search. Click Print on the File menu. Click OK. Hand in the printout.

5 Shelly Cashman Online Click Using Computers: A Gateway To Information, World Wide Web Edition on the Shelly Cashman Student Center Web page (`http://www.bf.com/scstudnt.html`). Scroll down and click Chapter 14. Complete the activities listed.

Figure 14-28

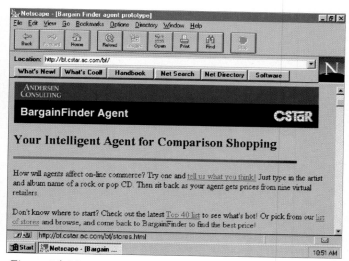

Figure 14-29

Virtual Reality

Virtual reality (VR) is the use of a computer to create an artificial environment that can be experienced by the user. The reality of the artificial environment and the extent the user can interact with it depends on the software and type of hardware used. Desktop virtual reality uses personal computers to display what appears to be a three-dimensional view of an environment such as an office or a home. Using a pointing device, such as a mouse or joystick, the user can simulate moving through the environment; for example, from room to room.

Immersion virtual reality uses additional equipment that makes the user feel as though he or she is actually in the simulated environment. This additional equipment includes a head-mounted display and may also include data gloves or complete body suits.

The following figures illustrate software and hardware used in virtual reality and some of the current applications.

Figure 1

The Virtual Windtunnel Project at NASA Ames Research Center uses a three-dimensional virtual reality display of aircraft and air flows. Different colors indicate different temperatures. Using the stereoscopic boom display from Fakespace Labs, shown in the lower left corner, the user can simulate walking around the aircraft to view the air flows from different angles.

Figure 2

Doctors at Kaiser-Permanente Medical Group worked with engineers at Division Inc. to develop a virtual reality method of helping people overcome a fear of heights. At the start of a Virtual Therapy session, the patient sees the display shown in the photograph. Using a hand-held device to indicate direction, patients can move from the patio, across a plank, and walk along a suspension bridge over a deep gorge. At any time they can look down and experience a sensation of height. Patients that have completed the virtual therapy have been able to more quickly complete their real world treatment, which includes a 15-story ride in a glass enclosed elevator.

Figure 3

Ciné-Med is one of several companies that have created virtual reality systems allowing doctors and medical students to practice surgery on a virtual patient. Ciné-Med's Virtual Clinic includes a fiberglass torso into which surgical instruments can be inserted. The progress of the operation is displayed on a monitor, just as it would be in real surgery.

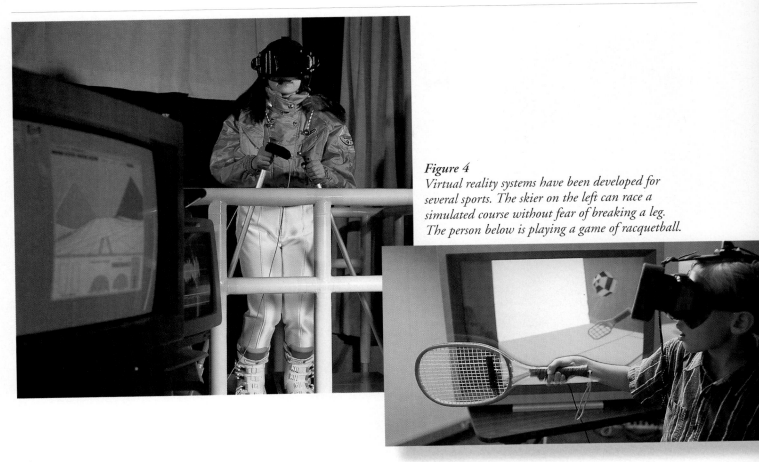

Figure 4
Virtual reality systems have been developed for several sports. The skier on the left can race a simulated course without fear of breaking a leg. The person below is playing a game of racquetball.

Figure 5
The force feedback virtual reality system, developed at the University of North Carolina, allows the user to examine chemical structures and search for places where other molecules could be joined.

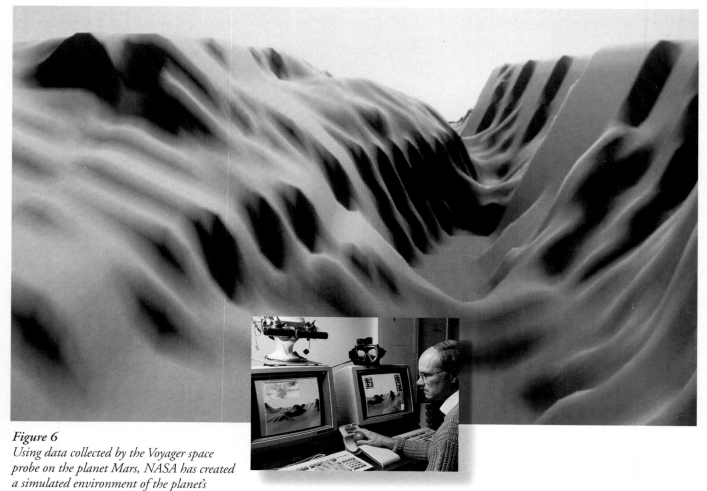

Figure 6
Using data collected by the Voyager space probe on the planet Mars, NASA has created a simulated environment of the planet's surface.

Figure 7
This virtual reality system was developed by the Hines Illinois Veterans Administration Hospital to help design apartments for people who use wheelchairs.

Figure 8
Architects and space planners use virtual reality systems to allow clients to view offices and homes before they are built.

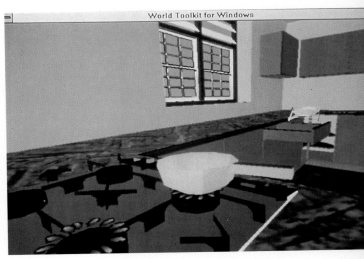

Figure 9
In this virtual kitchen, created for British Gas using software from Sense8 Corporation, cupboards can be opened and closed, cooking pots moved, and the stove's burners turned on.

Figure 10
WalkThrough is a three-dimensional software package from Virtus Corporation that allows a user to create and then explore a virtual environment.

Figure 11
Hanging on the wall are some of the many data gloves and body suits that can be worn to transmit a user's motion to a virtual reality system.

Figure 12
This picture shows a virtual reality financial application designed to track the movement of stocks in several international markets. Each grid represents an industry group, such as oil or autos, in a particular financial market, such as Hong Kong. The small chips within the grids represent individual stocks. The chips spin and blink to indicate buy or sell opportunities. The color of the chip indicates whether the stock has gone up or down from the day before. The distance a chip rises above the surface shows its relative performance to other chips.

Figure 13
Software from Worldesign was used to create these views of the Seattle, Washington harbor area showing the before and after views of a development project. The software allows users to drive or fly through the simulated environment.

INDEX

Operational decisions: Decisions made by operational management that involve an immediate action such as accepting or rejecting an inventory delivery or approving a purchase order. **10.6**

Operational management: Management level that makes operational decisions and provides direct supervision over the production, clerical, and non-management staff of an organization. **10.6**

Operation code: A unique value typically stored in the first byte in a machine language instruction that indicates which operation is to be performed. **4.18**

Operations group: Information processing employees responsible for operating the centralized (computer center) equipment and network administration including both data and voice communications. **14.4**

Optical character recognition (OCR), *see* **OCR**

Optical codes: In source data automation, codes that use a pattern or symbol to represent data, such as a bar code. **3.11**

Optical disks: Storage medium that uses lasers to burn microscopic holes on the surface of a hard plastic disk;able to store enormous quantities of information. **6.19**

Optical mark recognition (OMR): Input devices that are often used to process questionnaires or test answer sheets. Carefully placed marks on the form indicate responses to questions that are read and interpreted by a computer program. **3.12**

Optical memory cards: Storage devices that can store up to 1,600 pages of text or images on a device the size of a credit card. **6.22**

Optical recognition: Devices that use a light source to read codes, marks, and characters and convert them into digital data that an be processed by a computer. **3.11**

OS/2: IBM's operating system designed to work with 32-bit microprocessors. In addition to running programs written specifically for OS/2, the operating system can also run programs written for DOS or Windows. **8.13**

Output: The data that has been processed into a useful form called information that can be used by a person or machine. **1.7, 5.2-32**

Output devices: Most commonly used devices are the printer and the computer screen. **1.8**

Outsourcing: Process in which companies hire outside firms to provide information systems support for a contracted fee. **10.7**

Overvoltage: Occurs when the incoming electrical power increases significantly above the normal 120 volts, which can cause immediate and permanent damage to hardware. **13.12**

Owner: The higher level record in a network database. **9.15**

Packet switching: In communications networks, individual packets of information from various users are combined and transmitted over a high-speed channel. **7.24**

Page: In virtual memory management, the fixed number of bytes that are transferred from disk to memory each time new data or program instruction are required. **8.8**

Page composition and layout: In desktop publishing, the process of arranging text and graphics on a document page. **2.10**

Page definition language: In desktop publishing, language describing the document to be printed that the printer can understand. **2.11**

Page makeup, *see* **Page composition and layout**

Page printers: Nonimpact printers that operate similar to a copying machine to produce high-quality text and graphic output. **5.14**

Page scanner: An input device that electronically captures an entire page of text or images such as photography or art work. The scanner converts the text or image on the original document into digital information that can be stored on a disk and processed by the computer. **3.10**

Pages per minute (ppm): Measure of the speed of printers that can produce an entire page at one time. **5.15**

Paging: In virtual memory management, a fixed number of bytes (a page) is transferred from disk to memory each time new data or program instructions are required. **8.8**

Palmtop computer: Small computers that often have several built-in or interchangeable personal information management functions, such as a calendar to keep track of meetings and events, and an address and phone file;they do not have disk storage devices and usually have a nonstandard keyboard. **1.10**

Parallel conversion: Continuing to process data on the old system while some or all of the data is also processed on the new system. **11.23**

Parallel ports: Ports most often used to connect devices that send or receive large amounts of data such as printers or disk and tape drives. **4.15**

Parallel processing: The use of multiple CPU's, each with their own memory, that work on their assigned portion of a problem simultaneously. **4.20**

Parent record: In a hierarchical database, a record that has one or more child records. **9.14**

Parity bit: One extra bit for each byte that is used for error checking. **4.4**

Partition(s): Portions of memory allocated by operating system into fixed areas. **8.7**

Partitioned disk: Hard disk is divided into separate areas called partitions before it is formatted. **6.9**

Pascal: A programming language developed for teaching programming. Pascal contains programming statements that encourage the use of structured program design. 1.35, **12.23**

Passive matrix: LCD screens that use fewer transistors; one for each row and column. **5.21**

Password: A value, such as a word or number, which identifies the user. In multiuser operating systems, the password must be entered correctly before a user is allowed to use an application program. The password is usually confidential. **8.10, 13.5**

Paste: In word processing operations, an option used after performing either the cut or the copy command, where the text is placed elsewhere in the document. **2.6**

PC cards: Small, credit-card sized cards that fit into PCMCIA expansion slots, used for storage, communications, and additional memory. **6.19**

PC-DOS: Operating system developed by Microsoft Corporation for IBM and is installed by IBM on systems that IBM sells. **8.12**

PCMCIA (Personal Computer Memory Card International Association) cards: A special type of expansion slot that can be inserted into a personal computer, used for additional memory, storage, and communications. The small fitting into the expansion slot, called PC cards, are the size of credit cards. **4.13**

PC network specialist: Employee who installs and maintains local area networks. **14.4**

PCs, *see* **Personal computer(s)**

PC support specialist: Employee involved with end user computing group who installs and supports personal computer equipment and software. **14.5**

PDA, *see* **Personal digital assistant**

Peer-to-peer network: Local area network that allows any computer to share the software, data, or hardware (such as a printer) located on any other computer in the network. **7.23**

Pen computers: Specialized portable computers that use a pen-like device to enter data. **1.11**

Pen input devices: Allows the user to input hand-printed letters and numbers to record information. **3.7**

Pen plotters: Plotters used to create images on a sheet of paper by moving one or more pens over the surface. **5.24**

Performance monitoring: During the maintenance phase of the information system life cycle, the ongoing process of comparing response times, file sizes, and other system performance measures against the values that were estimated when the system was designed. **11.25**

Periodic reports: Reports that are produced on a regular basis such as daily, weekly, or monthly. Also called scheduled reports. **5.4**

Peripheral devices: The input devices, output devices, and auxiliary storage units that surround the processing unit. **1.9**

Personal communicator, *see* **Personal digital assistant**

Personal computer(s): The small systems that have become so widely used in recent years. Depending on their size and features, personal computer prices range from several hundred to several thousand dollars. **1.10**

Personal Computer Memory Card International Association, *see* **PCMCIA**

Personal digital assistant (PDA): Small pen input device designed for workers on the go;often has built-in communications capabilities that allow the PDA to use voice, fax, or data communications. **1.11,** 1.38, 14.12

Personal identification number (PIN): A numeric password, used to access computer system. **13.6**

Personal information management (PIM) software: Helps users keep track of miscellaneous bits of personal information. Notes to self, phone messages, and appointment scheduling are examples of this type of software. **2.24**

Phased conversion: Used with larger systems that can be broken down into individual modules that can be implemented separately at different times. **11.24**

Physical design: In the information system life cycle, the logical design that was created during the analysis phase is transformed into physical design, identifying the procedures to be automated, choosing the programming language, and specifying the equipment needed for the system. **11.17**

Picture elements, *see* **Pixels**

Pie chart: A graphic representation of proportions depicted as slices of a pie. **2.16**

PHOTO CREDITS

CHAPTER 1 *Figure 1-1,* (top) International Business Machines Corp.; (center) International Business Machines Corp.; (bottom left) International Business Machines Corp.; *Figure 1-3,* © Henry Blackham:*Figure 1-4,* International Business Machines Corp.; *Figure 1-5,* International Business Machines Corp.; *Figure 1-7,* © Henry Blackham; *Figure 1-9,* (a) Omnidata; (b) Hewlett-Packard Co.; (c) Toshiba America Information Systems, Inc.; (d) Zeos International Ltd.; (e) International Business Machines Corp.; (f) EO Inc.; (g) © Frank Pryor/Apple Computer Inc.; (h) © Mosgrove Photo/Apple Computer Inc.; (i) International Business Machines Corp.; (j) International Business Machines Corp.; *Figure 1-10,* Dell Computer Corp.; *Figure 1-11,* International Business Machines Corp.; *Figure 1-12,* International Business Machines Corp.; *Figure 1-13,* Cray Computer Corp.; *Figure 1-14,* Cray Research; *Figure 1-17,* CompUSA Inc.; *Figure 1-21,* Hewlett-Packard Co.; *Figure 1-22,* Hewlett-Packard Co.; *Figure 1-24,* International Business Machines Corp.; *Figure 1-25,* International Business Machines Corp.; *Figure 1-26,* International Business Machines Corp.; *Figure 1-27,* International Business Machines Corp.; *Figure 1-28,* Stock/Boston; *Figure 1-29,* Hewlett-Packard Co.; *Figure 1-30,* International Business Machines Corp.; *Figure 1-31,* International Business Machines Corp.; *Figure 1-32,* International Business Machines Corp.; *Figure 1-33,* © Frank Pryor/Apple Computer; **TIMELINE** *Page 1.32,* (top left) Iowa State University, News Service Photo Dept.; (top center left) Iowa State University; (top center right) Iowa State University; (top right) University of Pennsylvania Archives; (bottom left) Harvard University Archives; (bottom center left) Dept.of Navy; (bottom center right) Massachusetts Institute of Technology; (bottom right) Dept of Navy; *Page 1.33,* (top left) Institute for Advanced Studies; (top center) UNISYS Corp.; (top right) UNISYS Corp.; (bottom left) Dept.of Navy; (bottom center); Massachusetts Institute of Technology; (bottom right) International Business Machines Corp.; *Page 1.34,* (top left) International Business Machines Corp.; (top right) © Stuart Bratesman; (bottom left) Integrated Circuit Corporation; (bottom center left) International Business Machines Corp.; (bottom center right) Computer Museum; (bottom right) InfoWorld; *Page 1.35,* (top left) Digital Equipment Corporation; (top center left) © Shelly R.Harrison; (top center right) Intel Corp.; (top right) Intel Corp.; (botom left) Apple Computer, Inc.; (bottom center left) Apple Computer, Inc.; (bottom center right) Apple Computer, Inc.; (bottom right) VisiCalc; *Page 1.36,* (top left) Microsoft Corp.; (top right) International Business Machines Corp.; (bottom left) Apple Computer, Inc.(bottom right) Compaq Computer Corp.; *Page 1.37,* (top left) Time Magazine; (top center left) Lotus Development Corp.; (top center right) Lotus Development Corporation; (top right) International Business Machines Corp.; (bottom left) Intel Corp.; (bottom right) Microsoft Corp.; *Page 1.38,* (top left) Apple Computer, Inc.; (top center) Apple Computer, Inc.; (top right) Intel Corp.; (bottom) Environmental Protection Agency (EPA). **CHAPTER 2** *Figure 2-10,* © Fredrik D.Bodin; *Figure 2-25,* © Curtis Fukuda; *Figure 2-38,* (c) © Fredrik D.Bodin; (d) © Fredrik D.Bodin. **CHAPTER 3** *Figure 3-1,* © Henry Blackham; *Figure 3-2,* (a) International Business Machines Corp.; (b) International Business Machines Corp.; *Figure 3-3,* (a) Microsoft Corp.; (b) © Phil Matt; *Figure 3-5,* International Business Machines Corp.; *Figure 3-6,* Texas Instruments Inc./Temelin McClain PR; *Figure 3-7,* Suncom Technologies Inc.; *Figure 3-8,* (a) International Business Machines Corp.; (b) International Business Machines Corp.; *Figure 3-9,* GRID System Corp.; *Figure 3-11,* International Business Machines Corp.; *Figure 3-12,* International Business Machines Corp.; *Figure 3-13,* Compaq Computer Corp.; *Figure 3-14,* Compaq Computer Corp.; *Figure 3-15,* Hewlett-Packard Co.; *Figure 3-16,* Logitech Inc.; *Figure 3-17,* International Business Machines Corp.; *Figure 3-19,* (a) © Ed Kashi/Dell Computer; (b) Hewlett-Packard Co.; (c) © Paul Shambroom/Science; *Figure 3-20,* (right) Scantron Corp.; *Figure 3-23,* © Fredrik D.Bodin; *Figure 3-24,* NCR Corp.; *Figure 3-25,* Cooper Tire; *Figure 3-26,* Cimlinc, Inc.; *Figure 3-27,* International Business Machines Corp.; *Figure 3-29,* Texas Instruments Inc.; *Figure 3-31,* Videolabs Inc.; *Figure 3-32,* © Fredrik D.Bodin; *Figure 3-35,* © Gary Payne/Gamma Liaison; *Figure 3-38,* The Image Bank. **CHAPTER 4** *Figure 4-1,* © Henry Blackham; *Figure 4-8,* © Phil Matt; *Figure 4-9,* Intel Corp.; *Figure 4-10,* International Business Machines Corp.; *Figure 4-13,* © Phil Matt; *Figure 4-15,* © Alan L.Detrick; *Figure 4-20,* © Phil Matt; *Figure 4-21,* MegaHertz Corp.; *Figure 4-22,* © Phil Matt; *Figure 4-26,* © Tom Pantages; *Figure 4-35,* Courtesy of Paul DuBois, Hermes Engineering NV. **MAKING A COMPUTER CHIP** *Page 4.35,* (1) Index Stock Photography; *Page 4.36* (2) © Frank Wing Photographer; (6) Intel Corp.; (7) C-I Photography; *Page 4.37,* (5) Photo Researchers, Inc.; (9) International Business Machines Corp.; (10) © David Scharf; *Page 4.38,* (11) © L.Manning/Westlight; (12) International Business Machines Corp.; (13) C-I Photography; (14) © Chuck O'Rear/West*light*; (15) Dr.Jerry Burgess/Science Photo Library; (16) © Peloton & Associates, Inc./Westlight. **CHAPTER 5** *Figure 5-5,* Radius Computer Corp.; *Figure 5-6,* International Business Machines Corp.; *Figure 5-7,* AT&T; *Figure 5-10,* International Business Machines Corp.; *Figure 5-11,* © Peter Menzel; *Figure 5-12,* © Ed Kashi; *Figure 5-13,* © Gerry Gropp/Sipa Press; *Figure 5-15,* © Eric Futran Photography/Liaison International; *Figure 5-17,* Epson America, Inc.; *Figure 5-18,* Printronix; *Figure 5-24,* Hewlett-Packard Co.; *Figure 5-25,* Lexmark; *Figure 5-27,* Hewlett-Packard Co.; *Figure 5-28,* Siemens Nixdorf Printing Systems; *Figure 5-29,* CalComp Inc.; *Figure 5-30,* (a) Seiko Corporation; (b) Zebra Technologies Corp.; (c) Citizen America Corp.; *Figure 5-32,* Portrait Display Labs; *Figure 5-34,* Evans & Sutherland Computer Corp.; *Figure 5-36,* NEC Technologies Inc.; *Figure 5-37,* International Business Machines Corp.; *Figure 5-38,* Toshiba America Information Systems, Inc.; *Figure 5-39,* NEC Corp.; *Figure 5-42,* TRW Inc.; *Figure 5-43,* Electrohome Corp.; *Figure 5-44,* Hewlett-Packard Co.; *Figure 5-45,* Hewlett-Packard Co.; *Figure 5-46,* Eastman Kodak Co.; *Figure 5-48,* MusicWriter, Inc.; *Figure 5-49,* © Hank Morgan/Science Photo Library. **CHAPTER 6** *Figure 6-2,* © Phil Matt; *Figure 6-7,* © Phil Matt; *Figure 6-10,* Hewlett-Packard Co.; *Figure 6-11,* International Business Machines Corp.; *Figure 6-12,* Quantum Corp.; *Figure 6-13,* International Business Machines Corp.; *Figure 6-19,* © Phil Matt; *Figure 6-20,* MAC USA; *Figure 6-22,* 3M Corp.; *Figure 6-23,* 3M Corp.; *Figure 6-24,* International Business Machines Corp.; *Figure 6-28,* © Phil Matt; *Figure 6-30,* 3M Corporation; *Figure 6-31,* Symmetrix Inc.; *Figure 6-32,* Storage Technology Corp.; *Figure 6-33,* Dallas Semiconductor; *Figure 6-34,* © Phil Matt; *Figure 6-35,* LaserCard Inc.; *Figure 6-37,* © Phil Matt; *Figure 6-38,* © Kerry Klayman/U.C.Irvine; *Figure 6-39,* © Kerry Klayman/U.C.Irvine; **CHAPTER 7** *Figure 7-1,* © HMS Images; *Figure 7-2,* (b) MCI International Inc.; *Figure 7-3,* © Peter Hendrie/The Image Bank; *Figure 7-4,* Lotus Development Corporation; *Figure 7-5,* Klynas Engineering; *Figure 7-9,* © Henry Blackham; *Figure 7-12,* The Image Bank; *Figure 7-13,* © Don Lowe/Tony Stone Images; *Figure 7-14,* © Jim Zuckerman/Westlight; *Figure 7-16,* Photonics Inc.; *Figure 7-24,* Photos © Henry Blackham; *Figure 7-26,* © Fredrik D.Bodin; *Figure 7-27,* Hayes Microcomputer Products Inc.; *Figure 7-28,* Photos © Henry Blackham; *Figure 7-31,* Photos © Henry Blackham; *Figure 7-32,* Photos © Henry Blackham; *Figure 7-33,* EDS Corp.; *Figure 7-34,* Photos © Henry Blackham; *Figure 7-35,* Photos © Henry Blackham; *Figure 7-36,* Photos © Henry Blackham; *Figure 7-37,* North American Van Lines. **THE INTERNET** *Figure 1,* NCSA of University of IL; *Figure 4,* BBN Communications Corp. **CHAPTER 8** *Figure 8-9,* Photos © Henry Blackham; *Figure 8-13,* Apple Computer Inc.; *Figure 8-14,* International Business Machines Corp.; *Figure 8-16,* Berkeley Systems Inc.; *Figure 8-17,* NeXT Computers Inc.; **BUYER'S GUIDE** *Page 8.29,* (a) International Business Machines Corp.; (b) © Phil Matt; (c) © Phil Matt; *Page 8.30,* (a) Environmental Protective Agency (EPA):(b) Dell Computer Corp.:*Page 8.33,* (a) Curtis Inc.; (b) © Phil Matt; (c) American Power Conversion Corp.(APC); (d) MicroSolutions Computer Products, Inc.; *Page 8.34,* Curtis Inc.; *Page 8.35,* © Phil Matt. **CHAPTER 9** *Figure 9-20,* © Jay Freis/The Image Bank; *Figure 9-23,* Bank Marketing Group. **CHAPTER 10** *Figure 10-7,* © David Young-Wolff/Photo Edit; *Figure 10-8,* © Catherine Noren/Stock Boston; *Figure 10-9,* COMSHARE, Inc.; *Figure 10-13,* Ford Motor Co. **CHAPTER 11** *Figure 11-14,* PC Magazine; *Figure 11-15,* © Ed Kashi; *Figure 11-16,* © Phil Matt; *Figure 11-21,* © Richard Pasley; *Figure 11-22,* Bachman Information Systems Inc.; *Figure 11-23,* © Jim Pickerell/West Light. **CHAPTER 12** *Figure 12-13,* U.S.Naval Archives. **MULTIMEDIA** *Opening Page,* © David Wagner/Phototake NYC; *Figure 1,* International Business Machines Corp.; *Figure 2,* (left) International Business Machines Corp.; *Figure 3,* Deep River Publishing; *Figure 4,* Books That Work; *Figure 5,* Books That Work; *Figure 6,* Microsoft Corp.; *Figure 7,* Microsoft Corp.; *Figure 8,* Medio Magazine; *Figure 9,* (left) Mayo Clinic; (right) A.D.A.M.Software; *Figure 10,* (right) © Ed Kashi. **CHAPTER 13** *Figure 13-1,* Photos © Henry Blackham; *Figure 13-6,* Recognition Systems; *Figure 13-7,* Checkmate Software Inc.; *Figure 13-8,* © Moss Warner Communications; *Figure 13-9,* Business Software Alliance; *Figure 13-10,* QuickSoft, Inc.; *Figure 13-13,* Curtis Inc.; *Figure 13-17,* Cynthia Satloff; *Figure 13-21,* Olivetti Research Ltd.; *Figure 13-22,* Photos © Henry Blackham. **CHAPTER 14** *Figure 14-1,* © Ed Kashi; *Figure 14-2,* © Ed Kashi; *Figure 14-4,* © Michael Newman; *Figure 14-5,* © Robert E.Daemmrich; *Figure 14-6,* © Ed Lalio/Liason International; *Figure 14-8,* Datamation; *Figure 14-11,* © Peter B.Young/The Interface Group; *Figure 14-12,* © Phil Matt; *Figure 14-13,* Arcmate; *Figure 14-16,* (a) Toshiba America Information Systems, Inc.; (c) International Business Machines Corp.; (d) Prosignia VS; (e) International Business Machines Corp.; *Figure 14-19,* Ford Motor Company; *Figure 14-23,* Microsoft Corporation; *Figure 14-24,* 3-D Systems; *Figure 14-25,* © Henry Blackham. **VIRTUAL REALITY** *Figure 1,* Fake Space Inc., Photo Court, NASA Ames Research Center; *Figure 2,* Division Incorporated; *Figure 3,* Ciné-Med; *Figure 4,* (upper) Caroline Parsons, The Gamma Liaison Network; (lower) Jack Menzel, Autodesk Inc.; *Figure 5,* (left) Peter Menzel VR, University of North Carolina; (right) Peter Menzel VR, University of North Carolina; *Figure 6,* Peter Menzel, NASA Ames Research, Moffett AFB, CA VR; Mars data from Voyager, Lewis Hitchner; *Figure 7,* David Sutton Picture Group; *Figure 8,* Gamma Liaison; *Figure 9,* Sense8 Corporation; *Figure 10,* Virtus Software; *Figure 11,* Peter Menzel VPL Research Wall; *Figure 12,* VR Financial; *Figure 13,* Worldesign.